SELLING DESTINATIONS

SELLING DESTINATIONS

GEOGRAPHY FOR THE TRAVEL PROFESSIONAL

FOURTH CANADIAN EDITION

MARC MANCINI
West Los Angeles College

THOMSON
NELSON

Australia   Canada   Mexico   Singapore   Spain   United Kingdom   United States

THOMSON

———✦———

NELSON

Selling Destinations: Geography for the Travel Professional
Fourth Canadian Edition
by Marc Mancini

Associate Vice-President, Editorial Director:
Evelyn Veitch

Executive Editor:
Veronica Visentin

Senior Acquisitions Editor:
Kevin Smulan

Marketing Manager:
Nigel Corish

Senior Developmental Editor:
Joanne Sutherland

Content Production Manager:
Tammy Scherer

Copy Editor:
Lisa Berland

Proofreader:
Kelli Howey

Indexer:
Edwin Durbin

Senior Production Coordinator:
Kathrine Pummell

Design Director:
Ken Phipps

Interior Design:
Peter Papayanakis

Cover Design:
Glenn Toddun

Cover Image:
Cosmo Condina/
Stock Connection/
PictureQuest

Compositor:
Interactive Composition
Corporation

Printer:
Transcontinental

Library and Archives Canada Cataloguing in Publication

Mancini, Marc, 1946-
   Selling destinations : geography for the travel professional / Marc Mancini. — 4th Canadian ed.

Includes index.
ISBN 0-17-640722-7

   1. Tourism—Textbooks.
2. Geography—Textbooks. I. Title.

G155.A1M35 2006   338.4'791
C2006-902696-3

Contents

Preface

Does the sheer volume of things the travel industry expects you to know about the world overwhelm you? Do you ever wonder how that knowledge can be translated to real, everyday career experience? Then *Selling Destinations*—whether you're a student, trainee, or working professional—is written with you in mind.

Selling Destinations can be a quick way of bringing yourself up to speed on most major tourist destinations. It can be a powerful and rapid reference tool. And it can become a springboard to other, more specialized treatments of destination geography.

WHAT MAKES THIS BOOK UNIQUE

As you'll discover, *Selling Destinations* is a very different kind of geography book:

- **It approaches geography from a travel industry perspective.** Important tourist destinations receive detailed treatment in chapters of their own. Secondary destinations merit several pages or paragraphs in special "Potpourri" chapters. Facts and places that travel industry personnel rarely deal with are given only a passing reference (though the appendixes direct you to other reference sources that contain the information you'll need).

- **It treats geography as something the travel industry sells.** To be able to match visitors to destinations and services is the key to travel industry success. *Selling Destinations* underscores precisely how you can do this in your day-to-day work.

- **It makes reading about destinations fun.** Some say a geography book needs to be serious. That's nonsense. Your study of destinations can be academically rigorous *and* fun. That's why this textbook uses a breezy, magazine-style prose to make learning about places an enjoyable yet educational experience.

- **It uses many educational devices to make sure you remember what you read.** The biggest problem with most books is that you remember only about 30 percent of what you read. *Selling Destinations* addresses this problem in two ways. First, it limits itself to what you need to know to be a travel professional; it won't clutter your mind with obscure details. Second, its lists, headings, subheadings, graphs, tables, photos, and application activities serve to clarify and reinforce information. The result: You absorb a far greater percentage of what you read.

HOW THIS BOOK IS ORGANIZED

Selling Destinations' part-and-chapter structure is dictated by travel and touristic concerns.

- **The book is divided into six major parts.** Part I lays a sturdy geographic and sales foundation for all information to come. Parts II through VI cover the world's principal geographic areas: North America, Latin America, Europe, Africa and the Middle East, Asia, Australia, and the South Pacific.

- **A short introductory overview** opens each of Parts II through VI. Each overview is followed by several **in-depth chapters** on major touristic centres. (There are 28 such chapters in the book, each focusing on those destinations most visited by North American tourists.) Each part finishes with a **potpourri**

chapter that gathers together those remaining destinations not covered in an in-depth chapter.

- **Three useful appendixes** list typical lengths of time spent by tourists in major cities; research resources; and destination-related feature films. A detailed **index** follows.

- **Pronunciation guides** follow place names that are especially difficult. They're set off in brackets and spelled phonetically.

HOW EACH CHAPTER IS ORGANIZED

The organizational subheadings of *Selling Destinations* are critical to the book's sales-geography philosophy:

- An **Introduction** gives a historical, cultural, or visitor perspective on the destination. It also lists major geographic features, patterns of tourism, and languages spoken.

- **How Travellers Get There** discusses modes of transportation, national airlines (with airline codes), major airports (also with codes), and travelling times from Canada, if relevant.

- **Weather Patterns** analyzes seasonal weather and touristic patterns.

- **Getting Around** focuses on internal modes of transportation, both in broad subregions and within major cities.

- **Important Places** discusses touristic highlights and day-trip possibilities from central hub cities.

- **Possible Itineraries** lays out typical visitor travel patterns within the destination area.

- **Lodging Options** enumerates the lodging choices of a destination, including principal hotel chains and landmark hotels.

- **Allied Destinations** suggests the places that are easily combined with a primary destination as part of a larger itinerary.

- **Cultural Patterns** (where applicable) examines the local cultural behaviours of which travellers should be aware.

- **Factors That Motivate Visitors** analyzes why a person typically travels to the destination covered.

- **Possible Misgivings** enumerates those psychological barriers to a destination—perhaps valid, perhaps not—that a person may have, and how or if they should be countered. While the ability to get beyond objections is essential to travel agents, it's equally valuable to tourist-bureau, cruise, and tour personnel.

- **Sales Strategies** lists the extra services that a person may wish to arrange—the kinds that yield extra profits to almost all sellers of travel.

- **Activities** close each chapter. A **Map Activity** tests your knowledge of geographic places and their attractions. A **Case Study** permits you to apply your knowledge to hypothetical travellers. A **Creative Activity** challenges you to take a hypothetical situation in the travel industry and turn it into an innovative solution. Some describe actual scenarios you'd face in various segments of the travel industry. Others are more whimsical; these serve as springboards to deeper creativity. In all cases, the goal is to help you marshal all you know, to tap into your creativity—and to have *fun*. These Creative Activities also lend themselves readily to in-class group solutions.

WHAT MAJOR VISUAL ELEMENTS ARE USED

Selling Destinations features nearly 300 visual elements to enliven the information that it presents:

- You'll find more than 100 area, provincial/state, and country **maps.** As you read the text, you'll be able to follow along on the map; that way you'll instantly know where the place talked about is situated. The maps are simplified to give special attention to cities and areas that tourists frequent.

  Some chapter maps contain symbols. Following is a key to the symbols you will encounter.

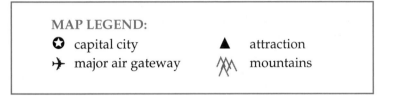

MAP LEGEND:
✪ capital city   ▲ attraction
✈ major air gateway   ⋀⋀⋀ mountains

- In many chapters you'll be able to consult a **"For Your Information"** box that summarizes geographic facts about a major destination, such as population, area, currency, languages spoken, history, and even on which side of the road visitors should drive.

- **"Climate at a Glance"** charts will enable you to rapidly determine the typical temperature, rainfall, and tourist season patterns of major world destinations.

- **"Qualifying the Traveller"** grid boxes will help you identify the types of people who are attracted to the major destinations.

- **"Travel Trivia"** boxes give you unusual, entertaining, surprising, or even weird bits of information that help round out your understanding of the industry and of the world.

- **Margin Notes** provide intriguing and/or offbeat tangents to the place being covered. These tips for travellers and bits of information will help you better understand each destination.

- **"Travelling the Web" icons** appear in the margin to indicate that additional information about an entry may be found on the *Selling Destinations* website.

THE *SELLING DESTINATIONS* WEBSITE

The website that accompanies this book, www.sellingdestinations.nelson.com, contains a wide variety of additional resources for both students and instructors. Creative Activities from the text are available to download and print. Quiz questions will allow students to test their knowledge of material from each of the chapters. Web links will be included to many tourist attractions, information on accommodation, transportation, online maps, atlases, and travel publications. The site will also direct you to useful travel-related tools on the Web and provide practical Travel Tips.

WHAT ISN'T INCLUDED

It would have been nice to include *everything* that the world has to offer to tourists, but that would have meant a publication bigger than a telephone book. That's why we've concentrated on the *essentials*. For the rest, a number of fine resources

—electronic or paper-based—can fill out your knowledge on something we may have chosen to leave out. Those sources are listed in Appendix B.

Selling Destinations deliberately avoids information that can become rapidly outdated or should more appropriately be looked up in standard, frequently revised sources (most of which are listed for you in the appendixes). Such information includes money conversion rates, visa requirements, and the like. This book also gives minimal attention to destinations that regularly suffer from political turmoil, terrorism, epidemics, and similar factors that make a place difficult or inadvisable to sell. Since a destination's touristic climate can change abruptly, we suggest that you consult Foreign Affairs Canada. Telephone 800-267-6788 or visit the Foreign Affairs website at www.dfait-maeci.gc.ca.

WHO SHOULD USE THIS TEXT

Selling Destinations is a geography book for those who sell, or who plan to sell, places. At first glance, it may seem to be primarily a study or reference work for travel counsellors, and it is certainly that. *But it will prove equally useful to you even if you're in another segment of the travel industry,* for two reasons. First, you need to know how travel agents deal with geography, since you depend on their ability to sell. Second, everyone in the travel industry, in one way or another, sells places. The insights and strategies that this book gives can be used by anyone who deals with the travelling public: travel supplier reservationists, travel agents, tour guides, sales representatives, cruise directors, corporate travel managers, and more.

HOW TO LEARN AS MUCH AS YOU POSSIBLY CAN

Learning about travel destinations is fun! But all those names . . .

Here are a few clues on how you can do your best when studying from *Selling Destinations*. One reminder: If your textbook is owned by your school, *you must not write in it*. If you yourself bought it, however, feel free to use all of the study strategies you're about to learn. Then keep your book for future reference. Consider it an investment. It'll be an extremely valuable resource in your work and, certainly, when you're planning your own future travels.

1. **Use the margins** to write comments, insights, reminders, and extra things your instructor tells you about.

2. **Fill out all the activities.** They're designed to help you reinforce and remember what you're learning.

3. **Use coloured highlighters** to underscore what you have trouble remembering. Key concepts are already boldfaced or italicized, so you have a head start. But using, say, yellow to highlight difficult concepts and blue to indicate things you're really having trouble with is a great way to study.

4. **Use index cards** to review. Imagine a question that could appear on a test and put it on one side of the card. Put the answer on the other side. Then shuffle the cards and use them to review. Put aside the cards you have trouble with and come back to them later.

TO THE INSTRUCTOR OR TRAINER

If you're new to *Selling Destinations*, welcome! You're now part of a family of over 400 educators who rely on our textbook to bring students and trainees up to speed on travel geography. If you've taught from *Selling Destinations'* first three editions, you'll notice some changes. We've retained what you've told us are the strongest features of our book while reshaping its voice to speak to the needs of all future travel professionals—not just travel agents. In this way, we can help you to better adjust to the swiftly changing landscape of travel education.

Selling Destinations—a combined textbook/workbook—was created with your pragmatic needs in mind. It can serve as your primary textbook; the many features listed above make it extremely effective when you're dealing with students or trainees who must round out their chequered knowledge of world geography. Or it may be used as a sales-application supplement to more conventional texts. It's well suited to compressed, one-semester geography programs, yet it lends itself easily to programs with multiple geography courses and even online distance-learning applications. As we mentioned, *Selling Destinations* works equally well for those of you who teach travel generically (for *all* travel career segments) and those who focus mostly on travel agent skills.

To further encourage your flexibility in using this book, each chapter is independent from the others. You can present chapters in whatever order you prefer. Note that "Part" sections, however, set the stage for what's to come and are therefore less adaptable to shifting.

A feature that will be especially useful to you is the *Instructional Resource Manual*, which amplifies the book and makes your teaching much easier. Among its contents: a set of behavioural objectives, teaching tips, answers to all textbook activities, supplementary research activities, blank maps for reproducing and for quizzing students, and an extensive test bank.

Information given in this textbook has been cross-checked against multiple sources, all of which are cited in the appendixes. Whenever possible, firsthand experience—that of the author or of various destination experts—has been used to buttress content. If you spot any changes or additions you feel should be made—an important new attraction, a changed hotel name, etc.—please send your comment to Dr. Marc Mancini at West Los Angeles College, 9000 Overland Ave., Culver City, CA 90230, USA. If we use it, we'll be pleased to credit you in our next edition.

ACKNOWLEDGMENTS

The author would like to thank Dawn Aitken of Humber College, whose diligent and thoughtful comments helped shape this Fourth Canadian Edition. Additional thanks go to Dawn for her outstanding work on the PowerPoint slides and the website that accompany this text.

And a special thanks to my research assistants, Robert J. Elisberg and Rob Kwortnik (first edition), and Karen Fukushima (first through fourth editions), for their efficient, thorough, and enthusiastic support throughout this project, as well as to Justus Ghormley for his wonderful photographs.

Marc Mancini

BASIC INGREDIENTS
Geography and How to Sell It

Here's a surprise: If you're in the travel business, you don't really sell travel. What you sell is *geography.* For example, if someone flies on a specific flight at a certain time and price, yes, they've bought *travel. They're going from one place to another.* But the act of travelling in an aircraft holds little pleasure. No, the reason that person is travelling is to get to a place, and places are what geography is all about.

To perform any travel-related sales job in a professional manner, you must be aware of at least some aspects of the places that travellers favour. Corporate travel managers; incentive operators; convention and meeting planners; tourist bureau representatives; hotel sales, marketing, and reservation staff; tour planners; cruise personnel; and airline employees—they all have to know their geography to do their job right.

The most obvious sellers of destinations are travel agents. That's why this book often examines the world through their eyes. But even if you're not a travel agent, you still need to know how they deal with geography, for virtually every person who serves the travel industry—including hospitality professionals—is somehow affected by how travel agents sell.

No matter what segment of the industry you're in, though, you'll profit enormously from a deep and lasting familiarity with the world you sell, the kind that the following chapters will give you. And don't forget that word *sell.* The object is not simply to inform people about a destination, which is worthwhile in itself, but to motivate them to *buy* that destination—with their hearts as well as with their wallets.

BASIC CONCEPTS OF DESTINATION

Selling a place is an art. It requires knowledge of the destination *and* of the traveller. The following five strategies will help you maximize your ability to sell a place.

1. You Must Know All the Relevant Facts about a Destination

Travel geography differs from all other forms of geography in this way: It concentrates on those features about a destination that affect travel and tourism. To know that people in Burundi speak Kirundi, that one of Burkina Faso's principal crops is groundnuts, and that Saskatchewan is Canada's leading producer of

The typical North American vacations with three other people for three days and three nights.

In 1970, women represented 1 percent of all business travellers. They now account for half.

Agawam, Massachusetts, has the United States' lowest zip code: 01001.

wheat may make you more culturally literate and certainly a winner at Trivial Pursuit. But will this knowledge help you in the travel industry? Probably not. The likelihood is very low that anyone will ever ask you about Kirundi, ground-nuts, or wheat. (For that matter, it's improbable that you'll ever encounter anyone going to Burundi or to Burkina Faso.)

On the other hand, to know that many Swedes speak English, that at least six Niagara Falls hotels now offer Falls-view rooms (all of them are on the Canadian side), and that opals are a good buy in Sydney *are* useful geography-related facts. Climate, transportation options, itinerary routings, hotel locations, and key attractions—these are things you need to know to motivate people's interests, to help shape their travel experience, and to sell and serve them effectively and well.

2. You Must Know What Kind of Traveller Favours a Destination

What's the biggest mistake that travel professionals make? To believe that what they like everyone else will like. Maybe you're the type of person who adores classical music, but hates lying on the beach. So you favour such destinations as Vienna and Milan, but not Hawaii or the Caribbean. After all, doesn't everyone enjoy a concert by the Vienna Boys' Choir or an opera at Milan's La Scala? No. Each place attracts its own type of visitor. Matching destination with traveller type is the key to a sensitive, efficient, and profitable sale.

How many "types" of travellers are there? What motivates them to travel? There are countless ways to slice the tourist "pie." One way is to separate them into **leisure** travellers (those who travel for pleasure) and **business** travellers. You can further subdivide each of these broad categories. Business travellers, for example, may go somewhere to attend a convention or to conduct business and may add on a vacation component to their trip.

Tourists whose primary motivation is leisure in turn can be subdivided into many types. One approach categorizes leisure travellers into 12 groups:

- **History buffs** primarily want to learn about a destination's past. They see travel as a way to experience what they've studied and read about.

- **Culture seekers** are fascinated by different ways of life. They're intrigued by how other people express their culture via distinctive customs, food, art, and so on.

- **Ethnic travellers** are like culture seekers, but they wish, above all, to explore the culture from which their ancestors came.

- **Religious pilgrims** seek an experience tied to their spiritual beliefs.

- **Environmental travellers** are drawn to scenery and the beauty of places and include two important subsets: ecotourists, who wish to see places, such as the Brazilian rain forest, where flora and fauna are endangered; and campers, who like to experience a natural place (though it might be from a well-insulated RV).

- **Recreational travellers** wish to participate in such "mass-appeal" sports as golf, tennis, snorkelling, or skiing.

- **Adventure seekers** prefer more demanding and hardy sports or activities, such as whitewater rafting, surfing, mountain hiking, or diving—frequently in off-the-beaten-path locations. Their tastes can even run to true physical challenges, such as mountain climbing or skydiving. This is called "hard" adventure travel, in contrast to more mainstream "soft" adventure tourism.

- **Entertainment seekers** are drawn to activities such as dancing, partying, gambling, and nightclub shows. Their tastes can also run to more "serious" entertainment, such as theatre and concert performances.

According to a Plog study, the four factors that make a destination a success are scenic beauty; warm, predictable weather; lots to do; and friendly, helpful people.

If forced to choose, most business executives would rather keep their vacation time than get a 10 percent salary raise.

About 25 percent of domestic business travellers add a leisure component to their trip. It's even higher for international travellers: 40 to 50 percent.

- **Shoppers** love to buy things on trips, and are perhaps a subset of the previous categories, since they view purchasing as entertainment or adventure.

- **Sensual travellers** wish to indulge their senses via, say, gourmet dining, sun-bathing, or a stay at a spa.

- **Status seekers** travel to trendy, often expensive destinations, and sometimes bring back significant purchases. They define themselves—both to themselves and to others—by the places they visit.

- **Interpersonal travellers** voyage primarily to socialize and meet people. An important subcategory is people who travel to visit family and friends—and often stay with them. This motivation accounts for the largest number of personal trips.

As you read this listing, did you think of a place that fits each kind of traveller? Did you think of someone you know who is the type described? Good, you're already thinking like a true travel professional. And did you imagine individuals who combine the traits of several or many categories? Great, because most people do travel for multiple reasons, even though one primary motivator may control their destination choices.

> To try your hand at matching traveller types to destinations, turn to the end of this chapter and do Activity 1.

3. You Must Know the Individual Client You Are Serving

Now imagine that you are, say, a travel agent. You do understand what kind of client favours a place. But are you able to identify that type of client when he or she comes to you for advice? In sales, the act of analyzing a client's needs and wants is called **qualifying** or **interviewing.** This is usually achieved by asking open-ended questions, called **probes.** Asking the right questions and listening carefully to the client's answer is the key to effective qualifying.

What kind of questions will you ask? At first, of course, you must determine the basics, such as traveller name, possible destinations, dates, budget restrictions, and so on. But then, you can probe, for example, to find out what the person does for a living. That might provide a clue. A university history professor might really enjoy the idea of going to Europe, but an Orlando vacation might leave him or her cold. Other possible probes: "Is your trip for business or pleasure?" (Business clients usually have much more focused travel plans.) "Are you an active outdoor person?" "Do you like adventurous places?" "Is this a family vacation?" "What was your favourite vacation and why?" A good way to probe is via contrasting questions: "Do you want to rest on your vacation or be active?" "Do you want to visit someplace exotic or a more familiar kind of culture?"

Note that such questions help you determine what traveller type you're dealing with—an essential step to match the person's needs with your recommendations. Failing to do so can lead to a mismatch—something sure to lead to dissatisfaction, complaints, or worse.

Qualifying isn't a skill used only by travel agents. Cruise, air, and tour reservationists often must clarify a caller's destination needs. Tourist bureau personnel are constantly assessing which offerings will appeal to potential visitors to the destinations they represent. Hotel concierges must recommend all sorts of destination-related experiences; the best ones ask hotel guests plenty of questions before "selling" their recommendation.

Thirty-eight percent of couples said they're more romantic on vacation than when they're at home.

A billion people will travel outside of their own country in 2010, according to the World Tourism Organization.

The world's deepest mine is Savuka, near Johannesburg, South Africa. Miners venture down 3.8 kilometres in search of gold.

Several other points bear discussion:

- Don't expect people who are thinking about a vacation to know exactly where they want to go. One study concluded that half of all travellers start out with only the vaguest idea of where to spend their vacation. The others do have a rather specific destination in mind, but they hope that you'll bring efficiency, quality, and insight to their trip.

- A person's primary motivation can change from one trip to the next. On one vacation, Mr. Jones may want to visit every major museum in Europe, but on the next, he'll want to kick back at an isolated beach resort.

- Always review travellers' needs with them before going on to make your recommendations. This tests whether you understand their needs and permits them to add to their list.

- When recommending, explicitly describe how a destination satisfies the person's wishes. It's not enough to say, "The Cayman Islands is where I think you should go." Put it this way: "You wanted to do some diving, not travel too far, and go in April. The Caymans have great diving, are only a two-hour flight away, and usually have great weather in April."

- Your recommendations should also convey a sense that you know the place intimately. Travellers realize that a travel professional can't have visited every place on the globe. But they do hope that in the absence of actual experience, you still "know your stuff" and have the equivalent of firsthand experience.

- Sprinkling little "insider tips" into your recommendations will help establish you as the professional that you are.

4. You Must Be Ready to Respond to a Person's Misgivings

Your descriptions of a place may be so powerful that closing the sale will be easy. But sometimes matching a person to a place isn't enough. Fears, either rational or emotional, may stand in the way: "A trip to Tokyo sounds great, but how will I be able to communicate with the Japanese?" "I'd like to go to New York City, but isn't it awfully expensive?" "An African wildlife safari sounds wonderful, but isn't it dangerous?"

Faced with such objections, a travel professional, when appropriate, provides sales-building responses, or **counters.** You should tell someone who worries about communicating in Japan that many of Tokyo's tourist-industry personnel speak some English. You can recommend less expensive hotels or weekend hotel packages to New York–bound travellers. An African wildlife safari is less intimidating if you counsel someone to travel as part of a tour offered by a reputable tour operator.

To allay misgivings isn't always the proper approach. Sometimes the objections a person brings up are so valid—say, the country really is too dangerous or is totally inappropriate in some other way—that you must say so and counter with a completely different destination. To simply dismiss an objection without thought is unprofessional and unethical, and could even trigger a lawsuit later on.

5. You Must Search for Enhancement Opportunities

Three general strategies permit you to enhance your company's profits from someone's trip, as well as enhance the traveller's experience. They're especially used in travel agency, car rental, lodging, and cruise sales environments:

- **Up-selling** allows you to improve the quality of the traveller's vacation while generally increasing your profits. Some examples: superior-category hotel rooms, first-class seats on a flight, a full-size car rental instead of a compact one, a more extensive **FIT** for a client. (FIT stands for foreign independent travel, but it often refers to any itinerary created from scratch, not just foreign

The coldest temperature reading ever taken—minus 89 degrees Celsius—was recorded in 1983 at Russia's Vostok Ice Station in Antarctica.

Rand McNally's first products were maps for bicyclists and railroad passengers.

ones.) Always start by recommending the best product that is reasonably appropriate to a person's needs, then work down. To start with budget recommendations and work up is a poor sales and service approach. Effective up-selling also is very much tied to geographic factors. For example, a hotel's appeal may come from its proximity to prime attractions, or to the ocean views its rooms afford (both geographic factors). Also, a person is far more likely to be tempted by a convertible car rental if the destination's weather is warm and inviting.

- **Cross-selling** requires you to offer "extra" products or services. For example, people often contact a travel agent only to book a flight. They haven't thought about anything else; they may even wait until they get to their destination to set up other services. This deprives the agent and the agency of potential income and the client of possible savings or convenience. Good travel agents offer to book hotels, car rentals, train trips, theatre tickets, city tours, meal plans, boat charters, travel insurance, airport-to-hotel transfers, and whatever else seems appropriate. They underscore the benefits of these services to their client's vacation plans. And they point out the advantage of booking these things in advance.

  Cross-selling is much simpler than it used to be: Computers now allow access to all sorts of services. Further, **all-inclusive packages**—combinations of services that can be booked with one call—have made cross-selling easy. Independent tour packages, escorted tours, all-inclusive resorts, and cruises enable agencies to draw profits from virtually everything their clients do—including eat and drink.

- **Follow-up** conversations with customers enable companies and their employees to find out how a trip went. This follow-up often yields geographically relevant insights. Follow-up surveys and client feedback enable cruise lines to rethink their itineraries, tour operators to identify hot new destinations, and airlines to apply for new routes.

  Let's say you're a travel agent. Follow-up will help you deepen your own destination knowledge. For example, a client could return from St. Martin and tell you that he couldn't get around the island without renting a car. In the future, you'll know to recommend a car rental to a St. Martin–bound tourist. Follow-up also cements the client–seller relationship, offers an opportunity to make amends for problems experienced during the trip, and opens the door to selling future trips to the client.

Are cross-selling, up-selling, and a follow-up sale manipulative? They can be, but only when you pressure someone into buying something he or she doesn't want or shouldn't have. Travellers often have vague, low, or unrealistic limits on what they want. Your job is to focus their plans, suggest ways to genuinely improve their vacation, and perhaps even save them a few dollars (since services arranged in advance or as part of a package are often less costly).

How Other Travel Professionals Sell Places

The five sales and service tactics we've examined primarily address the needs of a travel agent. But if you're contemplating some other career in the industry, these sales techniques will work for you, too:

- A cruise activities director may recommend and sell shore excursion tours.

- Airline reservationists can up-sell a caller to the comfort of business class on a long overseas flight.

- A car rental representative can suggest a convertible for the client's tropical vacation.

- A hotel clerk or concierge can make shopping, restaurant, and nightlife arrangements for the hotel guest.

A 0.77 kilogram hailstone fell on Kansas in 1970.

Fifty-two percent of travellers pick the restaurants they will eat in before arriving at their destination.

- Flight attendants often answer questions about that flight's destination or explain the many places where their airline flies (a key consideration for members of frequent-flyer programs).

- A tour conductor relates all sorts of facts about the destinations that the tour group will visit.

- An incentive trip planner can show corporate clients how certain add-on activities will enhance their employees' experience.

- A representative from a convention and tourist bureau can show an audience how the destination fulfills their expectations.

- A hotel's sales and marketing director must promote the geographic benefits of staying at his or her property: ocean-view rooms, proximity to attractions or businesses, easy access to public transportation, closeness to trails at a ski resort, etc.

- Even professionals in the food services industry must think about geography. Location is one of the key elements of whether a theme restaurant (e.g., Planet Hollywood) will succeed or fail.

So, the ultimate purpose of both sales and service in the travel field is this: to create the perfect match between the desires of a traveller and the assets of a place. But to do this, you must not only love places but also know them.

GEOGRAPHY—THE GREAT UNKNOWN

A 2600-year-old Babylonian tablet may be the oldest map of the world—or at least as much of the world as the Babylonians knew about.

Gil Grosvenor, chairman of the National Geographic Society, tells of a couple who once told him that they might be taking a cruise to Las Vegas (a desert-bound city). Writer S. J. Perelman relates that he once told a student that, on graduating from college, she should travel around the world. Her response: "I know, but there are so many places I'd rather see first!" Travel agents make embarrassing mistakes, too. A traveller was once found wandering around the airport in Oakland, California, asking where the New Zealand immigration officials were. His travel agent had mistakenly booked him on a flight to Oakland, instead of Auckland, his intended destination.

A *USA Today* poll discovered that one in seven Americans can't find the United States on a world map. One in five is unable to identify a single country on a map of Europe. One in four can't find the Pacific Ocean, even though it covers one-third of the surface of the earth.

In the late 18th century, England's Captain Cook became the first European to "discover" Hawaii. Yet a 17th-century Spanish map shows volcanic islands in the Pacific, just about where Hawaii lies. There's no record of any Spanish ship ever visiting there before Cook. The map remains a mystery.

No such poll has been taken among Canadians, but we can surmise that the results would be similar. To be living in this century and to be ignorant of the world is a shameful indictment of any nation's education system. But to be a travel professional and not to know geography is something else. Would you trust a physician who didn't know anatomy, a builder who didn't know how to read blueprints, or a bank teller who didn't understand math? Should the general public trust travel professionals who can't read maps, who don't know that summer comes to Australia in December, or who book clients bound for the nation of Colombia to the city of Columbia, South Carolina? That has happened, too.

But you can make a difference. You can decide to know the world you sell. And it starts right now with a commitment to understand the underpinnings of travel geography itself.

The Kinds of Maps

Maps are the blueprints of travel. Dozens of types of maps exist; here are the ones travel professionals work with the most:

FLAT MAPS. Standard flat maps are those we're most familiar with. They come in many varieties, with the "Mercator projection" (see Figure I-1) the most commonly used.

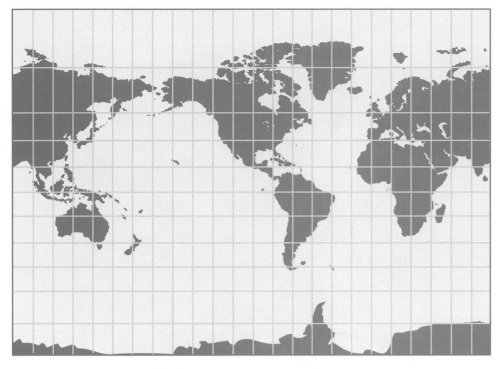

Figure I-1   Mercator Projection

Because you can't flatten out the curved earth, flat maps are somewhat distorted, especially when the whole world is displayed; extreme northern and southern areas may become grossly magnified. In Figure I-1, a typical map, Greenland appears to be the same size as South America. In reality, South America is more than eight times larger than Greenland. A way to remember: Maps that can lie flat, lie (i.e., they're inaccurate).

Flat maps mislead in a second way. If you draw a trip on such a map as a straight line—which seems logical—you'll be making a big mistake. On most flat maps, the shortest distance between two geographic points should be traced out as a *curved* line (often called a "great circle route" and always arcing toward polar regions). For example, the shortest route from Los Angeles to Cairo might appear, on a flat map, to be on Alitalia Airlines via Rome or Paris. But if you look at a polar projection map (see Figure I-2 on p. 10) or trace the route on a globe, you'll see that going on Finnair via Helsinki will be a bit shorter. Another surprise: From New York, the shortest way to Bangkok, Singapore, and Beijing is via Helsinki. So when looking at world maps, remember that curved routes are usually the most direct.

ROUTE MAPS. These are useful reference tools. Each airline often distributes a map that shows all the routes that it flies. This can be a handy visual aid if you're trying to keep a traveller on one airline for a trip, either for fare reasons or to help build up frequent-flyer miles. CAA also produces superb route maps, including some that give driving times between major cities.

GLOBES. Even though globes are awkward to use and lack detail, they're the most accurate maps around. Keep one handy. They're fun to play with and often help you plot out itineraries.

LOCATOR MAPS. These are often found in travel industry reference sources. Usually representing a small area, such as a city, they help you find the locations of attractions and hotels. Locator maps indicate places through a grid of numbers and letters rather than with the degrees of a conventional map (see Figure I-3 on p. 11).

MENTAL MAPS. A mental map represents the way you picture geography in your mind. Mental maps can be deceiving: The farther away a destination is, the more

For centuries, mapmakers and mathematicians struggled to determine how many colours were needed on a map so that no two countries with the same colour "touched." The answer to this math question was recently determined: four.

Each year, 20 000 pieces of luggage are lost by the airlines and never claimed. Most end up in a warehouse in Scottsboro, Alabama.

Figure I-2   Polar Routes
Source: Courtesy of Finnair

simple, closer together, and error prone the mental map becomes. For instance, people who have never been to Europe may think they can drive around to see most of its major cities in a week or two, that Paris is a day's drive from Rome, that a cruise on the Danube takes only a few days. In reality, Europe is bigger than Canada, Rome is more than 1500 kilometres from Paris, and the Danube is so long that most cruises last more than a week. For a well-known, amusing illustration of what a distant place seems like mentally, see Figure I-4.

Other Map Considerations

Several other map-related components have an impact on a travel professional's sales experience.

 Death Valley, 400 kilometres east of Los Angeles, recorded a temperature of 57°C on July 10, 1913.

HEMISPHERES. Everything north of the equator is called the Northern Hemisphere, and everything south, the Southern Hemisphere (see Figure I-5 on p. 12). Seasons

Figure I-3   Locator Map: San Juan, Puerto Rico

Source: Hotel and Travel Index/Reed Travel Group

Figure I-4   A Perspective

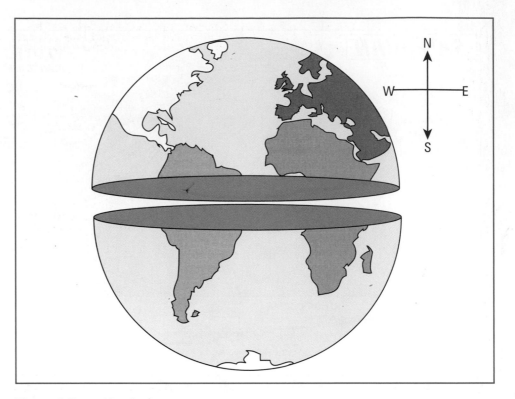

Figure I-5   Hemispheres

in the **Northern Hemisphere** are familiar to us: January comes in winter, and July in summer. But in the **Southern Hemisphere,** January has summer weather, July, winter weather. When selling travellers a Southern Hemisphere destination, keep these reversed seasons in mind. Remember, too, that the world is also often divided into a **Western Hemisphere** (North and South America) and an **Eastern Hemisphere** (everything else).

LATITUDE. Latitude is the distance measured north and south of the equator (expressed in standard geography as *degrees*). The farther away from the equator your destination, the greater the variations will be between seasonal temperatures and between hours of night and day.

For example, **Auyuittuq National Park** on Baffin Island, at a **polar latitude,** might be an intriguing destination for some in June and July. Why? Because that's when temperatures there are warmest and daylight is longest. Indeed, the summer midnight sun is a unique experience. But December and January would be a terrible time for such a visit, for darkness and bitter cold prevail. Remember that these seasonal days are exactly the opposite in the Southern Hemisphere. A trip to Antarctica, an exotic and increasingly popular journey, would be best in December or January, worst in June or July.

As one gets closer to the equator, seasonal and daylight differences become less pronounced. For instance, Nairobi, Kenya (in Africa), sits just south of the equator. Unlike Auyuittuq, where the average temperatures fluctuate more than 40°C between summer and winter, Nairobi—at a **tropical latitude**—sees a yearly fluctuation of only about 5°C and minimal variation of daylight. Areas between tropical and polar latitudes are called **temperate latitudes** and have neither pronounced nor minimal variations. Because of the absence of extremes, most major industrialized nations lie within this temperate zone.

By the way, most maps represent latitude lines (also known as parallels) as horizontal lines, measured in degrees. A good memory trick: LATitude lines are FLAT.

The earth's magnetic north pole (where compass needles point) is in Canada, about 1300 kilometres away from the actual North Pole. It also drifts constantly, moving about 16 kilometres per year.

Because of the angle of the sun's light, dusk and dawn near the equator are shorter than elsewhere.

Figure I-6   Time Zones

LONGITUDE. Longitude is the distance east and west of an arbitrary line, called the **prime meridian,** which passes through the Old Royal Observatory in Greenwich, England. Represented as vertical lines on most maps, longitude lines (like latitudes) are measured in degrees. Longitude will have less of an impact on your selling destinations, except in one respect: Time zones tend to parallel longitude lines (also known as meridians). Before the late 1800s, each city had its own time, determined by the sun-caused shadows on a sundial. Railroads found it next to impossible to create accurate schedules or timetables. So, in 1884, the world's major nations agreed to create 24 standard time zones, each extending over about 15 degrees of longitude (see Figure I-6). Because the prime meridian is located there, Greenwich became the reference point (called Greenwich Mean Time, or GMT). If it's 1 p.m. in Greenwich, it's five hours earlier, that is, 8 a.m., in Ottawa (expressed as –5); conversely, in Tokyo, it's 10 p.m. (expressed as +9).

Time zones aren't all that regular. For example, China—even though it extends through four theoretical time zones—observes only one time, that closest to Beijing, the capital. In other places, the zone's boundaries zig and zag around cities, islands, lakes, or mountains. India should have two time zones, but has averaged the two together. Instead of being, say, two o'clock in the west and three o'clock in the east, it's *two-thirty* across the entire country. Daylight savings time, when clocks are set forward to extend daylight into evening hours, complicates things even more. (Most of Saskatchewan, Arizona, Hawaii, and parts of Indiana don't even observe daylight savings time.)

A trip that crosses many time zones creates that tired feeling called **jet lag** and could affect the traveller in many other ways. A flight from Vancouver to Montreal takes about five hours, but the passenger, because of the time zones, arrives at a time that's about eight hours later. For example, a passenger leaving Vancouver at noon flies five hours and arrives at 8 p.m., Montreal time. That's why business travellers often book a morning departure for an eastward transcontinental flight; otherwise, they'd arrive at their destination late in the evening. For westbound

Russia is the world's largest country. It spans 11 time zones.

Canada spans six time zones: GMT –8 to GMT –3.5.

Figure I-7   International Date Line

travel, the problem is less severe: Someone leaving Montreal for Vancouver could depart at 1:30 p.m., fly for about five hours, yet arrive at 3:30 p.m., Vancouver time. Because it stretches out their workday, many business travellers count on this.

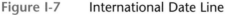

The International Date Line is on the opposite side of the earth from the prime meridian.

THE INTERNATIONAL DATE LINE. A rather challenging bit of time zone figuring involves the International Date Line, a vertical zigzagging line that bisects the Pacific Ocean (see Figure I-7). Crossing it requires a bit of complicated thinking, often expressed as "gaining a day" or "losing a day." Remember the following and you won't be bewildered: (1) When you cross the date line travelling westward, the day changes to the next day—for example, Tuesday, say, at 2 p.m. immediately becomes Wednesday at 2 p.m.; and (2) when you cross the line travelling eastward, the day changes to the previous day—Thursday becomes Wednesday, for example. The time of the day (except at midnight) means nothing. A traveller could cross at 2 p.m., 7 a.m., or 10 a.m. It's all the same. The day changes (but the hour remains the same).

Let's look at an example. Passengers flying from Vancouver westward to Tokyo on a Monday morning departure would arrive after about a nine-hour flight. But it would be Tuesday, because they crossed the date line. In turn, if they flew from Tokyo on a Saturday morning, they would arrive in Vancouver on Friday, again because they crossed the date line, this time west to east.

Because the flight is long and many time zones are crossed, the complications can be even greater. If you were to leave Vancouver for Tokyo at 11 p.m. on Wednesday, it would become Thursday an hour after departure, and you haven't even crossed the date line yet. A little later, you would cross the date line (on Thursday), at which point it would become Friday! So, you left on Wednesday and arrived on Friday, even though you flew only nine hours.

Confused? Don't worry. Airline schedules give arrival times that are already adjusted for time-zone crossings and for lost or gained days (indicated by some sort of symbol next to the time). If you're an airline reservationist or a travel agent, you won't have to do the complicated equations. But *do* make sure that you know which day the passenger will be arriving, or you may book his or her hotel stay for the wrong day.

ELAPSED FLYING TIME AND THE 24-HOUR CLOCK. One thing people often ask isn't always given in airline timetables: How long will a flight take? First, you must understand that time in the travel business is often expressed as a four-digit number: 7:00 a.m. is

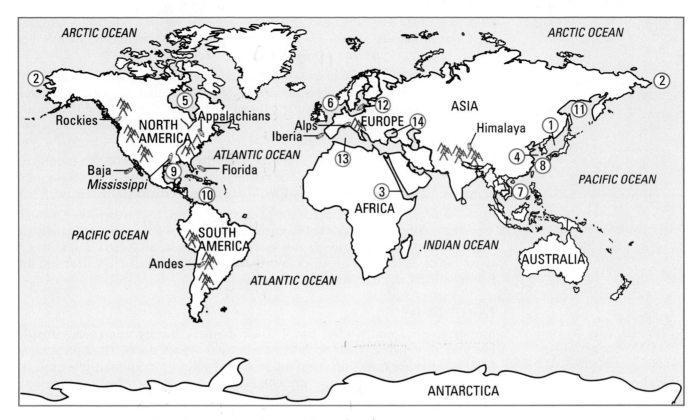

Figure I-8   Landforms and Waterways of the World: 1—Sea of Japan; 2—Bering Sea; 3—Red Sea; 4—Yellow Sea; 5—Hudson Bay; 6—North Sea; 7—South China Sea; 8—East China Sea; 9—Gulf of Mexico; 10—Caribbean; 11—Sea of Okhotsk; 12—Baltic Sea; 13—Mediterranean Sea; 14—Black Sea

0700, 11:25 a.m. is 1125, noon is 1200. Afternoon and evening continue up to the digit 24: 1:00 p.m. is 1300, 7:30 p.m. is 1930, midnight is 2400 (or 0000, to represent the beginning of the day).

To figure out elapsed flying time within one time zone, simply subtract the departure time of a flight from the arrival time. If a flight leaves Paris at 0800 and arrives in Lyon at 0900, the flight took one hour. If a plane leaves Edmonton at 1210 and lands in Yellowknife at 1345, the flight took one hour, 35 minutes.

What happens when time zones are crossed? Then it gets a bit more difficult, adding or subtracting the number of time zones. Many travel reference resources give charts that enable you to figure out complex elapsed flying-time problems. Fortunately, airline reservation systems compute elapsed flying time automatically.

Landforms

All destinations relate, in some way, to a landform. Let's now look at the principal landforms and how they're linked to the destinations you may deal with.

CONTINENTS. Continents are the major landmasses of the earth (see Figure I-8). There are seven continents. (Some people argue that there are only six; they think of Europe and Asia as one continent, *Eurasia*.) You'll likely deal most with **North America** and **Europe,** but **Asia, Australia, South America,** and **Africa** all boast destinations you may someday sell. Even **Antarctica** has become a destination for tourists via cruises from Chile, Argentina, and New Zealand.

ISLANDS. Because of their natural, isolated beauty, islands are often major destinations. Thousands of them cover the earth, but the most popular groupings are found in the **Caribbean,** in the **Mediterranean** (especially south and east of the Greek mainland), and throughout the Pacific (see Figure I-8).

Antarctica has the highest average altitude of any continent.

CAYS. Also called *keys,* cays are sandy coral islands that are low and small. Examples: the **Cayman Islands** and the **Florida Keys. Atolls** are also small coral islands, but they're usually ringlike and partially or totally enclose a lagoon.

PENINSULAS AND CAPES. Both of these are projections of land into the water. Generally, peninsulas are longer than capes. Among the peninsulas that are popular destinations are **Gaspé,** Quebec; **Baja,** Mexico; **Iberia** (which contains Spain and Portugal); and **Florida.** Some touristically important capes are **Cape Cod,** Massachusetts, and **Cape Canaveral,** Florida (see Figure I-8).

PANHANDLES. The term *panhandle* is often applied to a narrow portion of a country or state that "sticks out" into another. For example, Alaska's Panhandle extends southward into Canada and Florida's Panhandle protrudes westward into Alabama.

REEFS. Reefs are ridges of land that rise to or near the surface of water. They're often found just offshore. Composed of sand, rock, and coral, reefs can offer superb diving opportunities. Major reef diving and snorkelling areas lie off Australia's northeast coast; off the east coasts of Africa and Brazil; and throughout the Caribbean, the South Pacific, Indonesia, and the Philippines.

Mountains

Mountains profoundly affect travel. Their dramatic beauty impresses virtually every kind of visitor. Their snow-covered slopes attract skiers. Their forbidding heights can make travel slow and indirect. And volcanic mountains often put on quite a show (and pose an ever-present danger).

Mountains also affect climate. When moisture-bearing winds strike a mountain, precipitation often results at its peak and on its **windward** side. On the opposite side of the mountain, the **leeward** side, it's often much drier (see Figure I-9). For example, the winds that strike the Hawaiian Islands, and their volcanic peaks, generally come from the east and northeast. As a result, they create clouds, rain, and strong waves on the windward shores. On the other hand, most Hawaiian beach resorts are along the islands' western and southwestern shores, where it's most likely to be sunny. Another example: The westerly winds that flow into the Pacific Northwest often bring clouds and rain to Vancouver and Seattle—both of which are on the windward side of the Cascade Mountain Range. The area just east of these mountains (the leeward side) is more dry and sunny.

Figure I-9   Tropical Island Wind Patterns

There are all kinds of mountains: rugged ones, like North America's **Rockies,** Europe's **Alps,** South America's **Andes,** and Asia's **Himalaya;** old, worn-down ones, like the U.S. East Coast's **Appalachians;** and volcanic ones, like those of Hawaii, the Caribbean, Iceland, Central Africa, Japan, and the most volcanic nation of all: Indonesia.

Closely allied to a mountain is a **plateau.** A plateau is a broad, flat area that rises above the surrounding land and, because of its elevation, typically has cooler weather. (Mexico City is a prime example.) **Mesas** are smaller, steeper-sided versions of plateaux; **buttes** are even smaller, towerlike versions. The dramatic mesas and buttes of the American Southwest attract many tourists to that region's national parks.

Bodies of Water

Stop and think: Can you name one popular destination that's *not* near water? Not easy, is it? The majority of the places you'll sell are near bodies of water. It goes even beyond that. One example: Lodging's relationship with bodies of water usually affects pricing. A hotel right on Waikiki's beach sands can get much more money for its rooms than a hotel several blocks inland.

GULFS. Gulfs are large areas of ocean that penetrate into land. A good example is the **Gulf of Mexico. Bays** are similar to gulfs, but are generally smaller and less enclosed by land; **Chesapeake Bay,** in Virginia and Maryland, is an example. **Fjords** [FEE-YORDZ] are also inlets from the ocean or the sea; they are usually long, narrow, and lined with steep cliffs. The most dramatic ones notch into the coastlines of Norway, New Zealand, Chile, and Argentina.

Tourist sites are often associated with gulfs, bays, and fjords; beach resorts line the Gulf of Mexico's shores, and ships commonly cruise through the fjords of Norway.

RIVERS. Rivers provide significant cruise opportunities for you to sell. Currently, the most popular are North America's **Mississippi,** Europe's **Rhine** and **Danube,** Africa's **Nile,** and for the more adventurous, South America's **Amazon.** A **glacier** is

Ninety-seven percent of the earth's water is salt water.

Many glaciers are bluish. The reason: Refraction causes blue shades of light to be reflected off the ice, while all other colours are absorbed.

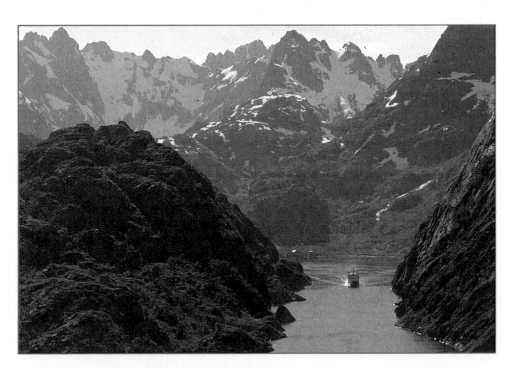

A Norwegian Coastal Voyage vessel passes through a fjord.
Courtesy of Norwegian Coastal Voyage

a sort of "river" of near-solid ice and compacted snow that flows very slowly down from high, cold places. In polar regions, a glacier may eventually tumble into the water, creating icebergs. Glaciers are often imposing tourist attractions, most notably in Canada, Alaska, Switzerland, Peru, and New Zealand. When a mass of ice sits, like a lake, over a broad area, it's called an **ice field.** The biggest ice fields (like those in Antarctica) are called **ice sheets.**

WATERFALLS. These dramatic cascades of water are magnets for tourists. Both **Niagara Falls** and Germany's **Rhine Falls** have been major attractions for centuries, while more remote ones—such as South America's **Iguazu Falls** and Africa's **Victoria Falls**—are becoming increasingly popular destinations.

People who intend to swim in the Dead Sea are warned not to shave. The sea's 33 percent salinity (ocean water is 3 percent) would cause stinging.

SEAS. Seas are large bodies of water, usually salty but sometimes fresh. They can be a region of water within an ocean, but usually some sort of land boundaries, such as islands or continental shoreline, partly or almost fully enclose a sea. Like gulfs, seas are often the site of resorts, cruises, and water-sport activities. Geographers count more than 50 seas. Among those most associated with tourism are the **Caribbean** and the **Mediterranean.**

The Great Lakes contain one-fifth of the world's fresh water.

LAKES. Lakes are smaller than seas, are usually fresh, and are mostly or fully encircled by land. They, too, often feature resort and recreation facilities. A few large saltwater lakes have been labelled seas, like the **Caspian Sea** and the **Dead Sea.**

LAGOONS. These are shallow bodies of water, generally separated from the ocean by reefs or barrier islands. Those in tropical areas often provide easy snorkelling opportunities.

BAYOUS. Bayous [BYE-yooz] are marshy or swampy areas. Those in Louisiana have become tourist attractions.

DELTAS. Deltas are the low, V-shaped areas at the mouths of rivers. Many important port cities, such as New Orleans (Louisiana) and Alexandria (Egypt) are located at deltas.

GEYSERS. Geysers are jets of steaming water that shoot high into the air. New Zealand, Iceland, and (in the United States) Yellowstone National Park have geysers that are tourist attractions.

SPRINGS. Springs occur where water flows naturally to the earth's surface. Spa resorts are often located near springs. One of the world's most famous spa resorts is Brenner's Park-Hotel & Spa in Baden-Baden, Germany.

Oceans

The Arctic is the world's smallest ocean.

These are the greatest bodies of water. There are four oceans: the **Atlantic,** the **Pacific,** the **Indian,** and the **Arctic** (refer back to Figure I-8). (It could be argued that there's only *one ocean:* All four oceans are connected and the boundaries among them are not clearly defined.) Ocean water sports, whether off a continental area (such as Florida) or around an island (such as Tahiti), attract many tourists.

One thing that's useful to those who sell travel is how to predict ocean water temperatures. This information isn't found in popular reference books or websites, yet tourists who look forward to swimming ask about it all the time. Three factors determine ocean water temperature: *season, latitude* (the nearer the equator, the warmer the ocean is likely to be), and *ocean currents.* This last factor is one of the hardest to predict. Yet knowing something about the Coriolis effect will help you make that prediction with greater confidence.

The **Coriolis effect,** among other things, makes oceans circulate in a clockwise fashion in the Northern Hemisphere and a counterclockwise manner in the Southern Hemisphere. The resulting currents enable water to pick up heat at the equator and carry it along; conversely, in the polar regions, the currents chill down and carry cold water away for some distance. If you look at Figure I-10 on p. 20, you'll see why ocean water off California is surprisingly cool, yet along the southeastern U.S. coast, it's comparatively warm. A significant variation: The shape of the north Atlantic permits warm water to flow along a **Gulf Stream** from

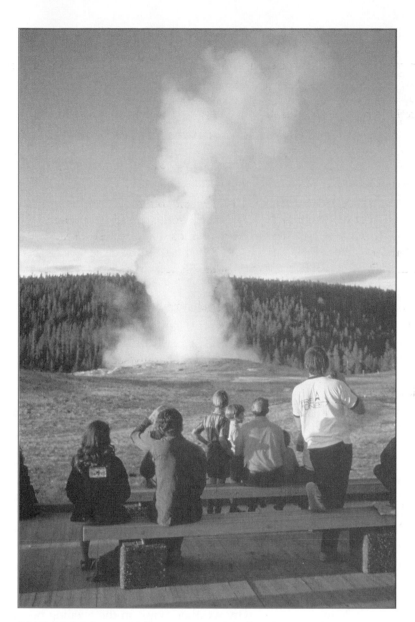

Old Faithful Geyser, Yellowstone National Park, Wyoming
Photo by Justus Ghormley

near the equator all the way to Great Britain. (That's one reason why London in the winter only occasionally gets really cold, while parts of Alaska and Canada, at the same latitude, are frozen.)

Generally, ocean water on the east coast of a continent tends to be warmer than ocean water on the west coast of that same continent. The water off, say, Australia's eastern Gold Coast resort area is much warmer than that off Perth, on Australia's western coast, though the two are only a few degrees different in latitude. That also explains why the water off the Galapagos Islands (which sit on the equator) is cooler than you'd expect. The northern-flowing currents carry water from the frigid Antarctic region.

Does the Coriolis effect determine temperatures in smaller bodies of water? Not really. The water temperatures of, say, the Mediterranean are governed largely by the seasons. Its water is chilly in the winter, but sunlight heats it up rapidly as summer approaches.

Two facts also worth knowing: (1) Seacoast locations have fewer extremes of temperature than those farther inland; and (2) regions that border cool ocean

About 80 percent of the earth's biggest earthquakes occur along the Pacific Rim.

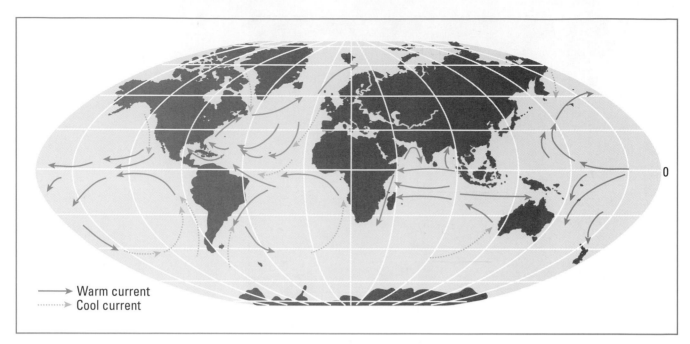

Warm current
······> Cool current

Figure I-10   Ocean Currents

currents (for example, California) tend to have a drier climate than those along warmer ocean waters (for example, Florida's east coast).

Winds

In 1934, a world's record wind speed of 370 km/h was recorded on Mt. Washington, New Hampshire.

The windiest city in the United States isn't Chicago, as many think, but Dodge City, Kansas.

The jet stream was not discovered until jet aircraft began flying at high altitudes.

Winds are among the most unpredictable of the geographically related events. If you've ever sailed a boat, you know that firsthand. But there are general earthwide patterns, especially for the prevailing winds that stream above the capricious surface breezes (see Figure I-11). Following are some of the major wind flows that affect the destinations a travel professional deals with.

THE WESTERLIES. The westerlies are winds that tend to blow around the globe from west to east in temperate areas between 30 and 60 degrees latitude, both in the Northern and Southern Hemispheres. Canada, the United States, and Europe lie within this belt. Now you know why weather maps on the evening news display weather flowing from west to east.

If you have cable TV, watch the Weather Network for 30 minutes. You'll be surprised at how many of the concepts you've just read about are referred to. How do the westerlies affect travel? First, the high-altitude, high-velocity core of these westerlies, the **jet stream,** is responsible for making east-to-west flights take longer. (A flight from Montreal to Vancouver, for example, takes at least 40 minutes longer than one from Vancouver to Montreal.) Second, western coastal regions, mostly within a 40-to-60-degree belt, tend to be rainier than eastern coastal regions, especially where mountains are involved. Some examples of regions with rainy west coasts: British Columbia, Oregon, Washington State, the Alaskan Panhandle, southern Chile, Ireland, Portugal, Croatia, and New Zealand.

Terrain, ocean temperatures, seasons, and many other factors conspire to create many exceptions to the above. To determine the rainfall patterns for key destinations, consult the "Climate at a Glance" charts sprinkled throughout the book.

THE TRADE WINDS. The trade winds are humid breezes that tend to flow from east to west. These winds are most pronounced in the tropical band between about 25 degrees north and 25 degrees south. North of the equator, trade winds often come from the northeast instead of the east, and south of the equator, they frequently come from the southeast. For complicated reasons, much of Africa and some tropical parts of Asia (especially India) don't always follow the east-to-west trade wind pattern.

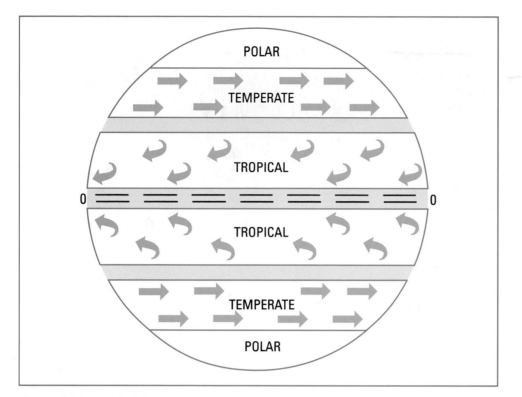

Figure I-11   Wind Patterns

But it does hold for Central and South America, for a good part of Australia, and especially for tropical islands.

When a tropical island is mountainous, the western coast is almost always leeward and therefore drier. This is where you should lodge visitors (refer back to Figure I-9). Because there are no mountains to squeeze the rain from the trade winds, flat islands are usually breezy and relatively dry. (A good example is Aruba, a flat coral island in the Caribbean.)

Storms

Storms often disrupt travel plans. Sometimes you can know when they're more likely to occur and thus recommend the best time to visit certain destinations.

HURRICANES. Hurricanes are among the earth's most violent storms. Usually born near the equator, hurricanes migrate in rather unpredictable patterns (see Figure I-12 on p. 22). They can cover hundreds of square kilometres with high winds (120 km/h or above) and heavy rains for a day or two in one place before moving on. When they're born near the Caribbean or Mexico, they're called hurricanes; when they originate in the western Pacific, they're called **typhoons.** The southward-heading ones around Australia and in the Indian Ocean are called **cyclones,** the official generic name for all such storms.

Hurricanes generally occur from June to November in the Northern Hemisphere, with about 80 percent of them coming in August, September, and October. (Of course, hurricane season brings not only the chance of vacation-damaging storms, but also bargain rates.) Cyclones almost never affect Europe, South America (except occasionally on its Caribbean shoreline), Africa (except for the region around Madagascar and Mozambique), or the western coast of Canada and the United States. Hurricanes also rarely maintain strength if they move far inland over a continent; instead, they degenerate into large rainstorms.

MONSOONS. Each year around summertime in certain parts of the world, winds reverse in such a way as to cause a lengthy, distinct, and heavy rainy season. This monsoon condition can dampen anybody's trip. India has torrential monsoon

On average, 1.6 hurricanes reach the United States each year.

Figure I-12   Hurricane Areas

rains from June to September; China's less intense season comes from May to September; and Korea sees quite a bit of rain in July and August. Northern Australia, Indonesia, and Singapore have monsoon-like conditions from December through March, whereas the south-facing parts of west Africa have a monsoon weather pattern from May to October.

Cloudbursts. Cloudbursts are heavy showers that occur suddenly. They're a major factor in the tropics. A typical pattern is for the morning to be sunny, the afternoon to be partly cloudy, and a heavy downpour to occur in the late afternoon or early evening. Visitors to tropical destinations should be warned to start the day as early as possible if they want to avoid the possibility of getting wet.

Other Aspects of Climate

There's a saying among meteorologists: "Climate is what you expect, weather is what you get." This does point out an important distinction: *Weather* refers to what's going on in the atmosphere at a given time and place; *climate* refers to the weather that prevails typically in a region at a certain time of the year. When you tell people that Acapulco is usually warm, dry, and sunny in January, you're talking about climate. When they return to tell you that it rained and was chilly for three of the seven days they were there, they're talking about the weather.

Travel professionals can't be expected to predict the weather. But they should know what climate will prevail. Climate is a critical traveller concern; knowledge of it can help to clinch a satisfying sale. Here are three facts you should keep in mind:

A **tsunami** is a massive wave, usually triggered by an earthquake, which can cross thousands of kilometres of ocean before devastating shorelines. The 2004 tsunami in the Indian Ocean was a prime example.

- **The higher a destination is, the cooler it will be.** Mexico City, which sits on a plateau, reaches an average high of only 23°C in July, whereas Manzanillo, a Mexican beach resort at virtually the same latitude (but at sea level) is typically in the low 30s in the same month. In a more extreme example, it can be snowing at Lake Arrowhead, a California mountain resort at a high altitude, while 30 kilometres away in Palm Springs, at a much lower altitude, vacationers are baking by their hotel pools.

- **The windier it is, the colder it will feel.** It could be –7°C in Moscow, but if it's not windy, the weather won't feel too uncomfortable. But if it's –4°C and the wind is whipping, it'll seem much colder. On the other hand, windy days can also be helpful. The trade winds in Hawaii can make a 30°C day feel absolutely wonderful.

- **When arranging a flight in which a stop or connection is involved, consider what the climate at the stopover city will be.** For example, for a January itinerary to South America, it might, if practical, be advisable to connect via a warm-weather city, such as Miami, rather than via New York, where winter weather could interfere with air travel. Conversely, in August, northern cities may make better stopovers than southern ones, where thunderstorms are more common.

Two other important points about determining the climate bear mentioning. First, carefully study the climate tables or graphs you use. Do they give rainfall in centimetres, as do those in this book? Do they list days with rain or days with no rain? Are temperatures given as average highs and lows, as record highs and lows, or as the average of the entire day? Second, make sure you find out if temperatures are measured in Celsius (used in Canada and most other countries) or in Fahrenheit (used in the United States).

Just for the record, to convert Fahrenheit to Celsius, subtract 32 from the Fahrenheit number, multiply by 5, and divide by 9. Or, to simplify things, memorize the following: 86°F is hot (30°C), 72°F is pleasant (22°C), 59°F is chilly (15°C), and 32°F is freezing (0°C). That way you can gauge most other Fahrenheit temperatures by comparison.

HUMAN GEOGRAPHY

Most of what you've read in this chapter has to do with **physical geography,** the study of the earth's land, air, and water. But studying the peoples of the earth, an equally noble discipline, is usually called **human** or **cultural geography.** Religion, food, politics, language, national boundaries, art, agriculture, economics, and even history all in some way affect geography. In the chapters that follow, we often bring up one or more of these considerations, for tourism is, after all, an activity of people, not of ocean currents or rocks.

One part of human geography that may bear some scrutiny right now is touristic patterns. People want to go to places for many reasons; climate, vacation time, and school holidays seem to be the most important factors. When tourism is buzzing in a place, it's called **high** or **peak season.** (It's also the most expensive season.) When tourists are fewest, it's called **low** or **off-season.** (Real vacation bargains can also be had.) And times in between, when neither a great many people nor a very few people are visiting, are called **shoulder seasons.**

In most places, fall and spring are shoulder seasons; some of the most satisfying vacations take place during shoulder seasons because the weather may be pretty good, rates aren't at their highest, and crowds are seldom seen. In temperate or arctic regions, high season usually takes place in summer, but tropical resorts peak in winter (with all those travellers wanting to get away from the cold). Conversely, for temperate and arctic areas, winter is the low season. One exception: ski resorts, which thrive at this time.

Holidays also profoundly affect travel patterns. In most countries, **people don't like to take regular vacations during family holidays,** such as Thanksgiving, Passover, or Christmas. They do like to fly to stay with family around these times, meaning that airfares are high, but hotels in most destinations are usually empty and offering bargains. One other interesting pattern: Travel falls sharply a few days after New Year's Day; January is bargain month in many places. But other holidays, such as the U.S. Fourth of July or Japan's Golden Week (April 29 to May 5), set off massive peaks of tourism. Most French and Italians leave their cities en masse in August for Riviera or Alpine vacations; thus, a sort of shoulder season exists in Paris and Rome at summer's end—when most business travel halts and when mostly foreign tourists are left to stay in these cities' hotels.

Make sure to consult each chapter's "Climate at a Glance" chart. In addition to climate, these charts show the destination's tourism patterns.

There are McDonald's franchises in more than 119 countries.

On the U.S. Atlantic Coast, Saturdays are 22 percent rainier than Mondays. One theory: It's a result of weekday car emissions.

The people of the earth speak about 3000 distinct languages.

One odd factor that affects tourism profoundly: the **"event" effect.** An event—either positive or negative—can create a strong, often disproportionate impact over a wide geographic area, and for a long time. Negative events produce the most dramatic (and often irrational) effects. The 1991 Gulf War wiped out tourism in Egypt, Morocco, and even Europe, though these places were hundreds, even thousands, of kilometres away. And the 1989 San Francisco earthquake reduced tourism for months across all of California. It's all about the public's misunderstanding of geography. Fortunately, the event effect can also be positive: The Olympics, a world's fair, or the Super Bowl can enhance tourism for years, not only at the venue city but also for the entire region or country.

Similar to the event effect is the power of imagery to affect destination choice. The tragic sight of jets flying into the World Trade Center towers in 2001 made New York City, in one poll, the city that travellers would most want to avoid. Indeed, those polled ranked it more dangerous than the Middle East. This sort of reaction, of course, is utterly irrational and eventually fades away, as positive images and experiences replace negative ones. For example, within about two years, tourism and business travel to New York City reached, then surpassed, pre–9/11 levels.

REFERENCE TOOLS

The 33 chapters that follow focus more precisely on the most popular places travellers want to visit. But even if you memorize every word in this book, there will be times when someone asks a question that you can't answer. For the most useful reference tools that may contain the information you seek, be sure to consult Appendix B of this book.

SUMMARY

Here's a summary of the most important sales-enhancing geographic facts in this chapter:

- Think "curved line" when you're deciding what route or airline to recommend for a long flight.

- Seasons in the Southern Hemisphere are the reverse of those in the Northern Hemisphere.

- When crossing the International Date Line from east to west, it becomes the following day; from west to east, it becomes the previous day.

- Winds called the westerlies flow west to east in most temperate parts of the globe, affecting weather and jet travel time.

- The trade winds flow more or less from east to west in the tropics.

- Mountainous tropical islands are usually drier on the western, leeward coast.

- Ocean water on the east side of a continent tends to be warmer than ocean water at the same latitude on the west side.

- Hurricane (cyclone) season in most places peaks in August, September, and October.

- Areas with monsoon conditions usually get rain during their summer season.

- The higher (in altitude) a destination is, the cooler it will be.

Someone once said, "Without geography you're nowhere." Well, you now know the underpinnings of geography. This is a great starting point. You're now ready to learn about those many "somewheres" that are essential to travellers. That's what the rest of this book is all about.

NAME _____   DATE _____

Qualifying the Traveller

Based on your current knowledge of geography, name one place, anywhere in the world, that you think might appeal to the traveller type named below:

TYPE	PLACE		TYPE	PLACE
1. History buff	_____		7. Adventure seeker	_____
2. Culture seeker	_____		8. Entertainment seeker	_____
3. Ethnic traveller	_____		9. Shopper	_____
4. Religious pilgrim	_____		10. Sensual traveller	_____
5. Environmental traveller	_____		11. Status seeker	_____
6. Recreational traveller	_____		12. Business traveller, garment industry	_____

Turn back to page 5 to continue with the sales portion of the text.

TRAVEL TRIVIA

THINGS GEOGRAPHERS DON'T AGREE ON

- Which is the world's longest river, the Nile or the Amazon.

- Whether Australia is an island or a continent.

- Whether the world's highest mountain should be measured from sea level (it would be Mt. Everest) or from the ocean bottom (it would be Mauna Kea, Hawaii).

- What exactly is the difference between a lake, a sea, and a gulf.

- Whether Europe and Asia form one continent or two.

- What distinguishes a cape from a peninsula.

DOWNTOWN CHICAGO

Hotel Location	Map Area
1 Allegro Hotel, Chicago	F4
2 Ambassador West Hotel	B5
3 The Belden-Stratford	A5
5 Best Western Grant Park Hotel	I5
6 Best Western Inn of Chicago	D6
7 Best Western River North	D4
10 The Blackstone Hotel	G5
11 Claridge Hotel	B5
12 Clarion Executive Plaza	E5
17 Doubletree Guest Suites Chicago	C6
18 The Drake	C5
19 Essex Inn	G5
20 The Fairmont Hotel	E6
21 Hampton Inn & Suites	D4
22 Hilton, Chicago Hilton & Towers	G5
23 Hilton, Palmer House Hilton	F5
25 Holiday Inn Chicago City Centre	D6
26 Holiday Inn Mart Plaza	E4
27 Hyatt on Printer's Row Chicago Loop	G5
28 Hyatt Regency Chicago On Chicago's Riverwalk	E6
34 Lenox Suites	D5
43 Quality Inn Chicago	F2
45 Regal Knickerbocker	C6
48 The Seneca Hotel-Chicago	C6
49 Sheraton Chicago Hotel & Towers	E6
51 Summerfield Suites Hotel	D5
53 The Talbott Hotel	C5
56 The Whitehall Hotel	C5

© •1998 Reed Elsevier Inc. 0498

Sched. Flight Time from:
Los Angeles - 4 hrs.
New York - 2 hrs.
Miami - 3 hrs.
Airport Transfers
O'Hare Int'l Airport to city center - 19 miles.
Midway Airport to city center - 10 miles.
Peak Convention Months
Jan. thru Nov.
Weather
Daily av. hi/lo
Dec. - Feb.   34/28
Mar. - May   57/39
Jun. - Aug.   82/64
Sep. - Nov.   63/47

Source: Hotel and Travel Index/Reed Travel Group

ACTIVITY 2

NAME _____   DATE _____

Reading a Hotel Locator Map

Study the locator map of Downtown Chicago on p. 26, then answer the following questions:

1. Which museum is at I-6 on the map?

2. A person has business at the Sears Tower. Which hotel is closest to it, Sheraton Plaza Chicago or Allegro Hotel?

3. It seems easier to lodge people near which of the following: the University of Illinois or Northwestern University?

4. A visitor to Chicago will be driving from the Hyatt Regency to Milwaukee, a city to the north. Which street and highways will he or she have to take?

5. A person wants to see the famous Water Tower. At which map coordinates is it?

ACTIVITY 3

NAME _____   DATE _____

Identifying Geographic Features

Below is a rendition of an imaginary tropical island in the Pacific. Letters identify the various geographic features. Match the features with the letter.

1. A peninsula: _____   6. A dry, leeward area: _____

2. The coolest area: _____   7. A lake: _____

3. A bay: _____   8. A coral reef: _____

4. A rainier, windward area: _____   9. A river: _____

5. A cape: _____   10. A fjord-like feature: _____

NAME _____   DATE _____

A Geographic Crossword Puzzle

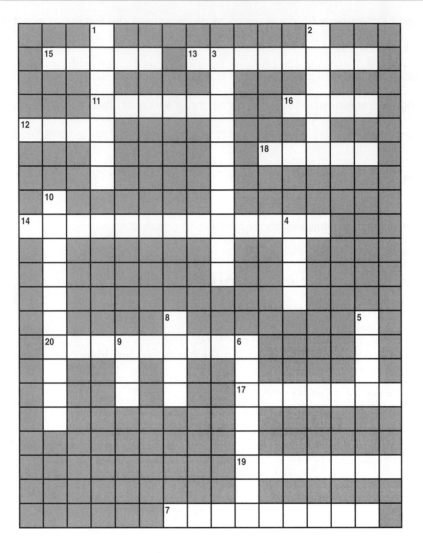

Down

1. A map with an A, B, C, 1, 2, 3 grid.
2. A state without daylight savings time.
3. The least-visited continent.
4. A European mountain range.
5. The number of oceans in the world.
6. The Gulf Stream is in the . . .
8. Thirty-two degrees Fahrenheit equals ___ degrees Celsius.
9. A hotel reference book.
10. Tropical winds.

Across

7. The direction the north Pacific's currents turn.
11. A month of hurricanes.
12. The side of a continent with cooler ocean temperatures.
13. Monday becomes Sunday if you cross the date line travelling . . .
14. The longitude line that passes near London.
15. The most accurate map.
16. What Cod is.
17. The dry side of a mountain.
18. You cruise down this river.
19. In the Caribbean it's a hurricane; in the western Pacific it's a . . .
20. A place with lots of volcanic activity.

NAME _____   DATE _____

Reading Climate at a Glance Charts

Examine the four charts on the next two pages, then answer the following questions:

1. Which season would probably provide the best overall weather for a business traveller to visit Calcutta?

2. Which of the four cities has the widest range between summer and winter temperatures?

3. Without looking at a map, determine which of the cities is clearly a Southern Hemisphere destination.

4. Which of the cities has the least monthly variation in rainfall?

5. Without looking at a map, which of these four cities would probably be closest to the equator?

6. In which month does Melbourne have its coolest temperatures?

7. Which city is the most likely to have snow in the winter?

8. Which two cities seem to have the greatest variation between daytime and nighttime temperatures?

9. What factor probably accounts for Quito's relatively low temperatures?

10. In one of these cities, it goes down to around 15°C at night in February. Which city is it?

11. What probably accounts for Calcutta's off-season for tourists?

12. Which month in Chicago will probably provide the best weather and temperatures, without hordes of tourists?

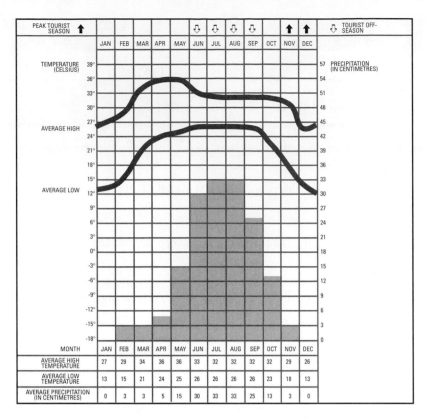

Climate at a Glance: Calcutta, India

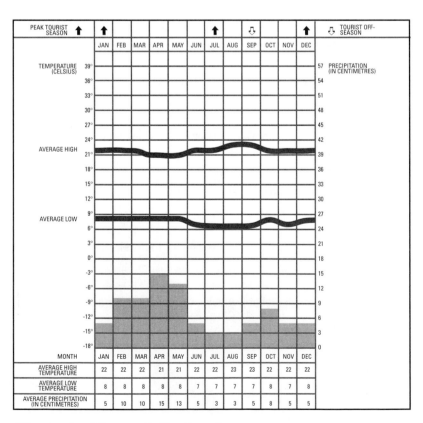

Climate at a Glance: Quito, Ecuador

MONTH	JAN	FEB	MAR	APR	MAY	JUN	JUL	AUG	SEP	OCT	NOV	DEC
AVERAGE HIGH TEMPERATURE	26	26	24	20	17	14	13	15	17	19	22	24
AVERAGE LOW TEMPERATURE	14	14	13	11	8	7	6	6	8	9	11	12
AVERAGE PRECIPITATION (IN CENTIMETRES)	5	5	5	5	5	5	5	5	5	8	5	5

Climate at a Glance: Melbourne, Australia

MONTH	JAN	FEB	MAR	APR	MAY	JUN	JUL	AUG	SEP	OCT	NOV	DEC
AVERAGE HIGH TEMPERATURE	-1	2	7	14	21	27	29	28	24	18	9	2
AVERAGE LOW TEMPERATURE	-8	-7	-2	4	9	15	18	17	13	7	-1	-6
AVERAGE PRECIPITATION (IN CENTIMETRES)	5	3	8	8	10	10	8	8	8	8	5	5

Climate at a Glance: Chicago, Illinois

NAME _____   DATE _____

Putting It All Together

Examine the world map below, then answer the questions by giving the letter or location on the map. You may use each letter only once; there will be some letters you won't use.

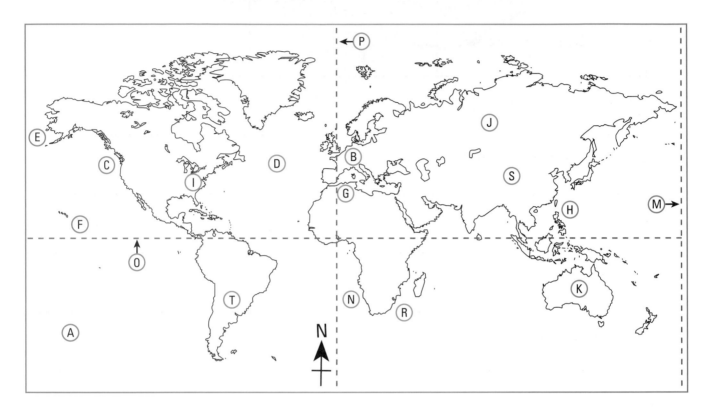

1. An area that, because of prevailing winds, has high rainfall.
2. An ocean where currents flow counterclockwise.
3. An area with many typhoons in the summer.
4. Cross it and the day changes.
5. The most popular overseas continent for North American travellers.
6. An African coast that has cool ocean water temperatures.
7. The country with the most time zones.
8. An area a jet would cross if flying from Vancouver to Japan.
9. A continent that has winter in July and has a cyclone season.
10. A place where prevailing winds typically come from the east.

NAME _____   DATE _____

Geography on the Web

Find at least one website that provides good information on each subject listed below:

e.g., Health issues/concerns for a specific country to be visited.
lonelyplanet.com/health/health.htm

1. Distances and routes between one place in Canada and another

   _____

2. The foreign embassies located in Ottawa

   _____

3. Predicted weather conditions for any place in the world

   _____

4. How to get an International Driver's Permit

   _____

5. Which cruise lines visit a certain port

   _____

6. Where a certain event will take place

   _____

7. Information on national parks in Canada

   _____

BEAUFORT
SEA

GREENLAND

BAFFIN BAY

Alaska Range

Great
Bear
Lake

LABRADOR
SEA

Great Slave Lake

HUDSON BAY

CANADA

Rocky

Lake Winnipeg

St. Lawrence River

Lake Superior

Mountains

Missouri River

Lake Huron

Cascade
Range

Lake
Ontario

Great
Salt
Lake

Lake
Michigan

Lake
Erie

PACIFIC OCEAN

Sierra
Nevada

Appalachian Mountains

Lake
Mead

Lake
Powell

UNITED
STATES

▲ Grand
Canyon

Colorado
River

ATLANTIC OCEAN

Rio Grande

Mississippi River

Hawaii

MEXICO

GULF of MEXICO

▲ Everglades

GULF of
CALIFORNIA

Florida
Keys

NORTH AMERICA
Charm of the Familiar

Think you know North America? Then where in Canada do cars appear to roll uphill backward? In what city is Disneyland located? Which North American region has the most thunderstorms yearly?

Maybe you knew the answers, maybe not. (The answers, in order: Magnetic Hill in Moncton, New Brunswick; Anaheim, California; central Florida.) The important point is this: Many people have only the haziest of images about any destination beyond a few hundred kilometres of their hometown. To serve travellers, you'll have to bring those distant images into focus. And you, yourself, will need to know North America just about as well as you know your own backyard.

That yard probably extends farther than you think. Geographers define North America as everything from Canada to the Panama–Colombia border. That includes rarely visited Greenland, the island nations of the Caribbean, and many southern countries, such as Mexico, Guatemala, El Salvador, Honduras, Costa Rica, and Panama. (We'll address these Caribbean and Latin American countries later, in Part III.) All you need to know about Greenland is that it's a self-governing territory of Denmark, its 2 175 429 square kilometres are mostly ice-covered, it supports only 56 000 people, and it draws few tourists.

So, in this Part II, we'll limit ourselves to Canada and the United States and save all North American countries between the U.S. and Colombia for later.

In most towns in Greenland, there are more dogs than people.

WHERE THE REGIONS ARE

Take a look at a map of North America. By far the broadest area is taken up by Canada, the world's second-largest country. **Eastern Canada** is composed of the **Atlantic provinces** (**New Brunswick, Nova Scotia, Prince Edward Island,** and **Newfoundland and Labrador**) and Canada's two largest provinces, **Quebec** and **Ontario,** which together form **Central Canada. Western Canada** includes **British Columbia, Alberta, Saskatchewan,** and **Manitoba.** (The latter three provinces are sometimes called the **Prairie provinces** or the **Prairies.**) Three northern territories cap off the country: **Yukon, the Northwest Territories,** and **Nunavut.**

Two U.S. states, both south of British Columbia, make up the **Pacific Northwest: Washington** and **Oregon.** Above them, and separated from them by British Columbia and Yukon, is **Alaska.** Below them are **California, Nevada, Utah, Arizona,** and **New Mexico**—often labelled the **Southwest.** (Occasionally, you'll hear of **California, Nevada, Oregon,** and **Washington** grouped as the **Far**

West.) Over 3200 kilometres to the southwest of the North American continent is the U.S. state of **Hawaii.**

The **Rocky Mountain** region is a buffer between the Pacific region and the middle of Canada and the United States. Which states make up the U.S. Rocky Mountain area is somewhat debatable—several of them qualify for inclusion in the Southwest, while others are considered part of the Great Plains area. For our purposes, let's say the Rocky Mountain states include, from north to south, **Montana, Idaho, Wyoming,** and **Colorado. Texas,** the second-largest U.S. state after Alaska, almost needs a category for itself, though it's often mentioned in the same breath with **Oklahoma,** which is just north of it. The flat agricultural area that stretches above Oklahoma is generally called the **Great Plains.** It's made up of, from north to south, **North Dakota, South Dakota, Nebraska,** and **Kansas.**

The **Midwest** encompasses many states, including **Minnesota, Wisconsin, Michigan, Iowa, Illinois, Indiana, Missouri,** and **Ohio.** (Yes, many of these states are in the eastern half of the United States, but they still call themselves Midwestern.) The **South** also covers a vast area. Its states are **Kentucky, Tennessee, North Carolina, Arkansas, Mississippi, Alabama, Georgia, South Carolina, Louisiana,** and **Florida.**

West Virginia and **Virginia** are occasionally labelled southern or can be classified with the **Mid-Atlantic** states: **New York, New Jersey, Pennsylvania, Maryland,** and **Delaware.** And between Maryland and Virginia is the **District of Columbia,** a "neutral" federal district that marks the U.S. capital, **Washington, D.C.** Finally, **New England** nestles in the northeast corner of the United States. Its members are **Maine, Vermont, New Hampshire, Massachusetts, Connecticut,** and **Rhode Island.**

A SATELLITE VIEW

Imagine you're in the space shuttle. You look down on North America. What do you see? A continent of sharp contrasts: the flat plains of the continent's centre, the worn peaks of the Appalachian Mountains, the permanent icecaps of the far north, or the barren deserts of the U.S. Southwest. Because these natural features (and other ones, like lakes, rivers, and oceans) have such a strong impact on travel plans, it's important to understand where and what they are.

Rocky beach on Hawaii's Big Island
Photo by Marc Mancini

Bodies of Water

Looking down from the space shuttle, you notice that the North American continent is flanked by three oceans: the **Atlantic Ocean** that lines the eastern shores, the **Arctic Ocean** that caps our continent, and the **Pacific Ocean** that laps against its western coast. Curving into Mexico and the U.S. southeastern border is the **Gulf of Mexico;** winds blowing over the Gulf help create the warm and often humid climate of that area. To the northeast, separating Canada from the United States, are the **Great Lakes: Superior, Michigan, Huron, Erie,** and **Ontario.** These lakes—and their shores—are important both to tourism and commerce. Toward the western side of the continent is another noticeable body of water, the **Great Salt Lake,** and to the north are several huge lakes: **Great Bear, Great Slave,** and **Lake Winnipeg.** Dominating this northern region is a very big body of water: **Hudson Bay.**

Look more closely and you'll spot several major rivers. The **St. Lawrence** slices into the continent's northeastern region. To the west, the **Columbia River** forms part of the border between Oregon and Washington. The **Mississippi River** divides the United States almost in half, starting up in Minnesota and travelling down through the Midwest and South to Louisiana, where it empties into the Gulf of Mexico. Even today, tourists can take a riverboat trip past its historic riverfront towns. The **Missouri River** starts in Montana and passes through the Great Plains states, finally merging with the Mississippi River in Missouri.

In the Southwest, the **Colorado River** winds from Colorado through Utah and forms part of the borders of Arizona, Nevada, and California; along the way, you'll see that it's been dammed, creating two lakes that are major recreation areas: **Lake Mead** in Nevada, and **Lake Powell** in Utah. The Colorado is also a popular rafting site for tourists. The **Rio Grande** marks off a large part of the country's southern border between Texas and Mexico.

Throughout North America, many smaller rivers and lakes help shape landscape. In the Atlantic provinces and New England, numerous inlets dig into the coastline and are popular recreation centres. Swampy bayous cover much of Louisiana, as do those of the **Everglades** in Florida. And Florida's collection of islands off its southwest coast, the **Florida Keys,** is a major tourist destination.

Ontario touches four of the five Great Lakes.

The largest lake entirely within Canada is Great Bear Lake.

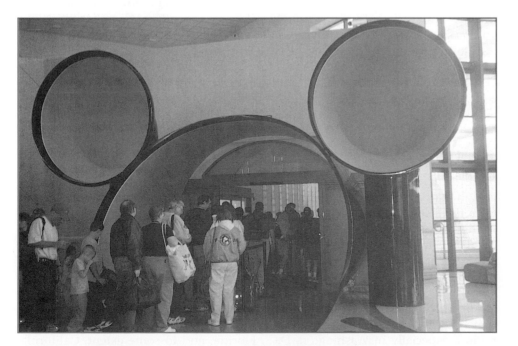

The embarkation gate to Disney's cruise ships, Port Canaveral
Photo by Marc Mancini

Mountains

Three mountain ranges loom over the North American landscape. They have a major effect on climate, travel conditions, and skiing. The impressive scenery they offer is a major factor for tourists. The weathered **Appalachian Mountains**—prime camping and hiking areas—rise in Pennsylvania, continue southwesterly down through Maryland, West Virginia, Virginia, Tennessee, North Carolina, and Kentucky, and end in northern Georgia. Other mountain ranges farther north, in New York, New England, Quebec, New Brunswick, and Newfoundland and Labrador, are popular summer tourist and winter skiing resorts. (Some geographers consider those northerly mountains an extension of the Appalachians.)

The **Rocky Mountains** run down the entire western length of North America, from Alaska to New Mexico, through Yukon, British Columbia, Alberta's western edge, Montana, Idaho, Wyoming, Colorado, Utah, and Arizona. One depression near the Rockies would be very noticeable from above: the cavernous **Grand Canyon** in Arizona. Along the west coast are two ranges (some consider them tributaries of the Rockies): the **Cascade Mountains,** stretching from northern California through Oregon and Washington to British Columbia, and the **Sierra Nevadas,** running most of the length of California. Like the Rockies, they both present great skiing and hiking opportunities. The Cascades continue northward from British Columbia into Alaska, where they become the **Alaska Range.** Between the Rocky and Appalachian Mountains are the flat lands of Canada's Saskatchewan and Manitoba, and the U.S. Great Plains and Midwest.

Climate

As a rule (and there are many exceptions), the southern portion of Canada and the northern portion of the contiguous United States have warm or hot summers, but cold snowy winters; whereas the southern region of the United States is mild to hot year-round. Because of this, southern portions of the continent tend to be all-year destinations, whereas tourism in the north is largely limited to the summer. Of course, skiers do head north in the winter, and October is prime foliage season there.

Winter in Alaska and Canada can be cold and harsh. However, late spring, summer, and early fall are surprisingly mild; and in southern Canadian cities, like Toronto and especially Vancouver, winter isn't as bitter as people might imagine.

Rainfall and humidity patterns vary widely across the continent. Rain is frequent in the Pacific Northwest and, often in the form of thundershowers, in the U.S. South and Southeast. The U.S. Southwest is dry and desert-like, with rain coming mostly in the winter months. Hurricanes are most likely along the Gulf and Atlantic coasts in the summer and fall.

TOURISM PATTERNS

Memphis, Tennessee's airport handles more cargo than any other in the world. The reason: It's FedEx's hub.

North American tourism patterns are probably familiar to you. In brief, summer is high season for most of Canada and the United States. (This high season extends from the last weekend of May to the first weekend of September.) One exception is the desert resorts in California, Arizona, and Nevada. These areas, where summer temperatures can be scorching, have their low season during June, July, and August.

Fall and spring are shoulder seasons for tourism in most places. Many travellers with flexible schedules (for example, retirees) profit from the lower rates and the cool (but not yet cold) temperatures that prevail. So, too, do conventions, which seem to flourish during this time. Easter, however, is a springtime high period, especially in Washington, D.C., Florida, and to some extent, California; students and families often travel during the week before or after this holiday.

October's fall foliage season is also a high period in many forested areas. And during spring, certain beach resorts are packed—the reason: It's spring vacation break at many colleges.

Winter is a low period for Canadian and U.S. tourism, except at ski resorts and at certain warm-weather places (for example, desert resorts). Special winter events, too, can draw crowds to cold-weather locations. For instance, Quebec City's Winter Carnival, the Festival of Lights in Niagara Falls, and New York City's pre-Christmas shopping opportunities serve as magnets for tourists.

NORTH AMERICAN DISTANCES

What is most striking to Europeans visiting North America? How big it really is. Even North Americans underestimate their continent's size. Why? The answers are many: The places are so familiar, air travel has compressed journey times greatly, and provinces and states are commonly seen as being parts of large blocks (for example, Ohio and Minnesota seem close to each other because they're both in the Midwest).

There's a flip side to this. Since cities like **Montreal, Toronto, New York, Boston, Philadelphia, Baltimore,** and **Washington, D.C.,** have strong identities, some people are surprised to find how close these cities are to one another. (For example, it takes only about five hours to drive from Montreal to Boston.) On the other hand, the central and western regions are so vast and uncrowded that distances between major cities are considerable. **Los Angeles** and **Portland,** for instance, even though in adjacent states, are more than 1600 kilometres apart; Toronto and **Winnipeg,** in adjacent provinces, are (by road) almost 2000 kilometres apart!

For all the continent's size, however, air service is so good between urban centres that distances seem short to travellers. And within regions, commuter airlines shrink those distances even more. On busy routes, fares can be very reasonable— even cross-country. However, if a route isn't greatly travelled, even if it's a short distance, prices can be high. Keep in mind that air travel isn't a cure-all for distance: Service between small towns can be limited or nonexistent.

North America's love of cars is well known, and many travellers will want to drive to their destination, especially in the compact U.S. Northeast. The network of highways is generally excellent, and so, too, are most provincial, state, and rural roads. Out west, though, the wide-open spaces truly are wide; direct major routes between secondary destinations aren't always possible to find.

Getting around *within* a city is another matter. Urban transportation in Canada is generally excellent, but in the United States it often leaves something to be desired. Your recommendations will vary according to the situation: a car rental for Los Angeles, taxis for New York City, streetcars and subways for Toronto.

In Canada, **VIA Rail** provides solid and dependable service, but its routes are somewhat limited. Although **Amtrak** offers some major routes in the United States (with high-speed service between Washington, D.C., and Boston), the train system there is geared more to commerce than to commuters. Trains aren't nearly as fast, nor the routes as diversified, as those in Europe. That's one reason why motorcoach tours and intercity buses (usually operated by **Greyhound**) are the ground transportation of choice for many travellers in the United States. Still, there *are* good rail routes throughout the country; special fares are commonplace; and train travel remains one of the great, romantic, scenic means of travel. Amtrak Vacations, a division of Amtrak, offers complete lodging–transportation packages that feature rail travel as one component.

Cruises have become a very common means of seeing North America. Among the most popular itineraries: New England and the St. Lawrence River, the Inside Passage in British Columbia and Alaska, and the Mississippi, along with its many tributaries.

Because the earth spins, if you're in North America you're travelling right now at about 960 to 1440 km/h.

Montreal, on the St. Lawrence River, is the world's largest inland port.

A number of "private" train experiences are offered across North America, especially in Alaska.

SOME MISCELLANEOUS CONSIDERATIONS

Here are a few items that may prove useful when dealing with people travelling within North America:

- The "hub-and-spoke" concept is important to North American air travel. Each airline has one or two cities where it has an especially large number of flights connecting. North America's busiest domestic hub cities, with the airlines that rely on them the most:

Atlanta (Delta)

Calgary (Air Canada)

Charlotte, NC (US Airways)

Chicago (American, United)

Cincinnati (Delta)

Cleveland (Continental)

Dallas (American)

Denver (United)

Detroit (Northwest)

Houston (Continental)

Las Vegas (US Airways)

Minneapolis (Northwest)

Montreal (Air Canada)

Philadelphia (US Airways)

Phoenix (US Airways)

Salt Lake City (Delta)

Toronto (Air Canada)

Vancouver (Air Canada)

New York City's 267 hectare La Guardia Airport could fit inside the 356 hectare terminal building at JFK Airport.

- For international departures, North American carriers concentrate on Toronto, Vancouver, Los Angeles, San Francisco, Miami, and New York City as hubs, though many other cities can serve as departure points for travellers heading to foreign places. These cities serve as hubs to domestic coastal and near-coastal cities, as well.

- Hotels in North America often have special reduced-rate packages with easy requirements, such as age, business, or membership in organizations.

- CAA makes available to its members free or low-cost maps and travel kits.

- The costs of staying in any North American city can vary enormously. Big cities (for example, New York) tend to be expensive; smaller cities (especially in the U.S. South and Midwest) tend to be less so.

- Most hotels in North America belong to chains, and each chain tries to maintain a certain quality level among all its properties. Though there can be *great* variation within a chain (especially Hilton, Sheraton, Hyatt, and Holiday Inn), here is what level each chain generally represents:

LUXURY	HIGH END	MID-RANGE	BUDGET
Four Seasons	Crowne Plaza	Clarion	Baymont
Peninsula	Fairmont	Delta	Best Western
Regent	Hyatt Regency	Doubletree	Comfort Inns
Ritz-Carlton	Inter-Continental	Embassy Suites	Days Inn
	Le Meridien	Hilton	Econo Lodge
	Marriott	Holiday Inn	Hampton Inns
	Omni	Hyatt	Howard Johnson
	Renaissance	Radisson	La Quinta
	Sheraton Resorts	Ramada	Quality Inn
	Sofitel	Sheraton	Red Roof
	Westin		Rodeway Inn
			Travelodge

NAME _____   DATE _____

Listed below are seven possible vacation trips throughout North America. Try to think of one or more persons you know who might enjoy taking each trip. Write down his or her name for each vacation and give several reasons why you think it would appeal to that person. If necessary, browse through Chapters 1 through 12 for additional information to guide you.

1. A seven-day riverboat cruise up the Mississippi River

2. A visit to Winter Carnival in Quebec City

3. A four-day stay in the Florida Keys

4. A week's stay in July at a Nova Scotia hotel that faces the Atlantic

5. A nine-day escorted motorcoach tour of Boston, New York, Philadelphia, and Washington, D.C.

6. A raft trip down the Colorado River

7. A weekend in Banff

TRAVEL TRIVIA

NORTH AMERICA'S DISTINCTIVE FOODS AND DRINKS

- Tourtière in Quebec
- Espresso in Seattle
- Beignets in New Orleans
- Chili on spaghetti in Cincinnati
- Key lime pie in Florida
- Cheese steak sandwiches in Philadelphia
- Stone crabs and black beans in Miami

- Hot-smoked salmon in B.C.
- Sourdough in San Francisco
- Sausages in Milwaukee
- Deep dish pizza in Chicago
- Beaver tails in Ottawa
- Quahogs, scrod, clam cakes, coffee cabs, chow mein, and chourico in southeastern Massachusetts

QUEBEC

LABRADOR

STRAIT OF BELLE ISLE

LABRADOR SE

▲ L'Anse aux Meadows N.P.

Long Range
Mountains

▲ Gros Morne N.P.

NEWFOUNDLAND

GULF OF ST. LAWRENCE

Conception Ba

Port aux Basques

St. John

Avalon
Peninsula

Edmundston

Caraquet

PRINCE
EDWARD
ISLAND

Cape Breton
Highlands N.P.

CAPE BRETON
ISLAND

NEW
BRUNSWICK

Cavendish

PEI N.P.

St. Pierre
and Miquelon

King's
Landing

Moncton

Charlottetown

Sydney

UNITED
STATES

Fredericton

Baddeck

Louisbourg

ATLANTIC
OCEAN

Saint John

Hopewell

Truro

St. Andrews

Grand-Pré N.H.P.

Campobello Is.

BAY OF FUNDY

Port Royal
N.H.P.

Peggy's Cove

Halifax

NOVA
SCOTIA

Lunenburg

Yarmouth

CHAPTER 1

Atlantic Canada

Legacy of the Sea

Who "discovered" Atlantic Canada? Officially, it was John Cabot, who claimed **Newfoundland** for the British Crown in 1497. But long before then, indigenous peoples, such as the Beothuks, had migrated there from Western Canada and Asian lands beyond. There's also strong evidence that explorer Leif Ericson or some other adventurous Viking reached the area more than 1000 years ago. Throughout the 17th century, a good part of the region was French territory (Acadia, or *l'Acadie*).

There are certainly no Scandinavian influences remaining in Atlantic Canada, but travellers will surely notice the confluence of British and Acadian French cultures when visiting the Atlantic provinces. (Acadia was the name given by France to Canada's easternmost regions. Many Acadians migrated to Louisiana, where they became known as "Cajuns.") With their scenic coastlines rimmed with fishing villages, lighthouses, and old churches, these diverse provinces hark back to another era, when times were simpler and the sea touched all.

The region's first Scottish settlers called the southernmost peninsular province **Nova Scotia,** or "New Scotland." Today, Nova Scotia is often labelled the nation's "ocean playground." To the west, bordering the U.S. state of Maine, is **New Brunswick,** an uncrowded haven for nature lovers best known for its diverse outdoor activities and distinct Acadian culture. East of New Brunswick is **Prince Edward Island,** the smallest of Canada's provinces and the most rural in terms of culture, scenery, and pace. (These three provinces are known collectively as the **Maritime Provinces.**) Finally, on Canada's far northeast coast, visitors will find Newfoundland and Labrador (the mainland portion, adjoining Quebec, is **Labrador;** the island below it is Newfoundland), a rustic wilderness province with friendly seaside villages, prime whale-watching sites, and many opportunities for outdoor adventure activities.

Though each of the Atlantic provinces has its own distinct history, culture, and "feel," they all share an intimate relationship with the sea. Visitors marvel at the beauty of the Canadian Atlantic coast, from the rugged, picturesque shorelines to the active, colourful harbour towns. They relish the sea's culinary offerings, especially the lobster and salmon, for which Canada's eastern provinces are justly famous. And they regularly comment on the "down home" hospitality of the locals they meet.

Newfoundland standard time is a half-hour ahead of the rest of Atlantic Canada and 90 minutes ahead of Eastern Standard Time.

New Brunswick is home to 70 picturesque covered bridges, including the world's longest at Hartland.

HOW TRAVELLERS GET THERE

Reaching Atlantic Canada by car or motorcoach requires a day's drive from Montreal—longer from Toronto. From Montreal, the primary highway is the **Trans-Canada,** route 20 (the Jean Lesage Autoroute), which passes Quebec City along the St. Lawrence River's south shore, and on to Rivière-du-Loup, at which point the Trans-Canada becomes Highway 185. An alternative route to Quebec City is Highway 40, the North Shore Autoroute, which follows the north bank of the St. Lawrence River. At the border of Quebec and New Brunswick, the Trans-Canada Highway becomes Highway 2 and leads to the town of Edmundston.

Montreal is also the connecting point for popular **VIA Rail Canada,** the national railroad service. The trains make stops in the Maritime cities of **Moncton,** New Brunswick, and **Truro** and **Halifax,** Nova Scotia.

Though the nearest major Canadian air gateway is Montreal (YMQ), several of the Atlantic provinces are conveniently served. The primary cities are **Saint John** (YSJ), New Brunswick; Halifax (YHZ), Nova Scotia; and **St. John's** (YYT), Newfoundland and Labrador. Smaller airports are found at **Sydney** (YQY), Nova Scotia, and Moncton (YQM) and **Fredericton** (YFC), New Brunswick.

Finally, several cruise lines sail from Montreal or Quebec City to the Atlantic provinces and on to New England, New York, and other U.S. Eastern Seaboard ports (and vice versa). The majority of these cruises take place during fall foliage season, though some operate during parts of the summer and, very rarely, in the spring.

WEATHER PATTERNS

The Atlantic provinces exhibit a climate pattern that can range widely (see Figure 1-1). Indeed, at any given time each province can have totally different weather; in summer, for example, northern Newfoundland and Labrador can see

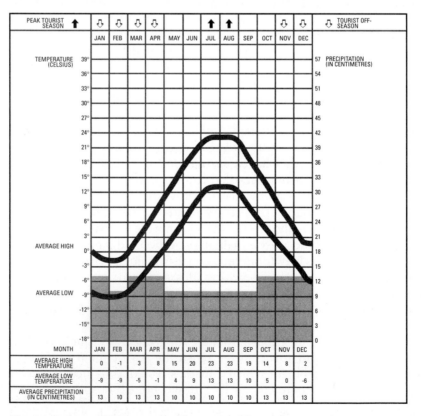

Figure 1-1 Climate at a Glance: Halifax, Nova Scotia

its temperatures drop into the 10°C range, while Nova Scotia may experience temperatures in the 30s. Travellers should bring sweaters or jackets for those cool and possibly damp nights, especially when visiting the coastal areas. Also, cold and rain aren't year-round features of the Atlantic provinces, as many believe; warm, sunny days are common in the summer. Of course, the winter months can be bitterly cold, particularly in Newfoundland and Labrador, with frequent snow-falls. (It can even snow in October or May.) That may appeal to cross-country skiers, but it might prove harsh for all but hardy, outdoors-oriented visitors.

The number of tourists increases sharply around the last week of June and tapers off around Labour Day. For this reason, May, June, or September are attractive times to visit, since the weather can still be quite pleasant, the attractions are uncrowded, and bargains are common. October can also be very special: Fall foliage bursts into magnificent colours and warm, Indian summer days are not uncommon.

Allergy sufferers will find a visit to Atlantic Canada's coastal areas quite a relief, even during the spring.

GETTING AROUND

One of the best ways to see Atlantic Canada is by car or motorcoach. The region is noted for numerous scenic drives, especially along the coast. For those in more of a hurry, the excellent Trans-Canada Highway enters Atlantic Canada from New Brunswick at Edmundston, then continues past Fredericton and Moncton on to Amherst, Truro, and New Glasgow, Nova Scotia. From New Glasgow, the Trans-Canada travels either to **Charlottetown,** Prince Edward Island (which is connected to the mainland by the 13 kilometre Confederation Bridge), or to Sydney, Nova Scotia, where the highway connects (via ferry) to **Port aux Basques,** Newfoundland. The Trans-Canada's final point is the nation's easternmost city, St. John's, Newfoundland.

The inter-island ferry system operates year-round and connects most of the region's major cities. The ferries are a particularly interesting mode of transportation, especially during whale-watching season and summer months (when reservations may be needed). Ferry rides, though, can be time-consuming. For example, the North Sydney–Port aux Basques run takes nearly six hours. For access to the provinces' more remote areas, air service is the more efficient alternative.

Though train service is available only to a few cities in New Brunswick and Nova Scotia, VIA Rail Canada offers connecting motorcoach service to Prince Edward Island and Newfoundland and Labrador. In addition, several major and regional Canadian bus companies, including Greyhound and Acadian, provide transportation to many cities and towns in Atlantic Canada—even to some very remote regions of Newfoundland and Labrador.

IMPORTANT PLACES

Tourists tend to visit only certain parts of Atlantic Canada, and the seaside attractions of the coast, with their fresh salt air and cool breezes, are particularly popular destinations. Atlantic Canada offers remarkable natural views and tends to be uncrowded, which appeals to those who want to relax, take in the sights, and enjoy the history and beauty at a leisurely pace. The region's highlights follow.

During July and August, advance lodging reservations (even for campsites) are a must.

Nova Scotia

Almost completely surrounded by water, Nova Scotia boasts a string of more than 65 seaside fishing villages and towns. Connected to New Brunswick only by a narrow isthmus, the province borders the remarkable **Bay of Fundy,** which has tides that average more than 14 metres—the greatest in the world. Nova Scotia is also the focal point of Canada's fishing industry, and is a province significant in

The Bay of Fundy recorded the greatest tide change in history: 21 metres.

history, music (especially Celtic music), and literature. Its best-known attractions are:

- **The Cabot Trail** of Cape Breton Island, a 300 kilometre sightseeing drive that loops along Nova Scotia's northernmost point, and famous as one of the most scenic drives in North America. With its rolling green hills and rugged coastal cliffs, the trail is not only visually remarkable but also winds past several interesting attractions. The Cabot Trail is one of 10 sightseeing routes in Nova Scotia's **Scenic Travelway** system. These drives are clearly marked for touring, and often offer stunning scenery, interesting museums, wilderness parks, hiking trails, lookouts, festivals, old forts, stately churches, bed-and-breakfast inns, heritage sites, recreational areas, and more.

- **Alexander Graham Bell National Historic Site,** in Baddeck, at the beginning of the Cabot Trail. The world's most comprehensive museum on Bell's scientific and humanitarian achievements, this Baddeck attraction is a must-see.

- **Cape Breton Highlands National Park.** With its waterfalls, landscape, beaches, and spectacular cliffs, the park is a playground for nature lovers, sightseers, and hikers.

- **Fortress of Louisbourg,** on Cape Breton Island. This National Historic Site is a superb restoration of the town and fort as it appeared 250 years ago, complete with authentically costumed staff, soldiers, and artisans.

- **Port-Royal National Historic Site**, near the southwest coastal town of Annapolis Royal. The park's **Port-Royal Habitation** is an exact replica of the fur-trading post built by Samuel de Champlain and Pierre Du Gua de Monts in 1605. Nearby is **Fort Anne National Historic Site and Museum,** with a preserved fortress.

- **Grand-Pré National Historic Site** (the setting for Longfellow's famous poem, *Evangeline*). The park commemorates the exile of the Acadians in the mid-18th century.

◎ Canada's only post office in a lighthouse is at Peggy's Cove.

- **Peggy's Cove,** just a short distance from Halifax. This beautiful, picture-perfect fishing village, complete with an old lighthouse and fishing wharves, may be the most frequently painted site in all of Canada. Many visitors stop just outside the village for a picnic lunch along the shore.

- **Old Town Lunenburg,** west of Halifax, is a UNESCO World Heritage Site that features buildings dating back to 1760. Lunenburg's Fisheries Museum of the Atlantic examines the fishing heritage of Canada's Atlantic coast. Among the exhibits are vintage fishing boats, which visitors can board.

- **Halifax.** The capital of Nova Scotia features numerous museums, landmark buildings, galleries, shops, restaurants, and a casino. Although it is the largest city in the Atlantic provinces, Halifax retains a small-city ambience and certainly much of Nova Scotia's cultural and maritime past, yet has become a vibrant, contemporary city as well. Tourists often visit the **Maritime Museum of the Atlantic, Province House,** and **Halifax Citadel National Historic Site.** The **Pier 21 National Historic Site** marks the place where more than a million immigrants gained entry into Canada. Attractive options include a stroll along the harbour or a harbour cruise on the *Bluenose II* fishing schooner—an exact replica of the famous international sailing champion (its image can be found on the Canadian dime). **Alexander Keith's Brewery,** North America's oldest working brewery, offers tours.

New Brunswick

New Brunswick, along with parts of Nova Scotia, is deeply marked by its Acadian influences. Like Nova Scotia, the province has strong maritime roots and abundant water sports, beaches, and seafood eateries. It, too, serves as a base to

◎ Seafood is the regional delicacy, especially fresh lobster, salmon, scallops, crabs, Malpeque oysters, and herring.

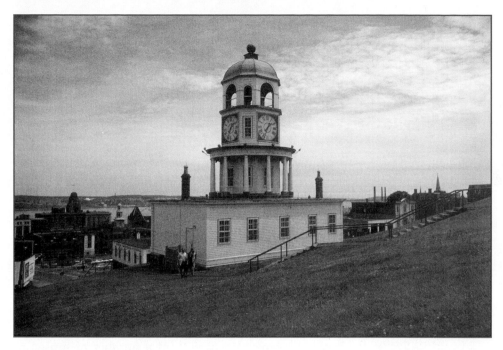

Old Town Clock, Halifax
Copyright COREL

whale-watch and to experience the Bay of Fundy's remarkable tides. (Two hundred billion tonnes of water come and go with each tide.) Acadian culture is important here. New Brunswick also has more lighthouses than anywhere else in Canada. Its most famous cities and attractions are:

- The port city of **Saint John,** Canada's oldest incorporated city. Saint John boasts several museums and landmarks, such as the **New Brunswick Museum** (shipbuilding exhibits) and the **Old City Market** (in operation since 1876). Particularly interesting is a visit to the **Moosehead Breweries** and the **Reversing Falls**—a natural phenomenon that occurs when the Saint John River flows backward due to the Bay of Fundy tides.

- **Fredericton.** The riverfront provincial capital, and one of the most attractive cities in Eastern Canada, is rich in history. The city features numerous churches (including the Gothic-style **Christ Church Cathedral**), Victorian homes, an old British military post (known as **Officer's Square**), museums, art galleries (such as the **Beaverbrook Art Gallery**), and live entertainment venues.

- **Kings Landing Historical Settlement** (in Kings Landing) and **Acadian Historical Village** (in Caraquet). These are both excellent restorations of typical New Brunswick villages, with buildings relocated from other parts of the province. Staff in period costumes demonstrate what life was like in an 18th-century Acadian village and a 19th-century Loyalist village (Kings Landing).

- The city of **Moncton** is best known for several natural oddities that are nearby, including **Magnetic Hill** (where things seem to roll *up* inclines), the awesome tides of the Bay of Fundy (at low tide, tourists can walk along what is, in effect, the ocean floor), and the **Tidal Bore** (twice daily, tidal changes in the Bay of Fundy cause a modest "wave" to surge upstream in the Petitcodiac River).

- A half-hour drive from Moncton is the **Hopewell Rocks Ocean Tidal Exploration Site,** where the Bay of Fundy's tides created the sandstone pillars called "flowerpots." Here, visitors may walk on the ocean floor at low tide. An

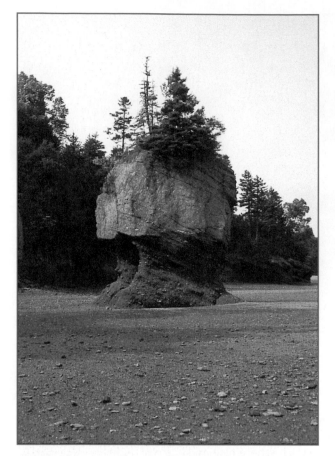

The Hopewell Rocks, New Brunswick
Courtesy of Mas Kikuta

interpretive centre explains the Bay of Fundy's tides, as well as the history of the area.

- A short ferry ride from the historic seaside town of **St. Andrews** brings travellers to **Campobello Island,** the summer home of former U.S. President Franklin D. Roosevelt. The island also has a golf course.

Prince Edward Island

Also known as **P.E.I.,** this is Canada's smallest province—a little more than 170 kilometres long and 70 kilometres across at its widest point. The pace on the island is slow and relaxed, and unless visitors choose to while away the hours on the beach, golf (there are several courses), or go clamming in tidal areas, P.E.I. can be toured in a day, with stops at fishing villages and several attractions, including:

- **Charlottetown,** P.E.I.'s historical centre and provincial capital. It was here, in **Province House,** that the idea of a united Canada was first discussed in 1864. Charlottetown is a picturesque waterfront city with quaint shops and cafés, and a number of museums and cultural sites, including the **Confederation Centre of the Arts,** built as a memorial to the Fathers of Confederation. The centre is also host to the Charlottetown Festival, which features a musical production of *Anne of Green Gables* (based on the famous novel by P.E.I. native Lucy Maud Montgomery).

- **Cavendish.** Just a short drive from Charlottetown, this white-sand beach town is best known for **Anne of Green Gables House,** which is open to the public, and several associated attractions.

 The readers of *Score* magazine have rated P.E.I. "Canada's Best Golf Destination."

 The northern lights occur 240 nights a year in Labrador.

- **Prince Edward Island National Park,** popular for its camping facilities, beaches, water sports, hiking and bicycling trails, and uncrowded "red" sand beaches.

Newfoundland and Labrador

The northernmost of the Atlantic provinces is a genuinely rustic wilderness area, with more than 16 000 kilometres of coastline (and locals who sometimes sound like they're speaking with an Irish accent!). The island of Newfoundland and the mainland portion, known as Labrador, are noted for colourful coastal fishing towns that seem unchanged from a century ago. For those who like to explore, the province has much to offer, including the ruins of early settlements, fossil and rock hunting along the eastern shore, summertime scuba diving among the more than 20 000 shipwrecks (including a German U-boat that sank in **Conception Bay** during World War II), iceberg watching, and that cutest of birds, the puffin. Other activities and attractions are:

- **St. John's,** the provincial capital and a lively port city on the far east coast, noted for its nautical history, old churches, and fantastic seafood. **Water Street,** one of North America's oldest streets, is a prime shopping destination. **George Street** may have Canada's largest concentration of pubs and live music venues. Historical sites near St. John's include **Signal Hill National Historic Site** and **Torbay.** St. John's is a popular cruise port.

 The iceberg that sank the *Titanic* came from Iceberg Alley.

- **Whale-watching,** either by boat tour or from the shores of **Avalon Peninsula** or Labrador. Twenty-two species of whales and dolphins, including the great humpback whale, visit Newfoundland and Labrador's shores during the spring and summer. Nature lovers will also be impressed by the area's ecological reserves, which are home to large colonies of puffins, gannets, kittiwakes, and other sea birds. Whales (and icebergs) can also be seen in **Iceberg Alley,** 400 kilometres southeast of Newfoundland.

- **Outdoor activities:** Sea kayaking, sailing, hiking, mountain climbing, and alpine and cross-country skiing are just a few of the many options. Less adventurous travellers might take walks among cliff-top lookouts and unspoiled beaches for a remarkable view of the occasional offshore iceberg.

- **Gros Morne National Park** on Newfoundland's west coast and **L'Anse aux Meadows** [lance oh MED-doze] **National Park** on the island's northern tip, both UNESCO World Heritage Sites. Gros Morne is noted for its stunning scenery—cliffs and fjords best viewed through hiking or boat tours. L'Anse aux Meadows has the distinction of being the first UNESCO site and is home to the only validated Viking settlement in North America—the legendary Leif Ericson probably "discovered" it. Several original sod-roof buildings have been rebuilt.

- **St. Pierre and Miquelon Islands,** about 25 kilometres off Newfoundland's southern coast. France's last holdings in North America, these two islands have bistros, cafés, and New Orleans–like architecture. They can be reached by plane from St. John's, Halifax, or Sydney, or by boat.

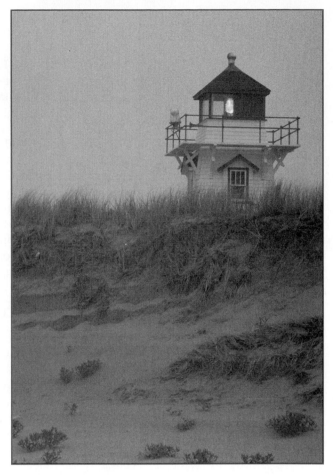

Visitors are drawn to the grassy dunes and dozens of picturesque lighthouses on Prince Edward Island.
Copyright COREL

POSSIBLE ITINERARIES

For those who have only a few days in which to see Atlantic Canada, a stay in just one province may offer a less rushed experience. Nova Scotia is a popular choice for such a short visit. For a multi-day itinerary plan, a tour of the three lower provinces is ideal, because the distances involved aren't overly great. Transport to and from locations via ferry is an offbeat way to travel and to see the coastlines. A one-week tour might take visitors from New Brunswick to P.E.I., then to the west coast of Nova Scotia, along the breathtaking Cabot Trail, and finally to Halifax. Those who have only a week may have to forgo Newfoundland and Labrador, unless they travel there by plane.

LODGING OPTIONS

The diversity of Atlantic Canada is reflected in its accommodations, ranging from fine hotels (many found along the coast), such as those of the Canadian-based **Fairmont, Delta,** and **Rodd** chains, to bed-and-breakfasts (sometimes known in Newfoundland and Labrador as hospitality homes), to campgrounds. Most major international chains have properties in each province.

Many pubs and restaurants offer "Maritime Kitchen Parties" that feature local Celtic entertainment.

Lodging choices that have a unique character or service bundle, such as the following, can enhance the trip:

Nova Scotia: **Delta Barrington** (Halifax)—a restored property in the historical area, that's connected to terrific shopping; **Prince George Hotel** (Halifax)—linked to the World Trade and Convention Centre via a tunnel; the **Casino Nova Scotia Hotel**—with many rooms with waterfront views; the **Prince George Hotel**—located next to the World Trade and Convention Centre; the **Westin Nova Scotian**—a historical property; the **Keltic Lodge** (Ingonish Beach in Cape Breton Highlands National Park)—boasting a difficult 18-hole golf course and a scenic waterfront/ countryside setting.

New Brunswick: **Fairmont Algonquin** (St. Andrews)—a historic landmark hotel featuring a Tudor-style façade, public golf course, and kilt-wearing, bagpipe-playing bellboys; **Delta Brunswick** (Saint John)—an excellent location near the Market Square shopping and dining complex; **Red Rose Mansion** (Saint John)— a 1904 mansion near Rockwood Park; **Delta Beausejour** (Moncton)—featuring Acadian decor and cuisine.

Prince Edward Island: **Delta Prince Edward Hotel** (Charlottetown)—a property that overlooks the waterfront. **Rodd Crowbush Golf & Beach Resort** is Atlantic Canada's only five-star resort.

Newfoundland and Labrador: **Fairmont Newfoundland** (St. John's)—in a prime downtown location.

Finally, bed-and-breakfast lodging (including some in old manors and mansions) has become a popular option throughout Canada's Atlantic region, both in the countryside and in major cities.

ALLIED DESTINATIONS

Due to its proximity to the U.S. East Coast, Atlantic Canada lends itself to add-on travel packages to New England or New York, thus providing an expanded itinerary. With the Atlantic Ocean or St. Lawrence River as passageways, the Atlantic provinces are perfect destinations for summer cruises. Major cruise lines operate seasonally from Quebec City or Montreal, call on several Atlantic ports, and continue on to Boston, New York City, or other U.S. Eastern Seaboard ports (the cruise can also start in the United States and finish in Montreal or Quebec City). Several ferry services also connect Yarmouth, Nova Scotia, to Bar Harbor or Portland, Maine.

Other options include train packages (VIA Rail Canada connects from Atlantic Canada to Amtrak train and/or bus service via Montreal to Washington, D.C., New York City, and outside Boston) or motorcoach tours of the north Atlantic seaboard. Someone from the Western provinces might wish to visit both Central Canada and Atlantic Canada on one extended trip.

FACTORS THAT MOTIVATE VISITORS

Atlantic Canada has a very specialized tourist appeal. Here are some of the reasons for going there:

- The area's natural beauty is stunning, especially along the shore and into the wilderness.

- The people are well known for their friendliness and hospitality.

- The region is of considerable historical importance.

- Great bargains are available, especially off-season.

- The leisurely pace will appeal to those wishing to get away from it all.

- There are abundant opportunities for outdoor activities, such as fishing, golfing, boating, camping, bicycling, hiking, and swimming.

- Coastal cities and towns offer an appealing shopping and dining scene, as well as the opportunity for quiet beach walks and sightseeing.

- The region is famous for its fresh seafood.

- Cruise possibilities are numerous.

POSSIBLE MISGIVINGS

Though Atlantic Canada has much to offer, potential visitors may have concerns and questions that you should address, such as:

- "Isn't it foggy and cold there?" Summers are generally mild, with average daytime temperatures in the low 20s. Fog is not uncommon, though, especially in the mornings, and evenings can be brisk. Atlantic Canada is not for those who think a tropical vacation is the ultimate.

- "Is there more to see than just fishing villages and lighthouses?" The coastal towns are what give Atlantic Canada its charm, but they are not the only attractions the region has to offer. Such unique sights as the Bay of Fundy, the Reversing Falls, icebergs, humpback whales, Louisbourg, and St. John's are sure to intrigue potential visitors. In addition, there's a broad array of landmarks, museums, historical attractions, and cultural centres.

- "I like fine food, but there's not much beyond seafood in Atlantic Canada." Yes, seafood lovers will thoroughly enjoy Atlantic Canada, but the region has much more to offer. P.E.I. and New Brunswick have large farming areas, providing a bevy of fresh meats and produce. In addition, the Acadian, British, Scottish, and French cultural influences guarantee a diversity of cuisine.

Qualifying the Traveller
ATLANTIC CANADA

FOR PEOPLE WHO WANT	HIGH APPEAL	MEDIUM APPEAL	LOW APPEAL	REMARKS
Historical and Cultural Attractions		▲		
Beaches and Water Sports		▲		Water a bit chilly for swimming
Skiing Opportunities			▲	
Lots of Nightlife			▲	Some in Halifax and St. John's
Family Activities		▲		
Familiar Cultural Experience	▲			
Exotic Cultural Experience			▲	
Safety and Low Crime	▲			
Bargain Travel		▲		Especially off-season
Impressive Scenery	▲			
Peace and Quiet	▲			
Shopping Opportunities		▲		Pewter in New Brunswick and Nova Scotia
Adventure		▲		
To Do Business		▲		Incentive and meeting destination

Pewter goods made in Pugwash, Nova Scotia, are known worldwide.

- "I like an active, exciting vacation. Spending a week driving along scenic routes would get repetitive." Though sightseeing by car or tour bus is one of the best ways to see the spectacular scenery, that's not the only way to get around. Suggest travel by ferry or even bicycle. Also, there are lots of interesting stops along Atlantic Canada's byways, quaint restaurants, craft shops, photo opportunities, and plenty of great scenery.

SALES STRATEGIES

Most experts concentrate their sales efforts on the kind of traveller who can appreciate Atlantic Canada: ecotourists, history buffs, outdoors types, and those who love scenery. Such visitors are drawn to the beauty of the coastal areas, the historical sites, and the quiet allure of a fishing village at sunset. Since the region's greatest asset is its scenery, lodging on the beaches of P.E.I. or on a Nova Scotia cliff top overlooking breaching whales is especially attractive.

An excellent way to increase the profitability of an Atlantic Canada vacation is a cruise or a tour package that combines the region with New England or New York. Cross-sell opportunities include motorcoach tours, ferry rides, boat tours, and, of course, car rentals.

Festivals and special events are major draws for visitors. Virtually every festival in Atlantic Canada takes place during the summer. The Charlottetown Festival (P.E.I.) runs from May to October, and features a musical production of *Anne of Green Gables.* Nova Scotia boasts a showcase of the "best street performers from around the world" at the Halifax International Busker Festival in August. The Shediac Lobster Festival (Shediac, New Brunswick) is a July party featuring lobster-eating contests.

NAME _____   DATE _____

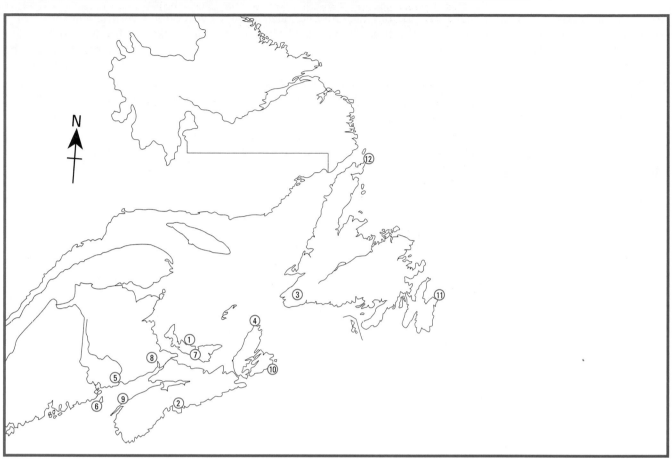

A traveller wants to visit the places listed below. Which number represents each on the map?

PLACE/ATTRACTION		IN WHICH CITY/PROVINCE?	NUMBER ON MAP
A.	The capital of the southernmost Atlantic province	A.	A.
B.	The Cabot Trail	B.	B.
C.	The Bay of Fundy	C.	C.
D.	L'Anse aux Meadows	D.	D.
E.	Fortress of Louisbourg	E.	E.
F.	Charlottetown	F.	F.
G.	Anne of Green Gables House	G.	G.
H.	The easternmost provincial capital	H.	H.
I.	Magnetic Hill	I.	I.
J.	Reversing Falls	J.	J.

NAME _____   DATE _____

You're a travel agent. Guy and Diane LeBlanc of Hull, Quebec, have come to you often over the years for help with their vacation plans. Now that they've retired (he was a city bus driver, she worked at the National Arboretum), they've become avid travellers and prefer leisurely sightseeing to sunbathing on a crowded beach. They're making plans for a seven-day, early-summer vacation. Last year, their cousins, who live in Boston, visited Nova Scotia and loved it. The LeBlancs also heard plenty about Nova Scotia from their son, who now lives in Stamford, Connecticut, but who used to work in St. John's. They are concerned, however, that there won't be enough to do or see. How might you provide them with information and suggestions for creating an Atlantic Canada vacation?

Circle the answer that best suits their needs.

1. What might you offer to enhance their vacation?

    A New Brunswick/Nova Scotia motorcoach tour   A train tour

    A car rental   A cruise

    Why?

2. Let's assume that they rejected your first suggestion. What would be your second recommendation?

    A New Brunswick/Nova Scotia motorcoach tour   A train tour

    A car rental   A cruise

    Why?

3. Keeping in mind their interests, what would you stress that would make a trip to Atlantic Canada most appealing to them?

    Numerous historical attractions   Scenic travelways

    Cultural uniqueness   The fact that their cousins liked it

    Why?

4. If the LeBlancs decide to visit only one province in Atlantic Canada, which one would you recommend?

    Nova Scotia   Prince Edward Island

    New Brunswick   Newfoundland and Labrador

    Why?

NAME _____   DATE _____

You're the owner of a small tour company offering packages that operate mainly during the peak summer season and winter skiing months. The upcoming spring shoulder season tends to be slow, so you're developing tour package ideas to entice your customers to take advantage of the off-season discount rates. Since spring and early summer are the months when whales visit the shores of Atlantic Canada, you're considering a whale-watching adventure tour concept.

You've checked your computer database and discovered that a significant number of past clients expressed an interest in ecotours. Might a whale-watching tour be just the vacation for these people? Since it's a targeted group, you've decided to use a focused direct-mail campaign to reach the prospective travellers. The show-piece of the mailing will be a threefold brochure, which you will design in-house.

Find two or three brochures that you believe to be effective and isolate their key elements. Consider the best use of intriguing headline and body copy, photographs, reply information, brochure colour, etc. Also take a look at several websites that target whale-watching travel. Keep in mind the varying time restraints of your customers. What tour options would you include? What features and benefits would you highlight? After analyzing these points, create your own threefold brochure. You may create it via handwriting, drawings, cut-out photos, or computer—whatever it takes to convey what a final version might look like.

TRAVEL TRIVIA
UNUSUAL GEOGRAPHIC FACTS ABOUT CANADA

- Canada is almost as large as all of Europe.

- At the height of the gold rush, Dawson City had a population of 30 000. Today, about 1200 people live there.

- The entire population of the Northwest Territories and Nunavut could fit comfortably into Toronto's Rogers Centre.

- The area around Lindbergh, Alberta, contains enough salt to meet Canada's needs for the next 2000 years.

- The island of Newfoundland has a population of 485 000 humans and 110 000 moose.

- There are so many lakes in Saskatchewan that you could fish in a different one every day for 250 years and still have some left over.

- Captain Kidd's treasure is said to be buried on Oak Island in Nova Scotia's Mahone Bay (but no one has found it—or even a map—yet).

- P.E.I. exports almost half of the world's supply of Irish moss, a sea-weed used in toothpaste and ice cream.

- The first mechanical lift, the first chair lift, and the first automatic snowguns in North America were all built on Quebec's slopes.

LABRADOR
SEA

MANITOBA

HUDSON
BAY

JAMES
BAY

ONTARIO

QUEBEC

LABRADOR

Kenora

Lake
Superior

Gaspé

Percé

Gaspé
Peninsula

Magdalen
Islands

Saguenay R.

PRINCE
EDWARD
ISLAND

Tadoussac

Quebec
City

Rivière-du-Loup

Laurentian
Mountains

Sudbury

Ottawa R.

Mont
Tremblant

St. Lawrence R.

Beachburg

Trois-Rivières

Algonquin
Park

Gatineau

Montreal

U N I T E D

Ottawa

Eastern Townships

NOVA
SCOTIA

Lake
Huron

Kingston

Upper Canada
Village

Mennonite
Country

Toronto

Thousand Islands

NEW
BRUNSWICK

Hamilton

Lake Ontario

Lake
Michigan

Stratford

Niagara
Falls

Windsor

Lake Erie

S T A T E S

Ontario and Quebec

A Tale of Twos

The provinces of **Ontario** (bordered by Manitoba to the west) and **Quebec** (bordered by Newfoundland and Labrador and New Brunswick to the east) offer a remarkable choice of travel experiences. You can view this region as a place of duality, of pairs, of twos. For example, these are the nation's two biggest provinces (Quebec is the largest), covering more than 1.6 million square kilometres. They contain Canada's two largest cities: **Montreal** (Quebec) and **Toronto** (Ontario), home to more than one out of every four Canadians. The provinces also boast two nationally significant cities (Canada's capital, **Ottawa,** Ontario, and history-rich **Quebec City,** Quebec) and two of North America's most remarkable natural attractions (the **Thousand Islands** and **Niagara Falls,** Ontario).

The duality of Ontario and Quebec is further illustrated in each one's character and ambience. Nowhere in Canada is the interplay of French and English cultures more prominent than it is in Quebec and southeastern Ontario. Here, too, are bustling metropolitan centres, yet calm, pristine, natural retreats are nearby. Even the major cities exhibit a dual nature: from cosmopolitan and modern to quaint and historic. Ontario and Quebec will surely satisfy those tourists wishing to experience Canada's diversity.

One final comment: Although Ontario and Quebec are most often referred to as "Central Canada," one look at a map shows that they're not central at all! (Manitoba seems a more likely choice.) The term "Central" applies more to the centre of demographics and economics than to the geographic centre.

HOW TRAVELLERS GET THERE

Air service to Central Canada is extremely convenient, with frequent flights to the region's primary gateways of Toronto (YTO) and Montreal (YMQ). Passengers bound for Toronto will most likely land at **Lester B. Pearson International Airport** (YYZ). Travellers to Montreal fly into **Pierre Trudeau** (formerly Dorval) **International Airport** (YUL), where all scheduled flights land. Ottawa (YOW) also has an airport for flights throughout the country. Quebec City (YQB) has more limited service. Travellers who are interested in visiting Niagara Falls might consider flying to Buffalo, New York (BUF), which is closer to the falls than Toronto (which is 90 minutes from the falls). Keep in mind, though, that this option will require visitors to go through Customs twice.

The **Trans-Canada Highway,** which is 7821 kilometres long, links St. John's, Newfoundland, with Victoria, British Columbia. As the world's longest national highway, it's a primary route for travellers coming from the east into Quebec. From Edmundston, New Brunswick, Route 2 enters Quebec, where it becomes Highway 185, and continues to **Rivière-du-Loup** (129 kilometres) becoming Highway 20, then south to Quebec City (208 kilometres). From Montreal to Windsor, most travellers find the Macdonald-Cartier Freeway, also known as Highway 401, more convenient and efficient. People travelling west from southeastern Ontario to **Kenora** follow Highway 17. Kenora is 2000 kilometres from Toronto and 2130 kilometres from Ottawa.

VIA Rail Canada's western transcontinental train service, the **Canadian,** has departures three times a week from Vancouver through the Canadian Rockies (via Jasper, Edmonton, and Saskatoon) to Winnipeg, one of the line's hub cities, and on into Ontario, where Toronto's elegant **Union Station** also serves as a hub. The Canadian is a stainless-steel train that has been restored to its original 1950s style. It features sleeper cars, lounges, a dining car, and a domed sightseeing car.

Though the southern portions of both Ontario and Quebec are almost entirely bordered by water (the St. Lawrence River and the Great Lakes), virtually no public transportation plies these waterways. One notable exception: A few cruise lines make seasonal sailings along the St. Lawrence River from (or to) the Atlantic Ocean and points southward (very rarely do they travel farther west than Montreal).

WEATHER PATTERNS

Winters tend to be quite pronounced in Central Canada, with a nearly permanent layer of snow on the ground from December through March. Temperatures in southern Ontario can be somewhat more moderate, however, thanks to the tempering effects of the Great Lakes. However, eastern Ontario and Quebec experience harsh winters, with temperatures sometimes reaching –30°C!

Summer months (marked by a tourist season that runs from late June to the beginning of September) are usually warm, with occasional spells of hot and humid weather. Temperatures drop quickly in the fall. Indeed, chilly nights often occur as early as the third or fourth week in August, a condition that Toronto locals know as "Exhibition weather," so called because the city's annual Canadian National Exhibition, or CNE, begins in mid-August. Autumn in Ontario and Quebec is a time of brilliant fall foliage and brief spells of mild Indian summer weather. (See Figures 2-1 and 2-2.)

Though the tourist off-season generally runs from September to early May, the winter months hold appeal for some, especially skiers. In addition, Quebec City is a draw in February when the annual winter festival, Carnaval de Québec, takes place.

GETTING AROUND

The world's longest street is Ontario's Yonge [pronounced YOUNG] Street, which stretches 1896 kilometres out of Toronto.

Traversing Central Canada by car, even during the winter months, is usually problem-free, due largely to the Trans-Canada Highway. From Manitoba, the Trans-Canada runs east through southwestern Ontario (at some points the highway also skirts the north shores of Lake Superior and Lake Huron). At **Sudbury,** a city located in Ontario's "near north," the Trans-Canada splits, with Highway 69 heading southeast toward Toronto and Highway 17 heading east toward Ottawa. Drivers should note that the Trans-Canada does *not* pass through Toronto; a provincial highway (the 400) connects the two. The main artery between Toronto and Niagara Falls is the Queen Elizabeth Way, or QEW, which also is not a part of the Trans-Canada system.

The Trans-Canada passes through Ottawa and continues east to the Ontario/Quebec border, where it becomes Highway 40. The 40 is a direct route to Montreal, from which Quebec City–bound travellers may take the Trans-Canada Highway 20 (the Jean Lesage Autoroute) northeast to Quebec City on the south

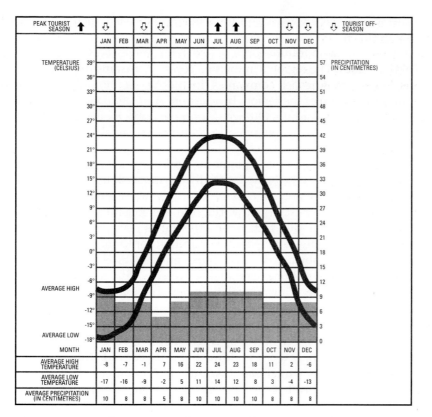

Figure 2-1   Climate at a Glance: Quebec City, Quebec

MONTH	JAN	FEB	MAR	APR	MAY	JUN	JUL	AUG	SEP	OCT	NOV	DEC
AVERAGE HIGH TEMPERATURE	-8	-7	-1	7	16	22	24	23	18	11	2	-6
AVERAGE LOW TEMPERATURE	-17	-16	-9	-2	5	11	14	12	8	3	-4	-13
AVERAGE PRECIPITATION (IN CENTIMETRES)	10	8	8	5	8	10	10	10	10	8	8	8

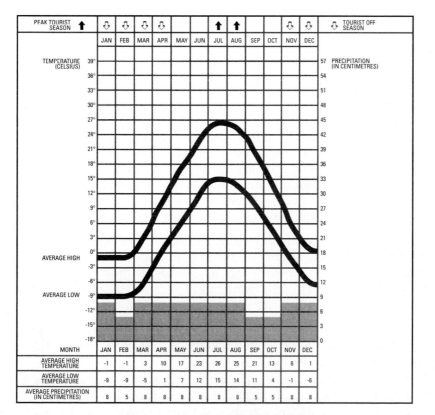

Figure 2-2   Climate at a Glance: Toronto, Ontario

MONTH	JAN	FEB	MAR	APR	MAY	JUN	JUL	AUG	SEP	OCT	NOV	DEC
AVERAGE HIGH TEMPERATURE	-1	-1	3	10	17	23	26	25	21	13	6	1
AVERAGE LOW TEMPERATURE	-9	-9	-5	1	7	12	15	14	11	4	-1	-6
AVERAGE PRECIPITATION (IN CENTIMETRES)	8	5	8	8	8	8	8	8	5	5	8	8

side of the St. Lawrence River or continue on Highway 40, which travels northeast along the north shore.

Many other transportation options exist for travel between Quebec's and Ontario's key cities. The region's numerous commuter trains make frequent inter-city runs. Several motorcoach companies (including Greyhound) travel the populated southern portion of the region. In addition, Air Canada schedules numerous daily flights between Toronto, Ottawa, Montreal, and Quebec City. St. Lawrence Cruise Lines, based in **Kingston,** Ontario, features a steamship replica that cruises the St. Lawrence River.

Travel within the key cities is superb. As in any major city, auto traffic in Toronto and Montreal can be busy, especially during rush hours, but public transportation is convenient and extensive. The subway systems in Montreal and Toronto are among the best in the world, and are considered models of cleanliness, safety, and efficiency. In fact, when other cities plan to build a subway, they often send representatives to Montreal and Toronto to see how it's done. Moreover, where the subways don't go, buses and, in Toronto, streetcars do. Taxis and car rentals are also options for travel.

Some truly unique transportation experiences are available in Central Canada. Quebec City is known for its rides via *calèche,* or horse-drawn buggy—a particularly romantic way to see the city's historic area. In addition, a funicular railway connects the Lower and Upper Towns of Quebec City. When visiting Ottawa, visitors may enjoy a cruise down the 170-year-old **Rideau Canal,** which bisects the city. During winter months, this nine kilometre canal becomes the world's longest skating rink; even business people sometimes use this thoroughfare to skate across town to their offices. (The canal is constantly groomed by the National Capital Commission, so it's always in great shape.)

IMPORTANT PLACES

Ontario and Quebec feature some of North America's most intriguing places. Here are the most popular:

Toronto

Toronto is a culture-filled metropolis that designer and visionary Buckminster Fuller once called "the only modern city that works." Ontario's provincial capital and the largest city in Canada, Toronto is known for its broad ethnic diversity. Dozens of ethnic neighbourhoods and enclaves, such as Chinatown, Greek Town, and Little Italy—Toronto may have more Italian-speaking people than any city outside of Italy—give the city a truly cosmopolitan feel.

The city's restaurants offer the best in fine food and ambience, and the theatre and arts scene is diverse, ranging from serious drama to standup comedy. (Toronto is a spawning-ground for countless internationally known comedians.) Besides New York and London, Toronto stages more live theatre and dance than any other English-speaking city. Among its many attractions are:

- **The CN Tower,** the world's tallest free-standing structure (553 metres tall) and the city's most recognizable landmark. An outdoor observation deck and a revolving restaurant provide panoramic views of Toronto. On a clear day, visitors can see plumes of mist rising from Niagara Falls, almost 100 kilometres away.

- **Toronto City Hall,** with its curving office towers and saucer-shaped council chamber, and the nearby **Eaton Centre,** a vast indoor space that features 350 restaurants and shops.

- **Rogers Centre** (formerly SkyDome), home to the Toronto Blue Jays (baseball) and the Toronto Argonauts (football). Rogers Centre has the world's first fully retractable roof (it can open or close in less than 20 minutes) and a hotel that overlooks the playing field.

Montreal's Mt. Royal Park was designed by Frederick Law Olmsted. He also designed New York's Central Park, the U.S. Capitol Grounds, and the parks lining the U.S. side of Niagara Falls.

Forty kilometres north of Toronto, in Kleinberg, is the McMichael Art Gallery, which houses one of Canada's richest collections of paintings by the renowned Group of Seven.

- **The Air Canada Centre,** located right downtown, the home of the Toronto Maple Leafs (hockey) and the Toronto Raptors (basketball).

- **The Hockey Hall of Fame** (located on the northwest corner of Front and Yonge streets), a shrine to the heroes and history of the nation's most popular sport.

- **The PATH Downtown Walkway,** a 27 kilometre underground walkway that links office buildings, hotels, subway stations, and 1100 shops and restaurants.

- **The Royal Ontario Museum,** Canada's biggest, featuring five million exhibits, artworks, and artifacts. Among the special attractions are a Chinese tomb, a gallery of dinosaur skeletons, a superb display of 20th-century design styles, a noteworthy Egyptian collection, and a bat cave.

- **Casa Loma** (completed in 1914), a cavernous, eccentric, medieval-style castle with 98 rooms and even secret passages. It may look familiar to you; it's been a location for countless movies and TV shows.

- **Historic Fort York,** official site of the founding of Toronto more than 200 years ago. It features restored barracks and other buildings, plus costumed soldiers who re-enact Canadian military life of 1812.

- **Toronto Zoo** (one of the world's largest), designed to re-create natural animal habitats.

- **The Ontario Science Centre,** showcasing scientific and technological achievements, and featuring many interactive exhibits.

- **Paramount Canada's Wonderland** amusement park—the largest theme park in Canada, with more than 60 rides (including several large rollercoasters) and live shows. It's located close to Toronto, in Vaughan.

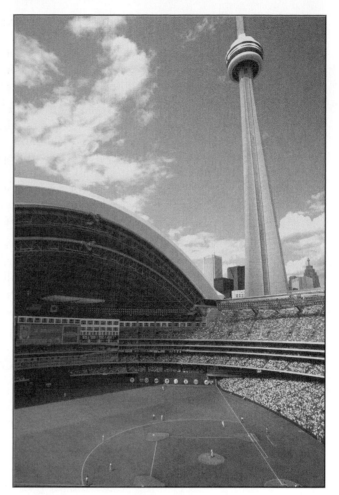

Toronto's CN Tower and Rogers Centre are two of the city's most recognizable landmarks.
Copyright COREL

Toronto's Bata Shoe Museum has perhaps the world's biggest display of historical footwear.

The first person to go over Niagara Falls in a barrel was a woman, Annie Taylor.

Toronto is within a one- to two-hour drive of several notable attractions, each of which is perfect for a one-day excursion or longer trip. Among the most visited are:

- **Niagara Falls,** known for more than a century as a destination for honeymooners, and one of North America's best-known attractions. Niagara Falls, which is about a 90-minute drive southeast of Toronto, is really three falls: **American Falls** and **Bridal Veil Falls** on the New York side, and the **Horseshoe Falls** on the Canadian side. The best views of the Niagara cascades are from Canada, where several observation towers provide awesome vistas onto the roaring 57 metre drop. Two other (and dramatic) ways to experience the falls are from the *Maid of the Mist* boat and from the **Journey behind the Falls** tunnels. During the day, rainbows are often created in the falls' mist; at night, the falls are lit for spectacular views. The **Whirlpool Aero Car** is a cable car suspended over the whirlpool caused by the river's "right turn" 3.25 kilometres from the falls. For the more adventurous, a high-powered jet boat challenges the lower Niagara River's rapids and whirlpool.

  Several attractions also look back on the eccentric history of Niagara Falls, from its tightrope walkers to daredevils who have challenged its plunging waters in barrels. The city of Niagara Falls is now also the site of two huge and popular casinos. En route to the falls from Toronto is the city of **Hamilton** (home to the **Royal Botanical Gardens** and **Dundurn Castle**) and a broad stretch of fruit orchards, vineyards, and wineries. The Niagara area has several vineyards boasting award-winning vintages, some with 4- and 5-star restaurants.

- **Niagara-on-the-Lake,** an arts-and-crafts community and historical town close to the falls. A highlight of the area, the annual **Shaw Festival,** runs from April to November and is the world's only live theatre devoted to George Bernard Shaw's work. Nearby are vineyards, where visitors can try the award-winning icewine, and the **Welland Canal Locks,** passageways that are filled with (or emptied of) water to facilitate the movement of large ships travelling between Lake Ontario and Lake Erie. (To see a huge tanker rise or fall a dozen or so metres in a matter of minutes at the Lock 3 viewing complex is a unique experience.)

- **Stratford,** a picturesque town southwest of Toronto and for about 50 years host of the critically acclaimed annual **Stratford Festival,** which runs from April to November. Plays by Shakespeare and others are staged in three theatres.

- **Mennonite country,** a popular rural area in southwestern Ontario that's great for a unique, one-day drive. In the towns of St. Jacobs, Elmira, and Elora, tourists can see "Old Order" members of this religious sect who still drive horse-and-buggies, wear old-style garb, and sell their crafts via local stores.

- **The Thousand Islands/Kingston** area, a popular spot for pleasure cruising, swimming, and fishing. East of Toronto, this scenic region is called the Thousand Islands because of the 1865 limestone and pink-granite islands that dot the local waters. The Thousand Islands is located where the St. Lawrence River flows out of Lake Ontario, and may be visited via tour boat from Gananoque [gan-ah-NAH-kway], Rockport, Lansdowne, or Kingston (where **Fort Henry** was built in 1812 and was recently restored as a military museum). Kingston also has many bed-and-breakfasts and is home to Queen's University. A key stop on most Thousand Island tours is **Heart Island** (in U.S. waters), where wealthy New York millionaire George Boldt built a never-completed castle for his wife.

Ottawa

Canada's national capital is Ottawa, though some of the sightseeing opportunities are found in neighbouring **Gatineau (Hull)**, Quebec, just across the **Ottawa River.** The combined area is known as the **National Capital Region.** Ottawa is a less visited tourist destination than Toronto or Montreal, but it provides a relatively uncrowded, relaxed, and charming visit, with an increasingly vibrant ambience. The city is noted for its spacious parks, canal cruises (and winter ice skating), and museums. Ottawa is also very conducive to walking and exploring by foot.

Visitors will find touring Ottawa to be very convenient. Most attractions are located within the **Parliament Precinct,** an area dotted with numerous government buildings, museums, memorials, and galleries, as well as two visitor information centres. Seeing Ottawa by motorcoach tour provides an overview of the city's prime sights and attractions, which include:

- **The Parliament Buildings.** These magnificent neo-Gothic structures, overlooking the Ottawa River, are particularly striking at night. (From May to September, the skies around **Parliament Hill** are lit by a sound-and-light show.) During the summer, visitors can also view the morning **Changing of the Guard** ceremony, a re-enactment of the British tradition. The **Peace Tower,** on the Centre Block (the central Parliament building), has an observation deck that provides great views of the Capital Region and beyond. Tourists visit the

The July 1st Canada Day celebrations take place in the capital as well as across Canada.

The Changing of the Guard, Ottawa
Copyright COREL

tower on a Parliament tour in order to see the structure's interior highlights. Also in the Centre Block is the visually stunning **Library of Parliament.**

- **Museums** (near Parliament Hill): the **National Gallery of Canada** (featuring a large collection of paintings, sculpture, photographs, and other works of art from around the world, housed in an architecturally striking glass building); the **Canadian War Museum** (with exhibits recounting the nation's military past); **Bytown Museum** (celebrating Ottawa's past and located in the city's oldest building); the **Canadian Museum of Contemporary Photography** (a museum with more than 160 000 photos on display); the **Royal Canadian Mint**; and the **Currency Museum of the Bank of Canada** (with coins and cash from around the globe).

- Somewhat farther from the city's centre: the **Canadian Museum of Nature** (a family museum with animal, bird, and dinosaur exhibits, housed in a castle-like structure); the **Canada Aviation Museum** (with a collection of vintage and modern aircraft); and the **Canada Science and Technology Museum** (with an especially impressive collection of mighty railroad steam engines).

- **Gatineau, Quebec** (just across the Ottawa River from Ottawa), home to the **Canadian Museum of Civilization,** a striking waterfront building that showcases Canadian culture and history. Within the museum are the **Canadian Children's Museum** and the world's only combined Imax and Omnimax film theatre. Also in the city is the **Casino du Lac-Leamy,** which has a very popular restaurant.

- **Gatineau Park,** just north of town, with bike paths, fishing, canoeing, and scenic lookouts.

- **Byward Market,** an open-air farmers' market and arts-and-crafts showcase that's been an Ottawa tradition for over 160 years. It's great for exploring, with its unique shops, cosy restaurants, and street performers.

- **Rideau River, Canal, and Falls,** more than 190 kilometres of linking lakes, canals, dams, and locks. Built between 1826 and 1832, the Rideau Canal (part

The "Diefenbunker," built near Ottawa to house government officials in the event of a nuclear war, is now open to the public.

Watch a ship or boat go through a lock. Ottawa has several small locks; bigger ones can be found near Montreal, Niagara Falls, and several places in Ontario.

of which is quite near the Parliament Buildings) is an engineering marvel. **Winterlude**—one of Canada's largest winter festivals—takes place during February on and around the Canal.

Potential day trips from Ottawa include **Upper Canada Village** (a living history museum re-creating a St. Lawrence Valley town of the mid-1800s—located southeast of Ottawa in Morrisburg); **Algonquin Provincial Park** (a huge wilderness park located 250 kilometres west of Ottawa, and popular with those who like to fish, hike, and canoe); and whitewater rafting on the Ottawa River near **Beachburg,** Ontario.

Montreal

Only a two-hour drive from Ottawa is Quebec's major city, Montreal, the second-largest city in Canada. A confluence of cultures with a distinct European character, Montreal is one of the largest French-speaking cities in the world (most locals speak English, too). It offers a foreign travel experience in a nearby metropolitan setting. The city is more than 360 years old and represents an unusual mixture of Old World charms and modern influences. Here one can find everything from historic churches set along cobblestone streets to soaring glass skyscrapers.

This city of more than three million residents blends a remarkable array of cultures and attractions. Dining is a favourite pastime, and with thousands of restaurants to sample, visitors can experience virtually any culinary style. The city also has a vibrant nightlife, with concerts, theatres, nightclubs, and eateries. And, of course, Montreal is a major sports centre, having hosted the Summer Olympic Games in 1976, as well as boasting a proud hockey tradition (the Montreal Canadiens is Montreal's NHL team). The **McCord Museum of Canadian History, Montreal Museum of Fine Arts,** and the **Pointe-à-Callière Montreal Museum of Archaeology and History** are noteworthy. Among Montreal's other notable attractions are:

- **Old Montreal (Vieux Montréal)**, a richly historic area in the heart of downtown, near the St. Lawrence River in the old port section (now a summer entertainment complex). This 38-hectare area is very walkable and retains an Old World charm. It's known for great shopping, restaurants, outdoor cafés in the summer, and nightlife.

- **The Basilica of Notre Dame (La Basilique Notre-Dame de Montréal)**, a Gothic cathedral built in 1829. Its stony exterior is rather dull, but its vast interior features large, delicate stained-glass windows, a 5772-pipe organ, an intricate main altar, and some truly remarkable blue-and-gold-highlighted woodwork. An evening sound-and-light show illustrates the history of the city and the church.

- **Mont-Royal Park,** featuring a 233-metre-high lookout that provides incredible day or night views of the Montreal skyline, the St. Lawrence River, and distant mountains.

- **St. Joseph's Oratory (Oratoire St-Joseph)**, a huge domed basilica located at the base of Mont-Royal Park. The older lower section of the basilica is said to have been the site of many miracle cures.

- **The underground city (la ville souterraine)**, a weatherproof, subterranean downtown with passageways that interlink more than 2000 shops and restaurants. (It's especially popular during the winter months.)

- **Expo Islands** in the St. Lawrence River, site of Expo 67 (the 1967 World's Fair). The islands contain several parks, shopping areas, and an amusement park (**La Ronde**) that's especially popular with families. A few of the old Expo structures have been converted to new attractions or sporting venues, such as **Montréal Casino**, a province-operated casino.

- **Olympic Park,** site of the Olympic Games and still used for major sporting events. **Olympic Stadium,** an all-weather stadium, features the world's tallest inclined tower (175 metres high). The former Velodrome (now called the **Montreal Biodome**) now houses an ecology centre, complete with varied ecosystems, animals, fish, and birds. Tours of the Olympic Park complex are available.

Among **day trips** are:

- **The Laurentians (Les Laurentides),** a chain of mountains 90 minutes north of Montreal, with engaging scenery, lakes, and great winter skiing. Within and around the Laurentians are several well-known resort areas, each with unique characteristics and abundant outdoor activities. **Mont-Tremblant,** a popular ski resort since 1939, is the highest peak in the mountain chain and has a variety of trails to suit every skill level. **St-Sauveur-des-Monts** is a favourite ski destination for local Québécois. (In the summer its water parks are quite popular.) **Val-David** is an arts enclave boasting an array of winter sports activities.

- **The Eastern Townships** resort area, one hour south of Montreal. This scenic lake and mountain region is a popular vacation area, boasting clusters of quaint towns and a variety of outdoor activities, including cross-country and downhill skiing, snowmobiling, and snowshoeing in the winter, and sailing, hiking, swimming, bicycling, and horseback riding in the summer.

- **The Magdalen Islands (Îles-de-la-Madeleine),** a chain of a dozen islands in the middle of the Gulf of St. Lawrence. Though closer to Prince Edward Island, these islands are part of Quebec and offer a remote getaway. Accessible via plane from Quebec or Nova Scotia, ferry from P.E.I., or passenger vessel (the *Voyageur*) from Montreal, the Magdalen Islands have secluded beaches and excellent seafood.

Quebec City

About a three-hour drive northeast of Montreal is Quebec's provincial capital, Quebec City. It could be visited as a long day trip from Montreal, though visitors will appreciate the city more fully if they spend several days there. Unlike most other cities, Quebec City is famous less for its individual attractions than for being one itself.

The first French settlement in North America, Quebec City was originally built as a walled fortification and is the continent's only walled city north of Mexico. Most of the city sits atop and around a rocky palisade overlooking the St. Lawrence River and has an architecture and ambience reminiscent of 17th-century coastal French towns.

The second-largest city in the province, Quebec City has a distinctly European feel, with its cobblestone streets, historical stone buildings, interesting museums, cozy outdoor cafés, and seductive bistros. Among the city's attractions are:

- **Old Quebec (Vieux Québec),** a restored section of the original walled city, and a living museum of French-Canadian history. A guided tour via horse-drawn *calèche* or a walking tour provides such sights as the massive **Fairmont Château Frontenac,** a 110-year-old landmark hotel, which initiated the baronial château-style hotel design that the railroads repeated across Canada; the **Notre-Dame-de-Québec Basilica (Basilique Notre-Dame-de-Québec),** a centuries-old cathedral with a white-and-gold interior; and the **Citadel (La Citadelle),** a huge star-shaped garrison (the largest in North America) that sits high above the St. Lawrence and features a morning Changing of the Guard ceremony in the summer. Visitors love Old Quebec's romantic charm, captured in the 17th- and 18th-century buildings that line its streets—both at the foot of and atop the city's cliffs—and in the wide variety of restaurants, cafés,

Trois-Rivières, a historic industrial city, can be an interesting stop on Route 132, which connects Montreal with Quebec City.

Meat pies (*tourtières*) and maple-syrup pies are French-Canadian specialties.

Roosevelt and Churchill planned the Normandy Invasion in the Château Frontenac.

The Château Frontenac, a 110-year-old landmark hotel, is among the impressive sights of Old Quebec.
Copyright COREL

and shops. By virtue of its rich history and culture, Old Quebec was named a world heritage site by the United Nations in 1985.

- **National Battlefields Park (Parc National des Champs-de-Bataille),** 100 hectares of parkland marking the site of the Battle of the Plains of Abraham. It was here that in 1759 a British victory ended official French claims to Canada. Tourists may drive to the park or walk along **La Promenade des Gouverneurs,** a picturesque walkway leading along the length of the Citadel to the plains. The park is home to the **Musée du Québec,** an art museum partially housed in a former city jail, and an observatory offering city and river views.

Among possible **day trips** from Quebec City are:

- **Ste-Anne-de-Beaupré,** a small town (34 kilometres northeast of Quebec City) famous for the huge Catholic shrine of the same name. The church is visited by millions annually and is reported to have been the site of numerous miraculous healings.

- **Montmorency Falls,** several kilometres north of Quebec City, featuring an 83 metre drop. Much narrower than Niagara but 1.5 times as tall, Montmorency has terrific views from both the base of the falls and the top. It's particularly impressive in winter, when the spray freezes, forming a large ice slide.

- **Mont-Ste-Anne,** site of numerous World Cup skiing competitions. Just 43 kilometres from Quebec City, this popular ski resort has more than 60 trails and a dozen lifts, and is best known for its 17 illuminated trails for night skiing.

- **Île d'Orléans,** an island linked by a bridge to northern Quebec City, and a favourite getaway spot for local Québécois. The island offers visitors fantastic views of Quebec City, as well as an array of century-old churches and unique restaurants.

Roadside homemade-bread stands are a delight on the drive eastward from Quebec City.

Visiting a "sugar shack," or "*cabane à sucre*," is a must-do experience here in early spring when the sap is running.

These destinations are popular extensions to a Quebec City trip:

- **Tadoussac,** located on the north shore of the St. Lawrence River (approximately 225 kilometres northeast of Quebec City). From June to October, the mouth of the river is a noted feeding area for whales.

- **Gaspé Peninsula (Gaspésie)**, a beautiful rural region with rolling hills, Breton-like fishing villages, and quaint little shops (especially those selling wood carvings). The **Gaspésie Park** is especially popular with hikers, campers, and nature lovers (moose and the rare wood caribou populate the area). The waterfront villages of Gaspé, located on the south shore of the St. Lawrence River and the western shores of the Gulf of St. Lawrence, offer a step back in time. The area is known as a prime spot for whale-watching, and the town of **Gaspé** is home to the only wooden cathedral in North America, **Cathédrale du Christ-Roi.** Southeast of Gaspé is the town of **Percé,** noted for the dramatic waterfront views of its famous "pierced" **Percé Rock**—a huge boulder (90 metres high) jutting out of the coastal waters.

POSSIBLE ITINERARIES

Because of the varied cities, settings, attractions, and activities available in Central Canada, it would be difficult to do the entire area in anything less than two weeks. A tourist could do one week in each of the provinces or spend five to seven days enjoying one of the following combinations:

- Toronto and Niagara Falls are easily combined, with an excursion northeast to see the Thousand Islands.

- For those in a hurry, Montreal can serve as a hub for day trips to Ottawa and/ or Quebec City. By car, Montreal is about two hours away from Ottawa and three hours from Quebec City. Trains are just a little faster.

- Visitors could also fly into Ottawa, spend two days there, then drive to the Thousand Islands (one-day stay), east to Montreal (three to four days), then north to Quebec City (two days), where they'll catch their departing flight.

- For skiing enthusiasts, Montreal is close to several major resorts in the Laurentians. For shorter trips, a visit to Quebec City followed by skiing at Mont-Ste-Anne would be a good choice.

LODGING OPTIONS

Central Canada boasts a diversity of accommodations. Six major hotel chains— **Fairmont, Delta, Four Seasons, Hilton, Marriott,** and **Sheraton**—have multiple facilities in Toronto, Montreal, and throughout the region. In addition, mid-price and budget chains are well represented. For those who would prefer something a little different during their stay, the numerous bed-and-breakfasts that can be found in even the smallest towns are quite popular.

Toronto has a wealth of top-flight hotels. A **Four Seasons** and an **Inter-Continental** anchor the city's trendy shopping and dining neighbourhood of Yorkville. Canada's biggest hotel, the **Delta Chelsea,** has nearly 1600 rooms, and is a popular lodging choice for families. Another huge facility, the landmark **Sheraton Centre,** looms over City Hall and Nathan Phillips Square, which fronts it. It has almost 1400 rooms, more than 60 shops, and many restaurants and bars nearby. Another landmark, the venerable **Fairmont Royal York,** has 1365 rooms, numerous restaurants and bars, and a strategic downtown location across from Union Station. **Le Royal Meridien King Edward,** more than a century old, is also an elegant choice. In the Harbourfront area are **Westin Harbour Castle** and **Radisson Plaza Hotel Admiral.** Finally, one of the more interesting lodging

Here's a wonder that Torontonians, but few tourists, know about: the Toronto Islands. Visitors who take the short, inexpensive ferry ride from Harbourfront to this park-like setting will find picnic areas, bicycle trails, relaxing beauty, a children's amusement park, and unparalleled views of the city.

options is the **Renaissance Toronto Hotel Downtown,** a 350-room hotel that's part of the home stadium for the Blue Jays and the Argonauts. Sports fans are intrigued by the idea of staying in one of the 70 rooms that overlook the playing field.

Despite Niagara Falls' reputation as a tourist draw, most hotel rooms in the area are not terribly high priced—except those with a falls view (which are worth it!). Falls-view hotels are clustered in two areas: at the base of Clifton Hill (better views of the American Falls) and on the cliff area above the Canadian Horseshoe Falls, near the newer casino. In the first group are the **Sheraton on the Falls** and the venerable **Brock Plaza.** Among the second group are two with exceptional views: the **Niagara Fallsview Casino Resort** and the **Embassy Suites.** Other hotels in this area with good falls-view rooms are **The Oakes,** the **Renaissance,** the **Hilton,** and the **Radisson.** Remember, some of these properties offer only partial views and some rooms have no view of the falls. Other value-priced, motel-like lodging (with no views) are found primarily along Clifton Hill and Lundy's Lane.

Ottawa has several good hotels, including one of the most famous in the country—the **Fairmont Château Laurier.** This landmark facility resembles a castle and is often mistaken for one of the Parliament Buildings. The hotel has a marvellous location overlooking the Rideau Canal. Other fine choices are the **Sheraton Ottawa** and the **Westin Ottawa,** located a few blocks from Parliament Hill near the Rideau Canal.

Like Toronto, Montreal has a very large selection of fine hotels from which to choose. The **Ritz-Carlton** and **Marriott Château Champlain** are upscale properties in prime spots. The **Hilton Montreal Bonaventure** is noted for its business-district location, underground network of shops, and uniquely landscaped gardens. The aging but still famous **Fairmont Queen Elizabeth (La Reine Elizabeth)** is Montreal's largest facility, with more than 1000 rooms. Other "name" hotels include **Delta, Omni Mont-Royal, Loews Hotel Vogue, Le Centre Sheraton, Le Meridien Versailles,** and **Inter-Continental.**

Quebec City is often associated with its most celebrated hotel (perhaps the most famous hotel in Canada)—**Fairmont Château Frontenac.** The hotel itself is an attraction (it even offers tours), with its distinctive Renaissance-château architecture, towers, and superb views of the St. Lawrence River, which can be seen from many rooms or from the Dufferin Terrace. Business travellers enjoy lodging in the **Loews le Concorde.** Offering panoramic views, this hotel sits on the highest point in the city and has a revolving rooftop restaurant. The **Hilton Quebec** also affords excellent city views. Perhaps Canada's most unusual lodging: the **Ice Hotel,** located 30 minutes from Quebec City. It consists of a series of connected "igloos" and operates from January through early April each year. Everything— the walls, tables, even the beds—is made of ice.

ALLIED DESTINATIONS

Central Canada presents a variety of options for extended vacations to other Canadian regions and some major U.S. cities. From Quebec, Atlantic Canada is easily accessed via the Trans-Canada Highway, which enters the region at New Brunswick. VIA Rail Canada also accesses Atlantic Canada from its hub at Montreal.

Those travelling from Toronto to Niagara Falls, Ontario, often continue to Niagara Falls, New York, and approximately 32 kilometres farther into New York State to the city of Buffalo. A drive west along the northern shores of Lake Erie will eventually take travellers down to Detroit, Michigan. Along the way, tourists can stop at Canada's southernmost city, Windsor, which is connected to Detroit by a tunnel that travels under the Detroit River. Windsor has a number of popular shopping malls and is noted for being the site of Ontario's first casino.

One-third of Canada's population live within 160 kilometres of Toronto.

Windsor, Ontario, is actually *south* of Detroit, Michigan.

FACTORS THAT MOTIVATE VISITORS

The following are a few reasons tourists may find Ontario and Quebec to be attractive travel destinations:

- Bargain travel and lodging rates can be found during the off- and shoulder seasons (note that major winter events like Carnaval de Québec may impact lodging rates).

- The Montreal–Quebec City area is "foreign" yet familiar to visitors.

- Winter-sports opportunities (especially downhill and cross-country skiing, skating, and snowmobiling) are plentiful.

- Public transportation (especially the subway systems) is efficient and convenient.

- Major cities provide many opportunities for culture seekers, gourmets, and history buffs.

- The major metropolitan centres are relatively close to vast wilderness areas and numerous sites of great natural beauty.

- Ottawa, Montreal, Toronto, and Quebec City, with their museums and historical attractions, offer an educational benefit to family vacations.

POSSIBLE MISGIVINGS

For all of Central Canada's positive attributes, some people may have concerns about the region that you'll have to address:

- "What is there to do or see, especially in the winter?" Toronto, Montreal, and (to a lesser extent) Quebec City and Ottawa are energetic, lively, good-sized cities. Even in the off-season, Toronto and Montreal bustle with activity. There's great skiing in the region and a handful of winter events that are a huge draw.

- "Toronto and Montreal are big cities—that's a bit overwhelming." Toronto and Montreal are Canada's two largest cities, but they're unlike many big metropolitan areas. Both cities are remarkably clean and safe. In addition, each has a superb public transportation system that makes travel within each city easy and convenient.

- "I don't enjoy cold weather; don't Quebec and Ontario have terrible winters?" As in most of the country, winter in Central Canada can be severe, but the larger cities are also adept at preparing for, and dealing with, inclement winter weather. For instance, Montreal and Toronto have extensive underground transportation, shopping, entertainment, and dining options that are generally unaffected by the weather.

- "My family loves going to the beach in the summer; Ontario and Quebec don't have much to offer in this area." Though these provinces are not known for their beaches, there is excellent boating and many chances for sun-worshipping at numerous sites along the St. Lawrence River and Lake Ontario (for example, the Thousand Islands, the Gaspé Peninsula, and the Toronto Islands). If water sports are what the family enjoys, you might suggest one of the many resorts in the Laurentian Mountains (for example, Mont Tremblant, Gray Rocks, or Mont-St-Sauveur/Avila), which are dotted with hundreds of lakes. The Wasaga Beach and Collingwood areas in Ontario also are very popular summer beach destinations.

- "I'd love to see Niagara Falls, but isn't it a tourist zoo?" Though July is truly hectic, things slow down a bit in August. Suggest late spring or early fall

Qualifying the Traveller
ONTARIO AND QUEBEC

FOR PEOPLE WHO WANT	HIGH APPEAL	MEDIUM APPEAL	LOW APPEAL	REMARKS
Historical and Cultural Attractions	▲			Especially Ottawa and Quebec City
Beaches and Water Sports			▲	Only on lakes in mid-summer
Skiing Opportunities		▲		Several resorts; not on par with Rockies
Lots of Nightlife	▲			Especially Toronto and Montreal
Family Activities		▲		
Familiar Cultural Experience		▲		Especially Ontario
Exotic Cultural Experience		▲		Quebec has strong French culture
Safety and Low Crime	▲			Even in big cities
Bargain Travel		▲		Especially off-season
Impressive Scenery		▲		Waterfalls and mountains; fall foliage
Peace and Quiet		▲		Outside cities
Shopping Opportunities	▲			Toronto, Quebec City, and Montreal
Adventure		▲		
To Do Business	▲			Many major companies and government offices headquartered here

instead. Remind potential visitors that other wonderful attractions in the area (for instance, Niagara-on-the-Lake) are less "touristy," even in July or August.

- "Isn't there political turmoil in Quebec?" The separatist movement, for now, remains dormant. Canada is a relatively safe and peaceful country, where locals are especially friendly to visitors.

SALES STRATEGIES

The dual nature of Quebec and Ontario offers numerous opportunities to a wide cross-section of travellers. Because of the diversity of cultural, sports-related, and historical attractions available in the provinces, there are also many cross-sell and up-sell options to consider, such as river cruises, motorcoach tours, VIA Rail

Bonhomme is the well-recognized ambassador of Quebec City's Carnaval de Québec.
Copyright COREL

Canada passes, ski packages, theatre or sports tickets, and city tours. In addition, the region's proximity to the northeast United States offers opportunities to cruise to New York City or Boston from Montreal.

Accommodations present considerable up-sell possibilities. The major cities have many fine hotels, featuring everything from above-average to ultra-high-end suites. Those who wish to stay in Niagara Falls should be up-sold to a falls-view room. Niagara Falls has a century-old reputation as a honeymoon destination. That reputation has become somewhat passé, although some about-to-be married couples will indeed consider the Falls area as a viable option. Remember: Honeymooners almost always prefer superior lodging. Niagara Falls has also become a major destination for families. Suggesting two rooms (one for the parents, the other for the kids) is a solid sales strategy.

Both provinces are noted for unique winter festivals, special events that can attract tourists even in off-season. Such festivals represent out-of-the-ordinary winter options for people seeking a different vacation and attraction experience. Three of the most famous are Niagara's **Festival of Lights** (November–January), when the icy surroundings of Niagara Falls glitter with colourful holiday bulbs; Ottawa's **Winterlude** (February), a celebration over three weekends featuring ice sculpture, races, and concerts; and Quebec City's **Carnaval de Québec** (February), two weeks of parades, fireworks, ice-sculpting contests, hockey games, skating, sledding, tobogganing, and canoe races on the icy St. Lawrence River.

Ontario also offers special events during the more temperate seasons: Toronto's **Caribana** (mid July–early August) is one of the world's largest Caribbean festivals, complete with parades and reggae music; Toronto's **Canadian National Exhibition** (mid August–early September) has been a national tradition for more than 100 years, attracting millions of visitors and featuring hundreds of amusement rides and games, arts-and-crafts stands, and concessions, plus big-name musical entertainment; and Ottawa's **Canadian Tulip Festival** (May) is a spring celebration complete with boat parades on the Rideau Canal, an arts-and-crafts show, music and dancing, and, of course, the blooming of several hundred thousand tulips donated by Queen Juliana of the Netherlands (who resided in Ottawa during World War II).

TRAVEL TRIVIA

ODDLY NAMED CANADIAN SPECIALITIES

- Caribou—a French-Canadian drink made of one part red wine to six parts grain alcohol
- Solomon Gundy—herring (Nova Scotia)
- Digby Chicks—smoked herring (Nova Scotia)
- Fiddleheads—the unopened fronds of the ostrich fern (Nova Scotia and New Brunswick)
- Dulse—dried seaweed
- Screech—a potent alcohol made in Newfoundland and Labrador
- Scrunchions—fried pork dish from Newfoundland and Labrador
- Ciapille—a French-Canadian pie containing fowl, game, or beef mixed with vegetables
- Beaver Tails—deep-fried pastries shaped like—you guessed it—beaver tails and served with condiments (sold in downtown Ottawa)
- Figgy Duff—steamed pudding with sauce

NAME _____   DATE _____

A traveller wants to visit the places listed below. Which number represents each on the map?

PLACE/ATTRACTION	IN WHICH CITY/PROVINCE?	NUMBER ON MAP
A. Château Frontenac	**A.**	**A.**
B. The CN Tower	**B.**	**B.**
C. *Maid of the Mist*	**C.**	**C.**
D. St. Josephs' Oratory	**D.**	**D.**
E. The Thousand Islands	**E.**	**E.**
F. Gaspé Peninsula	**F.**	**F.**
G. The capital of Canada	**G.**	**G.**
H. Site of Stratford Festival	**H.**	**H.**
I. Mont-Tremblant	**I.**	**I.**
J. Canada's southernmost city	**J.**	**J.**

NAME _____   DATE _____

You are helping a group leader plan a trip from Vancouver to Toronto to see the Blue Jays play in the World Series. Her group has 40 members—mostly well-educated, relatively affluent young couples and a few families with young children. They plan to see two ballgames and to stay in the area for five days.

Circle the answer that best suits their needs.

1. Based on your knowledge of Toronto's unique offerings (and those of nearby places), which of the following might be provided as a tour option?

   A train tour   A river cruise

   Car rental   Theatre tickets for a musical

   Why?

2. Which attraction(s) would you suggest as a visit for the entire group?

   Toronto Zoo   Paramount Canada's Wonderland

   Ontario Science Centre   Hockey Hall of Fame

   Why?

3. Where would you lodge the group?

   Brock Plaza   Château Laurier

   Renaissance Toronto   Four Seasons

   Why?

4. If the group wanted to venture just outside the metropolitan Toronto area, what day trip would you recommend?

   Visit to the nation's capital   The Laurentians

   Niagara Falls   The Eastern Provinces

   Why?

CREATIVE ACTIVITY

NAME _____   DATE _____

You're a travel agent based in Edmonton. It's been a few years since you studied Canadian history. Though you may not have every historical date committed to memory, you've got a solid grasp of the major areas, cities, and attractions that are significant to Canada's past. The client you just spoke to on the phone is going to challenge your knowledge and offer you an opportunity to plan an enriching (for the client and your agency!) itinerary.

You have an hour to prepare an itinerary for the client before he visits your agency with his wife and two children, ages 8 and 10. Though the client has stressed that this vacation is to be an educational one—a "living history" for his kids—you also want to make it exciting for all family members.

Map out a travel route for a 10-day driving tour of Quebec and Ontario. On your map, record the historical places you suggest as stops. On a separate notepad, write down, in point form, the historical significance of these attractions and any aspects that make them exciting or unique. Suggest a length of stay in each area. Also, consider novel transportation ideas (both to the region and within selected cities) and activities. The family plans to take the vacation in late June.

Be prepared to make your recommendations in class, describing and justifying them as you would to an actual client.

YUKON

NORTHWEST TERRITORIES

NUNAVUT

HUDSON BAY

Churchill

BRITISH COLUMBIA

Rocky Mountains

Peace R.

Fraser R.

ALBERTA

Athabasca R.

SASKATCHEWAN

MANITOBA

Lake Winnipeg

ONTARIO

Jasper Nat. Park

Edmonton

N. Saskatchewan R.

C A N A D A

Columbia Icefield

Columbia R.

Banff Nat. Park

Drumheller

Saskatoon

Lake Manitoba

Kamloops

Vancouver Island

Cache Creek

Whistler

Lake Louise

Calgary

Lower Fort Garry

Nanaimo

Vancouver

S. Saskatchewan R.

Assiniboine R.

Chemainas

Hope

Moose Jaw

Winnipeg

Victoria

Okanagan Valley

Waterton Lakes Nat. Park

Regina

Red River

PACIFIC OCEAN

U N I T E D   S T A T E S

CHAPTER 3

Western Canada

Anything and Everything

The provinces of **Manitoba, Saskatchewan,** and **Alberta,** together with their West Coast neighbour, **British Columbia,** are known as Western Canada. This categorization has as much to do with the region's personality as it does with its geography. Western Canada is a vast land of rugged openness from which its events and attractions seem to have grown: Where else in Canada would the **Calgary Stampede** or Saskatoon's **Western Development Museum's 1910 Boomtown** be more appropriate?

Indeed, Western Canada is an area of striking diversity, from the Pacific Ocean's shores to the Rocky Mountains; from the great rolling plains to the seemingly countless lakes of Manitoba. The region's biggest cities—**Vancouver, Edmonton, Calgary,** and **Winnipeg**—each manifest a thoroughly distinct character. And nowhere else in Canada can you find a greater range of climates, from the freezing cold northern areas most enjoyed by adventurers and polar bears to the felicitous weather that attracts tourists from around the world to Vancouver.

Understanding Western Canada's diversity is key to selling the area as a travel destination. You can certainly find something for everyone in the Western provinces.

HOW TRAVELLERS GET THERE

Visitors should enter Western Canada largely based on what they plan to see and do. For those who wish to take a leisurely driving tour, the **Trans-Canada Highway** Route 1 traverses all four provinces—a distance of more than 2500 kilometres. The Trans-Canada enters Manitoba's eastern border from Kenora, Ontario, and travels 204 kilometres west to Winnipeg, terminating in British Columbia at Victoria. For those who prefer land travel but would rather not drive, motorcoach tours or rail travel are an attractive option. **VIA Rail Canada** and a few private rail and motorcoach tour companies offer sightseeing packages of varied lengths (within specific areas in the region or, in some cases, across the country), with several departures weekly.

The most efficient and convenient access to Western Canada is by air. **Vancouver International Airport** (YVR) is the key Canadian gateway to the Pacific. In addition, Calgary (YYC) and Edmonton, Alberta (YEG), and Winnipeg, Manitoba (YWG), also have international airports. Carriers also fly to **Victoria**

International Airport, British Columbia (YYJ), **Saskatoon** (YXE), and **Regina,** Saskatchewan (YQR).

Another way to see parts of British Columbia is by cruise ship. Cruise travel along Western Canada's Pacific coast has become increasingly popular. Major cruise lines use Vancouver and Seattle as departure points for cruises along the Inside Passage and north to Alaska. Some cruise lines also combine cruises with motorcoach or rail tour packages to attractions in British Columbia and Alberta.

WEATHER PATTERNS

British Columbia (especially coastal Vancouver, in the southwest portion of the province) is Canada's most climatically temperate province. Vancouver's average high temperature in January is 5°C, versus an average high in Winnipeg of –14°C (see Figures 3–1 and 3–2). Snow is also far less common in Vancouver and Victoria (two or three mild storms in the winter) than in any other part of the country. British Columbia's mountain regions get plenty of snow, which is fine for skiing enthusiasts.

There are two tourist seasons in Western Canada: winter and summer. For most of the region, summer (June–August) is indeed the main tourist season—temperatures are generally pleasant during the day (though it can occasionally get hot) and rain is less common. Vancouver has a more extended season and attracts tourists year-round (though it rains often in the winter months, and showers are possible during the rest of the year). Vancouver's tourist season is heavily impacted by the cruise industry, which offers Alaska cruises from early May to late September.

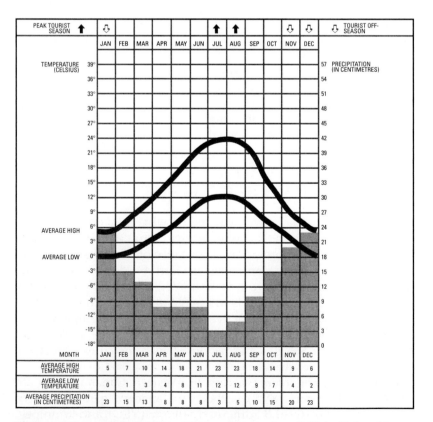

MONTH	JAN	FEB	MAR	APR	MAY	JUN	JUL	AUG	SEP	OCT	NOV	DEC
AVERAGE HIGH TEMPERATURE	5	7	10	14	18	21	23	23	18	14	9	6
AVERAGE LOW TEMPERATURE	0	1	3	4	8	11	12	12	9	7	4	2
AVERAGE PRECIPITATION (IN CENTIMETRES)	23	15	13	8	8	8	3	5	10	15	20	23

Figure 3-1   Climate at a Glance: Vancouver, British Columbia

PEAK TOURIST SEASON ↑	⇩	⇩	⇩	⇩		↑	↑			⇩	⇩		⇩ TOURIST OFF-SEASON

MONTH	JAN	FEB	MAR	APR	MAY	JUN	JUL	AUG	SEP	OCT	NOV	DEC
AVERAGE HIGH TEMPERATURE	-14	-11	-3	9	18	23	26	24	18	11	-1	-9
AVERAGE LOW TEMPERATURE	-25	-23	-15	-3	4	10	13	11	6	4	-11	-19
AVERAGE PRECIPITATION (IN CENTIMETRES)	3	3	3	3	5	8	8	8	5	5	3	3

Figure 3-2   Climate at a Glance: Winnipeg, Manitoba

GETTING AROUND

Travel by car across the four western provinces would require several long driving days, though the scenery along the way can be breathtaking (especially if travellers venture off the Trans-Canada occasionally). At times, the drive can be challenging, especially in the mountain areas of British Columbia and Alberta during winter and in the more northern latitudes. The Trans-Canada Highway connects most major cities, as well as key resort points in the Rockies, such as Alberta's **Banff** and **Jasper National Parks.** Car rentals are readily available at all major regional airports and cities (driving a rental car from one city and returning it to another isn't a good idea, though; huge drop-off charges may apply). In addition, there's frequent bus service throughout the region (even in the more remote northern regions, though to a lesser extent).

For more expedient travel, rail and air services are preferred interprovincial modes of transportation. VIA Rail Canada's Western Transcontinental train service—the **Canadian**—is the primary rail transportation through Western Canada. From Vancouver, the Canadian stops in major prairie cities such as Edmonton, Saskatoon, and Winnipeg, with continued service to Central Canada. You should note, though, that VIA Rail Canada travels through the Rockies mostly during night hours, thus passing through much of the scenery best seen during the day.

Private rail companies, on the other hand, time their departures and overnight stops to provide the best sightseeing opportunities during the daylight hours. **Rocky Mountain Railtours** departs from Vancouver and stops overnight in **Kamloops** before continuing northeast through the Rockies in the morning. (The trip can also be taken westbound, beginning in the Rockies and overnighting in Kamloops on the way to Vancouver.) **Royal Canadian Pacific** operates roundtrip excursions from Calgary.

Air Canada, WestJet, and, to a lesser extent, regional carriers, link the Western provinces. In addition to servicing the major city airports in the southern portions of the provinces, the smaller carriers fly to a variety of northern cities throughout the region.

Among the primary tourist destinations, transportation is varied. For example, two centres near Vancouver link southwestern British Columbia by numerous ferries to points on nearby Vancouver Island across the Strait of Georgia. In addition, the city has a good public bus service and relatively uncrowded streets (though weekday rush hours can clog things up). Motorcoach tours are an excellent way to see Vancouver and its environs.

Travel within the Edmonton/Calgary mountain area is supported by a good highway system and bus service. From Calgary, the Trans-Canada (Highway 1) travels west to the city of Banff. From Banff, Provincial Highway 93 runs northwest through the resort area of **Lake Louise** and on to Jasper National Park (from Lake Louise to Jasper, Provincial Highway 93 is called the **Icefields Parkway**). The Trans-Canada, Highway 16 (the **Yellowhead Highway**), picks up in Jasper, heading east to Edmonton. Finally, Highway 2 runs south from Edmonton to Calgary. Though VIA Rail Canada does not visit Calgary (the system runs farther north through Edmonton), Calgary is a stop for the private rail companies.

Virtually all of Saskatchewan's and Manitoba's cities and attractions are located in the southern portion of the provinces, which have an excellent highway system linking the major destinations. About 80 kilometres west of Winnipeg, Manitoba, the Trans-Canada splits into Highway 1 (west to Regina) and Highway 16 (northwest to Saskatoon). Frequent bus service is available between these locales, though car travel is probably the most convenient way to journey through this uncrowded area.

An interesting transportation service to sell is a helicopter tour of the Canadian Rockies. Vacationers are deposited on glaciers, alpine meadows, and mountain summits.

IMPORTANT PLACES

Western Canada is best known for its prime destination areas, Vancouver and the Canadian Rockies. The main attraction of these areas is their mountains and valleys—awe-inspiring sights when viewed from hotel windows, cruise ships, helicopter tours, or ski slopes. The less-visited destinations have their own appeal. The main cities in Alberta, Saskatchewan, and Manitoba feature unique cultural attractions, museums, special events, and sights. Plus, there's the pristine grace of Canada's lands—the prairies, forests, and lakes that teem with wildlife and draw hikers, campers, fishers, and nature lovers of all types. The region's main attractions follow.

Vancouver

Vancouver is one of the most friendly and pleasant cities in Canada. Tucked into British Columbia's southwest corner, the city is framed by mist-shrouded mountains and graceful bays, making it one of North America's most picturesque places to visit.

The city is an urban wonder and has become prosperous, thanks in part to the huge infusion of capital from Asia and its status as a major centre for television and movie production. The cruise industry has also enhanced Vancouver's popularity as a tourist destination, with large luxury liners and smaller "adventure" cruises sailing from the city's excellent deep-water port to a bevy of northerly attractions.

Denman Street in Vancouver's West End has a wide selection of ethnic restaurants and coffee shops.

Despite being Canada's third-largest city, Vancouver retains a romantic, small-city feel, with neat homes, tree-lined streets, and flowering gardens. Among the city's many sightseeing and entertainment opportunities are:

- **Gastown,** a restored section of the city's historic district. Long a popular tourist spot, Gastown's cobblestone streets are lined with jazz clubs, coffeehouses, restaurants, art galleries, and boutiques. Located in Gastown is the

Storyeum, a huge facility that traces the history of West Coast Canada. An off-beat sight: the town's unique steam clock, especially at the top of the hour. Locals feel that Gastown is becoming a little tacky, but out-of-town visitors may love it.

- **Stanley Park,** a 405-hectare expanse of greenery on the downtown peninsula, with magnificent scenery, many walking/jogging/biking trails, and numerous totem poles. Rimmed by **English Bay** on the west and the **Burrard Inlet** on the east (providing kilometres of beaches), Stanley Park features the excellent **Vancouver Aquarium,** the **Marine Science Centre,** a bird sanctuary, an amphitheatre, a children's farmyard, a rose garden, and numerous outdoor sports activities. Trolley shuttles (in the summer) and horse-drawn carriages (spring through fall) are interesting ways of getting around.

- **Granville Island,** a waterfront area with a popular indoor market, many restaurants, and plenty of people-watching opportunities. Fresh foods of all varieties—fruits, vegetables, seafood, meats, and baked goods—are sold in this festive marketplace, a favourite destination for tourists and locals alike.

- **Robson Street,** a shopper's paradise in the heart of downtown Vancouver, featuring upscale international boutiques, gourmet coffee shops and restaurants, and such sights as a skating rink, waterfalls, and gardens.

- **Canada Place,** Vancouver's convention centre and cruise port, originally built for Expo 86. The roof, resembling white sails unfurled, has become a city landmark. Indeed, the entire building reflects a nautical motif.

- **Harbour Centre,** featuring a 168-metre-high observation deck that affords excellent views of the city.

- **The University of British Columbia's Museum of Anthropology,** a first-rate museum that focuses on the history, art, and artifacts of First Nations culture.

- **Vanier Park,** home to several attractions (in addition to beautiful beaches), including the **Vancouver Museum,** the **H. R. MacMillan Space Centre**

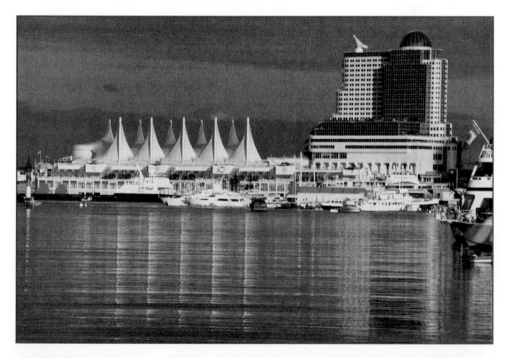

Canada Place in Vancouver is a convention centre and cruise port that was originally built for Expo 86.
Copyright COREL

(housing the **Gordon MacMillan Southam Observatory**), and the **Vancouver Maritime Museum.** The park is located across from the southeast shores of downtown Vancouver.

- **Chinatown,** the biggest Asian community in Canada and the second largest in North America (behind San Francisco). This neighbourhood boasts unique decorative architecture; a rich variety of restaurants, grocery stores, and shops; and distinct Asian gardens.

- **Grouse Mountain,** a popular skiing spot for Vancouver locals due to its proximity to the city (just 20 minutes from downtown). The 1.3 kilometre Skyride to the top of Grouse offers magnificent panoramic views of Vancouver and nearby mountains. Close by is the **Capilano Suspension Bridge,** a swinging 137-metre-long footbridge that spans a 70-metre-deep gorge and provides breathtaking views. This unusual attraction seems straight out of an Indiana Jones movie. Capilano's new attraction is the **Treetops Adventure,** a series of suspension bridges (some more than 30 metres high) linking the Douglas fir trees.

Vancouver offers several nearby destinations that warrant an extended stay in the area. The most popular are:

- **Vancouver Island,** which rests 39 kilometres off the western shores of the city of Vancouver. To reach it, travellers can take a 90-minute to two-hour ferry cruise from **Tsawwassen** (south of Vancouver) to **Swartz Bay** (near Victoria) or **Duke Point** (near **Nanaimo;** or **Horseshoe Bay** (north of Vancouver) to Duke Point. Though most visitors see the main sights in a long day, the Island merits a multi-day stay due to its many attractions and outdoor activities, especially fishing. In August and September, the Campbell River teems with salmon, and lake trout is abundant throughout the year. The island's parks and beaches are a haven for water-sports enthusiasts and nature lovers (there are several prime spots for whale-watching, and in late February Pacific grey whales can be seen passing the island on their way from Baja, California). The small town of **Chemainus** is famous for huge murals painted on the sides of buildings. The town also features First Nations art. A recent *Condé Nast Traveler* poll rated Vancouver Island as the number one North American island.

- **Victoria,** British Columbia's capital, located 48 kilometres southwest of Vancouver on Vancouver Island. This city of legendary beauty is famous for its "Old England" atmosphere. Victoria's most astonishing attraction is the **Butchart Gardens,** a privately owned park (open to tourists) that was once a limestone quarry. **Craigdarroch Castle** is a sandstone mansion open to the public. **Miniature World,** in the Fairmont Empress Hotel, is a quirky collection of more than 80 miniature scenes, including a "working" circus and an extensive miniature train layout. Though Victoria has a few notable museums (especially the **Royal British Columbia Museum**), the main attraction is the city itself—the Parliament Buildings, quaint streets, shops, and restaurants. A tour aboard a double-decker bus is a great way to get a feel for the city.

- **Whistler Resort,** the region's most popular ski resort, about a 90-minute drive north of Vancouver. Whistler and Blackcomb mountains are two of the tallest skiable peaks in Canada, and the resort area is usually rated among the top 10 in ski magazine reader polls. The runs and trails are varied, challenging skiers of virtually every skill level and style. Whistler's express lift makes the journey to the resort's peak a quick and comfortable ride. In the summer, its golf courses and summer ski schools are quite popular, too. The 2010 Winter Olympic Games will take place here and in Vancouver. In the summer, Whistler offers mountain biking, golfing, kayaking, white-water rafting, zip-trekking, and boarding.

- **Hope, Cache Creek,** and **Kamloops,** historic frontier towns located near or along Highway 1 (heading east through British Columbia's interior). Steeped in fur-trading and gold-prospecting lore, these towns are frequent stopover points for train or bus tours heading to Canadian Rockies resorts. Travellers through this region (the **Fraser Valley**) should take time to see **Fraser Canyon** and **Hell's Gate,** a stretch of the Fraser River noted for its turbulent waters and white-water rafting opportunities. A thrilling canyon cable-car ride provides a spectacular view of the river.

- **Okanagan Valley,** British Columbia's wine country. Beginning just north of the Canada–U.S. border (and east of Hope) near the town of **Osoyoos** is verdant countryside dotted with numerous wineries. Wine tours or festivals (such as the annual **Okanagan Wine Festival** in October) give visitors a chance to sample some of Canada's best vintages.

The Canadian Rockies

Every bit as scenic as the Alps, the Canadian Rockies are a magnet for both winter and summer visitors. Most of the region's attractions line Alberta's western boundary. Visitors usually start their trip from either Calgary or Edmonton (or on a train tour from Vancouver). The region's highlights include:

- **Banff,** a major resort area considered by many to be one of the world's most dramatic scenic spots. Located on the east side of the Rockies, Banff is Canada's first national park (1885) and its most popular. The extraordinary mountains, valleys, forests, glaciers, lakes, and waterfalls of Banff National Park provide astounding views, and the wildlife (that sometimes wander right into town) is impressive. In addition to the park's beauty, the area offers numerous recreational activities, such as horseback riding, golf, swimming, white-water rafting, mountain climbing, skiing, snowboarding, heli-skiing, and a gondola ride up Sulphur Mountain for awesome views. Within the park is a photographer's dream—Lake Louise. Fed by nearby glaciers, the lake's clear, turquoise-blue waters perfectly reflect the surrounding mountains. The **Lake Louise Ski Area** constitutes Canada's largest ski resort (Banff National Park also has two other major resorts: **Sunshine Village** and **Mount Norquay/Mystic Ridge**), with thousands of hectares of terrain for downhill and cross-country skiing.

Alberta's ski season begins as early as November and can extend into May.

Lake Louise
Copyright COREL

Chapter 3 Western Canada

- **Jasper National Park,** adjoining Banff National Park to the northeast and representing the largest mountain parkland in the world. The drive from Banff to Jasper on the Icefields Parkway offers dramatic mountain scenery, making the 290 kilometre drive an attraction in itself. Jasper is noted for its rich population of animals, as well as for the **Marmot Basin Ski Resort** and **Miette Hot Springs** (Canada's warmest natural springs). The park is the departure point for helicopter trips into the Canadian Rockies, both in Alberta and nearby British Columbia. Jasper and Banff serve as gateways to the Columbia Icefield.

- **Columbia Icefield,** an enormous collection of ice lakes and glaciers located on the Alberta–British Columbia border. Tourists can ride across the Athabasca Glacier in huge sightseeing tractors called Snocoaches.

- **Waterton Lakes National Park,** which together with Montana's Glacier National Park forms the Waterton-Glacier International Peace Park. Located about a two-hour drive south of Calgary, this beautiful area is noted for its rugged mountain scenery and waterfalls. Elk can be found traversing the streets in Waterton, and there are nowhere near the number of tourists found in other parks.

Calgary and Edmonton

Tourists visiting the Canadian Rockies may be so taken with the natural splendour of the area that they might be inclined to skip Alberta's more populated destinations: the cities of Calgary and Edmonton. Yet each is a must-see, with an atmosphere that combines their frontier pasts with modern business centres and entertainment complexes. Recommend:

⊙ Alberta's oil reserves are larger than those of Saudi Arabia.

⊙ Calgary has the best selection of cowboy fashions in the country.

- **Calgary,** a one-hour drive east of Banff and site of the 1988 Winter Olympic Games. The gateway to Alberta's ski resorts and presided over by a lofty tower, Calgary is a city with considerable character. Its boldness and brashness remind visitors of its early days as a cattle town and later transformation into an oil-boom town. Despite the many cultural, athletic, historical, and architectural attractions the city has to offer, Calgary is still best known for its biggest annual festival: the Calgary Stampede (July). This renowned rodeo showcases the world's best cowboys, buckin' broncos, chuckwagon races, and barbecued steaks. Those visiting Calgary at other times of the year might want to see **Heritage Park Historical Village** (a living-history village), **Canada Olympic Park** (one of the sites of the 1988 Games), and the **Calgary Zoo, Botanical Garden and Prehistoric Park** (the second-largest zoo in Canada). Tourists who want a taste of Calgary's nightlife should head for **Electric Avenue,** a vibrant area with several nightclubs. Sports enthusiasts can catch the Flames (hockey) or Stampeders (football) in action.

- **Drumheller** (about 90 minutes northeast of Calgary and often called Canada's "Badlands") is famous for the **Royal Tyrrell Museum,** a remarkable collection of dinosaur skeletons and exhibits. The **Drumheller Valley Interpretive Centre** (formerly the Drumheller Dinosaur and Fossil Museum) contains exhibits on dinosaurs and on the area's history. Two hours

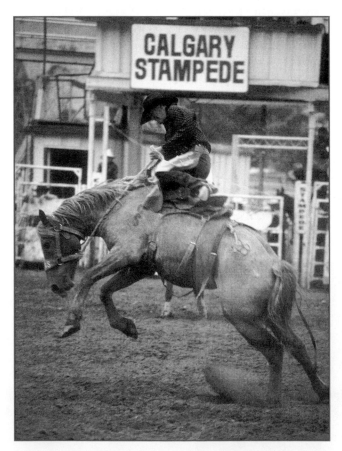

Calgary is best known for its biggest annual festival, the Calgary Stampede.
Copyright COREL

south of Calgary is **Fort Macleod** and nearby **Head-Smashed-in-Buffalo-Jump,** a park that details the hunting methods used by Plains First Nations, who killed buffalo by stampeding the animals over cliffs. The park is named after a young First Nations hunter who got caught in the stampede.

- **Edmonton,** the provincial capital and an important business city. Whereas Calgary is famous for its Stampede, Edmonton is most famous for the **West Edmonton Mall.** The 493 000-square-metre "mini city" contains more than 900 shops and eateries, and 26 movie screens. More astounding are such indoor surprises as roller coasters, an ice-skating rink (where hockey's Edmonton Oilers practise), lakes (one has a submarine ride), a huge wave pool and beach (with simulated surf), trained sea lion shows, a shark tank, and even a bungee-jumping platform.

- Among Edmonton's more educational or cultural features are the **Odyssium** (formerly the Edmonton Space and Science Centre), the **Provincial Museum of Alberta** (natural and human history), and the **Fort Edmonton Park** (a living-history village). In addition to the Oilers, sports fans can check out football's Edmonton Eskimos. Edmonton is known as "Canada's Festival City" for the dozens of major events it stages every year, including Klondike Days (July), the International Fringe Theatre Festival (August), and the International Street Performers Festival (July).

Saskatchewan

Saskatchewan is a land of unspoiled wilderness. Most of the province's southern territory consists of prairie, wheat fields, gentle hills, and lakes. Saskatchewan's main attractions are its parklands, which offer a full spectrum of summer and winter outdoor activities. Though the province lacks the towering natural wonders of neighbouring Alberta or the cosmopolitan allure of British Columbia, it boasts more museums and golf courses per capita than any other province. Museum-goers will want to visit:

The name *Saskatchewan* is derived from a Cree word meaning "swift-flowing river," a reference to the area's major river.

- **Regina** [ridge-EYE-nah], the provincial capital and Saskatchewan's primary business and cultural centre. Regina is best known as the headquarters and training ground for the **Royal Canadian Mounted Police.** Visitors to the **Training Academy** can watch the Mounties in their blazing red coats as they parade and drill on horseback. Regina has a number of notable museums, including the new **RCMP National Heritage Centre** (which encompasses the **Royal Canadian Mounted Police Depot and Centennial Museum**) and the **Royal Saskatchewan Museum.** Other city attractions include the **Saskatchewan Science Centre** (with an IMAX theatre) and **Wascana Centre** (a large recreational park).

- **Moose Jaw,** located 72 kilometres west of Regina. This city boasts a variety of unusual museums. Two of the more unique: **Sukanen Ship** (yes, a ship in the middle of Saskatchewan), **Pioneer Village and Museum;** and the **Moose Jaw Museum & Art Gallery** (First Nations art, crafts, jewellery, and clothing). Also of interest are the **Tunnels of Moose Jaw,** Prohibition-era underground passages that link businesses. (Chinese labourers helped dig these tunnels; many of their descendants remain.) In July, the Saskatchewan Air Show takes place: Moose Jaw is home to Canada's world-famous aerobatics squadron, the Snowbirds.

Moose Jaw boasts the world's largest moose statue.

- **Saskatoon,** Saskatchewan's largest city, located 257 kilometres northwest of Regina. The most visited of Saskatoon's several noteworthy museums is the **Western Development Museum's 1910 Boomtown,** a large living-history museum that showcases frontier life in Saskatchewan. Located just north of the city is **Wanuskewin Heritage Park,** which features 19 First Nation archaeological sites. The **University of Saskatchewan,** a beautiful campus overlooking the **South Saskatchewan River,** is home to the **Diefenbaker Canada Centre,** which displays artifacts of the well-known prime minister, as well as his gravesite.

Manitoba

Manitoba is known as the land of 100 000 lakes and rivers. Indeed, two of the province's most notable features are the massive Lake Winnipeg and Lake Manitoba (where locals go to "beach it"). Though Manitoba may boast few man-made attractions outside of the city of Winnipeg, the beauty of the province's diverse terrain is an attraction in itself. Those who enjoy outdoor activities (especially boating, fishing, and hunting) will find Manitoba to be both bountiful and beautiful. Among its primary attractions are:

- **Winnipeg,** the provincial capital and gateway to Western Canada. Because Winnipeg is located great distances from any other major city (Regina, Saskatchewan—576 kilometres west—is the closest), many might not consider it as a destination. Yet for those taking rail or driving tours across Canada's prairies, Winnipeg has several worthwhile attractions and entertainment offerings.

  The **Winnipeg Art Gallery** features the world's largest collection of Inuit art. The respected **Manitoba Museum** traces the province's historical and cultural development. Nearby is Winnipeg's **Chinatown,** a bustling neighbourhood that boasts excellent restaurants and a new cultural centre with a unique ornamental garden. Visitors to the **Royal Canadian Mint** can watch coins and currency being made. Winnipeg's oldest and largest park, **Assiniboine Park,** features a zoo, many outdoor activities, and a variety of gardens. The downtown shopping centre, **Portage Place,** contains numerous shops and dining spots, and is linked (via enclosed skywalks) with area hotels, theatres, and restaurants. Finally, **The Forks** in downtown Winnipeg combines a large public market with several attractions, including a working archaeological dig in the summer months. Winnipeg is also noted for its varied entertainment options, from the Winnipeg Goldeyes (baseball) and Blue Bombers (football) to the world-class Royal Winnipeg Ballet and Winnipeg Symphony Orchestra. There are numerous festivals throughout the year, including Folklorama (August), Winnipeg's largest; it's reputedly the largest multicultural event in the world.

- **Lower Fort Garry National Historic Site,** a stone fort built in the early 1800s. Located 30 minutes outside of Winnipeg in Selkirk, this park re-creates Manitoba's past as a key fur-trading centre.

- **Churchill,** a small northern Manitoba town on the south shores of Hudson Bay. Churchill's most famous residents are polar bears. The truly adventurous can reach Churchill by VIA Rail Canada or plane, and then take "Tundra Buggy" tours to campsites near the playgrounds of Canada's remarkable white bears (the best viewing is October through early November). For those visiting Manitoba in summer, Churchill offers boat tours to see beluga whales. Tours must be booked well in advance. Churchill also features the **Eskimo Museum,** with a fine collection of Inuit art and artifacts.

- **Lakes and provincial parks.** Scattered throughout the province are scenic parks that offer a full range of outdoor activities. Water sports, especially canoeing and white-water rafting, are summer favourites of locals and visitors alike. For those who enjoy fishing, Manitoba will seem like paradise. In addition to Lake Manitoba and Lake Winnipeg, the province has an astonishing number of unspoiled lakes, rivers, and streams, as well as dozens of vacation resorts and lodges that cater to anglers.

Lake Winnipeg is more than half the size of Switzerland.

Where Winnipeg's Portage and Main streets meet is called "the coldest corner in Canada." An underground concourse was built so people wouldn't freeze.

Winnipeg goldeye is a delicious, locally smoked fish.

POSSIBLE ITINERARIES

Tourists who lack the time for a long vacation would be hard put to see all of Western Canada's key sites in one trip. More likely, travellers will want to focus on a specific area and take day trips to outlying points of interest.

Vancouver offers the best options for multi-day, multi-destination vacations. For example, travellers may concentrate their visit on the city and Vancouver Island/Victoria (an especially popular summer itinerary). Excellent up-sell and cross-sell options are Inside Passage/Alaska cruises or sightseeing rail tours to the Rocky Mountains. A winter option could combine a few days in Vancouver with a side trip to the Whistler ski resort.

Banff National Park and its environs offer year-round opportunities for vacations of a week to 10 days. Active visitors (especially winter skiers or summer sports enthusiasts) and sightseers can choose from among Banff, Lake Louise, Jasper, or a combination of the three. For those seeking more diversified entertainment and cultural activities, the resort areas may be coupled with visits to Calgary or Edmonton.

LODGING OPTIONS

Hotel accommodations in Western Canada range from rustic lodges in Manitoba and Saskatchewan to the resort palaces of Alberta and the contemporary hotels of British Columbia. The region's most spectacular hotels are the château-style structures that were built across Canada around the turn of the 20th century by the Canadian Pacific Railway (and are now Fairmont hotels). These magnificent landmark hotels evoke a feeling of romance and grandeur that's changed little over the years.

Vancouver has a number of fine hotels, including several **Delta** properties, a **Four Seasons,** the landmark **Fairmont Hotel Vancouver,** the highly rated **Pan Pacific** and **Sutton Place** hotels, and **Hyatt Regency** and **Sheraton** hotels. For those wishing to stay on Vancouver Island, recommend the **Fairmont Empress Hotel** in Victoria. The Empress evokes the very essence of British Victoria, and has excellent views of the city's downtown and inner harbour. Afternoon tea in Palm Court is a great way to fully experience the hotel's (and city's) ambience.

Many visitors to Banff enjoy the world-renowned **Fairmont Banff Springs.** This dramatic, 770-room structure is perfectly suited to its surroundings—the majestic Rocky Mountains. An opulent resort, the Banff Springs has an incredible selection of recreational activities, dining and entertainment options, natural hot springs for soaking, and, of course, an unsurpassed site. Rooms with mountain views cost more, but are worth the price. The nearby **Fairmont Château Lake Louise** overlooks the shimmering lake of the same name. Though not as large (around 500 rooms) as the Banff Springs, this hotel is equally luxurious and offers similarly stunning views (though lake-view rooms are recommended, this feature is less important in winter when Lake Louise is frozen).

Other notable hotels in the region are Winnipeg's **Fairmont Winnipeg;** Calgary's **Fairmont Palliser, Sheraton Suites,** and **Westin;** Jasper's **Fairmont Jasper Park Lodge;** and Edmonton's **Fantasyland Hotel and Resort.** The Fantasyland Hotel is part of the West Edmonton Mall and features themed accommodations, such as a Roman Room (containing Greco-Roman art and a Roman tub), a Truck Room (featuring beds situated in the back of pickup trucks), and a Polynesian Room (complete with a waterfall and erupting volcano).

An offbeat alternative to traditional lodging is a stay on a farm, where guests become "farmers," helping the owners with daily chores and dining on wonderful, fresh food. This sort of "agritourism" is especially common in Saskatchewan.

ALLIED DESTINATIONS

For those interested in Alaska cruises, suggest 7- to 10-day, round-trip excursions from Vancouver into the Inside Passage that's shared by British Columbia and Alaska. (One-way trips through the Inside Passage, then into the Gulf Coast region to the Anchorage area are also common.) To see the glaciers, snow-capped peaks, dense forests, and animal life along the way can be an overwhelming experience. The Inside Passage is one of the most beautiful stretches of the entire cruise—and passes through a part of British Columbia that visitors rarely get to see.

BC Ferries also offers a cruise of the British Columbia portion of Inside Passage via car ferry. The trip runs north from Vancouver Island to **Port Hardy,** through the Passage, and on to **Prince Rupert.** For even shorter ocean trips, a ferry from Vancouver (or Victoria) to Seattle, Washington, takes about four hours.

Saskatchewan and Manitoba offer no obvious connections with other tourist destinations, even though they abut Montana and North Dakota in the United States. Winnipeg is a day's drive or short flight from Minneapolis, Minnesota, and is fairly close to Grand Forks, North Dakota.

Winnipeg is 1930 kilometres from Toronto, Ontario, the closest major Central Canada destination. One possible allied destination is a long day's drive (700 kilometres) east from Winnipeg to Thunder Bay, Ontario, located on the northeast shores of Lake Superior; Canada's third-largest port offers visitors interesting attractions (harbour cruises, old forts, and nearby amethyst mines), as well as recreational opportunities.

FACTORS THAT MOTIVATE VISITORS

Some tourists will be especially drawn to Western Canada. Here are some of the reasons:

- The area's natural beauty is stunning, especially in the Rockies, along the coast, and into the wilderness.

- Fishing, hunting, boating, camping, white-water rafting, golfing, and other outdoor-sports options abound.

- Wildlife is relatively easy to observe.

- Skiing is outstanding and ski resorts are a bargain compared to others of similar quality.

- Transportation along the southern portions of the area is convenient.

- The region offers a variety of ways to "get away from it all."

- First-rate restaurants and vibrant nightlife can be found in cities that are only minutes away from peaceful wilderness areas and parks.

- There are numerous cruise and tour possibilities.

POSSIBLE MISGIVINGS

Even those who would most enjoy a Western Canada vacation may have objections or misgivings. Among the concerns are:

- "What is there to see out there?" This will be the most common objection you'll hear. Paint a clear picture of whatever attractions you think will appeal to the would-be visitor: majestic scenery, uncrowded roads, natural wonders, great winter sports, and so on.

- "We'll need to drive too much between destinations." If someone wishes to see all of Western Canada, from Winnipeg to Vancouver, explain that considerable driving will, indeed, be involved. Though the Trans-Canada makes driving efficient and pleasant, other options, such as rail or air travel (especially across several provinces) may be more suitable. A more compact vacation requiring less driving time would be to visit only the southern portions of British Columbia and Alberta. Escorted tours also allow people to enjoy road travel while letting someone else do the driving.

- "We have a winter vacation planned. Is there anything else to do besides ski?" Skiing is the main reason to visit Western Canada in the winter, but it's not the only option. The Banff–Lake Louise area is tremendously beautiful in winter and offers tobogganing, skating, and shopping as well. A winter stay in one of the area's hotels can be very cozy and romantic. Finally, Vancouver and (especially) Vancouver Island enjoy less severe winters than the rest of the region, and Vancouver is a lively city year-round.

- "Aren't the resort areas expensive?" Choice rooms with a view in the best hotels will be pricey, especially during peak tourist seasons. Value seekers could stay in one of the smaller chalets or vacation during the fall/spring shoulder seasons. Compared to similar resort areas such as Aspen, Colorado, or the Swiss Alps, the Canadian Rockies' resorts represent excellent value.

Qualifying the Traveller
WESTERN CANADA

FOR PEOPLE WHO WANT	HIGH APPEAL	MEDIUM APPEAL	LOW APPEAL	REMARKS
Historical and Cultural Attractions		▲		Many small and medium-sized museums
Beaches and Water Sports		▲		Non–warm water activities
Skiing Opportunities	▲			Several world-class resorts
Lots of Nightlife		▲		Mostly Vancouver, Calgary, Edmonton, and Winnipeg
Family Activities	▲			
Familiar Cultural Experience	▲			
Exotic Cultural Experience			▲	
Safety and Low Crime	▲			Even in big cities
Bargain Travel		▲		Especially off-season
Impressive Scenery	▲			Greatest strength
Peace and Quiet	▲			Outside cities
Shopping Opportunities		▲		
Adventure		▲		Especially Alberta
To Do Business	▲			Especially Vancouver and its ties to Pacific Rim commerce

- "Isn't it boring?" Certain areas do lack major attractions or nightlife, but others have plenty of excitement. Calgary, for example, with its Stampede, professional sports teams, and country-western clubs, may appeal to excitement seekers. The West Edmonton Mall offers activities for the whole family. Vancouver is a large city with a wide array of cultural and entertainment options. For the truly adventurous, Western Canada's natural attractions offer many daring activities and sightseeing options.

SALES STRATEGIES

Several obvious recommendations can create a fine opportunity to augment profits from a trip to Western Canada. Among them are cruises, escorted tours, train trips, and ski packages. Travellers visiting Banff–Lake Louise should be up-sold to rooms with the best mountain or lake views. Consider also adventure tour options, such as helicopter tours, Snocoach rides through the Columbia Icefield, or charter fishing expeditions.

Few can resist the stunning natural grandeur of the Canadian Rockies, but special events or professional sports can also attract tourists; festivals are held frequently throughout the region, and most of the major cities host hockey and football games during the fall and winter months. The Calgary Stampede isn't the only summer festival in Western Canada. Other warm-weather events include Edmonton's **Klondike Days** (July), Winnipeg's **Folklorama** (August), Regina's **Buffalo Days** (August), the **Banff Festival of the Arts** (July–August), and Vancouver's **Pacific National Exhibition** (August and September).

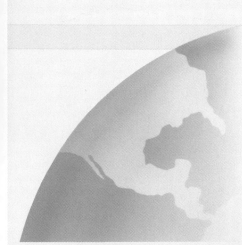

TRAVEL TRIVIA

MOST POPULAR REGIONS FOR FALL COLOURS

1. New England
2. Pennsylvania/Virginia
3. Canadian Rockies
4. Adirondacks
5. Pacific Northwest
6. Grand Canyon
7. Atlantic Canada
8. The Ozarks
9. The Great Smoky Mountains
10. The Great Lakes

Source: Carlson Wagonlit Travel Agents' Poll

NAME _____ DATE _____

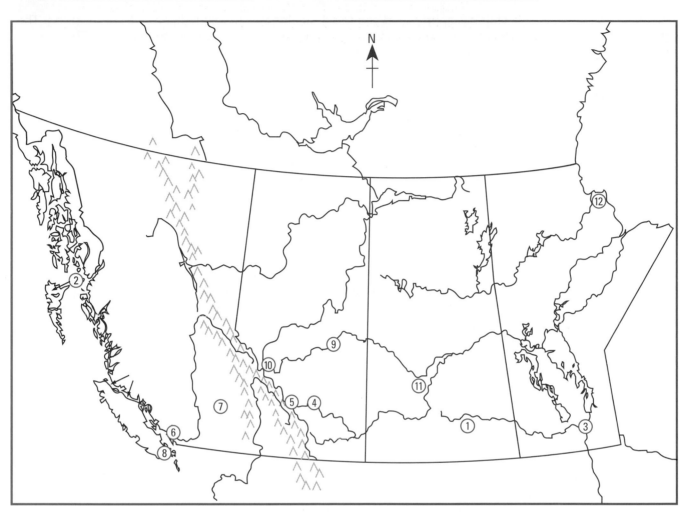

A traveller wants to visit the places listed below. Which number represents each on the map?

PLACE/ATTRACTION	IN WHICH CITY/PROVINCE?	NUMBER ON MAP
A. Château Lake Louise	**A.**	**A.**
B. A polar bear haven	**B.**	**B.**
C. The main cruise port	**C.**	**C.**
D. Home of the Royal Canadian Mounted Police	**D.**	**D.**
E. Columbia Icefield	**E.**	**E.**
F. Site of the Stampede	**F.**	**F.**
G. Site of a huge mall	**G.**	**G.**
H. Provincial capital with the Royal Canadian Mint	**H.**	**H.**
I. An island capital city	**I.**	**I.**
J. Wanuskewin Heritage Park	**J.**	**J.**

Chapter 3 Western Canada   **91**

CASE STUDY

The Winter Wonderland ski club has approached you to set up air travel to and lodging in Banff for skiing. The group, made up of about 15 couples, would prefer a weeklong trip and favour early spring skiing. They are open to suggestions for things to do while they are there.

Circle the answer that best suits their needs.

1. A good cross-sell you could make to them would be:

   Car rentals   A train trip to Vancouver

   Full ski packages   An Alaska cruise

   Why?

2. They could also travel up to Jasper. Which of the following activities might you recommend?

   A helicopter ride   White-water rafting

   A polar bear expedition   A shopping spree at a huge mall

   Why?

3. Where would you lodge the group?

   Château Frontenac   Château Lake Louise

   Banff Springs Hotel   Fairmont Palliser

   Why?

4. Which of the following natural attractions is most convenient to Banff?

   Hell's Gate   Columbia Icefield

   Big Moose Mountain   Lake Louise

   Why?

CREATIVE ACTIVITY

NAME _____   DATE _____

You are the events director for the Western Canada Tourism Bureau, a newly formed agency that works with municipal and provincial convention/visitor's bureaus to promote travel to the region. As one of your first projects, you have been asked to create a new festival or event to take place in fall (October or November).

The purpose of the new event is to create a spike in tourism during this typically slow period. Most regional events occur during the peak summer months or during the winter ski season. Other Canadian regions have developed successful special winter events that are unique to the area, such as Quebec City's Carnaval de Québec or Niagara Falls' Festival of Lights. These events not only attract tourists who would not otherwise make a winter visit but also create considerable excitement and participation opportunities for locals.

Based on your own knowledge of Western Canada and its unique destinations, as well as any information you might find in books or on the Internet, develop a multi-day event. Select a place in the region for this event and come up with a name and a list of activities, entertainment, and features. Explain why your idea is novel and appropriate for the region. Also, devise a brief promotional plan to outline how you would create awareness within the travel community of your new program.

ARCTIC
OCEAN

Queen
Elizabeth
Islands

BAFFIN
BAY

Point
Barrow

BEAUFORT
SEA

Auyuittuq
Nat. Park

Nome

Barnes Ice Cap

UNITED
STATES

Baffin Island

ALASKA

BERING
SEA

Alaska
Range

Fairbanks

Denali Nat. Park

Anchorage

Victoria
Island

Iqaluit

Dawson
City

Inuvik

Hudson Strait

GULF OF
ALASKA

YUKON

NORTHWEST
TERRITORIES

NUNAVUT

Kluane Nat. Park

Whitehorse

Watson
Lake

Great
Slave
Lake

Yellowknife

HUDSON
BAY

Skagway

Ft.
Simpson

Juneau

Nahanni Nat. Park

GLACIER
BAY

Sitka

BRITISH
COLUMBIA

HUDSON
BAY

Ketchikan

MANITOBA

C A N A D A

ONTARIO

ALBERTA

SASKATCHEWAN

Northern Canada and Alaska

Far North Adventure

The French philosopher Voltaire once called Canada "20 million acres of snow." Americans once labelled the U.S. purchase of Alaska, at 2.5 cents an acre, a "folly." Follies indeed. Northern Canada and Alaska are key to the wealth of the North American continent and are unique tourist destinations for truly adventurous travellers and lovers of nature.

Why does this chapter lump Canada's **Yukon, Northwest Territories,** and **Nunavut** with the U.S. state of **Alaska**? The reason is geographic. Northern Canada and Alaska form a physical cap to North America. The entire area has a certain similarity of climate, topography, and history. Still, the Canadian territories have their own cultural identity, and Alaskans pride themselves on their distinct way of thinking.

HOW TRAVELLERS GET THERE

Most people drive into the Yukon Territory, then Alaska, via the **Alaska Highway,** which ties into roads in northern British Columbia. The highway first enters the Yukon at Watson Lake and crosses into Alaska just west of the Yukon town of Beaver Creek. The Northwest Territories can be accessed by car via Highway 35 out of Alberta, which runs north through the town of Steen River before becoming Highway 1 (the **Mackenzie Highway**) at the Alberta–Northwest Territories border. Unlike the well-engineered Alaska Highway, roadways into the Northwest Territories (even sections of the Mackenzie Highway and the Yellowknife Highway, the main artery to Yellowknife, the territorial capital) are made primarily of gravel and can be hazardous during inclement weather.

For more comfortable highway touring, motorcoach travel is a good choice. Ferries and cruise ships are also a prime way of accessing Alaska. On the West Coast, vessels sail from Vancouver or Seattle to several spots on the Alaska panhandle.

Air service is the most convenient and efficient means of accessing the northern regions. Travellers can fly to **Yellowknife** (YZF) and **Inuvik** (YEV), Northwest Territories; **Iqaluit** (YFB), the capital of Nunavut; and **Whitehorse** (YXY), Yukon Territory.

Air travel to Alaska can be a little tricky. Major Canadian airlines have extremely limited service into the state. Instead, visitors will most likely fly to Seattle to connect to **Anchorage** (ANC), **Fairbanks** (FAI), or **Juneau** (JNU), the

Juneau, Alaska, covers the largest area of any U.S. state capital, but has the smallest population.

state capital. **Alaska Airlines** (AS), the state's well-known carrier, and several major U.S. carriers fly into Alaska.

WEATHER PATTERNS

◎ Buy a special bag to protect your camera from the cold of Northern Canada and Alaska.

Northern Canada and Alaska have very cold, harsh climates. Winters are snowy and freezing, with little sunlight and average daytime temperatures well below zero (see Figures 4-1 and 4-2). Rainfall is moderate throughout the year, except in the Alaska Panhandle, where Juneau is located and where rainfall, as in Vancouver, British Columbia, can be plentiful, especially in the late summer and during the fall.

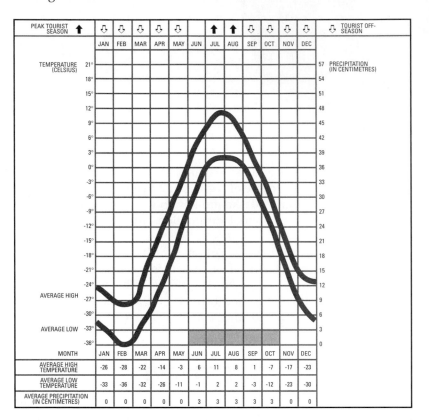

MONTH	JAN	FEB	MAR	APR	MAY	JUN	JUL	AUG	SEP	OCT	NOV	DEC
AVERAGE HIGH TEMPERATURE	-26	-28	-22	-14	-3	6	11	8	1	-7	-17	-23
AVERAGE LOW TEMPERATURE	-33	-36	-32	-26	-11	-1	2	2	-3	-12	-23	-30
AVERAGE PRECIPITATION (IN CENTIMETRES)	0	0	0	0	0	3	3	3	3	3	0	0

Figure 4-1   Climate at a Glance: Iqaluit, Nunavut

◎ Mosquitoes and biting flies can be a major irritant in Northern Canada and Alaska in the summer. Take insect repellent.

Tourist season reaches a peak in the short summer season (July and August), when daylight lasts for 20 hours or more in some areas. June and September attract budget travellers. Temperatures can rise into the upper 20s in some of the more southwesterly areas during the day, though nighttime temperatures may dip below freezing. Wind-chill factors can make even balmy days quite cool.

GETTING AROUND

◎ In some areas (especially in Nunavut and the NWT), gas stations are few and far between.

In more temperate months, the drive through most of Northern Canada and Alaska is a pleasant experience because traffic is virtually nonexistent (except on the Alaska Highway, which can get busy). For those who want to venture off the major roadways, though, it's quite a different story. Roads can leave something to be desired. Travellers in the north country may find small aircraft, helicopters, and seaplanes to be more efficient, though inclement weather can wreak havoc on schedules.

Two forms of transportation—trains and ships—are especially useful in Alaska. Train service between Anchorage and Fairbanks is very popular. Alaska has something called the "AlaskaPass": A one-time fee entitles clients to unlimited

Figure 4-2   Climate at a Glance: Anchorage, Alaska

MONTH	JAN	FEB	MAR	APR	MAY	JUN	JUL	AUG	SEP	OCT	NOV	DEC
AVERAGE HIGH TEMPERATURE	-7	-3	1	7	13	17	18	18	13	6	-2	-7
AVERAGE LOW TEMPERATURE	-14	-12	-9	-3	2	7	9	8	4	-2	-9	-14
AVERAGE PRECIPITATION (IN CENTIMETRES)	3	3	3	0	3	3	5	8	8	5	3	3

travel on certain ferries (numerous ferries criss-cross the region), buses, and trains. Travellers are very attracted to Alaska cruises: multi-day round-trip excursions from Vancouver or Seattle into the Inside Passage (or one-way trips through the Inside Passage, then into the Gulf Coast region to the Anchorage area). A cruise can also be done in reverse, starting in Anchorage and ending in Vancouver or Seattle. Passengers can even take plane or helicopter trips directly from locations near their moored ship. Note that Anchorage has three ports: Whittier, Seward, and the city of Anchorage itself.

IMPORTANT PLACES

What can travellers experience in the north country? Here is a list of places that are popular with visitors.

Northwest Territories and Nunavut

The vast Northwest Territories (NWT) and Nunavut (self-governed by the Inuit inhabitants) are Canada's northernmost regions. Their northern islands extend to within 800 kilometres of the North Pole. In the south, the NWT shares borders with British Columbia, Alberta, and Saskatchewan; Nunavut, with Manitoba and the great **Hudson Bay.** Though together the NWT and Nunavut cover more than 3.3 million square kilometres (just over one-third of Canada's land area) and span four time zones, their combined populations stand at little more than 64 000 total.

Collectively known as the "Land of the Midnight Sun," Nunavut and the NWT are bathed in daylight almost 24 hours a day during the summer months. Outdoor-sports enthusiasts, adventure seekers, and explorers are drawn to the region's abundant wildlife and expansive arctic wilderness. Among the main attractions are:

St. Jude's Cathedral in Iqaluit, Nunavut, is shaped like an igloo.

- **Yellowknife,** the capital of the NWT, located on the north shores of **Great Slave Lake.** Though Yellowknife has a few interesting museums (for example, the **Prince of Wales Northern Heritage Centre,** which features a collection of Inuit art), the city's greatest asset is the nearby lake, one of Canada's largest. In the summer, lake cruises and fishing are popular activities, as are the underground tours of local gold mines. Yellowknife also hosts several notable special events in the summer, including the **Canadian North Yellowknife Midnight Golf Classic,** the **Festival of the Midnight Sun,** and the **Raven Mad Daze** summer-solstice celebration.

- **Nahanni National Park,** nestled on the NWT's southwest border. Here visitors can camp beside a mountain, go white-water rafting, or hike in the park's deep canyons. Nahanni also features the massive **Virginia Falls** (twice the height of Niagara Falls) and several hot springs. The best way to reach the park is via a short flight from nearby **Fort Simpson,** a historic fur-trading outpost located at the end of Highway 1.

- For a truly outback experience, visitors can take a week-long summer cruise from Fort Simpson northwest up the tremendous **Mackenzie River** (Canada's longest river) into the Arctic Circle and the city of Inuvik (air travel to the city is also available). The centre of government for the western Arctic region, Inuvik is the largest Canadian community north of the Arctic Circle.

- **Baffin Island,** in Nunavut's far northeast, home to **Auyuittuq National Park.** The park features remarkable arctic scenery, summer midnight sun, hiking trails, and interesting wildlife. Unique Inuit carvings and art are available. On the island's eastern coast is Iqaluit [ee-KAH-loo-it] (formerly Frobisher Bay), the capital of Nunavut. From here, visitors can take a guided dog-sled trip, spending the night in an igloo.

⊚ The streets in Iqaluit have no names.

Yukon Territory

Gold fever in 1898 put Canada's Yukon Territory on the international map. With the Klondike gold rush, more than 100 000 fortune seekers poured into this frigid land. The Yukon retains much of the frontier spirit. Indeed, most of its major towns hark back to the days of gold prospecting and offer historical attractions

Virginia Falls

that retell the gold-rush story. That's one reason so many Alaska cruises feature a potential add-on, multi-day motorcoach visit to the Yukon.

The other reason is its scenery. Bordered to the west by Alaska, the south by British Columbia, and the east by the NWT, the region's mountains, canyons, forests, and wild, churning rivers provide numerous activities for outdoor adventurers and sightseers. And visitors certainly are impressed by summer's 24 hours of sun and winter's awesome display of the northern lights. Among the Yukon's main attractions are:

- **Whitehorse,** the Yukon's capital, transportation hub, and largest city. Whitehorse boasts a number of notable museums and shows, including the **MacBride Museum** (First Nations art and displays about the gold-rush years), the **Old Log Church Museum** (regional history), and **"Frantic Follies"** (a nightly summertime vaudeville revue that tells the Yukon gold story). Nearby natural attractions include **Takhini Hot Springs, Miles Canyon,** and the **Yukon River.** Popular activities include guided nature walks, river cruises through the canyon, and air tours.

- **Kluane** [clue-AH-nee] **National Park and Reserve,** a vast wilderness area (it's more than half the size of Switzerland) containing thousands of glaciers and the tallest mountain in Canada, **Mt. Logan.** Located in the southwest corner of the territory, just off the Alaska Highway, the park harbours varied wildlife and spectacular scenery.

- **Dawson City,** a frontier gold-rush city that re-creates the prospecting fervour that once shaped it. Located in the middle of the Yukon near the Alaska border, Dawson City can be accessed via the **Klondike Highway** (off the Alaska Highway). City highlights are **Diamond Tooth Gertie's Gambling Hall,** the **Dawson City Museum** (gold-rush exhibits), and several historical sites (gold-claims locations and dredges). Tourists can even pan for gold in the nearby Yukon River or at one of the various claim sites. Overall, Dawson City provides a real sense of "yesteryear" and excitement, combined with modern-day efficiencies. Like Whitehorse, Dawson City is also a gateway to many active experiences, such as canoeing, kayaking, cycling, and hiking.

The Yukon International Storytelling Festival takes place in Whitehorse in August.

Dempster Highway starts near Dawson City and continues on to Inuvik, NWT. It's the only public road in Canada to cross the Artic Circle.

Kluane National Park is popular with hikers and white-water rafters.
Copyright COREL

Alaska

In the far northwest of the North American continent (and only a few kilometres from Russia, to which it once belonged) is Alaska, the largest U.S. state at more than 1.5 million square kilometres. Despite its size, Alaska is sparsely populated.

Alaska appeals to those who love natural beauty, who can afford what could turn out to be a rather expensive trip, and who don't mind the prospect of a slow-paced (but certainly dramatic) adventure. All manner of boats and small aircraft at key towns provide ways to explore Alaska's pristine interior. Among the highlights of any trip to Alaska are:

- **The Inside Passage** cruise, which starts in British Columbia, with its striking views and interesting stops. Alaska ports include **Sitka** (featuring remnants of Russian influence), picturesque Juneau, **Skagway** (a key town in Alaska's gold-rush era), **Ketchikan** (a rustic centre of Native-American culture), and **Glacier Bay** (a remarkable place where passengers may see icebergs tumbling into the water from glaciers). Similar glacier experiences accessible to ships are at **Tracy Arm** and **Hubbard Glacier.** Smaller ports on Inside Passage cruises include **Icy Strait Point, Haines, Petersburg,** and **Wrangell.**

- **Juneau,** the state capital, located in a scenic harbour rimmed by mountains. Juneau has a few museums of note, but the real attraction is nearby **Mendenhall Glacier.** Recommend this dramatic site as part of a day trip from Juneau. Juneau is not accessible by car—only by plane, ship, or ferry.

- **Anchorage,** Alaska's largest city (over 40 percent of all Alaskans live here), which is close to major glaciers (the Portage Glacier is the best known) and parks. Other notable attractions include the **Alaska Zoo** (featuring arctic wildlife), **Earthquake Park** (a visible reminder of how the terrain shifted in the 1964 quake), the **Alaska Native Heritage Center** (focusing on Alaska's native groups), and the **Anchorage Museum of History and Art** (which traces the state's cultural history).

- **The Alaska Railroad,** a 573 kilometre trip between Anchorage and Fairbanks, which crosses several awe-inspiring national parks, most notably **Denali**

According to residents, Ketchikan is "five miles long, four blocks wide, and two blocks up Deer Mountain."
Copyright COREL

[den-AH-lee] **National Park,** home to grizzlies and **Mt. McKinley** (or Denali), North America's tallest peak. This journey is often part of a cruise-tour.

- **Fairbanks,** a gold-rush frontier town that features stern-wheeler trips on the *Discovery III,* old gold camps, **Pioneer Park** (formerly Alaskaland) frontier theme park, and the **University of Alaska** and its museum. Fairbanks is also a popular site in the winter for viewing the colourful northern lights.

- **Nome,** a northern gold-rush centre, and **Point Barrow,** the northernmost spot in the United States. Both places—known for their summer midnight sun—are often visited via plane as day trips from Fairbanks or Anchorage.

POSSIBLE ITINERARIES

Because Canada's northern regions are so vast and its roadways merely adequate, air travel is just about the only way to visit the Yukon, Nunavut, and the NWT in one vacation. Most people travel to just one of each territory's primary southern regions at a time.

One possible NWT itinerary: a flight to Yellowknife, followed by a long day's drive south to Fort Providence, then west to Fort Simpson. From Fort Simpson, it's a short flight to Nahanni National Park. Southern Yukon can be visited in the same manner, with a flight to Whitehorse followed by a drive west on the Alaska Highway to Kluane National Park.

A traveller can visit many Alaskan areas simply by day-tripping out of key cities such as Anchorage, Fairbanks, or Juneau. The most popular Alaska itinerary is an Inside Passage roundtrip cruise from Vancouver or Seattle to Juneau, or a one-way cruise beyond to Anchorage. Visitors not interested in cruising can fly to Anchorage, and then take a plane or train, or drive (via Highway 3, the George Parks Highway) from Anchorage to Fairbanks.

LODGING OPTIONS

In the Yukon, Nunavut, and the NWT, aside from a few standard-service inns or hotels found in the larger cities, accommodations tend to consist of rustic lodges or campgrounds with limited amenities. There are also quite a few bed-and-breakfasts.

Alaska has many hotels and motels, but they can be expensive, which is one reason cruises are an excellent option. One of the newer deluxe hotels is the château-style **Alyeska Prince Hotel** south of Anchorage in Girdwood. Those on the Anchorage–Fairbanks rail journey stay at various lodges at the trip's midpoint in Denali.

ALLIED DESTINATIONS

The Yukon, Nunavut, and the NWT are not logical extensions of any other destination, except for flights to or from Western Canada cities, such as Edmonton (for Yellowknife) or Vancouver (for Whitehorse). Tourists who travel to Northern Canada generally do so for fishing or hunting expeditions, as opposed to sightseeing journeys. Alaska (especially the southern panhandle area) lends itself to combinations with Washington State, British Columbia, and the Canadian Rockies.

FACTORS THAT MOTIVATE VISITORS

Northern Canada and Alaska hold a special attraction for certain kinds of tourists. Below are a few of the reasons for going there:

- The wilderness areas and glaciers are remarkable.

- People are friendly and welcome visitors.

- Outdoor-sports activities are challenging, adventurous, and plentiful.

- Wildlife is easy to observe and photograph.

- Fishing and camping opportunities are abundant.

- Open wilderness provides a chance to get away from it all.

- The First Nations and Inuit cultures lend an exotic feel to many destinations.

- The regional history (especially the gold-rush heritage) is well preserved in many towns.

- Cruises are a comfortable and convenient way to see Alaska's main sites.

POSSIBLE MISGIVINGS

- "Isn't it expensive?" Alaska can be expensive, but stressing the all-inclusive nature of a tour or cruise may be the right sales approach. Northern Canada is a travel bargain, especially in spring and fall.

- "Isn't it always cold up there?" Arctic winter weather (and much of the fall and spring) is freezing, both day and night, and requires special clothing

Qualifying the Traveller
NORTHERN CANADA AND ALASKA

FOR PEOPLE WHO WANT	HIGH APPEAL	MEDIUM APPEAL	LOW APPEAL	REMARKS
Historical and Cultural Attractions		▲		Gold-rush cities and towns
Beaches and Water Sports			▲	Fishing
Skiing Opportunities		▲		A few cross-country and downhill options in Alaska
Lots of Nightlife			▲	
Family Activities		▲		
Familiar Cultural Experience		▲		Can seem like another world
Exotic Cultural Experience		▲		First Nations/ Inuit cultures
Safety and Low Crime	▲			
Bargain Travel		▲		
Impressive Scenery	▲			Extremely varied
Peace and Quiet	▲			
Shopping Opportunities			▲	First Nations/ Inuit crafts
Adventure	▲			
To Do Business			▲	

Inuit art, soapstone sculptures, and leather-work are unique purchases here.

to deal with the frigid temperatures. Summer months, on the other hand, can be pleasant during the day, especially during the long stretches of near–non-stop sunlight.

- "It's too hard to get around." Alaska and the southern Yukon benefit from the Alaska Highway, though Nunavut, the NWT, and most other remote areas have rough roads, if any at all. Alternative transportation is varied but susceptible to the weather, making delays or cancellations common. Air travel is the best option, and charter flights can be arranged to most locations in the region.

- "What is there possibly to do up there?" Northern Canada and, to a lesser extent, Alaska lack many of the usual destination options. Those seeking the comforts of home, fine food, and varied entertainment probably shouldn't vacation in the Far North, unless, of course, they are visiting Alaska via a cruise. Outdoor enthusiasts will find endless options in even the most remote areas.

SALES STRATEGIES

Northern Canada and Alaska are sold most easily via package tours. Many Northern Canada adventure tours span a range of activities and destinations. Emphasize the value of an experienced tour guide when selling such packages. Car rentals are a good cross-sell for Northern Canada because travellers wishing to visit different locales will have to fly first, then rent a car to get around.

Alaska offers several up-sell opportunities, often involving cruises. Among the cross-sell options are motorcoach tours and guided tours of the state's parks.

Special events are prime motivators to travel and may entice tourists to visit the Far North during the colder months. Among the unique and exuberant festivals held in the fall and winter are Yellowknife's **Caribou Carnival,** featuring dogsled races and other snow sports (March), Whitehorse's **Yukon Sourdough Rendezvous Festival** (February) and **Frostbite Music Festival** (February), Dawson City's **Great Klondike International Outhouse Race** (September), and the **Iditarod Trail Sled Dog Race** (from Anchorage to Nome, held in March).

Hikers, mountain climbers, hunters, and other explorers should use the services of experienced tour guides, park rangers, or outfitters.

Prearranged package tours are the best way to see and experience Northern Canada. A variety of tours are available, from hunting expeditions, to white-water rafting trips, to dogsled adventures.

TRAVEL TRIVIA

WHO ARE ADVENTURE TRAVELLERS?

- 44 percent are single
- 55 percent are over 45 years old
- 80 percent have college degrees
- 31 percent travel as families
- 61 percent shop for local handicrafts

Adventure travellers rate camping as their favourite activity, followed by hiking. Hang-gliding is rated last.

Sources: Travel Industry Association; McRand International

MAP ACTIVITY

NAME _____   DATE _____

A traveller wants to visit the places listed below. Which number represents each on the map?

PLACE/ATTRACTION	IN WHICH CITY/ PROVINCE/STATE?	NUMBER ON MAP
A. Location of MacBride Museum; near Takhini Hot Springs	A.	A.
B. Scenic ocean cruise lane	B.	B.
C. Flights from here to Nahanni	C.	C.
D. Tallest peak in North America	D.	D.
E. Site of Outhouse Race	E.	E.
F. Northernmost U.S. point	F.	F.
G. Town on Great Slave Lake	G.	G.
H. Where Alaska Highway enters from British Columbia	H.	H.
I. Community at northern end of Mackenzie River	I.	I.
J. Northern end of many cruises	J.	J.

CASE STUDY

NAME _____   DATE _____

Doug and Roberta McKenzie love to travel but are unable to take long vacations due to the successful pub they run in Calgary. They both love sightseeing and outdoor activities, though Roberta has a fondness for creature comforts as well. They have less than a week to travel and plan to vacation in July. You suggest a journey north. They're intrigued by your idea and want to hear more.

Circle the answer that best suits their needs.

1. Where would you send the McKenzies and what would you suggest they do?

    Yellowknife fishing trip   Alaska cruise

    Alaska rail tour   Mackenzie River cruise

    Why?

2. How would you recommend they access their destination?

    By car   By rail

    By plane   By cruise

    Why?

3. Where would you lodge the McKenzies?

    A campsite   A hotel

    A lodge   Aboard ship

    Why?

4. What recommendations might the McKenzies appreciate?

    A gold mine tour   A rafting trip

    A helicopter tour   A car rental

    Why?

CREATIVE ACTIVITY

NAME _____   DATE _____

From the standpoint of where you live, where is Mexico City? Is it "up" or "down"? Though this seems like a simple question (Mexico City is south and therefore "down" on a map), Canadian travellers may have a different perspective.

According to a *National Geographic* study, some people view destinations not in terms of a world map, but rather in terms of the place they call home. Thus, residents of more northerly latitudes may mentally turn the world upside down, thereby envisioning southern points as being "up." Keeping this distinction in mind is important when planning itineraries for people who may differ from you in terms of the way they perceive destination positions.

As an exercise, look at the inverted map of North America below without turning the book upside down. Try to identify the 10 key cities in Canada and the United States from this new perspective. Write your answers in the space provided on the next page. Do you perceive the rest of North America in this manner, thinking of points south of Canada as "up" and the place you call home as "down"? If so, why? If not, why?

New England

The Cradle of Liberty

Ever heard stories of the Pilgrims stepping on Plymouth Rock, church lanterns signalling Paul Revere, and American Minutemen confronting Redcoats at Old North Bridge in Concord? You don't have to be American to know these stories—many Canadians have heard them, too (though perhaps with a different point of view). Mention New England and their minds will swirl with images both historical and contemporary: whaling ships, monuments, museums, white clapboard houses, and clambakes by the sea. These strong mental impressions define New England in almost everyone's minds. So it's no wonder that it's such a popular destination.

There's a wealth of cities, states, and attractions in the compact northeast corner of the United States. Northernmost is **Maine,** a sparsely settled state of wild, stark beauty. To the southwest of Maine are **Vermont** and **New Hampshire.** (To keep these two straight, remember that Vermont is shaped like a *V*.) Both states are mountainous and wooded, with many charming towns dotting the landscape. South of Vermont and New Hampshire is **Massachusetts,** the most visited of the New England states. Finally, in New England's south are **Connecticut** and **Rhode Island,** the smallest U.S. state.

Massachusetts has no cities named for saints. The reason: The founding Pilgrims and Puritans thought saints were too Catholic.

Boston cream pie is the official dessert of Massachusetts.

HOW TRAVELLERS GET THERE

Travellers will have to decide how they intend to get to New England. If it's by car, they'll enter through Ontario (via New York State), Quebec, or New Brunswick. If it's by air, they'll fly in on one of a half-dozen carriers that service the area. Cruise ships stop at New England cities on their way between New York City and Montreal. Rail service to New England is limited. Bus service is a good option for budget-minded visitors.

Most travellers bound for New England fly into **Boston**'s **Logan Airport** (BOS), but **Providence,** Rhode Island (PVD); **Burlington,** Vermont (BTV); **Manchester,** New Hampshire (MHT); or **Hartford,** Connecticut (BDL), are good alternatives. Why? Because Logan is a very congested airport. Moreover, Boston itself would be a difficult city to navigate on arrival day. Flying time to New England is about five to six hours from Vancouver, two hours from Halifax, and less than 1.5 hours from Toronto or Montreal.

Rhode Island is only 59 kilometres wide and 77 kilometres long, but it has 640 kilometres of shoreline.

WEATHER PATTERNS

"If you don't like New England's weather, wait a minute." That's a common saying locals use to describe their wildly changeable climate (see Figure 5-1). Winters are cold and snowy, especially in the mountain areas and away from the coast. Crisp, blue-skied winter days can be glorious. Early spring can be dreary, but May is usually a beautiful month. Summer temperatures are generally in the 20s, though very hot, humid spells occur more than New Englanders would like. Fall is especially beautiful; the fall foliage in October is justly famous.

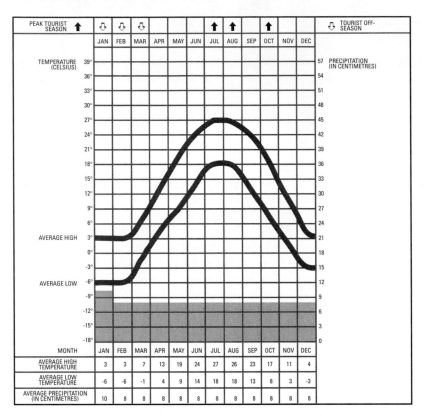

MONTH	JAN	FEB	MAR	APR	MAY	JUN	JUL	AUG	SEP	OCT	NOV	DEC
AVERAGE HIGH TEMPERATURE	3	3	7	13	19	24	27	26	23	17	11	4
AVERAGE LOW TEMPERATURE	-6	-6	-1	4	9	14	18	18	13	8	3	-3
AVERAGE PRECIPITATION (IN CENTIMETRES)	10	8	8	8	8	8	8	8	8	8	8	8

Figure 5-1 Climate at a Glance: Boston, Massachusetts

 Ninety-nine percent of all the wild blueberries in the United States grow in Maine.

Overall, New England's precipitation is about the same year-round. Multi-day storms are possible most of the year, except in summer, when rainfall tends to occur in short, intense downpours. Tourist season peaks in the summer months and again during fall foliage time, with a sharp drop-off, except for skiers, in the winter.

GETTING AROUND

The most scenic road on Cape Cod is 6A.

Boston's city transportation system—especially the "T" subway–train network—is extensive. To visit all of New England, however, visitors would do best to use a car. The highway network is superb and quaint rural roads are numerous. Traffic jams are uncommon, except in and around Boston, where they can be monumental, or during summer weekends and holidays, when certain roads that access popular vacation places (for example, Cape Cod and New Hampshire) get congested.

The most scenic ferry stop on Martha's Vineyard is Oak Bluffs.

For people who don't want to drive, a New England motorcoach tour is an appealing option. Budget vacationers like the region's excellent bus system. Amtrak connects Boston with several key New England cities. Distances are so short that brief commuter flights are useful only for those in a real hurry and willing to pay for it. Ferry service to the offshore islands of **Martha's Vineyard** and **Nantucket** can make for a pleasant day's outing.

IMPORTANT PLACES

Which places in New England are must-sees? It's a hard choice—there are so many. What follows are New England's most popular cities and attractions.

Boston

Boston is a graceful and historic city. Because its attractions are clustered in a compact area, visitors can walk the well-marked, five kilometre **Freedom Trail** and see most of the historical sites in a day. City tours and boat tours are also an excellent way for people to orient themselves to Boston. Cultural opportunities and fine dining experiences abound.

Among the sights that are "musts":

*   **Boston Common,** the oldest park in the nation, and the adjoining **Public Garden,** with its unique "swan boats."

*   **The Old State House,** the seat of Massachusetts's government.

*   **The Boston Tea Party Ship,** a full-sized replica of one of the ships involved in the well-known protest. A museum next door documents its history.

*   **Many museums,** especially the **Museum of Fine Arts,** the **Museum of Science,** the **New England Aquarium,** and **JFK Library and Museum** (south of the city on Columbia Point).

*   **Faneuil** [FAN-yule] **Hall Marketplace** (including Quincy Market), a restored complex of shops, dining facilities, and historical buildings.

*   **The U.S.S.** *Constitution,* nicknamed *Old Ironsides,* a 200-year-old frigate used in the War of 1812.

*   **Cambridge,** home to **Harvard University** and its own fine museums.

Among the **day trips** from Boston are:

*   **Salem,** the infamous seat of the Massachusetts witchcraft trials and the location of Hawthorne's *The House of the Seven Gables.*

The longest place name in the U.S. belongs to a Massachusetts lake: Chargogagmanchaugaugaugacharbunagungamaugg, which means "You fish on your side of the lake, I'll fish on my side, and nobody fishes in the middle."

Boston's subway system, constructed in 1897, was the first in the U.S.

The Italian food in Boston's North End is superb.

The Fig Newton is named after Newton, Massachusetts.

Old Ironsides, Boston, Massachusetts
Photo by Justus Ghormley

Chapter 5 New England

- **Plymouth,** with its universally known rock (it's a bit of a disappointment), replica of the *Mayflower,* and fascinating re-created settlement, **Plimoth Plantation.**

- **The Berkshires,** Massachusetts's western mountain range, with its breathtaking vistas, especially in fall foliage season, and its **Old Sturbridge Village,** a living history museum that captures New England as it was centuries ago.

- **Cape Cod,** potentially a stayover option in itself, which boasts superb beaches, and **Provincetown,** at the Cape's tip.

Vermont, New Hampshire, and Maine

These three northern states have much in common: forested hills, country inns, small towns, and dramatic scenery. Many of New Hampshire's attractions are only a little more than an hour's drive from Boston and could be made into a day trip. Most of this state's sites lie in the **White Mountains,** along old Route 3. **Mt. Washington,** whose summit can be reached by a cog railway, is New England's highest mountain, and **Laconia** is every visitor's idea of a New England town. **Portsmouth,** New Hampshire's former capital and its only seaport, is filled with many quaint homes, shops, and taverns.

Vermont is even more picturesque than New Hampshire, perhaps because it's less industrialized than its neighbour. It's a state of pristine lakes, covered bridges, and excellent ski trails. Many cute little towns dot two major highways; **Barre** [BARE-ree] (once the source of most of the nation's granite), **Montpelier** (the capital), and **Burlington** are along Interstate 89; and **St. Johnsbury** (noted for maple syrup) is on Interstate 91.

Maine is more than three times larger than any of its neighbour states, yet most of its area is dense forest and uncultivated brush. Maine's rocky coastline is breathtaking. This is best seen at **Bar Harbor,** the gateway to **Acadia National Park** and to cruises from Canada. **Boothbay Harbor** is a major boating centre.

Ben & Jerry's, in Waterbury, Vermont, offers tours of its ice cream factory.

There are more islands in the Maine archipelago than in either the Caribbean or Polynesia.

Acadia National Park
Vladimir Ivanov/Shutterstock

Kennebunkport is a charming summer resort that has attracted the likes of Booth Tarkington, Rachel Carson, and George Bush. **Kittery** is a well-visited ship-building centre, and **Brunswick** has many historic buildings.

As for skiing, **Killington** and **Stowe,** Vermont; **Sugarloaf,** Maine; and **Waterville,** New Hampshire, are highly praised. Other well-known ski resorts: **Mt. Snow** and **Okemo,** Vermont; and **Mt. Cranmore,** New Hampshire.

The Southern Coast

Many travellers make the mistake of treating this area as simply a road from New York to Cape Cod or Boston. Some of New England's finest attractions lie along its southern coast. From west to east, they are:

- **Mohegan Sun Casino** in Uncasville, Connecticut, and **Foxwoods Resort and Casino** in Ledyard, Connecticut, Native American–owned casino-hotels that bring Las Vegas–like glitz to New England.

- **Mystic,** Connecticut, a seaport that looks much the same as it did in its whaling heyday.

- **Providence,** Rhode Island's rejuvenated capital, with many restaurants, nightspots, and stately old houses near **Brown University.** On selected nights, a remarkable display, **Waterfire,** illuminates the city's riverfront area.

- **Newport,** Rhode Island, a gem of an attraction that features nearly a dozen great cliff-side mansions open to the public. (Two of the most impressive: **The Breakers** and **Marble House.**) Here, too, are the **Tennis Hall of Fame** and **Touro Synagogue,** founded in 1763. It's about 90 minutes from Boston.

- **New Bedford,** Massachusetts, where Melville's *Moby Dick* is set, with its restored downtown area and remnants of a once-booming whaling industry.

- **Martha's Vineyard** and **Nantucket,** Massachusetts, charming islands accessed by ferry from several southern Massachusetts ports.

The Trapp Family, of *Sound of Music* fame, owns a ski lodge in Stowe, Vermont.

Connecticut's official state insect is the praying mantis.

Stroll the Cliff Walk, a path that skirts the ocean and mansion lawns of Newport.

Marble House, Newport, Rhode Island
Photo by Marc Mancini

POSSIBLE ITINERARIES

One of the best collections of *Titanic* memorabilia is at the Marine Museum in Fall River, Massachusetts.

Visitors who plan to hub out of Boston or another city will need at least a week to fully sample New England. Tourists may also decide to stay over in several towns and cities, with their whole itinerary taking as much as two weeks. An appropriate itinerary would start in Boston; travel up into New Hampshire, Maine, and Vermont for a few days; and then head down through the Berkshires and continue south to Connecticut. The trip could continue along the south coast to Cape Cod, then back to Plymouth and Boston.

LODGING OPTIONS

The name *Connecticut* means "long river place" in the Mohican language.

Hotels and motels are plentiful in New England. Boston's luxury properties are expensive, as are those on Cape Cod; lodging in the summer outside Boston, though, can be reasonable. In fact, for those who intend to stay in only one or two cities and hub their way out to various attractions, a good option would be to lodge in and around Providence, **Fall River** (Massachusetts), or any one of Boston's outlying towns. Each of these is at a major juncture of highways. A well-developed network of inns and bed-and-breakfasts exists throughout New England.

ALLIED DESTINATIONS

The waters off New England used to have so many lobsters that the colonists would feed them to their chickens.

A trip to New England can be easily combined with a trip to the Mid-Atlantic region, especially to New York State and New York City (a little more than four hours' driving time from Boston). One option is to combine the trip with eastern Canada: Montreal is only about 480 kilometres from Boston, and Halifax, Nova Scotia, is but a short cruise from Bar Harbor, Maine.

FACTORS THAT MOTIVATE VISITORS

An offbeat attraction in Dedham, Massachusetts: The Museum of Bad Art.

Among the factors that will pique interest in New England are:

- It has a historic heritage and plenty of cultural and educational opportunities.
- Travel outside Boston, especially during the off-season, is quite affordable.
- Scenery—both seaside and mountain—is impressive.
- Driving around is very easy, especially outside Boston.
- The region is very close to Canada and New York.
- Cruises afford an efficient way to see the coastal towns.
- The fine food of the area (especially the seafood) has a renowned reputation and is reasonable.
- Excellent skiing facilities exist in Vermont, Massachusetts, and New Hampshire.
- The summer beaches and water-sport opportunities are quite good, especially along the southern coast and Cape Cod.
- The fall foliage season is beautiful. (Make sure to book early!)

POSSIBLE MISGIVINGS

The Borden house in Fall River, Massachusetts, where Lizzie Borden (may have) murdered her parents, is now a tourist attraction and bed-and-breakfast.

Even the most appealing destinations provoke a few misgivings. Here are some you're likely to encounter:

- "All that history and scenery will be boring." Suggest New England's beaches, ski trails, and the nightlife in Boston.

- "It's too expensive." Only Boston and a few other areas are costly. Lodge off-season or in off-the-beaten-path cities, such as Providence, Fall River, New Bedford, or Boston's outlying towns. Bargains can also be easily had in New Hampshire, Vermont, and Maine (except during fall foliage season).

- "I don't like to drive." Concentrate the visitor's plans in Boston so that public transit can be used. Suggest an escorted tour or a cruise.

- "New Englanders aren't friendly." The old notion of the stoic Yankee is out of date. In fact, many of today's New Englanders are of French-Canadian, Portuguese, Italian, African, or Irish descent. They're usually warm and hospitable to visitors.

- "I once flew into Boston and the place was frantic!" Suggest flying into Providence or other cities as an alternative.

Qualifying the Traveller
NEW ENGLAND

FOR PEOPLE WHO WANT	HIGH APPEAL	MEDIUM APPEAL	LOW APPEAL	REMARKS
Historical and Cultural Attractions	▲			Especially Boston area
Beaches and Water Sports		▲		Mostly summers
Skiing Opportunities	▲			Very good, but not alpine
Lots of Nightlife			▲	Boston mostly
Family Activities		▲		Experience history
Familiar Cultural Experience	▲			Well-known landmarks
Exotic Cultural Experience			▲	Some ethnic neighbourhoods
Safety and Low Crime		▲		Some crime in Boston
Bargain Travel		▲		Outside Boston and off-season
Impressive Scenery	▲			In mountains, along ocean
Peace and Quiet		▲		Especially northern areas
Shopping Opportunities	▲			Mill outlets for clothing
Adventure			▲	Mountain-related
To Do Business		▲		Especially in and around Boston, Providence

SALES STRATEGIES

There are more people of French-Canadian descent in the United States than there are French Canadians in Canada.

The best way to up-sell New England is to suggest an expansion of the planned itinerary or to bring up the idea of a motorcoach tour or a New England–Canada cruise. Some of Boston's lower-cost hotels leave something to be desired; a top-class hotel is advisable. A city or boat tour of Boston and, especially, a car rental are obvious cross-sell opportunities. If an upscale traveller has limited time, and especially if he or she doesn't want to drive, commuter flights between New England's points of interest could be an attractive option. Winter ski packages and fall foliage tours of New England are perennial bestsellers.

TRAVEL TRIVIA

UNUSUAL NORTH AMERICAN PLACE NAMES

Bald Head, Maine
Happy Jack, Arizona
Bat Cave, North Carolina
Lollipop, Texas
Medicine Hat, Alberta
Broken Arrow, Oklahoma
Clam, Michigan
Noodle, Texas
Couch, Missouri
Five Fingers, New Brunswick
Okay, Oklahoma
Toad Suck, Arkansas
Truth or Consequences, New Mexico
Asphalt, Kentucky
Hygiene, Colorado

Moose Jaw, Saskatchewan
Walla Walla, Washington
Black Gnat, Kentucky
Colon, Missouri
Cut and Shoot, Texas
Elbow, Saskatchewan
Porkee, Pennsylvania
Droop, West Virginia
Salvage, Newfoundland & Labrador
Funk, Nebraska
Tuna, Pennsylvania
Lithium, Missouri
Zzyzx, California
Moose Factory, Ontario
Egg Harbor City, New Jersey

MAP ACTIVITY

NAME _____   DATE _____

A traveller wants to visit the places listed below. Which number represents each on the map?

PLACE/ATTRACTION	IN WHICH STATE?	NUMBER ON MAP
A. Bar Harbor	A.	A.
B. Mystic	B.	B.
C. The Freedom Trail	C.	C.
D. The Berkshires	D.	D.
E. Mt. Washington	E.	E.
F. Cape Cod	F.	F.
G. Foxwoods	G.	G.
H. Montpelier	H.	H.
I. Newport	I.	I.
J. Plymouth	J.	J.

CASE STUDY

NAME _____   DATE _____

Mary and Jane Pepperidge grew up in Boston and now, after living 20 years in Toronto, want to return to New England during fall foliage season. They intend to fly to Boston and then drive around the countryside in a rental car. They're willing to spend extra money for the trip, though they also like value for their dollar. The length of the trip is not a consideration for them.

Circle the answer that best suits their needs.

1. When should they go?

   Late summer   September

   May   October

   Why?

2. In which of the following areas would they see great fall foliage scenery?

   Mystic   The Berkshires

   Cape Cod   Walpole Prison

   Why?

3. Which of the following cities would *not* have an airport that could serve as an alternative to Logan Airport?

   Providence   Burlington

   Hartford   Salem

   Why?

4. Which of the following would be *least* likely to appeal to these people?

   A stay at a seaside lodge on Cape Cod

   A fine hotel in Boston

   A side trip up Route 89

   Something better than a sub-compact car

   Why?

NAME _____   DATE _____

You're a travel counsellor at an agency that sells many trips to New England. Recently you saw a chart in an industry magazine that lists all the possible cross-sell items that could be offered to travellers. You want to create a list that you can consult whenever you send someone to New England. Check all the cross-sell items that you think could apply to a New England holiday. Then, go on the Internet. Find five New England companies that actually offer five of the activities you checked. Write each company's name next to the checked item.

_____ air sightseeing excursion	_____ hiking package	_____ rail pass
_____ attraction admission	_____ honeymoon package	_____ resort package
_____ balloon ride	_____ horseback riding package	_____ safari outing
_____ barge cruise	_____ hunting package	_____ sailing package
_____ bicycling tour	_____ insurance	_____ shopping tour
_____ boat cruise (limited)	_____ interpreter service	_____ shore excursion
_____ bon voyage party	_____ jeep rental	_____ ski package
_____ campground reservation	_____ kennel service	_____ snorkel package
_____ car rental	_____ limo service	_____ spa enrollment
_____ car rental insurance	_____ luau	_____ sporting event ticket
_____ city tour	_____ meal plan	_____ submarine ride
_____ concert	_____ meet-and-greet service	_____ tennis package
_____ convention arrangements	_____ meeting arrangements	_____ theatre ticket
_____ culinary classes	_____ motorhome rental	_____ theme park admission
_____ cultural event	_____ nightclub show	_____ tramway ride
_____ dine-around package	_____ nightlife tour	_____ transfer service
_____ dinner theatre	_____ passport photo service	_____ travel accessories
_____ diving package	_____ post-cruise land package	_____ traveller's cheques
_____ ferry transport	_____ pre-cruise land package	_____ video rental/sale
_____ fishing package	_____ private car	_____ walking tour
_____ gambling package	_____ private guide	_____ wedding package
_____ glass-bottom boat tour	_____ pub-hopping tour	_____ welcome party
_____ golf package	_____ raft adventure	_____ yacht charter
_____ helicopter tour	_____ rail excursion	

CANADA

QUEBEC

MAINE

Lake
Champlain

VERMONT

ONTARIO

Adirondack
Mountains

Lake
Placid

St. Lawrence

Alexandria
Bay

Lake
George

Thousand
Islands

NEW
HAMPSHIRE

Lake Ontario

NEW YORK

MASSACHUSETTS

Cooperstown

Albany

Rochester

Finger
Lakes

Niagara Falls

Woodstock

Hudson River

Hyde
Park

RI

Buffalo

Catskill
Mountains

CONNECTICUT

Watkins Glen

Corning

West
Point

Long Island Sound

Lake Erie

Tarrytown

Long Island

Delaware
Water Gap
N.R.A.

Newark

New York

PENNSYLVANIA

Trenton

Asbury Park

OHIO

ATLANTIC OCEAN

Camden

NEW
JERSEY

Atlantic City

MARYLAND

DE

WEST VIRGINIA

VA

Wildwood
Cape May

New York and New Jersey

Broadway and Boardwalk

What does a person imagine when he or she thinks of **New York City?** Great museums? Nightlife until dawn? Crowding? Broadway theatre? It'll be a complex vision, for sure.

There's plenty beyond "The Big Apple," too: **upstate New York,** the upscale beaches of **Long Island,** and the huge gaming casino-hotels along **Atlantic City's** Boardwalk.

First, a little geography: New York City is just off the Atlantic Ocean, between New England and the Mid-Atlantic States. America's most populous city, New York comprises five divisions, or boroughs; when travellers say, "New York," though, they usually mean not the entire city, but the borough-island of **Manhattan,** where the business and tourist action is. The other four boroughs are largely residential and industrial.

New York, of course, also refers to the entire state New York City is in. New York State, which stretches several hundred kilometres northward and westward from New York City, has many attractions of its own, including **West Point,** the **Catskill** and **Adirondack Mountains,** the **Finger Lakes,** and **Niagara Falls. Albany,** not New York City, is the state capital.

To New York City's south is the state of New Jersey. The 80-kilometre-long Jersey Shore is famous for its beaches. **Atlantic City,** the best known of its beach cities and famous for its gambling, is about a two-hour drive from Manhattan.

New Jersey was named for England's Duke of Jersey; New York for the English Duke of York.

Ausable Chasm, in upstate New York, is one of America's oldest private attractions.

HOW TRAVELLERS GET THERE

A vast network of highways, rail lines (including the high-speed Acela train), and air routes converge on New York City. Getting there won't be a problem. Choosing which airport to fly into might be a more difficult decision. **La Guardia** (LGA) is only 13 kilometres from downtown Manhattan, but the route between them can be slow moving, especially around rush hour. **Kennedy International Airport** (JFK) is farther out (24 kilometres), as is **Newark International** (EWR), in nearby New Jersey. Flying time from Western Canadian cities is less than five hours; from Eastern cities, less than two.

How to transfer from any of these airports to the city is even more complicated. Cabs and limousines (usually cars, not actual limos) are the favoured means of transportation, but they're expensive, especially from Newark. Rail lines now link Newark and JFK with transfer stations where passengers can catch trains to

Each year, 3800 horses, 400 000 frogs, and 250 million fish fly into JFK.

Manhattan's Penn Station. Share-a-ride cabs operate from La Guardia. Buses and minibuses also provide transfers from all three airports, and car rentals are an option as well.

What should you recommend? People in a hurry or on a budget should, if possible, fly into La Guardia, especially if they aren't arriving during rush hour. Newark is perhaps the best choice for travellers who can use the train, who won't be shocked by a hefty taxi fare, or who want to avoid stop-and-go traffic. Because of traffic and distance, JFK is rarely the best choice, yet it receives more flights (especially from a long distance, like Vancouver) than the other two; visitors may have no choice but to fly into this airport. (Fortunately the new train service makes JFK somewhat less arduous.) For those who want to drive into and around New York City, a warning: City traffic is intense and parking fees are astronomical.

Several smaller airports service New York City and the overall region. Atlantic City (ACY) has a modest but fast-growing airport; **Rochester** (ROC) serves the northern part of New York; and **Buffalo Niagara** (BUF) is often used by visitors to western New York State and Ontario. Many other New York cities have medium-sized airports. Rail lines and highways enter New York State and New Jersey from every direction. They are heavily used. For example, more than 90 percent of all visitors to Atlantic City arrive by car or bus.

A reminder: New York City is a major cruise port, with ships leaving for (and coming from) Canada, New England, Bermuda, and, occasionally, Europe and more southerly U.S. and Caribbean ports.

WEATHER PATTERNS

The Statue of Liberty wears 7.6-metre-long sandals, the equivalent of a women's shoe size 879.

New York State and New Jersey have typical northeastern U.S. weather: warm to hot summers and cold winters. Late spring and fall are extremely pleasant. Humidity can be a factor at any time of the year, with rainstorms or snowstorms in the winter and sudden thundershowers in the summer. Upstate New York has colder winters than New York City, often with considerable snow. New York City tends to be warmer than most cities, perhaps because all that concrete retains the heat. Precipitation can also wreak havoc in the city, causing traffic jams and making an available taxi almost impossible to find (see Figure 6-1).

As for tourist patterns, upstate New York and most of New Jersey peak in summer, with tourism dropping off as the cold sets in. Atlantic City is packed on weekends. New York City has virtually no off-season, except perhaps in January and, to some extent, on weekends.

GETTING AROUND

Of major U.S. cities, New York has the highest percentage of people who walk to work.

New York City has eight times more taxis than Los Angeles.

The Statue of Liberty was, in part, inspired by the Colossus of Rhodes, a huge statue that stood at the harbour entrance of Rhodes, a Greek island.

New York State and New Jersey have well-developed highway systems, but with many tolls. The train and bus systems are also quite convenient and are popular with New York commuters. One of the most popular short cruises out of New York City: a trip up the Hudson River.

The best way to get around New York City is by taxi; they're plentiful, relatively inexpensive, and fast. The subway and bus system is extensive and convenient. Contrary to what you may have heard, New York subways are relatively safe, especially during the day. A multitude of cars for hire and limos swarm through the city; they're a good choice for upscale visitors. New York is also a very walkable city, though only in certain areas and at certain times. Travellers should check with hotel staff before setting out on foot for a destination within the city.

Visitors to New York City can also get around by tour. Motorcoach tours are usually excellent (guides are licensed by the city) and the *Circle Line* boat tour that

PEAK TOURIST SEASON	↑	↓			↑	↑	↑	↑	↑			↓ TOURIST OFF-SEASON

Figure 6-1   Climate at a Glance: New York City, New York

MONTH	JAN	FEB	MAR	APR	MAY	JUN	JUL	AUG	SEP	OCT	NOV	DEC
AVERAGE HIGH TEMPERATURE	4	4	9	14	21	26	28	27	24	18	12	6
AVERAGE LOW TEMPERATURE	-3	-4	-1	6	12	17	19	19	16	10	4	-2
AVERAGE PRECIPITATION (IN CENTIMETRES)	8	8	10	8	10	10	10	10	10	8	8	8

circles Manhattan is famous. The ferry rides to the **Statue of Liberty, Ellis Island,** and **Staten Island** afford wonderful, inexpensive views.

IMPORTANT PLACES

This area's destinations can be divided into two categories: New York City itself, and New York State and New Jersey. Some of the latter category's attractions may be done as day trips from New York City, though most visitors who stay in Manhattan rarely take such day trips, except perhaps the Hudson River cruise.

New York City

New York City is astonishingly rich in attractions. Many, like **Chinatown** or the huge **St. John the Divine Cathedral,** are best visited as part of a city tour. Among the most popular attractions people visit on their own are:

- **The Statue of Liberty,** perhaps the world's most famous statue, and Ellis Island, both accessed by a ferry from Battery Park (or from Liberty State Park in Jersey City, New Jersey). Due to security and safety issues, visitors can no longer climb up inside the statue.

- **The Empire State Building,** whose higher levels afford the best views of Manhattan.

- **The United Nations,** one of New York's most graceful structures and an important world forum.

- **Rockefeller Center,** a "city of tomorrow" designed in the 1930s, with its famous skating rink (a café in the summer), the NBC Studio Tour, Radio City Music Hall (one of America's largest theatres), and nearby St. Patrick's Cathedral.

The world's largest cathedral (St. John the Divine) and largest synagogue (Temple Emanuel) are both in New York City.

The world's largest clock, the Colgate Clock, is in Jersey City. Its minute hand is seven metres long and weighs almost 1000 kilograms.

New York City has nearly 150 buildings over 50 storeys high.

Lightning strikes the Empire State Building about 25 times per year.

A fascinating tour of Radio City Music Hall is available.

Prometheus Fountain, Rockefeller Center, New York City
Photo by Marc Mancini

- **Superb museums,** most notably the **Metropolitan Museum of Art,** the **Museum of Modern Art** (MoMA), the **Guggenheim Museum,** and the **Museum of Natural History.**

- **Well-known neighbourhoods,** including **Greenwich Village, Chinatown, Little Italy, South Street Seaport** (a renovated riverside restaurant and shopping area), **Soho** (what Greenwich Village used to look like), neon-lit **Times Square** (vastly cleaned up), and **Central Park** (superb during the day, *not* advisable at night).

- **Ground Zero,** where the Twin Towers of the World Trade Center were destroyed by terrorists, has become an often-visited memorial site.

- **Abundant nightlife opportunities,** most notably the wealth of Broadway and off-Broadway plays and musicals, and major sporting events.

New York State

The rest of the state of New York is equally interesting. The following are the most popular with leisure travellers:

- **The Hudson River Valley.** Often called "America's Rhine," this picturesque route just north of New York City features many points of interest. Among them: **Tarrytown,** which captures the world of Washington Irving's *The Legend of Sleepy Hollow*; West Point, the U.S. military academy; and **Hyde Park,** best known for its Vanderbilt Mansion and the home of Franklin Roosevelt.

- **Long Island.** Stretching eastward from New York City and paralleling the southern New England coast, Long Island features excellent beaches, superb boating and fishing, many rental cottages, and mansion-dotted towns. It's more of a destination for New Yorkers, though, than for tourists from other regions.

- **The Catskills.** Northwest of Hyde Park is the Catskill Mountain area, long known for its old-time entertainment. Nearby is **Woodstock,** now an artists'

An urban legend: If you were to stay in Times Square, within a few days you'd see someone you know.

Central Park is larger than the nation of Monaco.

Three original stores—Macy's, Bloomingdale's and FAO Schwarz—are worth a special visit.

community, which was the site of the legendary '60s rock-music festival. Northeast of the Catskills is the state's capital, Albany, with its huge, stark complex of government buildings.

- **The upstate Lakes District.** Both **Lake Champlain** and **Lake George** are lined with resorts, hotels, old forts, and all manner of tourist attractions. In fact, things can get a little too touristy in both places. Here also are the Adirondack Mountains, which offer 2.4 million hectares of campsites, chasms, fishing, unspoiled hiking trails, and fall foliage. **Lake Placid,** within the Adirondacks, is a noted ski resort area that hosted the 1980 Winter Olympics. The very northwest part of the state borders Lake Ontario and the St. Lawrence River. Here are the **Thousand Islands** with many pleasing vistas, homes, and mansions—most often visited via half-day cruises out of the town of **Alexandria Bay.**

- **The Finger Lakes.** This region in the west-central part of the state delights photographers with its waterfalls, wineries, scenic vistas, imposing gorges, and 960 kilometres of shoreline. Also nearby: **Corning,** with its well-known glass factory and museum; **Watkins Glen,** famous for its gorge and auto racing; and the **Baseball Hall of Fame,** in **Cooperstown.**

- **Niagara Falls.** Although near Buffalo, New York, Niagara Falls is covered in greater detail in Chapter 2 (Ontario and Quebec). The New York side of the falls is not as dramatically beautiful as the Canadian side, nor is it where the best lodging is located. (Canada has all the falls-view properties.)

There are actually 1865 islands in the Thousand Islands.

Corning glassware can be purchased at a discount at the factory store.

Atlantic City

The first thing to strike visitors to Atlantic City is the familiar street names: Atlantic City inspired the board game Monopoly. The second thing to grab their attention: the intense strip of hotels, casinos, restaurants, amusements, shopping centres, and nightspots that line the Boardwalk. Beyond that, there's not much else to see; the beach is impressive and the convention centre vast, but the area away from the Boardwalk is poverty-ridden. Those who have spent time in Las

The Boardwalk, Atlantic City, New Jersey
Photo by Marc Mancini

Chapter 6 New York and New Jersey

Vegas may be a bit disappointed: Atlantic City isn't quite the attraction for high rollers and themed resorts that Las Vegas is. Indeed, most people who go to Atlantic City do so as a brief getaway from East Coast cities, to perhaps win a few dollars and to take in some first-rate entertainment.

The Jersey Shore boasts broad beaches, popular nightclubs, and much family entertainment, though it's not the beach resort area it was a hundred years ago. **Wildwood** is probably the best known town along the shore, with a half-dozen amusement areas and lively after-dark entertainment. **Asbury Park** is also well known as the place where many rock performers became famous. And a visit to **Cape May,** an astonishing collection of well-preserved Victorian buildings and houses, would be a delightful recommendation. Two other New Jersey options: **Camden,** with its impressive aquarium, and the ruggedly scenic **Delaware Water Gap National Recreation Area,** with its camping, hiking, and other outdoor activities.

POSSIBLE ITINERARIES

The New York Stock Exchange has a fascinating exhibition tour on weekdays.

It takes five to seven days to experience New York City, though the city's high cost may make such a stay quite expensive. A three- or four-day stay could enable visitors to see New York's principal highlights at a somewhat more reasonable cost. Atlantic City probably warrants no more than two days. A motoring tour of upstate New York could be done in about a week, with one or two days at such attractions as Niagara Falls, Lake Champlain, the Finger Lakes, or Lake George.

LODGING OPTIONS

One thing visitors must know: They'll pay about twice as much for lodging in New York City as they would for the same level of value in most other U.S. cities (though very good weekend "bargain" packages are often available). Rooms also tend to be small. The most popular, convenient, and safe lodging area in New York City is south and east of Central Park, though fine hotels are scattered throughout the midtown area. Hotels in the Times Square–Broadway theatre district are plentiful; many new properties have been built there and many older ones renovated. New York's downtown district—where the **Wall Street** stock exchanges, numerous corporate headquarters, and quite a number of tourist attractions are located— offers a few lodging choices.

Atlantic City is a comparative bargain. The glitzy, hulking properties along the Boardwalk can be pricey, but special three-day, two-night tour packages (especially on weekdays) are plentiful and may be a genuine bargain.

Accommodations across the rest of New Jersey and New York are generally reasonable, with the usual spectrum of hotels, motels, bed-and-breakfasts, and camping facilities.

ALLIED DESTINATIONS

All the following are within a day by land or an hour or two by air from the New York–New Jersey area: New England; southeastern Ontario; southern Quebec; Pennsylvania; Delaware; Maryland; Washington, D.C.; and parts of Virginia, West Virginia, and Ohio. Destinations in any of these areas are a logical extension of a New York–New Jersey stay. Remember, too, that New York City is a hub for cruises (especially to Bermuda and Quebec) and for flights to Europe, Africa, and, in some cases, South America. Travellers bound for these places often like the notion of a day or two in New York City as a way to break up a long trip.

Times Square, New York City
Photo by Marc Mancini

FACTORS THAT MOTIVATE VISITORS

Those who wish to visit New York City will probably want to do so for the following reasons:

- There's a remarkable wealth of tourist attractions.

- There are numerous transportation options into and out of the city.

- The shopping is extraordinary; as one brochure puts it, "If you can't find it in New York, it doesn't exist."

- New York City is home to more corporations and hosts more conventions than any other U.S. city.

- No city has a greater variety of choices for fine dining and nightlife.

- The city's museums are among the world's greatest.

- Christmastime is festive.

- There's a constant stream of major sporting events.

- The cultural, artistic, and entertainment opportunities are plentiful.

    People have a separate set of expectations for the rest of the area. Among the features that may attract them are:

- Camping and skiing opportunities, especially in the Adirondacks, and the great natural beauty of upstate New York and parts of New Jersey.

- The convenient system of highways, making driving easy.

- The beaches and water sports, especially on Long Island, the Jersey Shore, and in the upstate Lakes District.

- Gambling in Atlantic City and Native American–run casinos.

New York City has more than 10 000 hectares of parkland.

Each holiday season, nearly 300 000 people visit the Macy's Santaland in New York City.

POSSIBLE MISGIVINGS

New York and New Jersey are wonderful destinations. However, uninformed travellers often have reservations about going there, especially to New York City. Here are a few examples of misgivings and how to handle them:

 Half-price theatre tickets are available on the day of performance at Times Square.

- "New York City is too expensive." There are ways to reduce the cost of a New York City holiday. Recommend a shorter stay than they may have intended, thus cutting lodging cost; seek out weekend bargain rates at moderately priced hotels; emphasize the low cost of transportation to, around, and from Manhattan; mention discount theatre ticket prices; advise them to eat at coffee shops and delis rather than at full-blown (and full-priced) restaurants.

- "New York City is dangerous." New York City is a much safer place than it used to be. Emphasize that your lodging recommendation is in a safe area. Advise them to check with hotel personnel about when and where it's safe

Qualifying the Traveller
NEW YORK CITY

FOR PEOPLE WHO WANT	HIGH APPEAL	MEDIUM APPEAL	LOW APPEAL	REMARKS
Historical and Cultural Attractions	▲			Superb museums
Beaches and Water Sports			▲	Mostly for locals, Long Island is good
Skiing Opportunities			▲	Catskills and Adirondacks
Lots of Nightlife	▲			Superb theatre
Family Activities	▲			Famous tourist sites
Familiar Cultural Experience		▲		New York City *is* different
Exotic Cultural Experience		▲		New York City *is* different
Safety and Low Crime			▲	Not as bad as reputation
Bargain Travel			▲	Extremely expensive
Impressive Scenery			▲	Must go north of city
Peace and Quiet			▲	A noisy city
Shopping Opportunities	▲			Especially for luxury items
Adventure			▲	
To Do Business	▲			More corporate headquarters than any other city

to walk around. The terrorist attacks in 2001, of course, made New York City seem far more dangerous than it really was. The city's positive, inspiring, and romantic image has taken hold again.

- "New Yorkers are rude." The vast majority of New Yorkers are utterly thoughtful, cultured, and kind. New York, though, is a city on the go and a few people sometimes don't have time for niceties; it's no reflection on what they think of visitors.

- "Upstate New York sounds boring." The wealth of natural and manmade attractions is striking; even the most jaded can't help being impressed. If mentioning this doesn't work, maybe this is the kind of person who will flourish in New York City.

- "Atlantic City is only for gambling." The beach here and all along the coast is wonderful, the entertainment is excellent, nearby Cape May is an architectural wonder, and just watching gamblers can be an entertainment in itself.

SALES STRATEGIES

Up-selling hotels in New York City and Atlantic City is an attractive strategy, since budget properties in both places can provoke complaints. Outside these cities, car rentals and bus or train travel are appropriate services to offer to those not driving their own cars.

New York City offers many cross-sell opportunities. Airport transfers via limousine services are very popular. Theatre tickets, city tours, and boat cruises can be booked in advance. Suggest FIT extensions into allied destinations if the traveller's vacation time permits. Remember that business travellers may wish to extend their stay in New York City for leisure, perhaps with their families joining them. Also, cruisers are often open to a pre- or post-cruise package in New York City.

Major tour operators offer a gamut of tours to Atlantic City, New York City, and upstate New York. Ski packages to upstate resorts are popular, as well.

A great way to see New York City is on one of its double-decker tour buses.

TRAVEL TRIVIA

WHERE FAST FOODS WERE INVENTED

- Hot dog: New York City
- Sandwich: England
- Submarine sandwich: Groton, Connecticut
- Big Mac: Pittsburgh, Pennsylvania
- Pizza: Greece, Italy
- Fortune cookie: Los Angeles, California

- Chop suey: San Francisco, California
- Ice cream: China
- Ice-cream cone: St. Louis, Missouri
- Ice-cream soda: Philadelphia, Pennsylvania

Source: The History Channel

MAP ACTIVITY

NAME _____   DATE _____

A traveller wants to visit the places listed below. Which number represents each on the map?

PLACE/ATTRACTION	IN/NEAR WHICH CITY?	NUMBER ON MAP
A. An enormous waterfall	**A.**	**A.**
B. The Metropolitan Museum of Art	**B.**	**B.**
C. The Boardwalk	**C.**	**C.**
D. Hundreds of Victorian houses	**D.**	**D.**
E. South Street Seaport	**E.**	**E.**
F. St. John the Divine	**F.**	**F.**
G. A glass factory	**G.**	**G.**
H. A noted ski resort	**H.**	**H.**
I. A Thousand Islands cruise	**I.**	**I.**
J. Radio City Music Hall	**J.**	**J.**

NAME _____   DATE _____

Abe Farkas is a lawyer, and his wife, Susan, is a stock analyst. They live in Hamilton, Ontario, and want a three-day weekend getaway to Manhattan; they can leave late Friday afternoon and must return by Sunday night. They love theatre, fine dining, and museums. They have been to New York City at least a half-dozen times before.

Circle the answer that best suits their needs.

1. In which area should they probably stay?

   Downtown   The Broadway district

   Brooklyn   The Boardwalk

   Why?

2. Which would probably appeal to them the most?

   Theatre tickets   A cruise up the Hudson

   A car rental   A full-day tour

   Why?

3. Which recommendation would be correct?

   You should have breakfast at Tiffany's

   It'll be just a short walk from your hotel to Radio City Music Hall

   Visit Hyde Park, Manhattan's largest park

   While you're in Soho, you should go see the MoMA

   Why?

4. Which New York City attraction should you suggest that they visit?

   A Stock Exchange tour   A tour of the United Nations

   A Rockefeller Center tour   The Museum of Modern Art

   Why?

CREATIVE ACTIVITY

NAME _____   DATE _____

You're an executive with ACME Hotels, a chain of mid-priced lodging properties headquartered in Montreal. The company, which targets families with children, has decided to expand into New York State and New Jersey. The corporation has asked you to propose five cities to locate these hotels in. What would your five recommendations be, and why?

LOCATION	REASONS
1. New York City	**1.** Key American tourist city. New York City has need for more hotels that are family affordable. Large population within driving distance.
2.	**2.**
3.	**3.**
4.	**4.**
5.	**5.**

Pennsylvania, Maryland, Virginia, and Washington, D.C.

The Mid-Atlantic Medley

The Mid-Atlantic is a symphony of sounds: the mute ringing of the Liberty Bell in **Philadelphia,** Pennsylvania; the emotional strains of "The Star-Spangled Banner" written outside Fort McHenry near **Baltimore,** Maryland; wheels rolling along the cobblestones of the first American settlement in **Jamestown,** Virginia; or the old echoes of debate in **Washington, D.C.** The Mid-Atlantic region also embraces both New York and New Jersey (each covered in the previous chapter) and Delaware. So it's no wonder that this is one of the most popular tourist areas for Americans. (It attracts a significant percentage of visitors from other countries, too.)

Pennsylvania is the northernmost of the states to be covered in this chapter. Stacked south of it are **Delaware, Maryland,** Washington, D.C., and **Virginia.** In Pennsylvania, the **Pocono Mountains** resorts are in the northeast part of the state; in the very southeastern corner, on the eastern border, is Philadelphia; and west of this major city are the Amish of the **Pennsylvania Dutch country. Pittsburgh,** in the state's southwest, also has some interesting sights.

South of Pennsylvania Dutch country is Baltimore, Maryland, located on the west coast of **Chesapeake Bay,** just across from the eastern peninsula where the rest of Maryland and Delaware are. A short drive south of Baltimore, on the **Potomac River,** is the nation's capital, Washington, D.C. Most of the attractions that interest visitors to Virginia are found in the **Tidewater Virginia** region, the southeastern portion of that state: the colonial villages of **Williamsburg, Yorktown,** and Jamestown; **Virginia Beach;** and harbour communities such as **Newport News** and **Norfolk.** The beautiful **Shenandoah National Park** begins in northern Virginia and runs southwesterly through the state.

HOW TRAVELLERS GET THERE

Access to this busy, highly populated region is diversified and convenient. For air travellers, the major gateway into Philadelphia and much of Pennsylvania is **Philadelphia International Airport** (PHL). Western Pennsylvania's gateway is **Pittsburgh International Airport** (PIT). Flights to Baltimore land at **Baltimore-Washington International Airport** (BWI), which can also serve as a gateway to Washington, D.C. The nation's capital is also directly serviced by both **Ronald**

The Liberty Bell is probably smaller than you expect it to be.

Soft-shell crabs and crab cakes are Maryland delicacies.

Some "short-stop" D.C. attractions: the National Archives (with the Declaration of Independence and the Constitution), Ford's Theater (where Abraham Lincoln was shot), and, just across the street, Peterson House (where Lincoln died).

Reagan National Airport (DCA), which is almost downtown, and **Dulles Airport** (IAD), which is about 45 minutes away in Virginia. Most of these cities are, by air, about five or six hours from Western Canadian cities, and one to two hours from Toronto or Montreal.

There's also an extensive network of highways into the region for travellers who'll be either driving themselves or taking the bus, a good option for the budget-minded. Train service to Philadelphia, Baltimore, and Washington, D.C., is very good, too (especially Amtrak's high-speed train, Acela), though it's limited for the rest of the area.

WEATHER PATTERNS

The climates of Philadelphia and Baltimore are similar: hot and humid summers, with average high temperatures in the upper 20s, and cold, snowy winters, with average low temperatures of around zero degrees. Spring and fall are very pleasant. The Poconos are a little cooler, with cold and snowy winters. Summer is the main tourist season.

Washington, D.C., is renowned for its beautiful, temperate springs, when the cherry blossoms bloom (and student tours are everywhere). Summers are also well known, but for being humid and hot. These are by far Washington's two busiest tourist seasons (though tourism begins to drop off as early as August). Falls are pleasant, with some rain, and winters get chilly and a bit snowy (see Figure 7-1). Southeast Virginia has mild summers and fairly mild winters. September to May is the best time to visit here; summers are the most crowded. Fall is a particularly spectacular time to see the changing foliage of Shenandoah National Park.

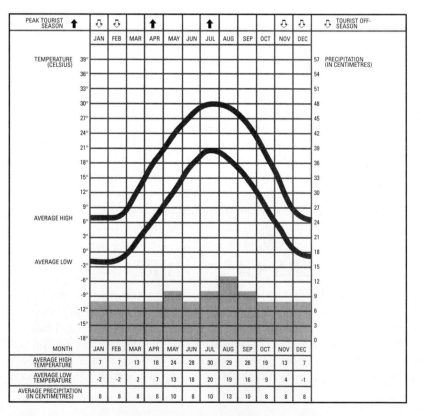

MONTH	JAN	FEB	MAR	APR	MAY	JUN	JUL	AUG	SEP	OCT	NOV	DEC
AVERAGE HIGH TEMPERATURE	7	7	13	18	24	28	30	29	26	19	13	7
AVERAGE LOW TEMPERATURE	-2	-2	2	7	13	18	20	19	16	9	4	-1
AVERAGE PRECIPITATION (IN CENTIMETRES)	8	8	8	8	10	8	10	13	10	8	8	8

Figure 7-1   Climate at a Glance: Washington, D.C.

GETTING AROUND

Most of the region's major cities are so close to one another that it's not usually necessary to fly between them. But for those who do fly, there are many airports, as well as major carriers and commuter airlines serving them. Train and bus connections are good. However, driving is probably the best way to get around. Traffic is heavy in the congested Mid-Atlantic corridor.

Once within a tourist centre, though, it's another story. The cities are large, and hectic urban driving conditions almost always prevail. Philadelphia is crowded, with limited parking and expensive taxis; however, Philadelphia does have a good subway and bus system. Washington, D.C., has limited parking and streets become one-way during rush hour. Taxis are inexpensive; the city has an excellent subway system and very good buses. Most major sights are fairly close to one another. As in Philadelphia, city tours are an excellent way for visitors to get around. Escorted tours through the Pennsylvania Dutch country are very popular. Cars aren't allowed in Colonial Williamsburg.

IMPORTANT PLACES

The historical sites of Philadelphia, Washington, D.C., the Williamsburg area, and Baltimore are this region's most popular. In addition, there are the lovely natural attractions of the Pennsylvania Dutch country, the Poconos, and Shenandoah National Park.

Philadelphia

Philadelphia was the first capital of the United States. It's where Benjamin Franklin, George Washington, Thomas Jefferson, and many other notable figures lived, worked, and founded a nation. Among its many attractions are:

- **Independence National Historical Park,** which comprises most of the city's famous sights. These include **Independence Hall,** where the Declaration of Independence was signed and the Constitution drafted; **Congress Hall,** where the first U.S. Congress met; and the **Liberty Bell,** which is housed in a

An almost exact reproduction of Independence Hall is at Knott's Berry Farm, in Buena Park, California.

The tradition in Philadelphia is to throw a penny on Benjamin Franklin's grave in the Christ Church graveyard.

Celebrating colonial heritage, Philadelphia, Pennsylvania
Photo by Justus Ghormley

glass pavilion near Independence Hall. Other park attractions: **Betsy Ross's House** (where legend says she made the first U.S. flag); **Christ Church** (the house of worship for Benjamin Franklin and George Washington); and **Franklin Court** (the grounds of Franklin's home).

If you're in Philadelphia during the Christmas season, visit Wanamaker's (now a Lord & Taylor department store) for the traditional light show and booming organ music under its famous bronze eagle.

- **Great museums,** including the **Franklin Institute Science Museum,** with its hands-on exhibits, a planetarium, and Franklin artifacts; the **Rodin Museum,** with the largest collection of Rodin's artwork outside France; the excellent collection of the **Philadelphia Museum of Art;** and one of the most unusual, rich, and eccentrically displayed collections in the nation, the **Barnes Foundation,** housed in a mansion-like structure on the outskirts of Philadelphia. (It will soon move to a downtown location.)

- **Fairmount Park,** with its scenic drives, bicycle routes, trails, and historical structures.

- **Philadelphia Zoo,** the nation's oldest zoo.

- **Valley Forge State Park,** just outside town, the famous site of George Washington and his troops' encampment.

- North of Philadelphia is **Reading** [RED-ing], which many consider the discount outlet shopping centre of North America.

Pennsylvania Dutch Country

The beautiful farmland of this area—about 80 kilometres west of Philadelphia—is home to the Amish and Mennonites, descendants of a strict German religious sect. (They weren't Dutch at all, but *Deutsch*.) The region's centre is **Lancaster,** which features several farmers' markets with banquets of justly renowned homemade food. Among the other interesting towns is **Hershey,** famous for its chocolate world exhibit, eccentric streetlight posts (they're shaped like Hershey Kisses!), and an enjoyable theme park.

It takes the milk of 50 000 cows to create a day's worth of chocolate at Hershey's main plant.

A half-day trip from this area is **Gettysburg National Battlefield,** where Abraham Lincoln delivered his famous address in 1863, commemorating the decisive U.S. Civil War battle that took place here.

The Pocono Mountains

Only two hours north of Philadelphia, this mountain resort area is popular in the summer (especially among honeymooners) and also in winter for skiing. The best of its ski resorts: **Big Boulder, Camel Back,** and **Jack Frost Mountain.** Nearby is the **Delaware Water Gap National Recreation Area** (which extends in from New Jersey).

Pittsburgh

This city, majestically located at the confluence of three rivers, was once picked as the United States' most "liveable" city. Pittsburgh boasts several major museums, including the **Frick Art Museum** and the **Carnegie,** a world-renowned centre for culture. (A number of museums in Pittsburgh have the name Carnegie attached to them.) Not far from Pittsburgh is **Fallingwater,** arguably the most famous structure ever designed by the great architect Frank Lloyd Wright.

Pittsburgh lost the "h" in its spelling in 1891, but after 20 years of protest, had it put back in 1911.

Baltimore

Baltimore has many treasures of its own: a symphony, fine museums (like the **Museum of Art,** with its post-Impressionist collection), the huge **National Aquarium,** and many renovated historical buildings. Among the other points of interest here are:

- **Fort McHenry National Monument,** where Francis Scott Key watched the battle that inspired him to write "The Star-Spangled Banner."

- The U.S.S. *Constellation*, an all-sail vessel that's the only U.S. Civil War–era military vessel still afloat.

- **Harborplace**, erected over Baltimore's old dock area, with nearly 200 restaurants, cafés, and shops.

Maryland's capital, **Annapolis**, is just 48 kilometres away. It boasts many restored 18th-century buildings, among them the colonial State House. The **U.S. Naval Academy** is here, too.

Delaware

The small state of Delaware contains several noteworthy attractions. **Winterthur Mansion and Gardens** in **Wilmington** is quite beautiful and worthy of a visit. Also of interest are the historical town of **Lewes,** the beach town of **Rehoboth,** and the restored sections of the state capital, **Dover.**

Washington, D.C.

The sights of the nation's capital are numerous and well known. But the city isn't always what everyone expects. Washington is a company town, and the business of the town is, of course, government. Among the many wonderful attractions are:

- **The Mall,** a long, park-like rectangle where many of the city's famous monuments are located, including the inspirational **Vietnam Veterans Memorial** and the obelisk-like **Washington Monument,** the tallest structure in the city. Nearby are the stately **Lincoln Memorial** (where Martin Luther King, Jr., made his "I have a dream" speech) and the graceful **Jefferson Memorial.**

- **The Smithsonian Institution,** the granddaddy of museums. Actually, the Smithsonian is a fascinating collection of separate museum buildings, many of them on the Mall. They include the huge **National Air and Space Museum** (which displays such gems as the Wright Brothers' aeroplane), the **Museum of Natural History,** the **Museum of American History,** and the **U.S. Holocaust Memorial Museum.** The red sandstone "Castle" houses the Smithsonian Information Center, which gives an overview of the Institution.

- **The National Gallery of Art,** on the Mall as well, with a vast collection of artwork from around the world.

- **The International Spy Museum,** which gives an overview of espionage and its historical applications.

- **Washington National Cathedral,** the sixth-largest cathedral in the world. One of its stained-glass windows commemorates the *Apollo 11* flight and contains a piece of moon rock.

- **Arlington National Cemetery,** just outside town (in Virginia), the resting place of some of the most famous names in U.S. history, and the location of a memorial to the crew of the Space Shuttle *Challenger* and of the **Tomb of the Unknowns.**

Maryland is the only state to have an official sport: jousting.

Wilmington, Delaware, was once a Swedish colony. Fort Christina marks the site.

When John Adams moved into the White House in 1800, it was America's biggest home.

Under the Lincoln Memorial is a rarely seen area where stalactites and stalagmites have formed.

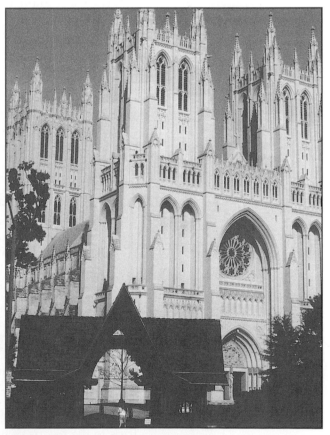

Washington National Cathedral, Washington, D.C.
Photo by Justus Ghormley

- **Capitol Hill,** where the seats of government are found. Visitors can tour the Capitol itself, where the Senate and House of Representatives meet; there's artwork throughout the halls, and the galleries are open to watch the legislative sessions. Visitors can also watch the proceedings in the nearby **Supreme Court Building** from October through June.

Not far from the city, and a popular half-day trip, is Virginia's **Mt. Vernon,** the plantation home of George Washington. **The National Air and Space Museum's Center,** near Dulles International Airport, has a huge collection of remarkable aircraft and spacecraft—most of which are here because there was no room for them at the museum's primary location on The Mall. And **Wolf Trap Farm Park,** the location of an internationally famous summer festival, is the first national park devoted to the performing arts.

Tidewater Virginia

Located in a triangular area along Chesapeake Bay, Tidewater is one of the most historic regions in the United States. The scenic **Colonial Parkway Drive** takes visitors through this beautiful area of colonial villages and plantations.

Williamsburg is the most popular Tidewater site, a lovingly restored 18th-century town with period craftsmen, taverns, horse-drawn carts, and a standing militia. Its preserved structures include the second-oldest college in the country, the **College of William and Mary,** with a building designed by famed architect Christopher Wren. Jamestown was the first permanent settlement in America; the **Jamestown Festival Park** harbours the three ships that brought John Smith's retinue across the ocean in 1607. Yorktown was where the final battle of the American Revolutionary War took place. **Yorktown Battlefield** has tours and a museum.

The most impressive and best-known plantations in the region are located west of Williamsburg and along the James River's north shore. A day trip just south of the Tidewater area is to the harbour towns of **Newport News,** with its Mariner's Museum, and **Norfolk,** where NASA's Langley Research Center offers fascinating aeronautical artifacts. Just south is the popular summer resort of **Virginia Beach,** which could merit a longer stay.

Another day trip is to **Richmond,** the historic state capital. Its attractions range from the Revolution—**St. John's Church** is where Patrick Henry cried out, "Give me liberty, or give me death"—to the U.S. Civil War, since the city was the capital of the Confederacy. Thomas Jefferson's mansion home, **Monticello,** is nearby.

Shenandoah National Park

This park—in Virginia but only 120 kilometres from Washington, D.C.—lies between the Blue Ridge Mountains to the east and the Shenandoah River to the west. The **Appalachian Trail** runs through the park, as does the beautiful 170 kilometre **Skyline Drive.** It's most crowded in the fall, when the forest colours are stunning. The famed **Luray Caverns,** with their remarkable stalactites and stalagmites, are nearby.

POSSIBLE ITINERARIES

For first-time tourists, nine days through historic Philadelphia, Washington, D.C., and Tidewater Virginia would permit a sampling of the area's attractions. For return visitors, several side trips would be worthwhile, including excursions into Pennsylvania Dutch Country, Baltimore, or the Virginia harbour towns. Short trips to the resorts of the Poconos or Virginia Beach would also be good suggestions. For those who just want to see Washington, D.C., five days or so would be enough to visit most of the major sights.

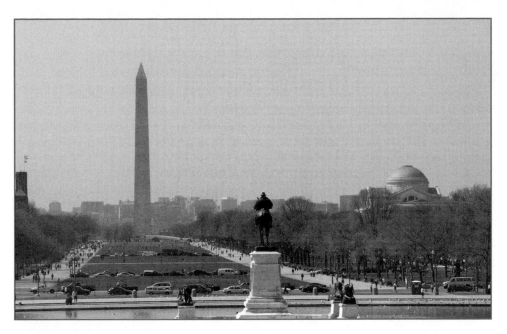

A view of The Mall, with the Washington Monument in the background, Washington, D.C.

Melanie Dayus/Shutterstock

LODGING OPTIONS

Every possible type of accommodation is available, from grand luxury hotels to budget motels. In Philadelphia, most hotels are around Rittenhouse Square and Logan Circle. In Baltimore, they're between the Civic Center and Center Plaza. In Washington, D.C., hotels are clustered north of the Kennedy Center and Lafayette Square; around Union Station; and along the Potomac, south of Reagan National Airport. For political buffs, two hotels stand out: The **Willard Inter-Continental** is where, legend has it, the art of lobbying began, and, of course, there's the **Watergate.** The **Hay-Adams Hotel** offers views of the White House across Lafayette Square. From Capitol Hill to the White House are many older, less expensive hotels. Many hotels and campgrounds are just outside the Tidewater Virginia area. In Williamsburg, the **Williamsburg Inn** is elegant and beautifully restored. Most hotels in Virginia Beach are along Boardwalk. Shenandoah National Park has a few lodges and many campgrounds.

This area also offers a wide selection of alternative lodging. Washington, D.C., contains some bed-and-breakfasts. Visitors to the Pennsylvania Dutch Country might enjoy staying in a Mennonite farmhouse. And guesthouses in the Tidewater Virginia area are popular.

English King Charles II originally wanted to call Pennsylvania "Sylvania," then added the name "Penn" to honour Admiral William Penn.

ALLIED DESTINATIONS

The Mid-Atlantic States are strategically located for those wishing to extend their trip to other areas. Pennsylvania borders Ohio to the west and New York to the north, which in turn leads to New England through Connecticut and Massachusetts. Keep in mind also that New York and Washington are jumping-off points for flights to Europe, so the area could be a side trip before such a long flight. Ontario is separated from Pennsylvania only by Lake Erie. Virginia borders West Virginia, Kentucky, North Carolina, and Tennessee, opening a gateway to the South.

Sir Walter Raleigh named Virginia in honour of Queen Elizabeth I, the "Virgin Queen" of England.

FACTORS THAT MOTIVATE VISITORS

Although U.S. history colours every corner of the Mid-Atlantic States, it's important to understand all the reasons that draw vacationers to the region. These include:

- Historical buildings, monuments, and sites are everywhere.

- Low airfares, convenient ground transportation, and reasonable lodging make the area a good bargain.

- The area brims with superb cultural attractions: great museums, symphonies, arts festivals, and the unique lifestyle of the Pennsylvania Dutch.

- The scenery is impressive, especially in Shenandoah National Park.

- There are very good winter and summer resorts.

- Skiing opportunities abound, especially at the Virginia resorts of Homestead and Wintergreen, or the Pocono ski areas of Jack Frost and Big Boulder.

- The area is accessible: Cities and attractions are fairly close together and are near many other parts of the United States.

POSSIBLE MISGIVINGS

As strong as the appeal of this area is, some visitors will have concerns that you may have to address:

- "Washington, D.C., is so hot and humid." It is, but only in the summer, and all buildings are air-conditioned. Spring and fall are particularly beautiful.

- "Except for its historic buildings, Philadelphia is dull." In fact, the city has a world-class orchestra, great museums, and a lively nightlife. This objection might also be raised about Washington, D.C., and more justifiably: The capital's nightlife is largely limited to dining, museums, and concerts.

- "There's not much to see in Baltimore." Besides being home to some important historical sites, the city is a great jumping-off point to Washington, D.C., and Philadelphia.

- "Tidewater Virginia is restored buildings and nothing more." Nearby are the harbour communities, Virginia Beach resorts, an amusement park, and the state capital of Richmond.

- "There's a lot of crime in Washington, D.C." The city is safer than it used to be, but, as in any large city, visitors should use caution. The tourist areas are very safe during the day and relatively so at night.

FOR PEOPLE WHO WANT	HIGH APPEAL	MEDIUM APPEAL	LOW APPEAL	REMARKS
Historical and Cultural Attractions	▲			Extremely high appeal
Beaches and Water Sports			▲	Must leave city
Skiing Opportunities			▲	Must leave city
Lots of Nightlife		▲		Good restaurants
Family Activities	▲			
Familiar Cultural Experience	▲			
Exotic Cultural Experience			▲	
Safety and Low Crime		▲		Crime mostly outside tourist areas
Bargain Travel		▲		
Impressive Scenery		▲		Impressive parks
Peace and Quiet		▲		Quiet at night
Shopping Opportunities			▲	
Adventure			▲	
To Do Business	▲			U.S. government related

SALES STRATEGIES

The region presents many opportunities to up-sell and cross-sell. City tours of Washington, D.C., and Philadelphia are popular and excellent ways to see those cities. Don't forget car rentals for those who prefer to drive. Booking an escorted tour of the Pennsylvania Dutch Country facilitates visiting the area; for a special tour of this part of the country, you might even suggest setting up a personalized guide. Coach tours of the Tidewater Virginia area can help tie those communities together. And keep in mind that many of the cities covered in this chapter are extremely close to one another; a vacation can be easily expanded by adding an additional destination to the already-planned trip.

TRAVEL TRIVIA

U.S. CITIES WITH DUBIOUS NAMES

Panic, Pennsylvania	Eek, Alaska	Hell, Michigan
Odd, West Virginia	Belcher, New York	Bad Axe, Michigan
Hemlock, Ohio	Looneyville, West VA	Hooker, Oklahoma
Pitts, Georgia	Needles, California	War, West Virginia
Boring, Maryland	Last Chance, Colorado	Roachtown, Illinois
Crummies, Kentucky	Terror Bay, Alaska	Muck City, Alabama
Tightwad, Missouri	Gross, Kansas	Girdle Tree, Maryland

MAP ACTIVITY

NAME _____   DATE _____

A traveller wants to visit the places listed below. Which number represents each on the map?

PLACE/ATTRACTION	IN/NEAR WHICH CITY/STATE?	NUMBER ON MAP
A. The Smithsonian Institution	A.	A.
B. A chocolate factory	B.	B.
C. The U.S. Naval Academy	C.	C.
D. Where "The Star-Spangled Banner" was written	D.	D.
E. Ford's Theater	E.	E.
F. A restored colonial village	F.	F.
G. The Liberty Bell	G.	G.
H. The Jefferson Memorial	H.	H.
I. Where Patrick Henry made his "Give me liberty" speech	I.	I.
J. Betsy Ross's house	J.	J.

CASE STUDY

NAME _____   DATE _____

Robert Townsend, a 34-year-old aerospace engineer from Winnipeg, is attending a November convention in Washington, D.C. The convention ends on Thursday. On Friday morning Mr. Townsend will meet with business clients, but after lunch he is free. He has already seen the standard historical D.C. sights on a previous trip, but he'd like to stay over, see more of the region, and fly back to Winnipeg late Sunday.

Circle the answer that best suits his needs.

1. Which would probably be the most appropriate service to set up in advance?

   A car rental   Tickets to Wolf Trap Farm Park festival

   A ski package   An escorted tour of the Pennsylvania Dutch area

   Why?

2. Which place to visit would probably be out of his geographic range?

   Richmond   Hershey

   Gettysburg   Pittsburgh

   Why?

3. Which attraction would probably be least appealing to Mr. Townsend?

   The Franklin Institute   The National Air and Space Museum

   Annapolis   Virginia Beach

   Why?

4. Though Mr. Townsend flew into DCA, he could probably fly back out of any of the following airports, except one. Which one?

   PHL   IAD

   BWI   LGA

   Why?

CREATIVE ACTIVITY

NAME _____   DATE _____

You're about to participate in an unusual scavenger hunt. The object: to take your photo next to seven attractions (described in clues) that are scattered throughout the Mid-Atlantic region. The clues will be given to all contestants at noon on the steps of the U.S. Capitol. The first person back to the steps with all seven photos will be declared the winner. (Their outing must be by car.) Using the following clues, try to name the attractions. You may have to consult other chapters or other reference tools to arrive at the answers.

YOUR PHOTO NEXT TO:	WHAT IS IT?	WHERE IS IT?
A bright kiss		
A famous Thinker		
Old pointy things		
Discounted Levis		
A cluster of stars		
Midshipmen		
The building that sank Nixon		

How long do you think it would take to win the contest? Consult an atlas or a road map, if you need to, and plot out a route for the most efficient path from place to place.

ALABAMA

GEORGIA

Amelia Island

ATLANTIC OCEAN

Destin

Tallahassee ✪

Jacksonville

Pensacola

Panama City

FLORIDA

St. Augustine

Cedar Key ▲

Daytona Beach

Sanford

Orlando ● ✈

Kennedy Space Center ▲

Cocoa Beach

Walt Disney World ▲

Port Canaveral ▲

GULF of MEXICO

▲ Cypress Gardens

Clearwater ● ✈ Tampa

St. Petersburg

Sarasota

Palm Beach

Captiva Island ● Ft. Myers

Sanibel Island

Naples

Ft. Lauderdale ✈

Port Everglades ▲

Miami ✈

Marco Island

Everglades National Park

Florida Keys

Key West

8

Florida

Where the Mouse Roars

Orlando wasn't much more than a sleepy little citrus town until a mouse showed up. *The* Mouse. Mickey himself. Walt Disney, creator of Mickey and much, much more, had long regretted not having bought up more land in Anaheim, California. Though Disneyland prospered there, its expansion was limited by the other entrepreneurs who surrounded the Magic Kingdom with hotels, motels, restaurants, and minor attractions. This time it would be different, Disney decided. His corporation bought up vast swaths of land, planned out extensive services, even envisioned an entire "city of tomorrow" where employees would live in futuristic happiness.

Most of Disney's dream—somewhat altered, but just as grandiose—has come true. Many other attractions also have sprung up around the Disney property. The result: The Orlando area has become one of the most popular vacation spots in the United States. And Florida, long a magnet for vacationers, has become the most visited state of all.

Florida is a flat peninsula, stretching southward into tropical waters: The Gulf of Mexico is on the west, the Atlantic Ocean on the east. Florida's east coast has been a resort destination for over a century. From north to south are the cities of **Jacksonville, St. Augustine, Daytona Beach, Cocoa Beach, Palm Beach, Ft. Lauderdale,** and **Miami,** to name a few. Extending southwestward are the **Florida Keys,** a string of bridge-connected, water-flanked islands that ends at **Key West.**

Florida's west coast, more recently developed as a destination, boasts several first-rate beach resorts, most especially around the tri-city area of **St. Petersburg, Clearwater,** and **Tampa.** The **Pensacola** area, in Florida's northwestern "Panhandle," corner, is also a major resort destination, especially for those also visiting Louisiana, Mississippi, or Alabama. It boasts some of the most beautiful beaches in North America. And, of course, almost dead centre in the Florida peninsula: **Orlando.**

HOW TRAVELLERS GET THERE

Many packages (usually including air, hotel, admissions, and car rental) to Orlando are available. Several airlines fly to Florida's other major cities, too. The state's busiest airports are Miami (MIA), Orlando (MCO), Tampa (TPA), and Ft. Lauderdale (FLL). Flying time to Florida is about three hours from Toronto and seven from Vancouver. Florida's airports (except perhaps Miami) are models of efficiency.

The most visited Disney theme park in the world is the Magic Kingdom at Walt Disney World.

According to one estimate, it would take 41 days to see all of the Orlando area's attractions.

Florida has the second-longest state coastline in the United States. (Alaska has the longest.)

An unexpected treat in St. Petersburg: The Salvador Dali Museum.

Several convenient train and bus routes lead into scenic Florida as well. An off-beat choice: **Amtrak** auto trains that carry the family car—and family—from Lorten, Virginia (just south of Washington, D.C.), to Sanford, Florida (north of Orlando).

WEATHER PATTERNS

○ On many of Florida's Atlantic beaches, you're permitted to drive on the beach itself.

Florida has extraordinary weather, especially in the winter, when daytime temperatures hover around 23°C, with only occasional rain. Days and certainly nights can be chilly; humidity can also make things uncomfortable, even at this cooler time of the year (see Figure 8-1). Summers are very hot and humid, with frequent brief but intense thunderstorms (and an occasional hurricane) from June through September. Fortunately for summer visitors, breezes temper the heat, especially along the coast.

MONTH	JAN	FEB	MAR	APR	MAY	JUN	JUL	AUG	SEP	OCT	NOV	DEC
AVERAGE HIGH TEMPERATURE	23	24	26	28	31	33	33	33	32	29	26	23
AVERAGE LOW TEMPERATURE	11	11	13	16	18	22	23	23	22	18	13	11
AVERAGE PRECIPITATION (IN CENTIMETRES)	5	5	8	8	10	20	20	18	18	10	3	5

Figure 8-1   Climate at a Glance: Orlando, Florida

Since people who live in colder climates visit Florida in the winter and families visit in the out-of-school summer period, there's no real tourist off-season in Florida, though the number of vacationers does drop off a bit in June, and September through November. Anyone going to Florida should avoid holiday periods, if at all possible, because of the crowds. Spring break, when students swarm to Florida, is especially frantic in beach cities.

GETTING AROUND

○ The highest mountain in Florida is Walt Disney World's Big Thunder Mountain.

In most places in Florida, a car rental is almost a must. Car rental prices here are extremely affordable. Car rentals are usually included in ITCs (offerings from inclusive tour companies). Bus travel is an option for those on a budget. One conceivable way to avoid a car rental or bus travel would be to stay in **Walt Disney World** (where monorails, boats, and shuttles take people from place to place) or in a single resort city and never leave, which can be an attractive option for some.

It's possible to fly between Orlando and Miami, or between several Florida cities and Key West. Several cruise lines call on Key West as part of a Caribbean cruise. The **Conch Train** in Key West takes visitors on an interesting 1.5-hour trip around this quaint island town.

IMPORTANT PLACES

Florida is best understood when divided into four principal tourist areas: Orlando, the Atlantic Coast Cities, the Miami–Florida Keys area, and the west coast. Each appeals to a somewhat different kind of person, as we'll see later.

 Florida is the number-one family destination in North America. (California is number two.)

Orlando

The Orlando area attracts more family vacationers than any other place. But it also appeals to couples, young people, older travellers, and even honeymooners. There are three distinct clusters of attractions in the Orlando area: Walt Disney World, non-Disney attractions in the Orlando region, and attractions that can be visited as day trips from Orlando proper.

Orlando has nearly 4000 restaurants.

Walt Disney World clearly dominates the area. Within its enormous boundaries—it's about 120 square kilometres—are hotel clusters, shopping and entertainment centres (especially **Downtown Disney**), campgrounds, animal sanctuaries, sports complexes, and water parks. Four Disney attractions, though, monopolize most visitors' attention:

- **The Magic Kingdom,** the ultimate theme park, usually tops any visitor's list. It's very similar to California's Disneyland, though it covers a much larger area.

- **Epcot** is, in effect, a permanent world's fair, with both national and corporate pavilions—all of them providing spellbinding entertainment. This is one of the most adult of Orlando's attractions and, during busy times, requires two days to fully experience.

- **Disney-MGM Studios** is a diverting look at how movies are made; it includes numerous attraction-rides and many buildings that are reproductions of Hollywood landmarks.

- **Disney's Animal Kingdom** is a 200 hectare cross between a zoo and a theme park. It stresses what we must do to preserve endangered species, but also boasts some exciting rides.

Outside Disney's vast empire are several other independent attractions, both major and minor. **Sea World** is the world's largest marine park. The **Universal Orlando Resort** requires two days to see. It's divided into two parks: **Islands of Adventure** (with thrill rides) and **Universal Studios Florida** (which has a character very distinct from Disney-MGM Studios). Connecting the two is **CityWalk**, a vibrant strip of stores, restaurants, and entertainment venues.

Other major attractions lie within about a two-hour drive of Orlando. To the east, near Cocoa Beach, is the **Kennedy Space Center,** the home of America's space program. Buses take visitors on a tour of the facility (and, on space shuttle launch days, to viewing sites); its excellent museum traces the history of man's exploration of the cosmos. To Orlando's south is the 94 hectare **Cypress Gardens,** one of North America's oldest theme parks. And to Orlando's west in Tampa is **Busch Gardens,** an extensive attraction that melds a zoo-like wild-animal preserve with an amusement park.

The Atlantic Coast Cities

In the late 1800s, several entrepreneurs decided to run railroad lines down from the U.S. Northeast and develop Florida into a resort vacation and retirement destination. Their plan worked. A sun-bleached string of towns and cities sprang up

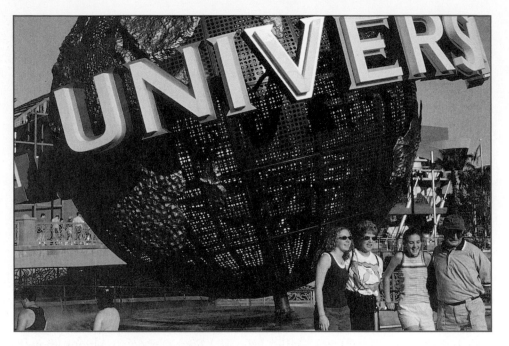

Universal Studios Florida, Orlando
Photo by Justus Ghormley

along the coastal routes; they still draw millions of visitors each year. Among the most important destinations, from north to south, are:

- **Jacksonville,** with its many cultural activities, sports events, nearby beaches, and, to the north, the offshore resort of **Amelia Island,** with its unspoilt beaches, golfing, and relaxed ambience.

- **St. Augustine,** the oldest city in the United States, with its old Spanish fort (the Castillo), historical restored streets, shops, and restaurants.

- **Daytona Beach,** the home of Daytona International Speedway, and one of the college vacation crowds' favourite haunts.

- **Cocoa Beach,** a smallish city with reasonable seaside lodging just a few kilometres from Kennedy Space Center. Close by is **Port Canaveral,** from which some cruises depart.

- **Palm Beach,** an upscale beach city with outstanding architecture, especially the old mansions along Ocean Boulevard.

- **Ft. Lauderdale,** with its long stretches of prime sand, 3000 eating establishments, and 40 000 registered boats. Nearby **Port Everglades** is a major departure point for cruises.

The Miami–Florida Keys Area

Miami—one of the United States' most exciting cities—has long been known for everything that is good and bad: On the plus side are the fabulous restaurants, fascinating architecture, rich cultural diversity, cruise opportunities, and picture-perfect beaches of **Key Biscayne** and **Miami Beach** (a separate city from Miami); negative factors include crime, racial conflict, and ethnic unrest. Though Miami's problems are well publicized, the city has also undergone an intriguing renaissance, becoming, among other things, one of the most visited cities for Latin Americans. You should counsel visitors to Miami to see the following:

- **Vizcaya Museum and Gardens,** a baronial home near **Coconut Grove** (Miami's famous artistic community) and upscale **Coral Gables.**

Amelia Island is the only U.S. territory to have served under eight flags. What are they? France, Spain, England, the Patriots of Amelia Island, Florida, Mexico, the Confederacy, and the United States.

The original Ripley's Believe It Or Not Museum is in St. Augustine. Among its displays: a London Tower Bridge model made out of 264 345 matchsticks, a clock made out of clothespins, and a painting made out of 63 pieces of toast.

Palm Beach has an unusual ordinance: no fast-food restaurants, movie theatres, neon signs, or car dealerships are allowed within city limits.

A rather unusual attraction near Miami: Monkey Jungle, where the visitors are in cages and the monkeys are outside.

- **The South Beach Art Deco District,** a vibrant strip of renovated old buildings that features trendy seaside eateries.

- **Little Havana,** a colourful and festive enclave of Cuban restaurants and shops.

- Several museums, including the **Museum of Science.**

- **Everglades National Park,** the swampy habitat of alligators, weird birds, and tourist air-boats, about an hour from Miami.

- **The Florida Keys**, a destination unto itself, with its 290-kilometre-long string of 32 islands, 42 bridges, and awesome seascapes that stretch out to the magical town of Key West. A drive from Miami to Key West, with stops, can easily take a half-day, so you should perhaps suggest lodging in Key West.

Florida's West Coast

Many interesting beach cities dot the Gulf of Mexico rim of Florida, yet Florida's west coast remains less known than its Atlantic side:

- **Ft. Myers,** a major port of sailing for those who love to fish.

- **The Resort Islands—Sanibel** and **Captiva** (off Ft. Myers) and **Marco** (off **Naples**)—with their fine fishing, seashell-laden beaches, and many upscale hotels and condos.

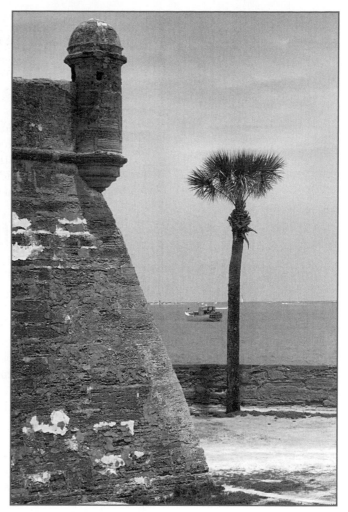

St. Augustine's Castillo de San Marcos is more than 300 years old.
Michelle Marsan/Shutterstock

An interesting activity in Key West: a guided tour of the Key West City Cemetery.

Over 90 percent of visitors to Florida have visited the state before.

Cruise ships, Miami
Photo by Marc Mancini

Chapter 8 Florida

- **Sarasota,** home of the **Ringling Circus Museum.**

- **Clearwater,** the west coast's prime beach community, only a short distance from the progressive metropolises of St. Petersburg (with several interesting museums) and Tampa (with its Busch Gardens).

- **Cedar Key,** a quintessential fishing village that's now also an artists' colony.

- **The Florida Panhandle,** which faces south onto the Gulf and is in Florida's northwest corner. Here can be found numerous beaches (some noisy and crowded, others pristine and preserved), fishing resorts, old Spanish-themed **Pensacola,** and Florida's capital, **Tallahassee** (which is inland). Among the beach resorts popular with Canadian travellers: **Panama City** and **Destin.**

POSSIBLE ITINERARIES

Probably the most popular itinerary for vacationers (especially families) requires about six or seven full days in Orlando, with three or four days in Walt Disney World and the rest spent visiting nearby attractions. Many people lodge at Walt Disney World and limit themselves to its attractions, especially on shorter trips. They would, however, miss the fascinations that lie outside Disney World's perimeter. For tourists who want to see everything in and around Orlando and have the time to do it, about 10 days should suffice.

An Atlantic-coast itinerary would require about a week, with travellers driving from Jacksonville to Miami and stopping along the way. Miami and the Keys merit six or seven days, as would a trip along Florida's west coast.

Some people will want to see all of Florida in a week. Explain to them that it's almost impossible. Suggest that they stay in Orlando or Miami and hub out. If they want to see the highlights of Florida, it might be possible to stay in Orlando for three days, then drive up to St. Augustine and down to Cocoa Beach for two days. From there, they could drive down to Miami and the Keys for four days, and up to the Clearwater–Tampa area for two. This results in an 11- to 12-day trip, but a very hectic one.

Remember that Miami and Ft. Lauderdale are major jump-off points for cruises and flights to South America and the Caribbean. Indeed, a short stay in Miami can be a welcomed add-on to someone's Caribbean plans. Packages that combine an Orlando vacation with a Bahamas or Caribbean cruise (usually out of Port Canaveral and some on Disney-owned ships) are also very popular with families.

LODGING OPTIONS

Lodging in Florida is comparatively inexpensive, especially in the Orlando area. Visitors can stay right on the Walt Disney World Resort property; there's everything from expensive to budget-priced accommodations. Guests staying at Disney-owned hotels are allowed early admission to the Disney theme parks. These hotels are themed; a unique example is **Disney's Animal Kingdom Lodge,** where guests in savannah-view rooms can watch animals, including zebras, gazelles, and giraffes, from their balconies.

Many fine hotels (usually part of well-known chains)—and a few awful ones—are located a few kilometres away. Some of the best are in the **Main Gate** area, and many are along **International Drive.** The Universal Orlando Resort also has interesting themed hotels (including the **Portofino Bay Hotel** and a **Hard Rock Hotel**) that adjoin its parks.

Miami has many downtown hotels (frequented by business travellers, people on pre- or post-cruise stays, and conventioneers), but most people will want to

Florida is a major destination for Canadians and Brazilians.

To avoid theme park lines: Arrive at morning opening time, walk to the far end of the park, and work your way back to the entrance.

Among U.S. cities, Miami has the greatest number of people who speak a language other than English at home.

In Coral Gables is a landmark working lighthouse. Yet it's kilometres inland.

stay on the long island of seaside property that is Miami Beach. For the upscale, recommend the super-deluxe properties in the Key Biscayne, Coral Gables, central Miami Beach, and **Bal Harbour** areas. The **Biltmore Hotel** in Coral Gables is a National Historic Landmark. The central Miami Beach district features one of the United States' most famous properties: the **Fontainebleau Hilton.** Those seeking moderate lodging should consider the "art deco district" and North Miami Beach "Motel Row." Be careful: The quality of lodging in both these budget areas varies enormously. Ritz-Carlton has many luxurious properties in Florida (in fact, it has more hotels here than in any other U.S. state). Throughout Florida are also many condominiums, several spas, and resorts. One of the most famous: the **Breakers,** in Palm Beach, is considered by some to be the most striking hotel in Florida.

ALLIED DESTINATIONS

The most obvious add-on to a trip to Florida is a voyage into the Caribbean by either ship or plane. A stay in Florida's Panhandle and, for that matter, all of Florida is easily combined with a New Orleans vacation. So, too, are any vacations spent in the southern states, especially in the Savannah, Georgia, area. Remember that there's considerable air service from Miami to South America. A short stay in Miami might be a way to break up a trip to this major tourist area.

FACTORS THAT MOTIVATE VISITORS

Florida boasts a wealth of tourist-motivating factors:

- It has a year-round tropical climate.

- A low-cost vacation is feasible.

- It's easily accessible by car, train, or plane.

- Many bargain ITC packages are available.

- There's an astonishing concentration of family attractions in the Orlando area.

- Deep-sea fishing and other sport opportunities abound.

- Florida is an air and cruise gateway to Latin America and the Caribbean. Its principal cruise ports are Miami, Port Everglades (Ft. Lauderdale), Port Canaveral, and Tampa.

- It's a major destination for students on spring break.

- Miami has great cultural diversity.

- A well-developed highway system criss-crosses Florida.

- Superior beach resorts are found along both the Atlantic and Gulf coasts.

Baseball fans can root for their favourite teams in Florida during Spring Training. (The Toronto Blue Jays train in Dunedin, Florida.)

POSSIBLE MISGIVINGS

As popular as Florida is, it also elicits certain predictable objections:

- "It's only for families and kids." Recommend any destination outside Orlando. Even in Orlando, Disney's Animal Kingdom and Epcot can be entertaining for adult visitors.

- "It's too hot and humid." Recommend a late fall, winter, or early spring visit.

- "There are no cultural opportunities." Miami appeals to culture seekers and Key West has many historical assets. Orlando's Epcot is a pop-cultural experience. But it is true that Florida, as a cultural destination, is not on par with, say, Europe.

- "I've been to Florida and the people aren't very friendly." This can be true, especially in Miami. But most Floridians are friendly and even engagingly upbeat.

- "Miami is crime-ridden." There's a bit of truth to this, but most areas—especially the upscale ones—are quite insulated from Miami's problems. Warn people to avoid driving off the tourist-beaten path and to remain alert and cautious when driving between the airport and their Miami lodging.

Qualifying the Traveller
FLORIDA

FOR PEOPLE WHO WANT	HIGH APPEAL	MEDIUM APPEAL	LOW APPEAL	REMARKS
Historical and Cultural Attractions		▲		Mostly Miami and St. Augustine
Beaches and Water Sports	▲			Along coast
Skiing Opportunities			▲	None
Lots of Nightlife		▲		Especially Miami
Family Activities	▲			Especially Orlando
Familiar Cultural Experience	▲			
Exotic Cultural Experience		▲		Mostly Miami
Safety and Low Crime		▲		Miami has some crime
Bargain Travel		▲		Especially Orlando
Impressive Scenery		▲		Seascapes and Everglades
Peace and Quiet			▲	Small towns only
Shopping Opportunities		▲		Mostly Miami and Palm Beach
Adventure			▲	Everglades
To Do Business		▲		Especially Miami

SALES STRATEGIES

Comprehensive packages are probably the best way to draw maximum profitability from an Orlando vacation: Typical packages include air, hotel, ground transportation, admissions, and maybe some meals. You should always try to up-sell lodging almost anywhere in Florida; even deluxe properties can be reasonable. Always offer to book car rentals, which are generally very reasonable. Offer a full-size or luxury car rental to a family. You can also book boat charters in advance for those who fish; the commissions can be considerable. You can suggest expansions of vacation plans with extensions into the Bahamas and the Caribbean, usually via cruises.

TRAVEL TRIVIA

TOP TEN U.S. AMUSEMENT PARKS BY ATTENDANCE

1. Magic Kingdom, Disney World, Florida
2. Disneyland, California
3. Epcot, Disney World, Florida
4. Disney-MGM Studios, Disney World, Florida
5. Disney's Animal Kingdom, Disney World, Florida
6. Universal Studios Florida, Universal Orlando, Florida
7. Disney's California Adventure, California
8. Islands of Adventure, Universal Orlando, Florida
9. Sea World Orlando, Florida
10. Universal Studios Hollywood, California

Source: Amusement Business magazine

NAME _____   DATE _____

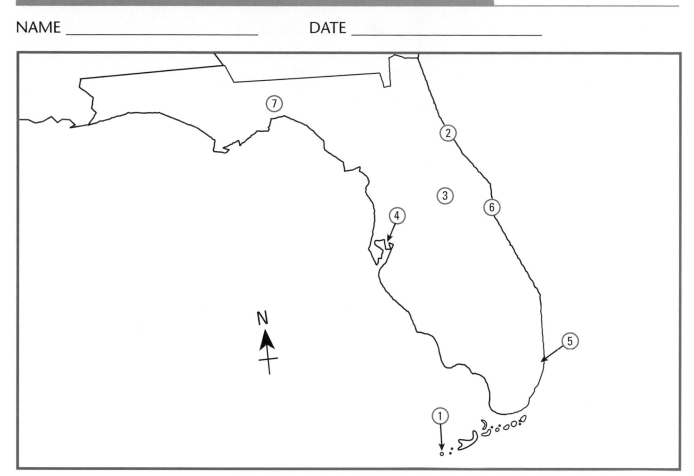

A traveller wants to visit the places listed below. Which number represents each on the map?

PLACE/ATTRACTION	IN/NEAR WHICH CITY?	NUMBER ON MAP
A. Epcot	A.	A.
B. Sea World	B.	B.
C. The Conch Train	C.	C.
D. The oldest city in the United States	D.	D.
E. Kennedy Space Center	E.	E.
F. Vizcaya Museum and Gardens	F.	F.
G. The Fontainebleau Hilton	G.	G.
H. Busch Gardens	H.	H.
I. Florida's Panhandle capital	I.	I.
J. Walt Disney World	J.	J.

CASE STUDY

NAME _____   DATE _____

Bart Beavis, 50 years old and recently divorced, is an outgoing individual who lives in Prince George, British Columbia. He wants to get away for his two-week vacation and is interested in Florida. He loves fishing, water sports, and sightseeing; a few of his buddies who live in Florida may join him for these activities. He's not a fan of idling on the beach, though, and he hates hot, humid, or stormy weather. He's prepared to spend a good sum of money on his trip.

Circle the answer that best suits his needs.

1. When would you suggest that he go?

    September   June

    Early May   Late August

    Why?

2. What would Bart not be able to easily do on his journey?

    Make a side trip to Nashville   Make a stopover in New Orleans

    Take a cruise   Take a side trip to Jamaica

    Why?

3. What would most appeal to Bart?

    A yacht charter   A train tour of Florida

    A Magic Kingdom package   An alligator hunt

    Why?

4. Which of the following cities should not be considered as a lodging spot?

    Ft. Lauderdale   Key West

    Ft. Myers   Orlando

    Why?

CREATIVE ACTIVITY

NAME _____   DATE _____

Travel and Leisure magazine once conducted an online poll to determine which cities, places, and attractions were "worth revisiting." The winner: Washington, D.C. (i.e., 40 percent said that Washington, D.C., merited a second trip). Why do you think those polled felt the way they did? Write your answer below.

Now, consider the following places. Do you think they merit a second visit? Again, write your reason in the space provided.

PLACE	YES OR NO?	WHY OR WHY NOT?
1. The Florida Keys		
2. Orlando		
3. The Kennedy Space Center		
4. Miami		

What three places in Canada and/or the United States, other than the ones above, do you think most merit a return visit? (Try to select at least one place in Florida.) Again, explain why.

PLACE

1.

2.

3.

CALIFORNIA

OREGON

IDAHO

WYOMING

Lake Tahoe ● Reno

Sonoma County
● Calistoga
Muir Woods
Napa ☆ Sacramento
Valley
San Francisco ● Oakland
● San Jose

Yosemite ▲
▲ Mammoth Mountain

▲ Kings Canyon
Sequoia ▲
National Park

Monterey
Carmel

▲ Big Sur

*PACIFIC
OCEAN*

▲ Hearst San Simeon

Sierra
Nevada

NEVADA

UTAH

Great
Salt
Lake

Colorado River

COLORADO

● Las Vegas

▲ Monument
Valley
▲ Painted
Desert

Santa Barbara
●

San Bernardino
Mountains

Grand ▲
Canyon

Williams
●

Flagstaff
●

Burbank
Los Angeles ● Ontario
Long Beach
Santa Catalina Island
Anaheim

▲ Lake Arrowhead
▲ Big Bear
Palm
Springs

Lake Havasu

Sedona
●
Meteor Crater

▲ Winslow
●

▲ Petrified
Forest

▲ Montezuma Castle

Carlsbad
● Escondido
San Diego

Colorado River

ARIZONA

NEW MEXICO

● Tijuana

MEXICO

Phoenix ☆ ● Scottsdale

*GULF of
CALIFORNIA*

Tucson ● Saguaro
▲ National
Monument

● Tombstone

TX

California and Arizona

Glamour and Grandeur

It all depends on whom you're talking to. Say the name "California" and the first thing some will think of is the glitz of **Hollywood** or the free-spirited sophistication of **San Francisco.** Others will conjure up the images of magnificent natural wonders like awesome **Yosemite** [yo-SEM-mih-tee] **National Park,** the rolling **Wine Country,** or the majestic redwoods.

California can be divided geographically into two areas, North and South, each with a distinct character. Southern California is largely desert and industrial, with **Los Angeles,** bordering the Pacific Ocean off its west coast, as its heart. The L.A. metropolitan area sprawls far south, through **Anaheim** (and the **Disneyland Resort**) and north, past the San Fernando Valley, home of **Burbank,** where many of the movie studios are found. In the very south is lovely **San Diego.**

Northern California is more mountainous and forested. Its centrepiece is the port city of San Francisco. South are the beautiful towns of **Monterey** and **Carmel,** and to the north is the Wine Country of the **Napa Valley** and **Sonoma County.** Yosemite National Park is east of San Francisco, near the Nevada border. Northeast of San Francisco, incidentally, is the state capital, **Sacramento;** it's not, however, much of a tourist centre.

California is connected on the southeast to Arizona. Largely desert (though there are mountains throughout its northern portion), Arizona has stunning scenery, notably in the areas around the **Grand Canyon** and **Sedona.** A bit south of Arizona's centre is **Phoenix,** the state's capital and cultural centre. Off in the southeast corner is **Tucson** [TOO-sahn], a city heavily influenced by Native-American culture.

In Arizona, you can drive past a place called Nowhere, a village named Eden, and a junction town called Why.

HOW TRAVELLERS GET THERE

Los Angeles is one of the country's easiest cities to reach by air. Most flights land at **Los Angeles International Airport** (LAX); however, **Burbank Airport** (BUR) is convenient for travellers who are staying in the San Fernando Valley or who prefer less-crowded terminals. There's also **John Wayne Airport** (SNA) in **Orange County** (for those visiting Disneyland and other attractions in that area), and **Ontario Airport** (ONT), east of L.A. **San Diego International Airport** (SAN), serves the most southerly part of California.

Flights to northern California are also numerous. The major gateway is **San Francisco International Airport** (SFO). However, many flights land at **Oakland** (OAK) and **San Jose** (SJC) as well.

One of the most bizarre attractions in the United States: Winchester Mystery House in San Jose, California. This rambling Victorian mansion has—among other things—stairs leading nowhere and windows that open onto other rooms.

○ Meteor Crater, outside Winslow, Arizona, is where a giant meteor crashed into the ground 22 000 years ago.

Most Arizona-bound travellers will fly into **Sky Harbor International Airport** (PHX) in Phoenix, though there's also a busy airport at Tucson (TUS). Flying time to all these destinations from Toronto or Montreal is about five to six hours; from Edmonton or Calgary it's around three and a half hours; from Vancouver it's around three.

A leisurely and scenic way of reaching the area is by train. **Amtrak** has lines to both Los Angeles and San Francisco that can be accessed from many cities across the United States (and from Vancouver via a bus–rail combination). One of the L.A. routes goes through **Flagstaff,** Arizona. Cruises access San Diego and L.A. on repositioning cruises from the Caribbean, Acapulco, Vancouver, and Hawaii. A rich complex of highways flows into Arizona and California from neighbouring states.

WEATHER PATTERNS

○ It snows in Los Angeles two or three times per century.

To describe the climates of California and Arizona is no easy task. The reason: Totally different climate conditions can exist within kilometres of each other. For example, a visitor to southern California can drive from the beach in Santa Monica to inland San Bernardino and into the nearby mountains, passing from pleasant, breezy beach temperatures through hot desert air, and into snow—all in less than two hours.

○ The Palace of the Legion of Honor in San Francisco is an exact reproduction of the one in Paris.

Four general climate patterns exist in California and Arizona. **Coastal California,** which includes the beach areas, tends to have warm but dry summers and pleasantly comfortable winters, with occasional rainstorms between November and March (see Figures 9-1 and 9-2). Fog along the immediate coast can occur anytime, though it happens less frequently in the fall (which may be California's most pleasant season). Nights are usually cool. Of course, the farther north a traveller goes up the coast toward San Francisco and beyond, the chillier the year-round

MONTH	JAN	FEB	MAR	APR	MAY	JUN	JUL	AUG	SEP	OCT	NOV	DEC
AVERAGE HIGH TEMPERATURE	18	19	21	22	23	25	28	29	28	25	23	19
AVERAGE LOW TEMPERATURE	7	8	9	11	13	14	17	17	16	13	11	9
AVERAGE PRECIPITATION (IN CENTIMETRES)	5	8	5	3	0	0	0	0	0	3	3	8

Figure 9-1   Climate at a Glance: Los Angeles, California

MONTH	JAN	FEB	MAR	APR	MAY	JUN	JUL	AUG	SEP	OCT	NOV	DEC
AVERAGE HIGH TEMPERATURE	13	15	16	17	17	18	18	18	20	20	18	14
AVERAGE LOW TEMPERATURE	7	8	9	9	11	12	12	12	13	12	11	8
AVERAGE PRECIPITATION (IN CENTIMETRES)	10	10	8	3	3	0	0	0	0	3	5	10

Figure 9-2   Climate at a Glance: San Francisco, California

temperatures become (and the greater the likelihood of fog). As Mark Twain put it, "The coldest winter I ever spent was a summer in San Francisco."

The second pattern occurs in California's **valleys and near-coastal areas** (for example, Anaheim). The climate is somewhat like coastal California, but with temperatures that run five to eight degrees warmer and with fog only rarely. The third pattern marks the vast, flat **deserts** of California and Arizona. Summer, early fall, and late spring feature extremely sunny, torridly hot, and bone-dry weather. Winter is much more pleasant, with warmth, sunshine, and only occasional rain (see Figure 9-3 on p. 166). **High-elevation areas** (for example, the Grand Canyon and California's mountain resorts) represent the last pattern: cold, snowy winters with warm daytime sun (even if there's snow on the ground) and pleasantly cool to warm summers.

Remember: California's ocean temperatures are chilly. As for tourist patterns, California enjoys major tourism year-round, with a slight thinning of crowds in the fall. The Grand Canyon's peak season is summer. The desert and ski resorts have their high seasons in the winter; rates plunge during the summer.

GETTING AROUND

Both California and Arizona have excellent freeway systems (though in both states, distances can be great). And, yes, California's massive freeway system in urban areas suffers awesome congestion. Many air connections tie the major cities together, especially along the Los Angeles–San Francisco corridor. For those who enjoy train travel, several Amtrak routes are convenient and scenic, especially the **Coast Starlight** (L.A. to San Francisco and beyond) and the **Pacific Surfliner** (from San Luis Obispo to San Diego). There are also train rides and cruises through California Wine Country.

Public transportation in Los Angeles is limited to a mediocre bus system and fairly new rail–subway lines. Because the city is so spread out, taxis can be

California's freeways used to be truly free. Some new routes charge tolls.

Buildings, roads, parking lots, and other structures in the United States cover an area the size of Ohio.

Chapter 9 California and Arizona

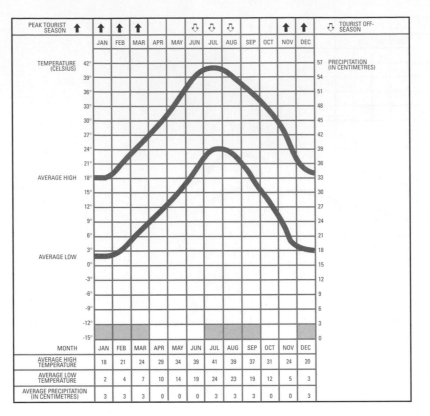

PEAK TOURIST SEASON ↑	↑	↑	↑			⇓	⇓	⇓			↑	↑	⇓ TOURIST OFF-SEASON
	JAN	FEB	MAR	APR	MAY	JUN	JUL	AUG	SEP	OCT	NOV	DEC	

MONTH	JAN	FEB	MAR	APR	MAY	JUN	JUL	AUG	SEP	OCT	NOV	DEC
AVERAGE HIGH TEMPERATURE	18	21	24	29	34	39	41	39	37	31	24	20
AVERAGE LOW TEMPERATURE	2	4	7	10	14	19	24	23	19	12	5	3
AVERAGE PRECIPITATION (IN CENTIMETRES)	3	3	3	0	0	0	3	3	3	0	0	3

Figure 9-3 Climate at a Glance: Phoenix, Arizona

expensive. City tours (especially past the homes of the stars) are popular. For most visitors, however, car rentals are the preferred way to get around. The highways are well laid out and the streets are wide. Rush hours (7 a.m. to 10 a.m. and 3 p.m. to 7 p.m.) can be truly awful.

San Francisco is much easier to get around, though the hilly streets can be difficult for cars and pedestrians. The excellent BART subway gets travellers around the Bay Area. And, of course, there are the famous and fun cable cars.

To get to the Grand Canyon from Flagstaff, visitors can either drive themselves on a beautiful (but slow) route or take a bus from the city's bus depot. In the summer season, the Grand Canyon Railway operates a vintage steam train from Williams, Arizona, 100 kilometres north to the Grand Canyon. (Vintage diesel trains are used the rest of the year.) One-day air excursions to the Grand Canyon from Las Vegas, Nevada, are popular. Phoenix, like L.A., is spread out; car rentals or the adequate bus system are the preferred options for getting around.

IMPORTANT PLACES

California and Arizona have a wealth of attractions. Here are the principal ones:

Los Angeles

Los Angeles is the heart of any trip to southern California and a magnet for millions of visitors yearly. A sprawling city of extremes, L.A. is the kind of place people either love or avoid like the plague. As befits the second-largest city in the United States, the Los Angeles area brims with first-rate attractions: theme parks, museums, beaches, nightlife, restaurants, theatre, and its own brand of glitz. Among the most popular attractions are:

- **The Disneyland Resort,** which is actually in Anaheim, about a half-hour from Los Angeles itself. It encompasses **Disneyland** (the granddaddy of theme parks), **Disney's California Adventure** (which celebrates the Golden State),

The most scenic cable car route is the Powell-Hyde line.

"Real" studio tours at Warner Bros., Sony, and Paramount are available.

Disney's California Adventure, Anaheim, California
Photo by Marc Mancini

and **Downtown Disney** (an entertainment, dining, and shopping district). Visitors could easily spend two days here.

- **Other theme parks,** like **Universal Studios Hollywood** (another must), **Knott's Berry Farm** (plenty of rides and famous foods), and **Six Flags Magic Mountain** (a more conventional theme park with a huge collection of thrill rides).

- **Grauman's Chinese Theater,** where movie stars' footprints are enshrined in cement. Nearby are the **Hollywood & Highland** shopping and entertainment centre (the home of the Academy Awards ceremonies) and the **Walk of Fame** (where star-shaped plaques honouring the famous are embedded in the sidewalk).

- **Beverly Hills,** with its posh Rodeo [roh-DAY-oh] Drive and mansions (which can be experienced via a "stars' homes" tour).

- **Excellent museums,** like the **L.A. County Museum of Art,** the offbeat **Museum of Contemporary Art,** and the **Getty Center,** perhaps the world's wealthiest museum.

- **The Queen Mary,** in nearby **Long Beach,** the former ocean liner now permanently docked as a hotel and tourist attraction. Some cruises depart from a terminal nearby. Long Beach boasts a good number of waterfront restaurants, hotels, shops, secondary attractions, and the world-class **Aquarium of the Pacific.**

- **The Venice Boardwalk,** with its assortment of beachside eccentrics (and those who come to see them). Three more trendy places to look, shop, and stroll: **Santa Monica's Third Street Promenade, The Grove** (next to Farmer's Market), and **CityWalk** (which adjoins Universal Studios).

Various **day trips** can be taken from Los Angeles, many of which can be extended into longer stays:

- **Catalina Island,** "26 miles across the sea from L.A.," exactly as an old song said. There are beautiful coves, mountains, hiking, buffalo herds, and boat and bus tours. (Officially it's Santa Catalina Island, but few people call it that.)

L.A.'s Farmer's Market is a favourite among locals for food and shopping.

A movie crew filming a 1912 Western brought buffalo to Catalina Island. When the shoot was finished, the buffalo were left to fend for themselves. Some of their descendants are still there.

- **Big Bear** and **Lake Arrowhead,** popular and pretty water-and-ski resorts, in the nearby **San Bernardino Mountains.**

A little farther out from L.A. and within an easy day's drive are some places that could make nice, short overnight stops of their own:

- **Palm Springs,** a fashionable desert resort. It's not quite as posh as it once was, but the resort complexes in nearby **Palm Desert** and **Rancho Mirage** are luxurious. During college spring break, it's a wild place indeed. A nearby attraction is an aerial tramway that takes visitors to the top of lofty **Mt. San Jacinto.**

- **Santa Barbara,** with its mission, boutiques, great ocean views, good small museums, and lovely gardens.

- **Sequoia** and **Kings Canyon National Parks,** with their famed towering redwood trees. These parks are about equidistant from San Francisco and Los Angeles.

San Diego

Some consider The Golden Door in Escondido (near San Diego) to be the finest spa in the United States.

There's an exact reproduction of Shakespeare's Globe Theatre in San Diego's Balboa Park.

Only a couple of hours south of Los Angeles is San Diego. Though close enough for a long, tiring day trip from L.A., this beautiful city—with its revitalized downtown core—should be seen on its own. Among its popular attractions are:

- **San Diego Zoo,** one of the world's greatest zoos. Most of the animals are kept in natural habitat surroundings, not cages. The zoo is actually just one part of **Balboa Park,** the city's centrepiece, with lakes, gardens, and many museums.

- **Sea World,** one of the world's great marine-life amusement parks.

Close to San Diego are:

- **San Diego Wild Animal Park,** a large animal preserve with tours.

- **Tijuana,** the Mexican city about 20 minutes away, across the border from San Diego. It's rather dirty and impoverished, but bargain hunters still love to go there. Most day visitors park their cars on the U.S. side and walk across the border to Tijuana.

San Francisco

San Franciscans dislike their city being called "Frisco."

The San Francisco telephone book lists restaurants by 57 nationality groups.

The Golden Gate Bridge isn't golden. It's painted burnt orange.

San Francisco's Lombard Street is the world's crookedest.

As Los Angeles is to southern California, so, too, is San Francisco the hub of central and northern California. San Francisco has wonderful restaurants, cutting-edge nightlife, and excellent symphony and opera. Among the attractions are:

- **Fisherman's Wharf,** a lively waterfront open-air market, with stalls selling that day's catch and the smells of sourdough bread permeating the air. This crowded district has excellent restaurants and interesting shops.

- **Ghirardelli Square,** a busy, fun shopping centre right near the Wharf that was once a chocolate factory. Several similar shopping complexes are also in the area.

- **Golden Gate Park,** a wonderful, huge recreation area with many lakes, several museums, and the beautiful **Japanese Tea Garden.**

- **Alcatraz,** the famed old prison in San Francisco Bay that the National Parks Service maintains as a tourist attraction.

- **Chinatown,** with the largest number of Chinese in any area outside of China. It gets crowded, but tourists enjoy walking among the pagoda-like buildings, checking out the import shops, and eating.

- **A few other attractions:** the oddly shaped **Coit Tower** on **Telegraph Hill,** crooked **Lombard Street,** and the Italian **North Beach** restaurant area.

Several areas outside San Francisco make for great **day trips:**

- **Monterey** and **Carmel,** to the south. These gorgeous towns have beautiful scenery, famous golf courses, and a lovely old mission. Monterey's aquarium is outstanding. The renowned **17 Mile Drive** is a must-see.

- **Muir Woods National Monument,** just to the north of San Francisco. This stunning park features walks among spectacular redwoods. On the way, a visitor could stop at **Sausalito,** a quaint waterfront town across the bay from San Francisco. Getting there offers a good opportunity to cross the **Golden Gate Bridge,** a world-famous landmark.

- **Hearst San Simeon State Historic Park,** with its famous ornate castle. It's a long day trip from San Francisco, at the southerly end of the scenic **Big Sur Coastal Road.** (It's actually closer to Santa Barbara.)

Most skiers know about **Lake Tahoe,** a popular resort on the Nevada border, just across from Reno, Nevada. It's about a four-hour drive from San Francisco. The Tahoe area contains a number of world-class ski resorts, including **Heavenly Valley, Alpine Meadows,** and **Squaw Valley.** To the south of the lake (nearer Yosemite) is the **Mammoth Mountain–June Mountain** ski area.

The Wine Country

Only an hour's drive north of San Francisco, Napa Valley and Sonoma County—the two biggest wine-producing regions in the United States—are commonly visited for several days on their own. The wineries have fascinating architecture; redwood forests and lovely little shops are all along the way. The Wine Country can be visited by car, train, or boat. The town of **Calistoga** is famous for its mineral springs and spas, which have attracted visitors since the 19th century.

Fairfield, California, is the home of the Jelly Belly. Factory tours are available.

Yosemite National Park

Yosemite is one of the most beautiful locales in the world, with numerous waterfalls and such justly renowned spectacles as **Half Dome** and **El Capitan.** This is a must visit for anyone near the area.

Yosemite's El Capitan cliff is more than one-and-a-half times higher than the CN Tower.

Bridal Veil Falls, Yosemite, California
Photo by Justus Ghormley

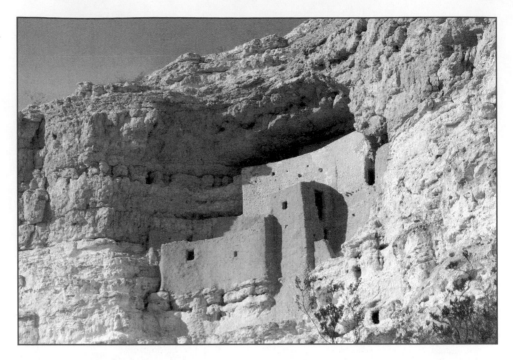

Montezuma Castle, Arizona
Bryan Busovicki/Shutterstock

Phoenix

This desert city (Arizona's capital) is surrounded by hulking mountains and is steeped in Native-American history. The city has several mega-resorts and all manner of dude ranches. Phoenix is also a baseball mecca from late February to early April, when major league teams train here.

Its most popular attractions include:

- **The adjoining town of Scottsdale,** with impressive upscale art galleries, resort hotels, golf courses, and shops specializing in Native-American crafts.

- **Architectural centres,** notably **Taliesin West** (the fascinating school created by Frank Lloyd Wright) and the **Cosanti Foundation** (the strangely wonderful, futuristic workshop of Paolo Soleri). Tours of both are available.

An attractive day trip is to Sedona, famed for its astonishing red cliffs; Sedona can be accessed by driving along the scenic Verde River valley, or from Flagstaff as part of a shorter, half-day trip through spectacular **Oak Creek Canyon.** Not far from Sedona is **Montezuma Castle,** the 800-year-old ruins of an ancient North American civilization, situated in the side of a cliff. To the west is **Lake Havasu,** most famous as the site of the relocated **London Bridge.** (There's nothing weirder than seeing this structure in the middle of the desert.)

Grand Canyon National Park

This is possibly the most famous natural landmark in the United States. It's breathtaking. The **South Rim,** which offers the best views, is the most popular area to visit and is jam-packed in the summer. The canyon's depths can be seen by hiking, riding on a mule, flying in a helicopter or plane, or rafting on the Colorado River. Hotel accommodations in the park are somewhat limited; most lodging is in Flagstaff (about 145 kilometres away).

Far to the northeast are the **Painted Desert** and **Petrified Forest National Park** (east of Flagstaff) and **Monument Valley** (northeast) with its ancient Native-

Eat in one of the several country-and-western restaurants on the outskirts of Phoenix. A western delicacy: rattlesnake (which tastes like chicken).

In Arizona, more boats are owned per capita than in any other U.S. state.

American ruins and familiar vistas. (Monument Valley appeared repeatedly in Western movies.)

Tucson

This city is extremely popular in the winter for its dude ranches, resorts, and the controversial, ecologically sealed community **Biosphere 2. Old Tucson Studios,** where many Westerns were shot, is just west of town. Several Tucson museums showcase Native-American art. The city is also near **Saguaro National Monument,** with its giant cacti. About 160 kilometres southeast of Tucson is **Tombstone.** Here's the Old West as it must have been, complete with the legendary **OK Corral, Boot Hill,** and the **Bird Cage Theater.**

POSSIBLE ITINERARIES

Where should first-time tourists to California go? Probably to either Los Angeles or San Francisco and their surrounding areas. There's enough to do close by Los Angeles and San Francisco to warrant a stay of five to seven days at each. Tourists often want to drive the coastal road between the two cities, but it's a long distance that's better done in two days, with a stop perhaps at Hearst Castle. Return visitors may prefer to get out of the urban centres and discover the riches of the state, exploring the southern California coastal communities or the desert for a week, or driving through the Wine Country and forestland of the north. Five-day excursions to Yosemite or the Grand Canyon and their surrounding areas are worthwhile trips of their own. A relaxing three to five days in Phoenix allows visitors to get away from it all.

What about an Arizona-only trip? Two itineraries are common. In the first, travellers fly into Phoenix and, taking a northerly route, visit the Petrified Forest, the Painted Desert and/or Monument Valley, the Grand Canyon, and Sedona. They might also detour to Lake Havasu, returning to Phoenix. This itinerary would take about a week. In the second, travellers stay in Phoenix for two or three days, then head south to Tucson, Tombstone, and Saguaro National Monument. This could be done in about six days.

LODGING OPTIONS

California offers an abundance of lodging choices. In Los Angeles, there's no real lodging centre; there are, however, hotel clusters around the L.A. Airport, Beverly Hills, Universal Studios, Marina del Rey, Century City, West Hollywood, downtown (more appropriate for some business travellers), and the Disneyland Resort in Anaheim. The **Beverly Hills Hotel,** with its famous bungalows, is where legendary movie stars have resided. The San Diego area also boasts some excellent hotels, especially the **Hotel Del Coronado,** an astonishing bit of wooden Victorian whimsy. Santa Barbara's **Four Seasons Biltmore** is a landmark.

In San Francisco, hotels tend to be based at Nob Hill, Union Square, Fisherman's Wharf, and on either side of Market Street. There are at least a half-dozen world-class hotels here, as well as many lesser-known gems. Yosemite has a wide range of accommodations, from hotels to tents and cabins; the **Ahwahnee Hotel** is rustic yet elegant, and a national landmark. For a change of pace, bed-and-breakfasts are popular in California, especially in the Wine Country.

Some Arizona resorts in the north close in the winter, whereas those in the south may close during summer months. Most hotels are open year-round, though, and may drastically lower their rates off-season. Lodging in the Phoenix area is clustered downtown and north of the city near the Metrocenter, as well as throughout Scottsdale. Frank Lloyd Wright designed the luxurious **Arizona Biltmore** resort. In Scottsdale is the **Phoenician,** a glitzy resort carved out of the side of a mountain. These and other Arizona hotel resorts attract conferences and

At San Luis Obispo's Madonna Inn, each room has a different theme. (The Cave Man room is the most popular.)

conventions. Dude ranches offer an intriguing lodging option, especially for horse lovers. **Grand Canyon National Park Lodges** include all the lodging properties within the park itself. Tucson has a surprisingly rich collection of upscale resorts (such as the **Canyon Ranch**) and ranches.

ALLIED DESTINATIONS

California is a good jumping-off point for the Pacific Northwest states of Oregon and Washington. It also borders Nevada and is a short flight to Las Vegas. California is a common stop for long flights to Hawaii and Asia. Both California and Arizona border Mexico, with cruise ships heading southward from L.A. to Mexico's Baja Peninsula, and beyond. Remember, too, that Arizona adjoins Colorado, New Mexico, and Utah (with its many national parks).

FACTORS THAT MOTIVATE VISITORS

The Spanish named California after an imaginary island, Califina, cited in a then-popular romance novel.

Among the diverse reasons that motivate travellers to southern California are:

- It has superb weather year-round.
- They want to see the "movie capital," Hollywood. (They also hope to bump into a movie star; good luck to them.)
- There's wonderful outdoor recreation available all year.
- Los Angeles, Long Beach, and San Diego are departure points for cruises to Mexico and, occasionally, the Panama Canal.
- The area brims with natural wonders.
- L.A. is a convenient way to break up a trip to trans-Pacific destinations.
- There's plenty to do at night in the major cities.
- Some of the finest theme parks are here.

Northern California appeals to people for altogether different reasons. They might prefer visiting here because:

- San Francisco is sophisticated yet has a small-town, European feel.
- There's the natural splendour of mountains and redwood forests.
- The Monterey–Carmel area has renowned golf courses.
- The climate is temperate.
- San Francisco has exciting nightlife and great restaurants.
- The Wine Country is a unique, almost European attraction.
- Northern California has world-class skiing; there are several less extensive ski resorts northeast of L.A., too.

  Arizona, too, has its own appeal:

- The Grand Canyon is a unique spectacle.
- There are several interesting resorts and ranches.
- Many Canadians head to Arizona in the winter, staying in retirement trailer parks, condos, and timeshares.
- Arizona hosts many conventions, especially in the Phoenix/Scottsdale area.
- It boasts an Old West and Native American ambience.

POSSIBLE MISGIVINGS

Some parts of California will set off warning bells for a few potential visitors. Arizona might raise some questions for others. Among concerns to address are:

- "People are weird in Los Angeles." Mention that the city is a melting pot of people and cultures. It's diverse, open, free-spirited, and friendly.

- "Driving in L.A. frightens me and there's no public transportation." City tours are very popular. Driving at times other than rush hour is usually easy. And there are buses, a subway, and a growing rail system.

- "Los Angeles is so smoggy." Late fall to early spring is much better than summertime. Coastal areas are also far less smoggy. There's 50 percent less smog in L.A. than there was two decades ago.

- "All there is in southern California is L.A." A short drive out of the city, and you can be in the desert, mountains, San Diego, or Santa Barbara—just for starters.

Qualifying the Traveller
SOUTHERN CALIFORNIA

FOR PEOPLE WHO WANT	HIGH APPEAL	MEDIUM APPEAL	LOW APPEAL	REMARKS
Historical and Cultural Attractions		▲		L.A. and San Diego museums
Beaches and Water Sports	▲			Water is cool
Skiing Opportunities			▲	Some in San Bernardino Mts.
Lots of Nightlife		▲		Mostly L.A.
Family Activities	▲			Especially theme parks
Familiar Cultural Experience	▲			A little different, but still U.S.
Exotic Cultural Experience		▲		Offbeat lifestyles and Hispanic influence
Safety and Low Crime		▲		Tourist areas safe
Bargain Travel		▲		
Impressive Scenery	▲			Mountains, desert, and ocean
Peace and Quiet			▲	Only desert and mountain towns
Shopping Opportunities		▲		Just about everything
Adventure			▲	Hiking, biking
To Do Business	▲			Key to the Pacific Rim

- "San Francisco has a lot of strange people." Like all stereotypes, this one holds little water. Yes, San Francisco is a somewhat counterculture city, but the diversity actually helps make it a more interesting place.

- "Arizona's too hot." Suggest the winter, when it's more pleasant in the south. In the summer, Arizona's northern regions are cooler than the southern ones.

- "There's nothing to do in Arizona." Phoenix is a very cultured city, but it takes energy to find that culture. Tucson and Tombstone are unique attractions.

- "The Grand Canyon is crowded." Suggest touring the North Rim rather than the South Rim, or going off-season.

SALES STRATEGIES

California and Arizona offer many ways to up-sell or cross-sell. A car rental is an obvious recommendation. L.A. city tours are very popular, since the city is so spread out. City tours are also a good idea in San Francisco. You might suggest that visitors extend their trip in southern California to include the Grand Canyon, Las Vegas, or Mexico (perhaps on a cruise). A popular winter activity is a whale-watching cruise; they most commonly depart from San Diego and Monterey. And around the Christmas holiday, the lavish, glorious **Bracebridge Dinner** is a long-standing pageant at the Ahwahnee Hotel in Yosemite; it must be booked far in advance by lottery.

For those going to Arizona, a river-rafting trip down the Colorado River through the Grand Canyon is spectacular. Helicopter or plane trips over the canyon are famous. Arizona is a popular resort state, and up-selling to a resort hotel could make this quiet state a great deal of fun.

Cruises to Mexico or repositioning cruises along California's coast are quite popular. Year-round, three- or four-day cruises to Ensenada, Mexico, and seasonal seven-day cruises farther south to other Mexican port cities mostly leave from San Pedro (L.A.'s port); Long Beach and San Diego are alternatives. Small-ship cruises and railway excursions can be sold to visitors wanting to tour the Wine Country in an unusual way.

NAME _____   DATE _____

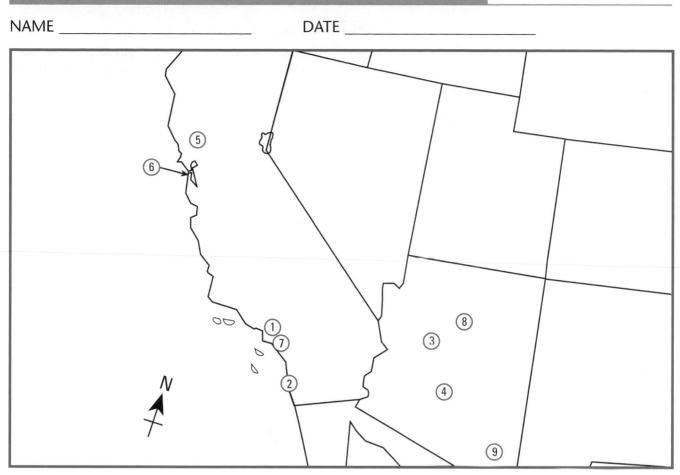

A traveller wants to visit the places listed below. Which number represents each on the map?

PLACE/ATTRACTION	IN/NEAR WHICH CITY/STATE?	NUMBER ON MAP
A. The OK Corral	A.	A.
B. Astonishing red cliffs	B.	B.
C. The Arizona Biltmore	C.	C.
D. Grauman's Chinese Theater	D.	D.
E. A mineral spring centred in the Wine Country	E.	E.
F. Lombard Street	F.	F.
G. Disneyland	G.	G.
H. A city near the Grand Canyon	H.	H.
I. Sea World	I.	I.
J. Alcatraz	J.	J.

CASE STUDY

Judi and Gordon Hayford, of Fredericton, New Brunswick, are taking their three teenage children on their first long-distance family trip—in this case, to Los Angeles. Their children have five days off during the March break. They're especially looking forward to Disneyland.

Circle the answer that best suits their needs.

1. What other attraction would you suggest for the family?

   Fisherman's Wharf   Montezuma Castle

   Universal Studios   Hearst Castle

   Why?

2. What area should the Hayfords probably lodge in?

   Hollywood   Anaheim

   Monterey   Palm Springs

   Why?

3. If they decided to leave L.A. and drive off on a one- to two-day trip, what place would you recommend?

   Yosemite   Sonoma

   Wally World   San Diego

   Why?

4. Which of the following would not be a good enhancement to their trip?

   A whale-watching cruise   The Bracebridge Dinner

   A car rental   A tour of the stars' homes

   Why?

CREATIVE ACTIVITY

NAME _____   DATE _____

You're driving down a lonely desert road outside of Palm Springs. Your car inexplicably stalls. Suddenly, a flying saucer lands next to you. A four-foot-tall green alien exits the craft and, in perfect English, says, "Human being! I wish to visit five interesting things in California and Arizona. No more, no less! What must I see? They must please me, or I will disintegrate you!" List your five responses below.

YOUR SUGGESTION   **YOUR REASON**

1.   1.

2.   2.

3.   3.

4.   4.

5.   5.

TRAVEL TRIVIA

TOP TEN U.S. PUBLIC GOLF COURSES

1. Pebble Beach, Pebble Beach, CA
2. Pacific Dunes, Bandon, OR
3. Bethpage (Black), Farmingdale, NY
4. Pinehurst (No. 2), Pinehurst, NC
5. Whistling Straits (Straits), Haven, WI
6. TPC @ Sawgrass (Stadium), Ponte Vedra Beach, FL

7. Bandon Dunes, Bandon, OR
8. Kiawah Island (Ocean), Kiawah Island, SC
9. World Woods (Pine Barrens), Brooksville, FL
10. Spyglass Hill, Pebble Beach, CA

Source: Golf magazine

Hanalei Bay
Princeville
Na Pali Cliffs
Waimea Canyon ▲ ●Fern Grotto
●Lihue
KAUAI
Poipu Beach

Sunset Beach
Waimea Bay ▲●Polynesian Cultural Center
▲Waimea Valley
Honolulu
OAHU
Hanauma Bay
Pearl Waikiki
Harbor Beach

Kalaupapa National Park
MOLOKAI
Iao Valley
Kaanapali ▲
LANAI **MAUI**
Lahaina
▲Kahului
Maui
Ocean ●Hana
Centre Haleakala▲

PACIFIC OCEAN

U.S. Mainland

HAWAII (Big Island)
Kohala Coast
▲Parker Ranch
Waikoloa
Mauna Kea ▲
●Hilo
Kona●
Kona Coast ▲Mauna Loa
Hawaii Volcanoes ▲Kilauea
National Park

Hawaiian Islands

PACIFIC OCEAN

Hawaii

Paradise Found

It must have been an astonishing trip indeed: Around 700 A.D., hundreds of natives from the Marquesas Islands in the South Pacific set sail in great double-hulled canoes and crossed more than 3200 kilometres of open ocean to arrive at what we now call the Hawaiian Islands. How did they know that the islands were there? Did they go back and forth many times, as legends insist? How did they interact with subsequent voyagers, who sailed in greater numbers from the Society Islands between the 11th and 14th centuries?

No one really knows. But we do know that tens of thousands of tourists now cross that same Pacific each week to visit Hawaii—in jets, of course. What they'll find there: perhaps the most sweet, gentle, and majestic islands in the world.

Don't assume, as do many, that there are only one or two islands. In reality, 312 Hawaiian islands stretch in an arc of almost 2500 kilometres in the middle of the Pacific. But only six, at the southernmost tip of the arc, attract visitors: **Kauai** [kah-WAH-ee], **Oahu** [oh-WAH-hoo], **Molokai** [mo-lo-KAH-ee], **Lanai** [lah-NAH-ee], **Maui** [MAU-ee], and **Hawaii** (also called Hawaii's Big Island). Each has its own personality: Kauai is the wettest and most tropical; Oahu is the bustling centre of tourism and commerce; Molokai and Lanai are sleepy little islands off the typical tourist path; Maui is an island of great resorts and breathtaking beauty; and Hawaii's Big Island boasts an active volcano and vast ranches.

HOW TRAVELLERS GET THERE

Dozens of North American and foreign carriers service the islands. Several airlines permit a traveller to stop off at no charge in Hawaii on the way to and from Asian or South Pacific destinations. Most flights from Toronto or Vancouver to **Honolulu, Oahu (HNL),** are nonstop or direct, with connections to the other islands. It takes six hours to get from Vancouver to Honolulu; eleven hours from Toronto. Some carriers operate nonstop flights from Vancouver to the other islands, as well. Occasionally, passengers can sail from Vancouver to Hawaii, especially when a cruise ship is repositioning itself, say, from Alaska to Asia.

WEATHER PATTERNS

Hawaii's climate barely varies all year (see Figure 10-1 on p. 180). The average high in August is 28°C and in January it's 25°C. Though it's generally humid, a strong east-to-west trade wind keeps the islands breezy and pleasant. It can get

Hawaii is the southern-most state in the United States, but Alaska extends farther west.

The statue of King Kamehameha was once lost at sea off the Falkland Islands, then retrieved and erected on Hawaii's Big Island.

Honolulu has the lowest air pollution of any major U.S. city.

Hawaii's climate is so varied that it offers 11 of the earth's 13 recognized climate zones. Only the Arctic and Saharan zones are missing.

MONTH	JAN	FEB	MAR	APR	MAY	JUN	JUL	AUG	SEP	OCT	NOV	DEC
AVERAGE HIGH TEMPERATURE	25	25	25	26	27	27	28	28	28	28	27	26
AVERAGE LOW TEMPERATURE	19	19	20	21	22	22	23	23	23	23	22	21
AVERAGE PRECIPITATION (IN CENTIMETRES)	10	8	5	5	3	3	3	3	3	5	5	8

Figure 10-1   Climate at a Glance: Honolulu, Hawaii

cool (around 18°C) at night in the winter, and it's liable to shower at any time—though rain is much more likely in the winter, which is, ironically, a peak tourist season. Summer, a time of minimal rain but greater heat, is also busy. Hawaii is least crowded in the spring and especially in the fall. Note: Hurricanes may occasionally reach Hawaii in late summer or early fall.

The weather does vary from place to place. The western, leeward side of each island tends to be dry (it's where most of the lodging is), whereas the windward side and central mountainous areas have more frequent rain. Kauai's tourist areas, especially, are quite wet. And **Mauna Kea** mountain, on Hawaii's Big Island, is snow-capped much of the winter and offers skiing (it's accessed by helicopter). So here's a unique opportunity for a real ski buff who loves the offbeat.

GETTING AROUND

Aloha Airlines (AQ) and **Hawaiian Airlines** (HA) provide inter-island flights, and swarms of small planes and helicopters fly tourists into the scenic but hard-to-access canyons of Hawaii's Big Island, Maui, and, especially, Kauai. Cruise ships act as "portable hotels" on cruises among the islands. Travelling by bus on Oahu is convenient, but for all other islands visitors should book a car rental. Atlantis Submarines provide an unusual way to experience the waters off Oahu and Maui. All manner of rides on outrigger canoes, yachts, and rubber boats can be arranged upon arrival.

IMPORTANT PLACES

Most tourists will already know of **Waikiki Beach,** which lies to the southeast of Honolulu's centre. But spending all one's time here is like visiting Niagara Falls and thinking you've seen Canada. Each of the main Hawaiian Islands offers a unique environment and wonderful experience.

On Kauai, no building is taller than a palm tree.

Seventy percent of all visitors to Hawaii rent a car for at least one day.

Waikiki was originally rocky. Most of its sand was imported from Molokai and, of all places, Manhattan Beach, California.

Oahu

This is the most visited island, the most populated one, the location of Honolulu (the state capital), and a central transportation hub. Most tourists stay in Waikiki, which offers many hotels, stores, and restaurants. (Most business is conducted in downtown Honolulu.) The island's sparsely populated **North Shore** is well known for its surfing. And its windward northeastern beaches, though often cloudy or rainy, are spectacular and uncrowded; on a sunny day they make for a wonderful alternative to the tourist-packed sands of Waikiki. Among Oahu's other principal attractions are:

- **The Polynesian Cultural Center,** near the town of **Laie,** with its villages, crafts, and shows that try to convey Pacific Island life; the presentation is polished and exuberant.

- **Hanauma** [hah-NOW-mah] **Bay,** a paradise for even novice snorkellers.

- **Pearl Harbor,** with its boat ride to the U.S.S. *Arizona* Memorial and to the retired battleship U.S.S. *Missouri*.

- **The Bishop Museum** (with its displays on the geology and culture of Hawaii) and **Iolani Palace** (the only royal palace in the United States), both within Honolulu city limits.

- **Waimea Bay** and **Sunset Beach,** two North Shore areas, with occasionally massive waves and always expert surfers; nearby is the lush **Waimea Valley Audubon Center** and picture-perfect falls.

Maui

An island of condos and resorts, Maui—Hawaii's second–most visited island—features a broad stretch of wonderful beaches along its western coast. Most notable is the **Kaanapali** area, a planned development dotted with numerous resorts and hotels, anchored by **Lahaina** [lah-HIGH-nah]. The island's northeast coast is tropical and spectacular. The island's major airport is at **Kahului** (OGG). Among Maui's attractions are:

- **Lahaina,** an old, picturesque whaling village. At its heart is a giant banyan tree that measures 400 metres in circumference.

- **The road to Hana,** a winding, overwhelmingly beautiful drive past waterfalls, pools, and vine-covered trees.

- **Iao** [ee-AH-o] **Valley State Monument,** a picturesque spot where a major ancient battle took place.

- **Maui Ocean Center,** a marine park with an underwater viewing tunnel.

- **Haleakala,** where a drive to the top offers spectacular views, especially at dawn to see the sun rise. Located in the centre of the island, Haleakala is the world's largest dormant volcano.

Hawaii's Big Island

Vast in size and with a wide variety of scenery, Hawaii's Big Island is a good recommendation for almost anyone (except those who seem chiefly attracted to Waikiki). The western **Kohala** and **Kona** coasts are rapidly developing resort areas. The island's largest city, **Hilo** (ITO), once a prime tourist destination, has somewhat lost its appeal and is now primarily a gateway to the volcanic area. For these reasons, Kona's airport (KOA) has become the choice (over Hilo's) for most tourists. Among the attractions are:

The statue of King Kamehameha near Iolani Palace, Honolulu

○ Rent a car on Oahu for at least one day and drive around the island, perhaps pausing at the beaches on the North Shore or the windward side.

○ Oahu's shopping is especially good at the Ala Moana Center and Ward's Warehouse.

○ Quiet Kailua and Lanikai beaches, on Oahu's windward coast, are considered by some to be the best beaches anywhere.

○ There are no billboards in Hawaii. A 1926 law banned them.

○ At the Big Island's Kealakekua Bay is a 528-square-metre area that was deeded to Britain for a monument to Captain James Cook. So you can literally swim from Hawaii to England in Kealakekua Bay.

Because of Kilauea's lava flow, Hawaii is the only U.S. state that's still growing.

- **Hawaii Volcanoes National Park,** with its steaming craters, most notably that of active **Kilauea** [kih-lah-WAY-ah]. Tourists should call ahead to find out if they can visit an active lava flow.

- **A drive from Hilo,** across the island's north shore, through the **Parker Ranch** area, and down through the moon-like lava field of **Waikoloa** [why-koh-LOH-ah].

- Many of the Big Island's beaches are rocky. For this reason, it offers fewer water-sport opportunities than do some of the other islands.

Kauai

Kauai is lush, moist, and dramatic—precisely what people picture a tropical island to be. Hotels are concentrated on the somewhat drier **Poipu Beach** area; in the area north and south of **Lihue** (LIH); and in the scenic **Princeville** area on the north shore. Among the attractions are:

- **The Fern Grotto,** with its beautiful fern-lined cliffs and cave. It can be accessed on a short boat cruise up the Wailua River. It's a popular site for weddings.

- **The Waimea Canyon,** a 23 kilometre, Grand Canyon–like spectacle that can be viewed from a road lookout, helicopter, or light plane.

- **The Na Pali Cliffs,** looming majestically over the island's nearly inaccessible northwest coast. Visitors can see them only if they hike, boat, or fly there.

- **Hanalei Bay,** a striking and serene area next to the resort city of Princeville.

Molokai and Lanai

The world's highest sea cliffs are on Molokai.

With their small populations, few attractions, and limited lodging choices, these islands should be recommended only to those who want to get away from it all or who are veteran Hawaii tourists who've seen the other islands. Molokai is famous for its **Kalaupapa** [kah-laow-PAH-pah] **National Historical Park,** once the site of a famous leper colony and sometimes accessed by a mule trip down a series of cliffs. Lanai, through most of its history, was one big pineapple plantation; it's

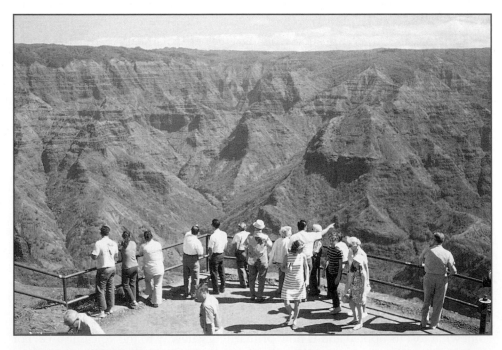

Waimea Canyon, Kauai
Photo by Justus Ghormley

perhaps the only Hawaiian Island where visitors can most easily mix with the locals. Several relaxed but upscale hotels are located on Lanai.

POSSIBLE ITINERARIES

First-time visitors should spend a week on one island or split time between Oahu and another island. More experienced Hawaii travellers may bypass Oahu to see those islands they're unacquainted with. A seven-day, four-island itinerary via cruise ship is a popular option.

LODGING OPTIONS

Virtually every major hotel chain has numerous properties on the islands, though **Sheraton, Hyatt, Hilton, Marriott,** and the Hawaii-based **Outrigger, ResortQuest** (formerly **Aston**), and **Castle** predominate. Sheraton owns many restored historical properties. Hyatt fills its resorts with fine art. Hilton has most of the truly huge resorts. **Ohana** is Outrigger's moderate level brand. ResortQuest and Castle have an unusually wide spectrum of properties, from budget to luxury.

Oahu has the most hotels, nearly all of which are concentrated along Waikiki Beach. Waikiki is a popular recommendation, especially for budget-minded travellers, since lodging is available at all price levels. Hotels and condos on the other islands tend to be somewhat more expensive, with few low-end properties. Maui's hotels are mostly clustered along its western coast, as are those of Hawaii's Big Island. Kauai's are along its wet southern and eastern sides, since the somewhat drier west coast is mostly cliffs. Molokai and Lanai have limited accommodations (though the Lanai properties are quite elegant).

Travellers may already know about certain Hawaiian properties, since several well-publicized hotels and resorts dot the islands. Oahu's list would be virtually endless, though the **Royal Hawaiian,** the **Moana Surfrider,** the **Halekulani,** and the **Kahala Hilton** are best known (and quite pricey). Three huge and extraordinary resort properties are located on the islands: the **Hyatt Regency** and the **Marriott** on Kauai, and the **Hilton** in the Waikoloa area of

Mark Twain once sat under the banyan tree in the Moana Surfrider's courtyard.

Diamond Head, Waikiki, Oahu
Photo by Marc Mancini

Hawaii's Big Island. Also on the Big Island are **Mauna Lani Bay** and **Grand Wailea,** with world-famous reputations for quality, and **Kona Village,** upscale huts perched on stilts.

ALLIED DESTINATIONS

Since the Hawaiian Islands are in the middle of the Pacific Ocean, no allied destinations are nearby. As we mentioned, however, travellers often go on from Hawaii to Southeast Asia, Australia, or New Zealand. There's also the possibility of continuing on to the South Pacific islands, including Tahiti and Fiji.

CULTURAL PATTERNS

A mystery: The first European to "discover" Hawaii was Captain Cook, in 1778. Yet a Spanish map created long before that indicates where the Hawaiian Islands are . . . .

People in Hawaii consume more Spam than do residents of any other U.S. state.

Luaus are touristy but fun. Try the poi (a paste made from taro root).

Even though Hawaii is a U.S. state, its way of life is much more relaxed; jackets and ties, for instance, are rarely worn. Also, visitors shouldn't expect primitive, South Sea Island conditions. Hawaii is a sophisticated, modern destination. Above all, don't refer to the U.S. mainland alone as the United States; Hawaii is also a part of the country. Hawaiians are very sensitive about this.

Hawaiians are becoming increasingly proud of their own history, and this is showing up in hotel decor, accuracy of entertainment, and the like. Visitors could read James Michener's *Hawaii*—or rent the movie based on it—to find out more about Hawaii's remarkable history and culture.

FACTORS THAT MOTIVATE VISITORS

Hawaii is a unique destination within the United States, and as such, there are unique reasons vacationers want to go there:

- They want to visit an exotic and romantic tropical paradise, but one that will still be relatively familiar.
- Hawaii affords a wide selection of accommodations, flights, independent tours, and natural attractions.
- Hawaiian fly-lodge-drive packages, especially those on Oahu, are available at all price levels.
- Hawaii's climate is predictably warm and pleasant, even when it's cold and wintry in Canada.
- Water sports and beach activities are readily available.
- The opportunities to practise other sports, such as hiking, tennis, golf, and horseback riding, are almost limitless.
- Visitors have a choice of the intensely busy nightlife of Waikiki or the more relaxed possibilities of the other islands.

POSSIBLE MISGIVINGS

Though Hawaii is, in many ways, a magical destination, there may be things about it that raise questions in a potential visitor's mind:

- "There's not enough to do." This type of person should be steered to Waikiki, an adventure tour or package, a major outer island resort, a cruise, or (perhaps) an escorted tour, especially if he or she is older and has taken tours before.
- "Hawaii is too touristy." Keep this kind of person away from Waikiki and on the outer islands.

Qualifying the Traveller
HAWAII'S BIG ISLAND

FOR PEOPLE WHO WANT	HIGH APPEAL	MEDIUM APPEAL	LOW APPEAL	REMARKS
Historical and Cultural Attractions		▲		Polynesian culture
Beaches and Water Sports		▲		Many beaches rocky
Skiing Opportunities			▲	Downhill on Mauna Kea
Lots of Nightlife		▲		In hotels
Family Activities	▲			Especially resort hotels
Familiar Cultural Experience	▲			U.S. state
Exotic Cultural Experience		▲		Asian influences are strong
Safety and Low Crime		▲		Petty crime in certain areas
Bargain Travel		▲		Everything from budget to luxury
Impressive Scenery	▲			Mountains, rain forests, seascapes, volcanoes
Peace and Quiet	▲			One of the quieter islands
Shopping Opportunities			▲	Much better in Honolulu
Adventure		▲		
To Do Business		▲		Key role between Asia and North America

- "I've heard it's expensive." Waikiki's budget hotels and low-cost independent tour packages may appeal to this traveller. Free tourist magazines are widely available and contain many discount coupons for food and entertainment.

- "There's nothing left of old Hawaii." Suggest a stay on Lanai or Molokai.

- "There's nothing cultural to see." Many small attractions underscore Hawaii's cultural heritage, but if someone's idea of a great vacation is visiting Europe's museums and cathedrals, Hawaii may indeed not be appropriate.

- "I'm too old to hang out and sun on the beach or at a pool all day." A surprising fact: More than half of those who visit Hawaii say they never spend much time on the beach. This type of visitor may enjoy a packaged escorted tour that involves sightseeing and will keep him or her occupied. Oahu and Hawaii's Big Island are especially appropriate.

- "Locals aren't friendly and there's a lot of crime." There's some resentment and crime against tourists, but it's rarely encountered. A little prudence can lessen the chance of an unpleasant experience.

- "Bugs are everywhere." As with any tropical destination, this is true. In rain-forest areas, the mosquitoes can be ferocious; visitors should take insect repellent. Roaches are indeed numerous; an occasional sighting even in luxury hotels or rental cars can be expected.

SALES STRATEGIES

More than half of the marriages performed in Hawaii are for nonresidents.

Hawaii can be a bargain destination, but often a low-cost hotel or subcompact car can undermine that dream vacation in "Paradise." Offer upgraded lodging; this is especially appropriate for Waikiki, where low-cost hotels may leave much to be desired. Ocean-view rooms are an upgrade that often appeals to guests. And for those going to Oahu for the first time, why not mention the possibility of a second or third island stay? Since they've gone that far, they likely will be receptive to having a longer and fuller Hawaiian experience. Here, knowledge of the distinct character of each island is imperative for a multi-island stay, since people may think that all the islands are the same. Car rentals are extremely useful on all islands. Even Oahu warrants one for at least a day. Up-selling someone to a convertible, jeep, or larger car may be an attractive strategy. And a multitude of cross-sell options (helicopter rides, dinner cruises, luaus, submarine rides, and so on) can often be booked and sold in advance.

About 20 percent more women than men visit Hawaii.

Finally, remember that independent tours and inter-island cruises (most operated by Norwegian Cruise Line) often enable you to secure bargains for visitors while deriving commissions from an entire package of services. There are escorted tours of the islands; such tours often appeal to seniors who prefer not to drive around or to simply bake on the beach.

NAME _____   DATE _____

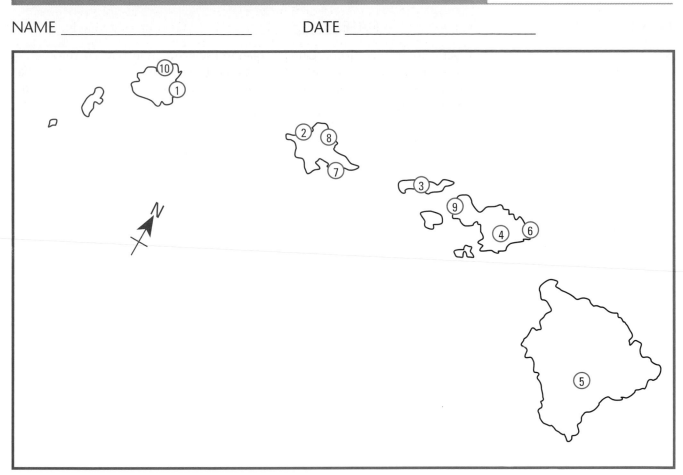

A traveller wants to visit the places listed below. Which number represents each on the map?

PLACE/ATTRACTION	ON WHICH ISLAND?	NUMBER ON MAP
A. Hana	A.	A.
B. The Fern Grotto	B.	B.
C. Waimea Bay	C.	C.
D. A mule trip	D.	D.
E. Princeville	E.	E.
F. The Halekulani Hotel	F.	F.
G. The Polynesian Cultural Center	G.	G.
H. Haleakala	H.	H.
I. Hawaii Volcanoes National Park	I.	I.
J. An old whaling village	J.	J.

CASE STUDY

NAME _____   DATE _____

Sharon and Marc, a couple in their early 30s from Windsor, Ontario, plan to honeymoon in Hawaii. They've been to Waikiki and didn't like it. They once visited Tahiti and loved its tropical splendour. Since this is a special trip, they're not afraid to spend money. They can take off only five workdays, but they want to get away from it all. They also want to stay in only one hotel during their trip.

Circle the answer that best suits their needs.

1. How many days would you recommend for their total trip, from departure to return home?

   Three   Seven

   Five   Ten

   Why?

2. If they went to only one island, which would you suggest?

   Maui   Corfu

   Kauai   Oahu

   Why?

3. If they wanted to see an active volcano, you could cross-sell a day trip air package to which island?

   Lanai   Oahu

   Hawaii   Kauai

   Why?

4. Which of the following would probably not be a good service to offer to book for Sharon and Marc?

   An escorted tour   A helicopter flight

   A hotel suite   First-class air reservations

   Why?

CREATIVE ACTIVITY

NAME _____   DATE _____

You're a reservationist for a large, British Columbia–based independent tour wholesaler to Hawaii. A caller has read an ad in the Sunday newspaper for a competitor's tour. The price is incredibly low: $599 per person, including air and six days in a hotel in Honolulu. The caller wants to know if you have something similar, since she's unfamiliar with the company in the ad, but knows yours well. She'll be travelling with her husband and 10-year-old son. This will be their 12th wedding anniversary.

You know you can't match the price and for a good reason: This is a bare-bones, cheapo trip that would almost surely displease the caller. The hotel might be in a poor location with no view, the available days might not be at a good time, etc.

What five possibilities might you suggest to the caller to convince her that you could offer her a trip that would cost more, but would offer so many more pleasing features (and make more profit for your company via your up-selling and cross-selling)?

For example: "We could offer you a hotel that's right on the beach and a room with an ocean view. Wouldn't that be much nicer? And it would cost you only $29 more per night."

1.

2.

3.

4.

5.

TRAVEL TRIVIA

SURPRISING FACTS ABOUT HAWAII

- Hawaiians didn't invent the ukulele. The Portuguese brought it to them in the 1880s.

- A new volcanic island is now forming underwater off the coast of the Big Island. It already has a name: Loihi.

- Though the first Pacific islands were "discovered" by Europeans in the early 1500s, the Hawaiian chain wasn't reached by them until 1778.

- Grass skirts aren't native to Hawaii. Micronesian immigrants brought them in the 1880s.

- The majority of Hawaii's land is owned by the U.S. government and by the descendants of five missionary families.

- The famous song "Aloha Oe" was written by Hawaii's last reigning monarch, Queen Liliuokalani.

American Potpourri (East)

Pretend you're a British tourist. What would be the best place to visit in North America? A city? An entire province or state? A manmade attraction? A natural wonder? The point is this: North America is a continent of vastly diverse attractions. There's something for just about everyone.

In the preceding chapters, you've read about major tourist centres in Canada and the United States. However, dozens of other locations we haven't mentioned yet are fiercely appealing to tourists. Indeed, this chapter and the next address many of the most popular cities in the U.S., including New Orleans, Chicago, Atlanta, Santa Fe, Seattle, and Las Vegas.

What follows isn't a compendium of every popular tourist attraction. Some, though wonderful, simply won't be places you'll be called on to book often. Others are visited mainly by business travellers, or by tourists who know the area well enough that they won't come to you for help.

There's a lot of information to digest about the U.S. That's why we've divided American Potpourri into two chapters: East and West. Read each chapter slowly and carefully. Highlight as many important points as possible. Follow along on the regional maps.

THE SOUTH

In many ways, it's unfair to gather all the southern states not covered in previous chapters into one collection, but we can make some generalizations about the South. Its many major cities have convenient air service, and an excellent network of highways criss-crosses the area. In fact, driving may be the best way to see the region.

The South's climate is generally temperate, especially along the coasts of the Atlantic Ocean and the Gulf of Mexico. Summers can be uncomfortably hot and humid; winters are chilly at worst, but pleasant. Spring can be a particularly beautiful time throughout the region—the magnolia blooms are legendary. Fall is very nice as well, but hurricanes and rain may occasionally interfere with the trip.

The South has many forests, rivers, and hills, especially where the southern **Appalachian Mountains** are prominent. Hiking, camping, and fishing are popular activities. The South is, in general, a rural land of quiet small towns; however, there are several sophisticated cities. Elegance, pride, and a strong sense of history are what the South is all about.

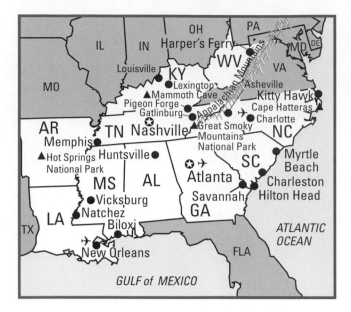

Important Places

The commercial, transportation, and convention gateway to the South is **Atlanta,** Georgia (ATL). Many other cities have large airports, including **Charlotte,** North Carolina (CLT), and **New Orleans,** Louisiana (MSY).

Among the most popular areas in the South are the following, listed clockwise by state, starting with Georgia:

- **Atlanta, Georgia.** This affluent, cosmopolitan city has impressive cultural venues for symphony, ballet, and theatre; the fascinatingly designed **High Museum of Art;** the many Olympic sports facilities; lovely magnolia tree–lined streets; and **Stone Mountain Park,** with its plantation, riverboat, small museums, and huge mountain carving of Confederate leaders. At the **Martin Luther King, Jr. National Historic Site,** visitors can attend services at the church where Dr. King preached.

- **Savannah, Georgia.** A beautifully restored and preserved city, Savannah has retained much of the charming heritage of the Old South. There are several museums and countless buildings in a three kilometre national landmark district that predates the U.S. Civil War.

- **The U.S. Space and Rocket Center.** This is one of the largest space museums in the country and is located in **Huntsville.** Alabama is noted for its grand old homes and wide spectrum of outdoor recreational activities.

- **Natchez, Mississippi.** This city boasts hundreds of pre–Civil War mansions that are best visited on one of the city's "pilgrimage" tours. (They occur only during certain seasons.)

- **Biloxi, Mississippi.** Gaming had made this port city a popular destination. However, Biloxi suffered serious hurricane damage in 2005. It is in the process of rebuilding.

- **Vicksburg, Mississippi.** Vicksburg is famous for its military park commemorating the famous U.S. Civil War battle.

- **New Orleans, Louisiana.** A 2005 hurricane and subsequent flooding devastated this low-lying city. It has already begun rebuilding itself and eventually will return to what made it one of the world's unique cities, with a strange, heady mixture of elegance, raucousness, great Dixieland jazz, and internationally renowned cuisine. The **French Quarter** is home to much of the city's entertainment, shopping, and dining. (It suffered little damage from the hurricane.) **Jackson Square** is the Quarter's focal point, and **Preservation Hall** features nightly jazz performances. A world-class aquarium is located here, and day and multi-day riverboat cruises are very popular. There are also tours of the surrounding bayou swamps and old, graceful plantations. The Tuesday before Ash Wednesday is when the spectacular, wild **Mardi Gras** festival is held. The astonishing floats used in the festival are then stored in a vast series of warehouses, called **Mardi Gras World,** an attraction open to the public.

- **Hot Springs National Park, Arkansas.** This famous resort has long been a favourite of vacationers. The **Ozark Mountains,** in northern Arkansas, have equally dramatic scenery and spas.

- **Nashville, Tennessee.** Nashville proudly calls itself "Music City USA," home of country music. Here's where tourists will find that great showcase for country-western music, the **Ryman Auditorium** (former home of the Grand

The airport at Charlotte, North Carolina, was one of the first airports to have rocking chairs.

Underground Atlanta is a subterranean shopping, entertainment, and dining area on the original 19th-century site of the city.

The world's oldest Holiday Inn is located in Clarksdale, Mississippi.

Try a *beignet* at the Café Du Monde in New Orleans.

Alma, Arkansas, the "Spinach Capital of the World," prominently displays a statue of Popeye.

Mardi Gras in New Orleans, Louisiana
Photo by Justus Ghormley

Ole Opry); the immense **Opryland Hotel** and adjoining **Opry Mills** (a huge entertainment and shopping mall); and a first-rate **Country Music Hall of Fame.** President Andrew Jackson's home, the **Hermitage,** is nearby, and the **Parthenon** (an almost exact reproduction of the one in Athens) sits in a Nashville park.

- **Memphis, Tennessee.** Like Nashville, this city is best known for its contributions to America's musical heritage. **Beale Street** boasts an active nightlife and many "blues" cafés. **Graceland,** the legendary home of Elvis Presley, features two of Elvis's private jets, a collection of his cars, his outrageously decorated mansion, and his burial site.

- **Pigeon Forge, Tennessee.** This town is home to the **Dollywood Theme Park** and a spectacular yearly "Winterfest" of lights. Pigeon Forge and nearby **Gatlinburg** (another quaint town) are just north of the **Great Smoky Mountains,** one of the most visited national parks in the United States.

- **Mammoth Caves National Park, Kentucky.** With its 480 kilometres of massive underground caves, this attraction is the world's largest cave system. Kentucky's two key cities, **Lexington** (famous for its horse farms) and **Louisville** (home of the Kentucky Derby), are gracious and charming.

- **Harpers Ferry, West Virginia.** This historic city is where John Brown made his ill-fated attempt to arm a slave rebellion. To its west are some of the South's most beautiful outdoor recreation areas.

- **Cape Hatteras National Seashore, North Carolina.** Cape Hatteras features remarkable scenery and excellent beaches. The Wright Brothers made the first plane flight from nearby **Kitty Hawk.**

- **Asheville, North Carolina.** Location of the largest home in the United States, the 250-room **Biltmore House,** built over 100 years ago by George Vanderbilt.

- **Hilton Head Island, South Carolina.** With 19 kilometres of superb beaches, wind-swept scenery, and countless opportunities for water sports, Hilton Head is one of the most popular resorts in the country. Like **Myrtle Beach,**

Ducks parade twice a day in the lobby of the Peabody Hotel in Memphis.

Paducah, Kentucky, is famous for its quilts.

Greenbrier, a luxury resort in West Virginia, has a once-secret military base buried beneath it.

another resort in this state, it draws golfers, tennis players, and families looking to vacation.

- **Charleston, South Carolina.** Charleston is one of the most elegant and charming cities in the United States; the **Battery** is its historical district of beautiful antebellum houses. **Fort Sumter,** where the first shots of the U.S. Civil War were fired, is off the coast. Tourists often visit the spectacular plantations and gardens that are near Charleston.

Sales Considerations

The Southern United States appeals strongly to travellers looking for music-themed experiences, water sports, historic sites, and a genteel way of life. The many offshore islands that stretch from Virginia through the Carolinas and down the coast of Georgia provide remarkable settings for a number of outstanding resorts.

The South offers convenient jumping-off points to other vacation spots. West Virginia is a gateway to Washington, D.C., Philadelphia, New York City, and beyond. Louisville is not far down-river from Cincinnati; in fact, Kentucky borders not only Ohio but also Indiana and Illinois. Louisiana is an excellent extension of a trip to Texas. And any of the coastal states could lead to a Caribbean holiday. Atlanta is a major destination for business travellers, so popular hotels should be booked ahead of time. All hotels should be booked far in advance for those interested in visiting New Orleans during Mardi Gras. Several river- and sea-going cruise ships call New Orleans their home port.

Remember: The South's great charm, strong tradition of preserving history, splendid outdoor recreation areas, and vital urban centres can each attract a different kind of traveller.

THE MIDWEST

The Hamburger Hall of Fame is in Seymour, Wisconsin.

The Midwest is what the region is best known as, but to some, this may seem like a misnomer. At the area's eastern end, Ohio could almost be considered a part of the East. Missouri was a part of the South during the U.S. Civil War. Even the area's westernmost boundary barely reaches the centre of the country. Perhaps a tourist might be more comfortable calling the region the Prairie States, but even that doesn't fully apply to much of the territory. And so, the Midwest it is.

Without question, the centrepiece of the Midwest is **Chicago,** Illinois, the third-largest city in the United States. Not only is it the major gateway to the region, but also its **O'Hare International Airport** (ORD) is one of the busiest in the United States. (Chicago's **Midway Airport** [MDW] is an alternative.) However, there are many other large Midwestern urban centres set within rich farmland and beautiful forests. Parts of Minnesota, Wisconsin, and Michigan are a bit hilly, offering some winter skiing possibilities, but for the most part the Midwest is flat.

It's very easy to fly into the Midwest, with major terminals not only in Chicago but also in **Detroit,** Michigan (DTW); **Milwaukee,** Wisconsin (MKE); **Cleveland,** Ohio (CLE); **Cincinnati,** Ohio (CVG); **St. Louis,** Missouri (STL); and **Minneapolis–St. Paul,** Minnesota (MSP). The highway network is excellent for car or bus travel; however, since the region is so very large, distances might make that prohibitive. Chicago is also the major hub of train travel in the country.

The Midwest can be hot in the summer and somewhat humid; winters can get quite cold and snowy. Spring is rainy and usually chilly. Fall is beautiful, especially when the leaves change.

An important note: Though such states as Minnesota and Michigan have beautiful and popular recreation areas, they depend mainly on local Midwesterners for their tourism. Scenic as they are, they're not likely to be destinations you'll deal with as often as others.

 Michigan has more lighthouses (116) than any other U.S. state.

Important Places

Beginning with Illinois in the centre and going clockwise from Missouri at seven o'clock, the most popular attractions in the Midwest include:

- **Chicago, Illinois.** This huge, cultured city is the Midwest's focal point. There's a world-class symphony, the renowned **Lyric Opera,** the **Goodman Theater** repertory, and **Second City** comedy—all centrepieces of its strong theatre community. Moreover, the city has superb museums. The most notable: the **Museum of Science and Industry,** one of the world's finest, with hands-on exhibits, an indoor farm, an underground coal mine, and a German U-2 submarine among its huge collection; the **Art Institute,** with its famous French Impressionist wing; the **Field Museum of Natural History;** and the **Shedd Aquarium.** The city also offers great shopping on the **Magnificent Mile** along North Michigan Avenue, and excellent ethnic cuisine.

Try deep-dish pizza where it was invented: Chicago.

- **Lincoln Country, Illinois.** This is the region where Abraham Lincoln lived. It includes **New Salem,** where Lincoln grew up and made his famous long walk to return a book, and **Springfield,** the state capital and Lincoln's home. The high-tech **Abraham Lincoln Presidential Museum** has recently opened in Springfield.

- **Hannibal, Missouri.** This charming town was Mark Twain's boyhood home.

- **St. Louis, Missouri.** The "gateway to the West" for 19th-century pioneers is commemorated by the famous **Gateway Arch.** The city's ornate cathedral has the largest collection of mosaics in the world.

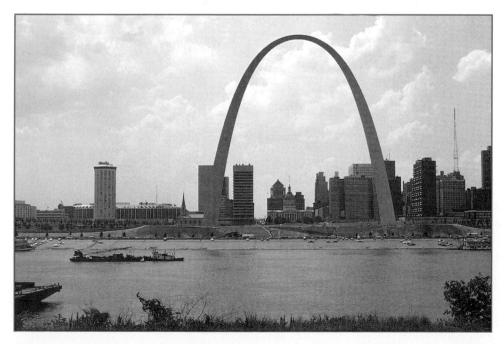

The St. Louis Arch, St. Louis, Missouri
Photo by Justus Ghormley

The most popular act in Branson is Japanese violinist Shoji Tabuchi.

Eskimo Pies were invented in Onawa, Iowa.

The Mall of America, with its 400 stores covering an area greater than 78 football fields, is in Bloomington, Minnesota. More people visit it each year than Walt Disney World.

Madison, Wisconsin, has the world's oldest continuously operating radio station (WHA).

- **Branson, Missouri.** This small town attracts millions of visitors a year with more than 30 entertainment venues. It's nestled in one of the most scenic areas of the Ozark Mountains. Visitors usually fly into Springfield, Missouri, then drive to Branson. Branson is one of the United States' most popular motor-coach tour destinations.

- **The Amana Colonies, Iowa.** This is a communal society of seven small towns founded by a strict European religious sect. There are good cultural museums, and excellent local food and crafts are available.

- **Minneapolis–St. Paul, Minnesota.** The twin-city area is justly proud of its excellent symphonies, opera, and theatre, especially the famed **Guthrie Theater.** Also here are a great zoo and several noteworthy museums. St. Paul celebrates a famous **Winter Carnival** each February.

- **Milwaukee, Wisconsin.** The most important city in the state has a new, architecturally daring **Milwaukee Art Museum.**

- **The Wisconsin Dells.** An hour north of the state capital of Madison and northwest of Milwaukee, this is an extremely popular recreation area where the Wisconsin River runs through scenic cliffs. Other impressive Wisconsin recreational areas include **Lake Geneva** and the **Door Peninsula.**

- **Mackinac Island, Michigan.** A charming and famous resort, the island has retained an Old-World feel. No automobiles are allowed here; people get around in horse-drawn carriages or on bicycles. The ornate **Grand Hotel** is wonderful; its 200 metre porch is legendary.

- **The Henry Ford Museum and Greenfield Village,** in **Dearborn, Michigan.** Some of the country's most famous edifices have been brought here intact, including those of Edison, Webster, the Wright Brothers, and Ford himself. This unique indoor-and-outdoor facility also includes a great collection of classic cars.

- **The Professional Football Hall of Fame,** in **Canton, Ohio.** This museum honours football's greats. Also in Ohio, just north of **Cincinnati,** is **King's Island,**

The State Capitol, St. Paul, Minnesota
Photo by Justus Ghormley

196   **Part II**   North America

NEL

the nation's most visited seasonal amusement park. **Dayton**'s **U.S. Air Force Museum** is the largest of its kind in the world. And Cleveland, on a beautiful lakeside location, is home to the immensely popular **Rock and Roll Hall of Fame and Museum.**

- **Indianapolis Speedway, Indiana.** The famous Indy 500 (Memorial Day), Brickyard 400 (early August), and U.S. Grand Prix (late September) auto races are held here. A museum traces the history of racing.

Martinsville, Indiana, is the world's largest producer of goldfish.

Sales Considerations

The Midwest can be an add-on to a driving trip of southern Ontario; Detroit is just across the border from Windsor. Ferries that take cars across the Great Lakes can save travellers a tremendous amount of driving time. Because it's so spread out, different areas of the Midwest also lead into trips to the U.S. East, the South, and the Great Plains. Chicago is a major business and convention destination, and business travellers may want to extend their visits or even bring their families along. The Midwest can be a particularly good area for those who seek a mix of rural vacation and urban culture.

TRAVEL TRIVIA

WHERE THE BRAND-NAME MUSEUMS AND TOURS ARE

- Corning Museum of Glass, Corning, NY

- Ben & Jerry's, Waterbury, VT

- Goodyear World of Rubber, Akron, OH

- Levi Strauss Museum, San Francisco, CA

- Crayola Factory, Easton, PA

- World of Coca-Cola, Atlanta, GA

- Jack Daniel's Distillery, Lynchburg, TN

- Louisville Slugger Museum and Factory, Louisville, KY

- Anheuser-Busch Museum, St. Louis, MO

- Boeing Aircraft, Everett, WA

- Hershey's Chocolate World, Hershey, PA

- Celestial Seasonings, Boulder, CO

NAME _____   DATE _____

A traveller wants to visit the places listed below. Which number represents each on the map?

PLACE/ATTRACTION	IN/NEAR WHICH CITY/STATE?	NUMBER ON MAP
A. The Rock and Roll Hall of Fame	**A.**	**A.**
B. The French Quarter	**B.**	**B.**
C. Graceland	**C.**	**C.**
D. The High Museum of Art	**D.**	**D.**
E. Mackinac Island	**E.**	**E.**
F. The Hermitage	**F.**	**F.**
G. Fort Sumter	**G.**	**G.**
H. The Museum of Science and Industry	**H.**	**H.**
I. The Guthrie Theater	**I.**	**I.**
J. The Ryman Auditorium	**J.**	**J.**

CASE STUDY

NAME _____ DATE _____

After the terrible damage done by a hurricane, the New Orleans business district and French Quarter are up and running. Most hotels have been reopened and are offering bargain rates to attract visitors back to New Orleans. Marcia Wilkinson's company has taken advantage of this and is holding a three-day business conference there. Marcia is eager to see the "new" New Orleans. The conference ends on a Friday and leads right into the Victoria Day weekend. Marcia's husband, Greg, has rearranged his schedule so that he can do some of his own business there and join her. These successful people in their late 20s have never been to the American South. The last time they did something like this was when Greg had to go to Boston, where they loved travelling around and visiting the historical sites.

Circle the answer that best suits their needs.

1. What attraction would you recommend they see?

   Harper's Ferry   The Ryman Auditorium

   Graceland   Jackson Square

   Why?

2. To where would you suggest they make a day trip?

   Savannah   Natchez

   Charleston   Lexington

   Why?

3. Which would not be an activity that could enhance their trip?

   A trip through the bayous   A one-day riverboat cruise

   A city tour   A trip through the Everglades

   Why?

4. To which historical site should they make an overnight visit?

   Hannibal   Fort Sumter

   Vicksburg Battlefield   Kitty Hawk

   Why?

NAME _____   DATE _____

Jurassic Park is a reality! Scientists have actually found a way to clone dinosaurs. But the investor who bankrolled the research wants to open the park not on an island off the coast of Costa Rica, but somewhere in Canada or the United States.

He has hired you to recommend where it should be located! You are given the following guidelines:

- It must be in a place remote enough that if the dinosaurs escape, they're unlikely to get very far or do any harm before being captured. Yet it must be close enough to lodging, transportation hubs, etc., to guarantee a considerable number of visitors. No tourists will be housed at the park. They'll have to drive, bus, or sail in from somewhere else.

- Climate, terrain, accessibility to foreign tourists, etc., should also be considered.

- You may consider any place in North America, even those covered in other chapters.

TRAVEL TRIVIA

NORTH AMERICA'S MOST SCENIC DRIVES

- Pacific Coast Highway (California Highway 1, U.S. 101), California
- Columbia Gorge Highway (U.S. 30), Oregon
- Coastal Highway (U.S. 1), Maine
- Going-to-the-Sun Road, Glacier National Park, Montana
- Skyline Drive, Blue Ridge Parkway, Virginia
- Million Dollar Highway (U.S. 550), Colorado
- Oak Creek Canyon Drive (U.S. 89), Arizona
- Highway 7, Arkansas
- The Cabot Trail, Nova Scotia
- Route 89, Vermont
- Icefields Parkway, Alberta

Source: Rand McNally Road Atlas *and others*

NAME _____   DATE _____

How's your knowledge of landmarks? Identify the city and/or country that each photo depicts. Write your answer on the line beneath each. Answers are at the bottom of this page.

1. _____

2. _____

3. _____

4. _____

5. _____

6. _____

7. _____

8. _____

9. _____

Photos by Marc Mancini

UNITED STATES

Washington, DC

ATLANTIC OCEAN

PACIFIC OCEAN

GULF of MEXICO

GULF of CALIFORNIA

Lake Superior

Lake Huron

Lake Michigan

Lake Ontario

Lake Erie

Florida Keys

Appalachian Mountains

Rocky Mountains

Cascade Range

Sierra Nevada

Missouri River

Mississippi River

Ohio River

Rio Grande

Colorado River

Lake Powell

Lake Mead

Great Salt Lake

ME
NH
VT
MA
CT RI
NY
NJ
DE
MD
PA
VA
NC
SC
GA
FL
WV
OH
KY
TN
AL
MS
LA
IN
IL
MI
WI
MN
IA
MO
AR
ND
SD
NE
KS
OK
TX
MT
WY
CO
NM
AZ
UT
ID
NV
CA
WA
OR

CHAPTER 12

American Potpourri (West)

In the American West, everything seems extreme: the vast plains, the towering mountains, the huge forests, the endless deserts. Even the cities can be overwhelming. Some of the country's most dramatic attractions, both natural and manmade, are here, too: Mt. Rushmore, the Stratosphere Tower, Yellowstone, and Carlsbad Caverns. Some of America's most extreme people live here, as well.

The American West isn't just about major destinations. It has its subtleties, too—modest places with remarkable personalities: Santa Fe, Sun Valley, Taos, and Telluride. Indeed, the Western U.S. is one of the most diversified and interesting places to visit in the world.

So let's look at those places we left out of previous chapters, those destination gems that warrant a special look.

THE GREAT PLAINS

The Great Plains states are rocky in the north but flatten out toward the south. Winters are cold and snowy, and summers are hot. The farther south you go, the higher the temperatures get. The interstate highway network is good but limited; and because there are fairly long distances between urban centres, driving should perhaps be recommended only to those who want to enjoy the rural scenery. There are no gigantic cities in the region, though **Omaha,** Nebraska (OMA); **Wichita,** Kansas (ICT); and **Kansas City,** Missouri (MCI), are of respectable size and interest. They're the main gateways to the area.

Important Places

The Great Plains region offers some famous attractions. Some of the most recognizable, from north to south, are:

- **Theodore Roosevelt National Park, North Dakota.** The park's badlands offer a beautiful rocky landscape and feature some of the largest bison herds in America. North Dakota is home to many other impressive recreation areas, wildlife preserves, and state parks.

- **Mt. Rushmore National Memorial,** just outside **Rapid City, South Dakota.** One of the country's most familiar tourist sites, Mt. Rushmore is where huge busts of four former U.S. presidents have been carved out of the mountainside. Nearby are three other attractions: **Wind Cave National Park, Jewel Cave National Monument,** and the surreal landscape of **Badlands National**

La Crosse, Kansas, has a barbed-wire museum.

Mt. Rushmore's sculptor originally intended to carve the four presidents' full bodies, not just their heads.

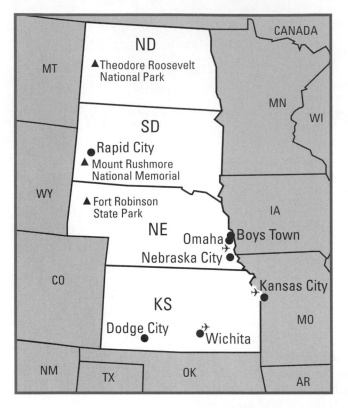

Park. To the north is **Deadwood,** a preserved Old Western town that sits in a canyon and that features gambling. And to the southwest another huge carving is being created: the **Crazy Horse Monument.**

- **Fort Robinson State Park, Nebraska.** This remote park is one of the most interesting in the Great Plains. The site of an old cavalry post, it's strategic to several lovely recreation areas and to intriguing prehistoric fossil beds.

- **Dodge City, Kansas.** The famous Western town, now restored, features the Boot Hill Museum, Boot Hill Cemetery, and historic areas like Front Street and the Long Branch Saloon. Another reconstructed cowboy town is **Wichita Cowtown.**

Sales Considerations

The Great Plains are wedged between the Midwest and the Rocky Mountain states, and offer a handy gateway from Canada. There's a pioneer history and spirit here, which may appeal to certain vacationers, especially Old West buffs. Anyone flying to the Great Plains should consider a car rental, since it's the best way to travel the great distances.

Kansas is 0.9997 flat, making it flatter than a pancake.

North Dakota has the lowest crime rate in the United States.

Oklahoma has one of the largest Native-American populations of any U.S. state.

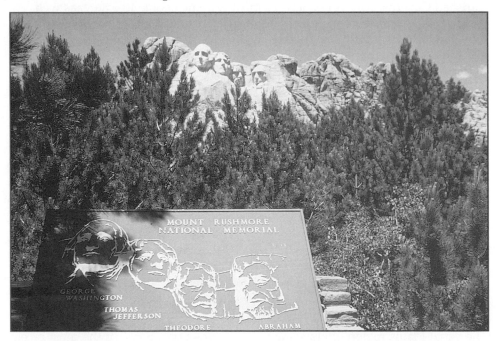

Mt. Rushmore, South Dakota

Photo by Justus Ghormley

TEXAS AND OKLAHOMA

These states are an anomaly. Together or separately, they could be considered part of the Great Plains, the Southwest, or even the South. Because these two states are so closely related, for tourism purposes it's best to look at them together.

Both states are quite hilly, though Texas has long stretches of desert in its southwestern region. The Gulf Coast on the southeast of Texas offers popular resort recreation areas. The climate in these two states is quite hot in the summer, with chilly winters; spring and fall are generally pleasant. Temperatures in Oklahoma are usually cooler. The eastern portion of both states tends to be rainier than the west, which is arid.

Texas is easily reached via major gateways in **Dallas–Fort Worth** (DFW) and **Houston** (IAH), with other airports in smaller markets. **Oklahoma City** (OKC) is the main air route into Oklahoma. A few major interstates criss-cross Texas, but because of the state's size, driving distances are long, and many areas don't have easy access. However, three important cities, Houston, **San Antonio,** and **Austin,** are reasonably close to one another.

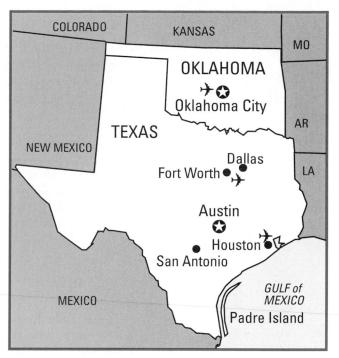

Important Places

Both states are renowned for their strong cowboy traditions. Texas, the second-largest state in the country, offers many attractions, the most popular of which are in Dallas, Houston, and San Antonio. These attractions include:

- **Dallas, Texas.** A cosmopolitan and sophisticated commercial centre, Dallas offers quite a few museums, the popular **Six Flags over Texas** theme park (in nearby Arlington), and a popular **Texas State Fair** in October. Its sister city, Ft. Worth, has some excellent Western art museums. Dallas is linked with the death of President Kennedy, and the **John F. Kennedy Memorial** commemorates the tragedy.

- **Houston, Texas.** The fourth-largest city in the United States, Houston is home to the **Lyndon B. Johnson Space Center,** NASA's training facility for astronauts and tracking centre for space flights (**Space Center Houston** houses the visitors' centre). Houston boasts the world's first indoor stadium, the **Astrodome.**

- **San Antonio, Texas.** This very popular city harbours the legendary centrepiece of Texas's struggle for independence: the **Alamo.** The **Riverwalk** is a unique attraction: A river several kilometres long, lined with dozens of restaurants and nightspots, twists and turns through the city's downtown.

- **Austin, Texas.** The state capital, Austin is famous for its music clubs and is the self-proclaimed bat capital of the world. (At sunset, 1.5 million bats set out for their evening hunting.)

- **Padre Island, Texas.** Actually two separate islands, Padre is made up of a pristine national seashore area and clusters of rapidly developing resort areas. Padre Island is 185 kilometres long and stretches from Corpus Christi to Port Isabel.

- **Oklahoma City, Oklahoma.** The capital of Oklahoma boasts the **National Cowboy and Western Heritage Museum,** with an excellent collection of Old West mementoes.

Sales Considerations

Texas is a logical gateway for those interested in a trip to Mexico. In addition, Houston is within a day's drive of New Orleans. Easily packaged with a trip to the Southwest, the region is particularly well suited for people who like Western history and the rugged outdoors. But don't be fooled: Dallas and Houston are both major urban centres, with sophisticated lodging (Dallas's **Mansion on Turtle Creek** is legendary). An interesting place to stay is at a ranch outside either of these cities.

A car rental is almost essential to get around the Dallas–Ft. Worth area.

Six flags have flown over Texas (thus the amusement park chain name). Whose flags? The United States, Mexico, Spain, France, Texas, and the Confederacy.

"Tex-Mex" cuisine is much spicier than Mexican food found elsewhere.

THE ROCKY MOUNTAIN STATES

Its name clearly defines the region's topography: rocky. From western Canada through the northern border of the United States, this massive mountain range twists down through the Rocky Mountain states. Areas of Montana and Wyoming also contain huge grasslands that spill over from the Great Plains. With its truly wide-open spaces, the area offers some of the most magnificent scenery and distant horizons in the country. The winters get quite cold and snowy, especially in the north, but summers are warm and pleasant. Surprisingly, eastern Wyoming and Montana, as well as southwestern Colorado, can get quite hot in the summer.

Denver, Colorado (DEN), serves as the main entrance into the area for air travellers. Driving, though it accesses dramatic scenery, can be difficult, especially in the winter when many mountain roads may be closed. Even under good conditions, interstate highway connections are few, and distances long.

Important Places

The natural wonders of this area represent many of the top attractions, which include (going from south to north and then turning west to Idaho):

Colorado means "red colour" in Spanish.

Between 1978 and 1992, 12 people were injured by bears in Yellowstone, and 56 by buffalo.

Montana is Latin for "mountainous."

- **Mesa Verde.** In the 13th century, Native Americans built cliff dwellings in the canyon walls of Mesa Verde (Spanish for "green table"). The archaeological sites here are among the best in the country.

- **Denver, Colorado.** With spectacular mountains as a backdrop, Denver has an interesting combination of modernity and Old West past. There are fine museums and excellent nearby skiing. **Rocky Mountain National Park** is 112 kilometres northwest of Denver, and the **U.S. Air Force Academy** is 105 kilometres to the south in **Colorado Springs.**

- **The ski resorts of Colorado.** One of the prime skiing areas in the country, Colorado has dozens of popular slopes, including **Aspen, Vail,** and **Telluride.**

- **Yellowstone and Grand Teton National Parks, in northwestern Wyoming.** Together, these two parks provide some of the most breathtaking scenery to be found anywhere in the world. Yellowstone, whose most famous attraction is Old Faithful geyser, was the world's first national park. Within the park are some fine lodges, which must be booked well in advance.

- **Jackson Hole, Wyoming.** Just south of the Grand Tetons, Jackson Hole is one of the country's top ski resorts. Here, too, is the Snake River, which offers many fishing and rafting opportunities.

- **Devil's Tower, Wyoming.** The United States' first national monument, it was featured in the movie *Close Encounters of the Third Kind.*

- **Little Bighorn Battlefield National Monument, Montana** (formerly known as Custer Battlefield). The famous battle took place here.

- **Glacier National Park, Montana.** With some of the most extraordinary scenery in the United States, the park has dozens of glaciers, hundreds of lakes, a huge diversity of floral life, and herds of virtually every large animal to be found in the country. Together with Alberta's Waterton Lakes National Park, it forms the Waterton-Glacier International Peace Park.

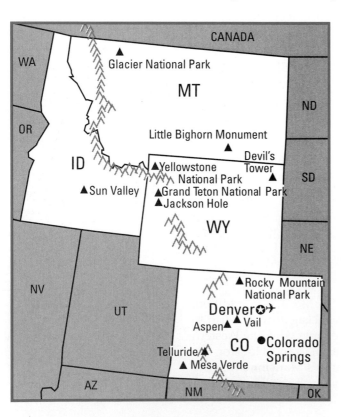

- **Sun Valley, Idaho.** In a region known for winter sports, Sun Valley was one of America's first great ski resorts.

Sales Considerations

Because many of the Rocky Mountain states could easily be considered parts of either the Great Plains or the Southwest, they clearly are excellent places to visit in conjunction with those areas. The great mountain ranges here will particularly appeal to those who ski or appreciate dramatic scenery.

THE PACIFIC NORTHWEST

Oregon and Washington, two of the best-loved states in the U.S., are notable for their lush farmland, rugged coastline, lofty mountains, high waterfalls, and charming towns. The region's coastal strip is especially rainy, particularly from late summer through early spring. The climate is temperate near the coast, but colder in the eastern mountains. **Seattle,** Washington (SEA), and **Portland,** Oregon (PDX), are the major cities here; they're also the major air gateways. Driving along the coast is actually the preferred mode of travel in the region, but venturing to the picturesque outer areas of the states can be more challenging, since the highway network is limited.

Important Places

This region covers only two states, but the overall beauty of the area is impressive. Its highlights include:

- **Seattle, Washington.** This cosmopolitan, beautiful city rests on Puget Sound. The **Space Needle** tower is the city's most recognizable landmark. Next to it is the **Experience Music Project,** an interactive music museum housed in an astonishingly shaped structure designed by architect Frank Gehry. Also part of the facility is the **Science Fiction Museum and Hall of Fame,** with the world's greatest collection of sci-fi movie props. Other attractions include the **Museum of Flight** (perhaps the Pacific Northwest's finest museum), **Pike Place Market, Pioneer Square** (a restored historical district), and, to the northwest, **Olympic National Park.** It's just a few hours' drive or ferry ride from either Vancouver Island or the city of Vancouver.

Oregon's Crater Lake is the deepest lake in the United States.

- **Mt. St. Helens, Washington.** The volcano that erupted in 1980 is now a starkly troubling national monument. Another volcano, **Mt. Rainier,** is a glacier-coated national park.

- **The Oregon Coast.** This area offers a breathtaking drive along the Pacific Ocean. Travellers can take a leisurely trip past grassy dunes, rugged cliffs, national forests, and picturesque towns.

- **Portland, Oregon.** The state's largest city has a restored old town and many impressive rose gardens. Nearby is the road along the **Columbia River Gorge,** with its towering cliffs and ribbon-like waterfalls. Many believe that this is one of the most beautiful drives in the United States. Along the Gorge, on the Washington State side, is **Maryhill,** where a château-like museum boasts a surprisingly rich collection of paintings and Rodin sculptures.

The Oregon Coast
Photo by Justus Ghormley

Sales Considerations

The Pacific Northwest combines naturally with a trip to western Canada. The region is also an excellent jumping-off point for cruises to Alaska. In addition, Oregon borders California to the south, and the Rocky Mountain states and their superb skiing opportunities lie directly to the east. (There's some skiing in Oregon and Washington, too.) River-rafting tours are very popular in the Pacific Northwest. Small cruise ships ply the area's waters.

THE SOUTHWEST

The Southwest is noted for its deserts and arid climate. However, its range of conditions is wider than this. Utah is extremely mountainous, as is the western portion of New Mexico. Summers get blisteringly hot in the desert area, whereas the mountains are cold and snowy in the winter. The major air terminals in these states are **Las Vegas,** Nevada (LAS); **Salt Lake City,** Utah (SLC); and **Albuquerque** [AL-beh-ker-kee], New Mexico (ABQ). It's common to drive from Albuquerque to **Santa Fe,** New Mexico, but most other sites are far apart and require long driving times.

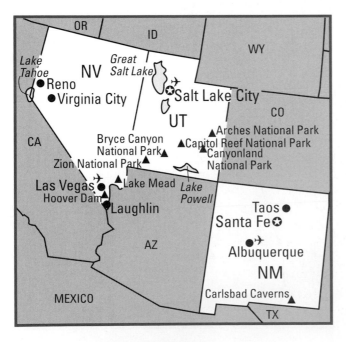

Important Places

The most popular places for tourists in the Southwest tend to be in California and Arizona. However, the remaining states in the region offer some superb attractions. Among them are Las Vegas (profiled in its own section) and the following places:

- **Reno, Nevada.** This little brother to Las Vegas also offers gambling and shows, though on a smaller scale. Reno is near the resort area of **Lake Tahoe** (which also has a few casinos). Other Nevada gambling centres are **Laughlin** (on the Colorado River near Arizona), which caters to an older, budget-seeking clientele, and **Primm** (at the California–Nevada border), which attracts budget-minded families.

- **Virginia City, Nevada.** Museums, mine tours, and mansions are attractions in this old mining town, where visitors stroll a wooden boardwalk street full of shops and saloons.

- **Utah's National Parkland.** Some of the country's most spectacular national parks are in this state: **Zion, Bryce Canyon, Arches, Canyonland,** and **Capitol Reef.** In southern Utah (and northern Arizona) is a popular recreational area, **Lake Powell.**

- **Salt Lake City, Utah.** The capital of Utah, Salt Lake City is the heart of the Mormon religion. The most important buildings are on and around **Temple Square.** Tours of the famous **Mormon Tabernacle** are available. The **Family History Library** is probably the greatest collection of genealogical resources in the world. It's open to visitors of all faiths. Salt Lake City was home to the 2002 Winter Olympics. Superb ski resorts—including **Snowbird, Park City, Deer Valley,** and **Alta**—are close by.

- **Santa Fe, New Mexico.** This absolutely charming capital city is famous as an arts and crafts centre. Native-American crafts are available everywhere; the dining facilities of the city—birthplace of "Southwestern cuisine"—are first rate. From July to August, the city hosts the internationally acclaimed **Santa Fe Music Festival.** To get to Santa Fe, travellers must fly into Albuquerque, then drive or bus to Santa Fe. (Air service into Santa Fe's modest airport is very limited.)

- **Taos, New Mexico.** This artists' colony is also one of the most popular ski resorts in the country. In addition, **Taos Pueblo** is a classic Pueblo village.

- **Carlsbad Caverns, New Mexico.** Its underground rooms (one of them could accommodate 11 football fields) and 34 kilometres of rocky passages carved out of the rock are renowned.

⊙ Many hotel rooms in Santa Fe come equipped with distinctive, funnel-shaped fireplaces.

Sales Considerations

The Southwest region is easily combined with a trip to Mexico or the Rocky Mountain states. The Southwest is of particular interest to those fascinated by Native-American culture. Skiers will be drawn here, as well. Keep in mind that Nevada's gambling cities are extremely popular for weekend trips (hotel rates are much lower on weekdays), and many special packages are available.

⊙ Visitors sometimes sprawl out at the point where Utah, Colorado, Arizona, and New Mexico meet, so they can say they were in four states at once.

Las Vegas, Nevada

A unique, desert-situated spectacle of neon, themed hotels, nonstop activity, and endless entertainment, Las Vegas has become one of the world's most visited cities.

WEATHER PATTERNS. Las Vegas is extremely hot in the summer, with daytime temperatures typically around 38°C. Because it's so dry, however, the heat—at least in short doses and with air conditioning in all buildings—is tolerable. Spring and late fall are much more pleasant. Daytime temperatures in the winter are around 16°C, but nights can be surprisingly cold and rain is a remote possibility.

TOURISM PATTERNS. Summer is somewhat of a shoulder season; late November through January usually sees the fewest visitors (and the best values). The rest of the year is very popular. Year-round, weekends are busier (and more expensive) than weekdays. Las Vegas is one of the country's top convention destinations.

GETTING THERE AND GETTING AROUND. Three- and four-night ITCs from Canadian cities are popular. Once in Las Vegas, visitors without a car can rent one (parking—even valet parking—is usually free), take taxis, or ride the local monorails and buses. Tours to nearby attractions are available.

About 150 couples get married in Las Vegas each day.

WHY PEOPLE GO. Gambling, entertainment, and quick weddings used to be the big draws. They're still very much factors in this town, "a place where you go to do the opposite of what you do at home," as writer David Lansing put it. However, lodging bargains (what you get for your money is often remarkable) and theme park–like hotels have made Las Vegas an attractive place for families. Major shopping venues are everywhere. Most of the large hotels stage lavish production shows and/or host world-famous performers. Dining choices are plentiful: World-class restaurants (with prices somewhat lower than they would be elsewhere), inexpensive coffee shops, fast-food outlets, and some absolutely astonishing buffets are just a few of the options.

Among the best buffets in Las Vegas: The Aladdin (now the Planet Hollywood Casino) and Mandalay Bay (Strip), Rio (off the Strip), and Main Street Station (downtown).

IMPORTANT PLACES. Las Vegas is a city where the hotel-casinos themselves are the attractions. (More about that next.) The 100-storey **Stratosphere Tower** is a more conventional attraction, but it too has lodging, gaming, shopping, amusements, and dining at its base (and some small but scary thrill rides at its top). Nearby are two interesting day trip destinations: the **Valley of Fire** (dramatic scenery) and **Hoover Dam.**

The 10 largest hotels in the United States are in Las Vegas.

LODGING. Las Vegas has over 130 000 hotel rooms and most of the world's largest hotels. Its lodging can be divided into three geographic regions: the Strip, Downtown, and peripheral hotels.

The six kilometre Strip (Las Vegas Boulevard South) features over 20 gigantic hotel-casinos, most of which are dramatically themed. Among them are **Mandalay Bay** (and its "beach" with artificial waves), the **Luxor** (a huge glass pyramid), **New York-New York** (with a scaled-down New York skyline), **Paris Las Vegas** (with its own Eiffel Tower), **Bellagio** (boasting a huge fountain show in its "lake"), **Caesars Palace** (like an ancient, decadent Roman city), the **Venetian** (yes, canals and gondolas), the **Mirage** (with erupting volcano), **TI-Treasure Island** (a show with sirens and pirates takes place in front every 90 minutes), and **Circus Circus** (a family property with rides and circus acts).

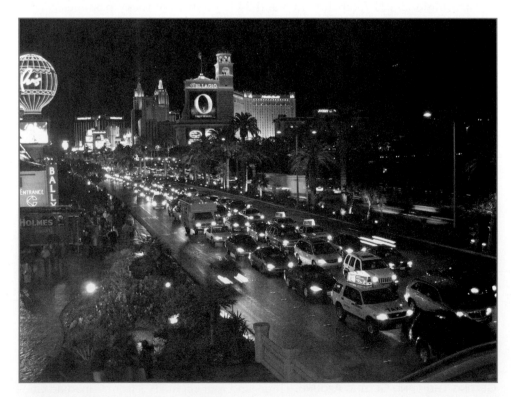

The Strip at Night, Las Vegas, Nevada
Stanislav Khrapov/Shutterstock

The Downtown area has lower-cost lodging and more modest casinos. Four blocks of its **Fremont Street** (seen in countless movies) is covered with a canopy made up of 2.1 million light bulbs that perform hourly sound-and-light shows each evening. There are more hotels and casinos near both Downtown and the Strip. Most of these are budget properties and are more modestly scaled. Two exceptions: the **Rio** (Mardi Gras themed) and the **Hard Rock Hotel** (trendy, with well-known performers).

SALES STRATEGIES. Air-hotel packages are a natural here. Enhanced lodging (e.g., a suite) is often very affordable, as are car rentals.

TRAVEL TRIVIA

TOP TEN SKI RESORTS IN NORTH AMERICA

1. Whistler/Blackcomb, BC
2. Snowbird, UT
3. Vail, CO
4. Squaw Valley, CA
5. Jackson Hole, WY
6. Mammoth, CA
7. Crystal Mountain, WA
8. Big Sky, MT
9. Aspen Highlands, CO
10. Fernie Alpine, BC

Source: Skiing *magazine*

NAME _____   DATE _____

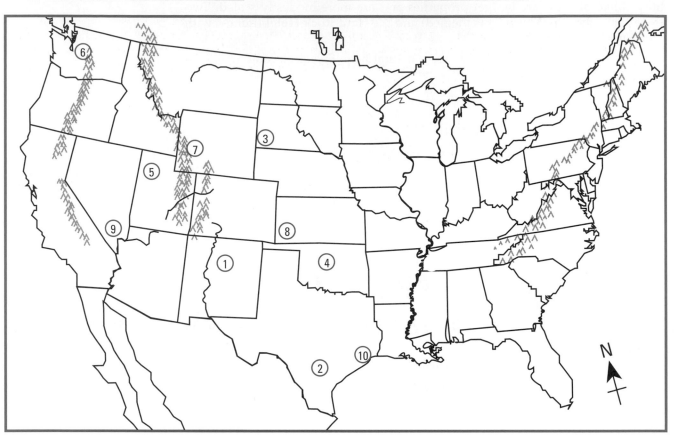

A traveller wants to visit the places listed below. Which number represents each on the map?

PLACE/ATTRACTION	IN/NEAR WHICH CITY?	NUMBER ON MAP
A. Mt. Rushmore	A.	A.
B. The Space Needle	B.	B.
C. Taos Pueblo	C.	C.
D. The Lyndon B. Johnson Space Center	D.	D.
E. Pike Place Market	E.	E.
F. Jackson Hole	F.	F.
G. Boot Hill	G.	G.
H. The Mormon Tabernacle	H.	H.
I. The Alamo	I.	I.
J. A glass pyramid, a volcano, and canals	J.	J.

NAME _____   DATE _____

Tiffany and Grant Mitchell are in their early 40s and live in Victoria. Grant's parents, who live in London, England, are coming to see them in February. Though the parents have travelled extensively and have toured British Columbia with Tiffany and Grant, they've never been to the United States. They've told Grant "they'd like to see something different," so Grant has decided to take them to Las Vegas for three days and perhaps extend that stay to at least one other destination.

Circle the answer that best suits their needs.

1. At which of the following lodging areas should they stay?

    The Strip   The Laughlin area

    Downtown   An off-Strip location

    Why?

2. They should expect weather similar to

    London in February   Frankfurt in November

    Athens in March   Nairobi in April

    Why?

3. What other city might appeal to them and be a real contrast to Las Vegas?

    Reno   Omaha

    Santa Fe   Seattle

    Why?

4. The parents have decided to come in June instead. Which national park might be the most interesting for them and wouldn't overly complicate their trip to Las Vegas?

    Yellowstone   Zion

    Mt. Rainier   Theodore Roosevelt

    Why?

CREATIVE ACTIVITY

NAME _____   DATE _____

You're a documentary filmmaker. You're currently scripting a one-hour special for The Discovery Channel called "America's 'Personality' Cities." You intend to choose 10 cities that have unusual character and distinctiveness. Your first five choices are San Francisco, New York City, Miami, Los Angeles, and Orlando. What would the other five be? Give reasons for your choices.

CITY

1.

2.

3.

4.

5.

REASON

1.

2.

3.

4.

5.

NAME _____   DATE _____

The Matching Game

Directions: Below is a list of places and attractions, some that we have covered and some that we haven't. There are all manner of connections among them. You have exactly 10 minutes to come up with as many connections as possible. (Items may be used more than once.) Write your answers below. Note: There are at least 20 possible connections. For example, the CN Tower and the Space Needle—both are tall towers.

Mt. Rushmore	Padre Island	Miette
Greenfield	Clearwater	High
Hudson	Washington, D.C.	Hilton Head
Yellowstone	CN Tower	Columbia
Aspen	Juneau	Santa Fe
San Diego	Citadelle	Sturbridge
Dulles	Williamsburg	Mt. Vernon
Space Needle	Shenandoah	Branson
San Simeon	Barnes Foundation	Stowe
Huntsville	Vizcaya	Dorval
Orlando	Takhini	Port Everglades
Louisbourg	Mackinac	Whistler
Carlsbad	Cape Kennedy	Ottawa
Monticello	Vancouver	Stone Mountain

UNITED STATES

ATLANTIC OCEAN

Baja Peninsula

GULF of MEXICO

MEXICO

GULF of CALIFORNIA

Sierra Madre Ranges

PACIFIC OCEAN

BELIZE

HONDURAS

GUATEMALA

NICARAGUA

CARIBBEAN SEA

EL SALVADOR

Lake Nicaragua

COSTA RICA

Orinoco River

Lake Maracaibo

GUYANA

SURINAME

PANAMA

FRENCH GUIANA

Canal

VENEZUELA

COLOMBIA

Galapagos Islands

ECUADOR

Amazon

BRAZIL

Andes

PERU

Lake Titicaca

BOLIVIA

Rio Paraná

Easter Island

Atacama Desert

PARAGUAY

Mountains

Rio de la Plata

CHILE

URUGUAY

Rio Uruguay

ARGENTINA

Strait of Magellan

Falkland Islands

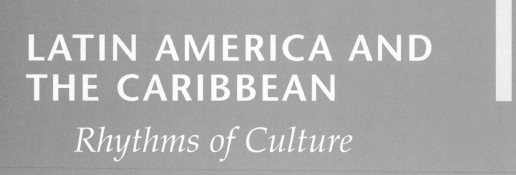

PART III

LATIN AMERICA AND THE CARIBBEAN

Rhythms of Culture

Read this sentence carefully: Mexico is South America's most popular destination, Costa Rica is that continent's hottest new place to visit, and Bermuda is perhaps the Caribbean's most gracious destination.

Find any mistakes? There are three: Mexico is *not* in South America; it's in North America. Costa Rica isn't in South America either; it's a Central American country. And Bermuda, though generally lumped together with the Caribbean islands, is actually in the Atlantic—at about the same latitude as Charleston, South Carolina.

For many of us, Latin America and the Caribbean are little-known, complex destinations. To be able to successfully sell these places, you'll have to bring their assets into better focus. Once you've done that, you'll realize that there's so much to sell: from ancient cultures to magnificent beach resorts; from jungles, islands, and mountains to cosmopolitan cities. The nations we cover in Part III can be as enticing as the pulse of the tango or the beat of a steel drum band.

The world's largest rain forest (the Amazon), driest desert (the Atacama), and longest mountain range (the Andes) are all found in South America.

WHERE THE COUNTRIES ARE

Mexico is the nation just south of the U.S. border. Continuing south (and connecting Mexico to the continent of South America) is the cluster of nations making up Central America. From north to south, they're **Belize, Guatemala, Honduras, El Salvador, Nicaragua, Costa Rica,** and **Panama.** Then comes South America. Except for **Bolivia** and **Paraguay,** both of which are landlocked in the centre of the continent, South America's countries are located almost in a circle along the coast: **Brazil** is by far the largest country in South America (indeed, slightly larger than the contiguous United States), occupying nearly half the continent as it protrudes to the east; continuing clockwise, we have **Uruguay, Argentina, Chile, Peru, Ecuador, Colombia, Venezuela,** and the **Guianas (Guyana, Suriname,** and **French Guiana).**

The geography gets more challenging when we examine the Caribbean islands. In Chapter 14, we'll fully sort out the Caribbean picture for you. For now, you should remember that the Bahamas and Bermuda are not officially part of the Caribbean islands. They're actually north of the Caribbean Sea, in the Atlantic. (They are, however, all generally viewed as part of the same sales market by the travel industry.)

A SATELLITE VIEW

From above, Latin America's landscape seems amazingly diverse. Two of the world's great natural wonders are obvious: the Amazon River and the Andes mountain range. Their impact on the region, as you'll see, is profound. Many lakes also dot the land, wide grasslands sprout up, rivers criss-cross the countryside, even a bleak desert area edges the continent's west coast. And, of course, there are thousands of islands, some floating isolated in the Caribbean Sea, others seemingly broken off from the South and Central American mainland.

Iguazu Falls
Photo by Marc Mancini

Bodies of Water

If you were in the space shuttle, you'd first notice the vast bodies of water flanking Central and South America: the **Pacific Ocean** to the west and the **Atlantic Ocean** to the east. The **Gulf of Mexico** is bordered by Mexico to its west and the United States to its north. Southeast of the Gulf is the **Caribbean Sea,** which opens onto the Atlantic.

Another gulf, though much smaller than the Gulf of Mexico, also stands out from your vantage point: Splitting the **Baja Peninsula** from the rest of Mexico is the **Gulf of California** (also called the Sea of Cortes).

Your eye will likely next be drawn to one of the world's major rivers, the **Amazon.** This mighty river runs from west to east across almost the entire breadth of northern South America, finally emptying into the Atlantic. Many tributaries flow into the Amazon, creating the massive Amazon Basin, which affects much of the continent's (and, for that matter, the world's) weather. It's here in the north that you can see South America's lush, tropical jungles. A few other major rivers are noteworthy. In the south, the **Rio Parana** and **Rio Uruguay** connect to the major estuary, **Rio de la Plata**, which in turn flows into the Atlantic. In the north, Venezuela's **Orinoco River** also empties into the Atlantic, just east of the Caribbean.

A few good-sized lakes interrupt the landscape. In Central America is **Lake Nicaragua.** As you gaze down to northern parts of South America, there's **Lake Maracaibo.** And finally, at the western bend of the continent is **Lake Titicaca,** a

There are no rivers on any of the 700 islands in the Bahamas.

popular resort area between Peru and Bolivia. Farther south, just east of the Andes, is the **Lake District** of Argentina; this is a major resort region.

The southwestern portion of the continent breaks up into a mass of islands (separated at its tip by the **Strait of Magellan**). Far west (3700 kilometres, actually) is **Easter Island,** a fascinating destination. Two other island groupings catch your eye: the **Galapagos Islands** (a popular expedition site), off the northwest coast; and the **Falkland Islands,** off the coast to the southeast, which sometimes serve as a stop for cruises bound for Antarctica.

One final feature is highly significant. Splitting the isthmus connecting Mexico and South America is the manmade **Panama Canal.**

Mountains

From your satellite view, there's only one major mountain range of any note. But what a range: the **Andes** begin in the northwest corner of South America and follow the western coast down to the very southern tip. These mountains greatly influence life in the western part of the continent. A few popular ski resorts can even be found in their southern reaches. One other range is apparent: Two branches of the **Sierra Madres** parallel Mexico's east and west coasts, finally joining south of Mexico City.

Climate

As a rule, the weather in much of Latin America and the Caribbean is hot and humid, with frequent summer afternoon cloudbursts (though winters in the south can get chilly). The Amazon Basin is extremely hot, humid, and rainy year-round. Mexico is also hot, but the central plateau area tends to be more temperate and dry. Mountain temperatures, of course, are colder. And on the west coast of South America, from the northern border of Chile southward for about 970 kilometres, is the **Atacama,** perhaps the driest desert in the world.

Ocean temperatures on South America's east coast are quite warm, though waters off the west coast can be chilly, since the prevailing currents carry water up from the Antarctic. Even the Galapagos Islands, which lie virtually on the equator, are surrounded by surprisingly cool ocean waters.

One other point must be made concerning the area's weather. Much of the region lies south of the equator, which bisects the northern part of South America. As a result, most of the continent has seasons that are *opposite* to those of the Northern Hemisphere: Summer is December through March, and winter (which tends to be the rainiest season) is June through September.

TOURISM PATTERNS

Of all the Latin American countries, Mexico attracts more visitors than any other. As a group, the Caribbean islands are the second most popular.

In South America, Brazil is by far the most visited destination. Second is Peru, with several world-class attractions; Argentina isn't far behind. In recent years, many other Central and South American countries have seen increases in the number of visitors.

LATIN AMERICAN DISTANCES

Because many people think of the region only in terms of its highly popular cities, such as **Rio de Janeiro, Buenos Aires,** and **Acapulco,** Latin America may seem far smaller than it is. In truth, it spills over two continents and covers an area several times greater than that of Canada.

All the major cities have very good air connections, which helps shrink the distances. In addition, many smaller cities within each country can be reached by air, since almost every country has its own national airline. Cruises are one efficient

Each autumn, millions of butterflies fly thousands of kilometres from all across North America to several small areas north and west of Mexico City, where they mate.

In a 1493 decree, the Pope decided which parts of South America should belong to Spain and which to Portugal.

Cruise ships docked in Nassau, The Bahamas
Photo by Marc Mancini

way to see Mexican and Caribbean beach resorts; ships also stop at many ports in Central and South America. A number of Mexican and Caribbean cruise patterns exist; we'll review them in Chapters 13 and 14.

As for South America, three cruise itineraries seem to predominate. The first starts in Florida or a Caribbean island, such as Barbados or Puerto Rico, sails past French Guiana, then up the Amazon River. The second begins from the same area, but bypasses the Amazon and continues down the coast, calling at several Brazilian ports along the way and, perhaps, ending in Argentina or Uruguay. The third is the most ambitious, entirely circling the continent.

There are other ways of getting around, but not all are efficient or comfortable; even when they are, the great distances to be covered may make them prohibitive. Tour travel is recommended.

Rail service, for example, is inconsistent, though there are a few fine and popular routes. Buses are for the more adventurous. In a few instances (usually between islands or through the river-crowded jungles), small boats and ships are the most useful way of getting around. They're slow, of course, but the scenery can be very beautiful.

Driving is always an alternative, too; plenty of rental cars are available. However, again, except for a few short distances over rather well-maintained roads (including the Pan-American Highway), this is a less likely recommendation. Major cities are *very* crowded and in rural areas roads often aren't in good shape; moreover, heavy rains commonly wash out the roads in some places.

Remember, too, that the climate plays an important role in travel. Tropical rains, hurricanes, or snow in the Andes can dramatically affect travel plans.

SOME MISCELLANEOUS CONSIDERATIONS

Latin America has a very distinct culture. Some important factors to keep in mind are:

- Spanish is the national language in most of these countries. (It's called Latin America because Spanish was derived from ancient Latin.) A few exceptions exist: Brazilians speak Portuguese; Belize's and Guyana's national language is English; Dutch is the official language of Suriname; and French Guianese speak French. The Caribbean is an even greater potpourri of languages, and all have been somewhat altered by African and Indian influences. However, English is widely spoken in the major cities and by most travel personnel.

- Some areas in Latin America are off-limits to photography. Visitors must be discreet when taking pictures (especially of government buildings) and when talking about politics.

- Economic inflation is a major problem in many Latin American nations. One way to offset this is by booking packages early, thus locking in prices.

- Political turmoil can flare up in many of these countries, turning an attractive destination into a dubious one. Keep up on the news and consult travel advisories.

- The concept of personal space and time in South America is different from that in Canada. Travellers are often surprised when a South American stands very close to them during a conversation. Though visitors should strive to be on time for an appointment, they shouldn't get offended if someone they are supposed to meet is late; time is very elastic here.

- In some South American countries, such as Chile and Bolivia, it's an insult not to hold eye contact with the person to whom you're talking.

- Crime is, unfortunately, a problem in some Latin American and Caribbean countries. Simple precautions and common sense will avert most predicaments.

- Many people mistakenly believe that all of the Caribbean and Latin America is a bargain. Not true. Venezuela and several Caribbean islands (for example, St. Martin) are somewhat pricey. On the other hand, Brazil, Peru, Argentina, Colombia, the Dominican Republic, and Cuba are bargains.

Market in Cuzco, Peru
Photo by Justus Ghormley

TRAVEL TRIVIA

THE WORLD'S TOP 10 CRUISE DESTINATIONS

1. Caribbean/Bahamas
2. Europe/Mediterranean
3. Alaska
4. Mexico
5. Hawaii

6. Trans-Canal
7. Trans-Atlantic
8. South America
9. Bermuda
10. Canada, New England

Source: Cruise Lines International Association

CREATIVE ACTIVITY

NAME _____   DATE _____

You work for a tour wholesaler that specializes in independent tours to Latin America. Anticipate five possible objections—either real or imaginary—that a customer might have to going to Latin America, then come up with information that might overcome each objection.

CUSTOMER OBJECTION

Example: I don't know Spanish. I'll have trouble being understood.

1.

2.

3.

4.

5.

OVERCOME OBJECTION WITH . . .

English is widely spoken in major cities and by most travel personnel.

1.

2.

3.

4.

5.

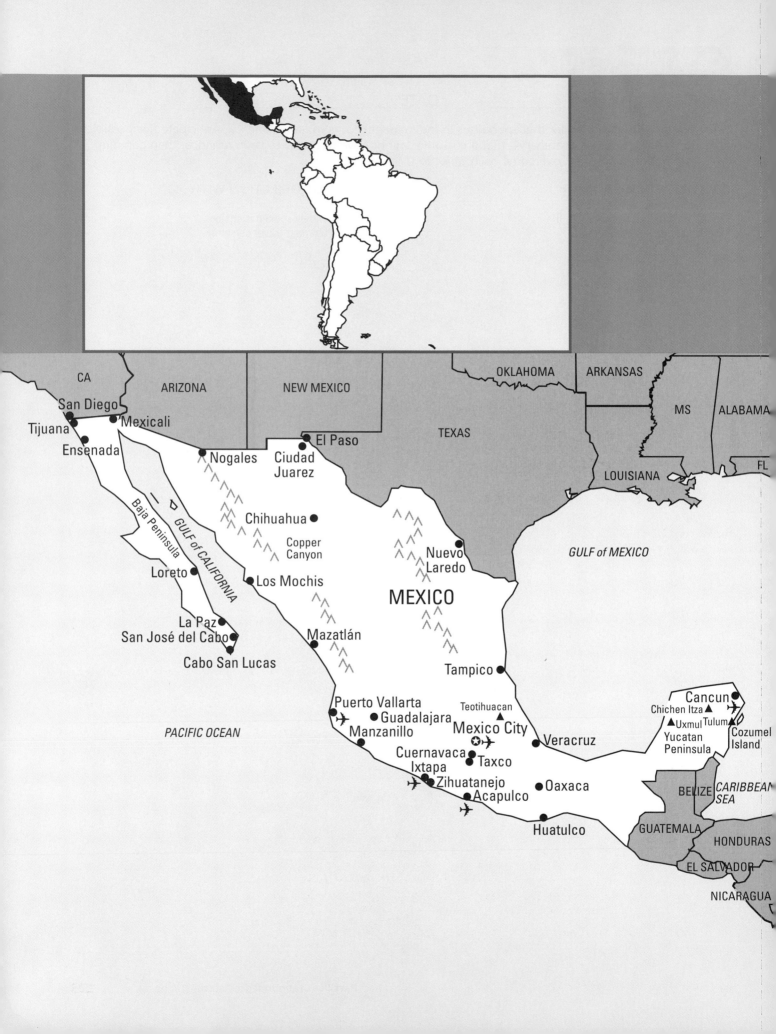

CA

ARIZONA

NEW MEXICO

OKLAHOMA

ARKANSAS

San Diego

Tijuana

Ensenada

Mexicali

El Paso

Nogales

Ciudad
Juarez

TEXAS

MS

ALABAMA

LOUISIANA

FL

Baja Peninsula

GULF of CALIFORNIA

Chihuahua

Copper
Canyon

Nuevo
Laredo

GULF of MEXICO

Loreto

Los Mochis

MEXICO

La Paz

San José del Cabo

Cabo San Lucas

Mazatlán

Tampico

PACIFIC OCEAN

Puerto Vallarta

Guadalajara

Manzanillo

Teotihuacan

Mexico City

Veracruz

Cancun

Chichen Itza

Uxmul

Tulum

Cozumel
Island

Yucatan
Peninsula

Cuernavaca

Ixtapa

Taxco

Zihuatanejo

Oaxaca

BELIZE

CARIBBEAN
SEA

Acapulco

Huatulco

GUATEMALA

HONDURAS

EL SALVADOR

NICARAGUA

CHAPTER 13

Mexico

Tropical Fiesta

Sure, every tourist has heard stories of how you can eat, drink, and dance all night at Mexico's beach cities, then take a siesta all day under the hot tropical sun. But there's much more to the country than that. Mexico, for example, is rich with historical attractions and archaeological sites. There are some drawbacks, though. The biggest problem: Poverty is widespread. Indeed, this may be the greatest misgiving people have about a trip to Mexico.

First, some geography. Mexico is quite large—about one-fifth the size of Canada—and it's not all palm-lined beaches. Mexico is a land of diverse landscapes: craggy canyons and cliffs, vast and arid deserts, dense tropical rain forests, and broad, high plateaux. Mexico is sandwiched between the United States to the north and Guatemala and Belize to the south. To the west are the warm waters of the Gulf of California (also called the Sea of Cortes) and the Pacific Ocean, and to the east are the even warmer waters of the Gulf of Mexico and the Caribbean Sea.

So much water is diverted from the Colorado River that by the time it reaches its mouth at the Sea of Cortes there's no water in it.

MEXICO

Capital: Mexico City

Area (square km): 1 972 400

Time Zones: GMT –6 to –8

Drive on: Right

Population: 106 000 000

Religion: Roman Catholic

Language: Spanish

Currency: 1 peso = 100 centavos

Electricity: 110 volts, 60 cycles AC

Capsule History: Mayas, Toltecs, and Aztecs rule, pre-1519; Cortés conquers, 1519–1521; Mexicans overthrow Spaniards, 1821; war with United States, 1846–1848; French invade and rule, 1861–1867; Juarez is president, 1855 and 1867; Civil War, 1920; major oil deposits discovered, 1975; political unrest, 1996; PAN party voted in, after 70 years of PRI party ruling Mexico, 2000.

For reference sources and suggested lengths of stay, see Appendixes A and B.

It's useful to divide the country into five major tourist areas. The **Baja** [BAH-hah] **Peninsula** stretches southward from California for nearly 1200 kilometres. On the northern part of Baja, just across the California border, is **Tijuana** [tee-WAH-nah], a city that's usually seen as a day trip from San Diego, California. Toward the southernmost tip are several small resort cities: **La Paz, Cabo San Lucas,** and **San Jose del Cabo** (as a group, they're often called **Los Cabos**). To Baja's east and south is a second major tourist destination, the **Mexican Riviera:** a string of resort cities that lines Mexico's long western coast.

The **Yucatan Peninsula,** which curves out from Mexico's east coast, is a third key destination and is often considered part of the Caribbean. **Cancun** [kan-KOON] is its chief resort. The Yucatan is also the location of many of Mexico's most dramatic ruins. West of the peninsula are **Veracruz, Tampico,** and other port cities that are less visited, except perhaps as a cruise stopover. But not all of Mexico's attractions are along the beach. The **Copper Canyon,** in Mexico's north-central area, is a fourth major destination. And the fifth is Mexico's **colonial region,** which includes **Guadalajara, Cuernavaca, Taxco** [TAHS-ko], and **Mexico City,** the nation's capital.

The meteor that helped kill off the dinosaurs probably hit the earth at the tip of the Yucatan Peninsula.

HOW TRAVELLERS GET THERE

Mexicana (MX), the country's national carrier, flies out of several Canadian gateways. (**Aeromexico** [AM], Mexico's other large airline, services the United States, but not Canada.) Quite a few Canadian and U.S. carriers, as well as charter companies, fly into Mexico; some people feel that service will be more reliable on these airlines than on Mexico's own. Unlike many countries, there's no real hub to the Mexican air system. There are enough connections that travellers can just fly into the cities they wish to visit. Among the principal airports: Mexico City (MEX), **Acapulco** (ACA), **Puerto Vallarta** (PVR), **Ixtapa/Zihuatanejo** (ZIH), and Cancun (CUN). Flying time to Mexico City from Toronto is about five hours; to Cancun is four hours.

To take a train, bus, or car into Mexico is usually inadvisable. Its trains and buses leave something to be desired, and driving can be perilous. (Visitors who get into an accident or break a traffic law in Mexico might be detained indefinitely in jail.) Cruises, usually out of Los Angeles or San Diego, are an extremely popular way to see **Ensenada,** Cabo San Lucas, and the Mexican Riviera. Mexico's Gulf-Caribbean ports—especially **Cozumel** and **Playa del Carmen** (Cancun's port)—are stops for cruises, usually on Western Caribbean itineraries.

WEATHER PATTERNS

Most people imagine all of Mexico to be hot and humid. Not so. Mexico City, for example, sits on a high plateau. The city can certainly be warm (though rainy) in the summer, but it's quite cool in the winter, with an average daytime high around 16°C in December. And at almost any time of the year, Mexico City is cool at night. The beach cities are indeed hot and humid in the summer and early fall, with frequent afternoon downpours and an occasional hurricane. (As you can guess, this is the season for travel bargains.) But winter, Mexico's high tourist season, is pleasantly warm and dry (see Figures 13-1 and 13-2). The only exceptions: the smaller resorts along the Baja Peninsula and on the Gulf of California, where winter air and water temperatures can be a bit chilly.

GETTING AROUND

In general, it's best to fly from place to place in Mexico. But there are a few exceptions: The Copper Canyon train ride is a first-rate trip. And several tour companies operate comfortable-enough motorcoach trips between the major beach resort of Acapulco and Mexico City, with stops at interesting towns in between.

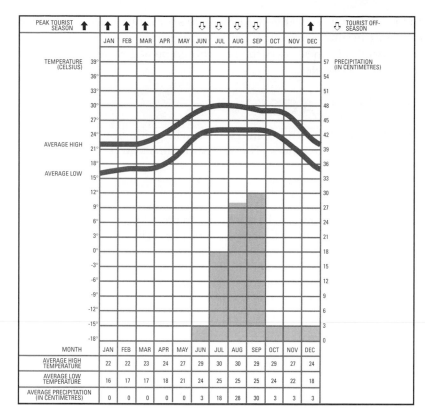

Figure 13-1   Climate at a Glance: Mazatlan, Mexico

MONTH	JAN	FEB	MAR	APR	MAY	JUN	JUL	AUG	SEP	OCT	NOV	DEC
AVERAGE HIGH TEMPERATURE	22	22	23	24	27	29	30	30	29	29	27	24
AVERAGE LOW TEMPERATURE	16	17	17	18	21	24	25	25	25	24	22	18
AVERAGE PRECIPITATION (IN CENTIMETRES)	0	0	0	0	0	3	18	28	30	3	3	3

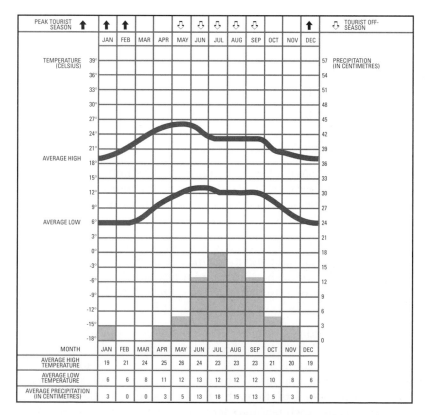

Figure 13-2   Climate at a Glance: Mexico City, Mexico

MONTH	JAN	FEB	MAR	APR	MAY	JUN	JUL	AUG	SEP	OCT	NOV	DEC
AVERAGE HIGH TEMPERATURE	19	21	24	25	26	24	23	23	23	21	20	19
AVERAGE LOW TEMPERATURE	6	6	8	11	12	13	12	12	12	10	8	6
AVERAGE PRECIPITATION (IN CENTIMETRES)	3	0	0	3	5	13	18	15	13	5	3	0

Getting around each city is relatively easy. There's a major subway in Mexico City, though taxis, as in all cities in this country, can be an inexpensive option. Beware: As with most things in Mexico, the fare should be negotiated in advance, especially if the taxi has no meter.

IMPORTANT PLACES

Carefully probe travellers' likes and dislikes. This will guide you in tailoring a Mexican vacation to their preferences. Those destinations you're most likely to deal with follow.

The Baja Peninsula

Visitors who intend to travel from San Diego to Tijuana must prepare to encounter a rundown environment as soon as they cross the border. (They should park their cars on the U.S. side and walk or taxi into town.) Tijuana, though, has become more attractive and isn't a seriously dangerous place, except perhaps at night. Why do people visit Tijuana? To bargain at the thousand little shops, to engage in the nightlife, and to say they've been to Mexico—if only for a few hours. Ensenada, a beach and college "party town" down the coast, is a frequent weekend getaway from southern California, either by car or by three- or four-day cruises out of Los Angeles or San Diego.

The area between Ensenada and the tip of Baja can be an arduous drive. It's better to fly either to **Loreto,** a quiet resort, or to the Los Cabos area, where tourists can visit and swim in several beautiful coves. The big attractions here are the superb deep-sea fishing and the many dramatic resorts that dot the 36 kilometre "corridor" between San Jose del Cabo and Cabo San Lucas.

The Mexican Riviera

Mexico has an astonishing 9600 kilometres of warm, tropical coastline. Most of its famous resorts are along the Pacific coast. From north to south, they are:

- **Mazatlan.** This mid-priced resort has a large harbour that easily accommodates big cruise ships. It's most famous as a fishing paradise, but also offers quite a few nonwater activities, including jungle tours, shopping, an aquarium, rodeos, and well-known Mardi Gras festivities. A ferry crosses daily from Mazatlan to La Paz, on the Baja Peninsula.

- **Puerto Vallarta.** Puerto Vallarta is more active than Mazatlan, with many fine hotels, a market, and superb beaches. Tours into the mountainous interior jungle are popular here, too.

- **Manzanillo.** The beach is small and the lodging choices limited. So why do people go to Manzanillo? Because **Las Hadas,** one of the world's most elaborate and romantic resort hotels, is located here. Deep-sea fishing is also excellent at Manzanillo.

- **Ixtapa** [is-TAH-pah]. A quieter and more exclusive beach resort than either Mazatlan or Puerto Vallarta, Ixtapa is a destination of great beauty. It offers several very good hotels, some shopping, and a few beaches. Nearby is the picturesque fishing village of **Zihuatanejo** [zee-wat-ah-NAY-ho], which also has lodging.

- **Acapulco.** This is the grand old resort of Mexico; it's been popular for many decades. A wall of large hotels lines Acapulco's many beaches; numerous nightspots, countless restaurants, and several moonlight cruises are available. And, of course, there are the famous cliff divers. The city has been spruced up, though beggars and pickpockets still patrol the streets and beaches. If Mexico is a fiesta, Acapulco is its brash featured act.

- **Huatulco** [wah-TOOL-ko]. This, Mexico's newest government-planned beach resort, faces a string of nine secluded bays and 16 kilometres of beach. Snorkelling is a prime activity.

The Yucatan Peninsula

Few destinations combine beaches and history so tantalizingly as the Yucatan Peninsula. Its chief city is Merida, but most travellers never see this bustling in-land urban centre. They usually arrive directly at Cancun. Among the peninsula's attractions are:

- **Cancun,** a vast government-planned seaside resort, boasting glorious beaches, dozens of first-rate hotels, many lively restaurants and nightspots, a wildlife reserve, and clean prosperity. The beach area south of Cancun has developed rapidly as well. Centred on the cruise port of Playa del Carmen, it often goes by the name **Riviera Maya.**

- **Cozumel Island,** not far off the coast from Riviera Maya and Cancun, also offers quite a few resort hotels, though the ambience is a bit more low-key. Cozumel has a few small Mayan ruins and is a haven for divers and snorkellers. It's reached by air, ferry, or cruise ship. In 2005, Cancun and Cozumel suffered considerable damage from a hurricane. However, the Mexican government put a priority on rebuilding the area.

- **The archaeological ruins** that dot the Yucatan, often seen on day trips via bus from Cancun. As dramatic as any in the world, they include **Chichen Itza** (with its well-known ball court and ancient observatory), **Uxmal** [oos-MAHL] (with an astonishingly steep pyramid), and **Tulum** (one of the only major ruins in Mexico to overlook the Caribbean Sea). The other ruins that are becoming increasingly popular to visit: Kabah, Sayil, Labna, Coba, and Dzibil Chaltun.

The Copper Canyon

Almost as dramatic as Arizona's Grand Canyon or Hawaii's Waimea, the Copper Canyon stretches through north-central Mexico. A train ride (which should be booked only through well-known tour operators) starts in **Chihuahua,** in the

The Aztec emperor Montezuma reputedly drank 50 cups of chocolate a day.

On Isla Mujeres (off Cancun), there's a cave where divers can actually pet sharks; the water's natural mineral content makes the fish groggy and therefore unthreatening.

Climbing a pyramid is popular, but the toughest part is coming *down.*

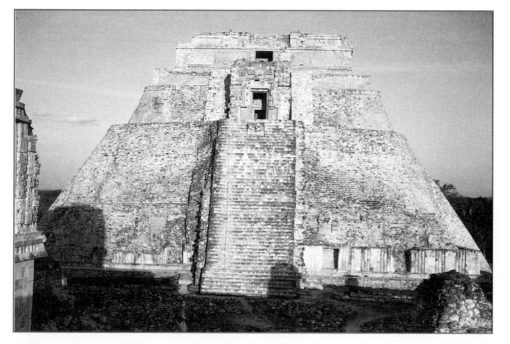

Uxmal
Photo by Justus Ghormley

The Copper Canyon train ride
Photo by William and Marie Rourke

north, and finishes in **Los Mochis,** on the Gulf of California. The multi-day Copper Canyon tours take passengers through dramatic scenery and make stops in various villages and towns along the way. Chihuahua is less than an hour's flight south of El Paso, Texas; Los Mochis is across the Gulf of California from La Paz and a relatively short flight from Mazatlan. In other words, you can easily combine the Copper Canyon trip with stays at Baja and Mexican Riviera resorts.

The Colonial Region

Oaxaca's Camino Real hotel is a converted convent.

Mexico was long a Spanish colony and briefly a French one; remnants of this colonial past mark many of Mexico's inland cities, most of which lie on the country's somewhat cooler central plateau. Among its most popular cities:

- **Guadalajara,** a city of lovely flowering parks, graceful European architecture, and one of Latin America's largest zoos.

- **Cuernavaca,** a charming town inhabited by many retired Americans. It has several interesting buildings, including Cortés's Palace. It's an easy day trip from Mexico City.

- **Taxco,** the "Silver City," often visited on a motorcoach trip between Mexico City and Acapulco.

Each year, on the evening of December 23, Oaxaca celebrates "The Night of the Radishes."

- **Oaxaca** [wah-HAH-kah], the most southerly of the Mexican colonial cities, best known as a centre for arts and crafts. It has an impressive church (**Santo Domingo**), a fascinating museum, and several nearby ruins (especially **Monte Alban**).

Mexico City

Only a few sights of Mexico City's colonial past remain; earthquakes, traffic congestion, exploding population, and smog have seen to that. Yet Mexico City has a European-like, cosmopolitan air that's unique in the country. And it does have many famous, first-rate attractions, including:

- **The National Museum of Anthropology,** one of the world's great museums, with its dazzling collection of Olmec, Mayan, and Aztec artifacts.

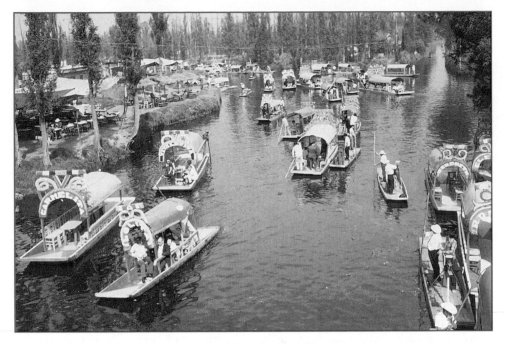

The Floating Gardens of Xochimilco, Mexico City
Photo by Justus Ghormley

- **The Zocalo,** a huge town square bordered by the city's dramatic cathedral and governor's palace.
- **The Floating Gardens of Xochimilco** [so-she-MEEL-ko], a charming attraction that visitors boat through. Popular with locals, it's all that's left of the system of canals that criss-crossed Mexico City in ancient times.

Several **day trips** from Mexico City are popular. The most interesting one takes you to the Toltec **Pyramids of Teotihuacan** [tay-oh-tee-wah-KAHN]—a major archaeological site about an hour away. America's first planned city, it housed 200 000 people in 500 A.D., and covered an area larger than imperial Rome.

The Border Towns

Many tourists envision Mexico through her border towns: Tijuana, Mexicali, Nogales (south of Tucson, Arizona), Ciudad Juarez (across from El Paso, Texas), and Nuevo Laredo (next to Laredo, Texas). Though these dusty, bustling places have their interesting points, they're hardly representative of the rest of Mexico.

POSSIBLE ITINERARIES

Booking a trip to any Mexican destination almost always requires the use of a wholesaler; the package is usually a bargain and Mexican hotels are more likely to honour a reservation made through a large tour company. The itinerary, therefore, will probably be shaped by a prearranged tour package. Mexico City, the Copper Canyon, or the inland colonial cities are almost always combined with a single beach resort in a four- to nine-day itinerary. You can also package together two beach resorts, though it would be good to set up a contrast, say, Acapulco with Ixtapa or Cabo San Lucas. People who prefer to stay at one place can book at a resort for anywhere from a weekend to a week. One-week ITCs to beach resorts are very popular; many are all-inclusive.

LODGING OPTIONS

Lodging in Mexico ranges from super-deluxe properties to budget hotels. To ensure clean, satisfying lodging, favour first-class and deluxe hotels whenever possible. Mexico's mid-priced chains include **Calinda, Fiesta Inn,** and **Real.** Upscale chains include **El Presidente, Krystal, Camino Real, Fiesta Americana,** and **Melia,** along with many prominent Canadian and U.S. hotel groups. Such hotels as Las Hadas (Manzanillo) and **Las Brisas** or **Princess** hotels (Acapulco) are world-famous. Remember: Modified American Plans (MAPs), where breakfast and one other meal are included in the room rate each day, are typical in Mexican hotels during high season.

Three other lodging options are open to travellers. **Club Med** has all-inclusive properties in many Mexican beach cities. Cruise ships offer lodging that moves from one resort port to another. And condos, timeshares, and private homes are a useful option for some.

ALLIED DESTINATIONS

Mexico's east coast resorts combine readily with vacations in the Caribbean, Texas, Louisiana, and Florida. Central and west coast destinations often precede or follow stays in California, Arizona, New Mexico, and Texas. Mexico can also be a stop-off point for journeys into Central and South America.

CULTURAL PATTERNS

Though it borders the United States, Mexico presents unique cultural experiences:

- The custom of *mañana* (putting off a task until tomorrow) persists. Don't confuse this with laziness. Time is perceived differently here; the pace is slower, more relaxed.

- A popular time to do business is during a long lunch. Business is commonly brought up after an extended period of socializing.

- If a traveller visits the home of a local, it's customary to bring a small gift.

- Mexicans give starting times for parties that are rarely observed. If a party is to start at 7 p.m., few will arrive before 8:30 p.m. This is especially true at beach resort cities.

- Almost anything is negotiable in Mexico, especially souvenir purchases. Don't be intimidated; what may seem like impatience, anger, or obstinacy in the seller is simply part of the "game." Counter with a price that's 50 percent of the original quote and work from there.

FACTORS THAT MOTIVATE VISITORS

A wide spectrum of reasons motivate a traveller to visit Mexico:

- The beaches are, in most places, glorious.

- All manner of water-sport options are available.

- Mexico is a shopping and lodging bargain, especially off-season.

- Archaeological treasures are everywhere. (In fact, one estimate claims that the jungle still covers 90 percent of all ancient Mayan and Aztec sites.)

- Air and cruise transportation into and around Mexico is convenient, plentiful, and relatively inexpensive.

- Super-deluxe resorts in Mexico are a bargain compared to similar properties in other parts of the world, especially in the summer off-season.

- The foreign, exotic culture of Mexico is less than a six-hour flight away from many Canadian locations.

- The winter weather is warm, dry, and inviting.

POSSIBLE MISGIVINGS

Mexico elicits both positive and negative reactions in potential visitors. Among the objections you may hear are:

- "I'll get sick." For possible intestinal problems—"Montezuma's Revenge" is genuine—travellers should consult their doctor about medication to take along. (Several over-the-counter remedies are highly effective.) And, of course, they should avoid drinking the water. Even brushing teeth with tap water or having ice cubes in a drink may cause problems. Coffee, tea, canned soft drinks, and bottled wine or beer are generally safe. Instruct travellers never to eat uncooked meats, fish, or vegetables and to eat only fruit that they peeled themselves.

Qualifying the Traveller
CANCUN

FOR PEOPLE WHO WANT	HIGH APPEAL	MEDIUM APPEAL	LOW APPEAL	REMARKS
Historical and Cultural Attractions	▲			Ruins are nearby
Beaches and Water Sports	▲			Warm, clear water
Skiing Opportunities			▲	None
Lots of Nightlife	▲			
Family Activities		▲		
Familiar Cultural Experience			▲	
Exotic Cultural Experience	▲			
Safety and Low Crime	▲			One of the safest Mexican destinations
Bargain Travel		▲		Expensive for Mexico
Impressive Scenery		▲		Primarily seascapes
Peace and Quiet		▲		Active, but not overwhelmingly so
Shopping		▲		Crafts markets
Adventure		▲		
To Do Business			▲	Low in Cancun (but high elsewhere in Mexico)

- "I don't speak Spanish." Many people in major cities and at tourist facilities speak English.

- "Mexico is poverty-ridden." Poverty and its symptoms—crime, corruption, street-begging, and unsanitary conditions—do plague many Mexican cities. Suggest Cancun, which is largely free of such problems. Self-contained mega-resorts such as the Acapulco Princess or Club Meds also can insulate tourists from most of the poverty.

- "The food disagrees with me." Mexican food has great diversity. Familiar North American–style food is available in many places. Nonspicy food is usually available in many locations, especially in the Yucatan.

- "The only time I can afford a Mexican vacation is when it's hot and rainy." Late spring or early autumn is a good compromise: Rain isn't as frequent, the weather may not yet be very hot, and low- or shoulder-season rates may still be in effect.

SALES STRATEGIES

Cruises, all-inclusive resorts, Copper Canyon packages, and high-season hotel MAPs maximize the potential profit from a Mexican vacation. Independent and escorted tours also offer efficient ways to profit from as many components as possible. Diving, fishing, or day-trip excursions can be booked in advance. Because most people are somewhat leery of budget or even moderate-class hotels in Mexico, the possibility to sell them superior or luxury accommodations is strong.

TRAVEL TRIVIA

PLACES WITH UNLIKELY NAMES

- Yucatan, Mexico—The response that natives gave to Spanish explorers who landed here; it means, "I don't understand you."

- Singapore—Means "city of the lion," even though there have never been any lions here.

- Cape of Good Hope—Near the southern tip of Africa, with intensely rough seas.

- Greenland—One of the coldest, snowiest places on earth.

- Iceland—Much less icy (and greener) than Greenland.

- Nome, Alaska—Miscopied from a map that indicated "Name?" at this spot.

- The Pacific—Called this by Magellan, who crossed at a time of no storms; of course, it has many dramatic ones.

- The West Indies—Columbus called the Caribbean islands this name because he thought he had reached the islands off the coast of India.

NAME _____   DATE _____

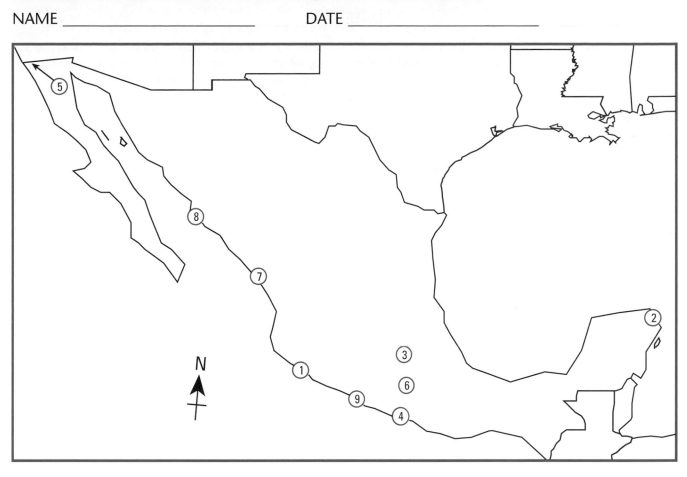

A traveller wants to visit the places listed below. Which number represents each on the map?

PLACE/ATTRACTION	IN WHICH CITY?	NUMBER ON MAP
A. A major Yucatan resort	A.	A.
B. City closest to San Diego	B.	B.
C. Resort near Zihuatanejo	C.	C.
D. The "Silver City"	D.	D.
E. A ferry crosses from La Paz to . . .	E.	E.
F. The Copper Canyon train ride begins in Chihuahua and ends in . . .	F.	F.
G. The Zocalo	G.	G.
H. Las Hadas Hotel	H.	H.
I. Cliff divers	I.	I.
J. Taxco is on the road between Mexico City and . . .	J.	J.

NAME _____   DATE _____

Ray and Connie Hernandez are a young couple in their late 20s. Ray is a successful electrician and Connie is a paramedic. Connie has just read a book, *Heritage of the Maya,* which has prompted her to consider spending an eight-day vacation at a Mexican destination. Ray wants mostly to relax: to enjoy some sun, perhaps do some snorkelling, eat well, and enjoy at least a little night entertainment.

Circle the answer that best suits their needs.

1. Which of the following hotels would be the poorest choice for them?

    Las Hadas   The Calinda in Cuernavaca

    The Acapulco Princess   The Fiesta Americana in Cancun

    Why?

2. Which of the following would be the best destination for them to explore their Mayan heritage?

    Cancun   Acapulco

    Manzanillo   Los Cabos

    Why?

3. Which would probably not be something they should consider?

    A Club Med vacation   A day trip to Chichen Itza

    A cruise   A stay in Mexico City

    Why?

4. Rain would definitely dampen things for the Hernandez couple. What month would be the best recommendation?

    September   April

    February   June

    Why?

CREATIVE ACTIVITY

NAME _____   DATE _____

Mexico has decided to release a series of 10 commemorative stamps that portray tourist-related places, landmarks, and activities for which the country is famous. If you were hired as a consultant, what 10 things would you recommend be put on the stamps? Use the Internet to find photos of your suggestions, with URLs. Be prepared to say why.

1.

2.

3.

4.

5.

6.

7.

8.

9.

10.

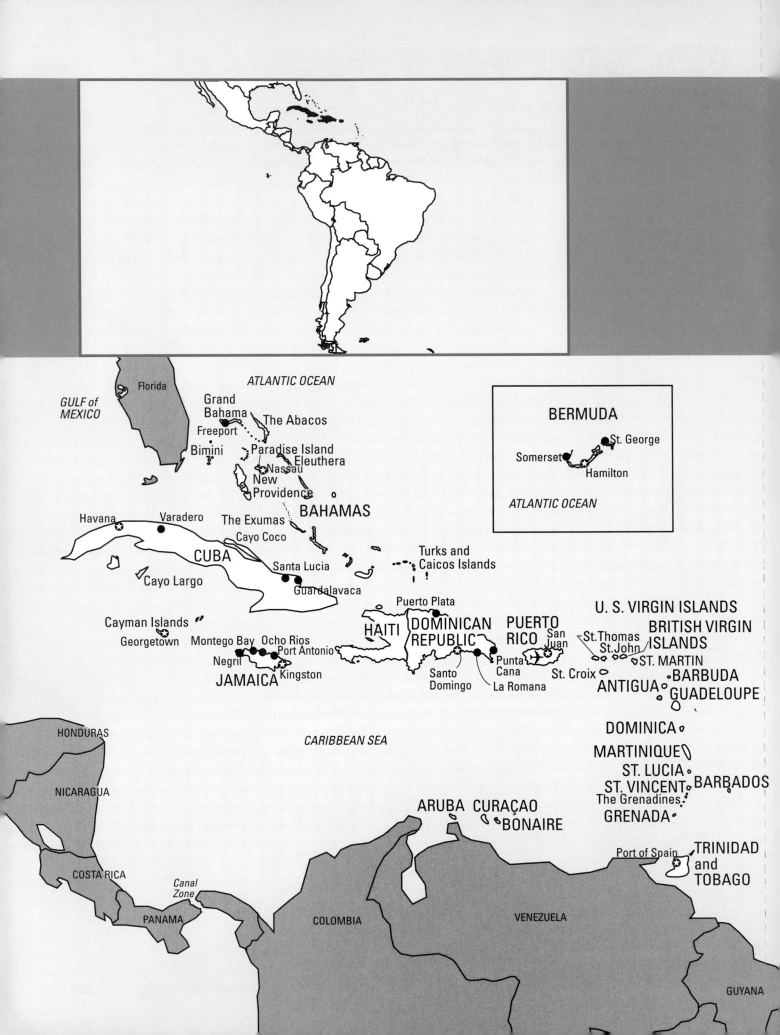

ATLANTIC OCEAN

GULF of MEXICO

Florida

Grand Bahama
Freeport
The Abacos
Bimini
Paradise Island
Eleuthera
Nassau
New Providence
BAHAMAS
The Exumas

Havana   Varadero
CUBA
Cayo Coco
Santa Lucia
Cayo Largo
Guardalavaca

Turks and Caicos Islands

Cayman Islands
Georgetown
Montego Bay   Ocho Rios
Negril   Port Antonio
JAMAICA   Kingston

Puerto Plata
HAITI
DOMINICAN REPUBLIC
Santo Domingo
La Romana
Punta Cana
PUERTO RICO
San Juan
St. Croix

U. S. VIRGIN ISLANDS
BRITISH VIRGIN ISLANDS
St. Thomas
St. John
ST. MARTIN
BARBUDA
ANTIGUA   GUADELOUPE

BERMUDA
Somerset   St. George
Hamilton
ATLANTIC OCEAN

CARIBBEAN SEA

DOMINICA
MARTINIQUE
ST. LUCIA   BARBADOS
ST. VINCENT
The Grenadines
GRENADA

HONDURAS

NICARAGUA

COSTA RICA

Canal Zone

PANAMA

COLOMBIA

ARUBA   CURAÇAO
BONAIRE

VENEZUELA

Port of Spain
TRINIDAD and TOBAGO

GUYANA

14

The Caribbean

A Sea of Nations

Let's face it, it's hard to master Caribbean geography.

Dozens of islands arc across this vast tropical region. Remembering which is where isn't easy. Furthermore, each island may have its own government, culture, value level, range of services and accommodations, topography, and language. To match a Caribbean destination to a traveller's needs takes great skill and knowledge. In this chapter we sort out and organize information about the Caribbean so that you'll feel far more confident about your understanding of the area and your ability to sell it.

A good way to start is to divide the Caribbean into six destination groupings. The first two, **Bermuda** and the **Bahamas,** aren't even part of the Caribbean, though many think of them as such. Bermuda is way off in the Atlantic, at about the same latitude as Charleston, South Carolina, and the Bahamas is a string of 700 islands that stretches southeastward from Florida into the Atlantic (and not into the central **Caribbean Sea,** which is farther south). Geographers label the third cluster the **Greater Antilles** ("greater" because most of the islands are large). Just south and southeast of Florida, they are, from left to right on the map, **Cuba;** the **Cayman Islands; Jamaica; Haiti** and the **Dominican Republic** (which together make up one island, Hispaniola); and **Puerto Rico.**

The fourth set of islands forms a crescent on the Caribbean's eastern side, starting near Puerto Rico and curving gently southward toward the shores of Venezuela. Because of their comparatively small size, they're called the **Lesser Antilles.** Trying to memorize them all would be quite a chore, so we concentrate on the most popular ones. They are, from north to south: the **Virgin Islands, St. Martin, Antigua, Guadeloupe, Martinique, Barbados,** and **Trinidad** and **Tobago** [tuh-BAY-go].

The fifth cluster of destinations is just northwest of Caracas, Venezuela: **Aruba, Bonaire,** and **Curaçao,** often called the **ABC Islands** because of their first letters. The Caribbean destinations forming the sixth group aren't islands at all; they're the mainland cities that encircle the Caribbean, especially those of Mexico, Colombia, Venezuela, Belize, Honduras, and Costa Rica. These latter destinations we treat under their respective countries' chapters.

Two historical notes: The Caribbean islands were once called the West Indies, since early explorers thought that they had arrived in India. And the origin of the word *Antilles* is shrouded in mystery, though it's certainly French and probably means "land near the continent."

HOW TRAVELLERS GET THERE

○ Almost half of all people who take a cruise each year do so in the Caribbean.

Visitors reach the Caribbean islands through major Canadian, U.S., and Caribbean airlines both scheduled and charter; several small commuter airlines companies (most out of Florida); chartered boats; and cruise ships. Cruise vessels have become the principal means of visiting the islands. They usually stop at several major ports and perhaps a few obscure, out-of-the-way ones. Four cruise patterns predominate: Short three- or four-day cruises into the Bahamas, almost always out of Florida; seven-day Eastern Caribbean or Western Caribbean sailings, again usually out of Florida; and seven-day Southern Caribbean cruises, mostly out of Puerto Rico. Longer itineraries also exist, and Caribbean cruises are often the final (or initial) leg of a trans-Canal cruise. Bermuda sailings are in a separate category: Usually seven days long, they generally depart from and return to New York City or Boston.

○ Set aside some local money for the airport departure taxes that are common at Caribbean airports.

Most flights to the Caribbean are from Toronto or Miami, though other mainland cities may serve as a point of departure. Travellers flying to the Caribbean should limit their trip to only a few islands (perhaps all serviced by the same airline). Otherwise, the airfares may turn out to be very high; inter-island flights can be quite expensive, especially when using more than one carrier or small local planes. A cruise is the best bet for tourists who want to visit multiple islands.

WEATHER PATTERNS

○ At one point the Caribbean is over six kilometres deep.

The Caribbean is a year-round destination. Winters are pleasant and dry, though Bermuda gets chilly and the southernmost islands (such as Trinidad and the ABC Islands) can still remain uncomfortably warm (see Figure 14-1 for one example). High tourist season extends from just before Christmas to around April, except for Bermuda, which attracts more people in the summer. Summers can be quite hot and humid almost everywhere in the Caribbean (and even in more northerly Bermuda), with fierce hurricanes tearing through the area mainly from July through

MONTH	JAN	FEB	MAR	APR	MAY	JUN	JUL	AUG	SEP	OCT	NOV	DEC
AVERAGE HIGH TEMPERATURE	30	30	30	31	31	32	32	32	32	31	31	31
AVERAGE LOW TEMPERATURE	19	19	20	21	22	23	23	23	23	23	22	21
AVERAGE PRECIPITATION (IN CENTIMETRES)	3	3	3	3	10	10	5	10	10	18	8	3

Figure 14-1 Climate at a Glance: Kingston, Jamaica

September. For this reason, summer and fall are considered off-seasons, with hotel rates dropping as much as 60 percent. (Again, it's just the opposite for Bermuda.)

Trade winds are important to the Caribbean's climate. They generally blow, as in all tropical regions, from east to west, bringing some relief even on the hottest days. The winds along the southernmost islands (e.g., the ABCs) are especially strong. Those islands with mountains (just about all of them except Bermuda, the Bahamas, the Caymans, and the ABC Islands, which are of coral, not volcanic origin—and therefore flat) tend to be drier on their western and, in some cases, northern shores.

GETTING AROUND

The means of transportation on each island are quite informal: mopeds, jeeps, buses, and car rentals. Off several islands, glass-bottom boats and even mini-submarines take tourists to view the underwater life. When reserving a car rental, remember to check whether the island is one of the many where traffic flows on the left, not the right; some people who normally drive on a trip won't if the driving is on the left. (If the island has a British heritage, it probably has left-side driving.) Remember, too, that tourists aren't allowed to rent cars in Bermuda; it's a way to control traffic.

Charter yachts are a popular way to get around the islands. The yacht-chartering capital of the Caribbean is the U.S. Virgin Islands, though some visitors charter vessels out of other islands or Florida. Generally, there are two options: a **crewed charter,** on which the yachting company provides all staff to operate the boat; and a **bareboat charter,** on which the renters actually do the sailing.

A few things to remember: First, Caribbean destinations aren't exactly into time and efficiency management. Their relaxed way of doing things can lead to lost reservations, especially for car rentals. The renter should have the confirmation number (and maybe even a photocopy of the confirmation, if possible). Second, taxis are very expensive on certain islands; visitors should determine the approximate price before getting in. Third, mopeds are a great way of getting around, but beware: People who aren't used to them frequently get into accidents.

IMPORTANT PLACES

Here's a thumbnail sketch of each major Caribbean and Caribbean-related island destination. There's also a section on some of the minor destinations.

Bermuda

Even though Bermuda isn't part of the Caribbean, it does share much with its southerly neighbours: fine beaches and resort hotels, gorgeous weather and the like. What makes Bermuda special, though, is how it differs from Caribbean destinations: its mixture of temperate and tropical climates (including all manner of vegetation), the surprising combination of formal and informal elements, the neat little houses with white coral roofs, the pink-sand beaches and azure waters that look straight out of a campy 1950s painting.

The coral roofs of Bermuda's houses help capture rainwater for home use.

Remember three things about Bermuda: The hotels are expensive (though less so in the winter); both the air and water are chilly in the winter, when the only bargains can be had; and most visitors get around in taxis or on mopeds because rental cars aren't allowed.

The capital of this English-speaking country is **Hamilton. St. George** and **Somerset** are historical towns. The island is dotted with several modest attractions, including a limestone cave, a lighthouse, and several churches. A politically stable and safe island, Bermuda is ideal for those who want a little formality and culture to go along with their beach vacation. It's also a popular honeymoon, incentive, and convention destination.

Bermuda's 110-metre-tall Gibb's Hill Lighthouse is made entirely of cast iron.

The Bahamas

Only 80 kilometres off Florida's southeast coast, the Bahamas are perfect for those who don't want to travel far from the mainland for their tropical vacation or who are first-time travellers to the area. Though the Bahamian chain is composed of hundreds of islands, only 22 are inhabited and even fewer attract tourists. The most popular Bahamian destinations are:

- **Nassau,** on the island of **New Providence.** This port city offers many opportunities to visit historical places, gamble, and shop (especially in and around its **Straw Market**). **Cable Beach,** 10 minutes from Nassau, is a major beach development with several large resort hotels.

- **Paradise Island,** a complex of resort and gambling facilities, reached by ferry or taxi from Nassau. Paradise Island is sometimes called the Bahamian Riviera. The **Atlantis** mega-resort is an attraction in its own right.

- **Freeport,** on the quiet island of Grand Bahama, another shopping treat. Freeport has no beaches, so to get some sun, tourists have to travel about eight kilometres to **Lucaya Beach** and its world-class golf course.

- **Bimini** [BIM-uh-nee], made famous by author Ernest Hemingway and a legendary place for fishing.

- **The Out Islands,** also called the **Family Islands,** lining the eastern Atlantic edge of the Bahamas. These relaxed and scenic islands are havens for yachting, sports-fishing, and diving enthusiasts. The principal ones are **Eleuthera,** the **Abacos,** and the **Exumas.** A few of the smaller islands have been converted into "private" islands, where cruise ships anchor for the day.

Cuba

Thanks to a considerable number of visitors from Canada and Europe, Cuba has begun to regain some of the lustre it had lost over the past four decades. New resorts continue to be constructed at key spots along its stunning shores, a few of Havana's faded buildings are being restored, and its people continue to be among the most friendly and warm in the entire Caribbean.

Most experts believe Columbus first landed in the New World at San Salvador Island in the Bahamas.

At Ardastra Gardens, you can see the world's only performing flamingos.

Paradise Island's original name was Hog Island.

A 14th-century European cloister was moved to Paradise Island in the 1920s.

Canada is Cuba's largest trading partner and source of tourists.

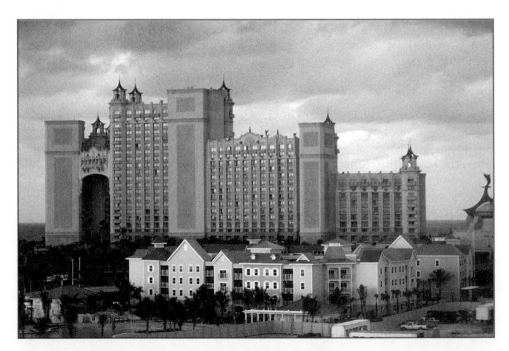

The Atlantis Paradise Island resort, The Bahamas
Photo by Marc Mancini

Cuba is far bigger than most people realize: It's over 1200 kilometres long. It has just about every geographic feature you can imagine: lofty mountains, deep valleys, meandering rivers, aqua waters, and those incredible stretches of seaside sand. There are historic and cultural attractions too, most of which can be found in the **Old Havana** district. The two most popular seaside resorts are **Varadero** (which has the greatest variety of lodging, dining, entertainment, and sports) and **Cayo Largo** (with great water-sports opportunities and a truly superb beach). Smaller but growing resorts are located at **Guardalavaca, Cayo Coco** (an offshore island), and **Santa Lucia.** Who is most attracted to Cuba? Water-sports enthusiasts, bargain hunters, and those interested in an environment that's markedly different from any other in the Caribbean. ITCs are most popular with the Canadian market.

The Cayman Islands

Another legendary place (especially for divers and snorkellers) is the Cayman Islands. It's a great destination, with some quaint (but expensive) restaurants and shops, dozens of water-sport opportunities, but virtually no scenery. (The Caymans are, in fact, large, flat coral reefs.) **Grand Cayman Island** and the capital, **Georgetown,** offer the most conventional diversions, including a **Maritime and Treasure Museum** that displays artifacts taken from the 325 shipwrecks that surround the island. Other Grand Cayman attractions: a **Turtle Farm** and **Stingray City,** where divers can swim with the ominous-looking yet gentle creatures. North of Georgetown is **Seven Mile Beach,** where most resort hotels are located. **Cayman Brac** and especially **Little Cayman** are small, tranquil islands that draw snorkellers, divers, and fishing enthusiasts in droves.

Jamaica

Jamaica, an island of wide terrain variations that's due south of Cuba, certainly has a high recognition factor. That can be both good and bad. Its reggae music, jungle waterfalls, and sweeping beaches have made it a major Caribbean destination. But it also has many social problems. Here's information that will help clarify the picture:

Jamaica was the birthplace of reggae (and of singer Bob Marley).

- **Negril** has become Jamaica's favourite beach. Once a hangout for counterculture types, it has become much more respectable and upscale. Nightlife here, though, is rather limited.

- **Montego Bay** is a major cruise port and air gateway. Shopping and nightlife are good, the **Rose Hall** tour is fascinating, but the beaches are so-so. Lodging here should serve as a base for excursions to the rest of the island, including to the **Blue Mountains** and to **Kingston,** the capital city. (Most travellers who fly into Kingston are visiting friends and relatives or are there on business.)

- **Ocho Rios** is another cruise port, with pleasant beaches, several outstanding hotels, and a dramatic mountain backdrop. Nearby is **Dunns River Falls,** Jamaica's most famous attraction. Here, a river cascades down a series of stone steps that visitors can climb, usually as part of a hand-holding "chain" of people.

- **Port Antonio,** a great beach area, has several minor attractions and one major one: the nearby **Rio Grande,** a river on which tourists can cruise on unusual bamboo rafts. (The shorter raft cruise is preferable; the three-hour cruise is a bit much.) Several other Jamaican rivers feature bamboo raft cruises. Visitors can get to Port Antonio from Kingston by car (a slow 100 kilometre drive), hotel shuttle bus, or air.

- Two hotel hints: Jamaican lodging taxes are very high. Many major all-inclusive resorts are here, including **SuperClubs** and several **Sandals** (for couples only) resorts.

The Dominican Republic

Amber jewellery is a speciality in the Dominican Republic.

Occupying the eastern two-thirds of the large island of Hispaniola is the Dominican Republic, a nation very much favoured by Canadians. The big draws here are the many golf courses, bargain prices, great beaches, casinos, and perhaps the best variety of historical sites in the Caribbean. **Santo Domingo** (the nation's capital, with a restored colonial district), **La Romana** (its **Casa de Campo** resort was designed by Oscar de la Renta), and **Puerto Plata** (home to **Fort San Felipe**) are ports on some Western Caribbean cruise itineraries. **Punta Cana**, a beach destination with several large resorts, is very popular with Canadian ITCs. Visitors who fly there will have plenty of accommodations to choose from: The Dominican Republic has the greatest number of hotel rooms in the Caribbean.

Puerto Rico

The world's largest radio telescope (seen in movies such as *Contact*) can be visited at Arecibo, Puerto Rico.

Two lodging options exist: to stay in bustling and historic **San Juan,** or at the resort beach complexes of **Palmas del Mar, Dorado,** or **Cerromar.** The most popular sightseeing attraction is **El Yunque** [YOON-kay], an 11 300 hectare rainforest. (It's a bit less impressive in the dry summer.) Nearby is **Luquillo Beach,** probably Puerto Rico's loveliest. **Old San Juan**'s historic ambience is worth experiencing, too, as is its adjoining **El Morro** fort. Many visitors are drawn to Puerto Rico's gambling casinos.

The Virgin Islands

Pusser's is a world-famous bar at Virgin Gorda.

One thing to know right away: There are *two* sets of Virgin Islands. The **British Virgin Islands,** sleepy little destinations, appeal primarily to yachters and divers, or to beach-loving vacationers who are seeking to really get away from it all. Two of its better known islands are **Tortola** (a haven for yachters) and **Virgin Gorda,** which features one of the Caribbean's most remarkable attractions, a pile of seaside boulders called **The Baths.**

The Sir Francis Drake Channel, within the British Virgin Islands, offers fantastic sailing.

The **U.S. Virgin Islands** are just west of their British counterparts. Sailing, fishing, and diving are also major attractions here, but these islands are livelier than the British islands. The U.S. Virgin Islands are relatively clean and prosperous. They can be accessed by boat from the British Virgin Islands or San Juan.

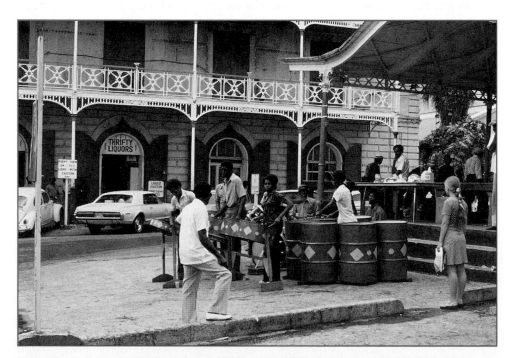

Steel drum band, St. Thomas, U.S.V.I.
Photo by Justus Ghormley

Three principal islands make up the U.S. Virgin Islands. Each has its own character and can be used as a lodging base:

- **St. Thomas** is where most visitors to the U.S. Virgin Islands stay. It's the most developed of the three, with the city of **Charlotte Amalie** [ah-MALL-yah] providing most of the tourist attractions and extensive duty-free shopping. St. Thomas is a convenient port for many cruise ships.

- **St. Croix** [CROY] is quieter than St. Thomas, though it harbours several minor but appealing points of interest. It's also a cruise port.

- **St. John** is the least developed of all. Its campgrounds (in a U.S. national park) are highly popular. St. John has the most dramatic scenery, with dense rain forests, sharp reefs, and extinct volcanoes. Ferries run between St. Thomas and St. John.

 Charlotte Amalie was the name of a Danish queen.

St. Croix is very popular with bicyclists.

St. Martin/Sint Maarten

St. Martin is perhaps the most unusual and satisfying of the Caribbean islands. Both France and the Netherlands govern it. The northern portion is French and the southern portion (where it's spelled *Sint Maarten*) is Dutch, but the island's informality leads to relaxed co-government over the entire island. The south is more commercialized, while the north is more relaxed, upscale, and scenic. There's a little sightseeing to do in St. Martin's two principal towns, **Philipsburg** (Dutch) and **Marigot** (French). But mostly it's the food, shopping, and sun that occupy visitors.

The town of Grand Case features some of the finest restaurants in the Caribbean.

Vacationers can also get away by plane or boat to one of the several attractive (but quiet) nearby islands:

- **St. Kitts:** a lush, flowery place

- **St. Bart's:** with fine beaches, gourmet restaurants, and rolling hills

- **St. Eustatius:** also called Statia, it has several historical points of interest and some good snorkelling areas

- **Saba:** a picturesque blend of seascapes and cottage-dotted hills

- **Anguilla** [an-GWILL-ah]: a favourite of many frequent Caribbean visitors for its fabulous beaches

Antigua

Usually pronounced "an-TEE-gah," not "an-TEE-gwah," this lush, tropical island and major cruise destination claims that it has a beach for every day of the year: 365. Antigua is well developed for its size, with many good hotels and casinos, and one unique historic attraction: **Nelson's Dockyard** at **English Harbour.** In the 18th century, Antigua was homeport to the British Caribbean naval fleet; Admiral Lord Nelson commanded it from English Harbour, which has been energetically restored by the Antiguans. Another attraction is sparsely settled **Barbuda,** a coral island 48 kilometres north of Antigua that boasts pink sand beaches reminiscent of those on Bermuda. Those who like sailing, diving, and get-away-from-it-all beaches may like a stay on Antigua. Many tourists visit it as part of a cruise itinerary.

Guadeloupe and Martinique

Both of these islands have much in common: French culture, volcanoes, deep green scenery, and so-so beaches. For those who want French ambience to go along with their water activities, both islands will be intriguing.

The largest cities, **Pointe-à-Pitre** (Guadeloupe) and **Fort-de-France** (Martinique), are *not* where most visitors stay. They're hectic and a bit run down. Major resort hotels aren't far away, though, and the all-inclusives are an excellent option,

For hikers, Guadeloupe offers the most extensive and well-maintained trails in the Caribbean.

especially since lodging and food can be quite expensive in the French West Indies. An island in this area for those who want a quieter tone: lush **Dominica** [doh-mih-NEE-cah], with waterfalls, mountains, and a boiling lake.

St. Lucia

Picturesque **St. Lucia** [LOO-shah] has excellent beaches and a well-known sight: the twin mountain peaks of the **Pitons.** Tourists can also visit an active volcano, mineral baths, plantations, a rain forest, and forts. The island is popular with honeymooners, hikers, bikers, bird-watchers, golfers, and water-sport enthusiasts. **Castries** is the capital and main cruise port.

Barbados

Barbados is the Portuguese word for "bearded ones." (The island's fig trees have a beard-like appearance.)

Most of the Caribbean islands have been tourist destinations for only a few decades. Not so Barbados. This most easterly of the Antilles has been attracting tourists for centuries. So it's not surprising that Barbados offers many small but fascinating historical attractions (including several plantations), as well as the usual great beaches, water-sport opportunities, small golf courses, and an underground wonder, **Harrison's Cave.**

Most people stay on the island's warm west Platinum Coast shore; the east can be windy and rainy. Who will most like Barbados? Those who want the calm, prosperous ambience of a very British, surprisingly formal island. Indeed, Barbados is quite reminiscent of Bermuda, but on a smaller scale.

Trinidad and Tobago

Mention these islands and you're sure to elicit visions of steel drum bands, calypso music, and limbo competitions. Among the Caribbean islands, Trinidad is one of the liveliest and most prosperous, with a broad selection of international cuisine, entertainment, and shopping. Nearby Tobago, on the other hand, is a quiet, fantasy-like desert island, accessed by ferry or flight.

Trinidad and Venezuela to the south are involved in oil exporting. This is where steel drums originated.

The locals in Trinidad seem friendlier to tourists than most, perhaps because poverty is less of a problem here. (But there is occasional unrest.) The principal city, **Port of Spain,** is filled with architectural surprises. The rest of Trinidad is best explored by car rental. Most of Trinidad's hotels are up in the hills, rather than on the island's only adequate beaches. Most of the upscale lodging is on Tobago.

The ABC Islands

The branches of *divi-divi* trees (on the ABC Islands) grow horizontally because of the strong winds.

Just north of Venezuela are Aruba, Bonaire, and Curaçao [koor-ah-SOW], the ABC Islands. Two things about these tidy little islands are surprising: They're very dry and desertlike, rather than lush; and they combine Dutch and Hispanic influences in a most unusual cultural blend. Aruba is best known for its fine beaches and casino-resort hotels, Bonaire for its superb dining and diving, and Curaçao for its fine dining, extensive shopping, and **Grotto of Hato** caves. Its beaches are only so-so.

The Portuguese gave Curaçao its name because sailors were *cured of* scurvy there.

Lodging choices are very good in Aruba and Curaçao, but limited in Bonaire. There are casinos on all three; the ABCs are quite popular among gamblers. Many flights connect the mainland to Aruba; fewer are available to Curaçao and Bonaire. Inter-island flights and ferries are also available.

Miscellaneous Islands

Here's a list of some of the less visited islands in the Caribbean:

- **Haiti,** on the western side of Hispaniola, is poorer and politically more unstable than its neighbour, the Dominican Republic. Its blend of French and African cultures, though, is intriguing. Haiti has become the folk-art capital of the Caribbean. Attending voodoo ceremonies is becoming a common tourist activity.

The waterfront, Willemstad, Curaçao
Photo by Justus Ghormley

- **Grenada** [grah-NAY-dah] (not to be confused with Granada, a city in Spain) is a sleepy little island with excellent beaches and a wide variety of water-sport activities. It's just north of Trinidad and Tobago, in the southern portion of the Lesser Antilles. Its nickname: The Spice Island.

- **St. Vincent and the Grenadines** are a collection of more than 100 islands, 160 kilometres west of Barbados. These casually formal destinations have great beaches, snorkelling, yachting, and a broad variety of volcanic landscapes.

- **The Turks and Caicos Islands** are, geographically, a southeasterly extension of the Bahamas (but under a different government). They have some of the same features of the Bahamas, but without the crowds. They're ideal for those who seek an isolated getaway or superb diving and yachting opportunities.

In the Turks and Caicos Islands, there are giant frogs called "mountain chickens."

POSSIBLE ITINERARIES

Since many people visit the Caribbean as part of a cruise, their itineraries will be predetermined. Other travellers might like to combine a stay on one island with a side excursion to another island. Remember, though, that air or sea connections between islands aren't always convenient. Concentrate on islands that are easily combinable yet contrasting: St. Martin with, say, Anguilla; Barbados with St. Vincent; or Antigua with Barbuda. Keep in mind that Caribbean cruises don't visit only islands but also mainland ports, especially in Central America. They also may visit ports that border the Gulf of Mexico, rather than the Caribbean. Also remember that the Caribbean isn't just about sightseeing. It's very much about *doing* things, too, like diving, playing golf, riding in a mini-submarine, hiking, kayaking, sailing, and biking.

Bermuda has more golf courses per square kilometre than any other nation.

LODGING OPTIONS

A few things to remember: First, good rooms are hard to get during high season; for last-minute types, a cruise is often the best option (if space is still available). Second, booking the highest affordable classification possible is usually best; budget lodging in most of the Caribbean is dicey. Third, more all-inclusive properties are located in the Caribbean than anywhere else in the world. The quality is relatively dependable, the activities endless, the beaches good, and the price (especially on some of the islands where food is costly) a bargain. Virtually every Caribbean island has at least one all-inclusive resort.

Most international hotel chains also have presences here. The two best-known lodging groups are Sandals and SuperClubs (SuperClubs has three main "brands": **Breezes, Grand Lido,** and **Hedonism.** The Atlantis mega-resort, on Paradise Island, Bahamas, is the largest hotel in the Caribbean area.

ALLIED DESTINATIONS

The Caribbean islands are a natural extension of a visit to Miami, New Orleans, Houston, Mexico, or South America. Disney Cruise Lines offers cruises combined with a stay at a Walt Disney World property—ideal for families wishing to cruise the region. And, of course, the islands are natural allied destinations for one another, as long as the air or sea connections are convenient.

CULTURAL PATTERNS

Montego Bay was once called the Bay of Lard.

The relaxed pace of the islands is renowned. This will present an especially unusual environment for business travellers.

- Though informality marks most of the Caribbean, some of the islands have a reputation for showing a genteel, conservative side, as well. For example, visitors shouldn't wear clothes that are too casual wherever they go; a few restaurants and nightspots may even require a jacket and tie for men and dresses or skirts for women.

- Those interested in experiencing the local lifestyle closely, perhaps even staying with a family, might consider either the **People-to-People** program in the Bahamas or the **Meet the People** program in Jamaica.

- A number of colourful festivals occur throughout the year in the Caribbean. The three most famous: the Bahamian **Junkanoo** (a Mardi Gras–like celebration on December 26 and January 1, but often beyond that), Trinidad's **Carnival** (just before Ash Wednesday), and Jamaica's **Reggae Sunsplash** (a music festival in August).

FACTORS THAT MOTIVATE VISITORS

Why do people visit the Caribbean? Here are some reasons:

- A tropical island stay beguiles almost anyone.

- The region features a wide variety of cultural experiences.

- No area in the world has more cruise options.

- The diving, fishing, and yachting possibilities are virtually endless.

- Many all-inclusive resorts dot the islands, as do several super-deluxe hotels.

- The weather is almost always warm.

- Several of the islands offer a great deal of nightlife and gambling opportunities.

- Shopping and lodging bargains are possible, especially in the off-season.

POSSIBLE MISGIVINGS

As popular as the Caribbean is, some people will have concerns:

- "The islands are unsafe." Political unrest and petty crime plague some of the islands, but in most destinations, serious problems arise only once in a while. Those worried about this should visit more stable islands, such as Bermuda or the Bahamas.

- "What about hurricanes?" For those with this concern, the winter months or cruises are popular; ships can usually reroute their itinerary in response to a hurricane's predicted path.

Qualifying the Traveller
THE CARIBBEAN

FOR PEOPLE WHO WANT	ANTIGUA	ABC IS.	BAHAMAS	BARBADOS	BERMUDA	BR. VIRGIN IS.	CAYMAN IS.	CUBA	DOMINICAN R.	GUADELOUPE	HAITI	JAMAICA	MARTINIQUE	PUERTO RICO	ST. LUCIA	ST. MARTIN	TRINIDAD	U.S. VIRGIN IS.
Cultural Attractions	✓	✓	✓	✓	▲	✓		✓	▲	✓	▲	▲	✓	▲		✓	▲	
Lots of Nightlife		✓	▲	▲				✓	✓		▲	▲		▲			▲	✓
Familiar Cultural Experience			✓					✓						✓				▲
Safety and Low Crime	✓	✓	✓	▲	▲	✓	✓	✓							✓		✓	
Impressive Scenery	✓			✓	▲	✓		✓	✓	▲		▲	✓	✓	▲	✓		✓
Peace and Quiet	✓	✓	✓	✓		▲	✓				✓				✓	✓		✓
Shopping Opportunities		▲	▲	✓	▲		✓	✓		✓	✓	✓	▲	✓		▲	✓	▲
Gambling	✓	▲	▲					✓	✓	✓			✓	✓		✓		
Sailing	▲		▲		▲								✓		✓	✓		▲
Diving	▲	✓	▲	▲	✓	▲	▲	✓		✓	✓	✓	✓		▲	▲	✓	▲
Fishing	✓	✓	▲	✓	✓	✓	▲	✓	▲	▲	✓	▲	✓	▲	✓	✓	✓	▲
Friendly Locals	▲	▲	✓	▲	✓	✓	✓						✓	✓	✓	✓	▲	✓
Cleanliness	✓	✓	✓	▲	▲	✓	▲									▲		✓
Golfing		▲	✓		▲				▲			▲		▲				✓
Hiking			✓					✓	✓	▲		▲	▲	✓	▲		✓	✓
To Do Business		✓	▲		✓	▲								✓		▲	▲	✓

✓ = Better than Average ▲ = Excellent

- "Lying on a beach bores me." Cruises or all-inclusive resort lodging take care of that. Islands such as the Bahamas, Bermuda, Jamaica, Puerto Rico, and Trinidad are more lively than most.

- "Do they speak English?" About a third of the islands in this area are English-speaking. French, Spanish, and Dutch are spoken on other islands, but people involved in tourism usually speak English.

- "Aren't the islands rather dirty?" Poverty and squalor do plague a few of the islands, especially those with a Spanish or French heritage. The situation is better in many of the U.S.- or British-influenced destinations, such as Bermuda, Barbados, the Caymans, or the Virgin Islands.

- "Aren't many islanders resentful of tourists?" On some of the poorer islands, the constant flood of affluent visitors provokes a quiet—though apparent—resentment. On some of the smaller islands, such as Antigua, friendliness is the norm.

SALES STRATEGIES

Few destinations offer as many sales opportunities as the Caribbean. Cruises and all-inclusive resort packages yield commissions on virtually everything the traveller will do. Yacht charters, a popular option for many, can be booked in advance. Submarine excursions, helicopter flights, and dive packages can also be pre-arranged. Because of poverty, crime, and unrest, visitors usually offer little resistance to deluxe lodging. Car rentals are popular on some of the larger islands. (Taxis are the mode of choice on the smaller islands.)

TRAVEL TRIVIA

THE TOP HONEYMOON DESTINATIONS

1. Hawaii
2. Italy
3. Tahiti
4. Anguilla
5. Fiji

6. St. Lucia
7. Mexico
8. St. Barts
9. Jamaica
10. France

Source: Modern Bride *magazine*

NAME _____   DATE _____

A traveller wants to visit the places listed below. Which number represents each on the map?

PLACE/ATTRACTION	ON WHICH ISLAND?	NUMBER ON MAP
A. Negril	A.	A.
B. Nassau	B.	B.
C. Georgetown	C.	C.
D. Hamilton	D.	D.
E. Dutch and French culture	E.	E.
F. The easternmost part of the Lesser Antilles	F.	F.
G. St. Thomas	G.	G.
H. Nelson's Dockyard	H.	H.
I. El Yunque	I.	I.
J. Sister island to Tobago	J.	J.

CASE STUDY

NAME _____   DATE _____

Vickie and Larry Minkoff, who live in Brandon, Manitoba, want to go to the Caribbean to celebrate their 10th wedding anniversary. They want to get completely away from it all, though Vickie wouldn't mind at least two nights on a second island with plenty of nightlife. They have a week off from work. They're both experienced divers.

Circle the answer that best suits their needs.

1. Which island should be their principal, get-away-from-it-all destination?

   Nassau   Trinidad

   Little Cayman   Jamaica

   Why?

2. What relatively nearby island could serve as the lively second destination?

   Cuba   Tobago

   Jamaica   Anguilla

   Why?

3. Which of the following would probably be most appealing to them?

   A cruise   A four-day car rental

   A week at Club Med   Upgraded accommodations

   Why?

4. Which would be the most likely month for bad weather?

   March   September

   May   November

   Why?

CREATIVE ACTIVITY

NAME _____   DATE _____

Slogans are a key to promoting destinations. For example:

      Korea: More Than Seoul!

      Mexico: Something Old, Something New

      New Orleans: Come Join the Parade

Invent a clever and evocative slogan that could help sell each of the following destinations:

DESTINATION	SLOGAN
1. Bermuda	1.
2. The Bahamas	2.
3. St. Martin	3.
4. Aruba	4.
5. The Caymans	5.
6. Puerto Rico	6.
7. Grenada	7.
8. Trinidad	8.
9. Martinique	9.
10. Jamaica	10.

CHAPTER 15

Brazil

Where Everything Sizzles

What do people imagine when they think about Brazil? The blistering temperatures along the Amazon River? The frenetic Carnival atmosphere of **Rio de Janeiro**? Such sizzling images come easily to mind, but they're only part of the picture.

Brazil is a huge country. Larger than the contiguous United States, it covers almost half of the South American continent. Visitors to Brazil will encounter dazzling diversity: lush rainforests (so dense in places that sunlight can't even reach the ground); some of the world's greatest beaches (on 7408 kilometres of coastline, more than 1.5 times the distance from Montreal to Vancouver); and warm, cosmopolitan cities.

Brazil is shaped a little like a triangle, with the base at the top. The northern region's largely jungle landscape is dominated by the **Amazon,** arguably the longest river in the world. **Belem** is at the Amazon's mouth; **Manaus** is located in the interior, just upriver on the Amazon's major tributary, **Rio Negro** [NAY-gro]. Northeastern Brazil conveys a strong African influence, centred primarily in the city of **Salvador,** located in Bahia province. The southeast is the cultural, commercial, and industrial heart of the country: There you can find the joyous spirit of Rio de Janeiro and the international business of **Sao Paulo,** one of the largest

BRAZIL

Capital: Brasilia

Area (square km): 8 510 974

Time Zones: GMT –5 to –3

Drive on: Right

Population: 186 100 000

Religion: Roman Catholic

Language: Portuguese

Currency: 1 real = 100 centavos

Electricity: 110 or 220 volts, 60 cycles AC

Capsule History: Claimed by Portuguese, 1500; Dutch invade Brazil, 1630, and are driven out, 1654; Portuguese royal family lives here, 1808–1821; independence and monarchy, 1822; republic proclaimed, 1889; revolution, 1930, Vargas becomes dictator; Vargas overthrown, 1945; capital moved from Rio to Brasilia, 1960.

For reference sources and suggested lengths of stay, see Appendixes A and B.

Capitol buildings, Brasilia
Photo by Justus Ghormley

cities in the world. Brazil's southern tip is where most of its agriculture and coffee-growing is found. And finally, the central and western regions are largely lush wilderness, with the capital, **Brasilia,** at the centre. Though a modern, unusual city, Brasilia attracts few tourists.

⊚ Brasilia is laid out in the shape of an airplane.

The national language is Portuguese. Portuguese is indeed different from Spanish, but those who do speak Spanish should be able to get along fairly well (especially when reading signs, menus, and the like). English is widely spoken in the major cities.

HOW TRAVELLERS GET THERE

Brazil's national airlines are **Varig** (RG) and **VASP Airlines** (VP), but several other foreign and domestic carriers also serve the country. **Galeao International Airport** (GIG) in Rio is the main gateway into the country. Rio's domestic airport is **Dumont Airport** (SDU). There are also two major airports in Sao Paulo: **Guarulhos International Airport** (GRU) and **Viracopos International Airport** (VCP). Flying time is 10 hours from Toronto and 8 hours from Miami (where connections to Brazil are often made). In addition, Brazil has extensive air service throughout the country, with airports at most major destinations (including Manaus, by the Amazon). Another way to reach Brazil is via a long cruise from Miami, San Juan, or even New York City.

WEATHER PATTERNS

Brazil experiences three climate patterns. The Amazon Basin, which includes Belem and Manaus, has a year-round temperature range of 23 to 31°C, with high humidity and rain most of the year. (The period from June through November is less rainy.) The plateau area (where **Iguazu Falls** is located) can be hotter, but there's less rain and humidity, and nights can be cool. There's almost no rainfall here from May through September. The coastal region (e.g., Rio) is a little cooler (low to high 20s), with sea breezes to offset the humidity. Rain comes here from October through May, though showers can occur anytime (see Figure 15-1). Reminder: In most of Brazil, the seasons are opposite those in North America.

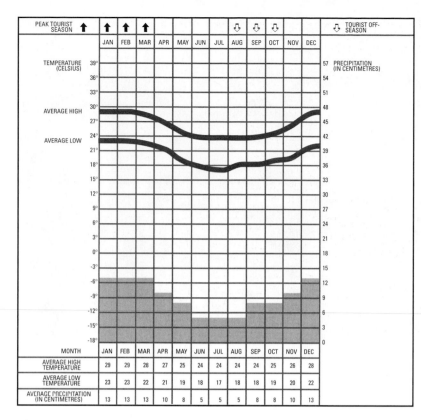

Figure 15-1   Climate at a Glance: Rio de Janeiro, Brazil

MONTH	JAN	FEB	MAR	APR	MAY	JUN	JUL	AUG	SEP	OCT	NOV	DEC
AVERAGE HIGH TEMPERATURE	29	29	28	27	25	24	24	24	24	25	26	28
AVERAGE LOW TEMPERATURE	23	23	22	21	19	18	17	18	18	19	20	22
AVERAGE PRECIPITATION (IN CENTIMETRES)	13	13	13	10	8	5	5	5	8	8	10	13

GETTING AROUND

There's extensive air service within Brazil. Intercity buses are less expensive, but probably not up to the standards visitors expect. Driving is no picnic either: Cities are very crowded, streets can be confusing, breakneck speed is the rule among drivers, and, outside the cities, heavy rains can wash out roads. Trains are very limited, except for a popular run between Rio and Sao Paulo.

In a country with extensive waterways and a long Atlantic coastline, ships and boats often represent an alternative means of travel. The most famous water journey is up the Amazon, all the way to Manaus. Many cruise lines include this adventurous trip as part of their South American itineraries.

Brazil's major cities feature inexpensive buses, but they can get very crowded. Taxis are a good way to get around. *Remis* (private cars) are considered safer and more reliable, but are more expensive than taxis. Tour packages to Brazil often include multiple forms of transportation.

IMPORTANT PLACES

Most visitors centre their Brazilian trip in one of three areas: around Rio de Janeiro, along the Amazon, and in the Salvador region.

Rio de Janeiro

Rio is one of the world's great cities. If it were only for the stunning location—oddly shaped mountains, a picturesque lagoon, and lush vegetation intertwine through the city, with superb beaches and the glistening Atlantic Ocean at its doorstep—Rio would be famous. But Rio offers more. It's a cosmopolitan city with rich culture, warm people, wonderful cuisine, and a frenetic nightlife, all wrapped in a casual yet elegant charm. Rio, though, isn't perfect: The city is very crowded;

The Amazon was named after female warriors who reputedly lived in a region east of ancient Greece. Supposedly, female warriors also lived in the Amazon Basin. Both stories are probably myths.

Soccer is a Brazilian passion. Attend a soccer match in one of Sao Paulo's or Rio's huge stadiums.

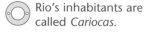

Rio's inhabitants are called *Cariocas*.

The ride to the top of Sugar Loaf, Rio de Janeiro
Photo by Marc Mancini

it has slums, plenty of petty crime, and, like all of Brazil, an unpredictable economy.

Among the most popular Rio attractions are:

- **Sugar Loaf,** the strangely shaped mountain that's the city's landmark. The summit offers beautiful views and is reached by cable car. It's best to go on a weekday; weekends are crowded and the waiting line for the cable car is long.

- **Tijuca National Park,** which claims to be the "world's largest urban, forested national park."

- **World-renowned beaches,** most notably **Copacabana** (the biggest) and two more trendy beaches: **Ipanema** [ee-pah-NEE-mah] and **Leblon.**

- **Excellent museums,** many of which can be found in **Flamengo Park,** including the **Museum of Modern Art.**

- **The Botanical Gardens,** which features a rich collection of plants and trees brought by Portuguese navigators from their many world voyages.

- **Corcovado Mountain,** serving as the base for the city's other famous landmark, the 36 metre, open-armed statue of **Christ the Redeemer.** The views from here are astounding.

- **Carnival,** a spectacular four-day festival starting the Saturday before Ash Wednesday and ending Tuesday evening. Visitors in the area at this time should not miss it. The city virtually shuts down, no one seems to go to bed, and anything goes.

Several **day trips** from Rio de Janeiro would add to a visit to this area:

- **Sao Paulo,** the business and industrial centre of Brazil, which is about 280 kilometres southwest of Rio. It has world-class international restaurants and shopping, some of South America's best museums, and a good nightlife. (Unfortunately, it also has considerable traffic and pollution problems.) The **Sacred Art Museum** has the largest collection of religious art outside the Vatican, while the **MASP** museum boasts a huge collection of Impressionist

Rio has the world's largest soccer stadium.

Never leave your valuables unattended on the beach.

The Feirarte, a great open-air market, is held on Sundays in the Ipanema area of Rio.

Since 1900, at least 19 indigenous groups in Brazil have become extinct.

Rio from Corcovado
Photo by Justus Ghormley

paintings. The zoo's great menagerie of animals from the Brazilian jungle is impressive. Visitors shouldn't carry valuables or go walking at night (taxis should be taken instead), since street robberies, sadly, happen far too often.

- **Guaruja** [gwah-ruh-ZHAH], a sophisticated beach town, actually a day trip from Sao Paulo.

- **Petropolis,** once the summer retreat for the emperor of Portugal, with its **Imperial Palace.** The 75 kilometre drive from Rio to Petropolis is very scenic.

- **Costa Verde,** the beautiful coastal area between Rio and **Santos** (a coastal village just south of Sao Paulo). The beaches here are much quieter than those in Rio.

- **Iguazu Falls** (spelled Iguaçu in Portuguese), a breathtaking attraction on Brazil's border which merits at least a two-night stay. To get there from Rio requires a short flight. Nearly 300 falls cover 4.2 kilometres and span an area much higher and wider than Niagara Falls. For movie buffs, this is where the film *The Mission* was shot. January through March is peak season, but it's also the hottest, steamiest time of year. August through October may be best for visiting Iguazu.

The Amazon

A trip up the Amazon promises one of the world's legendary tourist adventures. The river is about 6400 kilometres long and up to 13 kilometres wide. The dense jungles and lush rainforests are home to wildlife seen nowhere else on earth, with fishing villages and small islands dotting the river's length. There are also a few major cities along the way:

The Amazon Basin contains 20 percent of the world's fresh water.

- **Manaus,** deep in Brazil's hot interior, is a crowded city. Surprisingly, many Victorian buildings remain from the city's early rubber boom days. Today, the city is a free port with popular duty-free shopping; it's also a launch point for Amazon River boat trips to jungle lodges and for hunting expeditions. Manaus is also an inland stop for cruise ships.

The sites of Manaus include the **Teatro do Amazonas,** an ornate opera house built in 1892, where many of history's great opera singers and actors have performed; **Mercado Municipal,** a marketplace of fascinating design; interesting museums and zoos; and **Salvador Lake,** just outside town, a nature preserve with a remarkable array of wildlife. **The Wedding of the Waters,** 19 kilometres from town, is where the Amazon, the Rio Solimoes, and the Rio Negro meet. Each has water of a different colour, and the colliding swirls of separate hues provide a unique attraction. Half-day boat excursions can be taken from Manaus to visit this area.

- **Belem,** at the mouth of the Amazon, is home to a huge open-air market, **Ver-O-Peso,** which features all manner of items for sale. Lush parks and interesting old buildings decorate the city. The **Goledi Anthropology Museum and Zoo** has intriguing collections. A boat excursion to the ranches on the vast nearby island of **Ilha de Marajo** is popular.

- **Santarem** is a quiet city about halfway between Manaus and Belem. Although not offering anywhere near the attractions of those two cities, it's less crowded, less developed, and quite charming. A bit of trivia: Santarem was originally settled by people from South Carolina and Tennessee.

Salvador

Salvador once belonged to the Dutch.

Salvador, the capital of the **Bahia** district, is a baroque city with a strong African heritage. This coastal city, with perhaps the finest climate in the country, has excellent beaches, old neighbourhoods with winding streets, fine museums, and 365 churches. The city is built on two levels into a cliff, connected by the **Lacerdo Elevator.** The views are gorgeous, the locals are extremely friendly, and the unique African-European cuisine is great. And, like Rio, the city holds a festive Carnival for the four days before Ash Wednesday. Its most interesting sites include:

- **Many churches,** the finest of which are the **Basilica Cathedral,** a wonderful 400-year-old structure; the ornate **Church of St. Francis,** with a remarkable gold-leaf interior; and the **Church of Our Lord of the Good Ending,** whose congregation often wear the traditional clothes of their faith.

- **The Mercado Modelo,** with good buys on silver, rosewood, and fabric souvenirs.

- **Superb beaches,** the best of which are **Itapoa** and **Piata.**

    There are a few interesting **day trips** from Salvador:

- **Excursions** to the numerous islands off the coast. **Itaparica** is probably the best known; it's quiet, lovely, and virtually undeveloped.

- **Recife,** reachable from Salvador in a day, but probably requiring an overnight stay. This city has been compared to Venice because of its canals and bridges, though, unlike Venice, there's also normal vehicle traffic. There are many classical churches, an old fort, an 18th-century prison that's been turned into a shopping centre, and great beaches. The lovely artist colony of **Olinda** is nearby. Farther north is **Fortaleza,** a beach area that has grown in popularity.

POSSIBLE ITINERARIES

For first-time visitors, Rio de Janeiro is a must-see. A very common itinerary is to spend three or four days in Rio, fly to Iguazu for a two- to three-day stay, and continue on to Buenos Aires, Argentina. Travellers visiting Brazil for a second time might enjoy visiting the exotic Bahia region around Salvador for three or four days or could spend up to six days taking a cruise up the Amazon.

LODGING OPTIONS

Hotels in Brazil run the gamut from deluxe to budget, but the lower down the ladder you go, the greater the chance for disappointment. (Of course, during Carnival, everything is expensive.) The major luxury chains include **Othon** and hotels represented by **Leading Hotels of the World. Luxor** is a popular first-class chain. A few North American companies are also present in Brazil.

In Rio de Janeiro, the largest hotel grouping is along Copacabana Beach, with other clusters on Ipanema Beach, Leblon Beach, and upscale Gavea Beach. Lodging is expensive by South American standards, but less so than many other top resort areas around the world. The turn-of-the-century, deluxe **Copacabana Palace Hotel** is internationally renowned. Most Sao Paulo hotels are in the western part of the city. Visitors to Manaus should stay in the better-class hotels. Those staying in Salvador can save some money by lodging in hotels off the beach, since most of the finest beaches in the area, notably Itapoa and Piata, are out of town. At Iguazu Falls, the graceful **Hotel das Cataratas** is just a walk away from the falls and offers the only falls-view rooms on the Brazilian side. (One hotel also overlooks the falls on the Argentine side.)

An interesting alternative for lodging in Rio: furnished apartments, called *apartotels*, which have complete hotel services. There are also ranches and jungle lodges in many areas of the country.

Rio is a noisy city. A beachfront or interior room will shield you from the constant din.

ALLIED DESTINATIONS

Taking up half of South America, Brazil is the ideal connection to the other countries on that continent. To the north, it borders French Guiana, Suriname, Guyana, Venezuela, and Colombia. Peru and Bolivia are to its west. And to the south are Paraguay, Argentina, and Uruguay. In fact, the only South American countries it doesn't border are Chile and Ecuador. Brazil is also close to Central America and the Caribbean. A cruise, especially, would be an excellent way to extend a trip between those areas.

CULTURAL PATTERNS

Brazil is an adventurous, lively country. Understanding the customs here will go a long way toward making a trip, business or otherwise, even more rewarding:

- Brazilians are physically and emotionally open. Shaking hands, embracing, and so on are the rule.

- The OK sign in North America—made with the thumb and forefinger—is an obscenity in Brazil.

- Brazilians have a lax attitude toward time. Visitors should nonetheless be punctual for business appointments, even if they turn out to be the only ones there on time.

- To be invited to a Brazilian's home is an honour. Guests shouldn't plan to drop by for a brief visit; rather, they should be prepared to stay for many hours. It's also customary to arrive a little late. In addition, some small gift should be brought along. (An important note here, especially concerning flowers: Purple, in Brazil, is the colour of death.) Brazilians are very conscious of keeping their hands on the table when dining.

FACTORS THAT MOTIVATE VISITORS

Among the reasons that motivate people to visit Brazil are:

- Rio de Janeiro promises excitement, fun, fine dining, and much nightlife.

- There are great beaches throughout the country.

- Considering what its great cities offer, Brazil is a relative bargain.

- The locals are extremely warm, open, and friendly.

- The Amazon is adventurous and unique.

- There's great cuisine and good shopping (especially for precious stones).

- The history and culture of Brazil are fascinating.

- Rio's Carnival is world-renowned. Salvador's is almost as impressive.

POSSIBLE MISGIVINGS

The culture of Brazil offers up a very foreign experience. The concerns that usually arise are:

- "There's malaria, cholera, and other diseases in the Amazon." Most of the worst areas are well away from the typical tourist areas. Travellers should check with a doctor before coming here, get shots, and, if necessary, bring medication.

- "They speak Portuguese." Portuguese is somewhat similar to Spanish. More important, English is widely spoken in the major cities and by travel professionals.

- "I'm afraid to drink the water." Bottled soft drinks (including some very exotic Amazon fruit flavours) can be purchased everywhere. And Brazilian beer is excellent.

- "I won't like Brazilian food." Brazil is a mix of cultures. There is wonderful international cuisine. A special treat: *Churruscaria* restaurants that serve up barbecued meats carved at the diner's table.

- "The government and economy are unstable." Though this is true, it doesn't necessarily impact tourism.

- "There's a lot of street crime." Unfortunately, it's true. Common-sense precautions should be taken, such as leaving valuables in the hotel, dressing casually, keeping wallets protected, and not walking outside at night, except in clearly safe places.

SALES STRATEGIES

The unique qualities of Brazil lend themselves to special ways to up-sell and cross-sell a trip here. Because of the economic uncertainty and sometimes high inflation, an escorted tour package or cruise may lock in prices early, as well as help ease a vacationer's fears about travelling alone in such an exotic country. At the very least, booking city tours can be helpful, since driving in Brazilian cities is not recommended. (For that matter, driving *anywhere* in Brazil is not recommended.) Since intercity bus and train service is limited, flights between cities are preferable. Accommodations in lower-rated hotels can be risky; upgraded lodging should be the choice. For those visiting the Amazon, a boat trip is a must; a special excursion to the Wedding of the Waters would be a worthwhile addition. For those going to Iguazu Falls, a local helicopter tour or jet boat ride is exciting.

Qualifying the Traveller
BRAZIL

FOR PEOPLE WHO WANT	HIGH APPEAL	MEDIUM APPEAL	LOW APPEAL	REMARKS
Historical and Cultural Attractions		▲		Especially Rio and Amazon; Carnival
Beaches and Water Sports	▲			Legendary beaches
Skiing Opportunities			▲	None
Lots of Nightlife		▲		Especially Rio
Family Activities			▲	
Familiar Cultural Experience			▲	
Exotic Cultural Experience	▲			
Safety and Low Crime			▲	Petty theft common
Bargain Travel		▲		Air/hotel packages excellent
Impressive Scenery	▲			Seascapes and jungle
Peace and Quiet		▲		Cities noisy, but outlying areas not
Shopping Opportunities		▲		Semiprecious stones, rosewood, leather
Adventure	▲			Amazon and Iguazu Falls
To Do Business		▲		In large cities

TRAVEL TRIVIA

PLACES FAMOUS FOR PRE-LENTEN CARNIVALS

- Rio de Janeiro, Brazil
- New Orleans
- Venice, Italy
- Nassau, Bahamas
- Salvador, Brazil
- Oruro, Bolivia
- Caracas, Venezuela
- Beuel, Germany
- Trinidad
- Nice, France
- Martinique
- Corrientes, Argentina

MAP ACTIVITY

NAME _____   DATE _____

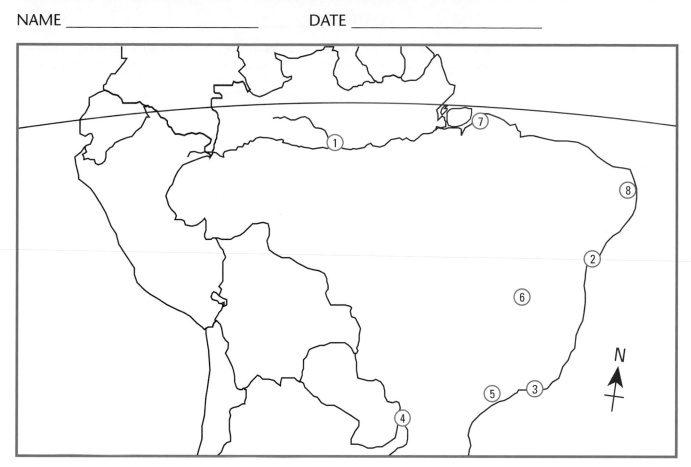

A traveller wants to visit the places listed below. Which number represents each on the map?

PLACE/ATTRACTION	IN/NEAR WHICH CITY?	NUMBER ON MAP
A. Teatro do Amazonas	**A.**	**A.**
B. Sugar Loaf	**B.**	**B.**
C. Itapoa Beach	**C.**	**C.**
D. Leblon Beach	**D.**	**D.**
E. Falls bigger than Niagara	**E.**	**E.**
F. Capital of the Bahia District	**F.**	**F.**
G. The Wedding of the Waters	**G.**	**G.**
H. Sacred Art Museum	**H.**	**H.**
I. Brazil's capital	**I.**	**I.**
J. Ipanema	**J.**	**J.**

CASE STUDY

NAME _____   DATE _____

Nancy and Mark Aston are in their early 40s, with a daughter in college. They haven't had a vacation in three years—since they went to Paris and enjoyed the fashionable city very much. After their daughter returns to school in the fall, they'll be spending 11 days in South America, split between Brazil and Peru. They're a professional couple and don't like hassles on their trips. They plan to base their Brazilian stay in Rio.

Circle the answer that best suits their needs.

1. Which special tip would not be appropriate?

   Be sure to see Carnival   Keep your valuables in the hotel

   Don't drive in cities   Take along an umbrella

   Why?

2. What good news could you tell the Astons?

   The beach at Itapoa, where you're lodging them, is beautiful.

   They're going during Brazil's bargain season.

   Since Nancy speaks Spanish, Brazil's national language, they should have no trouble.

   Like them, Brazilians dress conservatively.

   Why?

3. The Astons decide that they want to see the Amazon. Which city would you suggest they fly to?

   Salvador   Sao Paulo

   Manaus   Brasilia

   Why?

4. Which of the following services would not be good for the Astons?

   A city tour   A helicopter ride

   A boat cruise   A budget hotel

   Why?

CREATIVE ACTIVITY

NAME _____   DATE _____

At Epcot in Orlando, many nations maintain pavilions that reflect their heritage and culture. For example, Morocco has reproduced a bazaar; Mexico a Mayan pyramid (with a ride inside); France a café-lined street. If you were a pavilion designer for the Walt Disney Company (which owns Epcot), what concept would you propose if Brazil decided to set up a pavilion? Describe or even draw it below.

Belmopan ✪ **BELIZE**
GUATEMALA **HONDURAS**
Guatemala City ✪ ✪ Tegucigalpa
EL SALVADOR **NICARAGUA**
Managua ✪ *Lake Nicaragua*
COSTA RICA Canal Panama
San Jose ✪ Zone City
✪ Panama
PANAMA

CARIBBEAN SEA

✪ Caracas
Bogota *Lake Maracaibo* Georgetown
✪ *Orinoco River* Paramaribo
COLOMBIA ✪ ✪ **FRENCH GUIANA**
VENEZUELA Cayenne
Quito ✪ **GUYANA**
ECUADOR **SURINAME**

Galapagos
Islands

Amazon River

Andes

PERU

✪ Lima **BRAZIL**

Mountains

Lake Titicaca **BOLIVIA**
✪ La Paz

PACIFIC OCEAN

CHILE **PARAGUAY**
✪ Asuncion

Rio Uruguay

Easter Island **ATLANTIC OCEAN**

ARGENTINA **URUGUAY**
✪ Montevideo
Santiago ✪ Buenos Aires ✪
Rio de la Plata

Falkland Islands

STRAIT of
MAGELLAN South Georgia

CHAPTER 16

Latin American Potpourri

Too often when a traveller thinks of heading south, he or she will consider only certain well-known destinations: Rio, the Mexican beach resorts, or the principal islands of the Caribbean. Yet Central and South America boast many first-rate but little-known attractions, many off the beaten tourist track.

There's a waterfall over twice the height of the CN Tower, and another almost as wide as the Grand Canyon. There's the world's second-biggest coral reef, huge mysterious drawings on a vast plain, an island covered with oversized stone heads, and an abandoned city at 2400 metres in the Andes.

Do you know the names of these places? If not, you soon will. And you'll be able to use your knowledge to enhance the trip for anyone bound for Latin America.

◎ The Pacific Ocean is at the Panama Canal's *eastern* end.

CENTRAL AMERICA

The Central American isthmus, which connects Mexico to the South American continent, will probably be low on the priority list of most travellers. Though the land itself can be quite lovely and the weather tropical, the historical and cultural attractions are relatively undeveloped. More important: Some of the area's countries have been torn by enough intermittent wars and unrest to keep tourists away.

Air connections to and throughout Central America are the best bet for those who wish to visit the area. Car rentals are available and occasionally offer a good way to see the countryside; however, driving can be difficult in some places and dangerous in others. Bus service is widespread, but not recommended. Cruises may stop here as well, especially in **Costa Rica** and **Panama.** Indeed, cruises that pass from the Pacific to the Atlantic through the Panama Canal are quite popular.

Spanish is the national language in all Central American countries except **Belize** [beh-LEEZ], where

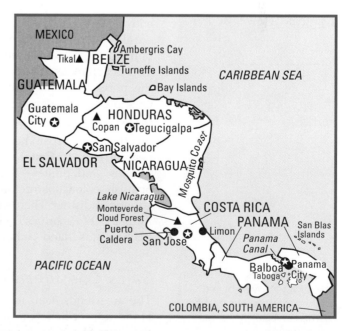

English is the official language. English, however, is commonly spoken by travel personnel throughout the region.

Important Places

Here are the countries, from north to south, you should know about:

GUATEMALA. Guatemala has had political instability. Its rich Mayan culture reached its high point at **Tikal** [tee-KAHL], an astonishing group of ruins that's right out of an Indiana Jones movie. Most of Guatemala's other ruins remain covered with earth and vines. **Guatemala City** (GUA), the capital, has several museums that explain Mayan civilization.

BELIZE. Belize is a tiny, politically stable country on the Caribbean coast with many Mayan ruins, meandering rivers, a lush jungle landscape, and some of the best diving spots in the world. It has become a popular stop for Western Caribbean cruises. Belize has the world's second-largest coral reef. At the reef's northern end is **Ambergris Cay,** with fine beaches, good fishing, and great diving. In the reef's middle are the **Turneffe Islands,** which feature what some consider the world's best dive site, the **Blue Hole.** The country strives to ensure that all new development is environmentally sensitive, most especially at its nature reserves.

HONDURAS. Honduras has a poor economy and has been affected, in the past, by fighting in neighbouring countries, some of which occasionally spills over its borders. However, tourism (especially from cruise ships) has helped its economy. Its capital, **Tegucigalpa** (TGU), is quite pretty. The town of **Copan** is renowned for its Mayan ruins. The **Bay Islands** off Honduras (especially **Roatan Island**) offer good dive sites, including one where visitors can dive with dolphins.

EL SALVADOR. El Salvador had been strife-ridden for many years, but is now courting tourism. This scenic, mountainous country has much to offer. There are fine beaches, Mayan ruins are everywhere, and the capital of **San Salvador** (SAL) is beautiful.

NICARAGUA. Nicaragua has also suffered on occasion from war and crime. The **Mosquito Coast** (the setting for the novel of the same name) lies on this country's Caribbean shore. Mayan ruins, abandoned gold mines, beach activities, and an old pirate settlement are among its attractions.

COSTA RICA. Costa Rica is the success story of Central America: It's stable, prosperous, and has decent tourist facilities. In the country's central highlands is the capital city of **San Jose** (SJO), which contains some interesting museums and churches, a lovely national theatre, and plenty of shopping. The climate here is pleasant. There are also interesting tours through the countryside and jungle: Costa Rica has a wealth of national parks and rain-forest reserves, which makes it appealing for ecotourists. The most famous of these is **Monteverde Cloud Forest Reserve.** Cruise ships call on the ports of **Limon** and **Puerto Caldera,** usually on Panama Canal itineraries. Offshore sports-fishing in Costa Rica is especially attractive.

PANAMA. Panama wavers between substantial tourism and no tourism at all; politics greatly affect tourism here. A common destination is **Panama City** (PTY), the capital, near the **Panama Canal.** This city—with a history strongly influenced by the Spanish, Indians, and pirates—is a popular cruise stop. Panama City boasts interesting Spanish colonial structures, old churches, and colourful plazas. **Balboa** is the American district: There's not much history to be found here, but it's safe and comfortable. Off Panama's Pacific coast is pretty **Taboga** Island; off its Caribbean side are the **San Blas** islands, a haven for Indian culture.

Sales Considerations

The area lends itself to cruises, particularly through Panama; along Costa Rica, Honduras, or Belize; or to some of the nearby islands. Book only the finest hotels in Central America. Tourists seriously interested in the local culture or ecotourism,

Belize was formerly known as British Honduras.

Costa Rica means "rich coast," based on the hope that there was much gold there. (There wasn't.)

Costa Rica's rainy season (May–November) is often interrupted in mid-July by the *canicula,* when rain nearly disappears.

those on cruises to South America or the Caribbean, or those who have relatives or ancestors from here will likely be the travellers visiting Central America. Vacationers who love fishing, secluded beaches, and diving are rapidly "discovering" Central America; its safer destinations are an appealing recommendation for those who've seen the more traditional ocean-oriented spots. A few fine resorts have opened or are under development in Central America. There are many ITC packages to Roatan Island, Costa Rica, Panama City, and the San Blas islands. Two-stay, city–beach tours in Costa Rica are also popular.

COLOMBIA

The legendary El Dorado, stocked with golden riches, was reputedly in this region. It has never been found. But with three Andes ranges, broad beaches, extensive coffee plantations, and an Amazon jungle, Colombia has a wealth of another kind. Unfortunately, the country's long history with crime may discourage vacationers from sampling its attractions.

For those who *are* interested, **Avianca** (AV) is the national airline, flying into the capital of **Bogota** (BOG), on an Andean plateau. Major airports are also in the Caribbean port city of **Barranquilla** (BAQ) and the resort port of **Cartagena** (CTG), once a walled fortress. Good air connections criss-cross the country, along with so-so rail service, crowded buses, and poor driving conditions. The national language is Spanish.

Bogota's residents live in a cool, spring-like, almost unchanging climate. The El Dorado tradition lives on here in the huge collection of the city's famous **Gold Museum.** A half-day trip from the city is **Zipaquira**, with its **"Salt Cathedral"** carved out of rock 137 metres below ground. Astonishingly large, it can hold almost 10 000 people. **San Agustin Park** is a 388-square-kilometre archaeological reserve dotted with stone monoliths. **Leticia,** accessible only by air or boat, is a gateway to Amazon adventure cruises. **San Andres Island,** about 480 kilometres north of Colombia, was the base of English pirate Captain Henry Morgan. (ITCs are a popular option on San Andres.)

Set elsewhere, the 8800 kilometre Andes would stretch from Madrid to Vancouver.

Venezuela named its unit of currency the bolivar, after Simon Bolivar.

VENEZUELA

Caracas, Venezuela's capital, lies in a northern Andean valley. Venezuela's other major geographic feature is the **Orinoco River,** which flows through the grassy plains (the *llanos*) into the Atlantic. **Simon Bolivar Airport** (CCS) in Caracas is the gateway into the country, though cruise ships also call on the nearby port of **La Guaira. Merida** (MRD) is the Venezuelan air gateway to the Andes, where visitors can ride the world's highest cable car. There's good air and bus service, but no train service to speak of. Though renting a car is easy, driving is difficult. *Por puestos* (taxis that pick up and drop off passengers along their routes, like a shuttle bus) are a popular way of getting around. Spanish is the national language.

The climate in Venezuela is very steady; in Caracas, for example, daytime temperatures average in the low to mid 20s year-round. Jungle areas are hotter and Andes destinations cooler. Venezuela has a dry season from December to early May, with moderate and occasional rainfall the rest of the year.

Important Places

Venezuela has a number of interesting destinations:

- **Caracas,** for the most part, is a handsome, modern city with many notable churches. It retains a strong Spanish influence and has an active, international nightlife. The birthplace and grave of Venezuela's national hero, Simon Bolivar (who helped free South America from Spain), is here. **Mt. Avila** offers great views of the city. **Colonia Tovar,** an interesting, German-like village, is nearby.

- **Angel Falls,** at 979 metres, is the world's loftiest waterfall. (It's nearly 18 times higher than Niagara Falls.) Located in the southeast jungle, and reached by plane, the area also has thousands of varieties of orchids.

- **Beach resorts** are found along the Caribbean coast. Two of the most popular are **Macuto,** not far from Caracas, and the very popular **Margarita Island** (in the Caribbean just east of the ABC Islands).

⊚ Angel Falls, which plummets from "Devil Mountain," was discovered by and named after an American, Jimmy Angel.

Sales Considerations

Venezuela is particularly convenient as an extension to a trip into the Caribbean. It's sometimes a stop on Southern Caribbean and trans-Canal cruise itineraries. Tourist services tend to be first-rate. An air tour to Angel Falls is an intriguing option; the drama of this attraction appeals to those who seek off-the-beaten-path experiences.

THE GUIANAS

⊚ The Dutch traded Manhattan for Suriname (originally Dutch Guiana).

⊚ The world's tallest wooden structure is Georgetown Cathedral.

These three very small countries—**Guyana** [guy-AH-nah], **Suriname** [SUR-eh-nahm], and **French Guiana** [ghee-AH-nah]—huddle together on the Atlantic coast. The Guianas are largely jungle, with many rivers (especially in Guyana) and savannahs. Guyana has a national carrier, **Guyana Airways** (GY), which flies into the capital of **Georgetown** (GEO); Suriname's national airline, **Suriname Airways** (PY), lands in **Paramaribo** (PBM), the capital. Other airlines service the region as well. The gateway into French Guiana is its capital, **Cayenne** (CAY). These three countries' ports are occasionally stops on Southern Caribbean or South American cruise itineraries. Train, bus, and boat are the easiest ways to get around; there are also some air connections. Rental cars are available, but driving conditions aren't good.

Each of these countries has its own national language: English in Guyana, Dutch in Suriname, and French (of course) in French Guiana. The climate is tropical, with conditions steadily humid and hot (though nights from December through February can get chilly). July through November might be the best time to visit here. May and June also have pleasant temperatures, but this is the rainiest season.

Important Places

Here are the most popular attractions in these exotic destinations:

- **Guyana** offers excellent trout and ocean fishing opportunities, and some interesting sites—notably in Georgetown. There's also **Kaieteur Falls,** which cascades down from a height of 226 metres.

- **Suriname** has a strong mix of cultures and religions, including Hindu, Muslim, and Catholic. In Paramaribo, a fairly sophisticated city, there are many interesting churches, marketplaces, and colonial buildings. Jungle excursions into Suriname's nature parks and reserves appeal to ecotourists. Suriname has occasional civil unrest.

- **French Guiana** is the least-developed country of the three. Its most noted attraction: a tour of the notorious penal colony **Devil's Island,** which is off-shore from **Kourou.** This is where French soldier Alfred Dreyfus was unjustly imprisoned at the turn of the 20th century. Devil's Island is a frequent stop for cruise ships heading to or from South America. On the mainland, jungle and river excursions are possibilities. But since poverty, heat, and crime are ever-present problems, such trips are suitable only for the hardiest of adventure travellers.

In the book *Papillon*, Henri Charrière wrote of his adventures as a convict on Devil's Island.

Sales Considerations

Since these are such challenging destinations, people who are not very adventurous travellers should visit the Guianas via a cruise or a well-established tour operator.

French Guiana is the launch site for France's aerospace program.

ECUADOR

Located in the northwest corner of South America, Ecuador borders the Pacific Ocean. The Andes mountain range shapes much of the country's geography. The climate stays fairly steady all year, though different areas vary greatly. The highlands—which include the capital, **Quito** (often called the City of Eternal Spring)—tend to have cool temperatures. The west coast—where **Guayaquil** is located—is much warmer, with highs in the 30s. Ecuador has a rainy season from January to April; the rest of the year it's very dry.

The national airline of Ecuador, **Ecuatoriana** (EU), provides service to **Mariscal Sucre International Airport** (UIO) in Quito and **Simon Bolivar Airport** (GYE) in Guayaquil, as do a few other carriers. Cruise ships dock at Guayaquil. There's good air service within the country. Visitors to the **Galapagos Islands** can fly to either **Baltra** or **San Cristobal** or take a boat there. Train service is limited in Ecuador, but there's a complicated series of connections between Quito and Guayaquil; the winding route through mountain

passes is spectacular. Buses are very crowded, and though car rentals are widely available, road conditions aren't good. Taxis are a good way to navigate cities. Spanish is the national language.

On Ecuador's Trans-Andean railroad, passengers are sometimes allowed to ride on the train's rooftop.

Important Places

Though Guayaquil is Ecuador's largest city, its attractions are limited to some interesting Spanish buildings and a few cultural museums. Ecuador has two major destinations: Quito and the Galapagos Islands.

Surrounded by immense mountains, Quito has a natural setting that few country capitals can match. A strong Spanish architectural influence marks the city. Quito boasts some fine museums specializing in pre-Columbian art, and a great many churches. The city's historical district, "Old Quito," is quite interesting.

The Galapagos Islands was where Charles Darwin did much of his research for his theories on evolution.

Panama hats actually originated in Ecuador.

A beautiful day drive will take visitors to **Mt. Cotopaxi,** a national park. A half-day trip is 24 kilometres north to the **equator,** which is marked with a monument; some interesting ruins are along the way. Farther to the north and south lie a string of colourful towns, each with a popular marketplace (**Otavalo** is the best known).

The Galapagos Islands possess some of the world's most remarkable wildlife. (Its famous giant tortoises are believed to be the world's oldest living animals.) The cindery islands are of volcanic origin, and a few active ones still exist. The Ecuadorian government sets a strict limit on the number of visitors to the Galapagos, so tours and trips should be booked well in advance.

Sales Considerations

Ecuador supplies one-quarter of the world's bananas.

Ecuador is less developed than some of the more popular nations in South America. However, it's also less crowded and is relatively stable. For ecotourists, the Galapagos are a must-see (usually as part of a cruise from the South American mainland).

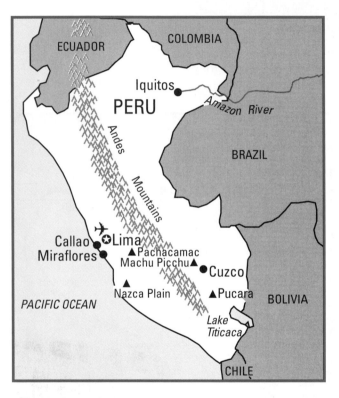

PERU

Few countries can boast as many well-known, first-rate attractions as Peru. Most tourists take **Aeroperu** (PL) or another carrier and land first in **Lima** [LEE-mah] (LIM) or, via cruise ship, in the port city of **Callao** [cah-YAH-oh]. They encounter a nation of dramatic contrasts: the warm, dry Pacific coast; the mighty Andes just inland (which can get quite cold during the June-to-September, south-of-the-equator winter); and the hilly, rainy jungles of the eastern lowlands, where the Amazon finds its source.

Important Places

Lima, which was the centre of Spain's New World government, retains much of its colonial architecture, especially at **Plaza de Armas.** The city brims with fine museums and several ornate churches (most notable is the **Church of St. Francis,** which has a vast system of catacombs beneath it). Nearby are **Pachacamac,** an Incan ruin; **Miraflores,** a charming beach town; and the **Nazca Plain,** whose huge mysterious designs drawn on the ground have intrigued archaeologists and tourists for decades. Visible only from the air, the drawings of animals, people, and geometric shapes are best seen via local charter plane expeditions that you can book in advance.

Soroche is what Peruvian locals call altitude sickness. It's the number-one problem for visitors to Peru.

Some hotels in Cuzco offer oxygen-enhanced rooms.

Cuzco, the former capital of the Incan Empire, is another of Peru's well-known destinations. About 640 kilometres southeast of Lima, it features ancient ruins, colonial mansions, several museums, a Renaissance-style cathedral, and a world-class hotel, the **Monasterio.** Not far is **Pucara,** an ancient Incan fortress. But Pucara pales in comparison to Peru's most remarkable attraction, **Machu Picchu.** Perched high in a dramatic Andes setting and hidden until it was rediscovered in 1911 by former U.S. Senator Hiram Bingham, Machu Picchu boasts more than 200 Incan temples, terraces, and residences. Most tourists visit it via a special morning train from Cuzco, returning in the late afternoon.

Iquitos [ee-KEE-tos], a city on the Amazon in northeast Peru, is the jump-off point for "Green Hell" boat tours up the Amazon River into the jungle.

Machu Picchu, Peru
Photo by Justus Ghormley

Sales Considerations

What draws visitors to Peru? The country's felicitous climate, accessible location, startling scenery, budget prices, and high-recognition attractions make it one of Latin America's easiest "sells." It's frequently an add-on destination to such bordering countries as Ecuador, Colombia, Brazil, Bolivia, and Chile. Many escorted tour packages are available to this "soft" adventure country.

There *are* problems related to a trip to Peru. As with many Latin American destinations, poverty leads to petty crime, terrorism, and health concerns—even in Lima and Cuzco. These problems, as well as inflation and limited hotel space, make booking packaged tours an advisable sales strategy. Since budget hotels leave much to be desired, up-selling to luxury-class accommodations is an attractive option. Travellers to the region should discuss with their physicians possible treatments for preventing or minimizing altitude sickness.

Bolivia's Aymara Indians were the first to cultivate the potato.

BOLIVIA

Located in the centre of the continent, Bolivia is one of the two landlocked countries in South America. (The other is Paraguay.) It's dominated by the Andes and is at extremely high altitudes; in fact, the thin air might be difficult for most visitors until they adjust. **La Paz,** the world's highest capital city, is in the far west-central portion of the country, not far from **Lake Titicaca.**

Visitors can reach Bolivia by air, landing at **El Alto Airport** (LPB) in La Paz. **LAB** (LB) is the national carrier, though other airlines service the country. The railway network is extensive, but trains are slow. There are air connections between major cities, as well. Because of the high altitudes, the climate in Bolivia is cooler than in the rest of South America; June through August, especially, is extremely chilly. The regions deepest in the mountains get quite cold. Spanish is the national language.

Important Places

The two main sites for tourists in Bolivia are around La Paz and Lake Titicaca. Here are some of the most popular attractions:

- **La Paz** is a modern, fairly sophisticated city. The main boulevard and hotel area, **El Prado,** provides fascinating markets of all kinds, including a legal "black market." The city also has many fine cultural museums. The drive to **Chacaltaya** mountain is breathtakingly stunning, but its steep and winding curves should be recommended only to the fearless.

- **Tiwanaku** (Tiahuanaco), with its famed ancient stone ruins and the unusual rock formations of the **Valley of the Sun,** is 64 kilometres from La Paz.

- **Lake Titicaca** is shared by Bolivia and Peru, though it's most commonly accessed from Bolivia. It's the highest navigable lake in the world. **Copacabana** is a popular, lively resort on its southwestern shore.

Sales Considerations

Bolivia is a beautiful country, but quite challenging. It should be recommended especially to more adventurous travellers. It's very well suited as an extension of a trip to Peru, since Lake Titicaca covers parts of both countries. Bolivia has begun to take advantage of its appeal to ecotourists. Many specialized tour companies are developing and selling adventure tours that appeal to hikers, campers, and lovers of nature. Because so much of Bolivia is at high altitudes, visitors may need some time to adjust.

PARAGUAY

Paraguay, just east of the Andes, is the second of South America's two landlocked countries. The capital city, **Asuncion** (ASU), is the gateway into Paraguay; buses are the most common means of getting around. The climate is hot from September to April, with rain possible at any time of the year. It's also fairly humid. From May through August, the temperature finally cools down to the lower 20s during the day. The national language here, too, is Spanish.

Important Places

Paraguay offers some pleasing attractions for those who visit it:

- **Asuncion** is a charming city. There's an odd, small-town feel here, with trees and gardens everywhere. The city's slow pace is especially evident during a three-hour siesta at midday. There are some churches, parks, and museums. A particularly charming train ride leads to the botanical garden and zoo. For cruise lovers, the Paraguay River connects Asuncion to Buenos Aires, Argentina.

- **The Golden Triangle** is the eastern farmland area of Paraguay. Visitors will find small, old villages throughout the Golden Triangle.

- **Iguazu Falls** is at Paraguay's eastern border. Very few tourists, however, access the falls from Paraguay, choosing instead Brazil or Argentina, which are more strategically located to the falls.

Sales Considerations

Since it's often missed on the larger "sampler" tours of South America's highlights, Paraguay is a good recommendation for travellers returning to this southerly

Because of the lack of oxygen at its 3810 metre altitude, La Paz is nearly fireproof.

The Mennonite sect, which is best known for its presence in southern Ontario and the prairies, also settled in Paraguay, Mexico's Copper Canyon, and the U.S. states of Pennsylvania and Ohio.

continent for a second visit. A jungle safari trip is often part of a more general escorted tour package. Paraguay is well known for its shopping opportunities. Because of holiday festivities, it's not advisable to go during December and January. May through September (winter) probably offers the most pleasant weather and the fewest crowds.

URUGUAY

Tucked between Brazil and Argentina, Uruguay is one of the most European countries of South America and one of the safest. For this reason, it's one of the continent's most visited nations. Its capital, **Montevideo** [mon-tay-vee-DAY-o] (MVD), on the southern coast, is where most visitors arrive, either by air or by cruise. One hundred and forty-five kilometres east is **Punta del Este,** the most famous beach resort on Uruguay's 320-kilometre-long "Riviera of South America."

Uruguay has a very comfortable, temperate climate. Its lengthy summer lasts from November until March. July is the coldest month, with daytime temperatures in the low teens. Rental cars are widely available and visitors might enjoy driving around the countryside. (Montevideo's traffic, though, can be insane.) There's also a good bus system. Spanish is the national language.

Important Places

Though small, Uruguay has some particularly interesting sites:

- **Montevideo** is a friendly and spacious city. Many of its most interesting buildings surround the **Plaza Independencia.** There are also very good parks, markets, and museums. The nearby resort town of **Carrasco** has excellent beaches and grand old mansions. And a half-hour away is **Tablada,** often called the "Town of the *Gauchos*."

- **Colonia** is about 115 kilometres west of Montevideo and a one-hour trip, via hydrofoil, from Buenos Aires, Argentina. The historic town preserves the cobblestoned and walled ambience of Spanish and Portuguese colonial times.

- **The "Riviera"** runs east from Montevideo. Punta del Este is its most popular resort. Trendy and lively, it offers gambling and has many nightclubs. Excellent fishing is nearby.

○ Montevideo is well known for its cuisine.

Sales Considerations

Uruguay is a good choice for people interested in exotic nature and for those who want to visit a South American country largely free of crime and political turmoil. It's also a wonderful add-on to a visit to Brazil and/or Argentina. Punta del Este is popular with sun-seekers who love "discovering" a new resort destination. Air day trips from Montevideo to Buenos Aires or to Iguazu Falls are potential cross-sell opportunities.

Many find the country's blend of cultures rather intriguing. (Uruguay, like Argentina, has many people of Italian and German descent.) This—and the availability of fine meats from Uruguay's ranches—makes for an especially diversified cuisine.

○ A hovercraft carries passengers between Buenos Aires and Montevideo.

ARGENTINA

Argentina, South America's second-largest country, is about one-quarter the size of Canada. The country shares its western border with Chile; the Andes serve as a border between the two. Its major city and capital is **Buenos Aires.** The popular beach resort **Mar del Plata** is south of Buenos Aires. The **Lake District** is in the western part of the country, near the Andes.

There's a very strong European influence in Argentina, where a local is almost as likely to have an Italian name as a Hispanic one. Though Spanish is the national language, English is widely spoken in the major cities. Buenos Aires is the gateway into Argentina for cruises and for flights, at **Ezeiza Ministro Pistarini Airport** (EZE). Flying time from Toronto is nine hours; from Vancouver it's 15 hours. **Aerolineas Argentinas** (AR) is Argentina's large national carrier, though many other airlines serve the country. Within Argentina, there's very good air service. There are also good bus and railroad networks. Car rentals are widely available, but distances can be long and challenging in some areas, and city traffic is hectic. The weather in Buenos Aires is wonderful: The summer months of December through February hit the high 20s and descend to the mid-teens at night. Winter (June through August) is cooler but still pleasant (see Figure 16-1).

Important Places

No visitor to Argentina should miss a stay in Buenos Aires, one of the world's great cities. Considered by some to be a South American Paris (some of the buildings even have grey mansard roofs), sprawling Buenos Aires is very cosmopolitan and has wonderful cuisine, top fashion, good museums, many parks, wide boulevards, and a lively nightlife. The city is also fairly safe for tourists. Notable attractions are:

Over one-third of all Argentineans are of Italian descent.

The tango originated in Argentina at the end of the 19th century.

On Calle Florida is a replica of Big Ben's tower, given to Buenos Aires by the city of London.

- **Plaza de Mayo,** the political heart of the city, with colonial buildings and the city's cathedral. Its **Casa Rosa** (Pink House) is a landmark government building.

- **Avenida 9 de Julio,** reputedly the widest boulevard in the world.

- **Colon Theatre,** a huge, world-class opera house that has hosted the likes of Toscanini, Nijinski, and Baryshnikov. Tours are offered regularly.

- **Diverse neighbourhoods,** such as **San Telmo,** the old colonial section with cobblestone streets, tango nightclubs, and markets. Another interesting neighbourhood to visit is **La Boca,** the Italian district, noted for its intensely coloured buildings, fine art galleries, alfresco dining opportunities, and lively restaurants.

- **Calle Florida,** a popular pedestrian-only street of shops and stores (including many leather manufacturers who will provide a custom-made coat in 24 hours).

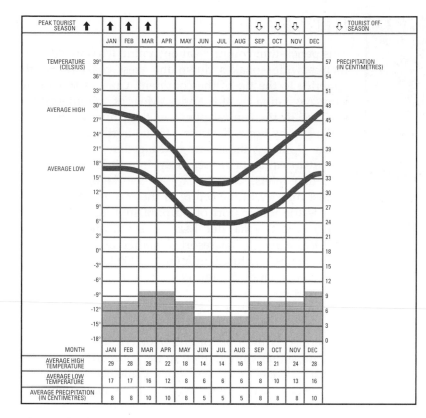

Figure 16-1   Climate at a Glance: Buenos Aires, Argentina

MONTH	JAN	FEB	MAR	APR	MAY	JUN	JUL	AUG	SEP	OCT	NOV	DEC
AVERAGE HIGH TEMPERATURE	29	28	26	22	18	14	14	16	18	21	24	28
AVERAGE LOW TEMPERATURE	17	17	16	12	8	6	6	6	8	10	13	16
AVERAGE PRECIPITATION (IN CENTIMETRES)	8	8	10	10	8	5	5	5	8	8	8	10

Some of Argentina's other destinations include:

- **Mar del Plata,** about 400 kilometres south of Buenos Aires, with eight kilometres of great beaches. There are hundreds of hotels, excellent shopping, and a huge casino.

- **Iguazu Falls,** probably the widest waterfall in the world. The falls are shared by Argentina, Brazil, and Paraguay, but are more often visited from Brazil.

- **The Lake District,** often compared to Switzerland. The town of **Bariloche,** just south of **Lake Nahuel Huapi** [nah-WEL wah-PEE], is a popular year-round resort; summer offers great fishing, whereas the winter season (from June through October) provides excellent skiing. Other major ski resorts are **Las Lenas** and **Chapelco.**

- **Patagonia,** a vast stretch of land in southern Argentina, is famous for its animals, birds, and rolling, largely unspoiled countryside. To its south is the **Strait of Magellan, Tierra del Fuego** (shared with Chile), and the port of **Ushuaia**—all of which are important ports on cruises around the tip of South America or to Antarctica.

Sales Considerations

Argentina will appeal to those who want a European flavour to their Latin American experience. It's safer than many other South American destinations, an important consideration for some. For those planning to travel around the country, an air package is ideal. Argentineans love sports of all kinds; sports packages are therefore an attractive cross-sell for Argentina-bound travellers. Tourists almost always visit one of the tango clubs in Buenos Aires, and it's usually worth the experience. Buenos Aires was once Latin America's most expensive city, but an unpredictable economy has made it a more reasonable destination.

Southern Argentina's indigenous people wrapped their feet in furs. So Spanish explorers called them *patagones,* or "big feet." Hence, Patagonia.

Gaucho ranches feature barbecued meals and horseback riding on the *pampas* (broad, grassy plains).

CHILE

This pencil-thin country—at one point, it's only 90 kilometres wide—snakes down the west coast of South America to the tip of the continent. Chile is separated from Argentina by the Andes. Most of the interesting sites are in the central plains of the country. The area is flanked by bone-dry desert to the north, whereas the south (split by the Strait of Magellan and reaching almost to Antarctica) breaks up into little islands and fjord-like inlets. Chile's capital, **Santiago,** is located almost directly in the centre of the country. Northwest of it is the major port of **Valparaiso** and the popular beach resort **Viña del Mar.** A bit farther north is **Portillo,** a major ski resort. Another of Chile's most famous sites is actually more than 3200 kilometres west of the mainland: **Easter Island,** with its mysterious, giant statues.

LAN-Chile (LA) and **Ladeco** (UC) are the national airlines and fly into the gateway of Santiago (SCL). Valparaiso is the port of entry for cruises. Air service and trains (basically limited to the southern part of the country) connect the major cities. Chile has an excellent bus system. Car rentals are widely available, though some of the conditions off the Pan-American Highway can be quite difficult. Spanish is the national language.

The weather in Santiago from November through March (summer) is pleasant and dry, but it can get hot. Winter gets chilly, dropping to as low as 2°C at night. Viña del Mar's climate tends to be milder throughout the year. On Easter Island, the weather is temperate, ranging between 16°C and 27°C.

Important Places

Santiago, surrounded by the Andes, offers beautiful scenery, lovely colonial architecture, and many modern structures. The city has good museums and an excellent planetarium. The most interesting sites include:

- **Plaza de Armas,** where many of the finest colonial buildings are found, including the huge cathedral and the **National Historical Museum.**

- **San Francisco Church and Colonial Art Museum,** a fascinating complex.

In addition to Santiago, Chile provides tourists with other wonderful places to visit, including:

- **Viña del Mar,** a very expensive, fashionable beach resort.

- **Portillo,** one of the world's finest ski resorts, open at full operation from June through September and on a more limited basis the rest of the year. A lively ski carnival takes place here in August (which, of course, is in the middle of winter!). Two other Chilean ski resorts are **Valle Nevado** (near Santiago) and **Chillan.**

- **Easter Island,** far off in the Pacific, with a volcanic, tree-stripped landscape. The most famous attractions here are huge statues, erected most probably for religious purposes. The island can be reached via air (a five-hour flight from the mainland of Chile) or cruise.

Chile is 4240 kilometres long and has no rivers of any size.

The leader of Chile's war of independence was named Bernardo O'Higgins.

Easter Island may have been the world's first manmade ecological disaster. The natives completely deforested the island.

Statues on Easter Island
© 2006 JupiterImages and its Licensors. All Rights Reserved.

Sales Considerations

For many years, Chile was under military rule. However, it's once again a democracy, and tourism is on the rise. The country provides opportunities for skiers as well as beach lovers. Expeditions to Easter Island are popular with culture seekers.

TRAVEL TRIVIA

TOP 10 WHALE-WATCHING AREAS

1. Patagonia, Argentina
2. Southern Ocean Whale Sanctuary, Antarctica
3. Bay of Samana, Dominican Republic
4. Campbell River, BC
5. Cape Cod, MA
6. Baja California, Mexico
7. Kaikoura, New Zealand
8. Cape Town to Cape Agulhas, South Africa
9. Shikoku, Japan
10. Lofoten Islands, Norway

Source: World Wildlife Fund

MAP ACTIVITY

NAME _____   DATE _____

A traveller wants to visit the places listed below. Which number represents each on the map on page 284?

PLACE/ATTRACTION	IN WHICH COUNTRY?	NUMBER ON MAP
A. Montevideo	A.	A.
B. Quito	B.	B.
C. Tikal	C.	C.
D. Cartagena	D.	D.
E. Machu Picchu	E.	E.
F. World's highest capital	F.	F.
G. Angel Falls	G.	G.
H. Buenos Aires	H.	H.
I. Santiago	I.	I.
J. The Golden Triangle	J.	J.

CASE STUDY

NAME _____   DATE _____

German and Leah Ruiz are a couple in their late 30s. Though they were both born in Canada, German's grandparents are from Venezuela and he has relatives there whom he's never met. The couple plan to take a 10-day trip; 6 days will be spent in Venezuela and the remaining time they'll spend in Buenos Aires. They don't have to worry about an itinerary in Venezuela; the relatives will take care of that. Buenos Aires is another matter and that's where they'll need some help.

Circle the answer that best suits their needs.

1. They want to visit an old Italian district known for its colourful houses. Where should they go?

    La Boca   Plaza de Mayo

    San Telmo   Portillo

    Why?

2. They'd like to squeeze in a natural wonder on their way from Venezuela to Buenos Aires. Which would be impossible for them to visit?

    Angel Falls   Iguazu Falls

    The Amazon   The Sea of Tranquility

    Why?

3. Which of the following services would be most appropriate for you to book for them in Buenos Aires?

    A cruise on Lake Titicaca   A city tour

    An Amazon cruise   A ski package

    Why?

4. They decide that they want to drive down the coast for a couple of days and spend some time at a beach resort. Which should it be?

    Mar del Plata   Punta del Este

    Viña del Mar   Villa D'Este

    Why?

NAME _____ DATE _____

A new *Star Wars* movie is in the works. Here's the plot: Luke Skywalker, now an old man, must find a successor to carry on the Jedi tradition. At the same time he is pursued by the evil clone of Darth Vader. First, Skywalker goes to a planet of mountains and ice. Then he travels to a hot, jungle planet. He leaves its lowlands, crosses a parched desert, and climbs to a mysterious ruined city in the cliffs, where a Yoda-like creature gives him many clues. But his pursuers catch up to him here. They chase him behind vast waterfalls and corner him in a fjord—

What? Did you think we'd give away the ending?! Anyway, you're the producer for this movie. You must find the necessary locations to shoot the scenes described. Why not shoot the entire film in Latin America? It will save money, and it has all the scenery needed.

In which Latin American place would you put up cast and crew for each location, assuming that you could take them by train or bus to and from the location each day? (Don't worry about the routing from base to location.) Assume flights are available to all places—no need to look up schedules.

SETTING	PLACE?
1. Mountains and ice	1.
2. Jungle	2.
3. Desert	3.
4. City in the cliffs	4.
5. Waterfalls	5.
6. Fjord	6.

What might be your flight itinerary for this shoot, assuming it starts and ends in Toronto?

The Matching Game

Directions: Below is a list of cities, attractions, etc., some that we have covered, some we haven't. There are all manner of connections among them. With your group, you have exactly 10 minutes to come up with as many connections as possible. (Items may be used more than once.) Place your answers below. Note: There are at least 20 possible connections; e.g., Sugar Loaf and Corcovado—both are mountains.

Dunns River	Bogota	Bariloche
Galapagos	Viña del Mar	Iguazu
Machu Picchu	Las Hadas	Sierra Madres
Las Brisas	Asuncion	Sugar Loaf
Angel	Corcovado	French Guiana
Copacabana	Andes	Easter
Plaza de Mayo	Chichen Itza	Cayman
Copan	Mar del Plata	Haiti
Portillo	Bonaire	Zocalo

ICELAND

NORWEGIAN SEA

SWEDEN

FINLAND

NORWAY

BARENTS SEA

BALTIC
SEA

ESTONIA

RUSSIA

GREAT BRITAIN

NORTH
SEA

SCOTLAND

DENMARK

LATVIA

LITHUANIA

NORTHERN
IRELAND

ENGLAND

NETHERLANDS

GERMANY

POLAND

BELARUS

IRELAND

IRISH
SEA

WALES

BELGIUM

CZECH
REPUBLIC

SLOVAKIA

UKRAINE

English Channel

LUXEMBOURG

Rhine

Alps

AUSTRIA

HUNGARY

MOLDOVA

ATLANTIC OCEAN

SWITZERLAND

SLOVENIA

CROATIA

The Danube

ROMANIA

FRANCE

ITALY

BOSNIA

ADRIATIC SEA

SERBIA

BULGARIA

BLACK SEA

GEORGIA

ANDORRA

Pyrenees

Corsica

MACEDONIA

ALBANIA

ARMENIA

PORTUGAL

SPAIN

Sardinia

TYRRHENIAN
SEA

IONIAN
SEA

GREECE

AEGEAN
SEA

TURKEY

IRA

Sicily

TUNISIA

MALTA

Crete

CYPRUS

SYRIA

IRAQ

MEDITERRANEAN SEA

LEBANON

ISRAEL

MOROCCO

ALGERIA

LIBYA

EGYPT

JORDAN

KUWA

SAUDI ARABIA

IV

EUROPE
Continental Flair

If a Canadian decides to voyage overseas, it will in all probability be to visit Europe (often called "the Continent"). Indeed, Europe is a magnet for tourists from all countries. Most of the top-10 destinations for world travellers are in Europe. Celebrated historical monuments, sun-baked beaches, sparkling ski resorts, landmark hotels, gourmet restaurants, intriguing cultures and people—Europe has all of these. Many jets criss-cross the Atlantic, so it's easy to get there. And once travellers arrive in Europe, they find an efficient network of railroads, highways, buses, motorcoach tours, and subways to get around. This broad array of services offers you, the travel professional, countless opportunities to enhance a person's European vacation.

According to the European Travel Commission, the number-one objection among Canadians to visiting Europe is the cost.

WHERE THE COUNTRIES ARE

Over 40 countries comprise Europe; many of them have their own language and way of life. Don't be intimidated, though. Their locations can be mastered easily, especially when you sort them into logical geographical groupings.

Look at the map. Across the north are the **Scandinavian countries: Iceland, Norway, Sweden, Denmark,** and **Finland.** (Greenland, a seldom-visited destination to the west of Iceland, is usually considered part of North America.) On the Baltic Sea, just beneath the Scandinavian Peninsula, are the **Baltic nations** of **Estonia, Latvia,** and **Lithuania.** In the northwest are the **British Isles,** which consist of **Great Britain** and **Ireland** (which isn't really British at all).

In western Europe are **France** and the **Benelux countries** (*Belgium,* the *Netherlands,* and *Luxembourg*), as well as the **Iberian Peninsula,** which features **Portugal** and **Spain.** Spain is also sometimes included as part of the **Mediterranean countries,** which curve along the northern shore of this legendary sea. Among them are **Italy, Greece,** and **Turkey** (which spills over from Asia).

Many cities in New York State are named after ancient Mediterranean cities. Some examples: Utica, Ithaca, Syracuse, Troy, Carthage, and Rome.

The Eastern European countries are **Poland,** the **Czech Republic, Slovakia** (also known as the Slovak Republic), **Hungary, Romania, Bulgaria,** and **Albania.** The former nation of Yugoslavia is also among these, but it has broken down into a series of smaller countries: **Slovenia, Croatia, Bosnia and Herzegovina, Macedonia,** and what remains of the original Yugoslavia (usually called **Serbia**). In the easternmost portion of Europe is **Russia** and its co-nations in the **Commonwealth of Independent States** (most of the former Soviet Union), which stretches well into Asia. And in the middle of Europe are the nations of Alpine Europe: **Germany, Switzerland,** and **Austria.**

Russia, Azerbaijan, and the United States have one thing in common: They're all split into two pieces by another country.

That's about all you need remember now. We'll mention Europe's smaller countries and principalities in the chapters that follow. Meanwhile, practise filling in a blank map of Europe to master where each country is situated. Do it over and again: You'll master their locations more quickly than you would expect.

A SATELLITE VIEW

If you were looking down from space, it would be impossible to tell one European country from another. Borders, after all, aren't painted across the face of the earth. But things like mountains, oceans, lakes, and rivers have long defined Europe's national boundaries. And these geographic features affect travel plans in major ways.

Bodies of Water

At the English Channel's narrowest point, only 34 kilometres separate Dover, England, from Cape Griz-Nez, France.

The first thing you'd see from a satellite would be the broad blue expanse of the **Atlantic Ocean,** which lies along Europe's western shore. In the north, the **Baltic Sea** separates Scandinavia from Russia and the Baltic States; and the **North Sea** cuts off Great Britain from the Benelux countries, Germany, and Scandinavia. The **Irish Sea** lies between Ireland and Great Britain. From space, the narrow blue line that separates Great Britain from France, the **English Channel,** wouldn't seem very significant, but it has been a critical body of water for centuries and is crossed by numerous ferries, hovercraft, and the Channel Tunnel (or "Chunnel").

And, of course, you'll easily make out the **Mediterranean Sea,** that long, azure feature that splits Europe from Africa. In several places, it stretches long fingers into Europe, including those of the **Adriatic** and **Ionian Seas** (between Italy, Greece, Croatia, and Albania) and the **Aegean Sea** (between Greece and Turkey). The Mediterranean is peppered with islands, many of which are beach or cruise destinations. Finally, the blue oval to the east is the **Black Sea,** a major resort for Eastern European and Russian tourists, as well as an increasingly popular destination for cruise ships.

If you have keen eyes, you could also spot a few major rivers criss-crossing Europe. The **Danube,** celebrated in literature and music, snakes its way eastward out of Germany through Eastern Europe and empties into the Black Sea. Down

The Danube Bend, Hungary
Photo by Marc Mancini

through Europe's middle is the **Rhine,** a river that finds its source in Switzerland and flows northward through Germany and the Netherlands, and eventually into the North Sea. Both rivers offer major cruise opportunities.

You may even be able to spot the lakes of northern Italy and of Switzerland, the fjords of western Norway, and the *lochs* (lakes) of northern Scotland. Many manmade waterways course through the continent, too: Barge rides on canals are an increasingly popular option for vacationers.

Mountains

It's critical to know where the mountains of Europe are; they have a significant impact on weather, travel times, and vacation activities. The most obvious are the **Alps,** the thick, lofty mountains that ripple across Switzerland, Austria, southern Germany, eastern France, and northern Italy. The **Pyrenees,** massive ridges that separate Spain from France, are important, too. Medium-sized mountains and hills are in many other areas; only Denmark, Poland, Hungary, and the Benelux countries are relatively flat.

There are about 40 000 ski runs in the Alps.

Climate

Europe's weather varies immensely according to latitude, altitude, and season. The Alpine mountain areas tend to be cold in winter and cool in summer. Skiers favour the winter, of course, but a surprisingly large number of vacationers visit in the summer. (Late spring or early fall, though, can be glorious and uncrowded.) Northern France, the Benelux countries, Eastern Europe, much of Germany, and the Alpine lowlands are similar to British Columbia: cool to cold in winter, with much dampness and cloudiness; cool to warm in the spring or fall. The Mediterranean rim is an all-year destination, though summers can get hot; winters are mild, but cold weather is not unheard of here. Mediterranean water temperatures are chilly and rain is more common in the winter months.

Precipitation also varies greatly. As you'd expect from what you learned in Part I, Europe's west coasts are wet; this is especially true of Norway's fjord area, the west coasts of Scotland and Ireland, northwestern Portugal, and the eastern shore of the Adriatic. There are also some very dry areas, especially southeastern and central Spain and the area northeast of the Black Sea. Rainfall in the rest of Europe tends to be like that of Atlantic Canada: humid and showery in the summer; rainy, snowy, or cloudy in the winter, with brief, welcome spells of crisp sunshine.

TOURISM PATTERNS

The United Kingdom is the most popular destination among North Americans, with France, Italy, and Spain not far behind. But these days, just about every country in Europe attracts both leisure and business travellers.

One important pattern: Europeans tend to take very long summer vacations, usually from mid-July to late August. And they generally head south to Spain, the French Riviera, Italy, and Greece. As a result, northern European cities seem somewhat empty at this time. Hotel room availability in central and northern Europe is therefore surprisingly good in late summer.

EUROPEAN DISTANCES

Because Europe brims with so many countries, it seems enormous. Yet Europe is smaller than Canada and is about the same size as the United States. A good comparison would be to think of each European nation as a geographic equivalent of a Canadian province or a U.S. state.

Europe is the smallest continent after Australia.

Remember, too, that certain cities in totally separate countries can, in reality, be very close to each other. For example, Brussels, the capital of Belgium, is less

A Scottish Cottage
Photo by Justus Ghormley

than a half-day drive or a 1.5-hour train ride from Paris; Paris is a mere one-hour flight from London; and Munich, Germany, is quite close to Salzburg, Austria.

Once Europe's compactness sinks in, however, it's easy to mistakenly think that travelling times within Europe are always short. Not so. Some nations—like Germany, Belgium, and the Netherlands—do have complex and modern highway systems; that's why car rentals are very popular there. On the other hand, Spain, Portugal, Greece, Ireland, Scotland, most of Scandinavia, and Eastern Europe have a more limited network of highways. As a result, to drive from, say, the Italian Riviera to Rome would take at least two days—even though the distance is about the same as from Toronto to Montreal, which (because of the highway system) is a five-hour drive.

Trains can be a direct and swift alternative, but not always. Europe's high-speed trains are a wonder: They whoosh from Paris to Geneva in 3.5 hours and at speeds approaching 320 kilometres an hour. On the other hand, Lisbon to Madrid (a distance equal to that of Paris to Geneva) takes a full 10.5 hours by train. Old tracks, curving routes, and awkward train connections can make some rail trips long and slow. For most tourists, this wouldn't be acceptable. (However, a slow, leisurely trip might be exactly what some want.) Several luxurious train excursions exist in Europe, including the most legendary of all: the Venice Simplon-Orient-Express. A principal route is London to Venice, but there are many alternative itineraries.

Cruises are very popular. Major cruise areas are the Eastern Mediterranean (including Greece, Turkey, and sometimes Israel and Egypt); the Western Mediterranean (Italy, France, and Spain); a route from Barcelona, Spain, along Portugal and France, and on to Great Britain; a British Isles itinerary; and several routings that call on ports in France, the Netherlands, Germany, Scandinavia, the Baltics, and Russia. Most European cruises are 7 to 14 days in length. In addition to cruise ships, Europe's waterways also feature small barges, large riverboats, and very large ferries, which sometimes offer overnight accommodations.

And what of aircraft? Of course they provide rapid European connections, though sometimes high-speed trains are just as fast. Air travel, however, doesn't provide those features that make train travel and motoring attractive: the scenery

The most famous high-speed trains are Eurostar (Transchunnel), ICE (Germany), TGV (France), X2000 (Sweden), AVE (Spain), and Pendolino (Italy).

along the way, travel unaffected by snow or fog (especially true for trains), and the option to stop and see some magnificent castle or fairytale town. One offbeat option: short or multi-day balloon trips, most often staged in France and Italy, but also available in Switzerland, Austria, and Turkey.

SOME MISCELLANEOUS CONSIDERATIONS

Certain bits of knowledge can help fine-tune your understanding of Europe. Here are a few considerations:

- Many European hotels are old and lack elevators, have small rooms, and feature only single-sized beds. Always check standard industry references before making reservations and make sure the lodging matches what the traveller wants.

- Eurailpasses are handy (though not quite the bargain they used to be) and an important item to cross-sell. These passes often cover airport transfers and ferries, too. Consult the Internet for rates, countries covered, services offered, and the like. First class is probably better for Canadian visitors, since in many countries second-class cars can be crowded, uncomfortable, or both. (The second-class Youth Pass is available for travellers under 26 years of age and may be a reasonable alternative.) Keep in mind that some privately run trains do not accept Eurailpasses.

Eurailpasses (and many single-country and regional passes) can be purchased only in North America.

- A single-country or regional train pass is a better value for a person travelling extensively in only one area. Some countries even offer rail–drive–lodging packages.

- Seeing Europe by car appeals to those who are used to driving when they vacation in Canada. It offers much more routing, scheduling, and sightseeing flexibility than do trains. The same applies to camper rentals, which have become an increasingly popular way of motoring through Europe. One warning, though: European driving—with its very high-speed highways, twisting secondary roads, narrow city streets, limited parking, many tolls, and high gasoline prices—can challenge the best driver. Also, travellers who rent a car in central or northern Europe may be told when they pick up the car that they cannot drive it in southern Europe, or that their insurance will not cover them in the south. It's important to know in advance if such conditions will apply.

Cars in most European nations tend to be small. The reasons: so they can navigate the very narrow streets in city centres; and because gasoline is much more expensive than in Canada.

- Most European countries have their own airlines, which offer regular service to major Canadian gateways and are partners in the frequent-flyer programs of North American carriers—a major consideration for some travellers.

- In the past, flights between countries in Europe were expensive. This has changed, however, as low-fare airlines have appeared throughout Europe.

- European carriers often offer fly–drive packages at substantially discounted rates.

About 60 cities and towns around the world promote themselves as "Little Switzerlands."

- Most major European cities are quite expensive, with Paris, Milan, Venice, London, and the Scandinavian capitals among the most costly in the world. Portugal, Ireland, Greece, Turkey, and some places in Eastern Europe are still relative bargains.

- In the following chapters, under "Lodging Options," you'll be reading about hotel chains that have major presences in Europe, such as Novotel, Le Meridien, Golden Tulip, and Mövenpick. Canadian and U.S. companies include Fairmont, Four Seasons, Sheraton, Marriott, Holiday Inn, Best Western, Hyatt, and Hilton. Be aware that there are many European hotels that are part of no official chain, but are represented by reservation organizations. For example, some of Europe's (and the world's) most exclusive hotels are booked via Leading Hotels of the World and Preferred Hotels. Even some hotels that *are* part of major chains can also be affiliated with these two organizations for the prestige it brings. A service that represents a broader range of hotel values in Europe is Utell International.

 Currently, the euro is used in 12 countries: Belgium, Germany, Greece, Spain, France, Ireland, Italy, Luxembourg, the Netherlands, Austria, Portugal, and Finland.

- Europe is striving to become a more unified political and economic unit. It has become easier for tourists to cross borders; intra-Europe flight costs are dropping, and more multi-country high-speed train lines have been built. Much of Europe has a single currency (the euro), standardized electrical outlets, uniform value-added taxes (VAT: taxes on goods and services), and passport-free travel. But longstanding traditions have made these tourism-facilitating breakthroughs a bit slow to achieve.

TRAVEL TRIVIA

YOU KNOW IT'S SPRING IN . . . WHEN . . .

- The Netherlands and Ottawa: The tulips bloom.

- Rome: Outdoor Easter Mass is celebrated at St. Peter's.

- Alaska: You hear the sound of ice breaking up on the rivers.

- Washington, D.C., and Tokyo: The cherry blossoms bloom.

- Sydney: People start planning their Christmas shopping.

- New York City: The Easter Parade takes place on Fifth Avenue.

- Guatemala: The Passion play is performed in the city of Antigua.

- Daytona Beach, Palm Springs, Fort Lauderdale, Clearwater, and South Padre Island: Students pour in for Spring Break.

- London: Someone first sights a cuckoo bird.

CREATIVE ACTIVITY

NAME _____ DATE _____

The kinds of people who prefer to visit Europe via rental car are different from those who wish to do so by train, plane, or ship. What do you think are the advantages and disadvantages of each way of getting around?

	ADVANTAGES	DISADVANTAGES
Car Rental:	1. Stop where/when you want	1. Dealing with traffic
	2.	2.
	3.	3.
Rail Travel:	1.	1.
	2.	2.
City-to-City Air Travel:	1.	1.
	2.	2.
Cruise Travel:	1.	1.
	2.	2.

ATLANTIC
OCEAN

SCOTLAND
*Loch
Ness*
Gleneagles
The Trossachs ● St. Andrews
*Loch
Lomond* ▲ *Firth
of Forth*
✈ ⊗ Edinburgh
● Glasgow
● Prestwick

Giant's Causeway

**NORTHERN
IRELAND**
Belfast ⊗

United

DONEGAL BAY

● Bundoran

Isle
of
Man

Kingdom
York ●

IRELAND
✈ ☆
GALWAY BAY Dublin
Cliffs of Moher ● Galway
Caernarfon

● Manchester

Mt. Snowdon
✈ ▲ Portmeirion
● Limerick
Waterford ●

*IRISH
SEA*

Snowdonia
National Park

ENGLAND

Stratford-
Upon-Avon

*Thames
River*

WALES Wye
Cardiff Valley

● Killarney
Ring of
Kerry
● Blarney ● Cork

Bath ● ● Canterbury
London Dover
Stonehenge ▲ ⊗ *Chunnel*
Windsor Greenwich
Salisbury ● Southampton

*NORTH
SEA*

Shetland Islands (Scotland)

NETHERLAN

● Calais

BELGIUM

ENGLISH CHANNEL

FRANCE

CHAPTER 17

Great Britain and Ireland

Foreign, Yet Familiar

Great Britain and Ireland may be perfect for a first visit for someone who hasn't yet been to Europe. Far across the Atlantic, they're distant and different enough to be intriguing, yet their language and familiar culture offer a sense of security and comfort.

How do England, Great Britain, and the United Kingdom differ? The *United Kingdom* is made up of four quasi-independent countries. Three of them constitute the island of *Great Britain:* **England,** the largest (about the size of New Brunswick and Nova Scotia combined), is to the southeast (the term *England* is sometimes used—incorrectly—for all of Great Britain); **Wales** is southwest; and **Scotland** is

Names in Great Britain aren't always pronounced the way they look. For example, the Scottish town of Kirkcudbright is pronounced "kuh-KOO-bree."

GREAT BRITAIN AND IRELAND

Capitals: GB: London
           IRE: Dublin

Populations: GB: 58 700 000
               IRE: 4 000 000

Areas (square km): GB: 244 700
                   IRE: 69 900

Religions: GB: Protestant
          IRE: Roman Catholic

Time Zone: GMT + –0

Language: English

Drive on: Left

Currencies: GB: 1 pound = 100 pence
              IRE: 1 euro = 100 cents

Electricity: 220 volts, 50 cycles AC

Capsule History: **Great Britain:** Rome invades, 1st century B.C.; Angles and Saxons invade, 5th century; England united, 11th century; Normans invade, 1066; Magna Carta signed, 1215; Church of England breaks from Pope, 16th century; formation of parliament, 18th century; World War I, 1914; World War II, 1939; first woman prime minister, 1979; greater autonomy given to Scotland and Wales, 1997.

Ireland: St. Patrick introduces Christianity, 432; Norsemen defeated, 1014; becomes separate republic, 1921.

For reference sources and suggested lengths of stay, see Appendixes A and B.

to the north. The fourth is **Northern Ireland,** across the Irish Sea on the northeast corner of the island of Ireland. (In this chapter we'll use the term *Great Britain,* since we're focusing on England, Scotland, and Wales.) The nation of **Ireland** is distinct from Northern Ireland. It's a separate country from the United Kingdom and feels very strongly about its independence.

A little less than half the size of the Yukon, Great Britain has two centres of tourism. **London,** a world unto itself, is a base for day trips in England; and **Edinburgh** [ED-in-bur-ro] is the heart of Scottish touring. Ireland has no real hub; visitors travel from town to town.

HOW TRAVELLERS GET THERE

There's extensive scheduled and charter service to London on domestic and foreign carriers. Most travellers arrive at **Heathrow Airport** (LHR), but **Gatwick** (LGW) and **Stansted** (STN)—which are farther out—also offer many flights. All three offer rail service into the city. Visitors heading directly to Scotland may fly into **Glasgow** (GLA), Edinburgh Airport (EDI), or even to **Manchester** (MAN), which lies halfway between London and Scotland. Travel time to London from Toronto is seven hours; from Vancouver or Calgary it's about nine hours. The national airline, **British Airways** (BA), flies throughout the world; **Virgin Atlantic** (VS) services North America and Europe; and **British Midland** (BD) flies domestically and to the Continent.

A hovercraft crosses the English Channel from Dover to France, and many ferries operate from other towns along both coasts. The **Channel Tunnel** (or "**Chunnel**") connects **Folkestone** (west of Dover) to Calais, France, and permits passengers to travel between Paris and London via the high-speed **Eurostar** train in under three hours.

Even though **Dublin** (DUB) is Ireland's capital and has a major airport, the country's principal air gateway is **Shannon** (SNN), outside **Limerick.** The national airline, **Aer Lingus** (EI), is the major carrier into Shannon, but its North American flights are from New York and Boston, so many Canadians choose charter carriers. Flights are six hours; some continue on to Dublin, which takes approximately 35 minutes more.

Cruises from Great Britain and Ireland to Spain, France, Germany, and other countries are numerous. England has three embarkation ports: **Southampton, Tilbury,** and **Tower** (in London itself). Cunard Line offers regularly scheduled cruise sailings from New York City to Southampton. Ships on repositioning or round-the-world cruises also often stop at ports in the British Isles.

WEATHER PATTERNS

Because of the warming influence of the Gulf Stream, Great Britain's generally moderate climate is similar to Vancouver's. The famous London fog is a memory of the past; it was actually smog, which has been brought under control. English summers hover around 20°C. Conditions change often between sunshine and rain. Winters are sharp (near 5°C) and wet, with occasional snow (see Figure 17-1). Most tourists visit between mid-April and mid-October; the peak tourist season extends from June to September. Scotland is cooler and rainier than England in winter, but summers are about the same. The best time to see Great Britain may be spring or fall, when the weather is still pretty good and crowds are somewhat thinner. The period just after New Year's is particularly slow; it's one of the only times to get bargains in London.

Ireland's weather is similar to Great Britain's, but runs slightly cooler, cloudier, and wetter. As a result, the tourist season is a bit shorter: May to September.

⊙ BritRail passes for unlimited train travel in Britain can be bought only in North America. The Eurailpass does not cover Britain (but does cover Ireland).

⊙ Luxurious Apsley House, once home of the first Duke of Wellington, is now open to visitors.

Figure 17-1   Climate at a Glance: London, England

MONTH	JAN	FEB	MAR	APR	MAY	JUN	JUL	AUG	SEP	OCT	NOV	DEC
AVERAGE HIGH TEMPERATURE	7	7	11	13	17	21	23	22	19	14	9	7
AVERAGE LOW TEMPERATURE	2	2	3	4	7	11	13	12	11	7	4	2
AVERAGE PRECIPITATION (IN CENTIMETRES)	5	5	3	5	5	5	5	5	5	5	8	5

Summers are in the upper teens, with frequent rain showers and fog (but long periods of daylight). Winters have more misty, rainy, or overcast days. It's hard to avoid precipitation here, but that's why the land is such a deep green. Ireland isn't called the Emerald Isle for nothing.

GETTING AROUND

Many airlines and flights connect the area's major cities. The excellent rail system links towns throughout Great Britain, as do many buses. (Some high-speed trains cover distances in half the time a car would.) Visitors can also reach Ireland by ferry, and once there, travel by train and bus.

London, despite its size, is easy for tourists to navigate. The subway system (called the Underground or the Tube) goes almost everywhere. Visitors can use two of the great transportation icons: the lumpy taxis and the red double-decker buses. (Though most double-deckers have been phased out, they are still used on two routes.) London is also a very walkable city.

What about driving? Car rentals are widely available, but mastering the art of tooling down the "wrong" side of the road is, without question, one of life's challenges. Actually, though, driving down a quiet country lane can be a joy—except for the odd, circular intersections called roundabouts—but in major cities there are saner ways for a tourist to get around.

City and multi-day tours are popular. Boats along the **Thames [TEMZ] River** in London are common, leisurely barge cruises through the countryside are delightful, and several cruise lines operate itineraries that call on English, Scottish, Welsh, and Irish ports.

Purchase multi-day discount transit passes at Tube stations in London. They save money and allow you to bypass the long lines waiting to buy tickets.

In 1300, the Pope declared that pilgrims should keep to the left on roads. The reason: so they could reach their swords easily if they passed a bandit. In the 1700s, the French began keeping to the right to let carriages go by. Napoleon spread the custom throughout Europe and it was copied by the newly formed United States. But the British never changed, nor did many of their colonies. Today, only 30 percent of the world travels on the left.

An especially interesting London pub is the Mayflower, which has on display an old copy of the passenger list of its namesake ship.

IMPORTANT PLACES

Great Britain and Ireland abound with charming cities, villages, and attractions. There are some unique treasures here, even a few that are tied closely to the history of Canada.

England

London—one of the largest and most lively cities in the world—offers a remarkable range of culture, history, and arts. First-time visitors will probably spend most of their time within the city. However, since London is also the central hub for seeing England, day trips offer veteran tourists even more opportunities. Return visitors to London will always find new plays to see (theatre tickets are reasonably priced), as well as unexplored museums, shops, and streets. Among the most important attractions:

- **The Tower of London,** home of the Crown Jewels, infamous prisons, and armouries. There are lots of tourists here and lots of historical pageantry, too. The Tower is, after all, one of Britain's top tourist attractions.

- **St. Paul's Cathedral,** the largest church in London, designed by Christopher Wren. In its Whispering Gallery, a word whispered to the wall can be heard clearly on the other side, over 30 metres away.

- **The British Museum,** a vast, legendary collection of such items as the Rosetta Stone and the Elgin (Parthenon) Marbles.

- **Buckingham Palace**'s Changing of the Guard, perhaps what tourists think of most when they think of London. Parts of the palace are occasionally open to tourists.

- **Westminster Abbey,** housing within its magnificent Gothic architecture the burial places of many of Great Britain's royalty, historical figures, and literary giants. Nearby are the **Houses of Parliament** and **Big Ben** (which isn't the famous tower or clock, but the bell).

In northwest London is the largest Hindu temple outside India.

Visitors can tour the interior of famous Tower Bridge.

Attending an Evensong service at a British cathedral can be a moving experience.

An exact reproduction of Shakespeare's Globe Theatre has been built in London near its original site.

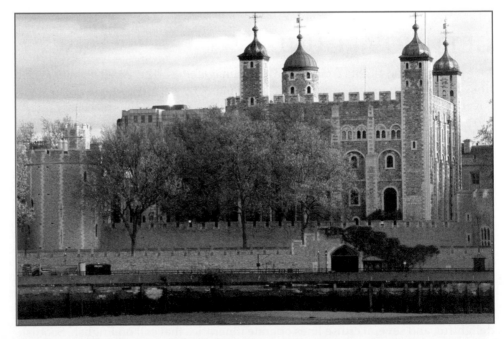

The Tower of London, London, England
Copyright COREL

- **The London Eye,** a tall, modern observation wheel on the south bank of the Thames. The 30-minute ride gives passengers great views of London and the surrounding countryside.

- **Several well-known shopping districts and stores,** including Harrods and Selfridges (two famous department stores), Oxford Street, Regent Street, and Covent Garden.

London offers a wealth of **day trip** options:

- **Stonehenge,** the strange, mystical circle of huge stones, a close drive to **Salisbury** (with its beautiful cathedral).

- **Stratford-upon-Avon** [AY-ven], a charming town that's Shakespeare's birthplace and home of the Royal Shakespeare Company.

- **Hampton Court Palace,** the expansive estate of Henry VIII, with its famous garden maze.

- **Windsor Castle,** home to Britain's monarchs for nearly 1000 years. It's the oldest inhabited castle in the world.

- **Greenwich** [GRIH-nij], just down-river from London, site of the **National Maritime Museum,** the **Old Royal Observatory,** and the clipper ship *Cutty Sark.*

- **Bath,** an elegant city of Georgian architecture and Roman baths.

- **Canterbury,** an ancient, picturesque city with a magnificent cathedral that's the centrepiece of the Church of England and the destination of the pilgrims in Chaucer's famous work *The Canterbury Tales.* Minutes away are the **White Cliffs of Dover.**

- **York,** a walled medieval city that boasts the **National Railway Museum** (the world's largest), **York Minster** (a huge Gothic cathedral with impressive

 When shopping, ask the salesperson about refunds on the VAT (a tax on all goods and services). Many stores participate in a service that mails you a cheque or credits your credit card account for the VAT on purchases over a certain amount.

In York, streets are called "gates," gates are called "bars," and bars are called "pubs."

The Old Weavers' House, Canterbury, England
Photo by Karen Fukushima

stained glass), the **Castle Museum** (with a re-created Victorian street), and the **Jorvik Viking Centre** (a reconstruction of the 10th-century Viking settlement that became York).

Scotland

Edinburgh, the capital of Scotland, has a regal, medieval ambience. It's a port city located on the Firth of Forth and is a good jumping-off point for the area. Among its best attractions:

The Edinburgh International Festival, the world's largest arts festival, is held in late August.

- **Edinburgh Castle** looks the way a person imagines a castle should look, looming high above the city and built out of the rock it sits on.

- **The Palace of Holyroodhouse** is the residence of Queen Elizabeth II when she is in the city; it retains an infamous association with Mary, Queen of Scots.

- **The Royal Mile** connects Edinburgh Castle and Holyroodhouse. It's the oldest and most historic area of the city.

Some of the best **day trips:**

- **The Trossachs** [TRAH-sacks], the area of Scotland's most beautiful moors and *lochs* (lakes), are a long drive and deserve more than one day.

- **Glasgow** is an industrial town, but with excellent theatre, fine arts, and the superb **Burrell Collection** museum. It's near famous **Loch Lomond** and is surrounded by very pretty countryside.

The British Open golf tournament, held in mid-July, is usually played in Scotland at St. Andrews or Gleneagles.

- **The Glasgow–Edinburgh area** is considered a virtual shrine for golfers. There are seven championship courses, including the legendary **Old Course** at **St. Andrews,** and **Gleneagles.**

- **Loch Ness** is well known for its often-sighted but never-found monster.

Wales

Though perhaps not as familiar as other parts of Britain, Wales nonetheless contains interesting sights. It's a land of mountains and castles, with a strong Celtic influence. Many residents of North Wales speak Welsh as their first language. Among the attractions in Wales:

The village with the longest place name in the world is in northern Wales: Llanfairpwllgwyngyllgogerychwyrndrobwllllantysiliogogogoch, known locally as Llanfair P.G.

- **Snowdonia National Park.** Steam trains climb to the summit of **Mt. Snowdon** for spectacular views of North Wales. Also in the park is **Blaenau Ffestiniog** [BLINE-ee fes-TIN-yog], a slate quarry centre with tours of the underground mines.

- **Caernarfon** [kyre-NAR-von]. The town is still partially encircled by its walls and is dominated by the huge castle where Charles was invested as Prince of Wales. Other impressive castles in northern Wales include **Conwy** (with a landmark suspension bridge nearby) and **Harlech** [HAR-leck] (built high on a rocky crag).

- **Portmeirion** [port-MARE-ee-on]. This extraordinary Italian-style village overlooking the sea was the setting for the 1960s TV series *The Prisoner.* It's now a hotel and is also famous for Portmeirion china.

- **The Wye Valley.** In this valley on the English border are many semi-ruined castles and churches, including well-known **Tintern Abbey. Hay-on-Wye** is a book-lover's dream; most of the town consists of second-hand bookstores. World-famous authors give readings at its annual literary festivals.

- **Cardiff.** The capital of Wales, Cardiff boasts a whimsically restored castle and the **Welsh Folk Museum** at **St. Fagans.** Buildings from all over Wales were reassembled here, providing a living history of the nation.

Giants Causeway
Copyright COREL

According to local legend, Giants Causeway was built by a giant.

Remember, too, that Northern Ireland, despite its political problems, still manages to attract many travellers. Visitors to Scotland or to Ireland often sidetrack for a few days to see Northern Ireland's scenic countryside or to play on its many golf courses. Giants Causeway, a natural formation of volcanic columns in the sea off Northern Ireland's north coast, is fascinating.

Ireland

Ireland has no true touring centre and is so compact, most visitors choose to see it via a car rental or motorcoach tour. Among the towns and attractions they visit:

- **Dublin,** the capital of Ireland, has a stormy and vibrant past. It offers a rich collection of medieval history, modern arts, and pubs. Among its attractions are **St. Patrick's Cathedral,** containing many monuments and plaques; **Christ Church**'s vaulted crypt; **Dublin Castle,** part of which dates back to the Celts; **Trinity College,** with a collection of old book treasures (including the Book of Kells); and the **National Museum,** holding one of the world's great gold collections (with some Bronze Age pieces).

- **Bundoran,** a popular resort, is located on **Donegal Bay.** Nearby is picturesque **Glenveigh National Park.**

- **Galway,** a beautiful and charming town on **Galway Bay,** is best visited by taking a relaxed walking tour. Just southwest of Galway are the spectacular **Cliffs of Moher.**

- **Limerick** is the first stop in Ireland after arriving at Shannon Airport. Historic, ancient architecture is everywhere, including **St. Mary's Church.**

- **Killarney** is renowned for its magnificent scenery of lakes, forests, and mountains. Nearby are **Bourne Vincent Memorial Park,** a national park; **Gap of Dunloe,** a stunning gorge; and the **Ring of Kerry,** a scenic drive past cliffs, mountains, lakes, and villages.

- **Cork** has extensive arts and cultural activities, including choral and drama festivals, ballet, and opera.

- **Blarney** is the town—about 10 kilometres from Cork—that's famous for its **Blarney Stone,** which is said to give the gift of eloquence to anyone who kisses it.

- **Waterford** is best known for its world-famous **Waterford crystal factory.**

POSSIBLE ITINERARIES

First-time visitors should spend about a week in London, including time for day trips through the area. The more experienced will still probably want to spend some time there before (or after) exploring the English countryside, Scotland, and Wales. Ireland could stand on its own for a full week. To visit the entire area of Great Britain and Ireland requires a stay of at least two weeks.

LODGING OPTIONS

Some of the most famous (and expensive) hotels in the world are in London's West End: **Claridge's,** the **Dorchester,** the **Ritz,** and the **Savoy.** Many interesting lodging alternatives exist, including bed-and-breakfasts, flats (apartments), manors and castles, and even working farms.

If conventional hotels remain the lodging of choice, there are other wonderful places to choose from, such as the very-English **Brown's** in London and the **Caledonian** in Edinburgh (though these, again, are costly). Among the most popular chains in Great Britain are **Millennium & Copthorne, Swallow, Moat House,** and **Thistle.** North American chains also have a large presence.

Ireland offers its own wide range of accommodations, and prices are lower than in Great Britain. There are still, of course, many first-class hotels, like Dublin's **Shelbourne** and **Burlington. Jurys** is a large Irish chain. However, like Great Britain, Ireland offers wonderful alternative housing. Notable among these are the spectacular **Ashford Castle** near Galway and **Dromoland Castle** near Limerick, both of which offer stunning grounds. Other castles and manors, as well as bed-and-breakfasts, farmhouses, and cottages, can be found.

ALLIED DESTINATIONS

Great Britain and Ireland are an ideal starting point for a visit to the rest of Europe. France, especially, is an easy connection. And just across the North Sea are Denmark and the rest of Scandinavia, the Netherlands, and Belgium. Travellers can get to these places via air, ferry, cruise, and (through the Chunnel) train.

CULTURAL PATTERNS

Yes, visitors find Great Britain and Ireland to be comfortable and familiar destinations. Nonetheless, these nations have distinct cultural patterns, as well. Here are a few tips:

- Business appointments must be booked well in advance.

- Honorary titles are *always* used, even among friends.

- Words for food are often different from those used in North America. *Pudding* can refer to dessert in general. *Biscuits* are cookies. *Beer* is generally bitter, dark, and tepid. (What North Americans call beer is known as *lager.*) *Crisps* are potato chips; *chips* are French fries.

- Don't talk shop over drinks and dinner unless a local does it first.

- The British are generally reserved and subdued. Politeness is still the standard here.

Members of the Irish rock band U2 own Dublin's Clarence Hotel.

London has over 150 000 surveillance cameras. If you walk around London for a day, cameras will capture your picture about 300 times.

Whisky is distilled in Scotland; *whiskey* (with an *e*) is distilled in Ireland.

- The peoples of Great Britain and Ireland are proud of their respective histories. Any visitor would do well to show an interest in these countries' pasts as well as current events.

- Promptness is important, especially for business appointments.

- When visiting the home of a local, it's not necessary to bring a gift; however, it's considered a thoughtful gesture. Any gift should be presented to the lady of the house.

- Scotland, Wales, and Northern Ireland are *not* England; they are all distinct regions of the United Kingdom. People here are very sensitive to these distinctions.

- Clearly, it's impossible and inappropriate to stereotype how people in each of these countries will act in every instance. There are, however, generalizations: Scotland tends to be more open, independent, and fun loving than England. Be careful about discussing religion and politics in Northern Ireland, where it's an extremely sensitive subject. And Ireland is generally a friendly, exuberant land.

FACTORS THAT MOTIVATE VISITORS

The major reasons for Canadians to choose these destinations are cultural ties and ease of language; however, there might be other reasons, too. Understanding them all is essential in setting up a memorable trip:

- There are more air connections from North America to London than to any other international city.

- Convenient public transportation and cruise options make the countries easy to get around.

- Picturesque villages are just about everywhere.

- A diverse span of accommodations and price levels is available.

- London is a major centre for cultural attractions and the theatre.

- Ireland is relatively inexpensive and can be the choice of budget-minded vacationers.

- The region is well known for its lush scenery.

- Many visitors have retained a close family association to Ireland and Great Britain and want to trace their roots here.

- The locals are known to be courteous and hospitable.

- And, yes, of course, English is spoken and the culture is familiar.

Some place names in Ontario show its Anglo-Celtic roots, such as Dublin, London, Stratford, and Windsor.

POSSIBLE MISGIVINGS

For any destination, including Great Britain and Ireland, people will always have concerns you'll have to address:

- "Driving on the left intimidates me." Public transportation is a widespread alternative.

- "Isn't the food really bland?" The best meals, especially in London, tend to be foreign; try Indian, Italian, Asian, or African restaurants. Even traditional English food has improved. The new cuisine emphasizes the fresh foods readily available throughout the country.

- "It's extremely expensive there." Bed-and-breakfasts are a reasonable alternative, as are tourist-class hotels. Suggest Scotland, Wales, Ireland, or the English countryside, where costs are much lower than in London.

- "I've been to London and seen everything." The many other areas of Great Britain and Ireland offer a wealth of options.

- "The political unrest in Ireland frightens me." The country of Ireland is calm. The problems have been in Northern Ireland and, even there, the chances are slim that tourists will be affected.

- "Ireland's so rainy." This is precisely why it's so green and beautiful, but for sun seekers there are better choices.

Qualifying the Traveller
LONDON

FOR PEOPLE WHO WANT	HIGH APPEAL	MEDIUM APPEAL	LOW APPEAL	REMARKS
Historical and Cultural Attractions	▲			London's chief asset
Beaches and Water Sports			▲	So-so beaches to south
Skiing Opportunities			▲	None
Lots of Nightlife	▲			Especially theatre
Family Activities		▲		Mostly sightseeing
Familiar Cultural Experience		▲		Foreign, but English-speaking
Exotic Cultural Experience		▲		
Safety and Low Crime		▲		Some visitors fear terrorism
Bargain Travel		▲		Some hotels are a bargain
Impressive Scenery		▲		Especially the countryside
Peace and Quiet			▲	Some parts quiet
Shopping Opportunities	▲			Antiques, china, woollens, legendary department stores
Adventure			▲	Outside of the city
To Do Business	▲			Many North American businesses are British-owned and vice versa

SALES STRATEGIES

The unique qualities of Great Britain and Ireland provide many selling opportunities. Motorcoach tours free visitors from the anxiety of driving on the left side of the road. Cruises call on most of the essential places, as well as a few less-visited ports. Lodging in castles might be that rare treat that makes a trip especially memorable. Barge cruises afford tourists a slow but special view of the country. Theatre packages in London solve the problem of getting tickets to hit shows. An overnight ferry ride to Scandinavia turns yet one more connection into an adventure.

And remember: For those who are hesitant about visiting Europe because it's a "foreign" place, Great Britain and Ireland are ideal choices. The familiarity of language and customs make this a comfortable recommendation, whether as a stand-alone destination or as a first stop on the way to other European countries.

TRAVEL TRIVIA

THE FIRST. . .

- *Hotel* was Low's Grand Hotel—Covent Garden, London (1774)
- *Airline* with scheduled passenger service was the St. Petersburg–Tampa Airboat Line of Florida (1914)
- *In-flight film* was *The Lost World*, on Imperial Airways (1925)
- *Travel agency* was the Thomas Cook Agency—Leicester, England (1841)
- *Tour* was conducted by Thomas Cook from London to Liverpool (1845)
- *American Express traveller's cheque* was cashed for $50 at the Hotel Hauffe—Leipzig, Germany—by William Fargo (1891)
- *Highway* was the Avus Autobahn—Berlin, Germany (1921)
- *Subway* was built in London (1860)

Source: The Book of Firsts

NAME _____   DATE _____

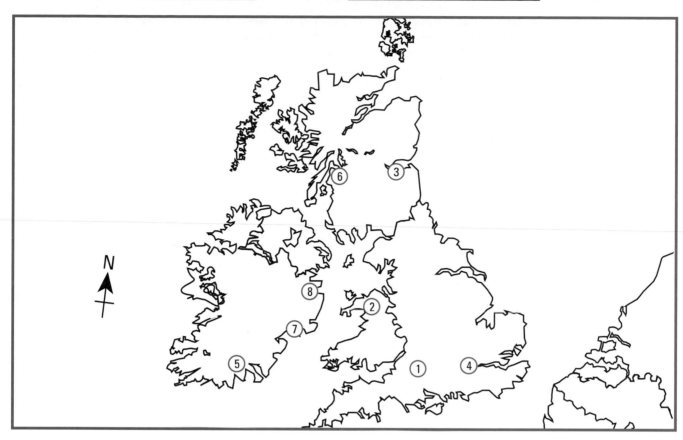

A traveller wants to visit the places listed below. Which number represents each on the map?

PLACE/ATTRACTION	IN/NEAR WHICH CITY?	NUMBER ON MAP
A. Stonehenge	A.	A.
B. Palace of Holyroodhouse	B.	B.
C. Italian-style village famous for china	C.	C.
D. The Blarney Stone	D.	D.
E. The Burrell Collection	E.	E.
F. St. Paul's Cathedral	F.	F.
G. A crystal factory	G.	G.
H. The Crown Jewels	H.	H.
I. Trinity College	I.	I.
J. The Royal Mile	J.	J.

CASE STUDY

NAME _____   DATE _____

Don and Karen Robinson are a couple in their late 30s, living in Red Deer, Alberta. They were in London 13 years ago, when they were first married; now, however, they have a 12-year-old son and are planning to return to the area. They would like to see some new sights, but don't want their son to miss out on anything. They have great curiosity and love theatre, but Karen is not very adventurous in travelling. They can take off five workdays. They're staying in a hotel in London's Mayfair district. (To do this case study fully, you'll need to do a little research, either on the Internet or in print resources.)

Circle the answer that best suits their needs.

1. How many days total would be best for their trip?

    Three   Five

    Eight   Ten

    Why?

2. On what area would you suggest they concentrate?

    London and environs   London and Scotland

    London and Ireland   Wales and Northern Ireland

    Why?

3. Which of the following would you not recommend?

    A trip to Stonehenge   A BritRail pass

    A barge cruise   A city tour

    Why?

4. Which of the following statements would be correct?

    You'll probably have a nice view of the Tower of London from your hotel room.

    Hyde Park will be just a short stroll from your hotel.

    Your hotel is right on the River Thames.

    The Royal Mile, where you're staying, is lined with wonderful shopping.

    Why?

CREATIVE ACTIVITY

NAME _____ DATE _____

You're studying to be a London city Blue Guide. Blue Guides are considered to be among the world's most knowledgeable tour guides. Using the Internet and/or reference books (refer to the appendixes for suggestions), answer the following questions regarding sights in London you'll have to be informed about.

1. How big is the "City of London"?

2. What is the Rosetta Stone?

3. What is Piccadilly Circus?

4. Where is London Bridge?

5. Whose statue is in Trafalgar Square?

6. Which art museum is housed in a converted power station?

7. Where does the Changing of the Horse Guards take place?

8. Who lives at 10 Downing Street?

9. Where was Anne Boleyn beheaded?

10. What is the Serpentine?

11. Where is Chaucer buried?

12. What is Hamleys?

13. Near which park is Madame Tussaud's?

14. When during the year does the Wimbledon tennis tournament take place?

15. Where is the *Magna Carta* kept?

Your research sources:

ENGLAND

Chunnel

GERMANY

BELGIUM

ENGLISH CHANNEL

LUXEMBOURG

Omaha Beach

Honfleur

Rouen

Reims

Arromanches

Giverny

Disneyland Paris

Deauville

Bayeux

Versailles

Paris

Normandy

Chartres

Fontainebleau

Alsace

Mont-St-Michel

Champagne District

Brittany

River Seine

Tours

Loire River

FRANCE

Dijon

AUSTRIA

Saumur

Beaune

SWITZERLAND

Lake Geneva

Burgundy

Alps

Evian

Annecy

Chamonix

Bay of Biscay

Medoc

Lascaux

Perouges

Mont Blanc

Lyon

St-Emilion

Bordeaux

Dordogne River

Val d'Isère

ITALY

Aquitaine

Rhone River

Grenoble

Provence

Toulouse

Avignon

Monaco

Nice

Biarritz

St-Paul de Vence

Grasse

Cap d'Antibes

Lourdes

Carcassonne

Cannes

Pyrenees

Marseilles

St-Tropez

SPAIN

MEDITERRANEAN SEA

Riviera (Côte d'Azur)

ANDORRA

CORSICA

18

France

The Movable Feast

Ernest Hemingway, in a bit of memorable phrasing, called **Paris** "a movable feast." The same can be said for all of France. Whether it's because of food, culture, language, or history, visitors bring back with them strong, fond memories of their feast-like visit to this rich country. Paris clearly is the focal point of most trips to France. However, to acquire a full appreciation of this country, you have to go beyond Paris. Indeed, its eight richly diverse regions could each merit a separate vacation.

FRANCE

Capital: Paris

Area (square km): 551 216

Time Zone: GMT +1

Drive on: Right

Population: 60 700 000

Religion: Roman Catholic

Language: French

Currency: 1 euro = 100 cents

Electricity: 220 volts, 50 cycles AC

Capsule History: Caesar conquers Gaul, 57–52 B.C.; becomes distinct country, 843; Louis XIV reigns, 1643–1715; revolution, 1789; Napoleon becomes emperor, 1804; Louis XVIII begins reign, 1815; second revolution, 1848; second empire, 1852; Germany invades, 1940; France liberated, 1944; de Gaulle begins rule, 1946; de Gaulle loses election after violent demonstrations and strikes, 1969.

For reference sources and suggested lengths of stay, see Appendixes A and B.

France is the largest country completely within Europe; it's about half the size of Ontario. Cosmopolitan, unique Paris sits in the north-centre of the country. Heading west (and counterclockwise) are the beaches of **Normandy,** with their seaside towns, war memorials, and medieval architecture. Below Normandy and Paris are the magnificent *châteaux* (castles) of the **Loire** [LWAHR] **River Valley.** South of the Loire region is the **Aquitaine** district, with its legendary wines, Roman ruins, and prehistoric sites. Along France's border with Spain are the **Pyrenees,** a place of scenery, shrines, and skiing. In southeastern France is the **Provence** region.

The French wine industry dates back to around 600 B.C.

Stretching along France's Mediterranean coast are the chic beaches of the **French Riviera,** also known as the **Côte d'Azur.** To the north are the fashionable ski resorts of the French Alps. Then, stretching northward toward Paris is France's **Eastern Wine Country,** including the **Burgundy** and **Champagne** districts. To the southwest, off the coast, lies the French island of **Corsica.**

English is commonly spoken by those in the tourist trade; however, though many citizens of this country have a strong command of English, they are *passionately* partial to speaking their own language.

HOW TRAVELLERS GET THERE

Many charter and scheduled carriers, both domestic and foreign, serve Paris, including the national airline, **Air France** (AF). Flights from Canada land at **Charles de Gaulle** (CDG). **Orly** (ORY) is Paris's other major airport. In addition, flights via Paris to the Riviera land in **Nice** at the **Côte d'Azur Airport** (NCE). **Lyon** [lee-OHN] (LYS) is a gateway to the Eastern Wine Country and the Alps.

Flying time to Paris from Toronto is seven hours. Travellers can get from London to Paris via a brief air flight (a little over an hour) or on the **Eurostar** train through the Channel Tunnel (under three hours). The high-speed **Thalys** train connects Paris with Brussels (Belgium) and Amsterdam (the Netherlands). Hovercraft and ferries connect southern England to various French ports. Cruise ships regularly call at ports on the Riviera, along the Atlantic Coast, and in northern France.

WEATHER PATTERNS

By and large, the climate of France is temperate. Paris has weather similar to London, though slightly warmer, ranging from the mid-20s in summer to near 4°C in winter. Temperatures do vary, however, in certain regions of the country. The Riviera's climate is somewhat similar to that of Los Angeles: summers in the high 20s and winters in the low 10s. In the Alps, winters are cold with snow—but then, that's exactly what skiers want (see Figures 18-1 and 18-2).

MONTH	JAN	FEB	MAR	APR	MAY	JUN	JUL	AUG	SEP	OCT	NOV	DEC
AVERAGE HIGH TEMPERATURE	6	7	11	16	19	23	24	24	21	15	9	6
AVERAGE LOW TEMPERATURE	0	1	2	5	8	11	13	13	10	7	3	1
AVERAGE PRECIPITATION (IN CENTIMETRES)	5	3	5	5	5	5	5	5	5	5	5	5

Figure 18-1   Climate at a Glance: Paris, France

MONTH	JAN	FEB	MAR	APR	MAY	JUN	JUL	AUG	SEP	OCT	NOV	DEC
AVERAGE HIGH TEMPERATURE	12	13	14	16	19	23	25	26	23	19	16	13
AVERAGE LOW TEMPERATURE	8	8	9	12	15	18	21	22	19	16	12	9
AVERAGE PRECIPITATION (IN CENTIMETRES)	5	5	8	5	5	3	3	3	5	13	10	10

Figure 18-2   Climate at a Glance: Nice, France

Who hasn't heard of April in Paris? It's famous. And rainy, which most people are surprised to learn. September is a better month to visit; the weather is usually nice and crowds are smaller. The main tourist season is June to September, peaking in July. Parisians go on vacation in August; the city empties and the Riviera gets packed.

GETTING AROUND

France has some of the finest transportation systems in the world. The **TGV** is a premier rail system with 300-kilometre-per-hour trains. For those who prefer to do their own driving, France has many good highways. Car rentals are readily available. And for flying within the country, **Air Inter** (IT) is the national domestic airline.

What the TGV is to France, the Metro is to Paris. One of the world's great subways, the Metro is simple to use: Each station has a map, and pushing a destination button lights up the best route. Paris buses are cheap but slow; the huge tour buses, though, give first-rate city tours. Taxis are a bit expensive and drivers can be selective about where they'll go. What about driving a car in Paris? Aggressive drivers, nonexistent lanes, and expensive parking make it a challenging experience. Beyond Paris, though, a car rental can be an attractive choice.

France offers adventurous travel alternatives. Bicycle tours through the wine regions and balloon trips over farmland and châteaux are quite memorable. Barges—with cabins onboard for passengers—cruise down the Loire and through the Wine Country. River Seine tours are a wonderful way to see Paris.

IMPORTANT PLACES

Think of France and you think of Paris. But the country offers many other regions, too, all of which should be considered when planning a trip.

Storms born in North Africa sometimes suck up Sahara sand. The storms then drift northward to France. The result: rainfall that coats southern France with sandy dirt.

The TGV covers the 400 kilometres between Lyon and Paris in two hours.

Toll roads are common in France. The roads, however, tend to be superbly maintained.

Motor homes are an increasingly popular way to visit the French countryside.

Paris

Lunch, not dinner, is the Parisian's main meal.

The French are fiercely proud of their culture and nowhere more so than in Paris. From history to arts, from architecture to haute cuisine and fashion, Paris has earned its reputation. The capital and largest city in France, the "City of Lights" is also the nation's business centre and perhaps the most romantic city in the world. The list of Paris attractions is lengthy. Among those that are must-sees:

- **The Eiffel Tower,** maybe the most famous icon of any city in the world. Built for the 1889 World's Fair, it rises high above the Seine and offers panoramic views.

- **Notre Dame,** the Gothic cathedral on the Île de la Cité, guarded by its stone gargoyles (best viewed by climbing up the staircase in one of the towers). The nearby **Sainte-Chapelle** church has stained-glass windows that are renowned.

Be aware of pickpockets—which include young children—in Paris.

Paris's Musée Rodin has virtually all of the great master's works, including *The Thinker.*

- **The Arc de Triomphe,** commemorating Napoleon's victories. The top offers a grand vista over Paris, especially down the **Champs-Elysées** boulevard to the **Place de la Concorde.**

- **The Paris Opera (Palais Garnier),** the ornate setting for *The Phantom of the Opera.*

- **Montmartre,** with its twisting streets, once the bohemian part of Paris. This district and its famous **Sacré Coeur** (a white marble basilica) are depicted in many famous Impressionist paintings.

- **The Louvre,** perhaps the greatest museum in the world. It houses such masterpieces as the *Mona Lisa, Winged Victory,* and the *Venus de Milo.* A half-dozen other great museums exist in Paris, including the **Centre Georges Pompidou,** with its modern art and bold exterior; and the **Musée d'Orsay,** a converted railway station with Impressionist works (including *Whistler's Mother*).

The foundations of the original Louvre Palace can be viewed in the museum's Sully Wing.

The following **day trips** from Paris are very popular:

- **Versailles** [vehr-SIGH], a sprawling, opulent palace with spectacular grounds.

- **Chartres** [SHART], one of the world's great medieval cathedrals, with its stained-glass windows.

Sacré Coeur, Paris
Copyright COREL

- **Fontainebleau,** the home of Napoleon, Marie-Antoinette, and many others, with its beautiful gardens.

- **Giverny** [zhee-ver-NEE], with its gardens made famous by the painter Monet. (His home is here, too.)

- **Disneyland Paris** and the adjoining **Walt Disney Studios,** east of Paris on the main route to Brussels, Belgium.

- **The Loire Valley,** best seen as a separate visit.

Normandy

This area along the English Channel will forever be a monument to the World War II D-Day landing. Beyond that, Normandy is a place of green farmland and medieval architecture. Among the attractions:

- **Omaha Beach,** the site of the Allied Invasion, is made up of what were originally three separate beaches. It is often seen along with **Arromanches** and its invasion museum.

- **Rouen** [roo-AHN], the "City of 100 Steeples," is famed for medieval architecture. Indeed, many of its 15th-century homes are still occupied.

- **Deauville** [doh-VEEL], a restored seaside resort, is to northern France what St-Tropez is to the southern Riviera. It has a 1.6 kilometre boardwalk.

- **Honfleur** is a highly picturesque fishing port, often depicted in paintings.

- **Bayeux** [bye-YOO] boasts a Gothic cathedral. The remarkable **Bayeux Tapestry,** housed in an adjacent museum, depicts the Battle of Hastings.

- **Mont-St-Michel** is a stunning fortified abbey from the 11th century—perched, like a spired silhouette, on a rock cut off from the mainland at high tide. Mont-St-Michel also borders the peninsula of **Brittany,** with its many castles and strange, prehistoric monuments.

> Across the English Channel is the British abbey, St. Michael's Mount, which was modelled after Mont-St-Michel.

The Loire Valley

Spread throughout the Loire River area are more than 100 majestic châteaux. The gateway of the area is the charming town of **Tours.** Some châteaux offer *son et lumière* (sound-and-light) shows at night. The sites you might recommend include:

- **The châteaux.** Among the most famous are **Amboise, Blois, Villandry,** and **Azay-le-Rideau.** If there's time for only one or two châteaux, the awesome **Chenonceaux** and **Chambord** are *the* ones to see.

- **Saumur,** famous for its **National Riding School,** many wine cellars, and, of all things, a mushroom museum.

> Some Loire Valley châteaux close between noon and 2 p.m., as do many other French attractions.

> Leonardo da Vinci spent his last years in Amboise.

The Aquitaine Region

The Aquitaine (also called Périgord) is one of France's most diversified tourist centres. It's famous for its vineyards, Roman ruins, prehistoric cave paintings, and *bastides* (quaint towns built on hillsides). Recommend the following:

- **Bordeaux** [bor-DOH], a sophisticated port city of parks, salons, bistros, casinos, and beaches.

- **The St-Emilion area,** in the heart of Bordeaux's Wine Country. The medieval town of St-Emilion itself is one of the most charming in all of France.

- **The Médoc,** another of the major wine regions, known for some of France's top vintages. More formal than St-Emilion, many of the estates have extremely grand châteaux.

A Loire Valley château
Photo by Justus Ghormley

The following **day trips** from the Aquitaine region are very popular:

- **The Dordogne** [dor-DOI-ing] **River Valley,** with its prehistoric cave paintings. The most famous, at **Lascaux,** are now closed to the public, but an exact reproduction can be visited nearby.

- **Biarritz,** a lovely beach town near the Spanish border on the Bay of Biscay. It's one of Europe's few surfing venues.

The Pyrenees

In the lofty mountains that separate France from Spain are several ski resorts. The shrine of **Lourdes** draws Catholic pilgrims seeking cures and is one of the most visited sites in France. As in the Aquitaine, a number of *bastides* dot the hillsides. The city of **Toulouse,** called the "Rose City," boasts Europe's largest Romanesque church. And **Carcassonne** is a huge, hulking medieval fortress of a town—the largest in all of Europe. Within its walls is the impressive **Castle of the Counts.**

The French Riviera

The Mediterranean-hugging Riviera offers an unusual blend of features. Its stunning beaches, wonderful weather, superb dining, and many art galleries have long enticed the jet-setting elite. It's also the most popular spot for the French themselves during their July and August holidays. Among the towns and attractions of the Côte d'Azur are:

- **Nice** [NEECE], the largest city on the Riviera, is crowded but still charming. Fine museums are around Nice, including the **Musée National Marc Chagall, Musée Matisse,** and **Museum of Modern and Contemporary Art.**

- **Cannes** [KAHN] is famous for its international movie festival, beaches, and boardwalk. With casinos and nightclubs, it's trendy and perhaps a bit noisier than other Riviera towns.

- **St-Tropez** [SAN troh-PAY] is very chic, but beginning to get crowded and just a bit aged. The 20th-century artwork housed in the **Musée de l'Annonciade** is excellent.

- **Cap d'Antibes** [CAHP dahn-TEEB] is for those looking for an especially luxurious seaside vacation. The nearby town of Antibes has a **Picasso Museum.**

- **St-Paul de Vence** and **Grasse** lie in the hills above the Riviera. St-Paul—a medieval village atop a hill—has many galleries, boutiques, fine restaurants, and the nearby **Maeght Foundation,** a world-class museum. Grasse is famous for its perfume factory.

You should advise visitors to take the following **day trips** from the French Riviera:

- **Marseilles** [mahr-SAY] is over 2500 years old. It's quite attractive, though a bit scruffy on the edges. Many museums dot this spirited city.

- **Monaco,** an independent principality close to the Italian border, is best known for its **Grand Casino** and for the **Monaco Grand Prix** auto race, held in late May. The road between Nice and Monaco goes through an area called the **Corniches,** a series of three winding roads—each at a different level. Along the way is a picture-perfect medieval town, **Eze** [AIZ], that rises above a steep cliff.

- The inland **Provence** [pro-VAHNS] **Region** features many spas and Roman structures (including the 2000-year-old **Pont du Gard** aqueduct). In **Avignon** [ah-vee-NYOWN] is the **Palace of the Popes** (where popes lived in the 14th century) and a bridge made famous by a children's song.

The French Alps

Skiers love the Alps for their winter facilities, and those who enjoy scenery are likely to visit at any time of the year. Among the towns that are the most visited are:

The Tour de France bicycle race takes place in July.

- **Chamonix** [shah-mo-NEE] (near **Mont Blanc,** one of Europe's highest mountains), a large, trendy resort town with spectacular views. There's also a casino.

- **Val d'Isère** [VAHL dee-ZARE], a charming village with fewer tourists. It's an ideal place for serious skiers.

The Pont du Gard, Provence

Photo by Justus Ghormley

- **Grenoble,** the site of the 1968 Winter Olympics. Accessible from Geneva, Switzerland, it's one of the most picturesque towns in the Alps.

- **Other world-class resorts,** including **Megève, Tignes,** and **Albertville** (site of the 1992 Winter Olympics).

- **Several charming cities,** including **Annecy** (the Flower City) and lakeside **Évian** (of the famous spa and bottled water).

The Eastern Wine Country

France's legendary Wine Country extends all the way from near Reims in the Champagne District, southeasterly through the **Alsace** region, and down through Burgundy into the Rhône River Valley. Among its major attractions, from south to north:

- **Lyon,** France's second-largest city and a centre of business and gastronomy. Nearby is **Pérouges,** one of Europe's best-preserved medieval villages.

- **Dijon,** another place of fine cuisine and the heart of Burgundy. Between Dijon and **Beaune** (a medieval town) are numerous wineries.

- The **Alsace** area, with its melding of German and French ambience. Here is the fabled **"Route du Vin,"** a 120 kilometre drive through vineyards and mountains.

- **The Champagne District,** another region of vineyards and wine cellars. It's anchored by the city of Reims. Several wineries in the area offer tours of their vast underground tunnel systems, where wines and champagne are left to age.

- **Reims,** at the northern tip of the Wine Country. Its Gothic cathedral is where most French kings were crowned.

POSSIBLE ITINERARIES

First-time visitors should spend a week in Paris—with day trips to Versailles, Chartres, and perhaps the Loire Valley. Seasoned tourists could put aside two weeks to visit a broader area. Starting in Paris, they could travel to the Loire, then continue down through the Aquitaine region, perhaps ending up in the Riviera.

Each area of France can easily sustain a five- to seven-day stay. In the winter France offers the skiing splendour of the Alps, and in the summer the pleasant beaches of the Riviera.

LODGING OPTIONS

The French pride themselves on having the best: haute cuisine, haute couture, great novelists, and trend-setting artists. France's hotels are no different: Some of the world's best are here. In Paris, many hotels are on the Right Bank, especially the areas just off the Champs-Elysées and near the Opera. Among them are the world-class **Ritz, George V, Bristol, Crillon,** and **Plaza Athenee.** On the Riviera, the **Negresco** in Nice is an official national monument.

The French government officially rates lodging, with four-star luxe as the highest rating, down to one-star. Alternatives to hotels are abundant. In Paris, for instance, visitors can rent apartments. In the countryside, farmhouses, castles, manors, and monasteries have been converted to upscale lodging facilities and have banded together into a network called **Relais et Châteaux.**

Many North American hotel chains serve France. Among the other major chains are the upscale **Sofitel, Le Meridien,** and **Concorde.** At the other end of the budget are the economy chains of **Hotel Campanile, Libertel, Mercure, Ibis,** and **Timotel.**

According to city measurements, the Périphérique expressway is the greatest source of noise in Paris. The Père-Lachaise Cemetery, where many notables are buried, is the city's quietest place.

Several hotels in the Loire region have rooms cut into rock cliffs. In effect, guests there stay in caves.

ALLIED DESTINATIONS

France borders Spain, Andorra, Italy, Switzerland, Germany, Belgium, and Luxembourg. The Netherlands is just around the corner, and Great Britain is right across the English Channel. Although closely related to France, Monaco has its own separate government. (It's officially a principality.) A France itinerary can be expanded to include any of these countries.

CULTURAL PATTERNS

The French are proud of their country's cultural heritage. This isn't limited to artistic endeavours but to all French customs. A business traveller, especially, wouldn't want to commit a *faux pas* (literally, a false step).

- The French prefer somewhat formal greetings. They regularly use such titles as *Monsieur, Madame,* and *Mademoiselle.* Once a French person knows someone, he or she may give the traditional kiss *by* the cheek. (The cheek isn't kissed, but the air next to it.)

- The French are proud of their language. Although many speak English, they far prefer French. Visitors should ask, *"Parlez-vous anglais?" not* "Do you speak English?"

- Visitors should be careful about using the OK sign. The thumb and index finger together means zero here, almost the opposite of what may be intended.

- Gift-giving should be done carefully. A business gift should not be embossed with a corporate logo; a hand-written note should accompany it; and flowers must be in an uneven number (not 13, though). Gifts that are intellectual or artistic in nature make a great impression on the French.

- The French admire promptness. On the other hand, the idea of standing in line is somewhat foreign to them.

The French rarely eat full breakfasts. Their *petit dejeuner* usually consists of rolls, perhaps orange juice, and coffee.

In Paris, it's against the law to honk your car horn except in an emergency; blink the headlights instead.

FACTORS THAT MOTIVATE VISITORS

Many would-be visitors know of France by its reputation. However, it's important to think about the reasons why the country truly intrigues them. Among these reasons:

- It's romantic.

- The cultural and artistic attractions are seemingly endless.

- The cuisine and wines are legendary.

- There are many airline flights into Paris.

- Easy public transportation makes it simple to get around.

- Winter skiing, especially in the Alps, is readily available.

- The beaches are trendy.

- Picturesque villages dot the countryside.

- The casino in Monaco offers gambling in sophisticated surroundings.

- Some want to see the cutting edge of fashion and arts.

- There's great shopping.

On a hot day, the Eiffel Tower is 15 centimetres taller than it is on a cold day.

One of France's greatest art collections is in a restaurant, La Colombe D'Or, next to St-Paul de Vence. The reason: Artists like Matisse, Picasso, and Modigliani would pay for their meals or a room here with one of their works of art.

POSSIBLE MISGIVINGS

No matter how graceful France might appear, visitors still have concerns. Here are the most common ones:

- "The French are rude." Parisians—like many big-city residents—can seem abrupt, but they're usually polite if treated with respect. Locals in the countryside tend to be friendlier.

- "All there is in France is Paris." There's also the Wine Country, Loire Valley châteaux, Normandy memorials and architecture, the Riviera, and the Alps.

- "They don't speak English and are intolerant of French that isn't flawless." Most people in any way connected to tourism speak English and prefer doing so to dealing with a foreigner's French—and they find Canadian French quite amusing.

Qualifying the Traveller
PARIS

FOR PEOPLE WHO WANT	HIGH APPEAL	MEDIUM APPEAL	LOW APPEAL	REMARKS
Historical and Cultural Attractions	▲			Superb museums
Beaches and Water Sports			▲	Must go to the Riviera
Skiing Opportunities			▲	Must go to the Alps
Lots of Nightlife	▲			Nightclubs expensive
Family Activities		▲		Mostly sightseeing and Disneyland Paris
Familiar Cultural Experience			▲	
Exotic Cultural Experience		▲		
Safety and Low Crime		▲		Petty crime
Bargain Travel			▲	In the countryside
Impressive Scenery		▲		Mostly in countryside
Peace and Quiet			▲	Side streets quiet
Shopping Opportunities	▲			Especially luxury items
Adventure			▲	Outside of the city
To Do Business		▲		Especially Paris, Lyon, and Marseilles

- "Traffic and parking in Paris is a problem." Public transportation is excellent, and there are many wonderful city motorcoach tours.

- "France is expensive." It's true that Paris and the Riviera (in spring and summer) are among the most expensive places in the world. However, bargains can be found (especially off-season). Other areas of France are generally more reasonable.

SALES STRATEGIES

The diversity of France generates many ways to up-sell and cross-sell. Balloon trips offer a spectacular way to see the country. Staying in a château would be memorable for just about anyone. Renting a car to drive through the countryside or booking train travel lets visitors see more than just the well-known highlights. Barge cruises, too, are a unique way of getting around. City tours of Paris make that sprawling city more manageable. A few extra days added on to a Paris trip will allow a tourist to visit the châteaux country or other regions. Cruises let you easily combine a trip to, say, the Riviera with visits to Italy and Spain.

Tours are offered of the sewers of Paris.

TRAVEL TRIVIA

WHERE THE FAMOUS PAINTINGS ARE

- *The Mona Lisa* (da Vinci)—The Louvre, Paris

- *The Starry Night* (Van Gogh)—Museum of Modern Art, New York City

- *The Last Judgement* (Michelangelo)—The Sistine Chapel, Vatican City

- *Syndics of the Drapers' Guild* (Rembrandt)—Rijksmuseum, Amsterdam

- *Three Musicians* (Picasso)—Museum of Modern Art, New York City

- *The Artist's Mother* (Whistler)—Musée d'Orsay, Paris

- *The Blue Boy* (Gainsborough)—The Huntington Library, Pasadena, California

- *Campbell's Soup Cans* (Warhol)—The Andy Warhol Museum, Pittsburgh, Pennsylvania

- *Luncheon on the Grass* (Manet)—Musée d'Orsay, Paris

- *The Last Supper* (da Vinci)—Santa Maria Delle Grazie Church, Milan, Italy

NAME _____   DATE _____

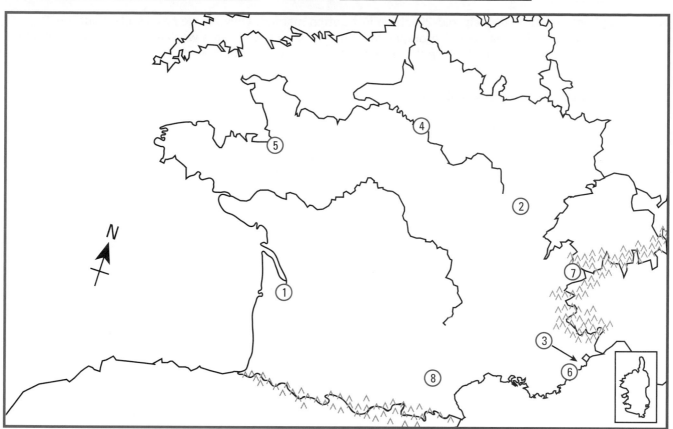

A traveller wants to visit the places listed below. Which number represents each on the map?

PLACE/ATTRACTION	IN/NEAR WHICH CITY?	NUMBER ON MAP
A. The Seine River	A.	A.
B. Sainte-Chapelle	B.	B.
C. An abbey on top of a rock	C.	C.
D. The Negresco Hotel	D.	D.
E. The heart of Burgundy	E.	E.
F. The Louvre	F.	F.
G. The site of a film festival	G.	G.
H. Mont Blanc	H.	H.
I. The Arc de Triomphe	I.	I.
J. The Castle of the Counts	J.	J.

CASE STUDY

NAME _____   DATE _____

Nicole and Matthew, both in their mid-20s, have just gotten married. Only Nicole has travelled outside Canada, and that was five years ago (through Great Britain). They each have a week off from work, but could possibly stretch the goodwill of their employers, considering the circumstances.

Circle the answer that best suits their needs.

1. What area would you suggest they concentrate on?

    Paris   Normandy

    The Riviera   Paris and the Loire Valley

    Why?

2. Which of the following tips should you not pass along to Nicole and Matthew?

    Go in April when the weather is best.   French trains can be very fast.

    Order prix fixe lunches.   *Bastides* can be seen in Aquitaine.

    Why?

3. Which of the following should you probably recommend?

    Taking a barge to Toulouse   Staying at the Negresco

    A first-day city tour   Visiting the Hermitage

    Why?

4. Which is not a day trip from Paris?

    Versailles   Fontainebleau

    Chamonix   Chartres

    Why?

CREATIVE ACTIVITY

NAME _____   DATE _____

You're the travel planner for Ice Cadettes, a skating show that has entertained audiences around the world for decades.

Experience has taught you that in order to turn a profit, only cities with a greater-metropolitan population of 300 000 or more are worth a visit. There's even a "divide-by-two" formula: Cities with 400 000 warrant two nights' performance; 600 000, three nights; and so on. The maximum the show stays in any city is seven nights.

The company has decided to stage Ice Cadettes in France. They want to spend no more than 40 days there. You also need one day off between each city engagement for travelling (by air, train, or road—as the distance warrants).

Below, write in the names of the cities in which Ice Cadettes will perform for this French road tour. Apply the day-population formula; look up the population of French cities in whatever reference sources you have access to. Also, try to make an itinerary that's geographically efficient. Don't have the group constantly flying back and forth across France. We've started you off, to show you what we want:

1. Fly into Strasbourg	15.	29.
2. Strasbourg	16.	30.
3. Strasbourg	17.	31.
4. Travel to	18.	32.
5.	19.	33.
6.	20.	34.
7.	21.	35.
8.	22.	36.
9.	23.	37.
10.	24.	38.
11.	25.	39.
12.	26.	40.
13.	27.	
14.	28.	

CHAPTER 19

Italy

Pisa and Pizza

How often have you heard a child confuse the words *Pisa* and *pizza?* Well, that child grows up and one day becomes a tourist. Even as adults, people think of Italy in terms of ancient ruins and pasta. The country, however, is much more; indeed, it's one of the richest experiences in Europe. Just pizza? Hardly. It's a banquet.

Italy is about half the size of Manitoba and is easily recognized by its famous boot shape. The country is so full of attractions that there's really no centre point to tourism. In fact, it could be said that there are *four* Italys: First, there's northern Italy, with its mix of mountains, lakes, and the **Italian Riviera;** then comes the Italy of great cities, including the art, history, fashion, and commerce of **Venice** (Venezia), **Florence** (Firenze), and **Milan** (Milano); next are **Rome** (Roma) and its environs, the country's political and cultural centre and once the hub of the world's most powerful empire; finally, there's southern Italy, with the area that surrounds **Naples** (Napoli), as well as the islands of mountainous **Sicily** and resort-lined **Sardinia.**

ITALY

Capital: Rome

Area (square km): 309 973

Time Zone: GMT +1

Drive on: Right

Population: 58 100 000

Religion: Roman Catholic

Language: Italian

Currency: 1 euro = 100 cents

Electricity: 220 volts, 50 cycles AC

Capsule History: Rome settled, about 800 B.C.; Roman Empire falls, 476–493; France, Austria, and Spain control parts of Italy, 1494–1815; Italy unified, 1861; Mussolini dictatorship, 1922–1943; free elections, 1946; many government changes and controversies since.

For reference sources and suggested lengths of stay, see Appendixes A and B.

HOW TRAVELLERS GET THERE

The major international gateways into Italy are **Rome-Fiumicino "Leonardo da Vinci" Airport** (FCO) and Milan's **Malpensa Airport** (MXP). Venice (VCE), Pisa (PSA), Florence (FLR), and Naples (NAP) all mostly handle shorter flights.

Alitalia (AZ) is Italy's national airline; the country is also served by several North American scheduled and charter carriers. Flying time to Rome from Toronto is 8.5 hours. Cruises also stop at dozens of Italian mainland and island ports. Indeed, Rome's **Civitavecchia** [chee-vee-tah-VECK-ee-ah] and Venice are two of the Mediterranean's busiest ports. Visitors can also drive into the country from the north, often via trans-Alpine tunnels.

WEATHER PATTERNS

Who hasn't heard of "sunny Italy"? It's a well-earned reputation, but Italy's climate is a little more complicated than that.

Italy has three climate patterns. The northern Alpine area has cold winters and mild, sometimes rainy summers. The region between Milan and Venice has hot, sunny summers, but winters are chilly and misty. The rest of Italy is like California, with dependably hot, dry summers. Winters are mild, with changeable, unpredictable weather (see Figure 19-1). Occasionally in the summer and fall, a hot, humid sirocco wind blows from the south, while in the winter, a hot, dry *foehn* wind from the north sometimes increases temperatures and lowers humidity in the Alps. Waters around Italy are pleasantly warm from May to October, but chilly the rest of the year.

June, July, and September are the busiest tourist months. There's a small drop-off in major cities in August, when Italian tourists head for other countries or for the Riviera.

⊙ Many attractions and most businesses, except restaurants, close between 1:00 p.m. and 3:30 p.m., but stay open as late as 8:00 p.m.

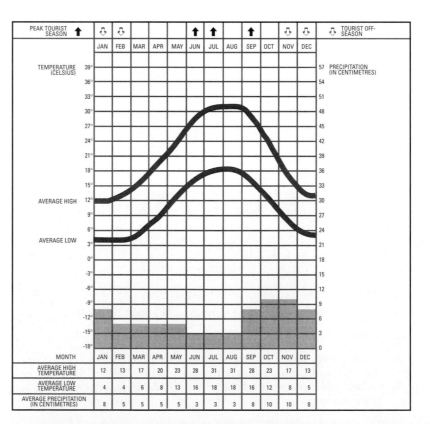

Figure 19-1   Climate at a Glance: Rome, Italy

GETTING AROUND

Italy's train system is inexpensive and fast, though efficiency is not its strong suit. The **Pendalino,** or **ETR,** is Italy's swiftest train. Travellers can also fly the short distances between major cities. Car rentals are readily available; however, Italian cities, especially Rome and Milan, are treacherous for "amateurs." Multi-day escorted tours or short city tours are good alternatives. Taxis are fairly priced, but they can be expensive for long distances, and cab drivers have been known to play loose with the meters.

In Rome, the subway and bus system are extensive, with many lines travelling beyond the city. Buses and trolleys are also good in Florence, but just so-so in Milan (which also has a subway).

A unique transportation system, of course, is found in Venice. No cars are allowed in the city. (Travellers driving to Venice must park in one of several huge garages on the city's perimeter.) Boats are the way to get around. The most famous, romantic, and expensive are gondolas. (If you want a singing gondolier, you'll have to pay extra.) Water taxis are fast but also expensive. *Vaporetti* are slow "water buses" and *motoscafi* are express ones.

○ Eurailpasses and Italy rail passes for unlimited train travel can be bought only in North America.

○ By law, Venice's gondolas must be painted black. The one exception: those owned by city officials.

IMPORTANT PLACES

Italy is a treasure-trove of diverse places to experience. Among its most popular cities and attractions are:

Rome

The Eternal City was originally built on seven hills along the **Tiber River;** its centre today is on the river's left bank. Rome is the political, cultural, and religious heart of Italy. Among its attractions are:

- **The Colosseum,** one of the most recognizable structures in the world. It's an ancient stadium where gladiators fought and Christians were martyred.

- **The Forum,** once the centre of the Roman Empire and now a broad area of ruins.

○ Recommend detailed guidebooks for each city. Many of Italy's attractions have poor signage and no guided tours.

○ *Trattorias* are less expensive for dining than *ristorantes* and offer very good food.

○ The Forum is best viewed from Capitoline Hill.

The Roman Forum
Copyright COREL

A 2000-year-old underground aqueduct feeds many of Rome's most famous fountains.

The Golden House, which was home to the Roman emperor Nero, has recently been opened to the public.

Visitors to St. Peter's must not wear shorts.

Best time to see the Sistine Chapel: at opening (bypass the museum, go straight to the Chapel, then work your way back) or in February.

The famous architect Frank Lloyd Wright applied for permission to build a home on Venice's Grand Canal. He was refused.

The view from the tower at St. Mark's is best at sunset.

- **The Spanish Steps,** a place where locals and tourists have gathered for centuries.

- **The Trevi Fountain,** of *Three Coins in the Fountain* fame. Throw a coin over your left shoulder and you'll return to Rome, says the legend.

- **The Pantheon,** renowned as a remarkably preserved domed Roman building from the second century A.D.

- **Vatican City,** actually one of the smallest nations in the world. The seat of Roman Catholicism and home to the pope, it's the site of **St. Peter's Basilica** (the largest church in the world) and the overwhelming **Vatican Museum.** Michelangelo's *Creation* is painted on the **Sistine Chapel** ceiling, his *Last Judgement* on its wall.

Outside Rome are wonderful attractions. Some popular **day trips:**

- **The Villa d'Este** in **Tivoli** is famed for its majestic, terraced water gardens and fountains. Nearby is **Hadrian's Villa,** a remarkable archaeological find.

- **Ostia Antica** contains the vast excavated ruins of an ancient port.

- **The Catacombs**—where early Christians secretly buried their dead—are located just outside town (there's a smaller version near the Via Veneto), as is the Roman Empire's principal road, the **Appian Way.**

Venice

Venice could never happen again. One of the truly unique cities of the world, it was built on 118 islands connected by 160 canals and more than 400 bridges. Located on the Adriatic, the city is expensive, with polluted waters and crowds of tourists (over two million each year, for a city whose population is less than 80 000). Yet a walk through its back alleys opens up a quiet, romantic, fragile world of another time. Among its attractions:

- **St. Mark's Square** is the city's busy gathering place. It's enclosed at one end by the fanciful **St. Mark's Basilica** and has numerous outdoor cafés, each with "duelling" orchestras.

- **The Doge's Palace,** near the basilica, reflects a Moorish architecture. It houses one of the world's great collections of maps and globes. The famous **Bridge of Sighs** is nearby.

- **The Rialto Bridge** is one of Venice's most photographed bridges. It crosses the **Grand Canal,** the city's main waterway.

- **The Lido,** a trendy, luxury beach resort, is on its own island across from the Grand Canal.

Here are some of the most popular **day** or **half-day trips:**

- **Murano** is a touristy island where glass has been made for some 700 years. (The sales push to buy can be very aggressive.)

- **Burano** is the quaint island-capital of lace making.

- **Padua** [PAD-yoo-wah] is a town with charming medieval buildings.

- **Verona** has noteworthy architecture and a renowned outdoor opera festival. "Juliet's balcony" is here, as well. Verona can also be visited en route to Milan or the **Lake District.**

Florence

A city of art and architecture with a strong intellectual community, Florence is where the Renaissance began and flourished in the 15th century under the Medici family. It's located on the **Arno River** in the beautiful **Tuscany hills.** This

A gondola in Venice
Photo by Justus Ghormley

international city remains, in many ways, a town of artisans and elegance. Among the many sites to see are:

- **The Duomo,** one of the most architecturally important cathedrals in the world. Started in 1256, it took 173 years to finish. One of the reasons for the delay: At first, no one knew how to engineer and build its huge dome.

- **The Galleria dell'Academia,** with its very fine collection of Florentine art, best known for Michelangelo's *David.*

- **The Church of Santa Croce,** where Michelangelo is buried.

- **The Vecchio Palace,** an opulent "town hall" built by the Medicis.

- **The Ponte Vecchio,** the renowned bridge over the Arno, lined with gold and jewellery shops.

- **The Pitti Palace,** a lavish home of the Medicis, which is so large it houses several museums.

- **The Uffizi Gallery,** a Renaissance palace housing one of the premier collections of art in Italy.

The following **day trips** from Florence are very popular:

- **Pisa** is world renowned, of course, for its leaning tower.

- **Fiesole** [FYAY-zo-lay] is a beautiful old Etruscan village. Plays are still performed in the amphitheatre, built in 80 B.C.

- **Siena** is a pretty Renaissance village in the hills of the Tuscany wine country.

The Italian Riviera

An extension of the French Riviera, the Italian Riviera offers stunning scenery along a mountainous coast. It's very crowded in the summer.

Portofino, an exclusive and high-priced resort town, is perhaps the most beautiful on Italy's Riviera. **Santa Margherita Ligure** and **San Remo** are popular beach resorts, as well. **Genoa** is a major Italian port and the birthplace of Christopher Columbus. It has many fine museums and Gothic architecture.

Duomo is an Italian term for any large cathedral.

Because of the noise from mopeds, it's best *not* to have a room facing a busy street in Florence.

Extra tips are expected for most service-related jobs. Waiters should be tipped a little in addition to the service charge on the bill.

San Gimignano, outside Siena, is famous among architects for its many medieval towers.

The Portofino Bay Hotel in Orlando, Florida, was built to look like Portofino, Italy.

The Duomo, Florence
Photo by H. Fukushima

Milan

○ Milan is closer to London than it is to the tip of Italy's boot.

Milan is the financial, business, fashion, and publishing centre of Italy. The city has a sophisticated cultural life and is the gateway to the Alps and the Lake District. Among the major attractions are:

- **The Church of St. Mary of Grace,** the location of da Vinci's restored *The Last Supper.*

○ To see its intricate carvings, go up to the roof of Milan's Duomo.

- **The Duomo,** an intricate marble structure and one of the world's largest cathedrals. The square that fronts it is famous for its pigeons.

- **La Scala,** perhaps the world's most famous opera house. Its season runs from December to June.

- **The Galleria Vittorio Emanuele II,** an ornate, glass-domed shopping mall built in 1861.

The Lake District

○ Aosta is off the tourist-beaten path, but has a picture-perfect location in the Italian Alps.

This Alpine region near Switzerland is one of magnificent scenery and charming villages. The many lakes and surrounding Alps are part of the same geologic development, which glaciers carved out millions of years ago. Among its key towns are:

- **Como,** on **Lake Como** (one of two main lakes in the district). Its notable structures include a 700-year-old palace and a Renaissance Gothic cathedral.

- **Stresa,** the largest town on the area's other major lake, **Lake Maggiore,** with beautiful villas.

- **Bergamo,** a two-level city. Its main plaza is surrounded by stunning medieval buildings.

Not far from the lakes are the ski resorts of the Italian Alps. Among the favourites are beautiful **Cortina d'Ampezzo** and **Courmayeur,** the area's largest ski resort, with a very busy nightlife.

Naples

Naples is crowded and a bit run down, but it does boast some interesting churches and museums. Though it may not be Italy's most popular place to visit, the region nearby offers fascinating attractions, including:

- **Mt. Vesuvius** and **Pompeii,** which had their histories intertwined in A.D. 79, when the volcano (now dormant, but potentially still active) erupted and buried the town. The ruins have since been excavated. A second nearby town, **Herculaneum,** was also buried. Like Pompeii, it has been uncovered and can be visited.

- **The Isle of Capri,** a trendy resort. Though there aren't many beaches, it's an area of charming villages and great vistas. Here, too, is the **Blue Grotto,** a watery cave of eerie azure light.

- **Sorrento,** which has long been one of the most beautiful, romantic, and famous resort areas in Italy. Unfortunately, it's becoming rather crowded, worn, and expensive.

- **Amalfi Drive,** along the peninsula of the **Amalfi Coast,** offering breathtaking views past cliffs, coves, and villages.

Sicily

Located just off the toe of Italy's boot, this beautiful island is mountainous and dry. It's excellent for water sports and has very good beaches. In the winter there's also some good skiing in the mountains. Among its attractions are **Mt. Etna,** a still-active volcano; **Taormina,** a charming and popular beach resort town; and **Palermo,** Sicily's seaport capital, with ancient buildings and Norman palaces.

Sardinia

About 160 kilometres off Italy's west coast, this sparsely populated island is known for its beaches and water sports, especially fishing. The beautiful country-side and picturesque villages hold remnants of many ages. Easily the most popular beach area on Sardinia is **Costa Smeralda** (the Emerald Coast), one of the trendiest luxury resorts in all of Europe.

POSSIBLE ITINERARIES

First-time travellers to Italy visit Rome and other great cities, perhaps Venice and Florence. A week is the bare minimum. Seasoned travellers will probably want to explore the other areas of the country, as well as spend perhaps a bit more in-depth time in the major cities. A week concentrated in any one area, such as the Lake District or the region south of Rome, is just about right. Two weeks in Italy, however, provides ample opportunity to visit several major regions and cities.

Ancient Romans placed chickpeas and bacon in sealed jars and exported them to the rest of the Empire. That's where our pork and beans comes from.

LODGING OPTIONS

There's a wide range of hotel chains to choose from in Italy. At the upper end are such organizations as **Atahotels, Starhotels,** and **Jolly Hotels** (many of whose hotels are more moderately priced than others). Many North American chains are also represented in Italy.

Hotels in Rome are concentrated around the rail station, the Spanish Steps, and the Via Veneto (famed for its many sidewalk cafés). In Venice, the best (and costliest) lodging is along the Grand Canal and near St. Mark's Square. Among the most famous: the **Cipriani, Danieli,** and **Gritti Palace.** Hotels in Florence are mostly to the north, along or near the Arno River. On Sicily and Sardinia, most of the accommodations are on the northern parts of the islands.

Although lower-rated hotels may present unwelcome surprises, Italy does offer wonderful alternative lodging, notably the chance to stay in old villas. Though some are expensive, many are moderately priced. ITC operators offer reasonable packages.

○ Request rooms in the oldest section of the Danieli.

ALLIED DESTINATIONS

Although most of the country is surrounded by water, Italy is bordered on the north by France, Switzerland, Austria, and Slovenia. The lovely and historic French island of Corsica is just off the west coast, and the island-nation of Malta is to the south of Sicily. Moreover, located as it is at the southern tip of Europe, Italy is also a perfect jumping-off point to Africa across the Mediterranean Sea. Nearby are Morocco, Tunisia, and Egypt. Note that many Eastern Mediterranean cruises start out in Venice, while Western Mediterranean cruises often begin at Civitavecchia.

CULTURAL PATTERNS

Italy has a rich, exuberant culture, but with traditions that can be quite different from those to which most Canadians are accustomed. Business travellers should pay close attention to the customs.

○ Address an Italian by his or her first name only when invited to do so.

- The daily pace is slower in southern Italy than in the north.

- Dinner can be a long, social event, but lunch is generally the day's biggest meal. Visitors shouldn't rush their meal and they should try their best to eat everything placed before them.

- When doing business, travellers should wear their finest clothes. In Italy, great clothing is a badge of success.

- It's appropriate for a guest to bring a small gift to an Italian home.

- The North American gesture for one (the index finger raised) means two in Italy, since the thumb is counted as one.

FACTORS THAT MOTIVATE VISITORS

For as diverse a country as Italy, it's important to understand precisely what motivates people to go there. Among their reasons might be:

- Some of the world's best-known ancient sites are here.

- The food is familiar and wonderful.

- The country serves as a centre for Christian religious pilgrimages.

- The culture is rich with opera, art, architecture, and history.

- There's the opportunity for water sports in summer and skiing in winter.

- There's great shopping.

- Many North Americans have their cultural roots in Italy.

- Some of the world's finest resorts are here.

- Italy is a major departure point for cruises.

POSSIBLE MISGIVINGS

For all Italy's attributes, certain concerns regularly arise:

- "Everything's so expensive." Italy is indeed expensive; pre-booked tours and cruises can blunt the cost a bit.

- "It's so disorganized." Book an escorted tour; the tour manager will deal with whatever problems may arise.

- "There's a lot of crime." Most are petty offences. But crime does happen, and normal precautions must be taken.

Qualifying the Traveller
ITALY

FOR PEOPLE WHO WANT	HIGH APPEAL	MEDIUM APPEAL	LOW APPEAL	REMARKS
Historical and Cultural Attractions	▲			Cities are virtual museums
Beaches and Water Sports		▲		Especially Riviera and Sardinia
Skiing Opportunities	▲			Northern Alps
Lots of Nightlife		▲		Especially Rome
Family Activities		▲		Mostly sightseeing
Familiar Cultural Experience			▲	
Exotic Cultural Experience	▲			
Safety and Low Crime			▲	Petty crime frequent
Bargain Travel			▲	Venice especially costly
Impressive Scenery	▲			Especially countryside and the North
Peace and Quiet		▲		In countryside
Shopping Opportunities	▲			Designer items, glass, gold, jewellery, high fashion, leather
Adventure		▲		
To Do Business		▲		

- "It's so hot." Spring or fall offers nice weather. Italy's northern regions are cooler.

- "Driving in cities is dangerous." Fine public transportation helps visitors get past this concern.

SALES STRATEGIES

Italy offers unique selling avenues. With city driving so treacherous, city tours and train transportation become especially attractive. For that matter, with so many different attractions in Italy, escorted tours or day trips can be excellent ways to see the country. So, too, are cruises, which often call on Italy's less visited areas (for example, Sicily and Sardinia) before continuing on to other countries.

Lodging in villas ranges from inexpensive to costly, but all offer a way to help make Italy memorable. Hotels along Venice's Grand Canal or with views in Florence may be expensive, but they're worth it. Their drama can cap off any guest's trip.

TRAVEL TRIVIA

ITEMS PURCHASED ON MOST RECENT TRIPS AMONG SHOPPING TRAVELLERS

- Clothing or shoes: 77 percent
- Souvenirs: 49 percent
- Books or music: 42 percent
- Specialty foods/beverage items: 41 percent
- Kids' toys: 39 percent

Source: Travel Institute of America

- Items/crafts by local population or unique to destination: 37 percent
- Jewellery or accessories: 36 percent
- Home accessories or furniture: 23 percent
- Home electronics: 16 percent
- Sports equipment: 15 percent

NAME _____   DATE _____

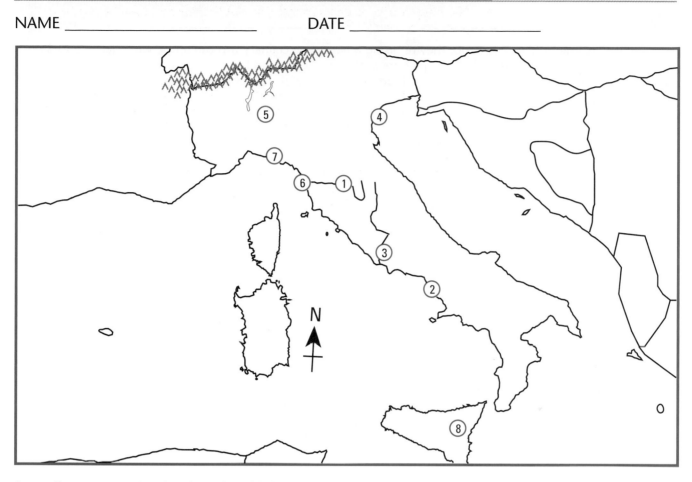

A traveller wants to visit the places listed below. Which number represents each on the map?

PLACE/ATTRACTION	IN/NEAR WHICH CITY?	NUMBER ON MAP
A. St. Mark's Basilica	**A.**	**A.**
B. The statue of David	**B.**	**B.**
C. The Trevi Fountain	**C.**	**C.**
D. Pompeii	**D.**	**D.**
E. La Scala Opera House	**E.**	E
F. Gondolas	**F.**	**F.**
G. *The Last Supper*	**G.**	**G.**
H. A leaning tower	**H.**	**H.**
I. The Doge's Palace	**I.**	**I.**
J. The Spanish Steps	**J.**	**J.**

CASE STUDY

NAME _____   DATE _____

Thomas and Jeannette Blair love food; they're taking a two-week culinary trip to Europe with Nancy and Sam Armato, who are also gourmets. Both couples are in their early 60s and have been to the Continent many times. What attracts them, in addition to the food, is the history of the cultures. They plan to go to Italy, France, and Spain.

Circle the answer that best suits their needs.

1. How many total days in Italy would you recommend for their trip?

   Two   Three

   Five   Ten

   Why?

2. Which of the following Italian destinations could you suggest?

   Costa Smeralda   Bimini

   Corsica   Santorini

   Why?

3. Which of the following tips would the couples find most useful in Italy?

   Vatican City is right next door to the Colosseum.

   Leave a tip, even when there's already one on the bill.

   Car rentals in Rome are inexpensive.

   Milan's Last Supper is its finest restaurant.

   Why?

4. Which of the following services should you not offer?

   A hotel suite   A city tour

   A luau   A Eurailpass

   Why?

CREATIVE ACTIVITY

NAME _____   DATE _____

Thanks to television, nearly a billion people see the Rose Parade each year. That's why so many countries sponsor Rose Bowl floats. This year, Italy will create a float. What do you think it should look like? Describe it very specifically or, if you're artistic, draw it below.

CHAPTER 20

Spain and Portugal

Everything under the Sun

Have you ever been faced with so many choices you didn't know where to begin? That's the problem with Spain. There are so many different cultures, climates, and topographies that it's almost impossible to determine where to start.

The one constant: all the sunshine. Though the climate changes in Spain from area to area, it's almost always a case of good, better, best. And though that fact may not be well known in Canada, Spain is one of the top vacation destinations for European tourists.

Actually, there may be a logical place to start in Spain: right in the centre of the map, at **Madrid,** the country's capital. If you view Spain as a clock, one o'clock would be **San Sebastian** (centre of the Basque region). Moving around the country clockwise, there's the beach resort of **Costa Brava,** followed by charming **Barcelona.** Off the coast in the Mediterranean Sea, at three o'clock, are the **Balearic** [bah-lee-AIR-ik] **Islands** of **Majorca** [mah-YOR-kah] and **Ibiza.**

There are two more exquisite beach regions: the **Costa Blanca,** along Spain's southeastern coast, and the **Costa del Sol,** along the southern coast. Then comes the mountainous area that most people imagine when they think of Spain—the **Andalusian** region, the home of bullfighting and flamenco. Centred in **Seville,** this area also includes **Granada.**

Spain is a little larger than Yukon. It's also only one part of what's known as the **Iberian Peninsula;** Portugal occupies the remainder. Bordering Spain on the west, Portugal is a bit larger than New Brunswick and P.E.I. combined. It, too, has its own beach resort area: the **Algarve** [all-GARVE-ah] on the southern coast. The capital of Portugal, **Lisbon,** rests up against the Atlantic Ocean. Several Spanish- and Portuguese-controlled islands lie far offshore in the Atlantic. The Portuguese **Azores,** about 1300 kilometres west of Lisbon, are gentle islands with a few spas and beach resorts. The **Madeira Islands,** also Portuguese, are farther south— 640 kilometres west of Morocco. And Spain's **Canary Islands** are southwest of the Madeiras.

In major tourist areas, English is spoken by many. Elsewhere, however, it's far less common; the national languages of Spanish (in Spain) and Portuguese (in Portugal) predominate.

Spain is one of the few countries whose capital is at its centre.

A hot, dry wind, called the *leveche,* sometimes blows from Africa across southern Spain and Portugal.

SPAIN AND PORTUGAL

Capitals: SP: Madrid POR: Lisbon	Populations: SP: 40 300 000 POR: 10 600 000
Areas (square km): SP: 512 514 POR: 91 645	Religion: Roman Catholic
Time Zones: SP: GMT +1 POR: GMT +0	Languages: SP: Spanish POR: Portuguese
Drive on: Right	Currency: 1 euro = 100 cents
	Electricity: 220 volts, 50 cycles AC

Capsule History: **Spain:** Part of Roman Empire, 201 B.C.; Barbarians invade, 412; Muslims invade, 711; Age of Discovery, late 15th through early 17th century; last Muslims defeated, 1492; defeat of Spanish Armada by British, 1588; republic declared, 1931; civil war, 1936–1939; Franco rules, 1939–1975; parliamentary system takes effect, 1982.

Portugal: Independence from Spain, 12th century; Age of Discovery, early 15th through early 17th century; world power, 1433–1581; republic, 1910.

For reference sources and suggested lengths of stay, see Appendixes A and B.

HOW TRAVELLERS GET THERE

The major gateway into Spain is Madrid's **Barajas Airport** (MAD), served by several North American carriers and **Iberia** (IB), the Spanish national airline. Flights originating from Toronto take at least 10 hours with connections. In addition, several carriers fly into **Malaga Airport** (AGP) on the Costa del Sol, and into Barcelona's **El Prat Airport** (BCN).

Flights to **Portela Airport** (LIS) in Lisbon can be booked on the Portuguese national airline, **TAP Air Portugal** (TP), and on a few North American and international carriers.

Tourists can also access the Iberian Peninsula from France via railroad and highways. Many ships end (or begin) their Western Mediterranean cruises in Barcelona. Several lines sail regularly from Great Britain, down Europe's Atlantic Coast, to ports in Portugal and Spain.

Spain's unlimited rail passes are available only in North America.

WEATHER PATTERNS

Most of Spain is very warm and dry in the summer, but during the rest of the year, three separate patterns occur. In the north and northeast, winters are a bit rainy, with plenty of snow in the mountains. Central Spain (where Madrid is located) has chilly winters, with frequent showers. (After all, the rain in Spain stays mainly on the plain . . .) (See Figure 20-1.) The coastal areas and Balearic Islands have a climate similar to southern California, with mild, occasionally rainy winters and hot, dry weather the rest of the year (when tourism is heaviest).

Portugal's climate has less temperature variation year-round, with more winter rain than in Spain (especially as one goes farther north). Water temperatures along the Algarve are warmer than on Portugal's Atlantic coast. (See Figure 20-2.)

Figure 20-1　Climate at a Glance: Madrid, Spain

MONTH	JAN	FEB	MAR	APR	MAY	JUN	JUL	AUG	SEP	OCT	NOV	DEC
AVERAGE HIGH TEMPERATURE	8	11	14	18	22	27	31	30	25	19	12	9
AVERAGE LOW TEMPERATURE	1	2	4	7	10	14	17	17	13	9	4	2
AVERAGE PRECIPITATION (IN CENTIMETRES)	3	5	5	5	5	3	0	0	3	5	5	5

Figure 20-2　Climate at a Glance: Lisbon, Portugal

MONTH	JAN	FEB	MAR	APR	MAY	JUN	JUL	AUG	SEP	OCT	NOV	DEC
AVERAGE HIGH TEMPERATURE	13	14	16	18	21	24	26	27	24	21	17	14
AVERAGE LOW TEMPERATURE	8	8	9	11	13	16	17	18	17	14	11	8
AVERAGE PRECIPITATION (IN CENTIMETRES)	8	8	8	5	5	3	0	0	3	8	10	10

GETTING AROUND

Spain is the second-largest country in Europe (only France is larger). Therefore, visitors may do better to fly from one area to the next, especially since the highway and rail systems aren't quite as extensive or efficient as in some other European countries. The Spanish national railway uses good equipment mostly on its high-speed long-distance **AVE** routes. Shorter runs can be slow and uncomfortable.

Trains in Portugal, however, are generally modern and comfortable (though the many daily runs on the pretty ride from Lisbon to the Algarve can get crowded). There's also a connection between Lisbon and Madrid. Buses are quite comfortable in Portugal. For those who want to drive themselves, car rentals in both countries are widely available—though a self-driving trip may not be prudent: Portugal and Spain have high accident and car break-in rates.

Cruises are a good way to see many of Spain's and Portugal's coastal and offshore sites, usually in combination with other European countries. In addition to Barcelona and Lisbon, ships call on the Balearic Islands, **Valencia,** the Costa del Sol, the Madeiras, and the Canaries (the latter two often in combination with Morocco).

Madrid has a good, inexpensive bus system and a fine Metro subway. Barcelona's buses and Metro are well run. Lisbon's subway, the Metropolitano, is good but not extensive. Taxis in Lisbon are reasonably priced.

IMPORTANT PLACES

Each region of Spain is virtually a world of its own. And Portugal, closely related, has its own unique charm and beauty. These countries offer a wealth of interesting cities and attractions.

Madrid

The largest city in Spain, Madrid is the centre of Castilian culture. Free enterprise, new personal freedoms, and burgeoning arts and industry have revitalized this beautiful and strong city. Among the major attractions:

- **The Prado,** one of the world's premier and most influential museums. Its collection of Spanish art, especially, is superb.

- **The Plaza Mayor,** an imposing square in the city's Old Madrid section.

- **The Royal Palace,** once home to King Charles III and today an art museum with one of the finest medieval arms exhibits in the world. A sound-and-light show takes place on summer nights.

The following **day trips** from Madrid are popular:

- **San Lorenzo de El Escorial,** an awesome monastery and palace. This sprawling 16th-century edifice, burial place of Spanish royalty, is 48 kilometres northwest of Madrid.

- **Avila,** a fully walled medieval city with an impressive cathedral and monastery.

- **Toledo,** a multicultured city with a famous cathedral. The beautiful town was home to the painter El Greco. Its **Alcazar** fortress was where the legendary leader El Cid was reputedly stationed.

- **Segovia,** a 2000-year-old town famous for its imposing castle and Roman aqueduct (which still provides water for some of the city's fountains).

Reservations should be made well in advance for the crowded Lisbon-to-Algarve train.

Though Portugal is small, its seafaring tradition enabled it to have a worldwide empire. Its former colonies include Macau (near Hong Kong), Brazil, Goa (in India), Formosa (now Taiwan), Angola, and Mozambique.

Spain was once considered the wealthiest and most powerful country in the world.

Tapas are hors d'oeuvres–like treats that Spaniards often combine to form a meal. They developed out of a 19th-century custom of topping glasses of sherry with toast to keep the flies out.

Madrid's Casa Boutin claims to be the world's oldest restaurant. It opened in 1725.

Over 3000 feasts and festivals take place each year in Spain.

San Sebastian

Built on three hills, San Sebastian lies at the heart of the picturesque Basque region, near the French border. The area is known for excellent cuisine—the city even has its own gastronomic academy. San Sebastian has fine beaches and an elegant casino, and is a popular summer resort. It's an excellent base for exploring the Basque country. Among possible **day trips** are:

- **Pamplona,** a charming, hilly village best known for the famous "running of the bulls" in July.

- **Bilbao,** a port city on the Bay of Biscay, with a Gothic cathedral and many museums. Most noteworthy: the architecturally daring **Guggenheim Museum.**

- **Guernica,** made famous by the Picasso painting (in the Museo Nacional Reina Sofía, in Madrid) memorializing the town's devastation in the Spanish Civil War.

Barcelona

The second-largest city in Spain, Barcelona was once a major seaport. The harbour has been renewed and the city today is also a thriving business centre and the heart of the distinctive Catalan culture. Barcelona is a city of diverse art museums, unusual architecture, fine music, and excellent food. Among the attractions that dominate this intriguing city are:

- **The Picasso** and **Miro Museums,** with collections that span the careers of each of these great artists.

- **La Rambla,** one of the great walking streets of Europe, with many little restaurants and shops.

- **Barri Gotic,** the old Gothic quarter, with 14th-century buildings and churches.

- **Montjuic Park,** with dramatic structures and gardens from the 1929 World's Fair and the 1992 Summer Olympics.

- **Sagrada Familia (Holy Family) Church,** a wonderfully bizarre edifice by architect Antonio Gaudi (who fashioned several other odd, striking buildings in Barcelona).

The following **day trips** from Barcelona are popular:

- **Montserrat** is the mountainous site of a monastery where pilgrims have come for 800 years. Housed here is a famous statue, the Black Madonna.

- **Andorra** is a charming, tiny country in the nearby Pyrenees, with great shopping buys.

Costa Brava

Among the beaches of this popular resort are busy **Lloret de Mar,** the more isolated **Playa de Canyelles,**

Most signs in Barcelona are in two languages: Catalan and Spanish.

Gaudi never created a blueprint for the Holy Family Church. He worked from a few rough sketches and simply instructed workers on what to build as they went along.

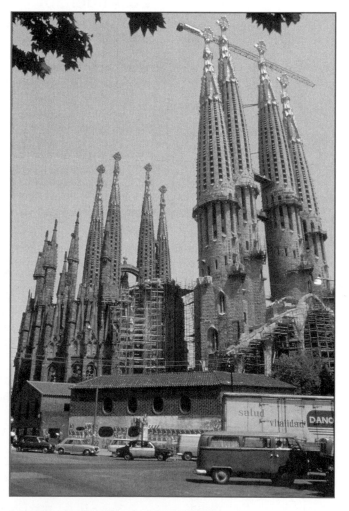

Sagrada Familia Church, Barcelona, Spain
Photo by Justus Ghormley

hectic **Tossa de Mar,** and luxurious **S'Agaro.** Other Costa Brava attractions include:

- **Ampurias,** with excavation sites of rare Phoenician ruins. There's also an impressive archaeological museum.

- **Figueras,** which houses the **Dali Museum,** ingeniously converted from an old castle.

Balearic Islands

Mayonnaise was invented on Menorca.

This group of Spanish islands is best known for the trendy and touristy resort island of Majorca. However, another island, Ibiza, has become popular with club-goers. **Menorca** and **Formentera** are also part of the Balearic group; their tourism is very low-key. Lodging is plentiful; there are twice as many hotel rooms in the Balearics as in all of Portugal.

Costa Blanca

The second of the mainland beach resorts, Costa Blanca is to the south of Barcelona. At its centre is the popular beach town of **Alicante.** The Costa Blanca is one of Spain's driest regions; it enjoys more than 3000 hours of sunshine a year.

Costa del Sol

Nightlife is important in Spain. Take in some musical and dance performance, such as the flamenco.

Located on the south coast, the Costa del Sol is one of the preeminent beach resorts in Europe. Highly developed with condominiums and high-rises, the area is known for having a very busy nightlife. Among its attractions:

- **Malaga,** the picturesque transportation centre of the area, is Picasso's birthplace and home to the Malaga vineyards. There's also the **Museo de Bellas Artes,** with a diverse collection including works by Picasso, El Greco, and Murillo.

- **Torremolinos** is the most popular (and crowded) beach town in the region.

- **Marbella,** the trendiest and most luxurious of the resorts, has been able to keep much of its Old-World architecture.

- **Nerja** became famous in 1975 when two children discovered its underground caves.

    Not far from the Costa del Sol are Granada and Seville. Tourists can visit them as day trips, but these cities are more commonly seen as part of a trip to Andalusia.

Andalusia

This mountainous region is the land of flamenco dancing, bullfighting, and lavish Moorish palaces. Among its cities and attractions:

- **Granada** boasts one of Spain's great structures, the **Alhambra,** a spectacular fortress and palace, built by the Moors and graced by some of the most famous gardens in the world.

- **Cordoba** is home to **La Mezquita,** a magnificent Moorish mosque so huge that a cathedral was later built inside it.

A highlight of Seville's cathedral is Christopher Columbus's tomb. Yet the Dominican Republic claims he is buried on their island.

- **Seville** has a 15th-century cathedral that is the world's largest medieval Gothic structure. The **Reales Alcazar** is a fortress remodelled to look like the Alhambra.

Lisbon

There are more people of Portuguese descent in New England than there are in Lisbon.

The capital of Portugal has an ancient history—possibly going back to the time of Ulysses, who legend says founded the city. However, Lisbon is also in many ways relatively new. An earthquake devastated much of the town in 1755 and since then

Monument to the Discoveries, Belem, Portugal
Photo by Justus Ghormley

it's been rebuilt. Lisbon is an easygoing place, gentle and less expensive than Madrid. Among the attractions you might recommend are:

- **The Alfama** and the **Barrio Alto,** famous for their cobbled streets and ancient medieval buildings. The **Baixa,** below them, is Lisbon's main shopping district.

- **Belem,** a riverside district that features the landmark **Tower of Belem,** the **Monument to the Discoveries,** and the white marble **Jeronimos Monastery,** a striking building whose sea-inspired architecture is unique to Portugal.

- **St. George's Castle,** a huge structure atop the city, with 10 towers, beautiful gardens, and great views.

- **Estoril,** a major seaside resort about 15 minutes from Lisbon.

A great **day trip** from Lisbon is picturesque **Sintra,** in the middle of the **Serra de Sintra mountains.** The **National Palace** and the sprawling **Pena Palace,** with its extravagant 200 hectare gardens, are located here.

In Lisbon, the Feast of St. Anthony revelry on the night of June 12 and all day June 13 is as festive as New Year's Eve.

The Algarve

The beaches of this south-coast resort area are quainter and quieter than those of Spain, though tourism to the region is escalating fast. Surrounded by high cliffs, the area is one of the most popular in Portugal. Its air gateway is the town of **Faro** (FAO). Among its towns are:

- **Lagos,** a walled seaside village with a rich history. It has wonderful beaches that are getting a little touristy.

- **Sagres,** a historical navigation centre. Vasco da Gama, Magellan, and Diaz all studied here.

- **Portimao,** with fine beaches. It has an active fishing trade and is fairly crowded.

- **Albufeira,** perhaps the busiest of the resorts. It's faster paced and has more of a nightlife.

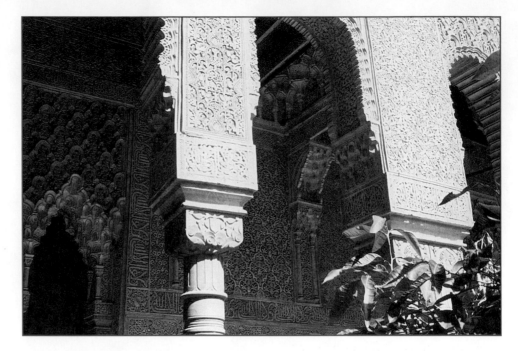

Arches of the Alhambra, Granada, Spain
Photo by Justus Ghormley

POSSIBLE ITINERARIES

First-time visitors to this part of Europe might enjoy a week that starts in Madrid before heading down to Seville and Granada or, instead, over to Barcelona. A few days could be added for one of the adjacent beach resorts. Return travellers could easily spend two weeks exploring: adding Portugal to a trip to Madrid, Seville, and the Costa del Sol; or including the Basque country with a trip to Madrid, Barcelona, and the Costa Brava. Furthermore, any beach resort or Balearic Island would make a wonderful four-to-five-day visit, or as a one-day cruise stop.

LODGING OPTIONS

Spain offers a wide range of accommodations; however, the lower-rated hotels may be a bit iffy. Many of the deluxe hotels are costly but very special.

Madrid's most famous lodging is the **Hotel Ritz,** an extraordinary Edwardian-style property. In Seville, there's the classically elegant **Alfonso XIII.** In Barcelona is another elegant **Ritz,** as well as the Old-World luxury of **Avenida Palace.**

The following chains offer the most lodging options in Spain: **Melia** (upscale), **Sol, NH,** and **Tryp.** Several North American and international hotel chains are also represented.

Alternative accommodations include the *paradores* (converted castles and monasteries that are fairly priced). The top among these are **Parador de Granada,** located actually inside the Alhambra; **Parador de Malaga Gibralfaro** in Costa del Sol, which is small and has a breathtaking view of the Mediterranean; and **Parador de Almagro,** on the way from Madrid to Seville, in Almagro.

Most of the world's major hotel chains have a few properties in Portugal. The country has a surprising number of opulent five-star hotels. An excellent alternative type of lodging here are the *pousadas*—inexpensive government-sponsored inns, many of which are castles.

ALLIED DESTINATIONS

At the very southern tip of Spain is British-controlled Gibraltar (and its famous rock) and across the Strait of Gibraltar is Morocco. Sandwiched between northern Spain and southern France is the tiny country of Andorra, a wonderful place to do some duty-free shopping.

CULTURAL PATTERNS

Though Western nations, Spain and Portugal present unique cultural challenges. Business travellers, especially, should be sensitive to a few unique customs:

- An invitation to a Spanish home is often made out of courtesy and shouldn't be accepted until one's host insists.

- Visitors should bring a small gift to a Spaniard's home. They may receive a gift in return, which should be opened on the spot.

- Many businesses close from 1:30 p.m. to 4:30 p.m. in Spain for siesta; in Portugal, they close from noon to 3 p.m.

- Dinner is served very late in Spain, where restaurants often do not open until 9 p.m. and don't fill until 11 p.m.

- One's appearance is given meaningful attention in Spain and shouldn't be taken lightly; visitors should dress carefully and well for business occasions.

- After a meal, diners must place their utensils together on their plate. To do otherwise would suggest that they weren't satisfied.

- Punctuality is not high among Spanish and Portuguese virtues. Yet the Portuguese do expect people to arrive on time for meetings (even if they start late).

> The only language related to Basque is a language spoken in Pakistan.

FACTORS THAT MOTIVATE VISITORS

Among the reasons a vacationer might be eager to visit Spain and Portugal are:

- The weather is sunny and beautiful.

- The countryside can be inexpensive, with great bargains for shopping and lodging. Portugal is an even greater bargain than Spain.

- The locals are extremely friendly.

- Portugal has some great golf courses.

- Both countries are easily accessible from North America.

- Water sports, beach activities, and cruise opportunities are readily available.

- The food is wonderful (though different from the Hispanic foods northern Americans are familiar with).

- There's rich cultural and artistic diversity to be found.

POSSIBLE MISGIVINGS

Of course, as with any country, would-be visitors have concerns about Spain and Portugal. Among these concerns are:

- "It's much too hot in summer." Northern Spain is cooler than the rest of the Iberian Peninsula. The heat elsewhere tends to be dry.

- "It's crowded in the summer." The beach resorts are indeed crowded in the peak seasons. Vacationers can visit at a different time, find a less famous beach, or choose another area of the country.

- "The Basque separatist groups commit terrorist acts." The few incidents that occur make the news. The chance of a tourist being affected is slim.

- "It's expensive." Madrid and Barcelona—once bargains—have become pricey. However, many secondary Spanish cities and most of Portugal are less expensive.

- "There's a great deal of petty crime there." Unfortunately, there's crime in most big cities of the world. Normal precautions will reduce risk.

Qualifying the Traveller
SPAIN

FOR PEOPLE WHO WANT	HIGH APPEAL	MEDIUM APPEAL	LOW APPEAL	REMARKS
Historical and Cultural Attractions	▲			World class museums
Beaches and Water Sports	▲			Both southern and eastern shores and islands
Skiing Opportunities		▲		Northern mountains
Lots of Nightlife		▲		Especially Madrid and Barcelona
Family Activities			▲	
Familiar Cultural Experience			▲	
Exotic Cultural Experience	▲			
Safety and Low Crime		▲		Much petty crime
Bargain Travel		▲		
Impressive Scenery	▲			Seascapes and countryside
Peace and Quiet		▲		In countryside
Shopping Opportunities		▲		Leather, lace, pottery
Adventure		▲		
To Do Business		▲		

SALES STRATEGIES

Lower-rated hotels can be unpleasant, so more highly regarded lodgings can make the difference between a successful and an unsuccessful trip. Deluxe hotels in Spain are expensive but luxurious and special. *Paradores* can make a visit memorable. Because of the size of Spain, especially, tours can be appropriate. On the Costa Brava or Majorca, chauffeured cars are a much safer way of getting around the dangerous, winding roads. Motorboats or cruises along the coast and to the islands are also an enjoyable way of seeing the country.

TRAVEL TRIVIA

MUSEUMS WITH THE GREATEST COLLECTIONS OF PICASSO PAINTINGS

- Metropolitan Museum of Art, New York
- Centre Georges Pompidou, Paris
- The Hermitage, St. Petersburg, Russia
- The Kunstmuseum, Basel, Switzerland
- Musée Picasso, Paris
- Museu Picasso, Barcelona
- Museum of Modern Art, New York
- National Gallery, Prague, Czech Republic
- National Gallery of Art, Washington, D.C.
- Philadelphia Museum of Art, Philadelphia

MAP ACTIVITY

NAME _____   DATE _____

A traveller wants to visit the places listed below. Which number represents each on the map?

PLACE/ATTRACTION	IN/NEAR WHICH CITY?	NUMBER ON MAP
A. The Alhambra	A.	A.
B. Transportation hub of the Costa del Sol	B.	B.
C. The Prado	C.	C.
D. The major city closest to Andorra	D.	D.
E. The Baixa	E.	E.
F. Picasso Museum	F.	F.
G. The Alfama	G.	G.
H. The town where the bulls run	H.	H.
I. The world's largest medieval Gothic church	I.	I.
J. The busiest of the Algarve's resorts	J.	J.

NAME _____   DATE _____

Mary-Jo and Bud Reid, in their early 30s, are planning a three-week trip to Europe, concentrating on Spain. It's their first visit there and their first big vacation in five years, so they're willing to spend money.

Circle the answer that best suits their needs.

1. How many days would you recommend for Spain?

   Three   Six

   Seven   Fourteen

   Why?

2. Which of the following countries would you be least likely to combine with a trip to Spain and Portugal?

   Morocco   Gibraltar

   Andorra   Grenada

   Why?

3. If they especially wanted to see a bullfight and flamenco dancing, where would you suggest Mary-Jo and Bud go?

   Granada   San Sebastian

   Ibiza   The Spanish Riding School

   Why?

4. Of the following tips you could propose to Mary-Jo and Bud, which would be most useful?

   Visit the Prado in Ibiza.   Shop at midday.

   Go in July.   Plan to eat late dinners.

   Why?

CREATIVE ACTIVITY

NAME _____   DATE _____

Your Halifax-based public relations company has been hired to create the tourist promotional campaign for the Iberian Tourist Office, which represents Spain, Portugal, and all of their islands.

You've decided to "target" your market to figure out which kinds of Canadian travellers are most likely to find Spain and Portugal appealing. You create the grid below to guide you.

Fill out the grid, circling a number according to the given rating system. Give your reasoning in the right column. (An example is provided.)

KIND OF TRAVELLER	APPEAL (5 HIGHEST, 1 LOWEST)					COMMENTS
Sun-and-fun types	(5)	4	3	2	1	Mediterranean beaches and Balearic Islands
Value seekers	5	4	3	2	1	
Quick-getawayers from Canada	5	4	3	2	1	
Families with children	5	4	3	2	1	
Single travellers	5	4	3	2	1	
Cruisers	5	4	3	2	1	
Affluent travellers	5	4	3	2	1	
Ethnic tourists	5	4	3	2	1	
Ecotourists	5	4	3	2	1	
Business travellers	5	4	3	2	1	
People seeking seclusion	5	4	3	2	1	
People who take tours	5	4	3	2	1	
Art lovers	5	4	3	2	1	

CHAPTER 21

Germany

Romantic Roads

Germany is a culture-rich land of fairytale sights. Whether driving the **Romantic Road** or cruising the **Rhine River,** visitors can discover charming hamlets, delicate or imposing castles, and, in at least one city, people who—on occasion—still dress in medieval clothing.

Germany was divided into two separate governments after World War II, but was reunified in 1990. German, of course, is the national language, though many Germans do have a good command of basic English.

When people think of Germany, the area they probably envision is **Bavaria,** in the south. With **Munich** [MYOO-nik] (München) as its centre, this is the land of Alpine terrain, oom-pah bands, beer halls, and mountain skiing. Meandering north from Bavaria is the Romantic Road, so named because of its enchanting medieval villages. Running down the west side of Germany is the legendary **Rhineland,** with its stunning scenery along the Rhine River. This leads into the **Black Forest,** found in Germany's southwest corner.

Binoculars are essential for a Rhine cruise.

GERMANY

Capital: Berlin

Area (square km): 356 841

Time Zone: GMT +1

Drive on: Right

Population: 82 400 000

Religions: Protestant, Roman Catholic

Language: German

Currency: 1 euro = 100 cents

Electricity: 230 volts, 50 cycles AC

Capsule History: Germanic tribe, the Franks, controls Europe, A.D. 800; Treaty of Verdun (843) and of Mersen (870) set German boundaries; Reformation, 1547; country divided by war, 1618–1648; Frederick rules Prussia, 1740–1786; Bismarck dominates, 1862–1890; Germany reunified, 1871; World War I, 1914–1918; Hitler, chancellor, 1933; Holocaust begins, 1938; World War II, 1939–1945; Germany divided, 1945; communist influence reduced, 1989; reunification, 1990.

For reference sources and suggested lengths of stay, see Appendixes A and B.

Cutting east to west across the country's centre are the rolling hills and magical palaces of the **Castle Road.** Nearby, in the middle of Germany, is **Frankfurt.** The flat, northern part of the country is less visited by foreign tourists; travellers do go to **Hamburg,** but it's mainly for business. And **Berlin,** once divided, has regained its status as Germany's preeminent city.

HOW TRAVELLERS GET THERE

The major gateway into Germany is **Frankfurt Airport** (FRA). **Munich Airport** (MUC) and **Dusseldorf Airport** (DUS) are also used heavily. Secondary airports are in Berlin (BER), Hamburg (HAM), and **Stuttgart** (STR).

Germany's airlines are **Lufthansa** (LH) and **L.T.U. International Airways** (LT). The country is also well serviced by North American scheduled and charter carriers. Flying time from Toronto is eight hours.

Hamburg is an important port of arrival and departure for cruises to the British Isles, Scandinavia and the Baltics, and other European destinations. **Passau** is a launch point for Danube cruises into Eastern Europe.

WEATHER PATTERNS

Summer days are very pleasant, with temperatures in the low 20s, but nights can drop to the low teens (see Figure 21-1); temperatures in Bavaria can run even cooler. Winters are cold and often overcast or foggy, with rain and (especially in Bavaria) snow. Indeed, when the sun comes out, it seems as if every German heads outdoors. Fall and spring are chilly, but in general quite lovely and less crowded. Summers are the peak tourist season, whereas winters see a drop-off in tourism. One exception: The Alpine area gets very busy in the winter with skiers.

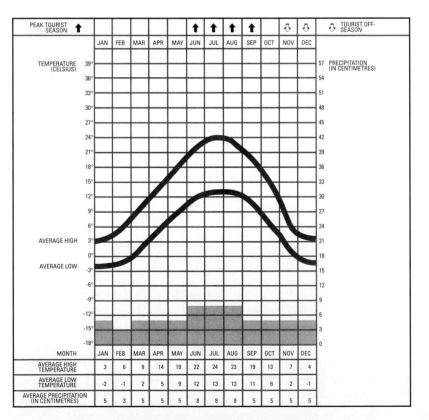

MONTH	JAN	FEB	MAR	APR	MAY	JUN	JUL	AUG	SEP	OCT	NOV	DEC
AVERAGE HIGH TEMPERATURE	3	6	9	14	19	22	24	23	19	13	7	4
AVERAGE LOW TEMPERATURE	-2	-1	2	5	9	12	13	13	11	6	2	-1
AVERAGE PRECIPITATION (IN CENTIMETRES)	5	3	5	5	5	8	8	8	5	5	5	5

Figure 21-1   Climate at a Glance: Frankfurt, Germany

GETTING AROUND

Germany's rail system is one of the world's finest—so good that it often beats travelling between cities by air, though most major cities have excellent airport connections. Travellers can even get off their plane and get on a train, since rail terminals are located at several airports. The **autobahn** is a wonderful way to travel through Germany. On some of its stretches, speed limits are nonexistent or only "suggested." Car rentals are widely available. Tourists who plan to buy a German car can order it before leaving home, pick it up at the factory in Germany, and then drive the vehicle around the country.

Rhine River cruises have been popular for well over a century. Cruises down the Elbe (from Hamburg to Dresden and on into the Czech Republic) provide a creative way to sightsee in eastern Germany.

In Munich, the U-Bahn is a very good subway system that connects with the S-Bahn local trains. There's also a well-run bus system. Taxis tend to be a little expensive. Berlin is usually reached by air, car, or train.

On the autobahn, stay in the slower right-hand lanes—unless you're prepared to hurtle along at breakneck speeds.

Germanrail Tourist Cards and Eurailpasses can be bought only in North America.

IMPORTANT PLACES

Though most people think of Germany in terms of Bavaria, the country's many regions are diverse in their attractions.

Bavaria

Surrounded by the **Alps,** Bavaria is a robust area, with picturesque castles and medieval villages. The heart of Bavaria is the region's capital, Munich.

Like the rest of Bavaria, Munich is a lusty place, with beer halls, cabarets, and a lively nightlife, especially during the renowned **Oktoberfest** celebration. It's also, however, a sophisticated city with world-class opera and symphonies, high fashion, excellent museums, and important centres of learning. This 800-year-old riverfront city appeals to almost everyone. Among its best attractions are:

- **The Marienplatz,** the heart of Munich, a town square with its famous glockenspiel clock.

- **The Deutsches** [DOY-ches] **Museum,** the world's largest science and technology museum.

- **The Hofbrauhaus,** a renowned huge, lively beer hall.

- **Nymphenburg Palace,** a 17th-century castle with vast gardens and a museum. Located just outside town, it also houses a china factory.

Here are some interesting **day trips:**

- **Fussen** [FEW-sen] is famous for the spectacular castles built by King Ludwig II. Just about every country has a castle that claims to have inspired the one in Disneyland, but **Neuschwanstein** [NOYSH-vahn-shtine], the most remarkable of Fussen's castles, is *the* one.

- **Oberammergau** has put on its legendary Passion play since the 1600s. The drama is presented the first year of every new decade.

- **Dachau** is a stirring and disquieting memorial to the victims of Nazi concentration camps.

- **Garmisch-Partenkirchen** was the site of the 1936 Winter Olympics. It's a modern yet charming town—beautiful in summer and a premier Alpine ski resort in the winter.

Street names change often in Munich, and these names are very long. Always carry a street map with you.

Munich's Oktoberfest begins in late September and runs through the first week of October.

Fasching, usually held in February or March, is the Munich version of wild Mardi Gras revelry.

In the 17th century, the villagers of Oberammergau vowed to stage the Passion play every decade to give thanks for being spared during the Black Plague.

The Romantic Road

Beginning in Fussen, in the heart of Bavaria, and winding north nearly 320 kilometres to **Wurzburg,** the Romantic Road is a string of medieval cities and Roman

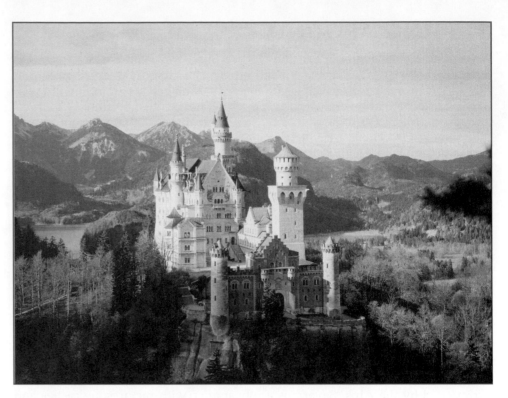

Neuschwanstein Castle, Bavaria

© 2006 JupiterImages and its Licensors. All Rights Reserved.

ruins. Suggest a visit by car or motorcoach tour. Among the attractions you might recommend are:

- **Nordlingen,** a town where, on market day, villagers often dress in period clothes from the Middle Ages.

- **Dinkelsbuhl,** a walled city with fanciful houses.

- **Rothenburg** [ROTE-en-burg], perhaps the finest preserved medieval village in all of Europe.

The Castle Road

Stretching west to east from **Mannheim** to **Nuremberg** (Nürnberg), the Castle Road is a path of castles and fortresses dating to medieval times. It's also a fine wine district. The route can be driven or taken as part of a cruise along the **Neckar River.** More commonly, this area is visited as part of a shorter version, from Mannheim to **Heilbronn.** Among its key towns are:

- **Heidelberg,** home to one of the world's great universities. Its medieval castles and churches are the setting of the operetta *The Student Prince.*

- **Rothenburg,** the well-preserved medieval town.

- **Nürnberg** (or **Nuremberg**), remembered as the site of the World War II war-crimes trials. It's also famous for its gingerbread, toymaking, medieval structures, and massive **Christmas Market** in December.

Although not precisely on the Castle Road, **Worms,** a historical town associated with Attila the Hun and Martin Luther, has the oldest synagogue in Germany and is the centre for Liebfraumilch wine.

In Rothenburg's oldest structures, tourists regularly bump their heads on overhead beams and door overhangs. The reason: People were much shorter when Rothenburg was built.

A small German–English dictionary is especially useful when ordering from a menu; remember to bring one along.

The Rhineland

The 1328 kilometre Rhine is one of Europe's oldest trade routes. The Rhineland proper is generally considered to stretch from **Mainz** to **Koblenz,** though some feel it goes all the way up to **Cologne** (Köln). Winding its way past charming villages, castles high on cliffs, and vineyards, this river passes through the region from which many German legends spring. Though the Rhineland can be seen by train or car, perhaps the most popular way of visiting this scenic area is on a cruise. Most cruises are run by **KD German Rhine Line** and range from a half to a full day. Other companies operate four- to eight-day trips (the multi-day cruises cover more of the river and use ships with overnight accommodations). Among the Rhineland's most interesting towns are:

- **Cologne,** with its renowned 12th-century Gothic cathedral and beautiful stained-glass windows.

- **Rudesheim,** a charming but touristy wine centre.

- **Bonn,** the capital of the former West Germany and the birthplace of Beethoven.

- **Dusseldorf,** a fashionable city with an active nightlife and good shopping.

Near the Rhineland is Frankfurt, the main air gateway to Germany. Although not a major tourist destination, the house of famed author Johann Wolfgang von Goethe is here, as are a few nice museums, a good opera company, and Gothic buildings.

The Black Forest

This beautiful region is rich with mountains, meadows, deep valleys, cool lakes, and dense forests. Beginning south of Frankfurt and continuing down to the thoroughly charming town of **Freiburg,** the area is particularly noted for spas,

On the banks of the Rhine River is the Lorelei Rock. According to legend, a siren (sea nymph) would sing to lure sailors to the rock, where they'd shipwreck and drown.

Lake Constance, at the border of Germany, Austria, and Switzerland, is also called Bodensee.

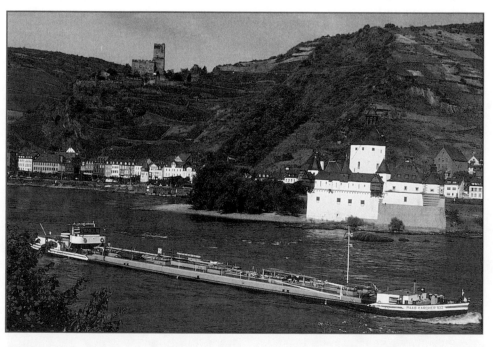

On the Rhine River
Photo by Justus Ghormley

cuckoo clocks, and ski resorts. Among the towns associated with the Black Forest are:

- **Stuttgart,** with its art and automobile museums, ballet and opera companies, and the nearby **Mercedes-Benz car factory.**

- **Baden-Baden,** one of the world's oldest and most famous spas, with an elegant casino.

- **Furtwangen,** with a unique clock museum.

When a city has the word *baden* in its name, it usually means that it has a spa.

Berlin

This city sits in Germany's northeast corner, in the middle of what was East Germany. It's a dynamic centre of culture, with a world-class orchestra, noted theatres, and some of the finest museums in Europe. Among its attractions:

- **The Wall** (or what little is left of it), the infamous 48 kilometre structure that once prevented East Berliners from going to the West.

- **The Reichstag,** the original, ornate German parliament building, now capped with a modern glass dome.

- **Charlottenburg Palace,** a grand, opulent structure built in the late 17th century.

- **East Berlin** (which used to be a separate area), with many worthwhile attractions. Sights include **Unter den Linden,** the soul of the city and its main boulevard, lined with linden trees and many historic buildings; the **Brandenburg Gate,** which once linked East and West Berlin; and an entire island of museums. Among the most visited of these museums is the **Pergamon Museum,** which boasts two astonishing structures that, piece by piece, were relocated here: the **Pergamon Altar** (a temple dedicated to Zeus in the second century B.C.), and the **Processional Way and Gateway of Ishtar** (from ancient Babylon).

- **Sans Souci Palace,** a monument to the fanciful and elaborate excesses of the Rococo architectural style. Located in nearby **Potsdam,** Sans Souci sits in a charming park.

The Pergamon Altar, Berlin
Photo by Marc Mancini

Eastern Germany

This formerly communist region has opened itself wide to tourism. In addition to Berlin, Eastern Germany features two other intriguing places:

- **Dresden** is a jewel of a city. Firebombed into near-oblivion during World War II, Dresden rose from the ashes and is largely rebuilt. Its palaces, art galleries, and opera are first rate.

- **Leipzig**'s musical heritage is legendary. This graceful city is most often associated with composer Johann Sebastian Bach.

POSSIBLE ITINERARIES

Because it borders so many countries, Germany is often included as part of a larger trip. First-time visitors should either spend at least five days exploring the Romantic Road and Bavaria, or take a few days on or along the Rhine. These destinations can, of course, be combined for a longer stay.

Return travellers may like to explore areas they haven't seen yet, such as the Black Forest or the Castle Road. A trip to Berlin would also be fascinating. You should keep in mind that Germany is very rich in attractions and can easily be visited in-depth for two weeks on its own.

LODGING OPTIONS

Germany can be a fairly expensive country to visit, and lodging is a large part of that cost. Germany's luxury chain is **Kempinski Hotels.** For those looking for something less costly, **Queens, Dorint,** and **ArabellaSheraton Hotels** are available. **Steigenberger** hotels range from first class to deluxe. Quite a few North American chains are present, as well. In Munich, hotels are clustered south and east of the rail station. In Berlin, many hotels are near the **Europa Centre.**

Germany offers assorted lodging alternatives. Many castles have been converted into hotels; they're beautiful, but can be expensive. **Gast im Schloss** is an association of somewhat reasonable castles that you might want to look into. In addition, spas (especially in the Black Forest) are popular. For those on a budget, *pensions* offer pleasant and inexpensive lodging.

ALLIED DESTINATIONS

Germany is centrally located in Europe, which is one reason it's often combined on a vacation with other countries, both by land and by sea. It borders Denmark, Poland, the Czech Republic, Austria, Switzerland, France, Luxembourg, Belgium, and the Netherlands. Switzerland and Austria, because of their similar cultures and proximity to Bavaria, are the most frequent add-ons to a trip to Germany.

CULTURAL PATTERNS

Located in the heart of the continent, Germany represents a rich mixture of Western European traditions and Eastern European ways of thinking. With the major changes this area has undergone in recent years, it's particularly important that business travellers, especially, are sensitive to its cultural diversity:

- Germans tend to be somewhat reserved. First names should be used only when one has been given permission or knows the person well; if uncertain, a visitor should follow the lead of the person to whom he or she is talking.

- Germans often hold strong opinions and will challenge others to defend their own. Be prepared to address questions that may arise.

- Punctuality and thoughtfulness (for example, acknowledging a birthday) are very important to Germans.

- It's considered rude to talk with one's hands in one's pockets.

- Prepare for an unusual custom: To show their appreciation at the end of a meeting, Germans will often bang their fists on the table.

FACTORS THAT MOTIVATE VISITORS

Among the reasons for wanting to visit Germany might be:

- Bavaria's scenery is spectacular.

- Germany is very accessible, clean, and organized.

- The country is filled with cultural riches and architectural landmarks.

- The people are friendly.

- The food is wonderful and hearty.

- Hamburg is a major cruise port and the Rhine is an important cruise waterway.

- There are lively festivals.

- Winter sports facilities are extensive, especially for skiing.

POSSIBLE MISGIVINGS

As spectacular as Germany is, some may feel reservations toward this destination. Among their concerns:

- "It's expensive." Yes, but there are bargains, and certain areas, like the Romantic and Castle roads, can be a bit less costly. All-inclusive tours help minimize unexpected costs.

- "The Nazis caused World War II and the Holocaust. Neo-Nazi sentiments still exist." This is a very sensitive topic. Some people, indeed, will *never* want to go to Germany. For those who might, but have some reservations, a visit to the Dachau Memorial might be appropriate. A new generation now leads the country and only a small (but vocal) few still harbour Nazi-like sentiments.

- "Germans are a cold people." In fact, the locals are quite friendly toward visitors.

- "They don't speak English." Germans are very well educated, and many people do indeed learn English as a second language.

- "It's so far from Canada." Germany is almost as close as Paris and is closer than Rome; a trip can easily be combined with one of those cities.

- "The weather's bad and there are no sun resorts." The weather is nice in the summer. A Bavarian resort or spa may be just fine; otherwise, Germany may be the wrong place for sun-and-fun types.

Qualifying the Traveller
GERMANY

FOR PEOPLE WHO WANT	HIGH APPEAL	MEDIUM APPEAL	LOW APPEAL	REMARKS
Historical and Cultural Attractions	▲			
Beaches and Water Sports		▲		Scenic lakes
Skiing Opportunities	▲			Bavarian Alps
Lots of Nightlife		▲		Mostly Munich
Family Activities		▲		Primarily sightseeing
Familiar Cultural Experience			▲	
Exotic Cultural Experience		▲		
Safety and Low Crime	▲			
Bargain Travel			▲	
Impressive Scenery	▲			Especially in south
Peace and Quiet		▲		Only in countryside
Shopping Opportunities		▲		Steins, cameras, cuckoo clocks, porcelain
Adventure		▲		
To Do Business		▲		

SALES STRATEGIES

Germany's strengths lend themselves to a great many sales enhancements. For instance, staying in a castle high above a forest, though expensive, would be magical. A cruise down the Elbe, Rhine, or Neckar may be the best way to see those regions. Spas have long been popular in Germany, and they're now catching on with Canadians. Because there's so much history spread out across the country, an escorted tour or river cruise might be perfect for some. City tours (especially of Berlin) are a good option.

A rail pass, too, provides efficient travel among Germany's far-flung attractions. Car rentals, because of the autobahn system, appeal to many. And "European Delivery" Mercedes and BMWs appeal to the upscale.

TRAVEL TRIVIA

EUROPE'S MOST FAMOUS SPAS

- Incosol (Costa del Sol), Spain
- Baden-Baden, Germany
- Albena, Bulgaria
- Biotherm Spa (Deauville), France
- Centro Benesere (Lake Maggiore), Italy

- Clinic La Prairie, Switzerland
- Évian (Lake Geneva), France
- Karlovy Vary, Czech Republic
- Sandanski, Bulgaria
- Thermal Hotel, Hungary
- Wiesbaden, Germany

Source: TravelAge *Magazine*

MAP ACTIVITY

NAME _____   DATE _____

A traveller wants to visit the places listed below. Which number represents each on the map?

PLACE/ATTRACTION	IN/NEAR WHICH CITY?	NUMBER ON MAP
A. Charlottenburg Palace	A.	A.
B. Europe's best-preserved medieval town	B.	B.
C. Neuschwanstein	C.	C.
D. The Marienplatz	D.	D.
E. An automobile museum	E.	E.
F. The university town where *The Student Prince* is set	F.	F.
G. The Hofbrauhaus	G.	G.
H. Goethe's house	H.	H.
I. The remains of the Wall	I.	I.
J. The Deutsches Museum	J.	J.

NAME _____   DATE _____

Clark and Ellen Griswold and their two teenage boys are planning a 21-day excursion to Germany, France, and Italy. The parents have been to France and Italy, but it's their boys' first trip to Europe. With four people travelling for three weeks, they don't plan to be extravagant, but they do want to be comfortable.

Circle the answer that best suits their needs.

1. How many total days in Germany would you recommend for their trip?

    Three   Six

    Fifteen   Twenty

    Why?

2. If they want to concentrate on only one area, which would you suggest?

    The Castle Road   Bavaria

    Eastern Germany   Vienna

    Why?

3. Which region should they visit if they want to take a cruise, as well as see some castles?

    The Lowenbrau River   The Elbe River

    The Loire   Rhineland

    Why?

4. If they wanted to see medieval towns, to which of the following should they *not* go?

    Rothenburg   Nordlingen

    Garmisch-Partenkirchen   Dinkelsbuhl

    Why?

CREATIVE ACTIVITY

NAME _____   DATE _____

Which German city should you recommend to a traveller who likes each of the following? (Be prepared to justify each choice.)

FOR TRAVELLERS WHO LIKE . . .   **RECOMMENDED CITY:**

1. Medieval history   1.

2. Recent history   2.

3. Drinking wine   3.

4. Visiting castles   4.

5. Skiing   5.

6. Cuckoo clocks   6.

7. Christian religious pageantry   7.

8. Literature   8.

9. Spas   9.

10. Festivals   10.

AUSTRIA

HUNGARY

SLOVENIA

ITALY

★ Zagreb

ROMANIA

Belgrade ★

BOSNIA AND
HERZEGOVINA

CROATIA

ADRIATIC SEA

Sarajevo ★

YUGOSLAVIA
(SERBIA)

BULGARIA

Dubrovnik ●

BLACK SEA

Straits of Bosporus

ALBANIA

MACEDONIA

Istanbul ● ✈

Tirana ★

Salonika ●

Sea of Marmara

Ankara ★

TURKEY

Meteora ●

AEGEAN
SEA

Izmir ●

Corfu

GREECE

▲ Ephesus

Cappadocia

Delphi ●

Kusadasi ●

Pamukkale ●

Athens ★

Mykonos

Bodrum ●

Antalya ✈

Corinth
Canal

Olympia ▲

Delos

Santorini

SYRIA

Peloponnese
Peninsula

Epidaurus ●

Marmaris ●

Cape
Sounion

Knossos

Rhodes ●

IRAQ

Crete ▲

IONIAN SEA

CHAPTER 22

Greece and Turkey

An Odyssey of Culture

Homer's classic tale *The Odyssey* is perhaps the most famous adventure story ever told: It traces the travels of Odysseus through some of Western civilization's most famous places. Present-day travellers can take the same trip—with fewer obstacles. The land of *The Odyssey*—the Eastern Mediterranean from Greece and its islands to Turkey—remains as classic today as it was in the time of Homer.

Greece, which altogether is about the size of New Brunswick and Nova Scotia combined, spreads over a broad area. The country is made up not only of its mainland but also of more than 1400 islands. Turkey is larger: It's about half the size of Quebec. A small part of Turkey occupies a little portion of Europe, but most of the country is in Asia. The two sections are separated by the **Straits of Bosporus** (which connect the Black Sea with the Sea of Marmara and, eventually, the Aegean).

Most tourists are interested in three areas: **Athens** and the region around it, the **Greek islands,** and western Turkey. Northern Greece, with cities such as **Salonika** (also called Thessalonika) and **Meteora** (with its hilltop monasteries), is interesting, but somewhat off the beaten path. **Istanbul,** Turkey, is a fascinating, unique city often visited on cruises. Other Turkish destinations are the ports of **Izmir** and **Kusadasi,** and the inland ruins. In both countries, English is spoken by those in the tourist trade.

Greece and European Turkey are often cited as part of a larger group called the **Balkans.** The Balkans include Bulgaria (treated in Chapter 23), **Albania**, **Slovenia, Croatia, Bosnia and Herzegovina, Serbia,** and **Macedonia.**

Turkey is 3 percent in Europe and 97 percent in Asia.

It can get hot when touring; bring bottled water along.

HOW TRAVELLERS GET THERE

Olympic Airlines (OA) is Greece's national airline and flies into the country's main gateway in Athens (ATH). A few North American airlines fly here, as well. Secondary airports operate on the islands of **Corfu** (CFU), **Mykonos** (JMK), and **Rhodes** (RHO). **Turkish Airlines** (TK) flies into Istanbul (IST) and **Antalya** (AYT).

Most Canadian tourists to Greece, however, visit the Greek islands and Turkey via cruises, most of which operate from May to October. During the other months the seas can be very rough; cruise opportunities, therefore, are limited beyond the high summer season. Most cruises arrive at Athens's **Piraeus** (the Mediterranean's number-one cruise port) or Istanbul.

GREECE AND TURKEY

Capitals: GR: Athens TURK: Ankara	Populations: GR: 10 700 000 TURK: 69 700 000
Areas (square km): GR: 131 935 TURK: 779 452	Religions: GR: Greek Orthodox TURK: Islam
Time Zone: GMT +2	Languages: GR: Greek TURK: Turkish
Drive on: Right	Currencies: GR: 1 euro = 100 cents TURK: Turkish lira = 100 kurus
	Electricity: 220 volts, 50 cycles AC

Capsule History: **Greece:** Ancient Greece reaches peak, fifth century B.C.; Roman colony from second century B.C.; Greece becomes Turkish (Byzantine Empire) province, 1460; wins independence, 1827; becomes kingdom, 1832; becomes republic, 1924; monarchy restored, 1935; Italy and Germany invade, 1941; liberated, 1944; military rule, 1967–1974; new republic, 1975.

Turkey: Captured by Alexander the Great, fourth century B.C.; Romans establish Ephesus, first century B.C.; Constantine founds Constantinople, 330; Muslims begin converting country to Islam, 11th century; Ottoman Empire established, 15th century; becomes republic, 1923; economic and political problems, late 1970s; military rule, 1980–1983; returns to civilian rule, 1983.

For reference sources and suggested lengths of stay, see Appendixes A and B.

WEATHER PATTERNS

Sudden strong winds often occur in the seas southeast of Greece. (They're what blew Odysseus off course.)

Greece is renowned for its wonderful temperate weather (see Figure 22-1). Summers are hot and dry, in the low 30s, whereas winters can drop into the low teens, with occasional rain and gusty winds. Coastal areas and the islands are cooled slightly by their proximity to the water. Northern Greece runs about five degrees cooler than the south. Summer is the peak tourist season. Spring and fall are good times to visit; the climate is still lovely and the country is less crowded. Tourism drops off in the winter, when bargains are available (and the waters get chilly).

Turkey has almost the same weather patterns as Greece. Istanbul, like Salonika, has cool winters and warm summers, with some winter rain and occasional summer showers. Izmir is like Athens—with hot, dry summers and cool, more humid winters; spring and fall are pleasant shoulder seasons.

GETTING AROUND

Olympic Airlines connects most major cities in Greece. However, cruises are the most common form of transportation among the islands, and many well-known cruise lines operate there. Inter-island ferries are also a way to get from island to island; most leave the mainland from Piraeus.

On the Greek mainland, the rail system is extensive, but not the best way for tourists to get around; English isn't commonly spoken, which can make trips difficult. There are, however, excellent trains from major European cities to Athens. Buses are not recommended for anyone but seasoned travellers. That goes for travel within Athens and Istanbul, as well, where a ride can be a crowded adventure. Taxis are inexpensive and a good way to get around. Car rentals are widely

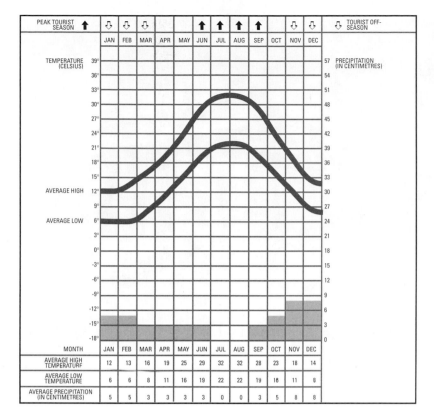

| PEAK TOURIST SEASON ↑ | ⇩ | ⇩ | ⇩ | | | ↑ | ↑ | ↑ | ↑ | | ⇩ | ⇩ | ⇩ TOURIST OFF-SEASON |

| | JAN | FEB | MAR | APR | MAY | JUN | JUL | AUG | SEP | OCT | NOV | DEC |

Figure 22-1   Climate at a Glance: Athens, Greece

MONTH	JAN	FEB	MAR	APR	MAY	JUN	JUL	AUG	SEP	OCT	NOV	DEC
AVERAGE HIGH TEMPERATURE	12	13	16	19	25	29	32	32	28	23	18	14
AVERAGE LOW TEMPERATURE	6	6	8	11	16	19	22	22	19	16	11	8
AVERAGE PRECIPITATION (IN CENTIMETRES)	5	5	3	3	3	3	0	0	3	5	8	8

available; they're best for excursions beyond Athens. One small warning: Greece has among the highest traffic accident rates in Europe.

Most tourists get around Turkey via cruise ship or on escorted motorcoach tours to the interior. Turkish Airlines services the major cities. Buses and trains connect many cities in Turkey. And, as in Greece, car rentals (outside the major cities) and taxis (within them) are viable alternatives.

IMPORTANT PLACES

Most of the best-known sights of Greece are located in the southern part of the country. On the mainland, there are the attractions of Athens and its environs and, for the seafaring, the magnificent Greek islands. For those venturing farther, Turkey offers many intriguing spots to visit.

Athens

Athens is the heart and soul of Western civilization. Philosophy, architecture, drama, and democratic government took root in Athens 2500 years ago. The people of Athens are warm and friendly. The pace of the city can be either relaxed or frenetic, according to the situation. Things can become almost like a nonstop party, especially when both locals and tourists dance late into the night to *bouzouki* music in the taverns. Among the attractions of Athens:

Most ancient Greek buildings and statues were originally painted in bright colours.

- **The Acropolis** is one of the world's most magnificent and inspiring places. Towering over the city, this rocky hill is covered with monuments and temples. At the top is its main temple, the legendary **Parthenon,** many of whose treasures can be found in the **Acropolis Museum.** (The Parthenon has probably influenced more buildings in the Western world than any other.)

Chapter 22   Greece and Turkey

The Parthenon, Athens, Greece
Photo by Justus Ghormley

- **The Pnyx**—just below the Acropolis—was the gathering place of ancient Athens, where issues were publicly decided. A sound-and-light show is held here at night.

- **The Agora** was the commercial centre of ancient Athens. With fascinating ruins, the area is still active today. Even more active is the city's business and entertainment district, the **Plaka.**

- **The National Archaeological Museum** is a world-class museum with a rich collection of Greek art and culture.

    Athens is a hub for many memorable **day trips.** Among them are:

- **The Peloponnese Peninsula**, in 1400 B.C. the home of the Mycenean civilization, with the citadel of Agamemnon and an unusual structure called the **Beehive Tomb.** On the way from Athens to the Peloponnese is the **Corinth Canal,** begun by the ancient Romans and completed by Greece in the late 19th century.

- **Delphi,** amid magnificent scenery, where the shrine of Delphi once housed a renowned oracle of the ancient world. There are also other temples and an amphitheatre. The 11th-century monastery, **Ossios Lukas,** is close by.

- **Olympia,** where the well-preserved ruins of the first Olympic Games (held in 776 B.C.) are found.

- **Epidaurus,** famous in ancient times as a spa and a centre for drama. Its 14 000-seat amphitheatre, still in use today, is renowned for its stunning acoustics.

- **Cape Sounion,** with its **Temple of Poseidon** overlooking the rushing seas.

- **The Saronic Islands,** between Athens and the Peloponnese Peninsula, covered with fascinating ruins of fortresses and Doric temples, as well as beautiful forests.

The ancient Greeks believed that the centre of the world—and of the universe—was at Delphi.

The 2004 Summer Olympics took place in Athens, returning to the country where the Olympics were born.

The Greek Islands

Of the more than 1400 islands, about 150 are inhabited. Most of the islands are off the mainland's east coast in the Aegean Sea, although a scattered group lies to the west in the Ionian Sea. Most tend to be quite arid and none are really tropical looking. They're most often visited on cruises or by ferry.

- **Crete**—the largest Greek island—is a mountainous place with beautiful gorges, wonderful beaches, and caves to explore. The famous **King Minos's Palace,** dating back 3500 years, has been reconstructed in **Knossos.** There's also a good archaeological museum.

- **Mykonos** is a fashionable island with excellent beaches, abundant nightlife, and many churches. Bright, colourful, with whitewashed houses, it looks the way people most likely envision Greece to be.

- **Delos** is usually reached through Mykonos. Once a sacred island, Delos is small, but covered with ruins and grand temples honouring Apollo (believed by the ancients to have been born here).

- **Santorini** (sometimes known as **Thira**) is one of the most dramatically beautiful places on earth. The island is formed by the blown-out cone of a huge volcano, with blue water within, several excavation sites, and bleached white buildings lining the slopes of what remains of the volcano's rim. Historians believe that, in ancient times, the island's volcanic eruption killed most of its inhabitants and perhaps created a tsunami that destroyed other nearby places. This catastrophe, they suspect, may be the source of the "lost continent of Atlantis" tale.

- **Corfu,** off the mainland's west coast, is another trendy resort. Because it's more lush than Greece's other, drier islands, many call it the most beautiful spot in the country. It has great beaches, a lively nightlife, and a semiformal casino. There are churches, a palace, and a very good museum.

Delos may have more ruins per square centimetre than any other place in the world.

Santorini
Photo by Marc Mancini

- **Rhodes** lies off the coast of Turkey. At **Lindos** is a remarkable amalgam of Greek, Byzantine, European, and Turkish ruins, with a commanding view of the countryside and sea. There are excellent beaches, a busy nightlife, and the **Palace of the Grand Masters,** a fully restored 15th-century Crusader fortress. One of the Seven Wonders of the Ancient World, the Colossus of Rhodes (a giant statue that inspired the Statue of Liberty), stood here before being felled by an earthquake. None of it remains.

Turkey

Turkey is a remarkable blend of European and Middle Eastern influences. It has some wonderful sites for travellers to explore. Among the destinations are:

- **Istanbul,** the capital of the old Byzantine Empire, and once called Constantinople. Sultans' palaces, minarets, and two important mosques (the **Blue Mosque** and the much older **Hagia Sophia**) grace the city's skyline. Istanbul is an active city with bazaars and a busy nightlife. **Topkapi Palace** is renowned for its spectacular jewels, Muslim relics, and countless (but mostly empty) chambers. Nearby is the **Kumeli Fortress,** a huge 15th-century structure that overlooks the Bosporus.

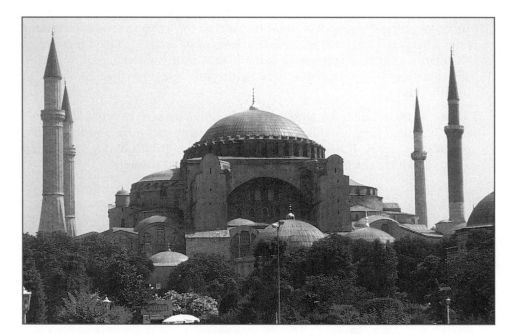

The Hagia Sophia, Istanbul, Turkey
Photo by Marc Mancini

- **The Turquoise Coast,** with its white sands and pine forests, facing both the Aegean and Mediterranean seas. It can be accessed by air (via Izmir or Antalya), charter yacht, or cruise ship (the principal ports are Izmir and Kusadasi). Among the Turquoise Coast's most visited seaside cities—often near ancient ruins—are **Bodrum, Marmaris,** and Antalya. The most important ruins, however, are at **Ephesus** (mentioned in the Bible), about 48 kilometres south of Izmir and about the same distance north of Kusadasi. There's no better place to experience what ancient Roman cities must have been like. Several other important (but less preserved) ruins are nearby at **Priene, Didmya,** and **Miletus.**

- **Inland Turkey,** including **Pamukkale,** with its hot springs and the white calcium terraces that look like "cotton castles"; **Cappadocia,** a place of hundreds of cave churches and dwellings; and **Ankara,** the nation's capital.

The Balkans

During the 1990s, there was great strife in this part of the world. Yugoslavia—rich in attractions and once a major tourist destination—broke up into a series of countries with conflict between various ethnic and religious groups. However, the region's conflicts have largely abated. The Balkans are once again becoming a viable destination.

- **Slovenia** is the most peaceful nation in the group. It has Alpine scenery, fine beaches, distinguished architecture, and bargain prices. The country's proximity to Italy makes it an intriguing add-on destination.

- **Croatia** borders the Adriatic Sea and has become a destination for many cruise ships on the way to or departing from Venice. **Dubrovnik,** a medieval port on the Dalmatian Coast, has been restored and is regaining tourist appeal. The capital city of **Zagreb** boasts many museums, art galleries and outdoor cafés.

  Dubrovnik is famous for its red tile roofs.

- **Bosnia and Herzegovina** was deeply affected by war. Its capital, **Sarajevo**— once a historic gem of a town and a major ski centre—was severely damaged but is being restored.

- **Serbia,** what remains of the original Yugoslavia, was also much involved in the fighting. Its capital, **Belgrade,** lies on the Danube and is famous for museums, cafés, and cabarets. **Macedonia** is considered by most to be an independent nation, by others as part of Yugoslavia.

- **Albania,** long a "mystery" country (it intentionally cut itself off politically from both East and West), has begun to court tourism. Its assets include Adriatic beach towns, Greco-Roman ruins, and the capital city of **Tirana.**

POSSIBLE ITINERARIES

Because of the length of time needed to get to Greece from Canada, travellers should ideally plan an extended visit.

However, if time is a constraint, first-time tourists can centre a weeklong trip in Athens and its environs. But to go to Greece and not experience its islands would be unfortunate. Nine days should be a minimum and 12 would be ideal. Travellers could see Istanbul and Kusadasi on an Eastern Mediterranean cruise, but to see Turkey in depth, visitors should take a week, starting in Istanbul, heading south to Pamukkale, then west to Ephesus, returning back to Istanbul. Return visitors would probably want to find new islands, explore old ones in greater depth, or take the occasion to see more of Turkey, including Ankara, Cappadocia, and Antalya.

LODGING OPTIONS

Greece's more upscale hotel chains include **Astir, Divanis,** and **Chandris.** Several North American companies have properties in Greece, as well. Several hotels face the Acropolis, providing a memorable view.

Fifty-nine percent of Greece's hotels are located on islands.

Some tourists prefer an alternative type of accommodation. There are beautiful villas throughout Greece, but they aren't bargains and many have maintenance problems. Other lodging choices include bed-and-breakfasts and spas.

In Turkey, such international chains as **Hilton** and **Mercure** predominate. Istanbul's better hotels cluster around Taksim Square (including the Hilton, with its fine view) and along the Bosporus. The famous **Ciragan Palace Hotel** was once a sultan's palace.

ALLIED DESTINATIONS

Since Greece, Turkey, and the Balkans are so far from Canada, visitors often choose to add on other nearby countries to their trip. Italy is a good add-on, as it's right across the Ionian Sea. Because the Middle East is just on the other side of the Mediterranean Sea, a trip to Israel or Egypt is a common add-on, as well. Remember that you can break up a trip to Greece or Turkey from Canada (especially the West Coast) by routing through many spots in Europe.

CULTURAL PATTERNS

Many vacationers are apprehensive about Greece and Turkey. And business travellers may have serious concerns about what will be expected of them in their daily contacts:

- Greeks and Turks are extremely hospitable to visitors. Hand-shaking is very important upon meeting someone.

- Many businesses close at midday for a few hours.

- A small nod of the head upward means *no,* not *yes.*

- If invited to visit a Greek home, bring a small gift as a token of appreciation. Also, if the host insists that you try a particular food, do so.

- Be careful about overpraising any item when visiting a Greek home. The host may feel obligated to present it as a gift.

- When on business, it's important to deal with the person who has the most authority. This isn't snobbery; it's the way Turkish society is structured.

- There is considerable political discord between Turkey and Greece. It's a subject that should be side-stepped, as should the conflicts among the other Balkan countries.

FACTORS THAT MOTIVATE VISITORS

To assume that tourists want to visit the area only because of its cultural history would be shortsighted. Among their many reasons might be:

- The culture and history of the region form the basis for Western civilization.

- It's one of the world's finest destinations for sunshine.

- Greece, Turkey, and the Balkans are comparatively inexpensive places to visit.

- Many water sports and cruise options are available.

- The people are extremely friendly.

- There are many shopping bargains.

Minnesota's Mall of America and the West Edmonton Mall—North America's largest—each have about 1000 shops. Istanbul's Covered Bazaar has more than 4000 shops.

POSSIBLE MISGIVINGS

The rewards of visiting these countries are considerable. However, they may not be for everyone. Among the concerns to address are:

- "I don't like long flights." Greece or Turkey can be part of a package that includes other nearby countries, breaking up the length of travel.

- "The area is dirty and there's so much poverty." Some of the Greek islands are quite upscale, as are certain areas in major cities.

- "There's terrorism there." The chances of being affected in Greece and Turkey are very small; on the islands, the odds are even lower. The Balkans seem to have quieted down, but conflicts could again arise.

- "It's so hot." The climate is temperate and dry most of the year. Humid heat is rare. Spring and fall are beautiful.

- "There's nothing to do there except see ruins." The nightlife can be quite impressive for those looking for excitement.

Qualifying the Traveller
THE GREEK ISLANDS

FOR PEOPLE WHO WANT	HIGH APPEAL	MEDIUM APPEAL	LOW APPEAL	REMARKS
Historical and Cultural Attractions		▲		Some ruins, but not major reason
Beaches and Water Sports	▲			
Skiing Opportunities			▲	None
Lots of Nightlife		▲		On larger islands
Family Activities			▲	
Familiar Cultural Experience			▲	
Exotic Cultural Experience	▲			
Safety and Low Crime		▲		
Bargain Travel		▲		
Impressive Scenery	▲			But not tropical or lush
Peace and Quiet		▲		On smaller islands
Shopping Opportunities		▲		Pottery, jewellery, leather
Adventure		▲		
To Do Business			▲	

SALES STRATEGIES

People visiting Greece should definitely take a cruise among the country's islands. And for a special way of getting from island to island, they may even go by yacht: A private one is expensive, but others will take up to 30 people and are more reasonable. Cruises calling on Istanbul and Kusadasi are also popular. City tours in Athens are a good way to see the town because public transportation isn't great. For seeing remote areas, car rentals and trains are always available (though, again, trains are not the best mode of transportation in Greece). Escorted tours are a very good option, too. Budget hotels throughout the region can leave something to be desired. Better accommodations are preferable. Most of the Balkans are appropriate mainly to those who *really* want something off the beaten path and don't worry about the conventional comforts or sudden political conflicts.

NAME _____   DATE _____

A traveller wants to visit the places listed below. Which number represents each on the map?

PLACE/ATTRACTION	IN/NEAR WHICH CITY OR ISLAND?	NUMBER ON MAP
A. King Minos's Palace	A.	A.
B. The Parthenon	B.	B.
C. Site of a famous oracle	C.	C.
D. The Blue Mosque	D.	D.
E. A small island near Mykonos	E.	E.
F. The Temple of Poseidon	F.	F.
G. Where the first Olympic Games were held	G.	G.
H. A resort island off Greece's west coast	H.	H.
I. Topkapi Palace	I.	I.
J. A city on a volcano rim	J.	J.

NAME _____   DATE _____

Every year, Jason St. Amand, a high school history teacher, takes a vacation. This year, the 32-year-old resident of Nanaimo, British Columbia, wants to go to Greece. Since he has his summers free, his schedule is very flexible. Though he doesn't have a great deal of money to spend, he has enough to make such a long trip worthwhile. Jason is single.

Circle the answer that best suits his needs.

1. Which place would you not recommend he visit?

   Athens   Crete

   Mykonos   Salonika

   Why?

2. If he decided to lengthen his trip, which city would be the least likely for an additional stop?

   Martinique   Istanbul

   Rome   Cairo

   Why?

3. Jason's hotel is near the Acropolis. Which of the following would be the farthest away?

   The Plaka   The Parthenon

   The National Archaeological Museum   The Temple of Poseidon

   Why?

4. Which would be the best month for him, all things considered?

   September   June

   November   August

   Why?

NAME _____   DATE _____

A contest! A travel magazine prints the grid below. It contains at least 18 words that refer to Greek or Turkish places. The words can read left-to-right, top-to-bottom, or diagonally. They can even be backwards—right-to-left, or bottom-to-top. Circle every word you can find and list it the bottom.

```
Z  O  R  B  A  C  R  H  O  D  E  S
M  Y  K  O  N  O  S  E  L  B  A  O
A  S  C  D  S  R  L  H  A  I  R  N
R  A  S  R  K  F  U  Y  X  P  I  E
M  N  U  U  A  U  M  P  M  I  M  R
A  T  S  M  E  M  S  E  A  P  Z  A
R  O  E  L  U  B  N  A  T  S  I  K
I  R  H  I  H  P  L  E  D  N  T  A
S  I  P  M  I  K  I  T  A  A  A  L
S  N  E  H  T  A  D  E  L  O  S  P
P  I  T  A  N  K  A  R  A  S  T  I
S  O  U  N  I  O  N  C  O  M  O  P
```

TRAVEL TRIVIA

FAMOUS RUINS

- Ephesus, Turkey
- Angkor Wat, Cambodia
- Machu Picchu, Peru
- Mayan ruins, Guatemala, Mexico, Belize
- Luxor, Egypt

- Petra, Jordan
- Rome's ruins
- Wye River Valley, Wales
- Fatehpur Sikri, India
- Lindos, Greece

Source: America Online's Travel Center

CHAPTER 23

European Potpourri

Collectors of countries—that's what tourists bound for Europe often are. Their motto: The more countries we see during our trips, the better. Sometimes, that's easy: A visit to Germany is readily combined with one to **Austria** and **Switzerland;** a trip to France can be easily side-tracked to **Belgium;** the **Netherlands** lends itself logically to a side trip to **Denmark** and on to the **Scandinavian countries** or to the **Baltics.** (Of course, travellers can also choose to spend an entire vacation in just one country for a more in-depth experience.)

It's very probable that a tourist will consider adding at least one of above-mentioned destinations to his or her itinerary. So you need to know them especially well. Here goes.

BELGIUM

One of the three Benelux nations, Belgium could be a robust addition to a European itinerary. Its capital, **Brussels,** is only one and a half hours northeast of Paris by train or five by car. It's easy to get around this nation, not only because it's relatively small and flat, but also because an efficient system of highways, trains, bus routes, canals, and small rural roads criss-crosses it. Those who prefer driving will find Belgium a good choice.

SN Brussels Airlines (SN) is Belgium's national air carrier, but many airlines fly into Brussels (BRU). (In fact, Brussels is a prime European gateway.) **Eurostar** trains run between Brussels and London via the Chunnel in less than two and a half hours. The climate is mild, with cool days in winter (snow is infrequent) and mildly warm summers. The area has a tendency toward fog, drizzle, and rain. French and Flemish are spoken here, but English is also commonly understood in key tourist cities.

Important Places

Brussels is a convenient base for visiting all of Belgium. The city bills itself as a "living museum" and it's certainly that: Medieval structures are everywhere. But modern buildings have shoved their way into this fast-paced city. Brussels is, therefore, not the uniformly quaint city that people may imagine. To discover that quaintness, tourists must visit some of Belgium's outlying towns. The following attractions are the most important in Brussels:

On certain feast days, the entire Grand Place is covered with flowers.

- **The Grand Place** [PLAHS], reputed to be Europe's most beautiful town square and the model for Munich's Marienplatz.

- **The Manneken-Pis,** the fountain with a statue of a small boy "relieving himself." The statue is often dressed in different outfits (it has a wardrobe of over 250).

- **Several museums,** especially the **Museum of Old Masters** and the **Museum of Modern Art.**

- **Erasmus House,** a classic 16th-century home and garden.

- **City tours** of Brussels, a particularly appropriate choice, since the city features dozens of small, fascinating attractions scattered about that tourists might miss on their own.

To really see Belgium, **day trips** out of Brussels are essential. Here are some highlights:

A great way to see Bruges is by sightseeing boat.

- **Bruges** [BROOJ], one of Europe's best-preserved medieval cities, often called the "Venice of the North" because of its many canals.

- **Ghent,** a picturesque city of flowers, gardens, and bridges.

- **Antwerp,** well known as an outlet for diamonds, but also graced by many museums, galleries, and churches.

- **The Ardennes** [ar-DEN] **Forest,** with its handsome vistas and Battle of the Bulge memorials.

Sales Considerations

There are more than 2000 chocolate shops in Belgium.

Belgium is a logical extension of a vacation in France or the Netherlands. It's especially appropriate for people who like tours. The country is also a shopper's paradise: Belgian chocolates, linen, ceramics, and precious stones are well known. Since Brussels is a major destination for European government officials and business executives, its hotels tend to fill up—especially on weekdays. Book lodging, therefore, well in advance. Tours, both escorted and independent, are a great way to obtain hard-to-get hotel space.

THE NETHERLANDS

Another Benelux country, the Netherlands (also called **Holland,** though technically Holland is only the western part of the country) conjures a ready image of tulips, windmills, dikes, and canals. The Netherlands is indeed a congenial destination, though its climate is often damp and its days gloomy.

Forty percent of the Netherlands lies below sea level.

Getting to **Amsterdam** (AMS), the centrepoint of Dutch culture, is easy. The national carriers **KLM** (KL) and **Martinair** (MP) have frequent and convenient service, as do many other airlines. In fact, Amsterdam is one of Europe's major gateways. Most Dutch attractions are within a day's trip from Amsterdam—accessed by convenient rail and bus service, as well as by a well-developed highway system. The locals speak Dutch, though knowledge of English is widespread.

Important Places

Amsterdam is the must-see city of the Netherlands. Its most important attractions are:

- **The Rijksmuseum,** with its magnificent collection of Dutch Masters.

- **Anne Frank House,** where the famed young diarist hid from the Nazis for two years.

- **Van Gogh Museum,** with the world's finest collection of works by the noted Dutch artist.

- **Rembrandt House,** where the artist lived and worked for two decades.

Venturing into the countryside provides a good sense of the country. Key places include:

- **Delft,** the world-famous pottery and tile centre.

- **Haarlem,** a well-preserved old city. Nearby are the vast **Keukenhof tulip fields,** which bloom in April and May.

- **Zaanse Schans,** with its concentration of working windmills.

- **The Northern Hamlet Route,** which features many small, delightful towns.

- **The Hague,** a splendid city (and home of the **World Court**) that boasts the **Madurodam,** a city fashioned in miniature.

The Dutch buy more books and bicycles per capita than any other people in the world.

W W W

The number-one weekend getaway for the Dutch is the beautiful city of Maastricht, a culinary and shopping magnet.

A windmill in the Netherlands
Photo by Justus Ghormley

Sales Considerations

Virtually every type of vacationer will find the Netherlands appealing, except perhaps those exclusively drawn to beach resorts. One possible objection: The country has a well-founded reputation for permissiveness. Drugs, prostitution, and pornography are tolerated and in many places legal. Yet the Dutch are a peaceful people. It's unlikely that visitors will find trouble unless they go looking for it. Two other points: The Netherlands has an unusually extensive system of camping facilities, and diamonds are a shopping speciality.

SWITZERLAND

Central and small, Switzerland boasts no real tourist hub city (like, say, England's London). Gingerbread hamlets, silvery lakes, and dazzling vistas dot this entire mountainous Alpine country. You might be able to get a handle on Switzerland by dividing it up into its three linguistic areas: the German-speaking north, central, and east; the French-influenced west; and the Italian-inspired south.

The Swiss are known for their efficiency; transportation to, within, and from Switzerland operates with clock-like precision. **Swiss** (LX) is the national carrier; both **Geneva** (GVA) and **Zurich** (ZRH) are major air gateways. Not even Alpine peaks interfere with the country's superb rail and highway system; giant tunnels bore through wherever appropriate. Except for its high mountain areas, Switzerland has a pleasant climate. Summers can even be quite hot (especially in the south), but without the humidity that makes other destinations uncomfortable. The *foehn* wind also sometimes brings unseasonably warm and dry weather to Switzerland's mountain valleys; it may occur in any season.

Important Places

Though small in size, Switzerland has distinct regions. It's important to understand their differences:

- **Northern and eastern Switzerland** is anchored by Zurich, Switzerland's largest city and its financial centre. Not far away is one of Europe's most visited natural attractions, tumultuous **Rhine Falls.** Also in northern Switzerland—on the Rhine, near both the French and German borders—is **Basel,** with its many first-rate museums, an excellent zoo, and spectacular winter carnival. **St. Gallen** is a picturesque Alpine city that is often a stopover between Zurich and Innsbruck, Austria.

- **Central Switzerland,** just southwest of Zurich, is often called the **Interlaken District.** The city of **Interlaken** itself would perfectly satisfy the expectations of what tourists think of a Swiss town: cute chalets, imposing clocks, and views of the **Jungfrau Mountains.** The country's charming capital, **Bern,** with its arcaded streets, fountains, and mascot bears, is to the west. Nearby is **Lucerne,** a medieval lakeside city whose landmarks include the **Lion Monument** and **Chapel Bridge.**

- **Western Switzerland** feels far more French. Most of the attractions border **Lake Geneva,** including **Lausanne** [low-ZAN], **Chillon** [shee-ON] (a famous, dank castle), **Montreux** (the site of many music festivals), and Geneva itself (whose most recognizable feature is the **Jet d'Eau** fountain, a geyser in the lake).

In Switzerland, Swiss cheese is called Emmentaler cheese.

In 1471, in Basel, Switzerland, a chicken was arrested, tried, found guilty, and burned at the stake. Its crime: It laid an egg so brightly coloured, it was judged to be possessed by the devil.

In a little town 48 kilometres south of Zurich is a huge surprise: the ornate church monastery at Einsiedeln.

The Lion Monument, Lucerne, Switzerland

Photo by Karen Fukushima

- **Zermatt** highlights the part of Switzerland that borders Italy to the south. Located at the foot of the well-known **Matterhorn** mountain, this town is quaint and car-free. Farther to the east but still along the border is the **Lake District,** which more fully captures the Italian influence on Switzerland. Chief lake cities are **Lugano** and **Locarno.**

Usually there's enough snow on the Matterhorn to ski in summer.

Sales Considerations

With its ski areas, palm-lined southern lakes, beautiful villages, and cities filled with culture, Switzerland is a genuinely easy country to sell. Sports enthusiasts especially relish the thought of a trip to Switzerland—which offers many opportunities for boating, hiking, and, of course, skiing. The prime Swiss ski resorts are:

- **Zermatt,** a massive winter-sport development.

- **St. Moritz,** a pricey resort in Switzerland's southeast, and beautiful **Arosa,** which is nearby.

- **Gstaad,** a resort beautifully set in a valley in southwestern Switzerland.

For those who prefer trains, the **Glacier Express**—which slices through some of Europe's most spectacular countryside between Zermatt and St. Moritz—is a must. And for lovers of service and luxury, Switzerland's fine hotels are a strong selling point.

AUSTRIA

Though small (it's slightly larger than New Brunswick), Austria ranks as a first-rate tourist destination. About 70 percent of its surface is mountainous, making it a prime ski destination. Its strategic position—bordering Germany, Switzerland, and Italy—makes it easily combinable with these major destinations. Its cultural legacy is rich, especially in music. Try to think of Austria without imagining the strains of Mozart, Strauss, and Haydn. You probably can't.

Austrian Airlines (OS) and other carriers connect into Austria's two principal cities, **Vienna** (VIE) and **Salzburg** (SZG). Rail transportation into and within the country is good. The climate is better than most people expect. Late spring, summer, and early fall are temperate, with occasional hot and dry *foehn* winds in south-facing valleys. Winters are very cold and snowy in the high Alpine regions, but other areas are surprisingly mild. Austria is a German-speaking country, though many locals know some English.

Important Places

Austria boasts many intriguing destinations, but three top the list: Vienna, Salzburg, and the Alpine ski resorts.

Vienna, Austria's capital, is a jewel-box of a city. Located in Austria's northeast corner on the legendary Danube River, it's filled with elegant palaces, graceful fountains, quaint cafés, huge museums, and world-class hotels. (The magnificent **Hotel Sacher** is famous for its tortes.) Yet imposing as it is, Vienna is a comfortable, civil city. Among its must-sees are:

- **The Hofburg Palace,** whose Vienna Boys' Choir is world famous.

- **St. Stephen's Cathedral,** whose soaring Gothic spire is a Vienna landmark.

- **The Spanish Riding School,** with its renowned white Lipizzaner stallions. (They perform there only in the spring and fall.)

- **The Schonbrunn,** a palace often called the "Versailles of Austria."

- **The National Library,** whose main hall is a baroque architectural wonder.

- A day trip to **Melk,** where a huge Baroque monastery perches on a high ridge overlooking the Danube.

Vienna's many coffee-houses are the legacy of a 17th-century occupation by the Turks.

During World War II, the Lipizzaner stallions were rescued by the U.S. Army under the command of General George Patton.

Hofburg Palace, Vienna, Austria
Photo by Marc Mancini

Salzburg, near the German border (and not all that far from Munich), is a remarkable destination. Though Mozart moved from Salzburg at the age of 25, his spirit still breathes through this picture-perfect city. Its attractions include:

- **Mozart's Birthplace,** the apartment where he composed his earliest works.

- **Hellbrunn Palace,** a wonderfully eccentric place with "surprise" fountains that spritz visitors when they least expect it.

- **Mirabell Palace,** with its vast marble decorations and gardens.

- **Day excursions,** most especially to **Werfen,** with 40 kilometres of dramatic ice-lined caves; to **Hallstatt,** where visitors dress as miners and ride a tunnel train; and into the countryside on an ever-popular *Sound of Music* tour.

The Austrian Alps, with their superb skiing, are also celebrated summer destinations. Key resorts are at **Innsbruck, Kitzbuhel, Lech, St. Anton Am Arlberg,** and **Zurs.** This mountainous region is often called the **Tyrol.**

Sales Considerations

Austria is ideally combined with trips to its neighbouring countries; its powerful appeal makes it an ideal way to expand an itinerary. Vienna is a key stop on many tours and Danube cruises. Skiers often extend their trips with visits to Vienna and Salzburg; both cities offer lively cultural attractions, even in the dead of winter.

Austria appeals strongly to those who seek safety, comfort, and well-organized facilities. Lovers of music, art, food, and winter sports will be especially drawn to Austria. Some, however, remember its close relationship to Nazi Germany in World War II and for this reason find Austria an unappealing destination.

SCANDINAVIA

Held together by a common cultural heritage, the five countries of Scandinavia spread broadly across northern Europe. **Norway, Sweden,** and **Finland** compose the Scandinavian Peninsula, a fan of land that stretches from the North Sea on the west to Russia on the east. **Denmark** (a peninsula and series of islands that stretch northward from Germany) and **Iceland** (way out in the North Atlantic) round out this nation grouping. Most tourists who visit Scandinavia are from Germany; Scandinavia, however, is becoming a more popular destination for North Americans, due, in part, to its reputation as a very safe and organized place to visit.

Scandinavia is cold most of the year. In summer the weather is generally pleasant: Real heat is a rarity and daylight lasts from very early to very late. Precipitation isn't excessive, except on Norway's west coast, which is rainy and snowy. Iceland, despite its name, isn't impossibly cold. (On the other hand, Greenland, with its optimistic name, is downright glacial.)

Several national carriers service Scandinavia, including **Icelandair** (FI), **SAS** (SK), and **Finnair** (AY); many other carriers go there, too. Internal transportation is excellent, with a wonderful system of trains, ferries, steamships, cruise ships, buses, and subways. The one weak link: Except for certain areas, Scandinavia's roads tend to be rural and marked with hard-to-decipher signs.

Important Places

Here are Scandinavia's nations and what each has to offer:

DENMARK. Denmark, Scandinavia's most popular tourist destination, is a friendly little country; it's impossible to visualize it without thinking of Hans Christian Andersen's fairytales. It was also once an immensely prosperous nation; all that wealth brought fine castles, rich artistic achievements, enlightened government, and the ability to create the ultimate open-faced sandwich. **Copenhagen,** the capital, is the focal point of travel; city tours and day-trip excursions are popular enhancements. Most tourists visit the **Little Mermaid** statue and **Tivoli Gardens,** which served as a major early influence on Walt Disney's amusement park plans.

NORWAY. Norway is an outdoorsy nation with few real urban centres. Oslo, its cozy capital, features a **Viking Ship Museum,** the **Kon-Tiki Museum,** and **Vigeland,** a park of unusual sculptures. You should offer to cross-sell Norway's prime attraction: a cruise through the fjord area. Fjords are steeply cliffed inlets from the sea; they're majestic and humbling. Most local fjord cruises depart from the city of **Bergen,** which can be accessed via a scenic train ride from Oslo. Norwegian Coastal Voyage ships run year-round. Other cruise lines occasionally offer fjord cruises, as well. It's rainy along Norway's western fjord coast. Winter-sports enthusiasts also enjoy Norway. The Olympic centre at **Lillehammer** is especially popular.

SWEDEN. Sweden is a friendly, modern country, and **Stockholm,** its capital, is cosmopolitan and charming. Three highlights are the **Royal Palace,** the **Old Town district,** and the **Wasa Ship** (a 17th-century galleon that was hauled up from the bottom of Stockholm harbour). A day trip to **Uppsala,** a historic university town only about an hour north of Stockholm, is an interesting option.

FINLAND. Finland and its capital, **Helsinki,** are often thought of as merely a stopover to Russia and the Baltics. That's unfortunate, for Finland has a lot to offer. The **Lakeland Region** to Helsinki's north is truly picturesque. More adventurous travellers are drawn to **Lapland,** Finland's northern wilderness. (Lapland also extends across Norway and Sweden.) Helsinki itself has many interesting attractions; again, a city tour is an excellent option.

ICELAND. Volcanoes, geysers, earthquakes, boiling cauldrons—that's not what most visitors will expect, but that's exactly what they'll find in Iceland. Indeed, all this geothermal drama constitutes Iceland's prime tourist attraction. **Reykjavik,** the capital, has many appealing though modest architectural points of interest.

Sales Considerations

Lack of knowledge about Scandinavia is the major factor that prevents many people from considering it for a European vacation. Another objection may be the costliness of visiting Scandinavia; the budget-minded *can* visit these countries, but their choices will be limited. However, even moderate lodging is usually clean and comfortable. And hotel rates are surprisingly reasonable in summer, when business travel in Scandinavia drops and many residents head south for their holidays.

Would-be visitors may also worry about the language barrier, especially if they've seen or heard any of the Scandinavian languages, which are often quite incomprehensible to Canadians. But most Scandinavians know at least some English and love to practise it. Emphasize the clean, safe, friendly, and orderly nature of these countries. Suggest a fjord sailing, or the more extensive cruises that call on Scandinavia (usually out of Copenhagen, Stockholm, or ports in England or Germany). And remember that many Scandinavian airlines route their flights to the rest of Europe and to the Middle East through their capital cities; a brief stopover can often be easily arranged.

The original Legoland, a theme park made mostly of Lego toy bricks, is in Billund, about five hours by train from Copenhagen. England, Germany, and California have their versions, too.

In Helsinki is the Temppeliaukion, a large church carved entirely into a huge rock.

The most northerly capital in the world is Iceland's Reykjavik.

Danish, Norwegian, and Swedish are similar. But Finnish is from a different language family and Icelandic is so much like Old Norse, people there can easily read stories that were written almost 1000 years ago.

EASTERN EUROPE

To place the many Eastern European nations under one heading is probably unfair; each does have a distinct character. These former communist countries were long closed to outsiders. But most of the nations involved are now doing an excellent job of serving tourists.

Several national airlines service Eastern Europe, as do some North American and Western European carriers. Eastern European countries, though, are quite a long distance from Canada and often involve connecting flights.

Once visitors get there, they'll find it a bit difficult to get around on their own, since few locals speak English, and major highways are rare. Escorted tours are, therefore, about the best way to sightsee. A Danube cruise that starts in Germany or in Vienna and continues through much of Eastern Europe is an inspired way to visit the area's great cities.

We can divide Eastern Europe into two groups. The northern group includes **Poland,** the **Czech Republic, Slovakia** (also called the Slovak Republic), **Hungary,** and **Romania.** These nations are hilly, with cool-to-cold winters and mild summers (though areas of Romania can get hot). The southern tier of countries has a climate and topography more akin to Greece. They are the Balkan countries (which were covered in Chapter 22) and **Bulgaria.**

Important Places

POLAND. A rapidly changing country, Poland has taken on greater tourist importance of late. The following cities are the most visited in Poland:

- **Warsaw,** the capital, with more than 30 museums, many coffeehouses, casinos, and a restored old-town section.

- **Cracow,** a beautiful medieval town, 320 kilometres south of Warsaw. Near Cracow is **Auschwitz,** the former Nazi concentration camp that is now a museum.

- **Poznan,** with its 16th-century town hall and old market square.

THE CZECH REPUBLIC. This western portion of the former nation of Czechoslovakia is a magnet for tourists visiting Eastern Europe. Its scenery, spas, villages, ski areas, and hundreds of castles give it a wide appeal. Key cities and towns include:

- **Prague** [PRAHG], the capital, a city of elegant architecture, parks, and shopping. It has become one of the most popular cities to visit in Europe.

- **Cesky Krumlov** and **Tabor,** both ancient, atmospheric medieval towns.

- **Brno** [BUR-nah], with its mixture of ancient and modern attractions.

To the Czech Republic's east is Slovakia. Though less prosperous, Slovakia has potential, with its appealing villages, castles, mountains, and a splendid capital, **Bratislava,** that's often a stop on Danube cruises.

HUNGARY. A country rich in historical and cultural attractions, Hungary has become one of Eastern Europe's most popular tourist destinations. It's a romantic country with legendary food, lovely musical performances, many hot-spring spas, and hundreds of historical structures. Among Hungary's chief destinations are:

The Wieliczka Salt Mine, near Cracow, is filled with religious and historical carvings.

Czechoslovakia broke apart and became the Czech Republic and Slovakia in 1993.

Prague's Charles Bridge was built with egg-based cement.

- **Budapest,** a graceful city and the seat of Hungary's government. Its **Parliament building** is one of Europe's most elegant. The Danube bisects Budapest, creating two sections: Buda, all hilly and historical, and Pest, a centre of business and commerce. Almost all the rest of Hungary can be a day trip from Budapest.

- **The Danube Bend**, a short trip north of Budapest, with its picturesque scenery. Nearby is **Esztergom,** where Hungarian kings resided. A huge church is Esztergom's chief attraction.

- **Lake Balaton,** a resort-lined lake offering all manner of water sports.

- **Pecs** [PAYCH], a southern city blessed with an unusual blend of Turkish and European architecture.

ROMANIA. Romania, a mountainous nation that borders the Black Sea, has made a good effort to attract tourists. Most visitors are interested in the following:

- **Bucharest** [BOO-kah-rest], the capital, a city of huge palaces.

- **Brasov,** a medieval town at the foot of the Carpathian Mountains in Transylvania. A day trip away is **Bran Castle**—associated with a Count Dracula, who, though not a vampire, contributed to the legend through his merciless rule and violent cruelty.

- **The Black Sea Coast,** with its nearly 320 kilometres of coastline and flourishing resorts. Its key city is **Constanta,** a well-known cruise port.

BULGARIA. One of the smaller Eastern European countries, pleasant Bulgaria has the most ancient history of any Eastern European nation. Its best known attractions include:

- **Sofia,** the capital, with its Moorish and Byzantine influences. Near Sofia are many spas and monasteries, most especially the **Rila Monastery,** with more than 1000 frescoes painted on its exterior walls.

- **The Black Sea Coast,** with some 320 kilometres of sandy beaches and so many resort hotels that it's often called the "Second Riviera."

Sales Considerations

Eastern Europe appeals to those who have already seen the major attractions of the rest of Europe, who are seeking bargain travel (though several of its cities are expensive), or who may be drawn to this area for ancestral reasons. An escorted tour or a Danube River cruise are efficient options. Skiers and spa enthusiasts who seek more offbeat destinations may find Eastern Europe appealing. People who normally resist tours will gladly book one to any of these countries. Hotel rooms must be booked well in advance; Eastern Europe has somewhat of a lodging shortage.

THE COMMONWEALTH OF INDEPENDENT STATES AND THE BALTICS

Like Yugoslavia, the Soviet Union politically "came apart" in the post–Cold War era. Most of the "new" nations that resulted banded together to form the **Commonwealth of Independent States,** or **CIS** (though that title is not used much today).

A number of airlines serve these nations, most notably Russia's **Aeroflot** (SU) and **Transaero** (UN). Cruise ships call on Russia's St. Petersburg and the ports of the Baltic nations.

Russia is the biggest and most important country, touristically. The **Baltic nations,** huddled in the northwest, consist of **Estonia, Latvia,** and **Lithuania.** To their south are **Belarus, Ukraine,** and **Moldova.** Another group—wedged on an isthmus between the Black and Caspian seas—is composed of **Georgia, Armenia,** and **Azerbaijan.** A final group of countries with tongue-twisting names flows eastward from the Caspian Sea: **Turkmenistan, Uzbekistan, Kazakhstan, Kyrgyzstan,** and **Tajikistan.** These latter five, all Muslim influenced, belong more properly to Asia than to Europe.

Important Places

Let's take a look at the most likely destinations:

RUSSIA. This huge nation—the world's largest—stretches across 11 265 kilometres and 11 time zones. The disintegration of the Soviet Union put a brief damper on Russian tourism, but the many attractions that grace this area have now become quite popular. Its two most important cities to visit are:

- **Moscow,** the capital, with **Tretyakov Museum, Red Square,** and its most important attraction, the **Kremlin,** which contains government buildings and ornate churches. Two very different places—the Bolshoi Ballet and the Moscow Circus—are prime attractions. The **Cathedral of Christ the Savior,** which was destroyed in 1931, has been rebuilt. And **St. Basil's Cathedral** is a Moscow landmark.

- **St. Petersburg,** an elegant, Western European–like city and cruise port that boasts one of the world's great museums (the **Hermitage**) and Russia's own version of the Tower of London (the **Peter and Paul Fortress**). Several huge "summer palaces" outside St. Petersburg are well worth the visit.

OTHER CIS NATIONS. Which CIS countries are most likely to interest tourists? Here are a few:

- **Ukraine,** a country of great agricultural wealth, featuring two interesting cities: **Kiev** boasts many fine monasteries and churches, most notably **St. Sophia's.** And **Yalta,** on the Black Sea, is a resort town of surprising sophistication.

- **Georgia,** which has suffered much political infighting. Its cities of **Batumi, Sukhumi,** and **Tbilisi** used to be part of a popular itinerary through the southern part of the old Soviet Union. They are becoming viable destinations again.

- **Azerbaijan**'s capital of **Baku,** a Caspian seaside city that was also a popular tour destination before strife began in the region.

- **Uzbekistan**'s cities of **Bukhara, Samarkand,** and **Tashkent.** All three were important economic and religious centres located on the legendary "Silk Road" that connected Europe with China. As a result, fine architecture and good museums are everywhere.

THE BALTICS. The first three nations to break from the Soviet Union—Estonia, Latvia, and Lithuania—have energetically begun to court tourism. **Riga** (Latvia) and **Tallinn** (Estonia) have become major cruise ports. To accommodate land-bound travellers, these three nations have developed a "Via Baltica" road system that begins in Warsaw, Poland, and works its way northward near **Vilnius** (Lithuania), then on to Riga and Tallinn.

The world's busiest McDonald's is on Moscow's Pushkin Square.

The world's biggest bell is at the Kremlin.

Moscow's subways are surprisingly ornate, with marble and chandeliers.

St. Petersburg was called Petrograd from 1914 to 1924, changed to Leningrad in 1924, and was renamed St. Petersburg in 1991.

Kiev's St. Sophia's was patterned on the church of the same name in Istanbul.

Sales Considerations

The Baltics and Russia continue to be attractive destinations for those who want something a little different in their European vacations. Tours and cruises appeal to many visitors. Be alert for political instability in all these countries. Many Canadian "necessities" are in short supply and crime is a problem in the former Soviet Union (one more reason for an escorted tour).

LITTLE COUNTRIES

Ever wonder how a weeklong European tour could visit nine countries? The answer is simple: Europe is peppered with little countries, some of which are principalities under the protection of a larger country. Little countries make excellent day trips or places to pass through on a voyage from one major destination to another. Most emphasize their duty-free shopping opportunities. Here's a thumbnail sketch of each:

- **Andorra**—ruggedly perched in the Pyrenees on the border between France and Spain—offers wonderful scenery, good-sized ski resorts, quaint villages, and great duty-free shopping. It's most often visited as a day trip from Barcelona, Spain.

- **Cyprus,** in the far eastern portion of the Mediterranean, lost some tourism because of internal strife between its two ethnic groups, the Greeks and the Turks. (The island is divided between the two.) But peace talks may lead to an easing of the decades-long tension between the two sides. Cyprus is an air connection point between Europe and the Middle East, and a stop for several cruise lines. Among its attractions are the walled capital of **Nicosia,** the mosaic-decorated ruins at **Paphos,** the **Tomb of the Kings,** many beaches, and the availability of water sports.

- **Gibraltar** has a high recognition factor among travellers, though they may never have thought of visiting it. This British-influenced promontory is 6.5 square kilometres. Its caves, beaches, ruins, and monkeys (yes, monkeys) are its principal attractions. Gibraltar can be reached by ferry from southern Spain or Tangier, Morocco. It's included in many escorted tours of Spain and Portugal.

- **Liechtenstein** [LICK-ten-shtine], a 158-square-kilometre patch of land on the Swiss–Austrian border, has much of the same appeal of its two neighbouring countries: a prince's castle, hamlets, vistas, mountain paths, and chalets.

- **Luxembourg** sits squarely at the intersection of France, Germany, and Belgium. Dense forests, flowering meadows, and quaint towns cover its 2587-square-kilometre terrain. It's easy to reach Luxembourg from Brussels, Belgium; Reims, France; or Frankfurt, Germany. It's also an important air gateway to all of Europe.

- **Malta** is a cluster of islands about 100 kilometres south of Sicily. Its climate is ideal, its beach resorts many, and its historical attractions plentiful. Most visitors reach Malta from Italy by air or boat.

- **Monaco,** on the extreme eastern edge of the French Riviera and near Italy, has long attracted the upscale and is a popular stop for tourists travelling along the Italian and French coasts. It's well known as the gambling centre of Europe. **Monte Carlo** is its capital. The closest major city is Nice, France.

- **San Marino** is a rocky mountaintop country completely surrounded by Italy. (It's near the northeast Italian coast.) This, the world's oldest republic (founded in A.D. 301), is a frequent stop for travellers on their way from Venice to Florence. It's very close to the seacoast town of Rimini. Prepare visitors for the crowds they'll probably encounter there: San Marino is a major duty-free shopping area.

The Sovereign Order of Malta, which occupies a building in Rome and has 80 people, claims to be the world's smallest country.

Because of an incomplete peace treaty, Liechtenstein is still at war with Prussia, a nation that no longer exists.

The world's oldest free-standing stone structures are on Malta.

TRAVEL TRIVIA

SIGNS ENCOUNTERED BY TRAVELLERS

- Fur coats made for ladies from their own skin. (Sweden)

- When passenger of foot heave in sight, toot the horn. Trumpet him melodiously at first, but if he still obstacles your passage, then tootle him with vigour. (Japan)

- Our wine leaves you nothing to hope for. (Switzerland)

- We take your bags and send them in all directions. (Denmark)

- Swimming is forbidden in absence of the Saviour. (France)

- Please do not feed the animals. If you have any suitable food, give it to the guard on duty. (Hungary)

- Ladies may have a fit upstairs. (Hong Kong)

- Please leave your values at the front desk. (France)

- Because is big rush, we will execute customers in strict rotation. (Greece)

NAME _____   DATE _____

A traveller wants to visit the places listed below. Which number represents each on the map?

PLACE/ATTRACTION	IN WHICH COUNTRY?	NUMBER ON MAP
A. The Spanish Riding School	A.	A.
B. The town of Bruges	B.	B.
C. Cracow	C.	C.
D. The Anne Frank House	D.	D.
E. Zermatt	E.	E.
F. Budapest	F.	F.
G. A famous boys' choir	G.	G.
H. The port of Tallinn	H.	H.
I. The Kremlin	I.	I.
J. Tivoli Gardens	J.	J.

NAME _____ DATE _____

Mr. and Mrs. Navratilova—a wealthy retired couple in their 70s—have seen much of the world. They've just returned from an Alaska cruise, which they enjoyed very much. They want to return to Europe, though Mr. Navratilova complains he hates seeing things twice. They have already visited France, Great Britain, Scandinavia, the Alpine countries, Italy, and Greece.

Circle the answer that best suits their needs.

1. What area would you recommend to them?

   Norway   Eastern Europe

   The Greek islands   The little countries

   Why?

2. What primary means of transportation would you recommend?

   A Danube cruise   A rail journey

   A rental car   Flying from city to city

   Why?

3. What destination would probably be appropriate to combine with your recommendation?

   Czech Republic   Italy

   Austria   Sweden

   Why?

4. Which places would Mr. Navratilova probably not want to visit?

   The Rila Monastery and the Parliament in Budapest

   Chillon Castle and the Spanish Riding School

   Lake Balaton and the Hermitage

   Red Square and Prague

   Why?

CREATIVE ACTIVITY

NAME _____ DATE _____

You've been a tour conductor for years, taking groups of Canadians across Europe. You're very proud of your knowledge of European history and culture; many tour passengers on your motorcoach have commented on how you make the past come alive.

It's your day off. You live in Brussels and decide to sort through the cluttered attic of your recently deceased aunt, Marie-Louise Wells. Marie-Louise was the granddaughter of the famous British author and thinker H. G. Wells.

But what's this in a dark dusty corner? A weird contraption with a brass plate that says . . . this is a time machine! Could it be that what Wells wrote about is real? Attached is a note from your aunt. It tells you that, indeed, this time machine works. You can visit any person or place in the past. Though the machine's *time* range is unlimited, its distance is not. The farthest away, geographically, you can go from Brussels is 3500 kilometres. You must also return to Brussels after each single "time trip."

You decide on your first excursion to visit six famous people and places from the past. Your first trip will be to visit Mozart in Salzburg. What will the other five be? (You may need to use an atlas to calculate distances.)

PERSON	PLACE	REASON
1. Mozart	Salzburg	To see a young musical genius at work.

2.

3.

4.

5.

6.

NAME _____   DATE _____

The Matching Game

Directions: Below is a list of cities, attractions, etc., some of which we have covered, some of which we haven't. There are all manner of connections among them. With a group of fellow students, you have exactly 10 minutes to come up with as many connections as possible. (Items may be used more than once.) Write your answers below. Note: There are at least 20 possible connections. For example, Andorra and Gibraltar—both are small nations.

Hofburg Palace	Rothenburg	British Museum
Red Square	Turkey	Prado
Lillehammer	Yalta	Venice
Delft	Salzburg	Wasa
Malta	Madurodam	Ardennes
Istanbul	Santorini	Carcassonne
Courmayeur	Kitzbuhel	Bruges
Chillon	Grand Place	Hermitage
Andorra	Legoland	Albufeira
St. Peter's	Sherwood	Russia
Kiev	Parthenon	St. Moritz
Schonbrunn	Blarney	Waterford
Liechtenstein	Marienplatz	Gibraltar

ATLANTIC
OCEAN

FRANCE
ANDORRA
SPAIN
PORTUGAL

YUGOSLAVIA BULGARIA   BLACK SEA

ITALY   ALBANIA
GREECE   TURKEY   CASPIAN
                                    SEA   C.I.S.

Azores

Madeira
Islands

Canary
Islands

Strait of Gibraltar

MOROCCO

Atlas Mountains

TUNISIA

MALTA

MEDITERRANEAN
SEA

CYPRUS
LEBANON
ISRAEL

SYRIA

Jordan River

IRAQ   IRAN

AFGHANISTAN

PAKIST

WESTERN
SAHARA

ALGERIA

LIBYA

EGYPT

Suez
Canal   Sinai
        Peninsula

JORDAN

Gulf of Suez

KUWAIT

Persian Gulf

BAHRAIN QATAR

OMAN

MAURITANIA

MALI

Sahara

Desert

NIGER

Lake
Nasser

Nile

River

SAUDI
ARABIA

UNITED
ARAB
EMIRATES

ARABIAN
SEA

Cape
Verde

CHAD

RED
SEA

ERITREA

YEMEN

DJIBOUTI

SENEGAL

GAMBIA   Gambia River

GUINEA-
BISSAU

GUINEA

Niger River

BURKINA
FASO

BENIN

Lake
Chad

SUDAN

ETHIOPIA

SIERRA
LEONE

IVORY
COAST

NIGERIA

LIBERIA

GHANA TOGO

CAMEROON

CENTRAL
AFRICAN
REPUBLIC

SOMALIA

INDIAN
OCEAN

SaoTome & Principe

UGANDA

EQUATOR

Congo

River

Lake
Victoria

KENYA

EQUATOR

EQUATORIAL
GUINEA

GABON

CONGO

RWANDA

Seychelles

Cabinda

DEM. REP.
OF CONGO

BURUNDI

Lake
Tanganyika

Mt. Kilimanjaro

TANZANIA

Comoro
Islands

MALAWI

ANGOLA

ZAMBIA

Zambezi River

Lake
Malawi

MOZAMBIQUE

Victoria
Falls

MADAGASCAR

Mauritius

ATLANTIC
OCEAN

NAMIBIA

ZIMBABWE

Reunion

BOTSWANA

SWAZILAND

Kalahari
Desert

LESOTHO

INDIAN
OCEAN

SOUTH
AFRICA

AFRICA AND THE MIDDLE EAST

Savannahs and Sand

Africa and the Middle East: The birthplaces of human culture, yet perhaps the earth's last unexplored touristic frontier. Just about everyone has wished to visit the homelands of the Bible and the Koran; to travel back in time to the palaces and pyramids of ancient pharaohs; to trek across the ever-shifting dunes of the Sahara; to witness the awesome spectacle of vast, migrating herds; even to pay a quiet visit to a family of mountain gorillas.

But few travellers ever get to Africa and the Middle East. It takes stamina and spirit to pursue these destinations, but they are destinations that return their levy tenfold. People who venture here bring home powerful, eternal memories of these genuinely exotic places.

A shrine in Ethiopia claims to have the Ark of the Covenant.

WHERE THE COUNTRIES ARE

Africa is the world's second-largest continent, yet most people have only the dimmest ideas about what it contains or even where it is. Africa is directly south of Europe, across the Mediterranean Sea. Indeed, some of the countries in northern Africa can be visited as day trips from Spain, Italy, or Greece. And what of the Middle East? Though often in the headlines, this region's location is obscure to many. But there's no mystery: It's to the northeast of Africa and officially is part of Asia.

Africa and the Middle East theoretically offer many countries as options for travel. Some, however, are developing nations with meagre tourist facilities. Others, because of political turmoil, aren't attractive possibilities. Some are simply too small and don't offer enough places of interest. As a result, we concentrate on only those countries with which you'll most likely be dealing.

Remember, too, that things change quickly in Africa and the Middle East: Today's tourist hot spot can be abandoned at the first sign of political upheaval; sleepy little countries can suddenly begin courting tourism with a vengeance.

The many African nations can be grouped into seven sections. The first, **Northern Africa,** is a region of deserts, oases, and Islamic culture. The countries we'll cover are, roughly from west to east, **Morocco, Mali, Tunisia, Libya, Egypt** (which is sometimes grouped with the Middle East), and **Ethiopia.** The second region is just northeast of Egypt: the **Middle East.** Leisure travellers are most interested in **Israel** (and the self-governing **Palestinian territories**) and **Jordan.** Some travellers may have business that will take them to **Saudi Arabia, Lebanon,**

The part of Africa that sticks out on its east coast and includes Somalia and Ethiopia is called the "African Horn."

Depending on the criteria, Djibouti may be the hottest inhabited place in the world, and Aswan, Egypt, the driest.

Bahrain, and the **United Arab Emirates**—among others. Muslims may also, for religious reasons, be very interested in a trip to Saudi Arabia to visit the holy city of **Mecca.**

A third touristic region is the massive peninsula of **West Africa.** Highly influenced by French culture, these countries include **Senegal,** the **Gambia, Sierra Leone, Liberia,** the **Ivory Coast, Ghana, Togo, Benin,** and **Nigeria.** The fourth area, located just to the east of these nations, is often thought of as the **Central Safari Belt.** Its most visited countries: **Cameroon,** the **Democratic Republic of the Congo** (formerly Zaire), **Tanzania, Kenya, Rwanda,** and **Uganda.** A fifth magnet for tourism is the more southerly **Central Victoria Falls Region,** flanked by **Zambia** and **Zimbabwe.**

A sixth prime destination is **Southern Africa. South Africa** dominates tourism here, but **Namibia, Botswana,** and the small nations of **Lesotho** and **Swaziland** have become popular, too. The seventh and final category isn't an area at all. It comprises the many islands that lie off the shores of Africa. The best known are east of Africa in the Indian Ocean and include the **Seychelles, Madagascar,** and **Mauritius.** The others are northwest of Africa and can be stop-off points on flights between Europe and North America: the **Azores,** the **Canary Islands,** the **Madeira Islands,** and the **Cape Verde Islands.**

A SATELLITE VIEW

From space, Africa is a distinctive-looking continent. What would be its most prominent feature? Probably the **Sahara Desert,** which covers most of the continent's northern third. In addition, the **Kalahari Desert** takes up much of southern Africa. And most of the Middle East is desert as well, notably the **Sinai** region. Though too many Tarzan movies lead people to think of the remainder of Africa as jungle, much of the rest of the continent is actually grassy savannah and veldt, with rivers and a few large lakes here and there. Furthermore, most of Africa consists of flat coastal and plateau regions, though some major mountains rise up in the northwest and along the continent's eastern side. And the equator splits Africa almost directly across its centre.

The features of Africa and the Middle East are a major part of what makes these lands so adventurous and exotic. Those same features dramatically shape the conditions travellers face when they venture here.

Bodies of Water

Two oceans lie on either side of Africa: the **Atlantic Ocean** on the west and the **Indian Ocean** on the east. Along the northern boundary is the **Mediterranean Sea,** and dividing the continent in the northeast from the Middle East (which is connected to Europe and Asia) is the **Red Sea.**

Two large bodies of water, the **Black Sea** and the **Caspian Sea,** form partial boundaries between the Middle East and Europe. The **Persian Gulf** juts into the centre of the Middle East and flows directly into the **Arabian Sea,** which in turn divides the region from western Asia. In the area separating the Middle East from Africa, you'll also notice the **Suez Canal,** which connects the Mediterranean with the **Gulf of Suez.**

Though much of Africa is desert, there's quite a network of rivers. Indeed, some of the most famous rivers in the world flow here. Emptying into the Mediterranean is the mighty **Nile River,** which dominates northeastern Africa. The **Jordan River** courses through the western part of the Middle East (and runs into the **Dead Sea,** a popular resort area). Several major rivers flow off the west coast of Africa into the Atlantic, including the **Congo** and **Gambia** rivers. A major rainforest surrounds the Congo River basin. And the **Niger River** runs through northwestern Africa. Emptying at the east coast is the **Zambezi River,** which begins in

---

◎ Spanish is the official language of only one African nation: Equatorial Guinea.

◎ The Sahara is the hottest, largest, and most desolate desert on earth.

◎ The Black and Caspian seas are both almost entirely surrounded by land and therefore could technically be called lakes.

◎ Until a few thousand years ago, lions, elephants, and other large animals lived in North Africa. Because the Roman Empire captured them for its spectacles and because the area became drier, these animals disappeared from the area.

central Africa and flows southward, then eastward, tumbling at mid-point over mighty **Victoria Falls,** a major tourist destination. Victoria Falls is often visited in conjunction with stays in Zambia, Zimbabwe, or Botswana.

Africa and the Middle East have few lakes, but **Lake Victoria** is quite large and stands out in eastern Africa. Below it are a couple of long, thin lakes: **Lake Tanganyika** and **Lake Malawi.** In the north, just south of the Sahara, is **Lake Chad.** One warning: Water in Africa is generally for viewing, not swimming. As picturesque and even pure as the water may seem, bacteria and who knows what other creatures may lurk there. They may be harmless to locals (who often are resistant) but not to tourists. Ocean water is usually safe, but pollution and sharks can, in some places, be a danger.

Mountains

If you were to traverse Africa and the Middle East, it would become clear that they're not as mountainous as, say, Europe or Asia. Though much of Africa is very hilly or has plateaux, only two major ranges interrupt its surface: the **Atlas Mountains** in the northwest corner and the many mountains (most volcanoes) of the eastern regions. Indeed, lofty **Mt. Kilimanjaro,** the highest mountain in Africa, rises more than 5800 metres above sea level. One other prominent feature stands out: the **Great Rift Valley,** which begins in the Middle East and continues down to east-central Africa.

The Great Rift Valley is a treasure-trove of early human artifacts.

Climate

To fully describe the climate of Africa and the Middle East is a challenge. First, since the equator bisects Africa, the region has two seasonal patterns. North of the equator, the seasons are those that Canadians are used to: Winter is December through March, and summer is June through September. South of the equator, winter starts in June, summer in December. What about temperatures? Winters in the desert areas of northern Africa and the Middle East, as well as in southern Africa, are warm to cool, with chilly temperatures especially at night. Summers in

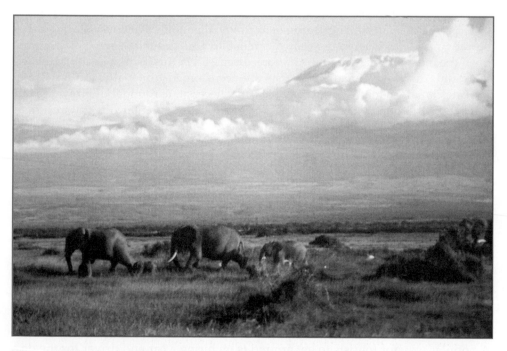

Mt. Kilimanjaro, Tanzania
Photo by William and Marie Rourke

the north can be broiling, though southern Africa's summers are relatively pleasant. As you get closer to the equator, however, temperatures tend to be warmer year-round, with only minor temperature fluctuations between summer and winter.

But altitude is a component, too. The plateau and mountainous areas of southern and eastern Africa tend to be cooler in general than land closer to sea level. (There are even snow-capped African mountains on or near the equator.) The Atlas Mountain region can also be quite cold in the winter, hence the ski resorts there. And what of rain? Northern Africa tends to be dry year-round, as is Namibia, on the southwestern coast. On the other hand, the coastal areas of western and central Africa are very rainy (here are the rain forests and jungles). The rest of Africa has moderate rainfall patterns. One final point: Rainy seasons vary widely from place to place in Africa. Certain countries near the equator, like Kenya, even have two distinct rainy seasons.

TOURISM PATTERNS

About one-tenth of the world's population lives in Africa.

The Middle East attracts more visitors than Africa. Among North Americans (and when the political climate is calm) Israel is the most popular destination, with South Africa a fast-rising second.

Political turmoil or a well-publicized crime against tourists in the Middle East or Africa usually impacts tourism intensely—not only in the immediate area of unrest, but thousands of kilometres away. For example, a 1990 crisis in Kuwait caused a 50 percent drop in tourism in Cairo, which is over 1280 kilometres away. Even Morocco suffered a major downturn, though it was thousands of kilometres distant from the Middle Eastern turmoil.

AFRICAN AND MIDDLE EASTERN DISTANCES

Africa and the Middle East span a vast distance. Africa alone is larger than South America and Europe combined. That, by itself, is enough to make point-to-point travel a major undertaking. Adding to the challenge is that, overall, the transportation networks here aren't always reliable. This is still a developing region. Even the most progressive of the nations discussed in this section haven't reached the standards most Canadian tourists are accustomed to. Finally, the politically delicate climate in many of the countries may necessitate roundabout travel plans. (Some governments, for instance, don't allow visitors to enter directly into their country from another rival nation; visitors have to reroute through a third, neutral country. Be sure to check government advisories on this.)

In short, travelling through Africa and the Middle East is an adventure. Travelling times can be easily miscalculated: A short direct road may be washed out or in poor condition. A simple flight between countries can become a circus of connections. In Africa and the Middle East, anything can change on a moment's notice.

In A.D. 900, the world's most populous city was Baghdad.

Most public transportation (specifically, buses and trains) should be viewed with healthy skepticism. The vehicles can be uncomfortably crowded; in many cases English won't be spoken. Taxis are a better bet, but the fares can be quite slippery. Rental cars are widely available. However, a car rental can present challenges, especially because road conditions are so uncertain; some areas might not even be safe to drive through or are poorly marked. Namibia and, especially, South Africa are among the few places where car rentals are a prudent option. A popular way for tourists to get around is by hiring a car and driver for the day, perhaps through their hotel's concierge, or to set things up via a reputable tour

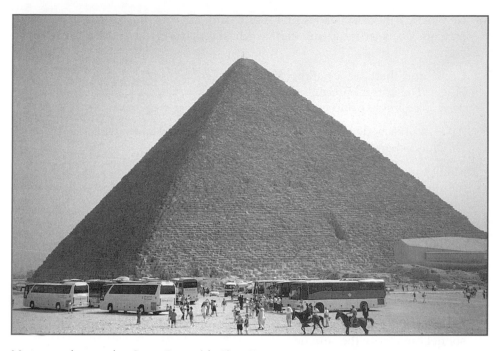

Motorcoaches at the Great Pyramid, Giza, Egypt
Photo by Marc Mancini

operator. And for visitors staying at a safari lodge, the hotel will provide a jeep, driver, and "tracker" to take them out on daily drives to see the wildlife.

Air travel to Africa and the Middle East has become easier. Though most itineraries must be built via European gateways, a few nonstop jets do fly from Canada. For example, Tel Aviv is a 12-hour flight from Toronto.

Perhaps the best option is an escorted tour and/or safari. Africa and the Middle East lend themselves ideally to such a mode of transportation, and even independent spirits may greatly appreciate how much easier their trips are when someone else handles the logistics. And what about air travel? Service is fairly good between major cities; however, scheduling can be uncertain.

Trains are a viable way of getting around in Egypt and South Africa. Indeed, South Africa's luxurious "Blue Train" is legendary, travelling between Cape Town and Pretoria. Cruises are even more reliable. Three cruise itineraries dominate: Morocco, Tunisia, and the Atlantic islands, often out of Spain; a routing that features Kenya and the Indian Ocean islands, often in combination with South Africa or, occasionally, India; and the highly popular Nile cruises.

The first beers were brewed in Ancient Egypt and Babylon.

One last thing to remember when setting up schedules: The weather can play an important part in transportation. Rainy seasons can wash out roads, hurricanes brush along Africa's eastern coast, and desert dust storms can make travelling difficult or dangerous.

SOME MISCELLANEOUS CONSIDERATIONS

People usually have a clear notion of only the most obvious destinations in this part of the world—the pyramids, for example, or Jerusalem. As for the rest—well that's another matter. Some situations you should be most aware of are:

- Health conditions here are often far below the standards to which many people are accustomed. Tourists should visit their physician before leaving on their trip to get appropriate inoculations and medicines.

- By North American standards, Africa and most of the Middle East are a bargain. Costs in Israel and certain Middle Eastern countries are somewhat higher.

- Crime and theft are a definite problem in some countries, decidedly not in others. The normal precautions should be taken. Begging, often by little children, is aggressive and common.

- AIDS has reached epidemic proportions in Africa (but not in the Middle East). Unsafe sex here is a potentially deadly mistake.

- Many tourists hear of wonderful exchange rates on the local black markets and decide to take advantage of the prices. But many nations here severely punish the practice. Indeed, the person offering that terrific exchange rate may be an undercover police officer.

- Similarly, drug use in many of these countries is a very serious crime.

- These destinations are informal. Yet tourists shouldn't dress too casually, especially when visiting temples and mosques. Shorts or sleeveless dresses are often a no-no.

- Bargaining at shops is usually lively and expected. But not always. Hotel personnel can clarify the situation.

- Africa and the Middle East can be very hot; insects are everywhere; malaria and polio are a problem, especially in West Africa. Sunscreen and insect repellent are essential.

- Outbreaks of lawlessness or political fighting sporadically occur across much of Africa. Keep abreast of travel advisories.

- Taking photographs is one of the great pleasures for many travellers. In many of these nations, however, certain sites (such as some government buildings or a special place of worship) may be off-limits. Visitors should ask about any restrictions when they reach their destination or consult a tour operator in advance.

The Sahara is growing. Its boundary is moving south at a rate of almost 50 kilometres per year.

Over half of the world's diamonds come from Africa's mines.

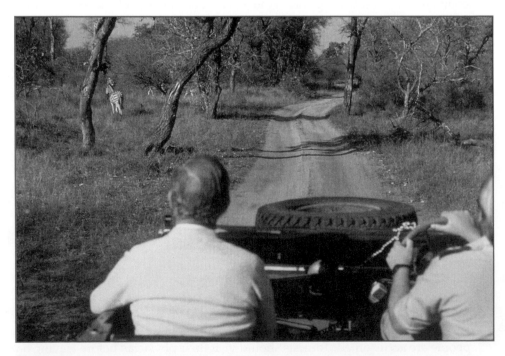

On safari
Photo by Justus Ghormley

- When booking a safari, find out how many vehicles are used per trip. A safari should have at least two vehicles travelling near one another, in case one breaks down, or should have a two-way radio to call another for help.

- Travellers should reconfirm their next flight, if practical, immediately on arrival—and in person, *not* by phone. Travellers must arrive for flights very early so they'll be at the front when boarding occurs. (Seat reservations are sometimes ignored.)

- The hotel chains with the largest presence in Africa and the Middle East include Hilton, Sheraton, Inter-Continental, Le Meridien, and Holiday Inn.

TRAVEL TRIVIA

WHAT THEY SAID

- "Everything in Africa bites, but the Safari bug is worst of all."—Brian Jackman

- "In the winter, Venice is like an abandoned theatre. The play is finished, but the echoes remain."—Arbit Blatas

- "Russia is the only country in the world you can be homesick for while you're still in it."—John Updike

- "Prague is like a vertical Venice—steps everywhere."—Penelope Gilliatt

- "Whether you go to Heaven or Hell, you still have to change in Atlanta."—old saying

- "I'm leaving because the weather's too good. I hate London when it's not raining."—Groucho Marx

- "Rome was a poem pressed into service as a city."—Anatole Broyard

- "He who rides the sea of the Nile must have sails woven of patience."—William Golding

CREATIVE ACTIVITY

NAME _____   DATE _____

You won the lottery! You can now indulge in your lifelong fantasy: to visit all seven touristic regions of Africa during a month-long trip. You have to plan your packing. What 10 special items do you think you'll need to bring, other than essentials (for example, don't list shirts, a toothbrush, and so on), for this African holiday?

ITEM

1. Binoculars

2.

3.

4.

5.

6.

7.

8.

9.

10.

REASON

1. To see distant animals at wildlife reserves.

2.

3.

4.

5.

6.

7.

8.

9.

10.

MEDITERRANEAN SEA

Mersa Matruh ▲   Alexandria ●   Port Said ●   ISRAEL

Suez Canal

Sinai
Desert   JORDAN

Giza ● ☆ Cairo
Sakkara ▲
Memphis ▲   Mt. Horeb ▲

St. Catherine's ▲
Monastery

Sharm
El Sheikh ●

Hurghada ▲

LIBYA   EGYPT   SAUDI ARABIA

*RED
SEA*

Nile River

▲ Karnak
Valley of ▲
the Kings ● Luxor

Esna ●

Edfu ●

Temple of ▲ ● Aswan
Kalabsha   ▲ Philae Island

Lake Nassar

Temple of Abu Simbel ▲

SUDAN

GULF of SUEZ

GULF of AQABA

Egypt

Riddles in the Sand

It's perhaps the most famous riddle of all time: the riddle of the Sphinx. "What is it," the Sphinx asked passersby, "that walks on four legs in the morning, two legs during the daytime, and three legs at night?" If travellers couldn't answer the question, the Sphinx would slaughter them.

The Sphinx was a mythical creature and the only big Sphinx left in Egypt is a stone statue, anyway. Fortunately, it doesn't ask tourists questions. But riddles do remain. How were Egypt's great monuments built? Why were they built? What was ancient Egypt really like? These are the riddles that continue to draw tourists today (and provide a seemingly endless topic for cable TV networks).

Egypt is located in the northeast corner of the African continent. It's a large country—about the size of British Columbia and Nova Scotia combined. Yet most of the population lives in the narrow, fertile **Nile River Valley.** Depending on how you measure, the Nile may be the world's longest river. (The Amazon is the other possibility.) The Nile flows south to north through the eastern portion of the country and empties into the Mediterranean Sea. The country's capital, **Cairo,** is on the Nile in northern Egypt. Indeed, most of the destinations that tourists are interested in—**Luxor,** in the centre of the country, and **Aswan,** in the south—are on the Nile. (Those who fly between cities will see an astonishing sight: a blue and green ribbon of a river cutting through the tan, dusty surface of Egypt.)

Western Egypt, which makes up the bulk of the country, is desert and largely uninhabited. The nation's eastern border is marked by the **Red Sea,** which (with the **Gulf of Suez** to the west and the **Gulf of Aqaba** [ACK-ah-bah] to the east) helps form the border of the **Sinai** (**Peninsula**) desert. The famous **Suez Canal** lies to the north, between the Gulf of Suez and the Mediterranean. Arabic is the national language, but English is widely spoken by tourist personnel.

The answer, incidentally, to the Sphinx's riddle is "man." For it's man who crawls on all fours during infancy, stands upright through the prime of life, and uses a cane in old age. The rest of Egypt's riddles are left for visitors to ponder on their own, during a fascinating journey to this faraway land.

The "Lower" Nile is in the north of Egypt, and the "Upper" Nile in the south.

Tolls paid by cruise ships and freighters going through the Suez Canal are a major source of income for Egypt.

HOW TRAVELLERS GET THERE

The national airline is **Egyptair** (MS), though other North American and foreign carriers also fly into the main gateway at **Cairo International Airport** (CAI). Travellers may also reach Egypt following a stopover visit in Europe; it takes five hours to fly into the country from Paris, for example. It's also possible to arrive in

It's believed that Alexander the Great is buried somewhere under Alexandria. No one knows where.

Egypt via ship; Egypt is a frequent stop on Eastern Mediterranean cruise itineraries, usually out of Piraeus (Athens) or Istanbul. The main port in Egypt is **Alexandria,** in the centre of the nation's northern coast. A secondary port is **Port Said** [sah-EED], on the Suez Canal.

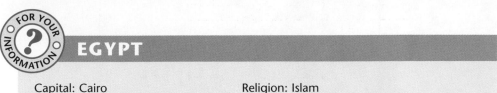

EGYPT

Capital: Cairo

Area (square km): 999 924

Time Zone: GMT +2

Drive on: Right

Population: 77 500 000

Religion: Islam

Language: Arabic

Currency: 1 Egyptian pound = 100 piastres

Electricity: 220 volts, 50 cycles AC

Capsule History: Upper and Lower Kingdoms united, 4000 B.C.; "Golden Age," 16th to 13th century B.C.; Alexander conquers Egypt, 332 B.C.; Rome takes over, 30 B.C.; Islam introduced, 641; Turks take over, 1517; Napoleonic occupation, 1798–1801; Suez Canal, 1869; British occupy, 1882; independence, 1922; monarchy ends, 1953; various Israeli–Egyptian wars, 1956–1973; fundamentalist unrest and acts of terrorism, 1993–1998.

For reference sources and suggested lengths of stay, see Appendixes A and B.

WEATHER PATTERNS

Most tourists to Egypt spend their time at destinations along the Nile, whose climate is far more comfortable than that of the Western and Sinai deserts. For example, the temperatures in Cairo during winter (the main tourist season) will reach only the low 20s and cool down to as low as 8°C at night (see Figure 24-1). Late fall can be pleasant as well, reaching 27°C or more. Visitors should avoid the summer, however, unless they're willing to put up with intense heat and air pollution in order to take advantage of bargain rates; the average summer highs are in the mid-30s, and it's dry (and it gets even hotter in southern Egypt). In addition, March through May is usually uncomfortable—not only because of shifting temperatures but also because of shifting sand; lung-searing winds (called the *khamsin*) can occur during this time. Rain, though, is unlikely to dampen a visit; it rains, on average, only one day a month in Cairo and a little more than that along the northern coast, where Alexandria is located.

GETTING AROUND

When setting up a camel ride, negotiate the price first and wait until the end to pay and tip. The same applies for trips in *feluccas* (small sailboats) and taxis.

The most popular way for tourists to get to their Egyptian destinations is on a Nile cruise. Sometimes they may also travel by plane; there are good connections between the major cities. Egypt also has adequate train and bus service. Travellers who decide to go by rail should take first class only; second class can be very uncomfortable. Ditto for the crowded buses that cross the country. (Those bus routes used predominantly by tourists are OK.) And remind visitors that donkeys, horses, and, yes, camels are commonly used for getting around in certain areas (especially around the pyramids). Escorted tours are a popular alternative.

		JAN	FEB	MAR	APR	MAY	JUN	JUL	AUG	SEP	OCT	NOV	DEC	
MONTH		JAN	FEB	MAR	APR	MAY	JUN	JUL	AUG	SEP	OCT	NOV	DEC	
AVERAGE HIGH TEMPERATURE		18	21	24	28	33	35	36	35	32	30	26	20	
AVERAGE LOW TEMPERATURE		8	9	11	14	17	20	21	22	20	18	14	10	
AVERAGE PRECIPITATION (IN CENTIMETRES)*		0	0	0	0	0	0	0	0	0	0	0	0	

Figure 24-1 Climate at a Glance: Cairo, Egypt

* Occasional rain, but never totalling more than 1.3 centimetres in any given month

Within Cairo, taxis are an inexpensive way to see the city. However, meters are often ignored; the cost of the ride should be firmly set at the beginning (and it often depends on the age, condition, and make of the vehicle!). Car rentals are widely available, but driving can be a nightmare of crowded streets and lonely desert roads. Many visitors hire a driver for the day; car rental companies and hotels can facilitate this. The jam-packed city buses should be avoided. There's an adequate subway system and visitors can also travel through the city by boat along the Nile.

IMPORTANT PLACES

Several remarkable destinations are typically on the tourist agenda.

Cairo

Located on the Nile, Cairo is a historic, bustling city (Africa's largest, by far). Visitors should be prepared for the squalor of certain sections of the area. Among Cairo's attractions are:

- **The Egyptian Museum,** near the Ramses Hilton Hotel, with perhaps the world's greatest collection of ancient Egyptian artifacts, including the mummies of most of the great pharaohs and the dazzling treasures of King Tutankhamun. It's best to get there early and to go directly to King Tut's room on the second floor, then to the mummy room, and on to the rest of the collection.

- **Great mosques,** the most notable of which are the ancient **Mosque of Ibn Tulun,** the renowned **Mosque of El Azhar** (near the old bazaar), and the colossal **Sultan Hassan Mosque.**

Over a million people live in structures within one of Cairo's cemeteries. It's called the "City of the Dead."

At Cairo's Egyptian Museum, you can actually look upon the face of Ramses II (mummified, of course), who may have been the pharaoh referred to in the story of Moses.

The most famous bazaar to see in Cairo is the Khan El Khalili.

- **The Citadel of Saladin,** a walled, hilltop fort built in the 12th century. Within it is the legendary **Alabaster Mosque,** the Citadel's central attraction.

- **Cairo Tower,** affording an excellent view of Old Cairo, New Cairo, and the pyramids (on a rare clear day).

- **The Museum of Islamic Art,** perhaps the finest exhibit of its kind in the world.

- **The Coptic Quarter,** with its old narrow streets, ancient Christian churches, and a museum. (The Coptic Church is an ancient Christian sect.)

- **The Three Great Pyramids and the Sphinx**—among the most renowned attractions anywhere—located in the town of **Giza,** just west of Cairo. The pyramids were one of the Seven Wonders of the Ancient World and they're the only "wonder" still in existence. The most famous is the pyramid of **Cheops.** The dramatic sound-and-light show (given in English on certain nights) is impressive. Early morning visits are good, too, since the heat is reduced and the crowds still thin.

A short day trip from Cairo is to **Sakkara.** Remarkable underground tombs and 14 pyramids are here, including the **Step Pyramid,** the world's oldest intact stone structure. Nearby is **Memphis,** which in ancient days was the capital of Egypt; brooding monuments and a huge statue of Ramses II are the attractions that remain from this city, now largely gone.

Luxor

 Thebes was also the name of the ancient Greek city-state conquered by Alexander the Great.

Upriver (south) from Cairo, Luxor features some of the most remarkable ruins in all of Egypt. In ancient days this city was known as Thebes. It was in the **Valley of the Kings**—across the river from Luxor—that King Tut's tomb was discovered. Other ancient pharaohs were buried here, as well. Though their tombs are now empty, the astonishing wall decorations remain. The area boasts two of the world's finest temple complexes: the **Temple of Luxor** and the nearby **Temple of Karnak.**

The pyramids were the tallest structures in the world until the Eiffel Tower was built in 1889.

Great Pyramid and Sphinx, Giza
Photo by Marc Mancini

The Step Pyramid, Sakkara
Photo by Justus Ghormley

Aswan

Farther upriver from Luxor, Aswan today is most recognized as home to one of the world's biggest structures: the **Aswan High Dam.** The temples on **Philae** [FIE-lee] **Island** provide the backdrop to a superb sound-and-light show. A number of excellent temples can be reached from Aswan; the best known is the towering **Temple of Abu Simbel,** where the figure of Ramses II is cut into a bluff. (The entire temple was cut into pieces—its original site was flooded when the Aswan Dam was built—and reassembled at its present location.)

Obelisks were first erected in Egypt. The world's tallest contemporary one is the Washington Monument, in Washington, D.C.

Nile Cruises

Cruises can be taken in either direction (or both), but it's most efficient to fly south and then cruise north with the current. For those with plenty of time, the week-long voyage from Aswan to Cairo is unforgettable. More common, however, is the shorter five-day trip between Aswan and Luxor. The ship will stop at such sites as **Esna** (with the **Temple of Khnum**) and **Edfu** (with the superbly preserved **Temple of Horus**). Passengers will also get a real feeling for everyday Egyptian life. Hotels operate most cruise ships; the cruise will include a cabin and most meals.

Even on the finest Nile cruise ships, stomach disorders are common.

Though these are the main destinations in Egypt, other areas draw tourists, including:

- **The Sinai Desert,** where many biblical sites are found, including **Mt. Horeb,** which some believe to be Mt. Sinai, where Moses received the tablets of the Ten Commandments. **St. Catherine's Monastery,** at the presumed site of the Burning Bush, is nearby.

- **Alexandria,** Egypt's second-largest city and its main cruise port. Though attractions are rather limited, there are some fine museums, a stunning new library, several palaces, and some ancient ruins. Divers have begun to find intriguing artifacts in Alexandria's harbour, some of which are now on display.

The original Library of Alexandria, established in 288 B.C., is said to have included all the knowledge of the ancient world.

- **Resorts,** most notably **Mersa Matruh** (on the Mediterranean, west of Alexandria), **Sharm El Sheikh** (at the southern tip of the Sinai Peninsula), and **Hurghada** [HOOR-gah-duh] (on the Red Sea), a fine snorkelling and diving site.

The Temple of Karnak
Copyright COREL

POSSIBLE ITINERARIES

Deciding on the length of stay in Egypt depends not only on the destinations to be visited but also on the mode of transportation. A good itinerary would be 10 days for first-time visitors. They would start in the area around Cairo and then fly to Aswan, where they'll take a ship downriver to Luxor, then return by air to Cairo. Experienced travellers may wish to take excursions to some of the lesser-known sites, visit the Sinai Desert, take a longer cruise, or even spend some time at one of Egypt's fine resorts.

LODGING OPTIONS

Budget accommodations in Egypt can provide guests with unwelcome surprises. Very good lodging, though, is reasonably priced. There's a wide selection of North American chains in Egypt, especially in Cairo. Perhaps the best hotel in Cairo is the **Marriott,** with a converted palace at its centre. Most Cairo bars and nightclubs are in the hotels. Few good hotels can be found outside Cairo, Alexandria, and Luxor.

Most of Cairo's lodging clusters around the Egyptian Museum and along the Nile. Quite a few hotels line the road to the airport. For those planning to spend much time exploring the Great Pyramids and the Sphinx, you might recommend accommodations in Giza, where there are several hotels and resorts. (The most famous is the **Mena House Oberoi.**) For those taking a Nile cruise, the ship acts as the hotel; passengers stay onboard at night.

The mummy of Ramses I, the father of Ramses II and a major pharaoh in his own right, had long been missing. In 2003 it was found, unidentified, in an obscure Niagara Falls museum. It has since been "repatriated."

ALLIED DESTINATIONS

It's not uncommon for a visit to Egypt to be combined with a trip to its neighbour, Israel, and to nearby Jordan. Egypt is also just across the Red Sea from Saudi Arabia. Because of the great distance to Egypt from Canada, visitors often prefer to break up the flight by stopping over in Europe for a few days before continuing. The country can also be seen as part of a Mediterranean cruise.

CULTURAL PATTERNS

Egypt's culture is different from what visitors are likely to be used to. This is most relevant to business travellers.

- The use of titles (for example, Doctor, Professor) is important when addressing people in Egypt. And dress is fairly formal and conservative.

- Parties, dinners, and other gatherings often don't start until 10 p.m. When staging a social gathering, have nonalcoholic beverages available for Muslim attendees.

- Building trust is important to Egyptians. As a result, visitors should be prepared to engage in extended conversation and coffee before starting a meeting. Even shopkeepers will offer customers a free coffee or cola.

- It's quite acceptable to ask an Egyptian about his or her opinion. However, to ask about personal matters is rarely done, except among close friends.

- If visitors are invited to someone's home, it's polite to bring a gift, and good manners to leave some food on their plates. (It's a sign of abundance.)

- When exchanging an item (such as food or a gift) with another person, never use the left hand alone; it's considered ill mannered.

- Many businesses close on Friday, the Muslim day of rest. Workweeks begin on Saturday and run through Thursday. Some places close completely (or early) on Sunday.

Many people expect small tips, called *baksheesh*, for favours that they've done; this includes letting their photographs be taken. Even museum guards may ask.

FACTORS THAT MOTIVATE VISITORS

Certain predictable reasons prompt people to visit Egypt:

- It has a unique and rich cultural history.

- Costs within the country are relatively low, and shopping is a bargain.

- The locals are friendly.

- It appeals to those who like cruises. Nile cruises are attractive to people who usually reject water travel because of seasickness; the Nile is quite calm.

- The weather is warm and pleasant during the winter.

POSSIBLE MISGIVINGS

A trip to Egypt is a unique experience. But it does generate concerns—some genuine, some unfounded:

- "Hasn't there been crime and terrorism directed against tourists?" Serious but sporadic incidents by terrorists have occurred and have dramatically impacted tourism, but overall, Egypt is an astonishingly crime-free country.

- "The hostilities in the Middle East worry me." Wars in the Middle East are not affecting Egypt.

- "I've been told that the water is very bad." Drink bottled liquids instead, and be careful with fresh fruits and vegetables.

- "There's widespread disease there." Check with a physician before making the trip and get any necessary shots.

- "It's blisteringly hot." Avoid Egypt during the summer; visit in the winter or late fall, when the weather is usually lovely.

○ Many of ancient Egypt's statues and carvings were hacked away by early Christians and, later, Muslims.

- "The country is dirty and crowded." Book a first-class or deluxe hotel, or take an upscale package tour. Cairo's traffic, smog, and crowds are real, though; those with this concern should perhaps stay only briefly in Cairo and move on to other Egyptian areas.

- "Aren't there aggressive salespeople and beggars everywhere?" Much of this is a sort of game that locals play to make a meagre living. Everyday Egyptians are among the most friendly, hospitable, and helpful people in the world.

Qualifying the Traveller
EGYPT

FOR PEOPLE WHO WANT	HIGH APPEAL	MEDIUM APPEAL	LOW APPEAL	REMARKS
Historical and Cultural Attractions	▲			Legendary sights
Beaches and Water Sports		▲		Seacoast resorts; Red Sea diving
Skiing Opportunities			▲	None
Lots of Nightlife		▲		In Cairo, especially in hotels
Family Activities		▲		Primarily sightseeing
Familiar Cultural Experience			▲	
Exotic Cultural Experience	▲			
Safety and Low Crime			▲	Safer than most tourists think
Bargain Travel		▲		After airfare, can be inexpensive
Impressive Scenery		▲		The Nile and desert
Peace and Quiet			▲	Cairo very noisy; rest of country is quieter
Shopping Opportunities		▲		Pottery, handicrafts, false antiquities, cotton items
Adventure	▲			
To Do Business			▲	Must understand the culture

SALES STRATEGIES

What's the most obvious way to enhance a trip to Egypt? By booking a memory-of-a-lifetime Nile cruise. An escorted tour is a good choice for those who feel a certain hesitancy about their visit. Because the flight to Egypt from Canada is so long, stopovers in Europe will break up the voyage. A trip to Egypt combines well with a visit to Israel or Kenya. Further, because many budget hotels can be unpleasant, better hotels are advisable. Cruises are a grand way to maximize profits from a traveller's trip.

TRAVEL TRIVIA

THE SEVEN WONDERS OF THE ANCIENT WORLD

- The Pyramids (Giza, Egypt)
- The Hanging Gardens of Babylon (near Baghdad, Iraq)
- The Statue of Zeus at Olympia (Greece)
- The Temple of Diana at Ephesus (Turkey)
- The Mausoleum (Helicarnassus, Turkey)
- The Colossus (Rhodes)
- The Pharos Lighthouse (Alexandria, Egypt)

MAP ACTIVITY

NAME _____   DATE _____

A traveller wants to visit the places listed below. Which number represents each on the map?

PLACE/ATTRACTION		IN/NEAR WHICH CITY?	NUMBER ON MAP
A.	The Temple of Karnak	A.	A.
B.	Cheops Pyramid	B.	B.
C.	Mosque of El Azhar	C.	C.
D.	Abu Simbel is usually visited from here	D.	D.
E.	A Red Sea resort	E.	E.
F.	The Valley of the Kings	F.	F.
G.	The Citadel of Saladin	G.	G.
H.	The Egyptian Museum	H.	H.
I.	The Sphinx	I.	I.
J.	The Aswan High Dam	J.	J.

CASE STUDY

NAME _____   DATE _____

Elizabeth and John Apicella enjoy the region around the Mediterranean. They've been to Italy and Israel and have cruised the Greek Isles, but they've yet to visit Egypt. This year, at last, they plan to go for 11 days.

Circle the answer that best suits their needs.

1. The Apicellas enjoy cruises. Which of the following do you suggest they take as a trip?

   Aswan to Luxor   Cairo to Aswan

   The Dead Sea   The Eastern Mediterranean

   Why?

2. While staying in Cairo, they want to see pyramids. To what town would you direct them?

   Uxmal   Giza

   Rhodes   Gaza

   Why?

3. Which of the following tips would *not* be a good idea to pass along to the Apicellas?

   Many businesses are closed on Fridays.   Pass gifts with the left hand only.

   Remove shoes before entering mosques.   Carry a lot of spare change.

   Why?

4. Which month would you suggest they go?

   May   June

   November   August

   Why?

CREATIVE ACTIVITY

NAME _____   DATE _____

Using only the Internet, see if you can find the answers to the following. Give the answer and the URL of the site where you found it.

1. Name three companies that operate cruises on the Nile.

2. Is it possible to take trips into western Egypt's Sahara? How would you do it?

3. Who was the architect of the Sakkara Pyramid and what else was he known—and venerated—for?

4. Your client lives in Yellowknife, NWT, and wants to fly to Cairo. Give three air itineraries you could offer, including the airlines you would use and the cities in which you would connect.

5. Do travellers need a visa to visit Egypt?

CHAPTER 25

Israel, Palestine, and Jordan

The Holy Lands

If Greece is the cultural heart of Western civilization, then the Holy Lands (Israel, Palestine, and Jordan), it can be argued, are its soul. Not only is this remarkable region the homeland of the Jewish religion, it holds a preeminent place among Christians—this is where Jesus lived. Moreover, **Jerusalem** is one of the holiest spots to those of the Islamic faith; for it's from here, Muslims believe, that Mohammed ascended to heaven. Perhaps what makes the region so emotionally unique is that it's where spiritual belief anchors itself to solid reality: The cities and sites where biblical events occurred and people lived are *right here.* They look almost exactly like you would imagine them.

This is a place of great contrasts and diversity, not only of religion and cultural history but also of topography; isolated and desertlike, it has been transformed into a flowering landscape. The fragile beauty and majesty of this region, praised in the Bible's poetic prose, continue to enchant visitors today.

Israel isn't as big as you might think; it's about the size of New Jersey. Bordered by the Mediterranean Sea on its west and surrounded by Egypt, Jordan, Syria, and Lebanon, the southern two-thirds of the country consists primarily of the **Negev Desert.** The capital, Jerusalem, is located in the north-central portion of Israel. Indeed, virtually all the major cities and tourist destinations are found in the north. **Bethlehem** is just southwest of Jerusalem, in Palestine. And a bit farther south is the historic site of **Masada,** near the major resort area of the **Dead Sea** (on the border with Jordan). **Tel Aviv,** Israel's second-largest city and a modern centre of commerce and culture, is on the central coast; many government offices and foreign embassies are here.

To the north, on the coast, is **Haifa,** Israel's primary seaport. Southeast and east of Haifa are the biblical sites of **Nazareth** and the **Sea of Galilee (Lake Tiberias).** The major city in the south of Israel is the port of **Eilat** (today a bustling resort destination) by the Gulf of Aqaba [ACK-ah-bah] and the Red Sea. The **Jordan River** marks much of Israel and Palestine's eastern boundary with Jordan.

The 1993 peace accords between Israel and the Palestinians gave self-governing status to parts of several regions taken over by Israel in previous wars. (See dotted areas on map.) The final form the governing will take, what areas it will extend to, and how it will impact tourism (as well as everyday life) still remains in dispute within the three "occupied" territories: the **Gaza Strip, West Bank,** and **Golan Heights.**

Jordan is nearly one and a half times the size of Nova Scotia. In addition to Israel and Palestine, it borders Syria, Iraq, and Saudi Arabia. Most of its cities

Much of Israel's early biblical history isn't all that precise. The traditional religious sites may or may not be exactly accurate; after so many centuries, no one really knows.

All Jews throughout the world have the automatic right to be Israeli citizens.

Many businesses close on the Sabbath (from sundown Friday to sundown Saturday).

ISRAEL, PALESTINE, AND JORDAN

Capitals: IS: Jerusalem
JOR: Amman

Populations: IS: 6 300 000
PAL: 3 800 000
JOR: 5 800 000

Areas (square km): IS: 21 501
PAL: 6220
JOR: 92 306

Religions: Judaism, Islam, Christianity

Languages: Hebrew, Arabic

Currencies: IS: 1 shekel = 100 agorot
JOR: 1 dinar = 1000 fils

Electricity: 220 volts, 50 cycles AC

Time Zone: GMT +2

Drive on: Right

Capsule History: Hebrew kingdom, 1000 B.C.; Rome takes control and rules 400 years, 63 B.C.; numerous invasions until A.D. 634–640, when Muslims take control; Crusaders arrive, 1099; Turks control, 1516–1917; Britain governs region as "Palestine," 1923–1948; Jordan becomes independent, 1946; Jewish state founded, 1948; wars between Israel and Egypt, 1956–1973; war between Israel and Lebanon, 1982–1983; Israeli–Palestinian Interim Agreement, 1993; major hostilities between Israelis and Palestinians, 2001–.

For reference sources and suggested lengths of stay, see Appendixes A and B.

(including the capital, **Amman**) and attractions are in the country's western regions, not far from its borders with Israel and Palestine.

In Israel, Hebrew is the national language, but Arabic is also an official language. Arabic is the national language of Jordan and Palestine, though Hebrew is spoken by many Palestinians. English is widely spoken in all three nations.

HOW TRAVELLERS GET THERE

The main air gateway into Israel and Palestine is Tel Aviv's **Ben Gurion International Airport** (TLV), which also serves Jerusalem. **El Al Israel Airlines** (LY), Israel's national airline, is considered one of the safest in the world; the security checks it employs are so extensive that a very early arrival for a flight is essential. Jordan's air gateway, **Queen Alia International Airport** (AMM) in Amman, is served by **Royal Jordanian Air** (RJ). Several North American carriers and many European ones service Israel and Jordan.

Flying times, often involving connections in Europe, are around 10.5 hours from Toronto and 18 hours from Vancouver. Many cruise ships on Eastern Mediterranean itineraries call on the ports of Haifa (gateway to Nazareth and the Galilee area) and **Ashdod** (gateway to Jerusalem). Many people visit Jordan by land from Israel and Palestine, or via the Red Sea port of **Aqaba.**

WEATHER PATTERNS

Sharav winds can bring very hot, dry weather in the late spring or early fall.

The region has two distinct climates. Western Jordan and Israel's Negev Desert, in the south, are hot—it's likely that only those heading for Eilat or Aqaba will want to spend time visiting here. In the north, the weather is pleasant year-round—though spring and fall are the best seasons to visit. (See Figure 25-1.) Summer can be hot and dry, with highs averaging around 30°C (dropping by up to 10°C at night). Summer rain is a rarity. Winter (which is somewhat a tourist off-season) gets cool and rainy. Average highs reach only the low teens (again, there's a big drop at night to as low as 5°C). Winter rainstorms are heavy but infrequent.

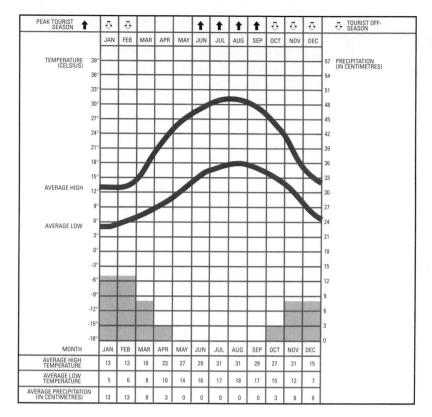

| PEAK TOURIST SEASON ↑ | ⇩ | ⇩ | | | | ↑ | ↑ | ↑ | ↑ | ⇩ | ⇩ | ⇩ | | ⇩ TOURIST OFF-SEASON |

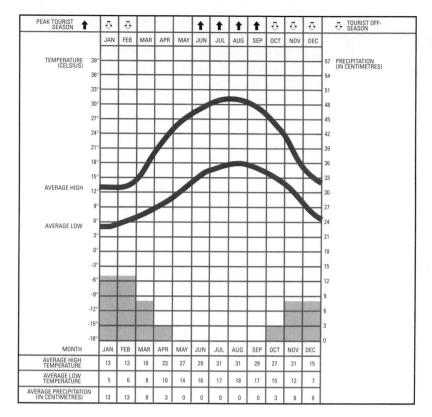

MONTH	JAN	FEB	MAR	APR	MAY	JUN	JUL	AUG	SEP	OCT	NOV	DEC
AVERAGE HIGH TEMPERATURE	13	13	18	23	27	29	31	31	29	27	21	15
AVERAGE LOW TEMPERATURE	5	6	8	10	14	16	17	18	17	15	12	7
AVERAGE PRECIPITATION (IN CENTIMETRES)	13	13	8	3	0	0	0	0	0	3	8	8

Figure 25-1   Climate at a Glance: Jerusalem, Israel

Some areas, like Jerusalem and Bethlehem, can even get snow. So all those Christmas cards that show biblical landmarks dusted with snow are more accurate than you might have thought!

GETTING AROUND

The bus system is quite good and fairly inexpensive in Israel and much of Palestine, both within cities and between them. Air service connects the major cities, but this is such a compact region that it's not really necessary for visitors to fly. The train network is limited. Roads are well maintained and car rentals are extensively available. To get around within cities, taxis are another good means of transportation. An alternative mode of transport between cities in Israel is a *sherut* taxi, which is larger than the regular cabs and takes more passengers. Tours, both in cities and over the whole region, are popular for North Americans.

Visitors can rent cars in Jordan, where rental prices are government controlled. Taxis are available in the major cities and can be hired for the day. Service cabs operate within cities and also connect major cities and towns; their fares are set by the government, and they tend to be less expensive than regular taxis. Buses (both government and private) and limousines operate within and between major cities and tourist sites.

IMPORTANT PLACES

Following is a list of the destinations that are most popular in the Holy Lands.

Jerusalem

This is perhaps the world's holiest city, home to some of the most sacred sites of the Jewish, Christian, and Islamic faiths. Jerusalem is located in the Judean hills.

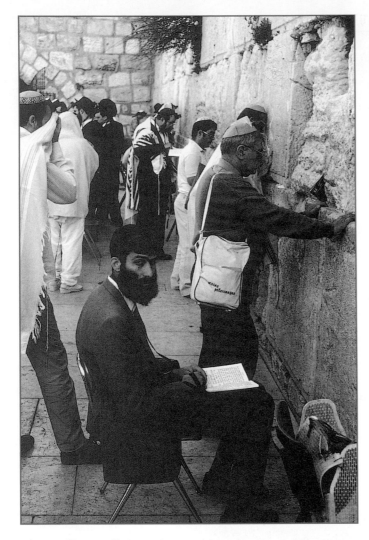

The Wailing Wall, Jerusalem
Photo by Justus Ghormley

◎ The same family (the Nusseiba family) has been in charge of opening and closing the Church of the Holy Sepulchre since A.D. 636.

Its attractions are sprinkled throughout the city; they can be categorized into two groups: those within the **Old City** and those outside. The Old City is a walled area, reached via several ancient gates (the most notable is the **Damascus Gate**); it's divided into Jewish, Christian, Muslim, and Armenian quarters, and is filled with historical and religious structures, ancient, narrow streets, and bustling markets. Among the many locations to visit in the Old City are:

- **The Wailing Wall** (or **Western Wall**), one of the most sacred sites in the world to Jews. It's all that remains of King Solomon's legendary Second Temple.

- **The Church of the Holy Sepulchre**, one of the most deeply sacred sites to Christians. The general location of Christ's crucifixion, burial, and resurrection is believed to be here.

- **The Dome of the Rock,** sacred to Muslims, the third of Jerusalem's most holy places. It's from here that Mohammed is believed to have risen to heaven. This site is also holy to Jews, as the Dome was built on the Temple Mount.

- **Via Dolorosa,** the supposed path Jesus took on his way to the crucifixion.

Outside the Old City, the popular sites of Jerusalem include:

- **Mt. Moriah,** the location where Abraham prepared to sacrifice his son, Isaac, according to God's wishes.

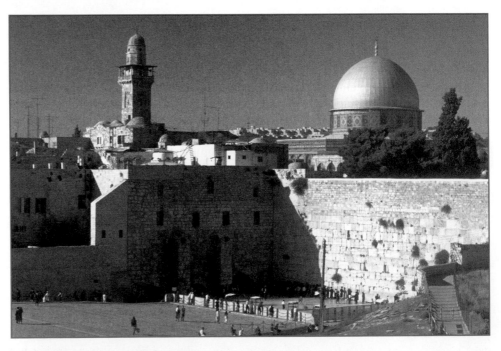

The Dome of the Rock, Jerusalem
Copyright COREL

- **The Dead Sea Scrolls,** held in the Shrine of the Book in the **Israel Museum.** These 2000-year-old scrolls, found in a cave by a shepherd seeking his lost goat (in 1947), have shed light on early Jewish texts and practices. The museum also contains works by Picasso, van Gogh, and Rodin. An instructive and inspirational museum is the **Museum of the Holocaust.**

- **The Mount of Olives,** with the **Garden of Gethsemane** and what is believed to be the tomb of Mary, Jesus' mother.

- **The Garden Tomb,** considered by many to be Jesus' actual place of burial, not the Church of the Holy Sepulchre.

- **Mt. Zion,** the tomb of King David, as well as where the room of the Last Supper is thought to be. A new addition is the **Chamber of the Holocaust.**

Among the superb **day trips** from Jerusalem are:

- **Bethlehem,** by tradition the birthplace of Jesus and also where King David was born. The **Basilica of the Nativity** at Manger Square supposedly sits on the place Jesus was born. Bethlehem is within the Palestinian West Bank.

The door to the Basilica of the Nativity was made very small so people couldn't ride their horses into the church.

- **Jericho** (also in the West Bank), considered the oldest city in the world, where Joshua fought the well-known battle. Northeast of Jerusalem on the Jordan River, it's now a favourite winter resort. Sites include Herod's Winter Palace and the Mount of Temptation. Nearby is Qumran, where the Dead Sea Scrolls were found.

- **Masada,** one of the world's great archaeological sites. This promontory is where nearly 1000 Jewish Zealots are purported to have barricaded them-selves against the Romans in A.D. 73, ultimately choosing mass suicide to enslavement. **King Herod's Palace** is at Masada.

Tel Aviv

This cosmopolitan city is the major centre of commerce and culture in Israel. Located on the Mediterranean coast, the area was nothing but sand dunes in 1900. Now there's a lively nightlife, many sidewalk cafés, and excellent shopping. Among its most interesting sites are:

Tel Aviv was the first capital of the modern nation of Israel.

- **Very good museums,** most notably the **Tel Aviv Museum** and the **Museum of the Diaspora** (for a compelling history of the Jewish people).

- **Independence Hall,** where David Ben Gurion declared Israeli independence in 1948.

- **Dizengoff Square,** with sophisticated shopping and cafés. Another inter-esting visit would be to the ancient adjacent town of **Jaffa,** which dates from the time of King Solomon. This old port, with its cobblestone streets, is now an artists' colony.

Haifa

Haifa is Israel's major cruise port. It has some interesting temples, particularly the **Bahai Shrine,** the centre of the Bahai faith. Biblical **Mt. Carmel** offers panoramic views; at the base of the mountain is **Elijah's Cave.**

Nazareth and the Sea of Galilee

These unique destinations in Northern Israel can easily be reached as a day trip from Haifa. **Nazareth** is the city where Jesus grew up, and is sacred to Christians. The **Basilica of the Annunciation** is, according to legend, on the spot where an angel told Mary that she was to be the mother of Christ. Other important sites are **Cana** (the site of one of Jesus' first miracles), **Capernaum** (with the ruins of a synagogue where Jesus may have taught), the legendary Sea of Galilee, and the Jordan River (where Jesus was baptized).

Visitors to **Tiberias** often try the town's famous St. Peter's Fish. Other popular destinations in northern Israel are the **Crusader's Underground City** at **Acre,** and **Safed,** once a vital centre for Jewish scholars, now an artists' colony with many fine synagogues.

Resorts

There are many popular resorts in the Holy Lands.

○ There are no fish in the Dead Sea.

- **The Dead Sea,** shared by Israel, Palestine, and Jordan, is a popular resort area. It's considered the world's largest natural spa. This is the lowest point on earth, and its waters are far saltier than those of the Great Salt Lake.

- **Netanya and Herzliya,** located in Israel between Tel Aviv and Haifa on the Mediterranean coast, are among the trendiest and most deluxe resorts.

- **Eilat (Israel) and Aqaba (Jordan),** at the northern tip of the Red Sea, offer excellent diving, snorkelling, sandy beaches, and especially beautiful coral reefs. Surrounded by mountains, Aqaba is also popular with mountain climbers.

○ Petra was used as the Holy Grail's resting place in the movie *Indiana Jones and the Last Crusade.*

Jordan

Jordan is often visited in conjunction with a trip to Israel and Palestine. Among the highlights not yet mentioned are:

- **Amman,** Jordan's hilly capital, with a notable archaeological museum and an old **Roman amphitheatre** still in use. Nearby are the ruins of the **Temple of Hercules** and many structures built by the Crusaders.

- **Biblical sites,** such as **Bethany** (where John the Baptist lived) and **Mt. Nebo** (where Moses is purportedly buried).

- **Splendid archaeological sites,** including astonishing **Petra,** a superb attraction with buildings carved out of a stone mountainside over 2000 years ago and accessed (via horse or on foot) through a long, dramatically narrow pass. Most impressive, too, are the ruins of an old Crusader fortress and castle at **Karak.** Greco-Roman ruins exist at **Jerash,** which presents a nightly sound-and-light show between April and October. The **King's Highway,** a 5000-year-old route mentioned in the Book of Genesis, connects many of the sites.

- **Wadi Rum,** with a "Valley of the Moon" landscape. The fort there is associated with Lawrence of Arabia.

The Treasury, Petra
Copyright COREL

POSSIBLE ITINERARIES

Seven days in the Holy Lands should be considered a minimum visit. After landing in Tel Aviv and spending a day or two there, visitors can head to Jerusalem for three or four days and explore the environs—including

Bethlehem. They then can head up to Nazareth and the Sea of Galilee, over to Haifa, and down the coast back to Tel Aviv for a couple of days. Return visitors or those wishing to experience more of the area outside Jerusalem can head into the Negev (and down to Eilat and Aqaba), explore Amman and Petra, and/or add some resort stops at the Mediterranean or Dead seas. It would be easy for a vacationer to fill up two weeks here.

LODGING OPTIONS

In Jerusalem, the largest clusters of hotels are around the Convention Centre and Independence Park, west and north of the Old City. One of the most famous hotels in town is the **King David,** offering great charm and elegance. Tel Aviv hotels are packed along the coast, south of the Atzma'ut Botanic Gardens. For alternative lodging, you might suggest an all-inclusive resort or a health spa. Many kibbutzes (collective farms) also offer accommodations for visitors. The Israeli Tourist Bureau can facilitate such a stay. Jordan has recently built many new hotels in Amman, near Petra, and along the Dead Sea coast.

It's against the law in certain hotels and restaurants to smoke during the Sabbath, from sundown Friday until nighttime Saturday.

ALLIED DESTINATIONS

The Holy Lands are an ideal gateway to the entire Middle East, bordering Egypt, Saudi Arabia, Syria, and Lebanon. European destinations are logical extensions of a trip to or from the region. Indeed, many Canadians who visit here stop off somewhere in Europe or North Africa.

CULTURAL PATTERNS

It's important that visitors to the Holy Lands, especially those travelling on business, understand the customs.

There are 1072 synagogues, 65 churches, and 59 mosques in Jerusalem.

- The Hebrew word *shalom* has at least three meanings: hello, goodbye, and peace.

- Israeli society is quite informal. Some examples: Ties are worn only for important occasions; titles are rarely used; schedules aren't strictly adhered to. A visitor should feel comfortable using an Israeli's first name soon after meeting him or her.

- Despite Israel's informality, Israelis expect precision in conversation, expect appointments to be met, and take few things for granted.

- Visitors should bring a small gift when visiting a Jordanian's home.

- When an Israeli invites a guest to his or her home, this is not an offer made lightly or out of a sense of politeness. It's an important gesture. It's not necessary to bring a gift, but a book is appropriate.

- Business dress is more formal in Jordan than in Israel. Men should wear a suit and tie for meetings. Though non-Muslim women aren't expected to cover their arms, legs, and hair as Muslim women do, they shouldn't wear very revealing clothing in public.

- The strife between Palestinians and Israelis is an explosive issue. Be very careful if you must discuss this topic.

- Jordanians are proud of their Arab heritage and are extremely hospitable to visitors.

FACTORS THAT MOTIVATE VISITORS

Among the reasons people are inspired to visit the Holy Lands are:

- The region is important to many different religious faiths. It boasts places many people have heard of from the time they were infants.

- The history, archaeology, and culture are fascinating.

- There are resorts and thermal spas.

- The climate in most places is extremely good.

- There's great opportunity for outdoor activities, including diving, desert trekking, and mountain climbing.

POSSIBLE MISGIVINGS

Though the Holy Lands provide some powerfully emotional reasons for people to visit, there are also some strong objections that can get in the way. A few of these objections and their counters are:

- "This is one of the most dangerous areas in the world." There's no denying the long history of war in the Middle East, primarily between Israel and the Palestinians. Relations between Palestinians and Israelis are sometimes good, and at other times quite tense. Keep up on news events in order to make appropriate judgments.

- "I'm concerned about airport and airline bombings." Because of the threat of terrorism, security at Ben Gurion Airport is probably the best in the world, as is the antiterrorist safety record of El Al Airlines. You could also suggest an Eastern Mediterranean cruise to someone with this worry.

- "The Middle East is unsanitary." Health conditions in the Holy Lands are very good, and it's safe to drink the water.

- "The flight here is too long." It is far, but it's quite near Europe. Travellers can break up the lengthy flight between Canada and the region with stopovers on the Continent.

FOR PEOPLE WHO WANT	HIGH APPEAL	MEDIUM APPEAL	LOW APPEAL	REMARKS
Historical and Cultural Attractions	▲			Sites appealing to Jews, Muslims, and Christians
Beaches and Water Sports		▲		Along Mediterranean
Skiing Opportunities			▲	Limited skiing in north
Lots of Nightlife			▲	Some in Tel Aviv and Jerusalem
Family Activities		▲		Primarily sightseeing
Familiar Cultural Experience			▲	
Exotic Cultural Experience	▲			
Safety and Low Crime			▲	Long history of strife; petty crime rare
Bargain Travel		▲		
Impressive Scenery		▲		
Peace and Quiet			▲	Jerusalem and Tel Aviv bustling
Shopping Opportunities		▲		Handicrafts, religious souvenirs
Adventure	▲			
To Do Business		▲		

SALES STRATEGIES

Located on the Mediterranean, Israel lends itself to cruises. Even though it's fairly easy to drive in this region, some may feel safer on an escorted tour.

Because the Holy Lands are so close to Europe, you might suggest a stopover there. There are some interesting camel ranches, of all things, in the southeastern region of Israel, which some might enjoy staying at for a few days. Several organizations set up short archaeological digs, and some tourists might jump at the chance to participate. Others might enjoy a nice rest at an all-inclusive resort, a dive package at Eilat or Aqaba, or a stay on an Israeli kibbutz. Pilgrimages, often arranged by and for church congregations, are very popular.

TRAVEL TRIVIA

TOP TEN FOREIGN MONUMENTS

1. Masada, Israel
2. Ephesus, Turkey
3. Petra, Jordan
4. El Escorial, Spain
5. Pompeii, Italy

6. Valley of the Kings, Egypt
7. Palace at Versailles, France
8. Westminster Abbey, England
9. Alhambra, Spain
10. Machu Picchu, Peru

Source: Condé Nast Traveller *readers' poll*

MAP ACTIVITY

NAME _____   DATE _____

A traveller wants to visit the places listed below. Which number represents each on the map?

PLACE/ATTRACTION	IN/NEAR WHICH CITY?	NUMBER ON MAP
A. The Dome of the Rock	**A.**	**A.**
B. Buildings carved in a mountainside	**B.**	**B.**
C. The Basilica of the Annunciation	**C.**	**C.**
D. The Wailing Wall	**D.**	**D.**
E. The Bahai Shrine	**E.**	**E.**
F. Associated with Lawrence of Arabia	**F.**	**F.**
G. The Museum of the Diaspora	**G.**	**G.**
H. Jaffa	**H.**	**H.**
I. The Church of the Holy Sepulchre	**I.**	**I.**

CASE STUDY

NAME _____   DATE _____

Deborah and Jerry Levin have wanted to visit Israel for years. This spring, they've saved up and are finally going for seven days. The couple, in their early 50s, has never travelled much, mostly through Canada. They've been to Mexico and the United States a few times and went to Europe about five years ago. They've been reading all manner of history books and watching videos to get ready.

Circle the answer that best suits their needs.

1. Which of the following services would be most appropriate for the Levins?

   A Mediterranean cruise   A moderately priced hotel

   A two-day stopover in Europe   A stay at a seaside resort

   Why?

2. Which of the following places would *not* be a good idea to recommend to the Levins for a day trip from Jerusalem?

   Bethlehem   Jericho

   Luxor   Masada

   Why?

3. Which of the following tips would be the best one for you to tell to the Levins?

   Go in August.   Drink bottled beverages.

   Do your shopping on Saturday.   Dress is very informal.

   Why?

4. In addition to experiencing the history of Israel, the Levins would like to enjoy some of the modern-day culture. Where should you direct them?

   Tel Aviv   Eilat

   Haifa   Babylon

   Why?

CREATIVE ACTIVITY

NAME _____ DATE _____

You're a Canadian filmmaker who's been hired by the Holy Lands Tourist Board to shoot a 15-second commercial for broadcast on Canadian television. You must start by creating a "shot" list of images that will go along with the music and narration that the Board has already decided upon.

Complete the list of shots below. (A few are already filled in.) Your images may be of people, places, or things.

SOUNDTRACK	IMAGES
Slow, romantic, full orchestrated music, with slight Middle Eastern allusions	1.
	2. Olive-treed garden
	3.
	4.
	5.
Music changes to peppy, intense, active beat	6.
	7. Cruise ship sailing into Haifa
	8.
Narration: "The Holy Lands: So much to see, so much to do, so much to relive."	9.
	10.
	11. Smiling children
	12.

SUDAN

ETHIOPIA

Lake Turkana

Rift Valley

KENYA

UGANDA

SOMALIA

▲ Samburu National Reserve

Lake Nakuru National Park ▲

▲ Mt. Kenya

EQUATOR

▲ Aberdare National Park

Lake Victoria

▲ Masai Mara National Reserve

✪ Nairobi

RWANDA

▲ Serengeti National Park

▲ Amboseli National Park

▲ Tsavo National Park

● Malindi

BURUNDI

Olduval Gorge ▲

Arusha ●

Ngorongoro Crater ▲

▲

● Mombasa
Shimoni

Lake Manyara National Park

Mt. Kilimanjaro ▲

Zanzibar

Dodoma ✪

TANZANIA

Dar es Salaam

DEM. REP. OF CONGO

Mafia Island

INDIAN OCEAN

ZAMBIA

Selous ▲ Wildlife Reserve

MALAWI

MOZAMBIQUE

Kenya and Tanzania

The Lion Sleeps Tonight

A herd of antelopes race and leap across the high grass of a seemingly unending savannah, as giraffes, zebras, and elephants rest at nearby watering holes. That one image defines both Kenya and Tanzania [tan-zah-NEE-ah]. These countries not only protect and preserve their wildlife but also have made a mission of it. Their wildlife reserves and national parks attract considerable trade. That income has fuelled their drive to become among the greatest natural refuges for animals in the world. The lions do indeed sleep here: in safety, in aloof majesty, and, unlike the title of the famous song, during the day as often as at night.

Kenya is located on the east coast of central Africa. Ethiopia lies to the north, Somalia and the Indian Ocean to the east. Uganda lies against Kenya's western border and Tanzania fronts the southern border.

About the size of Saskatchewan, Kenya is bisected by the equator. Also splitting the country, but from north to south, is the western region's **Rift Valley,** which continues south into Tanzania. **Nairobi,** the capital, is in south-central Kenya; most of the country's wildlife reserves can be reached in a few hours from here by road or by air. **Mombasa,** in the very southeast, along the coast, is Kenya's main seaport. Kenya also has nearly 640 kilometres of beaches along the warm waters of the Indian Ocean.

Tanzania is quite large: about the size of British Columbia. To Tanzania's north are Kenya and Uganda, and to the south are Zambia, Malawi, and Mozambique; across Lake Tanganyika to the west is the Democratic Republic of the Congo. Also to Tanzania's west are the small countries of Rwanda and Burundi. Like Kenya, Tanzania is bordered on the east by the Indian Ocean, and has even more beaches. **Dodoma,** in the centre of the country, is the capital. **Dar es Salaam,** the former capital, is the major seaport and air gateway.

There's a wide mix of cultures and tribes in Kenya and Tanzania. Kenya's national language is Swahili, though English is widely spoken. Swahili and English are the official languages of Tanzania.

 Don't even consider sneaking home ivory or wildlife items (such as skins). It's illegal and it encourages poaching.

Kenya has two marine parks in the Indian Ocean.

Though Swahili is Kenya's *national* language, English is the *official* language.

HOW TRAVELLERS GET THERE

The main gateway into Kenya is Nairobi, at **Jomo Kenyatta International Airport** (NBO). Flights also land in Mombasa (MBA). Travellers will most likely connect through Europe; since the flight to Kenya is so long, you might suggest a stopover. The national airline, **Kenya Airways** (KQ), and many international carriers fly

KENYA AND TANZANIA

Capitals: Kenya: Nairobi
TAN: Dodoma

Areas (square km): Kenya: 582 700
TAN: 945 087

Time Zone: GMT +3

Drive on: Left

Populations: Kenya: 33 800 000
TAN: 36 800 000

Religions: Traditional, Christianity, Islam

Languages: Swahili, English

Currencies: Kenya: 1 Kenyan shilling = 100 cents
TAN: 1 Tanzanian shilling = 100 cents

Electricity: 40 volts, 50 cycles AC

Capsule History: **Kenya and Tanzania:** First occupied by bushmen; herdsmen arrive from the north, Bantu tribespeople from the west, early A.D.; Arab traders settle coastal area, pre–Middle Ages; Portuguese explore, late 1400s.

Kenya: British occupy, late 1800s; British protectorate, 1895; British Crown colony, 1920–1963; Mau Mau revolt, 1952–1955; independence, 1963.

Tanzania: Portuguese and Arabs create Sultanate of Zanzibar, through mid-1800s; Tanganyika becomes German protectorate, 1886; becomes British protectorate, 1920; gains independence, 1961; merges with Zanzibar to become Tanzania, 1964.

For reference sources and suggested lengths of stay, see Appendixes A and B.

here, most notably European ones. Mombasa is a common cruise departure or return point for ships visiting the islands of Madagascar, Mauritius, and the Seychelles. Several European carriers land in Tanzania at **Kilimanjaro Airport** (JRO) or **Dar es Salaam International Airport** (DAR). **Air Tanzania** (TC) services travellers within the country. Tanzania is also often accessed by land via Nairobi (and vice-versa).

WEATHER PATTERNS

The equator bisects Kenya; however, because of its generally high altitudes, the climate in much of the nation is cooler than you'd expect in an equatorial country (see Figure 26-1). The desert-like northerly regions of Kenya tend to be drier and hotter than the southern highlands; temperatures are fairly constant year-round.

Nairobi, in the south, ranges from an average high in the low to mid-20s, to an average low around 12°C; the north runs about 5° warmer. The only truly tropical climate is along the coast, where Mombasa is located. The main tourist season is November through February, but July through September is also popular.

Kenya's rain pattern is quite unusual. There are two rainy seasons: March through May (Kenyans call it "the long rains") and October through early December (called "the short rains"). Tanzania's daytime temperature is fairly steady year-round, with days in the upper 20s, nights in the low 20s. Winter is the driest season; fall is the wettest. The mountain areas can get quite cold.

GETTING AROUND

Safaris are no longer taken to kill animals, but to photograph them.

Since most people visit Kenya or Tanzania to see the wildlife, the most common way for them to travel is by minibus, four-wheel-drive vehicle, or small

Figure 26-1 Climate at a Glance: Nairobi, Kenya

MONTH	JAN	FEB	MAR	APR	MAY	JUN	JUL	AUG	SEP	OCT	NOV	DEC
AVERAGE HIGH TEMPERATURE	25	26	25	24	22	21	21	21	24	24	23	23
AVERAGE LOW TEMPERATURE	12	13	14	14	13	12	11	11	11	13	13	13
AVERAGE PRECIPITATION (IN CENTIMETRES)	5	8	13	20	15	5	3	3	3	5	10	8

plane—usually as part of an organized safari tour (often booked through tour operators and/or hotels). Driving in Kenya and Tanzania is on the left. The roads are often narrow, and unpredictable road conditions may make driving an unwise idea. There's a fairly good rail system here. Buses in many places, however, are crowded and uncomfortable. In Nairobi, the taxi system is good: Visitors have the choice of taking normal everyday cabs, or *matatus*, which pick up passengers and go to more than one destination. Finally, hot-air balloon trips over the sprawling grasslands have become increasingly popular, often as part of a safari.

People often ask what a safari is like. In brief, the group heads out into the bush to sleep in comfortable lodges and sets out early in the morning along bumpy, dusty roads to spot the animals when they're most active. The vehicles sometimes leave the road to get to where the animals are; the vehicle roof opens, which permits passengers to view the animals from safety, yet at close range.

IMPORTANT PLACES

Most tourists visit Kenya in order to experience its remarkable wildlife. In fact, it helped pioneer travel safaris. Kenya has lost some of its tourism to Tanzania and other African countries. Nonetheless, it continues to have one of the most extensive tourism infrastructures in Africa.

Africa's tallest mountain and part of its largest lake are located in Tanzania.

Kenya

Nairobi, lying relatively near the equator, is a city of contrasts: at once sophisticated and primitive. A great many beautiful parks are here, along with a lovely forest preserve and an excellent aviary. The **Kenya National Museum** has a top collection of African arts and crafts, as well as a superb explanation of Kenya's prehistory. **Nairobi National Park** provides a wide range of animals in their natural habitat and serves as a quick "sampler" of the safaris beyond.

The national parks and reserves are beautiful year-round, especially when wildebeests and zebras are migrating. The Kenya Tourist Bureau can tell you when herds of a particular species will probably begin migrating. About 40 wildlife reserves exist in Kenya. The most popular of them are the following:

- **Masai Mara National Reserve**—perhaps the best of all—is the northern extension of the Greater Serengeti Plains and borders Tanzania in the southwest. A particularly wide range of animals gathers here, most notably zebra and wildebeest (both of which have renowned migrations through the region). Nearby is **Lake Victoria,** the world's second-largest freshwater lake.

- **Aberdare National Park,** in the central highlands, is noted for its waterfalls, rain forests, and banyan trees. **Mt. Kenya,** the second-highest mountain in Africa, is nearby.

- **Amboseli National Park** is on the Tanzanian border, southeast of Nairobi. In the early morning of a clear day, visitors can look across its flat borderland and see Mt. Kilimanjaro. Elephants are found in especially large numbers in Amboseli.

Tribespeople (who had never seen snow) thought Mt. Kilimanjaro was topped with salt.

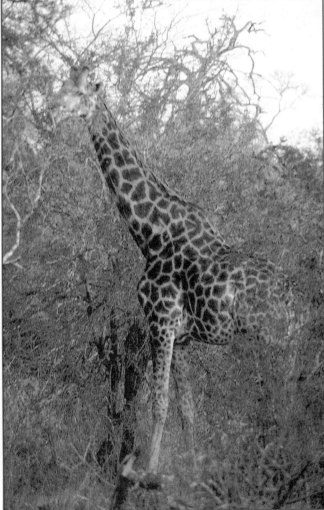

A giraffe feeding
Photo by Justus Ghormley

- **Tsavo** [TSAH-voh] **National Park** is in the southeast corner of Kenya, also on the Tanzanian border. It's Kenya's largest national park. Actually, Tsavo is closer to Mombasa than it is to Nairobi and may be more easily accessed from that coastal city.

- **The equator** is a popular destination. It's located a few hours north of Nairobi.

Among the other destinations that Kenya offers:

- **Samburu National Reserve** looks a little different from other wildlife reserves; it's hilly and has thick foliage. It also has particularly exotic animals, such as the blue-necked Somali ostrich, Grevy's zebra, and all manner of crocodile.

- **Lake Nakuru National Park** is a beautiful refuge for a variety of animals, especially birds. It's located in southwestern Kenya, in the Rift Valley, northwest of Nairobi. It's most noted for its grand flock of pink flamingos.

- **Mombasa** is Kenya's main cruise port. Largely a Muslim city, it has a great many mosques. Excellent crafts shopping and some fine beaches are nearby.

- **Coral reef beaches** are protected by the government. Easily accessible from Mombasa, there are some lovely towns near the reefs. **Malindi** and **Shimoni** are the most popular.

Tanzania

The large town of Arusha usually serves as the departure and return point for the multi-day safaris that visit Tanzania's many wildlife preserves.

The country's prime attractions lie mostly along the "Northern Crescent," which starts in Nairobi:

- **Serengeti National Park** is one of the world's most famous and finest wildlife preserves. Located in the north, this nearly 13 000-square-kilometre park is best known for its herds—especially wildebeests and zebras—which migrate during May and June, and again in September. Serengeti National Park is also famous for its black-maned lions. Relatively nearby is the renowned **Olduvai** [OLE-de-vay] **Gorge,** where Dr. Louis Leakey discovered some of the earliest known fossils of humans.

- **Other wildlife preserves** can be visited here, as well. Among the best: the huge **Selous Game Reserve,** noted for its elephants, and **Lake Manyara National Park,** a small reserve with spectacular pink flamingos.

- **Ngorongoro** [eng-gore-on-GOH-roh] **Crater,** 16 kilometres across, shelters large numbers of lions, zebras, elephants, and rhinos; visitors can view them in the crater from four-wheel-drive vehicles. Most lodges are on the crater's rim, affording a great view and chilly nights (because of the altitude). The animals here are used to tourists, so it's easy to get very close viewings.

- **Zanzibar,** a large and pretty island that once was an independent country, has fine, nearly empty beaches and interesting Arabic architecture, notably in **Stone Town.** (Wonderful beaches are also found at Dar es Salaam and **Mafia Island.**)

- **Lake Victoria** is in an extremely scenic area. But it's just for viewing, not for swimming (too many bacteria).

- **Mt. Kilimanjaro,** the highest mountain in Africa, is a stunning sight. Adventurous visitors can hike to its snow-capped top in about five days, either on their own or, preferably, as part of a hiking group. September, October, January, and February are ideal for such hikes, since clouds often obscure the mountain at other times. (The best view, though, is from Kenya.)

Lake Victoria has nothing to do with Victoria Falls, which is 1280 kilometres to the southwest on the Zambia–Zimbabwe border.

The snowcap and glaciers atop Mt. Kilimanjaro are receding. Global warming may be the cause.

Mt. Kilimanjaro in the background
Copyright COREL

POSSIBLE ITINERARIES

Tanzania's Selous Game Reserve is bigger than Switzerland.

Unlike most destinations, Kenya and Tanzania may be different each time a visitor arrives—depending on which herds are migrating and which animals can be seen. Because each area of the region specializes in different species, tourists can easily spend at least a week here. Travellers visiting Kenya could start in Nairobi, visit Masai Mara and Aberdare, then head up to Mt. Kenya and Samburu. Those who want to spend more time could add Amboseli and Tsavo, or Mombasa and the coral beach towns. Visitors to Tanzania use Arusha as a gateway to Serengeti National Park, Ngorongoro Crater, and Mt. Kilimanjaro. Extensions to this itinerary could include Selous Game Reserve, or the beaches of Zanzibar (which also boast historical sites) and Mafia Island.

LODGING OPTIONS

Princess Elizabeth was staying at the Treetops lodge when her father, King George VI, died. So she climbed up to her room as a princess and climbed down as queen.

Several major North American and European chains have hotels in the major cities of Kenya and Tanzania. What distinguishes lodging in both countries are the unique "lodges" that are near or in the wildlife reserves. Often built like large tribal huts—but more luxurious—these lodges offer wonderful meals, cultural entertainment, and the vehicles and guides that take visitors into the parks for wildlife-viewing safaris. Some are located near bodies of water or saltlicks—it's sometimes possible to see animals right near the guestrooms. **Treetops,** a famous lodge located in Aberdare National Park, is built into trees.

Treetops Lodge, Kenya
Photo by William and Marie Rourke

Kenya's largest lodging chain is **Serena.** However, most hotels and lodges in Tanzania and Kenya are independently owned and operated.

ALLIED DESTINATIONS

Most tourists travel between wildlife reserves via small, fixed-wing aircraft. The pilot will also serve as baggage handler and flight attendant.

If a trip to Kenya is to be extended, it most commonly would be to Tanzania, and vice versa. Most of the other countries in the region have political problems or limited tourist facilities, which make them improbable add-ons. (However Ethiopia, Uganda, Malawi, and the Democratic Republic of the Congo are beginning to attract visitors.) Two other major destinations, Israel and Egypt, can be a stopover on the way from North America, as can Europe.

CULTURAL PATTERNS

Most tourists visiting Kenya and Tanzania do so on an organized safari. Still, it's important that they understand the special traditions of the region.

- In Kenya, pointing with an index finger is very insulting; use the whole hand. Don't use the left hand alone when passing or receiving an item. (This is true in Tanzania, as well.)

- Be prepared to give hearty handshakes on greeting a Kenyan. A "soft" hand-shake is considered effeminate. So, too, is the use of cologne by men, especially to those Kenyans who live outside urban centres.

- Bring a gift when visiting someone's home. Socializing is often done at the end of the meal rather than beforehand.

- Some people feel that Tanzania now offers a better experience than does Kenya. Their belief: Tourism in Tanzania has been going on for less time than in Kenya. As a result, travel personnel are more eager to please and less jaded than those in Kenya.

The name *Tanzania* is a composite of Tanganyika (the country's original name) and Zanzibar.

FACTORS THAT MOTIVATE VISITORS

It's easy to figure out why people might want to visit Kenya and Tanzania. Among these reasons are:

- The wildlife is among the finest and most accessible in the world.
- Safaris are easily booked and provide safety in an adventurous environment.
- The culture is intriguing.
- Shopping choices are quite interesting.
- English is commonly spoken.
- Tanzania has sites of historical interest.
- There are lovely beaches.
- There's warm, pleasant weather year-round.
- Mombasa is a prime cruise embarkation and debarkation port.

Kenyans and Tanzanians greet people with the word *jambo!*

POSSIBLE MISGIVINGS

Kenya and Tanzania are beautiful yet challenging countries. Some typical objections are:

- "It's so far." Break up the trip with European or Middle Eastern stops.

- "There's a great danger of disease." Kenya and Tanzania can be quite safe, so long as the traveller checks with a doctor before leaving Canada and takes necessary precautions. And be sure to pack insect repellent and sunscreen.

- "African languages make it impossible to communicate." English is widely spoken in both countries.

- "The water and food can make you sick." Drink bottled liquids and make sure that food is properly prepared.

- "All there is to do is go on a safari." There are also some very nice coral beaches off the east coast. However, this may be the wrong destination for people who don't like safaris, though hiking, shopping, and cultural exploration are all valid reasons to visit these countries.

- "It's so expensive to get there." It can be expensive, but costs within the countries are reasonable. An all-inclusive package tour can help keep prices under control.

- "It's dangerous." Crime does occur, often with a great deal of publicity and usually in big cities, like Nairobi. Check on any advisories. An escorted safari with a reputable company minimizes danger.

SALES STRATEGIES

The best way to enhance a trip to Kenya or Tanzania is to book a package safari through a tour operator. For travellers who would rather take a less-structured trip, a private guide is a good alternative. A higher-class hotel is advisable; budget accommodations can be chancy. Because getting to Kenya and Tanzania takes so long and there's so much to see, tourists should lengthen their stay a few days to take full advantage of the region and to explore the less-visited reserves or coastal towns. A cruise would be a fine way to extend a trip. A multi-day stopover in Europe might be a good way to break up such a long flight from Canada. Finally, upscale travellers may wish to offset the long flight by flying in first or business class.

Qualifying the Traveller
KENYA AND TANZANIA

FOR PEOPLE WHO WANT	HIGH APPEAL	MEDIUM APPEAL	LOW APPEAL	REMARKS
Historical and Cultural Attractions			▲	Wildlife primarily
Beaches and Water Sports		▲		Near Mombasa; impressive coral reefs
Skiing Opportunities			▲	None
Lots of Nightlife			▲	Some in Nairobi
Family Activities		▲		Children love safaris
Familiar Cultural Experience			▲	
Exotic Cultural Experience	▲			
Safety and Low Crime			▲	Check news for recent information
Bargain Travel			▲	Airfare and safaris can be expensive
Impressive Scenery	▲			A little of everything
Peace and Quiet		▲		Quietest on wildlife reserves; though animals can get noisy at night
Shopping Opportunities			▲	Local handicrafts
Adventure	▲			Safaris
To Do Business			▲	

NAME _____   DATE _____

A traveller wants to visit the places listed below. Which number represents each on the map?

PLACE/ATTRACTION	IN/NEAR WHICH CITY OR PARK?	NUMBER ON MAP
A. The tallest mountain in Africa	A.	A.
B. The Kenya National Museum	B.	B.
C. Wildlife reserve in northern portion of Serengeti Plains	C.	C.
D. Mt. Kenya	D.	D.
E. The major cruise port of Kenya	E.	E.
F. National park near Olduvai Gorge	F.	F.
G. Crater with many animals in it	G.	G.
H. Kenya's air gateway	H.	H.
I. Gateway to Tanzania's animal preserves	I.	I.
J. A Muslim city with many mosques	J.	J.

CASE STUDY

NAME _____   DATE _____

Dr. Ernest Rollo and his wife, Anne, are a couple in their late 60s. They've always taken their annual vacation on their own. This year they want to go to Kenya, but are wary about travelling there alone, so they've decided to take a package tour. They can go only in February.

Circle the answer that best suits their needs.

1. They want to visit as many national parks as possible. Which of the following would they probably not go to?

   Amboseli   Aberdare

   Mombasa   Tsavo

   Why?

2. Which of the following tips would *not* be appropriate to pass along to the Rollos?

   You'll need to bring sweaters.   Zebra skins are great bargains.

   Exchange money only in a bank.   Drive on the left.

   Why?

3. Which of the following services would *not* be good for you to book?

   Business-class airfare   Accommodations in a lodge

   An Amazon cruise   A hot-air balloon trip

   Why?

4. The Rollos decide to extend their trip beyond just Kenya for a few days. What other nearby country might you suggest they visit?

   Tanzania   South Africa

   Morocco   Ivory Coast

   Why?

NAME _____ DATE _____

Do you think the following famous people would like visiting Kenya and Tanzania? Why or why not? What specifically would appeal to them?

1. Conrad Black (multimillionaire):

2. Jann Arden (singer-songwriter):

3. Don Cherry (sportscaster):

4. Ben Mulroney (TV host):

5. Jim Carrey (actor-comedian):

6. Your teacher:

TRAVEL TRIVIA

CULTURAL SURPRISES

- In Kenya, the verbal "tch, tch" sound is considered an insult.

- The North American "OK" sign is obscene in Russia.

- In Switzerland, asking for salt and pepper while dining is an insult to the cook.

- The North American hitchhiking sign is obscene in Yugoslavia.

- To drink ice water with a meal is a peculiarly North American custom.

- In France, a salad is served after the main course, not before.

- In Japan, one should accept a gift with two hands.

- In Muslim countries, to show the soles of one's shoes while seated is very rude behaviour.

ATLANTIC
OCEAN

○ Azores

Madeira
Islands

Canary Islands

Strait of Gibraltar

Atlas Mountains

TUNISIA

*MEDITERRANEAN
SEA*

MOROCCO

BLACK SEA

CASPIAN
SEA

LEBANON
ISRAEL

SYRIA

IRAQ

IRAN

ALGERIA

LIBYA

EGYPT

Jordan River

JORDAN

WESTERN
SAHARA

Sahara   *Desert*

*Lake
Nassen*

Nile

Gulf of Suez

Persian Gulf

BAHRAIN QATAR

SAUDI
ARABIA

UNITED
ARAB
EMIRATES

OMA

MAURITANIA

MALI

NIGER

CHAD

River

ERITREA

RED
SEA

YEMEN

*ARABIA
SEA*

SENEGAL

Niger River

Gambia River

GAMBIA

GUINEA-
BISSAU

GUINEA

BURKINA
FASO

NIGERIA

*Lake
Chad*

SUDAN

ETHIOPIA

INDIAN
OCEAN

SIERRA
LEONE

LIBERIA

IVORY
COAST

GHANA TOGO

BENIN

CAMEROON

CENTRAL
AFRICAN
REPUBLIC

UGANDA

*Lake
Victoria*

SOMALIA

KENYA

EQUATOR

GABON

CONGO

Congo

River

DEM. REP. OF
CONGO

RWANDA

BURUNDI

*Lake
Tanganyika*

Mt. Kilimanjaro ▲

TANZANIA

EQUATOR

Seychelles

ANGOLA

ZAMBIA

*Lake
Malawi*

MOZAMBIQUE

ATLANTIC
OCEAN

Victoria
Falls ▲

Zambezi River

NAMIBIA

ZIMBABWE

MADAGASCAR

Mauritius
Reunion

BOTSWANA

SWAZILAND

*Kalahari
Desert*

LESOTHO

INDIAN
OCEAN

SOUTH
AFRICA

African and Middle Eastern Potpourri

In describing the vast area that is Africa and the Middle East, writer John Gunther once said, "One travels like a golf ball, hopping from green to green." To Gunther, each "green" was a unique and exotic tourist destination: sacred sites, archaeological wonders, thundering waterfalls, great herds of exotic beasts. And such attractions aren't limited to the places we've already covered: Egypt, Kenya, Tanzania, Palestine, Jordan, and Israel. Africa and the Middle East constitute a huge region, one brimming with attractions. So, to make Africa as easy as possible for you to know, we've divided this chapter into eight important regions of tourism.

Many of the emerging nations discussed in this section suffer from political and economic uncertainties. Each country's political situation can become dangerous, and quite quickly. You should continually check government travel warnings on current situations and keep up on the news. Remember, too, that disorganization and unpredictable levels of service may mark emerging countries such as these.

MOROCCO

Canadian travellers are finding out what Europeans have long known: Morocco is one of Africa's most exotic yet accessible destinations. Often visited as a southern side trip from Spain or on a cruise, it's just a few kilometres across the Strait of Gibraltar. Most of its attraction-cities lie along the cool and dry Mediterranean coast, while inland are broad, hot deserts and the **Atlas Mountains.** French and Arabic are the principal languages.

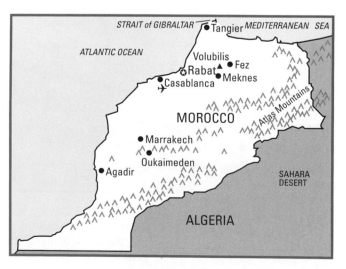

Important Places

*   **Casablanca** (CAS) is Morocco's air gateway. All the ambience made famous by the film of the same name—the dimly lit nightclubs, narrow streets, frenetic **Casbah**—is really here. Its **Great Mosque** is a noteworthy attraction and two churches—**Sacred Heart Cathedral** and **Notre Dame of Lourdes**—are impressive.

- **Rabat,** the capital, is a worthwhile day-trip destination from Casablanca. Nearby is **Chellah,** the site of Roman ruins.

- **Tangier,** just across from Spain and Gibraltar, has long been a prime port of entry. As a result, cultures have mixed freely, resulting in Tangier's renowned, diversified cuisine.

The world's oldest existing educational institution is a university in Fez. It was founded in A.D. 859.

- **Fez** is Morocco's oldest city and a major centre of the Islamic religion. Its *medina* (Arabic for marketplace), **Qarawiyin Mosque,** and old walled city section are usual tourist stops. Two major day trips from Fez: **Meknes,** often called the "Versailles of Morocco"; and **Volubilis,** the site of some of the best Roman ruins in North Africa.

- **Marrakech,** Morocco's most popular tourist destination, is usually reached by train from Casablanca. Its most fanciful attraction is **Djemaa el Fna Square**—with snake charmers, fortunetellers, food vendors, and nearby bazaar. Marrakech is also noted for its daily **Fantasia**—a feast of food, music, dance, and horse-mounted guards who, while firing their guns in the air, charge at people. Marrakech is also poised strategically between mountain and sea: **Oukaimeden,** an Atlas Mountain ski resort, is to the south; and **Agadir,** a beach resort, is to the southwest.

Marrakech has a legendary hotel, La Mamounia.

Sales Considerations

Morocco is relatively inexpensive, so it appeals to bargain hunters. It's sufficiently exotic for the adventurous, yet geographically and culturally close enough to Europe to make it appealing to more timid travellers. Street crime and health problems can be vexing; high-quality hotels, lodging in better areas, and escorted tours largely protect tourists from unpleasantness.

NORTHERN AFRICA

This region—much of it covered by the **Sahara Desert**—exhibits a strong Arab influence. Bordered to the north by the Mediterranean Sea, a few of its destinations are close enough to Europe to be booked as day trips from there. And east of Northern Africa is the Middle East—technically a part of Asia.

Important Places

Northern Africa's destinations are among the most unusual on the continent. We've already discussed Egypt (in Chapter 24) and Morocco (in the previous section). We now cover the other countries.

TUNISIA. On Africa's northern coast is Tunisia. Arabic and French are its national languages. With a long, winding coastline, much of the country is graced by a warm, breezy Mediterranean climate that's ideal for resorts; in fact, the first Club Med was built here. Winters can be rainy.

Tunis, the capital, occupies an area that in ancient days was the powerful city-state of **Carthage.** (You may remember from your history books how its general, Hannibal, nearly defeated the Roman Empire.) Today,

The ancient Coliseum at El Jem, Tunisia, rivals the one in Rome.

Tunis boasts excellent ruins (including those of Carthage), the **National Museum,** the **Bardo Museum,** the **Medina,** and the **Great Mosque.** It's also an occasional port for Mediterranean cruises. A visit to Tunisia often includes a visit to **Matmata,** an underground city where more than 10 000 people live. The island of **Djerba** has interesting ruins and beaches, and is very popular among Europeans. In the north is **Hammamet,** a modern beach resort.

LIBYA. Long considered a hotbed for terrorism, Libya has become more friendly with the rest of the world. As a result, some adventurous tour operators have begun to offer trips there. Libya has some notable ancient Roman sites.

○ Ninety-five percent of Libya is covered by sand.

MALI. Mali's national languages are French and Bambara. Not much English is spoken here and tourist services are somewhat unreliable. Its most famous city is Timbuktu, once one of the world's most inaccessible places. Timbuktu doesn't offer much to see—but then, that's sort of the point.

ETHIOPIA. Far to the east is Ethiopia, a mountainous, poverty-ridden country. It does feature some interesting mosques, tombs, palaces, and a good zoo in **Addis Ababa,** the capital. The ancient town of **Aksum** (a major religious site) features ruins, the country's crown jewels, the **Palace of the Queen of Sheba,** and the **Cathedral of St. Mary of Zion** (the *supposed* resting place of the Ark of the Covenant). Ethiopia is especially famous for its 11 remarkable churches carved out of solid rock. They're in the town of **Lalibela.** A visit to Ethiopia could coincide with a trip to Egypt or Kenya.

ERITREA. Eritrea has potential: Diving along its Red Sea coast is good and its capital, **Asmera,** has Italian-influenced architecture. The country has had on-again, off-again strife with its southern neighbour, Ethiopia.

○ Haile Selassie, Ethiopia's emperor from 1931 to 1974, once visited Jamaica and made such an impression that many Jamaicans still revere him deeply.

Sales Considerations

Northern Africa is strategically central to travel. The reason: It's just south of Europe (separated by only the Mediterranean), just west of the Middle East, and a gateway to the rest of Africa. Escorted tours, especially desert safaris, are popular here, since they wrap lodging and travel into one efficient package. This is a destination, though, that appeals mostly to bargain hunters, the adventurous, or those intrigued with desert culture. Its Mediterranean beaches offer some excellent opportunities for a resort stay, usually among European tourists.

THE MIDDLE EAST

The Middle East is one of the world's most newsworthy, volatile, and historically important regions. The political climate here fluctuates constantly. In normal times, tourists tend to gravitate toward Israel, Palestine, Jordan, and Egypt (all covered in previous chapters). Business travellers visit these countries, too, as well as those nations where oil is an important resource. The Middle East is bordered by Europe to the north, Africa on the west (in fact, Egypt—often considered part of the Middle East—is actually on the African continent), and Asia on the east. The Arabian Sea lies just to the south.

Chapter 27 African and Middle Eastern Potpourri

Important Places

Religious sites and historical landmarks—that's what the Middle East is famous for. We've listed key nations in their order of importance to travellers.

SAUDI ARABIA. Taking up the bulk of the Arabian Peninsula is Saudi Arabia. In a region known for its religious significance, the Islamic beliefs and laws in Saudi Arabia—the birthplace of Mohammed—are among the strictest. Jordan and the Red Sea are to its west, Iraq and the Persian Gulf to the east, and Yemen and Oman to the south. There's limited direct air service here via North American carriers; more direct service is available via national carrier **Saudia Airlines** (SV) and by several European airlines. The main gateway is the capital, **Riyadh** (RUH), in the centre of the country; travellers can also find international service on the western coast in **Jiddah** (JED), which is also the major port.

The climate in Saudi Arabia varies immensely from place to place, but daytime heat is a near constant. Temperatures in Riyadh climb from a spring and fall average in the mid-20s to the upper 30s in the summer; winters are cooler. Sandstorms can happen in any season. The national language is Arabic.

Some significant religious destinations exist here, especially for Islamic pilgrims. Remember that Saudi Arabia gets major business trade from Western countries.

- **Mecca,** Mohammed's birthplace, is the holiest city in the Islamic religion. This is a major pilgrimage destination—able-bodied Muslims must visit it at least once in their lives as part of a voyage called the *haj*—but it's closed to non-Muslim tourists. Two of the most sacred sites are the gigantic **Holy Ka'aba Shrine** and a huge mosque.

- **Medina,** where Mohammed is buried, is the second-holiest city to Muslims. Like Mecca, only Muslim pilgrims may enter the city.

- **Riyadh,** sitting in the middle of the desert, is a modern capital city. There are palaces, museums, and an old-city area.

- **Jiddah** is an interesting mixture of modern and old. There's lovely scenery, a good marketplace, several palaces, and an old-city quarter. Red Sea beaches are nearby. Snorkelling here is excellent.

- **Dhahran** is important to business travellers; it's a major oil field area on the Persian Gulf east coast, with nearby oases and good beaches.

THE UNITED ARAB EMIRATES. Sitting on the eastern tip of the Arabian Peninsula is the small country of the United Arab Emirates (or UAE). Seven emirates (each led by an emir, an Islamic chief or commander) united to form this nation, which is extremely oil-rich. Like Kuwait to the north, it's mainly a business destination, but there are some historic buildings and small beach resorts for leisure travellers. **Gulf Air** (GF) has served the UAE for a long time. The relatively new **Emirates Air** (EK) has become a major airline, with an extensive network of long-distance air routes into and out of its hub city, **Dubai** (DXB).

- **Abu Dhabi,** one of the Emirates and also the name of the capital of the UAE, has ancient ruins, an archaeological museum, and a popular open-air market. In addition, the city boasts a major Middle Eastern gateway at **Abu Dhabi International Airport** (AUH).

- **Dubai** (both a city and a UAE sheikhdom) has, in recent times, experienced astonishing growth. Its landmark building, the **Burj Al Arab Hotel,** rises just offshore, like some gigantic ship's sail. Some consider it one of the most stunning achievements of modern architecture. Most of the luxury chains also have properties in Dubai.

Though few Westerners visit Syria, it has two remarkable ruins: a 2000-year-old Roman city, Palmyra, and an 800-year-old Crusader castle, Crac des Chevaliers.

Over two million Muslims visit Mecca each year.

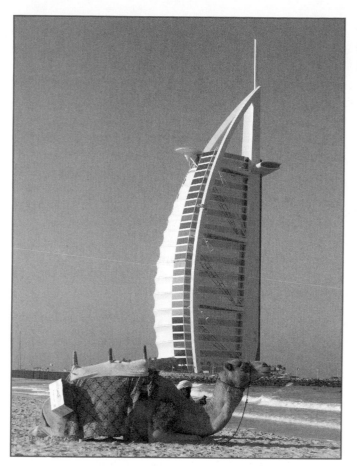

The Burj Al Arab Hotel, Dubai, UAE
Karen Kean/Shutterstock

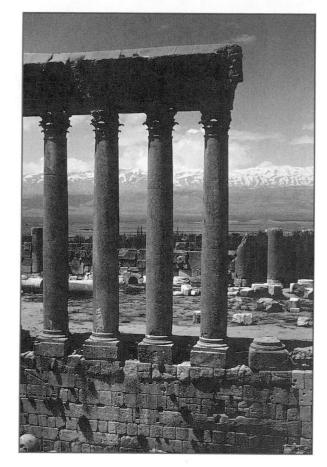

Ruins at Baalbek, Lebanon
Photo by Justus Ghormley

What attracts people to Dubai, other than business opportunities? Great shopping, safety, convenient air connections, and several historical attractions.

LEBANON. Located north of Israel and west of Syria, Lebanon was once one of the most popular tourist destinations in the region, but decades of strife virtually eliminated visitors. To some extent, that has now changed. Potential attractions are **Beirut,** the capital city once known as the "Paris of the Middle East"; **Tyre,** with the remains of the ancient Phoenician civilization; **Baalbek,** with well-preserved Roman temple ruins; and **Byblos,** one of the oldest towns in the world.

There are bears in the mountains of Lebanon.

BAHRAIN. Bahrain is a tiny, multi-island, oil-producing nation just off the east coast of Saudi Arabia in the Persian Gulf. Compared to many of its neighbours, the formerly British-dominated country is fairly sophisticated and has some active nightlife. **Bahrain Island,** where the capital city of **Manama** is located, has marketplaces, mosques, and interesting archaeological sites. Bahrain's shores have some good beaches.

Sales Considerations

Leisure travellers may avoid this region because of its political situation or the torrid climate. The Middle East will attract those who travel for religious or business reasons. It's also a prime location for those deeply interested in archaeology. Some good snorkelling, deep-sea fishing, and beach-resort opportunities exist here, though services aren't always up to Western standards. If political tensions ease, Iraq, Iran, and Syria—because their lands were so important in antiquity—could become viable tourist destinations.

The ancient Babylonian civilization was centred on what is today Iraq.

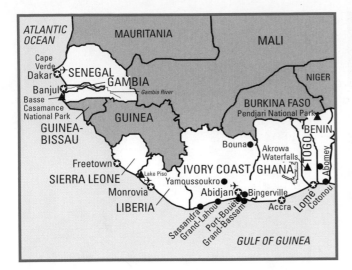

WEST AFRICA

This region—largely of French culture—lies in the most recognizable area of Africa: along the "crook" where the continent bends around the Gulf of Guinea.

Important Places

Though most of the nations in this coastal region are tiny, they offer many unique, seldom-visited attractions.

NIGERIA. The densely populated country of Nigeria is the most visited of western African countries, though most travellers come for business reasons (Nigeria is an oil producer) or are tourists from places other than Canada. Nigeria is often subject to political unrest.

SENEGAL. Steeped in Muslim culture, Senegal is the most westerly country in Africa. Several European carriers offer limited service to **Dakar** (DKR), the capital. Summers here are quite hot and August is particularly rainy; Senegal's winters are very warm, with almost no rain. The official languages are French and several local dialects.

Among the places you should be aware of:

- Dakar, a fairly sophisticated city on the central coast, was designed in a style reminiscent of Paris, with wide boulevards. Dakar is proud of its theatre, ballet, museums, and fine beaches. Popular day trip destinations include the historical harbour area of the **Island of Goree,** a place from which slaves were originally shipped out. Also, **Cape Verde** (not to be confused with the Cape Verde Islands, about 640 kilometres off the coast) profits from a rolling, volcanic landscape.

- **Cap Skirring** is a beach resort district not far from Senegal's best-known wildlife preserve, **Basse Casamance National Park.**

IVORY COAST. Also known as **Côte d'Ivoire** (its official name), Ivory Coast lies along the southern coast of Africa's western arm. The influence of French culture is even stronger here than in Senegal, and tourist services are well developed. There are limited flights from North America via a few European carriers. The gateway is the capital of **Abidjan** (ABJ). Ivory Coast has a hot climate almost year-round; winters are largely rain-free. French and various local dialects are the national languages. In recent times, Ivory Coast has suffered from political strife. Among its prime destinations:

- **Abidjan** is an active, fairly contemporary city; it's quite pretty and offers a zoo, palaces, a national museum, and gambling. It's often called the "Paris of Africa."

- **Luxurious (and expensive) resorts** can be found nearby in lovely **Grand-Bassam** (the country's former capital) and **Sassandra.**

- **Banana, pineapple,** and **coffee plantations** are fun attractions. They can be visited not far from Abidjan in **Bingerville** and **Port-Bouet.**

- **Our Lady of Peace** is a spectacular Roman Catholic cathedral—one of the largest in the world. Located in **Yamoussoukro,** this granite, glass, and marble structure cost more than US$200 million and was paid for by the country's then-president, Felix Houphouet-Boigny.

LIBERIA. Liberia began as a settlement of freed slaves from the United States. Its capital, **Monrovia** (founded in 1822), was named after U.S. President James Monroe. English is the official language; local dialects are also spoken. Monrovia boasts a fine museum and cultural arts centre. **Lake Piso** is in a beautiful area on the northwest coast. Liberia has recently suffered serious political turmoil.

Most African Americans are descendants of people who lived in West Africa.

Felix Houphouet-Boigny built the cathedral in Yamoussoukro because the city was his birthplace.

Liberia's flag looks like the U.S. flag, but with only one star.

Sierra Leone. On the west coast is the tiny nation of Sierra Leone. Settled by freed British slaves (English is one of its official languages), it is sometimes visited along with Liberia. Like its neighbour, it is also subject to political unrest. The capital, **Freetown,** is in a beautiful hilly area along the coast. A famous 500-year-old cotton tree stands near the fine **National Museum,** and several markets attract tourists. The country features wildlife preserves and several deluxe resorts.

The Gambia. The Gambia runs from the Atlantic Ocean through a thin slice of Senegal, along the **Gambia River.** English and tribal languages are spoken here. The country is best known as the starting point in Alex Haley's novel *Roots;* it remains a popular destination for African Americans. This former British colony has good beaches and fishing. **Banjul,** its quiet capital, is a base for trips through the country and along the river.

NASA upgraded Banjul's airport to accommodate possible emergency landings by the space shuttle.

Ghana. Well known for its colourful festivals is Ghana, with its capital, **Accra.** Scenic beaches (but with rough waters), oceanside castles and forts (which supported the slave trade), fishing, wildlife reserves, tribal ceremonies, and English-speaking locals account for Ghana's ever-increasing tourism.

Togo. The tiny nation of Togo is wedged along the southern coast of the western arm. The country is known for its beaches, casinos, and tribal culture. The capital, **Lome,** has much nightlife and an open-air market. The spectacular **Akrowa Waterfalls** is a bit of a challenge to get to from Lome.

Benin. Formerly a French colony, Benin has begun to attract tourism. The country is generally visited out of **Cotonou,** where some modest lodging is available. Among the most popular day trips from Cotonou: **Ganvie,** a city of canals and houses on stilts; **Abomey,** with several ancient structures and offbeat shopping; and two wildlife parks.

Voodoo began in Benin, not Haiti.

Sales Considerations

Though best known for wildlife safaris and the general friendliness of its people, West Africa presents some very good (and less-crowded) sites for adventurous tourists (though services are often below par). Beach resorts—some deluxe—dot the Gulf of Guinea. And ambitious travellers might like a trip up the Gambia River. Many of the nations here can be combined for an extended visit. Political unrest in some of these countries is often a problem; make sure to check current advisories.

THE CENTRAL SAFARI BELT

The central portion of the African continent can be divided into two sections: the Safari Belt and the Victoria Falls region. The Safari Belt, especially, is what many people imagine when they think of Africa.

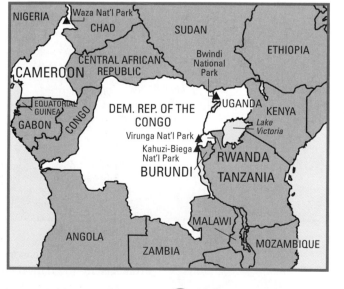

Important Places

Although Kenya and Tanzania are the most visited of the Safari Belt countries and are covered in their own chapter, they're not the only places with spectacular herds. The countries that follow are, in many ways, just as awe inspiring (though for the more adventurous). They're listed in order of importance to travellers.

Democratic Republic of the Congo (formerly Zaire and not to be confused with the Republic of the Congo, its neighbour to the west). Almost directly in the centre of the continent is the large Democratic Republic of the Congo. Once also known as the

Visitors to wildlife reserves hope to see Africa's "Big Five" animals: lions, leopards, rhinoceroses, elephants, and water buffaloes.

Belgian Congo, this is a nation of great tribal diversity (and rivalries). The country's transportation system is limited, there's political unrest, and, unfortunately, crime is common. **Virunga National Park** is the country's finest and most scenic wildlife reserve. **Kahuzi-Biega National Park** is one of the few places in Africa where you can see gorillas in the wild.

CAMEROON. Though considered part of central Africa, Cameroon lies on the hilly western coast, not far from the French-influenced West African nations. Less crowded than most other wildlife-reserve countries, Cameroon has a first-rate destination: **Waza National Park,** with its large herds of elephants.

RWANDA AND UGANDA. Most tourists to these two nations go to view mountain gorillas in the wild. The most popular parks for viewing these animals are **Parc des Volcans** (Rwanda) and **Bwindi National Park** (Uganda). Both countries have suffered from political unrest. They're sometimes combined with trips to their neighbours: Kenya and Tanzania.

Sales Considerations

This region will appeal to the most hardy and adventurous travellers: animal lovers, mountain climbers, and water-sports aficionados. Escorted safaris are obviously popular. A trip here could be extended to a visit to the Victoria Falls region. Remember that political turmoil, banditry, disease, and unpredictable tourist services can be potential problems for those headed for the Safari Belt; as always, check for political advisories.

THE CENTRAL VICTORIA FALLS REGION

South of the popular safari destinations of central Africa is another equally popular but vastly different area. The nations covered in this section are gloriously lush and the highlight is the awesome Victoria Falls.

Important Places

Its name tells most, but not all, of the story. Victoria Falls is one of the world's great natural sites. However, this region offers many other beautiful attractions.

ZAMBIA. Located almost directly in the centre of Africa's southern region is the landlocked country of Zambia (formerly Northern Rhodesia). **Aero Zambia** (Z9) and **Zambian Express** (OQ) are the national airlines. European carriers bring travellers here via flights from Europe. The gateway is **Lusaka International Airport** (LUN) in the nation's capital. Zambia lies below the equator, so its seasons are opposite those of North America. It's also mostly plateau country, so temperatures are less tropical than you'd think: around 30°C from September to December and in the low to mid-20s the rest of the year. Dry season extends from May to October. English and various tribal dialects are the national languages. Among the beautiful attractions in Zambia:

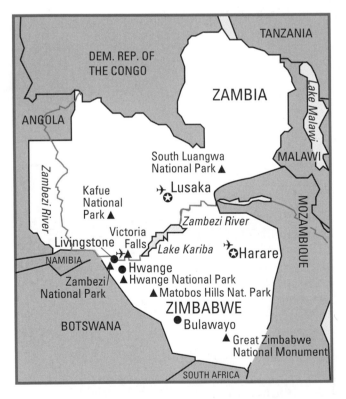

Victoria Falls is 1.7 kilometres wide.

- **Victoria Falls,** on the **Zambezi River,** is an awesome sight. Period. It's many times the width of Niagara Falls. Visitors must not miss it if they're anywhere near the area. (They'll usually stay overnight at nearby lodging.) The Zambian town closest to the falls is **Livingstone;** the **Livingstone Museum** houses memorabilia of Dr. Livingstone, as well as 300-year-old African maps.

- **Kafue National Park** is a huge area with elephants and more than 400 species of birds.

- **South Luangwa National Park,** in the Luangwa Valley, is perhaps one of Africa's most richly stocked animal preserves. It's best visited during dry season.

ZIMBABWE. Once known as Southern Rhodesia, Zimbabwe has had a troubling political situation for many years. Yet, located just south of Zambia, it offers many superbly beautiful destinations. There's limited service here from North America on European carriers, though more connecting flights leave from Europe directly. Zimbabwe's national carrier is **Air Zimbabwe** (UM). The main gateway is at **Harare Airport** (HRE) near the capital.

This south-of-the-equator country has seasons that are opposite those of North America. The climate is moderate: From November to February, temperatures reach the upper 20s and there'll be rain. Otherwise, the weather is cool and dry, around 20°C during the day. The low-lying areas (like Victoria Falls, the **Zambezi Valley, Hwange** [HWONG-gay], and **Lake Kariba**) will be warmer. The official languages are English and tribal dialects. Among the top attractions in Zimbabwe:

- **Victoria Falls,** as described earlier, is one of the most beautiful sights on the globe. Zimbabwe, in fact, offers a better vantage point of the Falls than does Zambia (seven-eighths of the Falls are on the Zimbabwe side). Access is through **Victoria Falls Airport** (VFA).

- **Zambezi National Park** lies along the shores of the Zambezi River. Visitors can stroll the riverbanks, take cruises, or travel via road to see the many types of wildlife that live here.

- **Hwange National Park,** Zimbabwe's largest wildlife reserve, is notable for its vast herds of elephants.

- **Matobos Hills National Park** offers fantastic rock formations, a rhino sanctuary, bushmen cave paintings, and the stunning gravesite of financier-colonizer Cecil Rhodes. It's usually accessed out of **Bulawayo.**

- **Great Zimbabwe National Monument** features the most impressive African ruins south of the Sahara. There are many theories about who built the vast stone structures—that's what makes this place so intriguing.

The ruins of Great Zimbabwe are 1200 years old.

Sales Considerations

Victoria Falls is what brings tourists to Zambia or Zimbabwe. When people visit the falls, they often take a "Flight of Angels." This aerial view of the rushing waters is stunning. Though there are animal reserves in the region, its main attraction is the spectacular scenery. But the adventurous will surely have a great time here: Safaris, walking tours, river rafting on the Zambezi, and boat excursions are all popular.

SOUTHERN AFRICA

Though the nation of South Africa dominates the region's tourism, quite a few other countries are here as well. Nestled into the very bottom of Africa, the area is bordered by both the Atlantic and Indian oceans, ending in the south at the famous, scenic, and often visited **Cape of Good Hope**, a geographic attraction that marks where the two oceans meet.

Important Places

With the elimination of its racial apartheid policy, South Africa—one of the most physically beautiful and westernized nations of Africa—has regained its popularity as a tourist destination. In fact, South Africa has become a destination that rivals Kenya and Tanzania. The other countries within or near South Africa (**Lesotho, Swaziland,** and **Botswana**) are attracting many visitors, as well.

SOUTH AFRICA. **South African Airways** (SA)—the national airline—flies to South Africa, Africa's southernmost country, as do several European carriers (for East Coast cities) and Asian carriers (an alternative for West Coast cities). Air gateways are **Pretoria** (PRV), the administrative capital, located in the northeast; **Johannesburg** (JNB); and **Cape Town** (CPT), the legislative capital, on the southwest coast. In addition, cruises that visit southeast Africa and its islands start or end at Cape Town.

South Africa's subtropical, southern California–like climate is pleasant all year, though September to November (spring) is best. South Africa is south of the equator and its seasons are opposite those of North America. Most of the country is dry; indeed, the **Kalahari Desert** covers much of the northwest. The **Drakensberg Mountains** (lying southeast and east) and interior plateaux tend to have cooler temperatures and some rain, which falls from May to September. The official languages are Afrikaans and English. Among the remarkable attractions in South Africa:

- **Johannesburg** (often referred to as Jo'burg), south of Pretoria, is an active city and the nation's gold-mining centre. There are tours and a museum at **Gold Reef City,** as well as other nearby mines. You can suggest a long day trip to **Kimberley,** the diamond-mining centre, where tours of the mines are offered. A few kilometres from central Johannesburg is **Soweto,** a township where the anti-apartheid movement began and ultimately triumphed. (Apartheid was a countrywide policy of strict racial segregation.) A popular museum here explains the history of apartheid. The hero of the anti-apartheid movement, Nelson Mandela, was imprisoned at **Robben Island,** also now a popular tourist attraction. Johannesburg serves as a jump-off spot for trips to most of South Africa's major wildlife refuges. It does, however, have a problem with crime. It's best to stay at a hotel that's located in the safer, upscale parts of the city.

- **Sun City,** a 90-minute drive northwest of Johannesburg, is sometimes known as the "Las Vegas of Africa." Its casinos, theme attractions, and resort hotels draw many visitors. Especially astonishing is the **Lost City Resort,** with fake ruins, a 25-hectare forest, simulated ocean waves, and the immense, ornate **Palace Hotel.**

- **Cape Town,** one of the world's most beautifully situated cites, lies near the edge of the Cape of Good Hope. It has fine museums, a couple of excellent botanical gardens, good beaches, vibrant nightlife, a busy waterfront shopping area, and several excellent hotels. **Table Mountain,** reached by cable car, provides grand vistas. There's an especially beautiful "Garden Route" drive from Cape Town to **Port Elizabeth,** which has excellent beaches and vistas. Several "wine routes" lie east of Cape Town—it's estimated that the region has over 3000 wineries.

- **Durban,** on the southeast coast, is a fashionable, multicultural resort that's very popular with vacationing South Africans. Its "Golden Mile" beach is lined with restaurants, gardens, and shops.

- **Kruger National Park,** in the northeast, is a massive, crowded wildlife reserve that matches those of Kenya and Tanzania for attracting foreign visitors. June through October are prime months for animal watching here.

The best time to take a safari here is in the winter, when more animals gather.

In South Africa, traffic signals are sometimes called "robots."

Afrikaans, a language spoken by many South Africans, was derived from Dutch.

Africa produces more gold and diamonds than any other continent.

The owner of the biggest hotel in Sun City also developed the giant Atlantis Paradise Island resort, in the Bahamas.

Zulu dancers in South Africa
Photo by Justus Ghormley

- **Zululand,** once a separate territory, provides five excellent wildlife reserves. Visitors learn about the Zulu culture at craft centres and the **Zululand Historical Museum,** and can even spend the night in a Zulu hut.

- **The Kalahari Gemsbok National Park,** which is quite remote, has a varied collection of animals. The desert boundaries cross over into Namibia and Botswana.

- **Sabi Sand**—a collection of private reserves—is perhaps the finest place in South Africa for wildlife viewing. Its most famous reserve is **MalaMala.** Adjacent to Kruger National Park, Sabi Sand is also less crowded than many of the public preserves. Luxurious safari lodges are available and animals are viewed from open vehicles, with some of the most close-up viewing of animals in all of Africa.

LESOTHO. Lesotho, sometimes called the "Switzerland of Africa," is surrounded by South Africa. Criss-crossing this tiny country are beautiful mountains, notably the **Maluti Mountains** (which offer ski facilities). **Sehlabathebe National Park** is quite impressive.

SWAZILAND. Like Lesotho, Swaziland is a small, independent, picturesque country. It harbours a surprising number of wildlife reserves.

NAMIBIA. Lying along the Atlantic and bordering South Africa to the northwest is Namibia. It's becoming a popular safari destination: **Etosha National Park** is a beautiful park and wildlife preserve, as is **Fish River Canyon National Park.** The **Namib Desert** landscape and wildlife are magnificent. **Skeleton Coast,** nestled in the north between the ocean and desert, is the historical site of many sunken ships and moon-like landscapes.

The Skeleton Coast got its name from the many ships that were wrecked and lost there.

BOTSWANA. Sandwiched between Namibia and Zimbabwe, Botswana has some of the finest and most uncrowded wildlife preserves in Africa, as well as a wide spectrum of accommodations, from upscale lodges to tented camps. Two parks in the north are especially well known: **Chobe National Park** (with around

The Okavango is one of the world's only inland deltas.

50 000 elephants) and **Moremi Wildlife Reserve.** The latter occupies a portion of the **Okavango Delta,** one of the greatest homes for wildlife in the world. Northern Botswana is relatively near Victoria Falls, too; a visit to Botswana's reserves is often combined with a trip to the falls. Botswana has the oldest democracy and perhaps the most stable government in Africa, and is especially concerned with preserving its wildlife.

Sales Considerations

Southern Africa will appeal to those who admire beautiful scenery, bargains, good weather, and safaris. There are also some world-class beach resorts and good skiing (though lodging tends to be simple, not luxurious). Gold- and diamond-mining tours are popular. (But diamonds here are no less expensive than elsewhere.) Reservations, especially at or near the wildlife reserves, need to be booked very far in advance. The **Blue Train** is legendary and offers a luxurious and unique way to see the region between Cape Town and Pretoria. The trip takes about 22 hours, with passengers sleeping overnight in one of the train's private compartments. (Each compartment has a bathroom and shower.) **Rovos Rail** operates vintage trains from Cape Town to Victoria Falls.

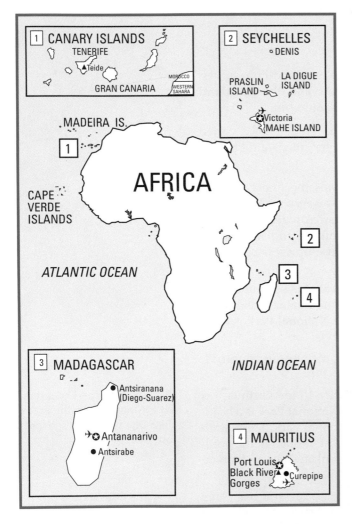

THE AFRICAN ISLANDS

In the Indian Ocean off the southeast coast of Africa are a number of islands that draw tourists; the largest of these by far is **Madagascar,** but others offer finer, more developed attractions. Indeed, **Mauritius** [moh-RIH-shus] is one of the world's more popular island destinations. There are also some islands off the northwest coast, most notably the **Canary Islands.**

Important Places

The islands that surround Africa are largely neglected by Canadian tourists. Part of the reason is that they're simply not well known. These islands are wonderful destinations and are growing in popularity. We've ordered them in their importance to travellers.

THE SEYCHELLES [say-SHELLS]. Sixteen hundred kilometres east of Kenya and lying northeast of Madagascar, the Seychelles is actually made up of nearly 100 tiny islands. There's limited service from North America by European carriers; **Air Seychelles** (HM), the national carrier, also flies from Europe, South Africa, and Singapore. The gateway is **Seychelles International Airport** (SEZ), near the capital of **Victoria** on Mahe [ma-HAY] Island. There's air service among the country's various islands.

The Seychelles' climate is generally warm and balmy, and its look is absolutely distinctive among tropical islands: unusually shaped granite boulders line many areas. Being south of the equator, its seasons are opposite those in North America. Creole English and French are the national languages in this British-influenced country. Among its finest sights:

- **Mahe Island**—the most populous—has great beaches, beautiful gardens, and a lovely, mountainous national park. Mahe offers especially superb snorkelling and diving. Suggest a car rental; the drive around the island is spectacular.

- **Praslin** [prah-LIN] **Island** has good facilities as well, to go with its wonderful scenery and beaches. Thirty-four kilometres from Mahe, it's reached by either boat or plane.

- **La Digue** [DIG] **Island,** a half-hour boat ride from Praslin, has spectacular rock formations at **Union Beach.**

- **Animal sanctuaries** can be found throughout the Seychelles; the most notable are **Bird Island** (with its thick, colourful flocks) and **Denis Island** (famed for its tortoises).

MAURITIUS. Mauritius lies 800 kilometres east of Madagascar. **Air Mauritius** (MK), the national carrier, flies here from Europe and Africa, and a few European airlines depart from their home countries, landing at **Sir Seewoosagur Ramgoolam Airport** (MRU) on the southeast coast. Spring and fall are lovely seasons here, with average temperatures in the mid-20s. June to August can get pretty chilly, whereas December through February is rainy. Once under British control, the dense population here is mixed, which is reflected by its official languages: English, French, Creole, and Hindi. Mauritius is a major getaway destination for European vacationers. It features some lovely attractions, including:

> Mauritius was home to the weird dodo bird, which became extinct shortly after Europeans settled the island in the 1600s.

- **Port Louis,** the capital, which is on the northwest coast. Fine museums, gardens, and an aquarium are located in Port Louis. There are some examples of interesting architecture and an enjoyable marketplace.

- **Abundant beaches and coral reefs.** The resorts are low-key and relaxed, the diving and deep-sea fishing excellent.

- **The Black River Gorges,** with beautiful views and gorgeous scenery.

- **Curepipe** [cure-PEEP], a fairly cosmopolitan town that offers excellent shopping.

MADAGASCAR. Madagascar, the fourth-largest island in the world, is almost the size of Saskatchewan. It lies east of Mozambique, about 385 kilometres from the coast of southern Africa. Formerly under French control, Madagascar has a wide variety of assets: rain forests, semideserts, mountains, and excellent beaches. It's very famous for its lemurs (primitive primates) and unique species of plant life. The national airline is **Air Madagascar** (MD). Attractions in the central capital and main gateway, **Antananarivo** (TNR), include a palace, a zoo, and botanical gardens. Not too far away is **Antsirabe,** which has interesting geothermal activity. **Antsiranana** (formerly Diego-Suarez) is on a very picturesque bay on the north coast. Remember that Madagascar's tourist facilities are much more limited than those on the nearby Seychelles.

> Eighty percent of Madagascar's plants are found nowhere else.

THE CANARY ISLANDS. In the Atlantic off the northwest coast of Africa are the Canary Islands. Provinces of Spain, they offer volcanic scenery, superb beach resorts, and a pleasant year-round climate, especially during the dry and warm summers. Its two most important islands are **Gran Canaria** and **Tenerife** (Spain's highest mountain, **Teide,** at 3700 metres, is here).

> Yes, canary birds are native to the Canary Islands.

Other islands off Africa's western and northwestern coasts are Portugal's **Cape Verde, Madeira,** and **Azores** islands. Of the three, only the Azores have any sort of major tourism. The Azores are most pleasant in the summer, with air temperatures in the mid-20s and water temperatures in the lower 20s. However, winters tend to be grey, wet, and chilly.

> Madeira wine is indeed named after the Madeira Islands.

Sales Considerations

Almost all the African islands have magnificent beaches and superb scenery. These islands are attractive to people looking for a warm, sunny destination with great water-sports opportunities and who are willing to traverse long distances to get there. Snorkelling and deep-sea fishing are ideal here. This is also a wonderful region for naturalists. The Seychelles Island Foundation offers special tours. Both the Atlantic and Indian Ocean island groups are often part of cruise itineraries; it's a great way to combine an island package with a mainland one.

TRAVEL TRIVIA

WHAT THEY USED TO BE CALLED

Current Name	Old Name
• Ethiopia	Abyssinia
• Democratic Republic of the Congo	Zaire, Belgian Congo
• Belize	British Honduras
• Mali	French Sudan
• Sri Lanka	Ceylon
• Bangladesh	East Pakistan
• Ghana	Gold Coast
• Suriname	Dutch Guiana
• Vanuatu	New Hebrides
• Iran	Persia
• Zambia	Northern Rhodesia
• Zimbabwe	Southern Rhodesia
• St. Petersburg, Russia	Leningrad, U.S.S.R.
• Thailand	Siam
• Tanzania	Tanganyika and Zanzibar

NAME _____   DATE _____

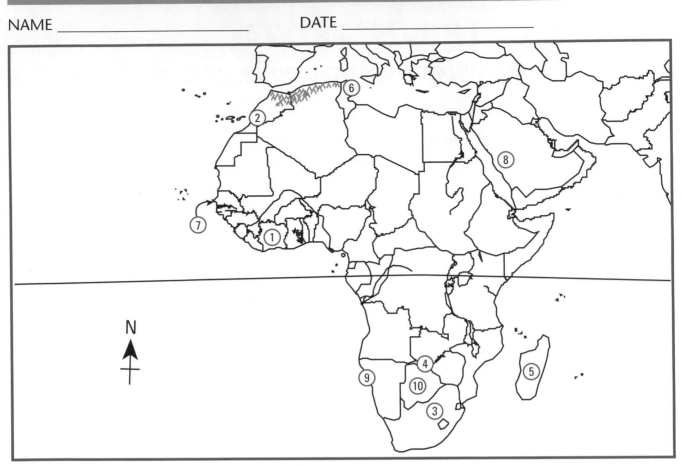

A traveller wants to visit the places listed below. Which number represents each on the map?

PLACE/ATTRACTION	IN/NEAR WHICH COUNTRY?	NUMBER ON MAP
A. Carthage	A.	A.
B. Victoria Falls and the Livingstone Museum	B.	B.
C. Djemaa el Fna Square	C.	C.
D. Our Lady of Peace Cathedral	D.	D.
E. Gold and diamond mines	E.	E.
F. Lemurs	F.	F.
G. The Island of Goree	G.	G.
H. Mecca	H.	H.
I. The Skeleton Coast	I.	I.
J. The Okavango Delta	J.	J.

CASE STUDY

NAME _____   DATE _____

Mike and Carolyn Robitaille usually take their vacations in Europe, but three years ago they tried something different: a safari in Kenya. The couple, in their early 50s, had a wonderful time. They loved the wildlife, and everything about the trip was so well organized that it was much easier than they thought it would be. They've decided to go back to Africa.

Circle the answer that best suits their needs.

1. Having gotten their feet wet, the Robitailles feel that it's time to get a little more adventurous. And as much as they enjoyed Kenya, they don't want to repeat the trip, preferring to see some different animals, if possible. Which country should they visit?

   South Africa   Morocco

   Niger   Ivory Coast

   Why?

2. They decide not to limit their experiences in Africa merely to safaris; they want to enjoy a different part of the continent's dramatic attractions, as well. To what scenic area should they extend their trip?

   Tarzan's tree house   Iguazu Falls

   Victoria Falls   Lake Tanganyika

   Why?

3. The Robitailles decide that, after all, they do prefer a more relaxed, less adventurous trip; it's been a hard year. They'd still like to see some wildlife, but also miss the charms of Europe and wouldn't mind stretching out on the beach for a few days. Where would you suggest?

   Bahrain   Zambia

   Ethiopia   Senegal

   Why?

4. What services would be appropriate for the Robitailles?

   An escorted tour   A budget hotel

   A stopover in South America   First-class rail tickets to Mauritius

   Why?

CREATIVE ACTIVITY

NAME _____   DATE _____

Ecotourism—tourism driven by a desire to see places in their natural state—has become a significant and profitable segment of the tour business. You're an itinerary planner for a tour company that has decided to sell a 15-day ecotour of Africa, starting and ending in Nairobi.

How would you construct the tour? Where would you go? Describe your tour below, remembering to set aside a day each time the group flies from one country to another. (Assume there are air connections between each place; no need to look them up.) And be sensitive to what ecotourists might want to see.

DAY	CITY/PLACE OR COUNTRY	ACTIVITY
1.	Nairobi	Orientation meeting for group; reception dinner
2.		
3.		
4.		
5.		
6.		
7.		
8.		
9.		
10.		
11.		
12.		
13.		
14.		
15.	Nairobi	Free day; departure late in day.

NAME _____   DATE _____

The Matching Game

Directions: Below is a list of cities, attractions, etc., some of which we have covered, some of which we haven't. There are all manner of connections among them. With a group of fellow students, you have exactly 10 minutes to come up with as many connections as possible. (Items may be used more than once.) Write your answers below. Note: There are at least 20 possible connections. e.g., Dakar and Nairobi—both are capital cities.

Lost City	Haifa	Sinai
Sultan Hasan	Alexandria	Zambezi
Dome of the Rock	Eilat	Mt. Kilimanjaro
Kalahari	Jomo Kenyatta	Okavango
Masai Mara	Dakar	Nile
The Ark	Mombasa	Sacred Heart
Zanzibar	Great Mosque	Ngorongoro
Ben Gurion	Serengeti	Hurghada
Ka'aba	Canary	Tel Aviv
Nairobi	Madagascar	Our Lady of Peace

KAZAKHSTAN

RUSSIA

MONGOLIA

Gobi Desert

Yellow River

NORTH
KOREA

*SEA of
JAPAN*

*YELLOW
SEA*

JAPAN

CHINA

▲ Mt. Fuji

SOUTH
KOREA

Himalaya
Mountains

AFGHANISTAN

Yangtze   River

*EAST
CHINA
SEA*

*PACIFIC
OCEAN*

NEPAL

PAKISTAN

BHUTAN

TAIWAN

Saipan
and
Guam

▲
Mt. Everest

BANGLADESH

INDIA

*Ganges
River*

BURMA

LAOS

M I C R O N E S I A

PHILIPPINES

*ARABIAN
SEA*

*BAY of
BENGAL*

THAILAND

VIETNAM

CAMBODIA

SOUTH CHINA SEA

*GULF
of
THAILAND*

BRUNEI

SRI LANKA

SINGAPORE

MALAYSIA

PAPUA
NEW
GUINEA

M E L A N E S I A

TAHITI
Part of POLYNESIA

Krakatoa
(on Island of
Rakata)

▲

INDONESIA

Solomon
Islands

Vanuatu

FIJI

TIMOR SEA

New Caledonia

*CORAL
SEA*

*INDIAN
OCEAN*

AUSTRALIA

Great
Dividing
Range

*TASMAN
SEA*

NEW ZEALAND

Southern
Alps

P O L Y N E S I A

ASIA AND THE PACIFIC

Rim of Mystery

In the great courts of Europe, word had spread about the fabulous riches—both cultural and physical—that existed off in the far, mysterious East. But no one truly knew what was there until Marco Polo travelled to the Orient and returned with stories and treasures that dazzled the Europeans of his day.

Asia and the Pacific still offer treasured opportunities to those who visit the far rim of the Pacific. Yet 700 years after the great explorer made his journey, the Far East is still poorly understood by travellers, even though they may drive Japanese cars, buy Korean DVD players, and watch Australian movies.

With the growth in trade among Pacific Rim nations has come a major growth in travel. Fifty years ago, most North Americans would never have considered visiting Asia or the Pacific islands—not only because of closed cultures but also because of the sheer physical logistics. However, with the advent of long-distance jumbo jets, the Far East is not much more than a half-day away.

In days past, even crossing the International Date Line was a major event—a celebration. Today, a pilot merely informs the plane's passengers about it—assuming, of course, that they hear him or her through their mid-Pacific doze.

WHERE THE COUNTRIES ARE

Tourists and geographers don't always think alike. For instance, where exactly does Asia start and Africa and Europe end? Most geographers consider every-thing to the east of the Red Sea and the Ural Mountains to be Asia—and that includes the Middle East, Turkey, and the majority of Russia.

However, the Middle East is often booked as part of a trip to Europe or Africa. Few tourists ever visit Russia in conjunction with a vacation to China; more likely, a Russian vacation is tied to a trip to Scandinavia. And Turkey is most commonly accessed as an extension of a Greek island cruise. As a result, we've covered some of Asia's 40 or so countries in previous sections, to relate them to realistic tourist itineraries.

What's the most obvious place on a map of Asia? **China,** which physically dominates most of the continent. It dwarfs **Mongolia,** which borders it to the north, and **North** and **South Korea,** which take up the peninsula on its north-eastern corner. (Communist North Korea is rarely visited by Westerners and there-fore won't be covered here.)

Off China's east coast is a string of island nations; from north to south: **Japan, Taiwan,** and the **Philippines.** Continuing south, you encounter the multi-island

The words "orient" and "oriental" come from the Latin word for the East, *oriens,* because Asia was to the east of the Roman Empire. This also explains the "Near East" (today's Turkey), "Middle East" (the now-Muslim nations beyond Turkey), and the "Far East" (China, Japan, etc.).

Sixty percent of the world's population lives in Asia.

Some scholars now suspect that Marco Polo never actually reached China, but made up many of his descriptions.

nations of **Indonesia** and **Malaysia,** along with **Singapore.** On the Southeast Asian mainland are **Thailand, Vietnam** (with its swiftly emerging tourism), and the less visited **Cambodia, Laos,** and **Myanmar** (better known by its traditional name, **Burma**). Below China and to the west of Southeast Asia is the large area known as the Indian subcontinent. From west to east, it includes **India, Nepal,** and **Bhutan** (as well as less-visited **Pakistan, Bangladesh,** and **Sri Lanka**). Also in Asia are five independent nations of the former Soviet Union. **Azerbaijan** and **Uzbekistan** are the most important of these.

The islands of the Pacific may seem to be a great distance from Asia, but some of them are much closer to the continents of Asia or **Australia** than to the Americas: **Papua New Guinea** and **Fiji** (both parts of Melanesia) are relatively close to Australia and Indonesia; the Micronesian islands of **Saipan** and **Guam** are to the east of the Philippines. For this reason, visits to Asia can easily be combined with stopovers at Pacific islands. Though the tens of thousands of Pacific islands are clearly much too numerous to mention, the major ones are (from west to east): **New Zealand, Fiji, Tahiti** (one of the Polynesian islands), and the state of Hawaii (which is closest—about five hours—to the North American mainland and which we covered in Chapter 10).

A SATELLITE VIEW

Looking down on Asia and the Pacific, it would be easy to distinguish the larger islands among the area's oceans and seas. The Asian continent is another matter; it blends into Europe and the Middle East (and therefore Africa, as well).

Perhaps the most noticeable feature of the entire region is how flat much of it is. Most of western China is desert (notably the **Gobi Desert**), as is the western two-thirds of Australia. Much of Southeast Asia, too, is flat rainforest.

However, the exceptions to this flatness are dramatic and have an overwhelming impact on the region (e.g., the Himalaya Mountains). To properly plan trips to this region, it's essential to fully understand the lay of the land.

Bodies of Water

As you would imagine, the **Pacific Ocean** is critical to this vast region. Moreover, the continent of Asia, being as large and geographically situated as it is, is ringed by an assortment of seas.

Beginning at the western part of Asia is India, which is bordered on its west by the **Arabian Sea,** on its south by the **Indian Ocean,** and on its east by the **Bay of Bengal.** Farther east is the **Gulf of Thailand,** in the midst of Southeast Asia; the Gulf, in turn, flows into the **South China Sea.**

The **Sea of Japan** separates Russia and the Korean peninsula from Japan. The **Yellow Sea**—which forms a bay between northeast China and Korea—empties into the **East China Sea,** which in turn merges into the South China Sea. Bordering this whole region to the east is the vast Pacific Ocean.

The Pacific encompasses most of the South Sea islands. However, other major waters here bear note: The **Timor Sea** separates northern Australia from Indonesia; the **Coral Sea** lies northeast of the continent; and dividing southeast Australia from New Zealand is the **Tasman Sea.**

Asia, Australia, and the Pacific islands have only a few major rivers. The **Yellow** and **Yangtze** wind and twist their way through the centre of China. They offer visitors a superb way of exploring the magnificent countryside. (There's also an important canal system in northeastern China that permits several popular excursions.) The **Ganges,** which flows through the northeast of India, is perhaps the most sacred river on earth, for Hindu pilgrims immerse themselves in its waters to spiritually cleanse themselves. Most of Australia's rivers are in its southeast corner. The **Murray** and the **Darling** are the two most important ones.

No one knows how many islands are in the Pacific Ocean. Geographers guess there are at least 20 000, and there could be more than 30 000.

Himalaya is the Sanskrit word for "abode of snow."

The Pacific Ocean is as large as all the continents put together—with room for another Asia.

The deepest place on earth is in the Mariana Trench. It's about 11 kilometres below the surface of the Pacific Ocean.

Singapore Harbour
Photo by Justus Ghormley

Mountains

The 3200 kilometre **Himalaya Mountain range** is the loftiest range in the world. To put this in its proper perspective, Himalaya's **Mt. Everest** is the world's tallest mountain: It's 2700 metres higher than the tallest mountain in North America, Mt. McKinley, and 2100 metres higher than the tallest peak of the Andes. Of the world's 50 tallest mountains, virtually all are in the Himalaya. The challenging Himalaya are considered by adventurous travellers to be the finest trekking and mountain-climbing territory in the world. The Himalaya ripple through the top of Pakistan, northern India, Nepal, Bhutan, and the Tibet region of China, covering an area greater than all of Germany.

In addition, a spine of volcanic mountains runs down the length of much of Japan, the most famous of which is stately **Mt. Fuji.** There are also many mountains of volcanic origin in Indonesia (where the legendary **Krakatoa** erupted) and in Australia, with its **Great Dividing Range** down the east coast. The **Southern Alps** rise above New Zealand's South Island. Parts of western China are also somewhat mountainous—though few tourists visit there.

Climate

Since parts of Asia and the Pacific lie both north and south of the equator, two distinct patterns exist: North of the equator, seasons are the same as those in North America; south, they're the opposite. An important point to remember: Though many think of this entire region as hot and humid, Australia and New Zealand are exceptions. They both have temperate weather. In the winter, New Zealand's mountainous South Island gets plenty of snow. In addition, the Himalaya and other high regions can have very cold weather. One more exception: Western China and western Australia have largely desert climates.

The Indian subcontinent, most of China, the islands of Japan and Taiwan (all of which lie north of the equator), and northern Australia (to the equator's south) have a subtropical climate. Summers in these areas are very warm and humid; winters are drier and more pleasant. A fully tropical climate can be found in those countries that flank the equator—most of Indonesia and all the South Sea

The correct term is *Himalaya,* not *Himalayas.*

Climbers who reach the top of Mt. Everest spend an average of only 32 minutes there.

islands—as well as in Southeast Asia, the Philippines, and Micronesia (north of the equator).

A final note: The region is famed for its monsoons, typhoons, and cyclones. Monsoons are long-standing summer rainstorms, usually associated with the Indian subcontinent and Southeast Asia. Typhoons are what hurricanes are called when they occur in the China Sea and west Pacific area. Cyclones (the generic name for hurricanes and typhoons) often whip along Australia's northeast coastal areas.

Tourism Patterns

Two words summarize the pattern of Pacific Rim tourism: *explosive growth*. It has not been unusual to see a doubling of the numbers of tourists in a matter of a year or two. As a result, major hotels are being built everywhere. China (including Hong Kong) is by far the most popular destination in Asia. Japan, South Korea, and Australia are also popular with North American travellers. In addition to the leisure segment, business travel accounts for much movement across the Pacific between North America and the Far East.

What of the Pacific islands? The U.S. state of Hawaii is number one, but surprisingly, the Micronesian islands of Guam and Saipan are in second place (most of their tourists come from Japan, though). Fiji is the most successful destination in Melanesia, and Tahiti leads the Polynesian islands in tourism. Hawaii, Tahiti, and Fiji are all common stopover points on trans-Pacific travel itineraries, both on planes and on repositioning cruises.

ASIAN AND PACIFIC DISTANCES

For travelling through Asia, the mode of choice for most tourists is the escorted tour. Driving a rental car is not a good idea (except in Australia and New Zealand). Asia's rural roads are sometimes primitive and they can be washed out; city traffic may be impenetrable. Asian languages are usually indecipherable to Westerners. These can be real problems if you're a car renter, especially if you get lost and can't read the signs. Some trains are comfortable, even luxurious. Buses—except those used on tours—are usually a challenge.

Even though many in these countries do speak English fairly well, the language is still a critical—and very real—obstacle. One way around this: cruises, which have become a popular option for visiting key port cities in Asia, Australia, New Zealand, and the Pacific islands.

For those who are travelling on their own, distances in some Asian countries can be great—giant China and India being the obvious examples. However, in many Asian countries, the major destinations tend to be clustered in distinct, limited areas: In China, for instance, the sites typically visited are almost entirely in the east.

The Pacific islands, on the other hand, don't pose that much of a problem. The inhabitants of many of the popular islands speak English; for many (Fiji and Guam, among others), it's an official language. These islands are relatively small, so taxis, car rentals, and (perhaps) buses will do.

Certainly, roads on the smaller islands may be primitive, but again, distances are comparatively minor. The only modes of transportation of any great importance among the islands are planes that hop from one island to the next, ferries that weave their way among clusters of islands, and cruise ships that connect the islands.

Visitors must fly between sites in Australia that are far apart, unless they have a lot of time to spare. Australia is very big: It's about the size of the contiguous United States. Its attractions (except for a notable few) are along the east and west coasts, with much of the inland area desertlike and sparsely populated. The majority of New Zealand's most popular attractions, too, tend to be conveniently

The Bullet Train, Japan
Photo by Brian Yokoyama

clustered. Train and bus travel in both countries (as well as in Japan) is excellent. Trains and buses are less predictable elsewhere, though luxury trains travel through India, and between Singapore and Bangkok.

SOME MISCELLANEOUS CONSIDERATIONS

Asia and the Pacific are often thought of as exotic. Usually travellers to this part of the world want some sense of security before they leave. Among the suggestions you can give are:

- Health conditions in some of these countries are far below the standard that most tourists expect. Travellers should check health advisories and visit their physician before leaving on a trip to Asia and the Pacific.

- Shopping in Asia, in Australia, and among the islands is of great allure to many tourists. The best prices on brand names can usually be found in Hong Kong, South Korea, and Singapore, while crafts are a bargain in almost all of these places.

- The engines of commerce are powerful in Asia. Nowhere in the world, these days, is business travel more important. The industrial nations of Asia, by the way, are often called "The Dragons."

- Bargaining on prices is extremely common, indeed almost expected, in many of these countries—though not in Japan, Australia, and New Zealand. Check with hotel personnel about local customs.

- Even though many locals understand English, visitors who are having a difficult time communicating should write out their questions. It's not uncommon for someone here to read English better than they speak it.

- Tourists who plan to take photographs in China and in Southeast Asia should check ahead of time to make sure it's not prohibited in the area they're touring.

- The water in Asian lakes, ponds, and rivers (including the mystical Ganges) is often filled with microbes that North Americans have no resistance to. Swimming in Asian waters is generally a bad idea.

- Many of the regions here offer only the most basic conveniences; however, Australia, New Zealand, and Japan offer great luxury and comfort.

- Uninformed tourists often think all Asian nations have the same general customs. Not so. Differences among Japanese, Chinese, Korean, Thai, and Philippine cultures are as pronounced as those among, say, French, British, Italian, and Greek cultures.

- Treks have become a popular form of adventure travel; several areas in China, India, Nepal, and Bhutan offer trekking tours, but only hardy travellers who are prepared to walk for hours at high altitudes and sleep in a tent should consider a trekking tour.

- Costs in this vast region vary widely. For example, Japan is expensive, while China, Thailand, and Southeast Asia tend to be bargains.

TRAVEL TRIVIA

TOP TEN TROPICAL ISLANDS

1. Maui, Hawaii
2. Kauai, Hawaii
3. Phuket, Thailand
4. Bali, Indonesia
5. Bora Bora, Tahiti
6. Big Island, Hawaii
7. Moorea, Tahiti
8. Oahu, Hawaii
9. St. John, U.S.V.I.
10. Bermuda

Source: Condé Nast Traveller *readers' poll*

CREATIVE ACTIVITY

NAME _____   DATE _____

Based on the information in this chapter and in other sources, which 10 different Asia/Pacific destinations would you suggest to someone looking for each of the following? Be prepared to justify your recommendations.

1. Hiking:

2. Dry, warm climate:

3. A river cruise:

4. A rarely visited tropical country:

5. Diving:

6. An exotic cultural experience:

7. A bargain vacation:

8. Luxurious accommodations:

9. A stopover between Vancouver and Sydney:

10. A country that can be seen on a one-day visit:

INDONESIA

SOLOMON
ISLANDS

Darwin

INDIAN
OCEAN

CORAL
SEA

GREAT
BARRIER
REEF

Cairns

NORTHERN
TERRITORY

NEW CALEDONIA

AUSTRALIA

QUEENSLAND

Sunshine Coast

Alice
Springs

▲ Uluru (Ayers Rock)

SOUTH
PACIFIC
OCEAN

WESTERN
AUSTRALIA

SOUTH
AUSTRALIA

Brisbane

NEW SOUTH
WALES

Gold Coast

Perth

Fremantle

Windsor

Hawkesbury River

NORTH
ISLAND

Adelaide

Blue Mtns.

Katoomba

Sydney

Auckland

Rotorua ▲

Canberra

Waitomo Caves ▲

VICTORIA

NEW ZEALAND

Melbourne

Wellington

Phillip Island

TASMAN SEA

Mount
Cook ▲

Christchurch

INDIAN
OCEAN

TASMANIA

MILFORD
SOUND

Queenstown

Lake Wakatipu

Fiordland
National Park

Te Anau

SOUTH
ISLAND

CHAPTER 28

Australia and New Zealand

Where Things Are Jumping

It was the late 18th century. European explorers were finally making serious excursions to the strange, distant lands of Australia and New Zealand. Other experiences had prepared them for much of what awaited them: fierce Maori [MAH-ree] warriors; the bleak, reddish, desert-like Outback; the Alpine peaks of New Zealand. Similar things they had seen before.

But nothing could prepare them for the animals they found in this "land down under": kangaroos that can leap a span of eight metres; the koala, a bear-like little creature that lives in (and on) eucalyptus trees; and the platypus, a mammal with webbed feet and a duck-like bill that lays eggs. Indeed, the platypus is so weird that European zoologists at first thought it to be a patched-together hoax sprung on them by prankish sailors.

Visitors of today still find the fauna and flora of these two countries astonishing. That and the friendly reputation of their people are a powerful magnet for tourism. Indeed, Australia and New Zealand were two of the genuine travel industry success stories of the 1980s and still continue to draw more and more tourists.

When you sell this area, remember that it's much more vast than people may imagine. The continent of Australia is about the size of the contiguous United States. (But its population is only 19 million.) To its west is the Indian Ocean; to the east are the Coral and Tasman seas, which in turn open onto the Pacific Ocean.

The principal cities on Australia's charming but less visited western shore are **Perth** and nearby **Fremantle.** The nearer east coast is a more popular destination. Here are, from the northern state of **Queensland** to the southern state of **New South Wales,** the **Great Barrier Reef,** a 2000 kilometre stretch of coral that's generally accessed from the city of **Cairns** (which Australians pronounce CANS); the **Sunshine Coast,** a beach resort area north of the key city of **Brisbane;** the **Gold Coast,** an even bigger, Miami-like beach area that starts about 80 kilometres south of Brisbane; **Sydney,** Australia's largest and liveliest city; and inland **Canberra,** Australia's capital. Along the southeastern coast are three popular destinations: **Melbourne, Adelaide,** and the island-state of **Tasmania.**

And what's in the middle? Several million square kilometres of bleak, desolate brush and desert, called the **Bush** and the **Outback.** Still, there are two Outback attractions that tourists visit: **Alice Springs,** a frontier town that's a showcase for the culture and art of Australia's original dwellers, the aborigines [ab-uh-RIDGE-uh-neez]; and **Uluru** (better known as **Ayers** [AIRZ] **Rock**), a massive red stone that's best seen in the crimson light of sunset. Even more remote (and less visited) is **Darwin,** a port on Australia's wet, tropical north coast.

Australia is the world's smallest continent.

The genuinely bizarre creatures down under make a zoo or animal park visit an essential activity.

Tasmania was a British penal colony whose nickname was "Devil's Island."

The Great Barrier Reef is so big it's visible from the moon.

Capitals: AUS: Canberra
           NZ: Wellington

Populations: AUS: 20 100 000
            NZ: 4 000 000

Areas (square km): AUS: 7 686 526
                    NZ: 268 655

Religions: Protestant, Catholic

Time Zones: AUS: GMT + 8 to +10
              NZ: GMT +12

Language: English

Drive on: Left

Currencies: AUS: 1 AUS dollar = 100 cents
              NZ: 1 NZ dollar = 100 cents

Electricity: 240 volts, 50 cycles AC

Capsule History: **Australia:** Aborigine ancestors arrive, 30 000 B.C.; Dutch land here, 1606; British James Cook explores, leading to a British claim of possession, 1770; island remains a British penal colony until 1850s; gold discovered, 1851; Commonwealth declared, 1901; Australia Act severs many ties with Britain, 1986; Olympics held in Sydney, 2000.

New Zealand: Maoris, a Polynesian group, arrive and settle, 1300s; discovered by Dutch, 1642; Britain annexes from Maoris, 1840; Maori wars, 1845–1870; gold rush, 1861; declared nuclear-free zone, 1984.

For reference sources and suggested lengths of stay, see Appendixes A and B.

New Zealand, about 1900 kilometres to Australia's southeast, used to be a more difficult sell, since it didn't elicit the strong mental pictures that Australia does. No more. *The Lord of the Rings* movies—mostly shot in New Zealand—helped the public visualize the country's intense beauty. It's logical to visit New Zealand along with Australia. Its **North Island** has rolling green hills and considerable geothermal activity. **Auckland,** New Zealand's largest city, is here; as is **Rotorua,** a centre of Maori culture and powerful, steaming geysers. **Wellington,** at the southernmost tip of North Island, is New Zealand's hilly and increasingly cosmopolitan capital. The **South Island** (where much of *The Lord of the Rings* was filmed) is dramatically mountainous and colder, with many fjord-like inlets. Its chief cities are **Christchurch** and **Queenstown.**

HOW TRAVELLERS GET THERE

Virtually everyone from North America who visits the "land down under" arrives via jet. It's a long haul, though; from the West Coast it's more than 11 000 kilometres. And for travellers flying from any point farther east, it'll be even longer. Many flights stop in Hawaii, Fiji, or Tahiti to refuel. In fact, it's often possible to break up the long trip by stopping over for a pleasant day or two at one of several South Pacific island destinations.

Most Australia-bound travellers arrive through one of three gateway cities: Brisbane (BNE), Sydney (SYD), or Melbourne (MEL). Those heading to New Zealand usually land at Auckland (AKL) or Christchurch (CHC). And don't forget that travellers will be crossing the International Date Line (and therefore changing days) while airborne.

Several North American airlines fly to the region. A traveller can also be booked on the countries' principal carriers: Australia's **Qantas** (QF) and

Air New Zealand (NZ). Cruise ships sailing from North America on repositioning cruises often cross the Pacific and terminate in New Zealand or Australia, where they'll begin to operate their "down under" summer itineraries.

WEATHER PATTERNS

Remember that the seasons in these Southern Hemisphere destinations are the opposite of those in North America: The coldest weather is in June, July, and August, while summer heat arrives in January and February (see Figures 28-1, below, and 28-2, p. 486). New Zealand's North Island has cool and occasionally rainy winters (June to August), but warm and sometimes humid summers (January and February). The South Island is somewhat colder all year, especially in the mountains.

Australia has a warmer and generally drier climate than that of New Zealand. Cities such as Melbourne and Sydney have wonderful warm summers and mild, chilly-water winters—with relatively modest amounts of rain year-round. (Melbourne is a bit drier than Sydney.) Brisbane and Perth are even warmer, with more rain. Cairns and especially Darwin have a tropical climate (somewhat like Florida's or Mexico's coastal regions) with hot and rainy summers (January to March) and warm, dry winters. The climate of Australia's vast interior is Sahara-like.

High tourist season is December, January, and February, when the locals take their summer holidays and snowbirds hope to get away from the cold. Bargain rates are most likely in June, July, and August, except in mountain resorts and Queensland, which (because of their weather) become winter getaways for Australians and New Zealanders.

A surprising 40 percent of Australia lies within the tropics.

Woollens are a relative bargain, but so are opals, which are mostly gathered and polished in Australia.

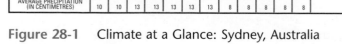

PEAK TOURIST SEASON ↑	↑	↑			⇩	⇩	⇩	⇩			↑	↑		⇩ TOURIST OFF-SEASON

	JAN	FEB	MAR	APR	MAY	JUN	JUL	AUG	SEP	OCT	NOV	DEC	
MONTH	JAN	FEB	MAR	APR	MAY	JUN	JUL	AUG	SEP	OCT	NOV	DEC	
AVERAGE HIGH TEMPERATURE	26	26	24	22	19	16	16	17	19	22	23	25	
AVERAGE LOW TEMPERATURE	18	18	17	14	11	9	8	9	11	13	16	17	
AVERAGE PRECIPITATION (IN CENTIMETRES)	10	10	13	13	13	13	13	8	8	8	8	8	

Figure 28-1   Climate at a Glance: Sydney, Australia

Chapter 28   Australia and New Zealand

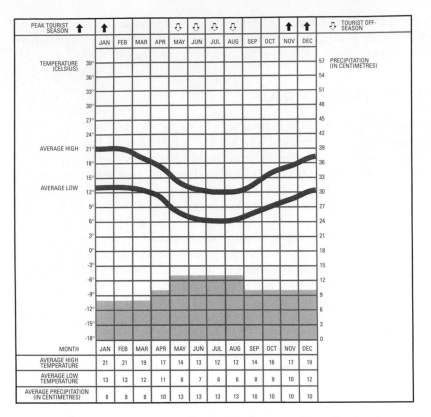

	JAN	FEB	MAR	APR	MAY	JUN	JUL	AUG	SEP	OCT	NOV	DEC
MONTH	JAN	FEB	MAR	APR	MAY	JUN	JUL	AUG	SEP	OCT	NOV	DEC
AVERAGE HIGH TEMPERATURE	21	21	19	17	14	13	12	12	14	16	17	19
AVERAGE LOW TEMPERATURE	13	13	12	11	8	7	6	6	8	9	10	12
AVERAGE PRECIPITATION (IN CENTIMETRES)	8	8	8	10	13	13	13	13	10	10	10	10

Figure 28-2   Climate at a Glance: Wellington, New Zealand

GETTING AROUND

Being so vast, Australia almost always requires air travel to get from one region to another. (It takes about four to five hours, for instance, to fly from Sydney to Perth.) Qantas and many regional airlines provide internal transportation. Ground transportation is also excellent, with a well-developed system of motor-coach and rail routes. Car rentals are an option, though driving is on the left (as is the case in most former British colonies). Several cruise lines service Australia, with stops at major port cities, or provide trips up the **Hawkesbury River.** Many tour operators offer excellent packages that can be booked ahead of time.

New Zealand's internal transportation options are much the same as Australia's. Since the country is relatively compact, however, visitors are more likely to drive around, take buses, or ride the train from one city to the next, especially on the North Island. (The South Island perhaps warrants flights between its more far-flung points of interest.) Cruises also call at the major New Zealand ports, often continuing on to (or coming from) Australia.

One final note: Each country boasts some rather famous train rides. In Australia, it's the **Indian Pacific** route (from Sydney to Perth) and the **Ghan** (from Adelaide to Darwin). Each affords a comfortable way of experiencing Australia's Outback. New Zealand operates its **Silver Fern,** which connects Wellington and Auckland.

IMPORTANT PLACES

Unlike some countries, Australia and New Zealand have clear-cut centres of tourism. Here are the most important:

Sydney

With nearly a fifth of Australia's population, Sydney is one of the world's most energetic, stylish, and progressive cities. Though Sydney is enormous in area,

New Zealand experiences about 400 earthquakes yearly. Almost all of them are so mild that they're not felt.

The Sydney skyline, with the Opera House and Harbour Bridge
Copyright COREL

most of its tourist sites are in a concentrated section near its fine harbour. Among the city's attractions are:

- **The Sydney Opera House,** an astonishing building with a design so unorthodox and original that it took years before anyone could figure out how to build it properly.

- **The Rocks,** the old, restored section of Sydney.

- **Kings Cross,** a nightclub, pub, and restaurant area that's Sydney's liveliest and rowdiest.

- **Harbour cruises** that afford a superb view of Sydney's lively waterfront area, hill-clinging skyline, and the landmark **Harbour Bridge.**

- **The Queen Victoria Building,** now converted into an attractive shopping centre.

- **Several nearby beaches,** including Bondi [BON-dye] and Port Jackson.

Short trips out of Sydney take visitors to **Botany Bay** (where Captain Cook's *Endeavour* anchored) and to several wild-animal parks (with up-close views of koalas and kangaroos). Similar parks exist throughout Australia. Three longer **day trips** can be recommended:

- **The Blue Mountains,** a scenic area that centres around the town of **Katoomba,** with its waterfall, railway (which travels steeply down into a valley), and skyway (a cable car that traverses between two cliffs).

- **Canberra,** Australia's sedate and isolated capital, which boasts some rather interesting modern architecture and a fountain jet not unlike Lake Geneva's.

- **Hawkesbury River cruises,** available out of **Windsor** (a city north of Sydney). Ships take passengers along the river's rugged gorges and into a national park. One- or two-day cruises are available.

Melbourne

Australia's second-largest city—a melting pot of diverse ethnic groups—is as cosmopolitan as any of the nation's urban centres. It's well known for its gardens

W W W

Because of its shape, the Sydney Harbour Bridge is called the "Coat Hanger." For a hefty fee, visitors can walk to the top of its high, arched superstructure.

The Blue Mountains got their name because of the blue haze given off by eucalyptus trees.

Melbourne is home to more Greeks than any other city in the world except Athens.

(Melbourne is sometimes called the "Garden City"), elegant stores, ever-present streetcars, sporting opportunities, and nearby ski resorts. Most hotels, restaurants, theatres, stores, and government buildings are within the city's "**Golden Mile**" district.

Just south off the coast from Melbourne is **Phillip Island,** one of Australia's most famous attractions. It's home to the "fairy" penguins—which, each day at dusk, march dutifully from the beach to their burrows. The area is well lit to ensure that tourists will see these creatures' waddling parade. (At certain times, though, the number of penguins dwindles, making for some disappointment.) Farther offshore is the island-state of Tasmania, with its slow pace, mild climate, and deep-green countryside.

Queensland

Queensland is to Australia what California and Florida are to the United States: a region of palmy splendour, striking seascapes, and booming growth. Queensland is vast: It's larger than Quebec. The state's principal points of tourism are, from north to south:

- **The Great Barrier Reef.** This 2000 kilometre strip is made up of hundreds of offshore coral islands. Resort hotels anchor many of the larger islands, and the diving, snorkelling, and marlin fishing here provide astonishing experiences. Cairns, at the Reef's northern end, is its principal gateway.

- **The Sunshine Coast.** This nearly 65 kilometre stretch of beaches, lakes, and mountains has a reputation for being less commercialized than its southerly competition. For vacationers who want relaxation or plenty of sporting opportunities, the Sunshine Coast is ideal.

- **Brisbane.** Queensland's capital is a lush tropical paradise, with superb landscaping and several animal sanctuaries just outside the city. It's about a 90-minute drive south of the Sunshine Coast.

- **The Gold Coast.** About an hour south of Brisbane, this beach resort area is Australia's most developed and crowded. It's somewhat reminiscent of Miami Beach, with many large hotels and resorts, as well as several family theme parks. (One well-known section is **Surfers Paradise.**) This is for the vacationer who wants seaside hustle and bustle, not a get-away-from-it-all vacation.

The Outback

The vast, arid, near-empty centre of Australia has an otherworldly quality that many visitors find absolutely intriguing. The art and culture of the aborigines, too, layer the region with even more mystery. Though vastly separate, two Outback attractions (usually reached by plane) probably merit attention:

- **Alice Springs,** a frontier town with many art galleries, and surrounded by an almost surrealist landscape of red hills and hard, flat desert. Many natural wonders are nearby.

- **Uluru** (Ayers Rock), a massive stone outcropping that's best seen at sunset, when its reddish hue is most striking. It's 300 metres high and 10 kilometres around, and is a holy site for aborigines. Nearby is the tourist oasis of **Yulara,** with its unorthodox, tent-like structures.

Perth

This, Australia's largest west coast city, is a sunny amalgam of parks, hills, and friendliness. Fremantle, a nearby town, is famous for its yachting, restored buildings, art galleries, and springtime flowers. Few Canadian tourists visit the Perth

Tasmanian devils do indeed come from Tasmania, but they hardly look like or behave like the cartoon character.

Off the coast of southern Queensland is the world's largest sand island: Fraser Island.

The Great Barrier Reef may be the largest living organism on earth.

Australians call people with red hair "bluies."

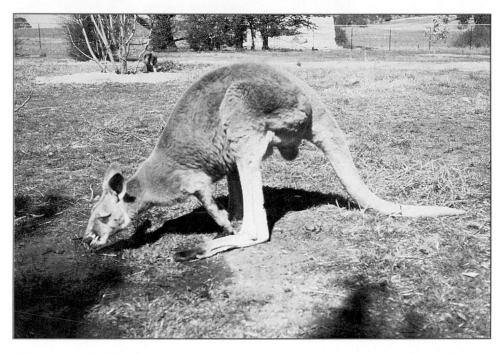

A kangaroo drinking water
Photo by Justus Ghormley

area, however, since it's a nearly 10-hour roundtrip from Australia's east coast. Still, Perth appeals to just about everyone who decides to see all of Australia.

New Zealand's North Island

New Zealand–bound tourists usually wish to see two cities: Auckland (New Zealand's largest city) and Wellington (its capital). Both cities, though lovely, are relatively small and quiet—the kinds of places with many little points of interest (best seen via a city tour).

Auckland's most notable sight is a waterfront theme attraction: **Kelly Tarlton's Antarctic Encounter and Underwater World.** Among the major attractions between Auckland and Wellington are:

- **The Waitomo** [why-TOE-mo] **Caves,** where thousands of glow-worms turn the ceiling of a deep grotto into a night-sky-like fantasy.

- **Rotorua,** a small city whose numerous features make it a must-see. First, Rotorua is an important centre of Maori native culture; its **Maori Arts and Crafts Institute** shows contemporary artists continuing the traditions of the country's first inhabitants. Second, Rotorua is the site of tremendous geothermal activity. Its thermal area boasts geysers, steam vents, and bubbling mud pots.

- **The Agrodome,** not far from Rotorua, an offbeat attraction where New Zealand's important sheep-raising industry is explained. It may sound boring, but it's not—visitors love it when 17 different kinds of "trained" sheep trot out to their appointed platforms on stage.

New Zealand's South Island

Colder, larger, and more mountainous than its northern neighbour, the South Island claims several world-class attractions. Christchurch (with its graceful peaks) and Queenstown (a scenic mountain resort town that boasts a very active nightlife) are both essential stops on a South Island itinerary. So, too, are the following:

A geyser in Rotorua, New Zealand
Copyright COREL

- **Mt. Cook,** with its awe-inspiring glaciers, most frequently visited via ski planes.
- **Milford Sound,** a dramatic, carved sea inlet that's part of New Zealand's picturesque **Fiordland National Park.**

Other possibilities: a visit to the **Te Anau** [TAY AH-now] glow-worm caves, a cruise on **Lake Wakatipu** (near Queenstown), or white-water rafting on any of several South Island rivers.

POSSIBLE ITINERARIES

Because Australia and New Zealand are so distant from Canada, vacationers, once they set out for this region, almost always wish to see as much as possible. Typical is a minimum 10- to 12-day itinerary that includes New Zealand's North or South Island and Australia's east coast, especially the areas around Sydney and Melbourne. Those with the time for a more extended vacation or on a second, in-depth trip will certainly want to see both of New Zealand's major islands and either Australia's west coast (with a stop at Alice Springs and Uluru) or the Queensland region. Finally, those seeking a tropical stay or wishing to drive often limit their stay to Australia's east coast, with perhaps a day or two in Sydney and the rest of the time along the Great Barrier Reef and the beach areas north or south of Brisbane.

LODGING OPTIONS

North American chains have a strong presence here, as do such local companies as Australia's **Rydges** and **Flag.** Both Australia and New Zealand have some deluxe properties (especially in Sydney and the Great Barrier Reef), but most of the accommodations in these countries tend to cluster at a mid-range, first-class level. Motels are popular; it's traditional here for motel rooms to have full kitchenettes, so this type of accommodation may appeal to families and the budget-minded. Home and farm stays can also be easily arranged—they're a wonderful option, since Australians and New Zealanders are among the world's friendliest people. Lists of farm and home-style accommodations are available from each country's tourist bureau.

ALLIED DESTINATIONS

Arranging a visit to any of the many Pacific islands that lie between North America and Australia or New Zealand is a wise and popular sales strategy. But other options exist. Singapore, Malaysia, Indonesia, and several other less-visited countries lie just to the north of Australia. Even Japan, China, the Philippines, and the nations of Southeast Asia are potential add-on destinations, since visitors are already flying across the Pacific and may feel that they might as well visit other transoceanic places if they have the time. Perhaps the most exotic option of them all: Antarctica. Several companies operate summer cruises from New Zealand to this bottom-of-the-world continent of ice.

CULTURAL PATTERNS

Most Canadians feel comparatively at home here. Yet Australia and New Zealand have their own customs:

- These are two friendly, very open nations, and visitors should feel comfortable about using first names in greetings.

- Though these countries are easygoing in their ways, customs are more formal than a visitor might expect. Punctuality, for example, is important in both countries. And New Zealanders tend to be more formal than Australians; for instance, they're likely to be restrained with strangers at first meeting.

- A gesture similar to the "thumbs up" sign is considered an obscenity here.

- Tipping in restaurants isn't common. As a visitor, you may wish to tip, but it's rarely expected.

- The food here was once considered bland. No longer. Foreign specialities have melded with post-British cuisine to create some wonderful culinary treats. Two major specialities: oysters and lamb-based dishes.

- Nightlife in New Zealand often features Maori-Polynesian entertainment. Australian nightlife ranges from informal pubs to several nightspots that pay homage to Australia's colourful frontier history, as well as to aboriginal music. It's all very touristy, but then again, the locals somehow give it an unjaded, gee-whiz treatment. (Visitors will probably tire of sheep-shearing demonstrations, though, which are done in so many tourist places that they'll half-expect the flight attendants to do it on the plane home.)

Vegemite is a yeast spread that Australians slather on their bread. (Frankly, it tastes awful.)

The word *kiwi* applies to a type of bird, a fruit, and a New Zealander.

FACTORS THAT MOTIVATE VISITORS

Awareness of what Australia and New Zealand offer is growing daily. Among the features you should emphasize are the following:

- Increasingly, New Zealand and Australia are being viewed as adventure destinations, both for soft adventure activities and "extreme" ones, such as bungee jumping and white-water rafting.

- Though distant and offbeat, Australia and New Zealand are culturally very accessible.

- The plants and animals are unlike those anywhere else in the world.

- The people are extremely friendly to tourists, have a wonderfully informal attitude, and speak English.

- Food and lodging are bargains, especially for those staying in motor inns.

- The Queensland beaches are superb and especially uncrowded north of Brisbane, and the diving along the Great Barrier Reef is legendary.

- New Zealand and Australia rarely feel hectic or crowded, except perhaps in Sydney and along the Gold Coast.

- The Aborigine and Maori cultures are intriguing. (However, they can be experienced only in certain areas, such as Alice Springs and Rotorua, respectively.)

- These countries bask in their most pleasant summer weather when many Canadians are shivering from winter's cold and are ready to get away for a warm-weather vacation.

- There's skiing in southeast Australia and in southern New Zealand, where many slopes are accessed only via helicopter.

- Both countries are extremely stable politically and have a relatively low crime rate.

POSSIBLE MISGIVINGS

Australia and New Zealand aren't for everyone. Here are some of the objections that may come up:

Perth is closer to Singapore and Jakarta than it is to Sydney.

- "It's too far." These countries are indeed a long flight from anywhere in Canada. You could break up the trip, however, by adding a stop in each direction (generally with little or no additional airfare) at a Pacific island resort. Travellers from the East Coast could pause a day or two in Vancouver, Los Angeles, or San Francisco.

- "It's too expensive." Airfares can be hefty, but bargain rates appear in the off-season. Once there, tourists can drive around, staying at motels or farmhouses.

- "We can't be away from work that long." If visitors limit themselves to one area of Australia or New Zealand, a roundtrip can be done in about nine days.

- "There's not all that much to see and do." You must explain the many wonders of this part of the world to offset such preconceptions.

- "We'd like to bring our children, but they'll have nothing to do." Again, most people don't know about Australia's beaches, New Zealand's family outdoor adventures, and so on. Furthermore, many children love animals, and both countries have plenty of weird ones. The one legitimate objection for families: the cost of airfare.

Qualifying the Traveller
AUSTRALIA AND NEW ZEALAND

FOR PEOPLE WHO WANT	HIGH APPEAL	MEDIUM APPEAL	LOW APPEAL	REMARKS
Historical and Cultural Attractions			▲	Some cities; Maori and aboriginal culture
Beaches and Water Sports	▲			In Queensland
Skiing Opportunities		▲		In southern mountains
Lots of Nightlife			▲	Sydney and Queenstown
Family Activities		▲		Children will find animals interesting; motor hotels plentiful
Familiar Cultural Experience		▲		
Exotic Cultural Experience		▲		Animals; Maori culture
Safety and Low Crime	▲			
Bargain Travel		▲		Flight expensive, but other costs reasonable
Impressive Scenery		▲		Bush and Outback impressively bleak; mountains and seascapes
Peace and Quiet	▲			In countryside
Shopping Opportunities		▲		Opals, woollens, leather
Adventure		▲		Especially in the Outback, areas near Darwin and South Island
To Do Business		▲		A common language facilitates business

SALES STRATEGIES

Expand a trip by suggesting that as long as they'll be going to Australia, why not add New Zealand, Fiji, Tahiti, or Hawaii? It will require just a short lengthening of their trip. Suggest a larger rental car, especially if the person expects to drive across Australia's vast stretches. Ski, cruise, and dive packages can all be sold in advance, as can city tours (especially appropriate in Sydney, Melbourne, and Auckland).

TRAVEL TRIVIA

MOST BIZARRE QUESTIONS TRAVEL AGENTS HAVE HEARD

- "When you travel to Australia do you have to fly backward or upside-down?"
- "Can I take a Greyhound bus to Europe?"
- "Do I need a visa for China? I prefer using MasterCard."
- "What time does the sun pass over the pool at the Flamingo Hilton in Las Vegas?"
- "Will there be any icebergs en route in the Caribbean?"
- "Could you book a room with an ocean view for me in Palm Springs?"
- "Can I take a seven-day Mediterranean cruise out of San Juan, Puerto Rico?"
- When an elderly lady was told she had to fly through Phoenix, she exclaimed, "Venus? I don't want to go to Venus!"

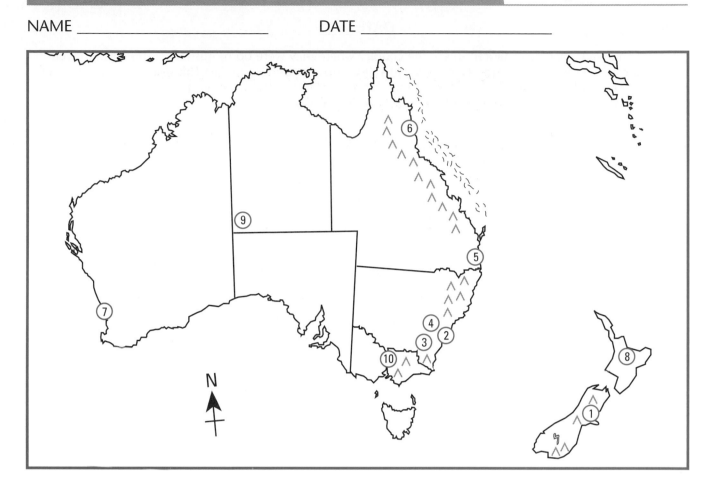

A traveller wants to visit the places listed below. Which number represents each on the map?

PLACE/ATTRACTION	IN/NEAR WHICH CITY?	NUMBER ON MAP
A. Australia's gateway to Queensland's beach resorts	A.	A.
B. A remarkable opera house	B.	B.
C. Fremantle's sister city	C.	C.
D. Geysers and steam vents	D.	D.
E. A famous rock	E.	E.
F. "Fairy" penguins can be seen south of this city	F.	F.
G. The Great Barrier Reef's air access city	G.	G.
H. The South Island's principal city	H.	H.
I. The Blue Mountains' principal city	I.	I.
J. Australia's capital	J.	J.

CASE STUDY

Geri Harding wants her two children to see the country where they were born, Australia. (The children were very young when the family moved from Sydney to Kamloops, British Columbia.) This will be a costly trip, so Geri would like to find some bargains. Geri can take as long as two weeks from her job as a high-school teacher. She wishes to go to Sydney and then travel around a bit by car.

Circle the answer that best suits their needs.

1. When would you suggest that they go?

   July   Christmas

   November   April

   Why?

2. Which of the following should you tell Geri about?

   The attractions in Sydney   The motor vehicles she can book

   The weather at the time she's going   The great driving distances between cities

   Why?

3. Which add-on foreign destination might be the most appealing to them?

   Fiji   Singapore

   Perth   Tokyo

   Why?

4. What might be the most appealing enhancement opportunity?

   Business-class flights   Sheep-shearing lessons

   A dive package   A larger-size car rental

   Why?

CREATIVE ACTIVITY

NAME _____   DATE _____

You're reading a magazine and see that Qantas is running a "Down Under Mystery Tour" contest. You're supposed to read the "Mystery Tour" description, guess each city or region the tour will visit, fill out the contest blank, then wait to see if yours will be chosen from among the correct entries to receive an all-expenses-paid trip. Here's the description:

> On the first few days you'll let off a little steam, have the wool pulled over your eyes, and see "stars" at noon. Two days later you'll pretend you're in Norway. Then it's across the water to someplace that everybody says is filled with cans. Next stop: a big reddish thing in the middle of nowhere. The next place is even stranger: It's for the birds, tuxedoed ones at that. We finish off with a drink on the Rocks.

PLACES THE TOUR WILL VISIT:

1.

2.

3.

4.

5.

6.

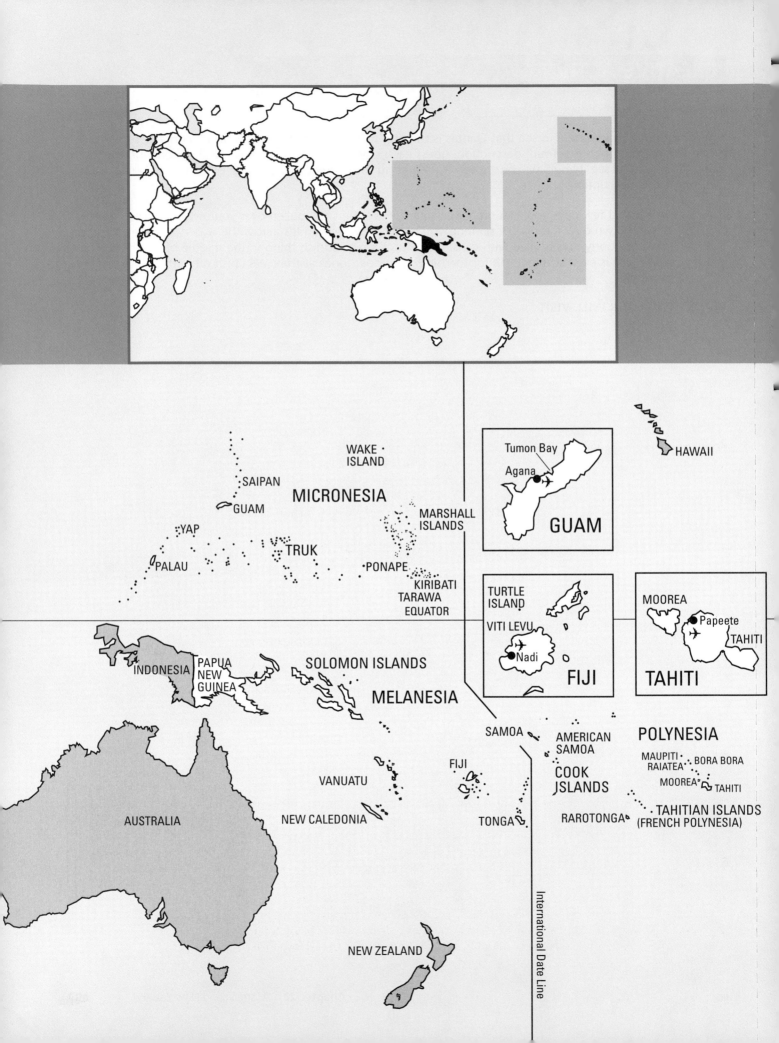

WAKE
ISLAND

SAIPAN

MICRONESIA

GUAM

MARSHALL
ISLANDS

YAP

TRUK

PALAU

PONAPE

KIRIBATI
TARAWA
EQUATOR

Tumon Bay

Agana

GUAM

HAWAII

TURTLE
ISLAND

VITI LEVU

Nadi

FIJI

MOOREA

Papeete

TAHITI

TAHITI

INDONESIA

PAPUA
NEW
GUINEA

SOLOMON ISLANDS

MELANESIA

SAMOA

AMERICAN
SAMOA

POLYNESIA

MAUPITI
RAIATEA

BORA BORA

MOOREA

TAHITI

VANUATU

FIJI

COOK
ISLANDS

AUSTRALIA

NEW CALEDONIA

TONGA

RAROTONGA

TAHITIAN ISLANDS
(FRENCH POLYNESIA)

NEW ZEALAND

International Date Line

CHAPTER 29

The Pacific

Fantasy Islands

How many islands dot the Pacific? Thousands. In fact, tens of thousands. Either coral or volcanic in origin, spreading across vast stretches of ocean waters, these islands have been the subject of fantasy to the Western mind since 1519, when the explorer Magellan first passed through them. No, you'll not have to learn all of their names and locations. Probably the world's foremost geography experts would have trouble doing that. Only about a dozen or so have become significant tourist destinations. Some of these islands or island groupings are independent countries. Others are under various levels of administration by France, Great Britain, the United States, and others.

The islands of the Pacific can be loosely divided into three regions. (The whole area is sometimes called **Oceania.**) North and northeast of Australia are the islands of **Micronesia.** Tourism in Micronesia is limited, except for **Guam** and **Saipan,** which appeal strongly to Japanese tourists. **Truk** [TRUCK], **Kiribati** [kir-uh-BAH-tee or kir-ih-BASS], **Yap,** and **Palau** (also spelled Belau) have an almost legendary appeal for divers.

Melanesia—so named for the natives' dark skin (*mela* means *dark*)—draws quite a few North American tourists, though the islands of this group appeal most strongly to Australians and New Zealanders. **Fiji** [FEE-jee] is by far the most popular, but **Papua** [PAP-yuh-wah] **New Guinea** and **New Caledonia** also have their devotees.

Polynesia is perhaps the best known of the South Sea island groups. Legendary for its romantic scenery, soft climate, and graceful native lifestyle, it extends, technically, all the way north to Hawaii (covered in Chapter 10), to Easter Island on the east, and to New Zealand on the west. We concentrate mostly on those dots of land to the immediate east of Melanesia—**Tahiti** and its nearby islands are the big draw here, but **Tonga, American Samoa, Samoa** (formerly Western Samoa), and the **Cook Islands** all have their admirers.

Two significant geographic lines cross the region. One is the International Date Line, which we spoke of in Part I of this book. It zigs and zags among the islands so that it crosses no major destination. (Otherwise, you could find yourself in another day just by crossing the street!) It zags just to the east of Tonga. As a result, Tonga is technically the place where each new day starts. (That's why some Tongan stamps proclaim, "Tonga—Where time begins.") The other significant line is the equator. In this chapter, we treat mostly those destinations south of it (they're called the South Seas), but remember that quite a few Pacific islands spill out north of the equator, including Hawaii and almost the entire area that is Micronesia.

HOW TRAVELLERS GET THERE

Several major North American airlines fly to these destinations from the West Coast and Hawaii, as do such foreign carriers as Qantas, Air New Zealand, Air France, and a number of Asian carriers. After travellers fly on a major airline to a principal gateway—**Papeete** [pah-pee-AY-tee], Tahiti (PPT); **Nadi** [NON-dee], Fiji (NAN); or Guam (GUM)—they'll need to hop aboard one of the dozens of local airlines to get to the less visited islands. Some of these connections will be cited later; remember, though, that air service in the region is in a constant state of flux.

Several tour operators specialize in air-hotel packages to the South Pacific; they can often save travellers hundreds of dollars—and booking and itinerary-planning time, as well. Cruise ships visit the area (sometimes on repositioning cruises) and all manner of ferries, yachts, and cargo ships unite the islands.

WEATHER PATTERNS

Since virtually every one of the Pacific islands lies within the tropics, the climate is relatively predictable: for Polynesia and Melanesia, May through October (winter season) is warm, fairly dry, and high tourist season, whereas November through April (summer season) is hotter, wetter, and sees a thinning of tourism. (Remember that Polynesia and Melanesia are mostly in the Southern Hemisphere, so their seasons are the reverse of North America's.) On the other hand, Micronesia—being largely north of the equator—has the best weather in its winter season, from November through March, when temperatures are milder. The Micronesian summer season (July to October) is rainy; hurricanes are a threat in the summer and fall.

Topography and location, though, can produce variations within these patterns. For example, visitors to Papeete (Tahiti) in August can expect it to rain only about one day a week, but someone visiting **Pago Pago** [PONG-o PONG-o] (American Samoa) during that same month may experience rain just about every other day. To predict the leeward (and, therefore, drier) side of a mountainous island is not always as easy to do as in other parts of the world, since this region stretches across several opposite wind patterns. In general, though, the rule we learned in Part I applies to these tropical islands: Western shores will tend to be drier and eastern shores will be rainier. For an example of a South Seas climate, see Figure 29-1.

Mosquitoes are ferocious and roaches are ubiquitous throughout the islands; bring repellent and get your inoculations against mosquito-borne diseases.

GETTING AROUND

When shopping, don't try to bargain for items. Among most islanders it's considered inappropriate.

Frequent flights and cruises connect the islands. On-island transportation is quite informal. Buses are usually a good option, since locals are often friendly and talkative. Mopeds and bicycles are a popular choice. Taxis are plentiful on the major islands, and visitors can often rent a car or taxi with driver for a day's sightseeing at a reasonable cost. How about car rentals? Well, they're available on the major islands; because of poor road conditions, a four-wheel-drive vehicle might be more practical. One thing to make clear: Don't expect the quality of service or efficiency of transportation to be anywhere near that of Canada's. Other options: helicopter rides, glass-bottom boats, and even horseback riding.

IMPORTANT PLACES

To bring some sense of order to this vast destination, we examine the principal islands according to their traditional cultural and geographic divisions: Polynesia, Melanesia, and Micronesia.

Figure 29-1 Climate at a Glance: Papeete, Tahiti

The chart shows monthly temperature and precipitation data for Papeete, Tahiti:

MONTH	JAN	FEB	MAR	APR	MAY	JUN	JUL	AUG	SEP	OCT	NOV	DEC
AVERAGE HIGH TEMPERATURE	32	32	32	32	31	30	30	30	30	31	31	31
AVERAGE LOW TEMPERATURE	22	22	22	22	21	21	20	20	21	21	22	22
AVERAGE PRECIPITATION (IN CENTIMETRES)	25	25	18	15	10	8	5	5	5	10	15	25

Polynesia

Polynesia—the word itself conjures up the scent of plumeria blossoms, the sounds of friendly voices, and the feel of warm, azure waters lapping at your feet. Visitors favour five Polynesian island groups:

THE TAHITIAN ISLANDS. The Tahitian Islands, also known as the Society Islands (an older term), comprise the western part of French Polynesia. Tahiti itself (with its capital, Papeete) is the principal gateway to the region's 130 or so islands. Papeete is a bustling little city, with an open-air market, several fine resorts, and a small museum displaying the works of French artist Paul Gauguin, who lived here. An interesting law—no building can be higher than a coconut tree—keeps Papeete and the rest of Tahiti free of view-spoiling high-rises.

There are many scenic areas on Tahiti itself, but even more dramatic scenery and the most extensive tourist lodging is on the nearby island of **Moorea** and on **Bora Bora** (which is 230 kilometres northwest of Tahiti). **Raiatea** and **Maupiti** have fewer lodging options, but are excellent get-away-from-it-all islands. One warning: French Polynesia is one of the most expensive island destinations in the South Pacific. Recommend French Polynesia to those who like water sports, all-inclusive resorts (which can blunt some of the high costs), and awesome scenery.

TONGA. Tonga has spectacular scenery—including several active volcanoes—and provides visitors with just about every water-sport opportunity available. Boaters love Tonga for its comparative absence of reefs. Tonga, which is still a monarchy, is made up of several islands; **Tongatapu,** where the capital is located, provides most of the modest lodging choices and, by Polynesian standards, is somewhat crowded. Travellers to Tonga will probably have to route through American Samoa, Samoa, Fiji, or Auckland.

AMERICAN SAMOA. Another mountainous (and picturesque) chain of islands, American Samoa has facilities even more limited than Tonga, but what is there feels

On French islands, locals often speak only French. But unlike many of France's residents, islanders will happily tolerate a tourist's high-school French.

In South Pacific hospitals, a significant number of injuries treated are coconut tree–related.

Cook's Bay, Moorea, Tahiti
Photo by Justus Ghormley

more American than Polynesian. In other words, it's appropriate for those who want to retain at least some of the feel and comfort of home. Deep-sea fishing is good here, as are hiking opportunities. Virtually all accommodations are in the town of Pago Pago. Travellers can fly to Pago Pago's airport from Fiji, Samoa, the Cook Islands, or Hawaii.

SAMOA. Samoa and its chief town, Apia, feel much more Polynesian than does American Samoa. Indeed, Samoa has the world's largest population of full-blooded Polynesians. Services, though, are limited; a growing influx of tourists may change that soon. For now, Samoa is still a bargain. Visitors can get here from Tahiti, Fiji, Tonga, American Samoa, or the Cook Islands.

THE COOK ISLANDS. Once sleepy and secluded, the Cook Islands are becoming more active, thanks to investment money from Australia and New Zealand. Rarotonga and Aitutaki islands have most of the hotels—several are deluxe. Most of the guests are from the lands down under, though the Cook Islands are increasingly popular with Canadian travellers. This would be an interesting, offbeat destination for those into snorkelling, diving, deep-sea fishing, or just beaching it. Travellers could be booked via Tahiti, Fiji, Samoa, or American Samoa.

Melanesia

Better known to Australians and New Zealanders (who are fairly close by), the islands of Melanesia are fast becoming destinations that appeal to Canadians. In some cases, they're destinations unto themselves, but more often they're stop-off points on the way to or from Australia and New Zealand. Two bits of trivia: Eighty percent of the Pacific's islander population lives in Melanesia, and nearly 1200 distinct languages are spoken throughout Melanesia—fortunately, English is one of them and it's spoken on many of the islands.

THE FIJI ISLANDS. The Fiji Islands have become among the most important of South Sea destinations. The large island of **Viti Levu** has many fine tropical hotels—especially on the west coast around Nadi (where the airport is located) and along the southern coast, which has come to be known as the **Coral Coast.** Hotels dot other shores of

Samoa was named after a sacred chicken.

Fijians are famous for their intricate tattoos and fire walking.

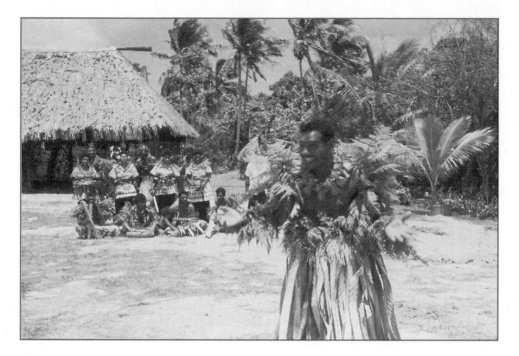

Villagers in Fiji
Photo by Justus Ghormley

Viti Levu, as well as those of other islands in the Fijian chain, including **Turtle Island,** a well-publicized, very expensive private resort. The rest of Fiji, though, is a comparative South Sea bargain and is quite popular with divers, shoppers, and culture seekers. (The islands' population is a not-always-harmonious blend of Polynesians, Indians, Chinese, and Europeans.)

PAPUA NEW GUINEA. Papua New Guinea occupies the eastern half of the large island of New Guinea, which lies north of Australia (the western half is part of Indonesia). This tropical destination is especially interesting for its native culture: Until fairly recently, some of its natives were Stone Age headhunters. A few areas of the country are quite modern, with many conveniences, but most are thoroughly primitive. Papua New Guinea is an expensive destination, political and social turmoil is frequent, and crime can be a problem. But divers love its offshore areas and nature buffs appreciate its huge variety of orchids and birds. Air connections are generally made through several Australian east coast cities, though flights also arrive from Singapore and New Zealand.

NEW CALEDONIA. New Caledonia is famous for two things: its superb diving (one of the world's largest barrier reefs lies offshore) and its capital city, **Noumea** [noo-MAY-uh]. Often called the "Paris of the Pacific," Noumea has a few elegant boutiques, some gourmet restaurants, and, not far outside town, a casino. Don't fall into thinking that this is another French Riviera; New Caledonia seems elegant only in comparison to neighbouring island destinations. Indeed, much of the island has a charming seediness about it. Yet, like other French islands, New Caledonia can be a rather expensive destination. A short flight northeast of New Caledonia are the islands of **Vanuatu,** with their impressive scenery, good diving, and surprising array of quality lodging.

New Caledonia means "New Scotland."

Bungee jumping originated on Vanuatu.

Micronesia

Thousands of islands, but all of them isolated and small—that's the best way to describe Micronesia. The islands of Micronesia weren't exactly household words until World War II, when news reports from Guam, Yap, Truk, and Saipan became

If you see geckoes (little lizards) in your room, encourage the creatures to stay. They chase insects while avoiding humans.

commonplace. In the period following the war, nuclear testing took place here; one site, the island of Bikini (part of the seldom-visited Marshall Islands), became permanently associated with a scanty form of bathing suit. Micronesia continues to be of military interest, but Canadian tourists are gradually finding out what Japanese tourists discovered decades ago: These islands are truly appealing destinations.

GUAM. Part of a collection of islands geographically known as the Marianas, Guam is Micronesia's principal destination. The U.S. military's growing presence here helps ensure air connections to Hawaii—and many Western amenities. Water sports and dramatic scenery are Guam's principal attractions. Most tourist facilities are around the capital, **Agana,** and on **Tumon Bay,** which is highly frequented by Japanese and Taiwanese tourists. Guam is also a gateway to most of the other Micronesian islands. Travellers who are into water sports, history (especially that of World War II), golf, and other comforts typical of Canada will find Guam appealing.

SAIPAN. Also part of the Marianas, Saipan is Micronesia's other well-developed tourist centre. It, too, owes its success to its reputation as a Japanese honeymoon destination. More so than Guam, Saipan is mostly geared to Japanese travellers, not Canadians. A strong point for most: It feels less military. Divers, windsurfers, golfers, and scenery lovers will find Saipan quite pleasing.

TRUK. Politically part of the Federated States of Micronesia (which also includes Ponape [PO-nah-pay] and Yap) and geographically part of the Caroline Islands, Truk is a legendary destination for divers. Here, the United States bombed and crippled the World War II fleet of Japan; 70 wrecks lie on the bottom of Truk's 64 kilometre lagoon harbour. Another diver's paradise in the Carolines (though accommodations are limited) is Palau, with its superb reef diving opportunities and picture-perfect tropical island scenery.

KIRIBATI. These flat atoll islands—stretching across almost 3200 kilometres of the Pacific—include the Gilbert and Phoenix island groups. Still relatively uncommercialized, Kiribati appeals to divers and others who want to get away from it all. Basic lodging is available on several islands, especially **Tarawa,** where the capital is located.

POSSIBLE ITINERARIES

There are two ways to consider the islands of the Pacific: as "pause-points" on the way to other places, or as a vacation's main destination. Polynesia and Melanesia can break up a trip to and from Australia and New Zealand. For example, travellers could fly to Fiji, where they might stay two or three days before they continue on to, say, New Zealand. They could then pause for a few days in Tahiti or Hawaii on the way back. Similarly, Guam or Truk could be a several-day pause between the mainland or Hawaii and such countries as Japan, China, the Philippines, Singapore, or any of the other Southeast Asian countries. Unfortunately, the flight connections may be a little difficult to arrange if the travellers need to use multiple airlines.

What of those travellers who want to visit only an island or combination of islands? It's best to keep them within one general island grouping. For example, a nine-day itinerary could include two flight days, four days on Moorea, and three days on Bora Bora. Another longer possibility would be to fly to Fiji for a three-day stay, then connect to two- or three-day stays in the islands to the east: Tonga, American Samoa, Samoa, or Rarotonga. Or hub out to the west, to such Melanesian destinations as New Caledonia and Papua New Guinea. Divers might enjoy a 9- to 14-day itinerary to the Micronesian islands of Guam, Truk, and Palau, with a more lively stay in Hawaii along the way. Cruises provide efficient itineraries between or among these island groupings.

○ Before World War II, Guam had no snakes. Now it has more snakes per square kilometre than anywhere else in the world.

○ Ask about tipping early on. On many islands, it's not the practice.

LODGING OPTIONS

The Pacific islands' range of accommodations is staggeringly wide. On Bora Bora, for example, you can stay in a deluxe hut that sits on piers over a lagoon; at an all-inclusive resort, like **Club Med;** or in simple, inexpensive bungalows. Among the Fiji islands is super-exclusive Turtle Island Resort, once featured on *Lifestyles of the Rich and Famous.* Or you can book into a New Guinean guesthouse run by the descendants of headhunters. For those seeking more conventional accommodations, many North American and international chains have properties throughout the Pacific.

At some of the over-water hotel properties, room service is delivered by canoe.

A few warnings: Even the most deluxe properties can be a bit disorganized and messy; reservations can be lost (bring a copy of the confirmation and pray); the locals on French islands sometimes don't speak English; bugs are everywhere in the tropics, including in the finest hotels; and some of the less-visited islands don't have anything but the most basic of lodging—one more reason to depend on independent tour packages that select hotels carefully and place more clout behind a guest's reservation.

In a poll of *Condé Nast Traveller* readers, the number-one factor that could spoil a tropical island vacation was a room overlooking a parking lot.

ALLIED DESTINATIONS

Polynesia and Melanesia are easily combined with trips to Australia and New Zealand. Micronesia can be a stopover to the Philippines, Singapore, Malaysia, and all of mainland Asia. You can also combine several islands into one vacation package, including some South Sea destinations that few tourists visit and that we've not mentioned here. For information on such islands (including Nauru, Niue, the Solomons, Tuvalu, Wallis, and Futuna), consult a more detailed resource.

CULTURAL PATTERNS

Each of these many islands has its own unique customs of which vacationers and business travellers alike should be aware. Among them are:

More languages are spoken in Papua New Guinea (700) than in any other country.

- In Fiji, time is informal and it may be acceptable to arrive quite late. Visitors to someone's home should remove their shoes before entering. The drink *kava* is often offered to guests; though it may taste harsh to Canadians, it would be considered rude to refuse it. (This also applies in Samoa.) When talking with a Fijian resident, crossed arms is a sign of respect.

- Though it's not necessary to tip in French Polynesia, small gifts are often given.

- In Samoa, an elaborate greeting is considered very respectful. It's rude for a person standing to sway while talking to a Samoan; indeed, almost all conversation is held while sitting.

- Completely give up the notion of punctuality or efficiency while in the islands; nothing here seems to work as it should. (Consider that at some small island airports, the air traffic controller is also the ticket-taker and the skycap!)

- To Tahitians, shaking hands is very important. Visitors to the home of a local should taste at least a little bit of everything offered and be prepared to eat with their fingers. And they should not praise any item in the home too highly; it may be presented as a gift.

FACTORS THAT MOTIVATE VISITORS

Among the motives that people may have for travelling among the islands of the Pacific are:

- They seek the legendary beauty and romance of the islands.

- They want to break up a long trans-Pacific trip.

- The climate is spectacular.

- Water-sport, beach, adventure tour, and cruise opportunities are widely available.

- The cultural differences are fascinating.

- It's a good way to visit many off-the-beaten-path, get-away-from-it-all destinations without too many inconveniences.

- The food is fresh and generally wonderful.

- Bargains can be had for those willing to put up with the barest of accommodations or with freighter transport.

- The scenery on the volcanic islands is dramatic.

POSSIBLE MISGIVINGS

Twice as many people are killed by falling coconuts than by sharks.

Perhaps you're in love with the South Pacific as a destination. Don't assume everyone else is. There are many potential objections to a South Sea vacation:

- "It's too expensive." This is a genuine concern; since most supplies are shipped to the islands, all costs are high, especially on French-governed islands. Suggest an off-season trip, when airfares are lower. Recommend one of the major islands, where a wide variety of services is available and air connections are easy. Suggest Fiji or Samoa, which are somewhat less expensive.

- "It's too far." The trip can indeed be long, with many potential connections if a lesser island is involved. A stopover in Hawaii can break up the initial long flight.

- "It seems too primitive for me." Suggest Fiji or Tahiti, where many conveniences are available.

- "I've heard of political unrest." On some islands, friction does sometimes occur between natives and the governing country or among different local factions. (This is especially true in Fiji.) Yet it seems that tourists are usually left alone here, even in revolutions. Still, check government advisories and give prudent, informed advice.

- "There aren't enough cultural attractions." The people and their way of life *are* the culture here, especially in the non-U.S. territories. If this is the type of person who loves Europe but not island stays, though, you may have to counter with a destination other than the South Seas.

- "We didn't like Hawaii and we won't like this." Find out why they didn't like Hawaii. Was it the overt commercialism? If so, perhaps the South Seas are exactly what they're looking for.

FOR PEOPLE WHO WANT	HIGH APPEAL	MEDIUM APPEAL	LOW APPEAL	REMARKS
Historical and Cultural Attractions		▲		Melanesian culture
Beaches and Water Sports	▲			
Skiing Opportunities			▲	None
Lots of Nightlife		▲		In hotels
Family Activities		▲		Families will enjoy it, but airfare prohibitive
Familiar Cultural Experience			▲	
Exotic Cultural Experience	▲			
Safety and Low Crime		▲		Some unrest
Bargain Travel		▲		Many bargains; flights costly
Impressive Scenery	▲			Seascapes, volcanic mountains, jungle
Peace and Quiet	▲			Much quieter than Hawaii
Shopping Opportunities		▲		Carvings, jewellery
Adventure	▲			Especially less-visited islands
To Do Business			▲	

SALES STRATEGIES

Independent tour packages and cruises are a sterling way to ensure maximum value and commission. All-inclusive resorts—common on some of these islands, not on others—often represent a good value. Dive packages, dive tours, and adventure jeep tours into an island's lush interior can often be booked in advance. Helicopter and even submarine rides are available on several islands. With someone who is worried about the quality of accommodations, up-sell to the best hotel possible and suggest an ocean-view room. For those who dread long flights, suggest business or first class.

TRAVEL TRIVIA

TOP TEN DIVE SITES FOR SERIOUS DIVERS

1. Great Barrier Reef
2. Micronesia (Truk/Palau/Yap)
3. Fiji
4. Solomon Islands/Vanuatu
5. Red Sea

6. Papua New Guinea/Irian Jaya
7. The Channel Islands (California)
8. Thailand/Myanmar
9. Galapagos Islands
10. Indonesia

Source: Beach Travel

MAP ACTIVITY

NAME _____   DATE _____

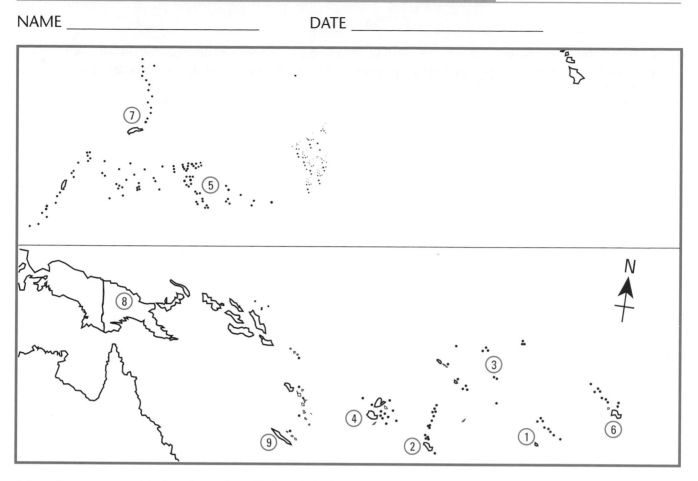

A traveller wants to visit the places listed below. Which number represents each on the map?

PLACE/ATTRACTION	ON WHICH ISLAND OR ISLAND GROUP?	NUMBER ON MAP
A. A monarch-ruled island	A.	A.
B. Nadi	B.	B
C. A Gauguin museum	C.	C.
D. Descendants of headhunters	D.	D.
E. Noumea, the Pacific Paris	E.	E.
F. Micronesia's gateway isle	F.	F.
G. Papeete	G.	G.
H. A legendary dive site from World War II	H.	H.
I. Pago Pago	I.	I.
J. Rarotonga	J.	J.

CASE STUDY

NAME _____   DATE _____

Larry Olson, who loves diving, comes to you with vague plans to visit some Pacific islands. His wife, Adrienne, is also somewhat of a diver, but still feels the need for a culturally interesting place. Since she tells you that in university she was a French major with an art history minor, you think of several possibilities. They tell you they can be away for as long as nine days. Mr. Olson, by the way, owns a large building materials firm and drove up to your office in a Mercedes.

Circle the answer that best suits their needs.

1. Where would you suggest as a primary destination?

   Truk   Palau

   Fiji   New Caledonia

   Why?

2. Which of the following would be a second destination that's nearby and would especially appeal to Larry?

   Tokyo   Tahiti

   The Philippines   Cairns

   Why?

3. Adrienne states that perhaps a hard-core diving trip could be postponed to another vacation, that this time it might be nice to stay at a Club Med and have a variety of activities. Larry agrees. What might you recommend?

   Bora Bora   The Thousand Islands

   Papua New Guinea   Samoa

   Why?

4. The Olsons like very comfortable lodging and you'd be glad to up-sell them to a fine hotel. Of the following, which would be the *least* likely to have a selection of deluxe hotels?

   Tahiti   The Cook Islands

   Fiji   Palau

   Why?

CREATIVE ACTIVITY

NAME _____ DATE _____

In the Creative Activity for Chapter 26, you judged whether a group of celebrities would like to visit Kenya and Tanzania. This activity is the reverse of that. Below are eight Pacific island destinations. Try to think of a famous person who might enjoy each destination (you must have a different celebrity for each one). Be prepared to explain how you arrived at your solution.

DESTINATION	CELEBRITY	WHY?
1. Moorea	1.	1.
2. Vanuatu	2.	2.
3. Tonga	3.	3.
4. Pago Pago	4.	4.
5. Papua New Guinea	5.	5.
6. Fiji	6.	6.
7. New Caledonia	7.	7.
8. Truk	8.	8.

CHAPTER
30

Japan

Pearl of the Orient

Mitsubishi, Toyota, Sony—these are names that the whole world knows. Yet until the 20th century, Japan—like some pearl hidden in an oyster—existed in almost complete isolation, a mystery to the world: small, unimpressive, largely unknown. Japan still is only a series of small islands in the shadow of that teeming behemoth, China. Yet a mere few decades after having faced defeat in World War II, Japan today powerfully influences world economics, business, and politics. It's a country of calm beauty and aggressive drive.

About the size of Newfoundland, Japan is bordered by the Sea of Japan to its west and the Pacific Ocean to the east. A spine of volcanic mountains runs along the western length of the country; indeed, most Japanese live along the country's eastern flank. One surprising fact: Japan is made up of not one, but more than 4000 islands. Only four, however—**Hokkaido** [ho-KYE-doh], **Honshu, Shikoku** [she-KOH-koo], and **Kyushu** [KYOO-shoo]—are populated to any great degree. And of those, it's Honshu, the largest, that dominates the country.

On Honshu, **Tokyo**—the world's largest metropolitan area—lies near the centre, on the east coast. **Kyoto,** an ancient city of great charm, rests in the

For buying electronic gadgets, visit Tokyo's Akihabara district, which packs 1000 shops into five square blocks.

FOR YOUR INFORMATION

JAPAN

Capital: Tokyo

Area (square km): 377 505

Time Zone: GMT +9

Drive on: Left

Population: 127 400 000

Religions: Buddhism, Shintoism

Language: Japanese

Currency: Yen

Electricity: 100 volts, 60 cycles AC

Capsule History: Contact with China, fifth century A.D.; first Shogun, 1185; Portuguese visit, 1542; trade between Japan and the West opens, 1854; parliamentary system, 1889; Pearl Harbor attack, 1941; Japan surrenders, after two atom bombings, 1945; full sovereignty, 1952.

For reference sources, and suggested lengths of stay, see Appendixes A and B.

south-central region of the island, and the port of **Osaka** (a major business destination) is just to its southwest.

Although the national language of Japan is Japanese, many people (especially travel personnel) speak relatively good English and are eager to communicate.

HOW TRAVELLERS GET THERE

Kansai Airport is on the world's largest man-made island. Unfortunately, it's slowly sinking.

Tokyo is Japan's gateway. **Narita** (also known as New Tokyo) **International Airport** (NRT) is where most international flights land. It's 69 kilometres to the northeast and the fares into Tokyo in regular taxis are incredibly expensive. Limousine buses, cars (booked in advance), and an express train are the best alternatives and can cost much less than a taxi would. Osaka's **Kansai International Airport** (KIX) is another popular option for Japan-bound travellers.

The world's tallest light-house is in Yokohama.

Nonstop service is available to Japan from Canada. Several North American carriers fly here, as do many international airlines, especially those based in Asia. **Japan Air Lines** (JL) is the national carrier; **All Nippon Airways,** also called **ANA** (NH), provides service as well. Flying time from Vancouver is 10 hours; from Toronto it's 13 hours. Japan is also a cruise destination. A few cruises start in **Yokohama,** just south of Tokyo, while others stop off at various Japanese ports (especially **Nagasaki**) as part of a longer Asian itinerary.

WEATHER PATTERNS

Japan's climate is temperate, though conditions are less than ideal; grey and drizzly days are all too common. (See Figure 30-1.) Summers are warm and humid, whereas winters are chilly. (Winter in Hokkaido and the northern portion of Honshu, however, is very cold.) Rain is common from March through October; only winter is relatively dry, with about five rainy (and occasionally snowy) days

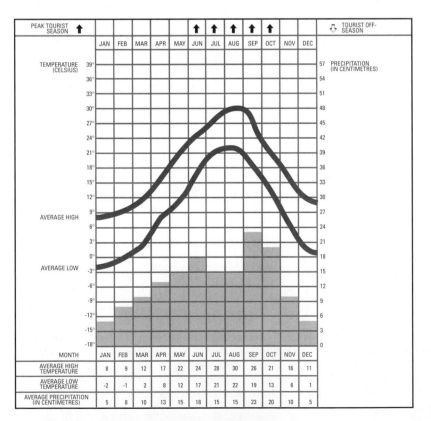

MONTH	JAN	FEB	MAR	APR	MAY	JUN	JUL	AUG	SEP	OCT	NOV	DEC
AVERAGE HIGH TEMPERATURE	8	9	12	17	22	24	28	30	26	21	16	11
AVERAGE LOW TEMPERATURE	-2	-1	2	8	12	17	21	22	19	13	6	1
AVERAGE PRECIPITATION (IN CENTIMETRES)	5	8	10	13	15	18	15	15	23	20	10	5

Figure 30-1 Climate at a Glance: Tokyo, Japan

per month. Spring is a legendary time to visit Japan; the cherry blossoms are in bloom, the temperatures are pleasant, and the rainy season hasn't quite reached its full strength. September to November can also be pleasant. Temperatures average in the upper teens during the day, and precipitation, especially in late fall, is less likely. (Typhoons bring heavy rains in early fall.)

A warning: Avoid travelling in Japan during major Japanese holiday periods because accommodations and transportation get very crowded. The days before and after New Year's are one such vacation time; mid-August (the Obon Festival) is another. Finally, Golden Week, April 29 through the first week of May, is the third big holiday period. Tourism thins out a bit during winter, but rates—especially hotel costs—don't drop very much. There's no real budget season in Japan.

GETTING AROUND

Japan Air Lines and ANA provide domestic flights between major cities. However, since most of the country's main tourist destinations are comparatively close to one another, air service may not be the most convenient mode of transportation. That honour falls to the famed bullet trains (*Shinkansen*), which hurtle down tracks at speeds up to 200 km/h. Every visitor to Japan should travel on at least a part of the bullet train route between Tokyo and Osaka: The *Hikari* train offers near-express service, whereas the *Kadama* provides more stops (especially helpful for tourists who wish to see the sights en route). The **Japan Rail Pass** is a useful option for those who intend to spend a good length of time in Japan; it allows unlimited rail travel and can be purchased only in North America. There also are regular service trains throughout the country, some of which are highly luxurious. (Note: A few trains are private and aren't covered by the Japan Rail Pass.)

Though car rentals are widely available, they're not the best idea. Because driving is on the left and most road signs are in Japanese, conditions can be extremely confusing. A better (though costly) alternative: a private car with driver or guide.

Tokyo and Osaka offer superb subways. The systems are frenetic, but not nearly as confusing as some might fear. (They're fairly well marked for Westerners.) Kyoto has a limited subway. Bus service in Japan is good and moderately priced. Avoid public transportation during rush hours. The kind of crowding that goes on may come as quite a shock.

Hailing taxis is not easy, especially late at night. Taxi stands are in many places, though.

During rush hours, Tokyo's subways have professional "pushers" who shove commuters into the packed cars.

IMPORTANT PLACES

Japan has many unusual places to enjoy. Keep in mind that the country is also an especially important destination for business travellers.

Japanese products aren't necessarily cheaper in Japan, but you'll probably find many items not yet available in North America.

Some of the rare shopping bargains: fine paper goods, toys, clocks, sugar novelties, children's clothing, and electric razors.

Tokyo

Tokyo, Japan's capital, is a paradox: futuristic yet deeply traditional; intensely crowded yet thoroughly efficient. It's Japan's centre of commerce, education, publishing, and entertainment, as well. This is a city of districts: The **Marunouchi** [mah-roo-NO-chee] district is where many corporations are found; **Shinjuku** [sheen-JOO-koo] is an entertainment and shopping district; Western, youth-oriented nightlife is in the **Roppongi** [roh-POHN-ghee] district; and the **Akasaka** is a centre for expensive nightlife and restaurants. Other major sites in Tokyo are:

* **The Ginza district,** one of the most recognizable areas of the city to Westerners. Its glittering neon shines on high-fashion shops, restaurants, theatres, and very expensive nightlife.

- **The Imperial Palace Plaza,** home of the emperor, in the centre of the city. Though the palace itself is closed to tourists (except on special occasions), the sprawling grounds are open; they feature a moat, park, and museum.

- **Tokyo Tower,** over 300 metres high, offering the best view of the city (as long as it's clear, which it seldom is).

- **Temples and shrines,** the most popular of which include the **Meiji Shrine** (with its sacred Shinto gardens) and the large, impressive **Asakusa Kannon Temple.**

- **The Ueno** [oo-EH-no] **district,** where several museums and a zoo are located. One problem for Westerners: Most of the signs are in Japanese only.

- **Tokyo Disneyland,** just outside the city. It's similar to its overseas cousins, but there are a few differences—some cultural, some practical. (For instance, "Main Street U.S.A." is covered with a canopy to keep out the rain.) Adjacent is **Tokyo DisneySea,** a maritime-themed amusement park.

Most visitors to Tokyo wish to travel out of the city and take some **day trips.** Among the attractions you can recommend are:

- **Nikko,** considered by many to be the most beautiful place in Japan. It's in a mountainous region two hours northwest of Tokyo by train. Its huge national park is spectacular, with glorious mountain views. The region is well known for the intricately carved **Toshogu Shrine** (the "see no evil" monkey carvings are here).

- **The Kamakura-Hakone region,** an hour southwest of Tokyo, often visited on the way to Kyoto and Osaka. Kamakura, an ancient government seat, is home to the **Daibutsu,** the Great Buddha (a 450 tonne statue more than 700 years old). Lake Hakone (also called Lake Ashi) provides a spectacular setting to view **Mt. Fuji,** the famous volcanic mountain. (That is, of course, if it's not shrouded in mist.)

There's an *indoor* ski facility near Tokyo.

Shoes should be removed before entering temples, homes, and rooms with straw tatami mats.

A gate in Nikko, Japan
Photo by Justus Ghormley

Kyoto

Surrounded by hills, this ancient, historical city—for 1000 years Japan's capital—is noted for its architecture, folk arts, and graceful beauty. Kyoto claims to have 2000 temples and shrines, not to mention many exquisite gardens. Kyoto's popular sites include:

- **The Imperial Palace,** the ancient royal residence dating to the 14th century. (Attendance is sometimes limited.)

- **Heian Shrine,** a vermilion-hued structure featuring exquisite gardens.

- **Nizo Castle,** a subtle 17th-century structure built for a shogun.

   The following **day trip** destinations are usually reached from Kyoto:

- **Nara,** the capital of Japan 1200 years ago and the origin of much of the country's art, religion, and government. It's only about a half-hour from Osaka and Kyoto. Its most famous attraction is the **Todaiji Temple,** considered the largest wooden structure in the world: It houses a 16 metre bronze Buddha. **Kasuga Shrine** has a lofty pagoda and a path lined with thousands of lanterns. Legendary is Nara's 520 hectare **Deer Park,** where the deer are so tame that they will nibble food right out of visitors' hands.

- **Hiroshima,** the first city ever to be devastated by a nuclear weapon. A very long day trip from Kyoto in southern Honshu, Hiroshima's **Peace Park** and other memorials are very moving.

Japan's largest park is in Nara.

Nara's deer are so aggressive that they'll poke into visitors' pockets and bags for food.

Osaka

Though often bypassed by tourists in favour of nearby Kyoto, Osaka—one of the main commercial and industrial centres of Japan—has much to offer. The city is one of the most frenetic in the world, with businesspeople constantly hurrying

Osaka's corporate centre is in the Nakanoshima district.

Osaka Castle
Chris McCooey/Shutterstock

from place to place and an astonishing array of stores and shopping malls. Among Osaka's main attractions are:

- **Osaka Castle,** a 16th-century structure that affords an excellent view of the city. A good museum is nearby.

- **Performances** of Kabuki drama, Noh theatre, and Bunraku puppet shows (all of which, frankly, can seem alien and perhaps boring to many Canadians).

POSSIBLE ITINERARIES

Japan is often visited as a business destination, but tourism is still quite important. The country is fairly compact, with most major attractions centred on Honshu island. First-time visitors could spend about a week here: a couple of days in Tokyo, a day trip to the Kamakura-Hakone area, and three or four days in Kyoto-Osaka-Nara. Return travellers may want to add visits to Nikko, Hiroshima, or the Imperial Villas. Some fine resorts are on the northern island of Hokkaido, including an excellent ski facility in **Sapporo,** where the 1972 Winter Olympics were held. (The 1998 Games took place in **Nagano,** on Honshu.)

LODGING OPTIONS

In Japan, beer can be purchased from vending machines.

Hotel accommodations in Japan are among the best run—and most wallet thinning—in the world. To save money, you might look into voucher programs sponsored by tour operators: Participating hotels are usually in the first-class and tourist-class categories and offer substantial savings. Another possibility is a business-class hotel; these offer quite small and very basic accommodations that are popular among Japanese businessmen, though they wouldn't be suitable for families. One other alternative: *ryokans,* or Japanese-style inns, which offer soaking baths and thin futon mattresses. (They also have Western-style rooms and tend to assume that foreign visitors prefer such accommodations.)

Tipping in Japan is considered inappropriate, except perhaps if a taxi driver helps with baggage. Tips *are* sometimes automatically added to a bill as a service charge.

Tokyo's hotels are scattered throughout the city. But the best ones are clustered in two places: the area around the Imperial Palace, and a section just west of the Shinjuku district. Plenty of lodging is available in the Narita Airport/ Convention Centre area.

Many North American and other international chains serve Japan. Among the best Japanese deluxe chains are **Okura, Akasaka, New Otani,** and **Rihga.**

ALLIED DESTINATIONS

Japan is just across the Sea of Japan from the nations of South Korea and China. Both are potential add-on destinations. Russia is also adjacent; most major Russian tourist destinations, however, are nearer Europe. The Philippines and the islands of Micronesia are sometimes add-on destinations for Japan-bound travellers. Southeast Asian countries such as Thailand, Malaysia, and Singapore aren't anywhere as close to Japan as many people imagine; however, considering the distance that most Canadians travel to reach Japan, it might be reasonable to recommend any of these nations to expand a trip. And don't forget: Hawaii may be a convenient way to break up a flight to or from Japan.

CULTURAL PATTERNS

The Japanese tend to dress conservatively. When doing business, dress in dark, muted colours.

Customs are of great importance in Japan. It's necessary that business travellers, and people on holiday, understand them.

- The Japanese are very formal in their introductions. Though handshaking is acceptable, bowing is still the custom; moreover, visitors should bow as low as they are being bowed to in return. Titles are commonly used when addressing one another, and first names are used only among the closest of friends and family.

- One's position holds great meaning in Japan and business cards are widely exchanged; make sure to bring some along, even if on vacation—you never know when a business contact will be made. (Bilingual cards are preferable and can usually be ordered through the hotels.)

- All dealings and relationships should be handled with restraint and reserve. And be sure to treat the elderly with the utmost respect.

- The Japanese are astonishingly helpful to foreign visitors. If you get lost, try to find someone who knows a smattering of English. That person will then probably escort you to wherever you're bound.

- This helpfulness extends to stores. Don't be surprised by all the attention you'll get from sales personnel.

- Bring a small gift when arriving at a business meeting or visiting a Japanese home; these gifts should be wrapped in pastel-coloured paper with no bows, and items that come in pairs (for example, pen-and-pencil sets) are often considered good luck. (By the way, over-complimenting an object in a Japanese home is a bad idea: It may be presented as a gift.)

- Though there's active nightlife in Japan, it doesn't go on until the wee hours. Because the subways don't run all night, restaurants and nightclubs close relatively early.

- If offered a gift, refuse once, modestly and calmly. Then accept it using both hands.

- Punctuality is important, especially for business meetings.

- The Japanese don't like to say "no" if it can be avoided. Instead, they often answer "maybe" or "it is very difficult." This is an important distinction to understand, particularly for travellers here on business, for they may misinterpret this to mean agreement with their position.

- Although individualism is prized in North America, the welfare of the group predominates in Japan.

- It's considered rude to point with one finger; use the whole hand.

- Business is almost never discussed until the participants have socialized considerably—sometimes for days.

FACTORS THAT MOTIVATE VISITORS

It's important to understand why someone might want to visit Japan. This is a wonderful country, but it's not for everyone. Some reasons for wanting to visit Japan are:

- It's a very important business destination.

- Japan has a unique, exotic, and ancient culture.

- Some visitors can trace their ancestry here.

- There's beautiful art and architecture.

- For an Asian nation, it's very Westernized and comfortable.

- Its level of service, efficiency, and creature comforts is astonishingly high.

- The countryside has great natural beauty.

The lyrics of the Japanese national anthem are over 1000 years old.

- It's an absolute heaven for golfers, though they may find courses to be somewhat smaller and more expensive than those at home.

- Japan is an extremely safe place to visit.

- The Japanese are incredibly helpful to visitors, who shouldn't be surprised if a local goes very much out of the way to help them.

- A full schedule of nonstop flights makes travelling from Canadian cities convenient.

POSSIBLE MISGIVINGS

Here are a few of the qualms that some people might have about Japan, and their counters:

- "Japan is extremely expensive, especially its food." Prices certainly can be high. This country is not for the budget conscious. However, there are many ways to keep costs down: You can book hotels through a voucher program or as part of a tour; travellers can get a Japan Rail Pass and take subways instead of cabs. As for food, beef is particularly expensive. Try eating at regular neighbourhood restaurants, sushi bars, and noodle shops rather than in fancy places. And, of course, tours—both escorted and independent—lock in prices and eliminate most financial surprises.

- "The Japanese language is terribly confusing." Many Japanese speak English, especially in business. English is often easier for many Japanese to read than to speak: If problems in communication do occur, you should write down what you wish to say.

- "I've heard that the Japanese don't get along with people who weren't born there." Travellers should know that the Japanese are exceedingly polite and gracious. Moreover, the country's relationship with North America is very good.

Plastic food in a restaurant window
Photo by Marc Mancini

- "Japanese culture is different; I'll feel lost there." Of all the Asian nations, Japan may be the most Westernized. Read a book on Japanese customs; it's a simple effort and tremendously helpful.

- "I know I won't like eating there; I've never liked sushi." Japanese cuisine is much more than just raw fish. For example, *yakitori* is skewered and grilled meats and vegetables, and *tempura* is deep-fried. There are many other styles as well, not to mention Western restaurants and fast food. One interesting custom: Restaurants display in the window the dishes they serve so that you can know what you'll eat. (The display food is, of all things, plastic, but incredibly realistic.) Menus are also posted outside.

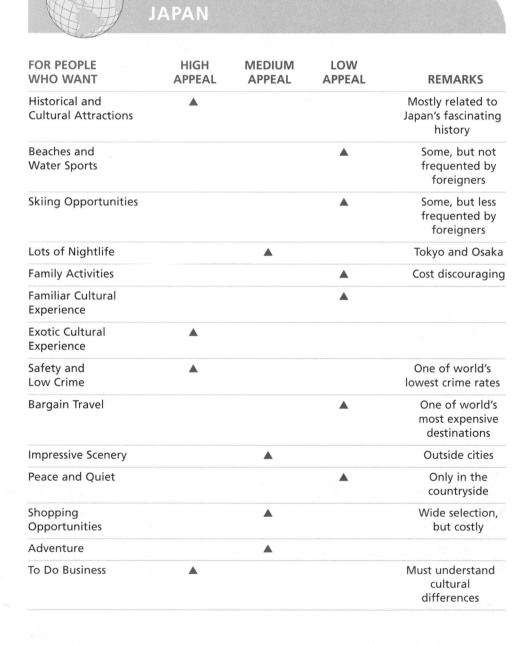

Qualifying the Traveller
JAPAN

FOR PEOPLE WHO WANT	HIGH APPEAL	MEDIUM APPEAL	LOW APPEAL	REMARKS
Historical and Cultural Attractions	▲			Mostly related to Japan's fascinating history
Beaches and Water Sports			▲	Some, but not frequented by foreigners
Skiing Opportunities			▲	Some, but less frequented by foreigners
Lots of Nightlife		▲		Tokyo and Osaka
Family Activities			▲	Cost discouraging
Familiar Cultural Experience			▲	
Exotic Cultural Experience	▲			
Safety and Low Crime	▲			One of world's lowest crime rates
Bargain Travel			▲	One of world's most expensive destinations
Impressive Scenery		▲		Outside cities
Peace and Quiet			▲	Only in the countryside
Shopping Opportunities		▲		Wide selection, but costly
Adventure		▲		
To Do Business	▲			Must understand cultural differences

SALES STRATEGIES

Because of its distance from Canada, Japan provides you with a wonderful option to break up the long flight by booking a stopover, like Vancouver, along the way. And since the country is so far away, some travellers might extend their trip—either within Japan or by visiting other nearby destinations. Because of Japan's unusual cultural, linguistic, and monetary conditions, vacationers are quite willing to consider all-inclusive escorted or independent tours. Though most tourists don't think of Japan as a resort or spa country, there are some fine ones here. A Japan Rail Pass is a good idea for those who intend to travel around the country over several weeks. Cruises are becoming a popular way to visit Japan's port cities.

MAP ACTIVITY

NAME _____   DATE _____

A traveller wants to visit the places listed below. Which number represents each on the map?

PLACE/ATTRACTION	IN/NEAR WHICH CITY?	NUMBER ON MAP
A. Toshogu Shrine and "see no evil" carvings	A.	A.
B. Imperial Palace Plaza	B.	B.
C. Todaiji Temple and tame deer	C.	C.
D. The Daibutsu (the Great Buddha)	D.	D.
E. Japan's capital for 1000 years	E.	E.
F. Nizo Castle	F.	F.
G. The Ginza	G.	G.
H. Peace Park	H.	H.
I. DisneySea	I.	I.
J. Heian Shrine	J.	J.

CASE STUDY

NAME _____   DATE _____

Jack Fujimoto has a small business that's just starting out and he's trying to land a major Japanese account. Though it's a stretch for his company, he's decided to fly to Tokyo for three days. As long as he has to go over anyway, the 40-year-old executive and his wife, Grace, have decided to extend this trip into a personal vacation; they may not have another chance for a while. She will fly over with Jack and they'll spend some extra days travelling around the country.

Circle the answer that best suits their needs.

1. What service would *not* be appropriate for the Fujimotos?

   A Japan Rail Pass   An independent tour

   A business-class hotel   A stopover en route

   Why?

2. Which of the following tips would benefit them?

   Buy a Japan Rail pass when you get there.   Take a cab from Narita Airport into Tokyo.

   Be prepared to dine relatively early.   Always tip at least 10 percent.

   Why?

3. How many days would you recommend for their pleasure trip after business is completed, if they go only to Japan?

   Five   Twelve

   Nine   Four score

   Why?

4. The Fujimotos decide that since they'll already be going as far as Japan, they might as well extend their trip three days to visit another country. They have to return to Tokyo for their flight home, so they don't want to travel too far. Which of the following destinations would *not* be appropriate for them to visit?

   Thailand   South Korea

   Hong Kong   Taiwan

   Why?

CREATIVE ACTIVITY

NAME _____   DATE _____

Since you're in the travel industry, your friends often ask you for free advice. But this time the request is unusual: Your neighbours' daughter will be on her school's team in a provincial geography competition. She's been told that one of the destinations that will be focused on is Japan, but that any other global destination may also come up. Can you help coach her?

You discover that she knows plenty about the world's cities and attractions, but not much about Japan. You give her a book on Japan to study. You also set up a little training exercise for her. You create a list of Japanese attractions and challenge her to come up with an equivalent somewhere else in the world. She must explain her choice. (You hope this will help her "connect" what she already knows about the rest of the world with what she's now learning about Japan.) You should also predict a possible answer for each, just in case she can't think of one.

JAPANESE PLACE/ATTRACTION	EQUIVALENT ELSEWHERE	WHY
e.g., The Imperial Palace	Buckingham Palace, London	Both homes to monarchs, rarely open to public.
1. Tokyo Tower		
2. Mt. Fuji		
3. The Ginza		
4. Hiroshima		
5. Osaka Castle		
6. Sapporo		
7. Tokyo Disneyland		
8. Yokohama		
9. Narita		
10. The *Shinkansen*		

TRAVEL TRIVIA

WORLD'S MOST POPULOUS ISLAND COUNTRIES

1. Indonesia
2. Japan
3. Philippines
4. United Kingdom
5. Taiwan
6. Sri Lanka
7. Madagascar
8. Cuba
9. Dominican Republic
10. Haiti

Source: Island Information, Joshua Calder

CHAPTER 31

Singapore and Thailand

Crossroads of Asia

The great trader ships of yesteryear must certainly have been a sight, with their sails billowing in the wind. Bound for China and India from the South Pacific, they had but one direct route: through the **Strait of Malacca** at the tip of the **Malay Peninsula.** Lying at the peninsula's southern end was the major port of Singapore, and just to the north was Siam. Today, Singapore remains one of the world's busiest ports, and Siam, now known as Thailand [TIE-land], has stayed—through wars, massive migration, and an unending onslaught of trade—a strong, independent nation. At the cornerstone of a continent, both glory in their rich mix of cultures. And for both their past and present, they represent two of the world's most intriguing destinations.

SINGAPORE AND THAILAND

Capitals: SING: Singapore
THAI: Bangkok

Populations: SING: 4 400 000
THAI: 65 400 000

Areas (square km): SING: 586
THAI: 513 428

Religions: Buddhism, Christianity, Islam, Taoism, Hinduism

Time Zones: SING: GMT +8
THAI: GMT+7

Languages: SING: Mandarin, Malay, Chinese, Tamil, English
THAI: Thai

Drive on: Left

Currencies: SING: 1 dollar = 100 cents
THAI: 1 baht = 100 satangs

Electricity: 220 volts, 50 cycles AC

Capsule History: **Singapore:** Founded as separate entity by Sir Stamford Raffles, 1819; separate British Crown colony, 1946; independence, 1959; part of Malaysian federation, 1963; separate republic, 1965.

Thailand: Separate identity beginning sixth century A.D.; British dominate, 1824; absolute monarchy ends, 1932; Japan occupies, 1941–1945; many refugees migrate into Thailand, 1978.

For reference sources and suggested lengths of stay, see Appendixes A and B.

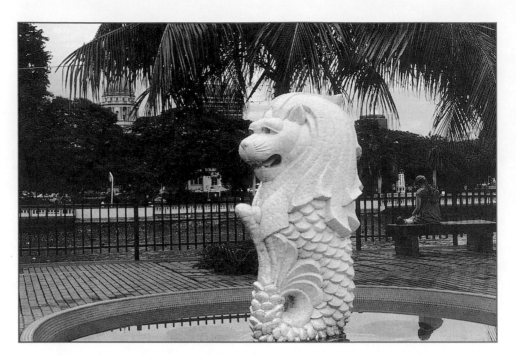

The symbol of Singapore: The merlion

Photo by Justus Ghormley

Food in Singapore, and especially in Thailand, can be very spicy.

Originally a British colony, Singapore is a unique island—it's both a city and a self-contained country. Thailand is approximately the size of Yukon. Its capital, **Bangkok,** lies slightly north of the Gulf of Thailand, just before the country thins out and winds its way down the peninsula. It's here that you'll find two of the country's popular resorts: **Pattaya Beach** on the south coast and **Phuket** [poo-KET] **Island** just off the west. **Chiang Mai,** the second-largest city, is in the hilly north.

Thailand's national language is Thai, though English is widely spoken, especially by travel personnel. In Singapore, because of the particularly diverse origins of its populace, there are actually several official languages: Malay, English (which is predominant in the business and travel industries), Mandarin Chinese, and Tamil.

HOW TRAVELLERS GET THERE

Two major gateways serve this region: Singapore and Bangkok. Singapore is accessed by its national carrier, **Singapore Airlines** (SQ), which flies into **Changi International Airport** (SIN) (praised by many as the world's finest airport), as do other North American and international airlines. Flights from Vancouver take nearly 18 hours. Singapore is also one of the world's busiest seaports and is a common embarkation and stopping point for cruises. In addition, Singapore is linked by causeway to the adjoining nation of Malaysia and can be reached from Malaysia by train. The national airline of Thailand is **Thai Airways** (TG); it and other North American and international carriers land at **Bangkok International Airport** (BKK). Cruises call near Bangkok and at Phuket.

WEATHER PATTERNS

The temperatures of these two areas are quite similar (see Figures 31-1 and 31-2). Both are generally hot and muggy year-round, with little variation in temperature. Singapore, particularly, is stunningly consistent, since it's so near the equator: It averages a high of around 30°C, down to around 24°C, 12 months a year. Though there's plenty of rain in every season, November to January are Singapore's wettest months. March and September are especially uncomfortable—cooling breezes are minimal or nonexistent.

Figure 31-1 Climate at a Glance: Bangkok, Thailand

Figure 31-2 Climate at a Glance: Singapore

Unlike Singapore, Thailand has relatively little precipitation from November through April; May through October are the rainiest months. The hottest months of the year are March through August, with highs in the mid-30s and lows in the low 20s. November through February is the coolest time, with temperatures somewhat lower—though it's still pretty warm (but nights can get chilly). Typhoons and monsoons can affect travel in the late summer and fall.

Tourism is fairly consistent year-round in Singapore, though the period from June through August draws more tourists than any other. The same situation prevails in Bangkok, though January and February are off-season—a surprising fact, since Bangkok weather is at its best in the winter. (It's because Thais leave Bangkok for the southern beach cities at this time of year; as a result, tourism peaks at beach resorts such as Phuket in the winter, in complete reversal of the patterns for the rest of the country.)

 There are stiff penalties in Singapore for jaywalking and littering, and smoking is prohibited in many public places.

GETTING AROUND

It's relatively easy to get around Singapore: Many taxis patrol the streets and they're reasonably priced. (The main business district has a restricted area during early hours for vehicles with a minimum number of passengers; those who are there mainly for business should be sure to check the restrictions.) The bus system can be confusing. Three-wheeled "trishaws" can be an unusual way to travel; settle on a price first.

Cars in Singapore cost five to six times their original, overseas value. Two families sometimes share one car.

Bangkok's canals are called *klongs*.

Thailand has a good bus system and fairly good trains. The roads are basically sound, but avoid them during the rainy season. In Bangkok, the hotel-run taxis are more expensive than private ones, but they're a little better. Because there are many canals through the city, river taxis can be a fun and inexpensive way to travel. The streets are crowded, so renting a car is a bad idea. Thailand's major cities are connected by air. And, of course, the two countries—and the nations around and in-between—are interconnected by flights and cruises. A luxury train, the **Eastern & Oriental Express,** makes the 1600 kilometre run between Singapore and Bangkok; some departures continue on to Chiang Mai.

IMPORTANT PLACES

Singapore and Thailand offer visitors a rich mix of cultures, superb scenery, and many ancient monuments. Tourism concentrates on the following areas.

Singapore

Singapore has the highest rate of personal savings and home ownership in the world.

Singapore is a very contemporary city—and one of Asia's most prosperous. (It's also the second-most densely populated country in the world, after Monaco.) It's one of the world's busiest ports and a major business destination. The 4.2 million residents are largely of Chinese descent; yet there remains a strong British influence left over from colonial days. Singapore boasts famous shopping, fine dining, active nightlife, and a well-scrubbed look. Among the most popular attractions:

- **Haw Par Villa** (formerly Tiger Balm Gardens), an offbeat attraction with grottoes, statues, amusement rides, and a superb view of the sea. Other gardens you should recommend are the **Japanese Garden,** the **Chinese Garden,** and the **Mandai Orchid Garden.**

- **Chinatown, Little India,** and **Arab Street,** charming, fun, and interesting neighbourhoods that offer excellent shopping and great food.

- **The National Museum,** which houses the renowned Aw jade collection.

- **The Singapore Zoological Gardens,** considered one of the world's finest zoos. It has a "night safari" so visitors can see nocturnal animals.

- **Jurong Bird Park,** a colourful and extremely large home to more than 3000 birds from around the world.

Among the several **day trips** from Singapore that you might want to suggest are:

- **Kusu,** a popular island resort. Turtles are a major attraction here. (According to legend, the island itself was a turtle at one time.)

- **Sentosa,** another active island resort located nearby, with many recreational activities and several major resort hotels. Also here is **Underwater World,** a US$20 million oceanarium.

- **Malaysia,** which begins just across the Strait of Malacca. **Johore Baharu** is the Malaysian town closest to Singapore; a bazaar and sultan's palace are its prime attractions. (We examine Malaysia—a major destination in its own right—more fully in Chapter 33.)

Bangkok

Bangkok is a chaotic, noisy, densely populated city, yet its spirit, friendliness, and heritage make it a top-class travel destination. The **National Museum** has an excellent and extensive collection of Oriental artifacts. However, what visitors notice first are the temples. Hundreds of them embellish the city skyline. Among the most popular sites are:

While visiting Malaysia in the 1960s, Jim Thompson disappeared under mysterious circumstances.

- **The temples**, of course (called *wat* in Thai). The most striking ones are the soaring **Wat Arun** (Temple of the Dawn), which offers a great city view; **Wat Trimitr** (Temple of the Golden Buddha), with its 4.5 tonne, solid-gold carving; **Wat Po** (Temple of the Reclining Buddha), with a 60 metre statue; and the beautiful **Wat Benchamabophit** (Marble Temple).

- **Cruises** on the city's meandering **Chao Phraya River** and canal waterways.

- **Jim Thompson's house,** the residence of an American silk merchant, which contains remarkable, beautiful Asian artwork.

- **The Grand Palace,** the royal residence, once a walled fortress. Also a part of the complex is perhaps Bangkok's most famous site, **Wat Phra Kaeo** (Temple of the Emerald Buddha).

- **The Pat Pong,** the city's notoriously wild nightclub, bar, and shopping district.

Not far from Bangkok lie several fascinating destinations for **half-day trips.** Those you should be most aware of are:

- **The Damnoen Saduak,** an aromatic floating fruit and vegetable market, about an hour southwest of Bangkok.

- **The Rose Garden Cultural Centre,** less than a half-hour west of the city, with its beautiful flowers, authentic dance performances, and array of outdoor activities. This is a comprehensive cultural experience that most visitors enjoy.

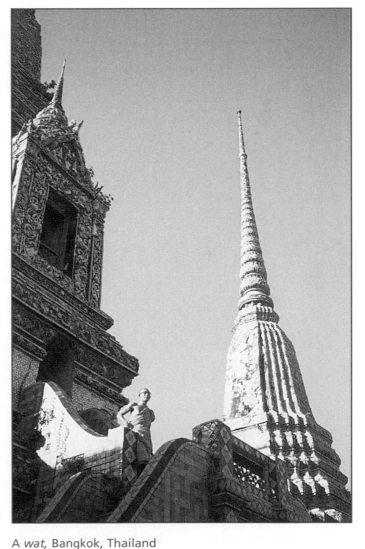

A *wat*, Bangkok, Thailand
Photo by Justus Ghormley

Among the **day trips** from Bangkok are:

- **The Bridge on the River Kwai,** which many will recognize from the famed movie. It really does exist; it's in **Kanchanaburi,** west of Bangkok. Allied prisoners of war were forced to build the bridge during World War II in order for the Japanese to move their supplies into Burma.

- **Nakhon Pathom,** with the biggest Buddhist monument in the country. Nakhon Pathom can be combined with the trip to the River Kwai bridge.

- **Ayutthaya** [ah-yoo-TYE-uh], Thailand's capital until 1767. North of Bangkok and usually accessed by bus or a river cruise boat, it offers interesting archaeological sites, ruins, and museums.

- **Tropical resorts,** most notably the world-class Pattaya Beach—a somewhat polluted and unsavoury, yet lively and (in most places) luxurious city that's a two-hour drive south of Bangkok; and Phuket—a lush tropical island with particularly lovely scenery and towns. Phuket is about a one-hour flight south of Bangkok. It seems to be going the same way as Pattaya: Overdevelopment and pollution are becoming a problem. Less crowded is **Ko Samui,** on the east side of the peninsula. Several of Thailand's beach resorts were hard hit by a 2004 tsunami, but reconstruction is helping them regain their vitality.

- Beyond Phuket are a number of dramatic, rocky, uninhabited islands that tourists can visit via a "long-tailed" boat. **Phang Nga** [PONG GAH] **Bay** is especially famous, with its gorges, caverns, and limestone pillars.

Chiang Mai

Located in the northwest corner of Thailand about an hour's flight from Bangkok, this compact walled town is the second-largest city in Thailand. It offers temples and museum art that are quite different from those of southern Thailand. The **Po Ping Palace,** which has beautiful gardens, is the summer home of the royal family. Chiang Mai is also an excellent base for trips through the nearby hills, national parks, teakwood forests, and tribal villages. Many modes of transportation are common: elephants, river rafts, and on-foot trekking. You should make sure, though, to book with a reputable guide or tour company; otherwise, this beautiful but primitive area can be unpleasant at best and dangerous at worst. The cities of **Chiang Rai** and **Mae Hong Son,** though less known, are perhaps better starting places for treks into the wilderness.

POSSIBLE ITINERARIES

For those travellers interested in visiting Singapore and Thailand as their sole destination (rather than as part of a larger tour of Southeast Asia), you should suggest a minimum of 10 days. Starting with two or three days in Singapore, they could then head up to Bangkok for a couple of days. A short jump to the north and to Chiang Mai would help round out the trip, as would a visit to one of Thailand's resorts, notably Phuket and the small offshore islands. Such a vacation could easily be extended, depending on how much the travellers would like to more fully explore the sites and ruins around Bangkok. Return visitors might wish to spend more time on the beaches.

LODGING OPTIONS

Singapore boasts an extremely famous inn, **Raffles Hotel,** a place of English colonial gentility. The **Goodwood Park Hotel** is a Singapore national landmark. In addition to these two legendary hotels, Singapore boasts a number of other world-class luxury hotels. Many hotels here are clustered in the **Orchard Road** and downtown areas. Most North American chains are present in Singapore.

A first-class chain headquartered in Thailand is **Dusit Hotels.** The **Siam Lodge Group** is moderately priced. Most hotels in Bangkok are located on and especially to the east of the Chao Phraya River. Bangkok, like Singapore, features several hotels world-famous for their level of luxury and service. Phuket also has some super-deluxe lodging, especially the **Amanpuri Resort Hotel.** One interesting practice at many Thai hotels: Christmas Eve and New Year's Eve lodging requires a supplementary charge for a mandatory dinner-celebration at the hotel.

Tipping is uncommon in Singapore and Thailand (though it may be included on restaurant and hotel bills as a service charge).

ALLIED DESTINATIONS

The most obvious allied destination for Singapore and Thailand is Malaysia, which is sandwiched between the two countries. Burma (Myanmar) also borders them, as do Laos and Cambodia, though political turmoil may make it less likely that you'll book these countries. Nearby are Vietnam, the Philippines, Indonesia, and the island of Borneo. Parts of China and India are also a fairly short jet trip away. Thailand and Singapore are commonly reached as part of cruises of Southeast Asia.

CULTURAL PATTERNS

The customs of Thailand and Singapore will likely seem unfamiliar to most Westerners. Business travellers, especially, will want to understand the traditions of those with whom they will be dealing.

- When visiting Thailand, always return a *wai* greeting (where one's hands are held together at the chest like a prayer and then a slight bow is given).

- Certain gestures in Thailand and Singapore carry meanings different from those in Canada. For instance, never point a finger or foot toward another person.

- Remember to remove shoes before entering a temple. Female visitors should dress modestly and cover their heads when visiting religious attractions.

- Don't pause on the doorsill of a house; this is where Thais believe a spirit lives. Guests shouldn't feel obligated to bring a gift when visiting. Moreover, they shouldn't overcompliment one of their host's possessions: It may later be presented to them.

- Never pat a Thai child (or for that matter, an adult) on the head.

- Both countries expect punctuality for meetings.

FACTORS THAT MOTIVATE VISITORS

Among the reasons to visit these countries are:

- The culture is intriguing.

- The food is superb.

- They are easily visited as part of a cruise.

- The countryside is beautiful.

- The weather is consistently warm all year.

- There are several first-rate beach resorts and super-deluxe hotels.

- The people are friendly toward tourists.

- Singapore, especially, is one of the cleanest and most modern cities in Asia and a comfortable one for people apprehensive about the Far East.

POSSIBLE MISGIVINGS

Here are a few of the objections some may have about the area:

- "It's polluted and crowded." Bangkok and Pattaya are indeed choked with traffic and pollution. Suggest only a short stay in Bangkok and more time in the countryside. Singapore is spotless.

- "I hear there are guerrillas and in-fighting in Thailand." Most of the dangerous areas are away from tourist areas. If the itinerary emphasizes Bangkok and the major cities, visitors will likely be safe, though parts of Bangkok and Pattaya Beach are a bit rowdy and seedy.

- "Southeast Asians dislike Westerners." In fact, the locals are extremely friendly.

Qualifying the Traveller
THAILAND

FOR PEOPLE WHO WANT	HIGH APPEAL	MEDIUM APPEAL	LOW APPEAL	REMARKS
Historical and Cultural Attractions	▲			Especially Buddhist temples
Beaches and Water Sports		▲		Excellent, but less known outside Asia
Skiing Opportunities			▲	None
Lots of Nightlife	▲			Lively and even notorious
Family Activities			▲	
Familiar Cultural Experience			▲	Western amenities but exotic locale
Exotic Cultural Experience	▲			
Safety and Low Crime		▲		
Bargain Travel		▲		Especially outside Bangkok
Impressive Scenery		▲		Wide variety
Peace and Quiet		▲		Outside Bangkok
Shopping Opportunities	▲			Silks, precious stones, gold, antiques, wood items
Adventure		▲		Especially in the Chiang Mai region
To Do Business		▲		Singapore more so than Thailand

- "I don't like to rough it." Singapore is quite modern and Bangkok has most Western conveniences. However, excursions out of Chiang Mai shouldn't be recommended to such a person.

- "I'm afraid of drinking the water." The water in Singapore is very safe; in Thailand, drink only bottled beverages.

- "The Thai language is strange and I can't read their signs." English is widely spoken in Thailand and Singapore, especially by travel personnel. Many signs in Thailand have English printed along with the Thai words.

SALES STRATEGIES

The region is a particularly good one for packaged tours—either city tours of Singapore or hosted tours of Thailand—and they are the best way to fully comprehend each place's cultural complexities. And because Malaysia is situated directly between these two countries, you could easily cross-sell a trip to Kuala Lumpur and Malacca. In addition, Vietnam, the Philippines, and Indonesia are nearby, as are some other interesting destinations; you might suggest that travellers extend their visit, as long as they're in the area. Because low-end hotels can be risky, higher-rated accommodations are far preferable. Cruises are a way to package these two destinations into an efficient, high-commission package.

TRAVEL TRIVIA

PLACES WITH DRAMATIC VIEWS

- The Masada Plateau, Israel
- Machu Picchu, Peru
- The Pali Lookout, Oahu
- St. Mark's Campanile, Venice
- The Empire State Building, New York City
- Mont Royal, Montreal
- The 10th floor of the Samaritaine Department Store, Paris
- Telegraph Hill, San Francisco
- Swissotel Stamford Hotel (70th floor), Singapore

- Mulholland Drive, Los Angeles
- Victoria Peak, Hong Kong
- Pincio Hill, Rome
- The Eiffel Tower, Paris
- The Roof of St. Peter's, Vatican City
- The Skylon Tower, Niagara Falls
- Borobudur Tower, Indonesia
- Corcovado Mountain, Brazil
- Great Wall of China, Badaling

A traveller wants to visit the places listed below. Which number represents each on the map?

PLACE/ATTRACTION	IN/NEAR WHICH CITY?	NUMBER ON MAP
A. Wat Arun	A.	A.
B. Po Ping Palace	B.	B.
C. Haw Par Villa	C.	C.
D. The Bridge on the River Kwai	D.	D.
E. Jim Thompson's house	E.	E.
F. One of Asia's cleanest cities	F.	F.
G. The former Thai capital	G.	G.
H. Raffles Hotel	H.	H.
I. A Thai island resort	I.	I.
J. The Grand Palace	J.	J.

CASE STUDY

NAME _____   DATE _____

Karen Wise, age 29, will fly to Singapore in January on business. She hasn't had a real vacation in almost two years and has decided to stay in the area for eight days. She has money to spend and is interested in fairly active sightseeing. She's used to comfort, though, and doesn't particularly care to rough it.

Circle the answer that best suits her needs.

1. She wants to stay at a fine hotel while in Singapore, preferably one she's heard about that's English colonial style. Which of the following would be best?

   Raffles Hotel   The Amanpuri Resort

   The Victoria Princess   Underwater World

   Why?

2. What cultural suggestion would *not* be appropriate for you to give to her?

   Never point a finger at a Thai.   Try to return a *wai* greeting.

   Don't ever jaywalk.   Meetings rarely start on time.

   Why?

3. Karen decides that because she's been working so hard, she'd like to kick back and relax for a few days in Phuket. Which of the following should you tell her?

   It will be high season.   Rent a car and do a day trip to Bangkok.

   Thai food is very mild.   Visit Jim Thompson's house.

   Why?

4. This business trip is a special one; Karen doesn't expect to get back to the area for quite a while. She'd like to see as much as possible. What destination could you suggest she add to her trip (from Singapore up to Thailand), without too much inconvenient flying?

   Burma   Malaysia

   Indonesia   Micronesia

   Why?

CREATIVE ACTIVITY

NAME _____   DATE _____

You've taken tests on travel geography. Now is your chance to make a test. Pretend that you're a teacher and create a 10-question, multiple-choice quiz on Singapore and Thailand. Make sure your questions cover important information, use travel-related language, and are creative. Indicate the answers on a separate answer key. (Your instructor may ask you to swap tests with another student.)

For example: Which of the following would *not* be an easy add-on destination to Singapore?

a) Thailand   b) Benin   c) Malaysia   d) Indonesia

1.

2.

3.

4.

5.

6.

7.

8.

9.

10.

China

Of Red and Gold

Two colours—red and gold—hold positions of great symbolic importance to the Chinese. In ancient times, red signified good luck, and gold was a colour exclusive to the emperors. Today, these hues have taken on other meanings. Red is often used to refer to China's communist regime, begun under Mao Zedong. And gold is the perfect colour to symbolize the money currently pouring into the vast, yet largely untapped, market that is China. And now that Hong Kong has become part of China, it is money, not an emperor, that rules.

China—or, more officially, the People's Republic of China—is a noteworthy land, not merely for its history, culture, size, and population; it's remarkable, as well, that so important a nation is so poorly known to outsiders. China is the world's third-largest country, slightly smaller than Canada; its population is over 1.3 billion (almost 40 times greater than the Canadian population). One-fifth of all the people in the world live here, providing a potentially huge marketplace for investors, both Chinese and foreign.

China has only one time zone, though it spans six.

Virtually the entire Chinese population lives in the arable eastern half of the country; the west is mountainous, sparsely populated, and extremely dry. Bordered on the east by Russia, North Korea, the Yellow Sea, the East China Sea, the Pacific Ocean, and the South China Sea, it's easiest to envision the major cities of China as if on the rim of a left-facing crescent. At the one o'clock position of the crescent, in northeast China not far from the coast, is **Beijing** (formerly Peking), the capital. Heading clockwise, **Shanghai,** the largest city and main port, is located at three o'clock. In the southeast is **Guangzhou** [GWANG-JOE], the city closest to **Hong Kong** and with the most contact with the West. **Macau** [muh-COW] (sometimes spelled Macao) is a close neighbour to Hong Kong.

China's recorded history goes back 4000 years.

Guilin, considered by many to be the most beautiful area of China, is near the crescent's bottom. Out at the crescent's far tip, at about seven o'clock, is mountainous **Tibet** in the Himalaya. Considered to be the basis of the Shangri-La legend, Tibet is a popular tourist destination. It's on the south-central border and is more often visited as part of a trip to Nepal and India. And in the centre of this Chinese crescent are the astonishing archaeological treasures of **Xian** [she-AHN], the ancient capital of China.

Many regional dialects are spoken in China, but the main languages are Mandarin and Cantonese. Not many people here understand English, though some of the major tourist personnel may be helpful. This is one of the reasons escorted tours are almost always the mode of choice on a visit to China. English is spoken by almost everyone in Hong Kong.

CHINA

Capital: Beijing	Religions: Buddhism, Confucianism, Taoism
Area (square km): 9 560 249	Languages: Mandarin Chinese, English (in Hong Kong), Cantonese and Portuguese (in Macau)
Time Zone: GMT +8	Currency: China: 1 yuan = 100 fen H.K.: 1 Hong Kong dollar = 100 cents Mac: 1 pataca = 100 avos
Drive on: Right	Electricity: 220 volts, 50 cycles AC
Population: 1.3 billion	

Capsule History: Feudal states unite, 246–210 B.C.; arts flourish, 618–907; Mings rule, 1368–1644; Manchus invade and rule, 1644; Hong Kong ceded to Britain, 1841; Korea, Taiwan, and other areas ceded to Japan, 1895; Boxer rebellion, 1900; republic declared, 1912; communists take power, 1949; Tibet annexed by China, 1951; Red Guard revolts, 1966–1967; Mao dies, 1976; student revolt quelled, 1989; Hong Kong merges into China, 1997; Macau merges into China, 1999.

For reference sources and suggested lengths of stay, see Appendixes A and B.

HOW TRAVELLERS GET THERE

The two main Chinese gateways are **Hong Kong International Airport** (SAR) and Beijing's **Capital International Airport** (PEK). There is some direct service to Beijing from Canada by both domestic and international carriers, as well as by China's two national air carriers, **Air China** (CA) and **China Eastern Airlines** (MU). Both domestic and international carriers, including Hong Kong–based **Cathay Pacific** (CX), also serve Hong Kong. North American travellers will face long flights, often with connections. Flying time to Hong Kong or Beijing is about 14 hours from Vancouver and about 19 hours from Toronto; it takes 11 hours from Honolulu, a frequent stopover for cross-Pacific trips. A flight from Hong Kong to Beijing takes 2.5 hours; from Tokyo, it's 3.5 hours.

Shanghai and Hong Kong are also very popular ports for either extended cruises or general boat arrivals from Japan. China can be reached via train from Russia (which borders the country to the north). And travellers may access China from India, Nepal, or Vietnam.

WEATHER PATTERNS

China produces more cotton and tobacco than any other country in the world.

The climate in much of China is similar to that of the United States, though the temperatures tend to be more extreme: hotter highs and colder lows. Generally, the north is colder and the south (except for Tibet, which can be extremely cold) is warmer, rainier, and more humid. Late fall to early spring can bring dust storms in the north, while monsoon rains sweep across the south coastal regions in late summer and early fall. Western China is very dry.

Beijing has a wide swing of temperatures, not only from season to season but also from morning to night. From March to May and again from September to November, the highs average in the upper 20s; nights, however, can drop below zero. Summer in Beijing can be very hot—as high over 30°C during the day—whereas winter ranges from near zero to –10°C. A somewhat hot rainy season takes place from June through August, making spring and fall the best times to visit Beijing.

Figure 32-1   Climate at a Glance: Hong Kong, China

MONTH	JAN	FEB	MAR	APR	MAY	JUN	JUL	AUG	SEP	OCT	NOV	DEC
AVERAGE HIGH TEMPERATURE	18	17	19	24	28	29	31	31	29	27	23	20
AVERAGE LOW TEMPERATURE	13	13	16	19	23	26	26	26	25	23	18	15
AVERAGE PRECIPITATION (IN CENTIMETRES)	3	5	8	13	30	41	38	36	25	13	5	3

The climate in Hong Kong and Guangzhou is much steadier (see Figure 32-1). Late fall, winter, and early spring are particularly nice, with temperatures in the mid- to upper 10s. Summer can be brutal: From May to September there's plenty of rain, occasional typhoons, high humidity, and daytime temperatures around 30°C.

As for tourism patterns, China generally sees a drop-off of tourism from early December to early April. Spring and fall are high season, with summer a slightly off-peak time.

GETTING AROUND

China is so huge, air transportation is often the best way to get around. Air China, China Eastern, and Hong Kong–based **Dragonair** (KA) are the primary domestic air carriers. As for train travel, you should book a top-class soft berth. It's a bit expensive, but it's clean, comfortable, and worth the extra cost. Tourists can't rent a car (except in Hong Kong). You can book a driver with a car in advance, however; in fact, you can get a car, driver, and guide for a surprisingly reasonable price. Boat cruises are a popular way to travel along the **Yangtze, Li** [LEE], and **Yellow** rivers, as well as portions of the ancient **Grand Canal.**

Within most cities, taxi service is good, but get a cab from a hotel; long waits anywhere else are common. (This is why it's often a good idea, on reaching the destination, to ask the driver to stay and keep the meter running, even if it might cost quite a bit.) Buses are very crowded.

Hong Kong is a different matter. The subway system is excellent and easy to use, with English signs and diagrams. Taxis are plentiful. Ferries are the easiest way to get around the harbour—the historic **Star Ferries** are renowned. Buses and double-decker trams are crowded, but visitors should take the cog railway up to **Victoria Peak** for the best view of the city. Rickshaws in Hong Kong are for tourists only and are very expensive. (Make sure to settle on a price first.) And car

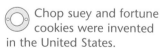 Kublai Khan had much of the Grand Canal constructed.

Chop suey and fortune cookies were invented in the United States.

rentals are an option, though Hong Kong is so compact and crowded that renting a car isn't always a good idea.

IMPORTANT PLACES

China offers superb, exciting, and dramatic destinations. Here are the most important ones:

Beijing

Beijing, the capital of China, is the country's economic and cultural centre. Like many of China's major cities, it's extremely crowded. There's some good and diverse shopping in the city. Many temples are scattered throughout Beijing, and the zoo here is noted for its pandas. But it's the grand and graceful structures of Beijing that clearly stand out. Among them are:

- **The Imperial Palace** (once known as the Forbidden City), the home of 24 Chinese emperors. Commoners were not allowed inside (hence the "forbidden" city). One of the world's greatest attractions, this walled complex covers 100 hectares and encloses 800 structures—each more dramatic than the last.

- **The Temple of Heaven,** a complex of structures whose pagoda-like **Hall of Prayer for Good Harvests** houses what may be China's most exquisite room.

- **Tiananmen Square,** the largest public square in the world and the centrepiece of Beijing. Here Mao raised the flag of the People's Revolution. A giant portrait of him still looms over this 40 hectare plaza. The **Great Hall of the People,** site of the National People's Congress, sits on the western side of the square. Opposite it are the **Museum of Chinese History** and the **Museum of the Chinese Revolution.**

Beijing offers several **half-day trips,** including:

- **The Great Wall,** a structure that's perhaps even more spectacular than people imagine. This architectural wonder is, from end to end, more than 4500 kilometres long. That's greater than the distance from Vancouver to Quebec City.

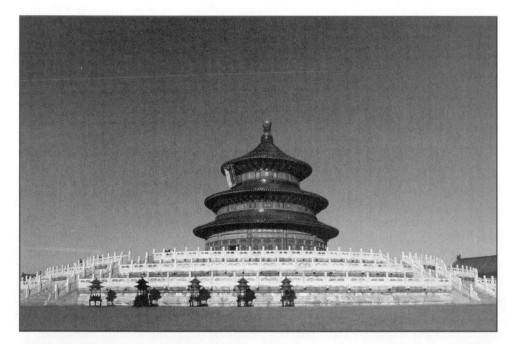

The Temple of Heaven, Beijing
Wang Sanjun/Shutterstock

However, because the ever-winding wall is full of twists and turns, it's actually about 16 000 kilometres long. The most popular site to visit this 2300-year-old structure is at **Badaling,** 76 kilometres from Beijing. To walk along the wall's top is unforgettable—but also exhausting, for in Badaling it snakes up and down some rather steep hills.

Legend says that construction workers who died on the job were buried in the wall.

- **The Ming Tombs,** at **Shin San Ling,** usually combined with a visit to Badaling. Thirteen emperors are buried in its cavernous but now largely empty halls.

- **The Summer Palace,** on the outskirts of Beijing, in use for more than 1000 years. The central palace and its extensive grounds are elegantly situated on a lake. One of the oddest sights here is a stone "boat" built with navy monies by an empress.

Shanghai

Shanghai is the largest city in China and its major port and commercial centre. Because it was one of China's first international ports, Shanghai is one of the nation's most cosmopolitan cities. Its skyline is now dominated by many dramatically modern high-rises, visible symbols of China's new, booming economy. There are attractive gardens, such as the **Yu Yuan** (Mandarin's Garden), open markets, museums, a children's palace, the **Bund** (a European-like, water-skirting boulevard), a zoo with pandas, and the famous Shanghai Acrobats. Among the other sites are:

Bund sounds German, but it's actually a word from India that means "an embankment used to control the flow of water."

- **Pudong New Area,** across the river from the Bund, affording great views of Shanghai.

- **The Temple of the Jade Buddha,** a particularly beautiful structure, with a 2 metre white jade Buddha brought from Burma.

- **Longhua Park,** a charming area that houses the ancient **Longhua Temple and Pagoda** and a well-known jade-carving factory.

- **The Shanghai Museum,** which contains one of the world's best collections of Chinese furniture, brass, and jade. The **Shanghai Art Museum** contains more contemporary works.

There are several interesting destinations near Shanghai. In fact, since many of these lie along the 1000-year-old Grand Canal, the best way to enjoy them might be via cruise. Among the most popular **day trips** are:

- **Suzhou** [SOO-JOE], a city known for its many gardens (the **Humble Administrator's Garden** is anything but humble), as well as numerous canals. Suzhou has also been renowned for silk since the Sung Dynasty. The **Yunyan Pagoda** at **Tiger Hill** is a popular stop.

- **Wuxi** [WOO-SHE], a city of gardens, canals, and pagodas.

- **Hangzhou** [HAWNG-JOE], an exceptionally pretty city. Though its temples, canals, and lakes alone would make Hangzhou scenic, the city's abundance of gardens are what really make it stand out.

The Yangtze River

This legendary river (called Changjiang in Chinese) is a popular cruise destination; there's superb scenery along several parts of its 5500 kilometre length. Though the river can be reached by a short flight from Shanghai to **Wuhan,** it's best to start farther west, at the historical city of **Chongqing** (also known as Chunking) and travel downriver to the east, ending at Wuhan. The 189 kilometre stretch known as the **Three Gorges** is dramatic and spectacular, as the river wends its way through the mountains. Unfortunately, a new dam has been built and the

In its upper stretches, the Yangtze is 3050 metres above sea level.

rising water will soon make the Three Gorges far less impressive and may sharply reduce tourism to this region.

Guangzhou

Because it's only 130 kilometres from Hong Kong, Guangzhou (better known to North Americans as Canton) has had much contact with Westerners. Guangzhou is a very active trading and commercial centre. This is a frequent destination for business travellers; in fact, its Trade Fair attracts huge crowds from all over the world. (Check with Chinese travel authorities about the dates: Many business travellers will want to go at that time; everyone else will want to avoid it.) Guangzhou boasts great shopping, some fine temples, a museum of history, and an excellent zoo (of course, with pandas).

Guilin

Guilin offers exceptional, strange beauty—many consider it to have the most spectacular scenery in China. Li River cruises, which depart from Guilin and generally last six hours, float past dreamlike rock formations that look like something out of a surrealist painting. Or as one Chinese poet put it, "The fantastic peaks grow like a jasper forest, the blue waters ripple like silken gauze." One of Guilin's major attractions is **Reed Flute Cave.**

Xian

Xian is the ancient capital of China. Until recently, that was its sole claim: enough to attract interest, but not enough to make it a major destination. All that has changed. And it all begins with a legend.

An old epic poem extolled the riches of Qin Shi Huang Di, China's first emperor. It detailed the fabulous wealth he had buried with him, guarded by 7000 soldiers. For centuries this was viewed as a mere artistic and political myth. But no more. In the 1970s a farmer struck something in the soil by accident. It proved to be a life-size terra-cotta statue of a soldier. Hundreds upon hundreds of other statues of soldiers in full battle dress, horses, and wagons were excavated. Archaeologists suspect even more wonders are to be discovered in Xian (the Chinese are taking their time to be extremely careful); the artifacts that have already been found are now exhibited in a giant, roofed excavation. Other sites of interest in Xian include:

- **The Wild Goose Pagoda,** a famous structure from the seventh century.

- **The Imperial Tomb of Qin Shi Huang Di,** with its stunning underground vaults and tombs.

- **Banpo Museum,** at the site of a 6000-year-old prehistoric village.

Tibet

Once an independent country, Tibet is a very mountainous, underdeveloped area of China in the Himalaya. The air is thin here: The average altitude is around 4600 metres. **Lhasa,** the capital city, is Tibet's major attraction. Nestled in a valley, Lhasa was once home to the Dalai Lama, who resided in the huge, nine-storey **Potala Palace.** The seventh-century **Jokhang Temple** is the holiest Buddhist temple in Tibet and attracts masses of pilgrims.

Hong Kong

Hong Kong, which had been a British colony, was returned to China in 1997. This port city is a place of legendary shopping, where you can buy electronics, custom-tailored suits, gems—you name it—and entrepreneurial Hong Kong will sell it to you, cut-rate. Hong Kong has two principal districts: **Hong Kong Island** and **Kowloon Peninsula** (which probably offers the best lodging and shopping). The

The lhasa apso dog, which comes from Tibet, was named after the city of Lhasa.

It's hard not to buy a custom-made suit before leaving Hong Kong. Measurements will be taken one day and the completed suit delivered to the hotel the next. Hong Kong's most famous tailor shop is Baron Kay's.

A floating restaurant in Aberdeen, Hong Kong
Photo by Justus Ghormley

One Hong Kong experience that's a *must:* a meal aboard one of the huge floating restaurants (though they're certainly not the best restaurants in Hong Kong).

predominant languages are Cantonese and English. Among Hong Kong's attractions are:

- **Aberdeen,** a floating village on Hong Kong Island. People live here on junks, sampans, and fishing boats. There are also floating markets and restaurants.

- **Victoria Peak,** for the best view of the city. It can be reached via the "peak tram" cog railway. Another way to see the Hong Kong skyline is via a junk ride.

- **Stanley,** an upscale district, with a popular open-air market.

- **The Golden Mile,** a portion of Nathan Road in Kowloon, is lined with Hong Kong's best hotels and shopping.

- **The Star Ferries,** boats that carry passengers across the dramatic harbour. Other means of transportation exist here for this purpose, but the Star Ferries are too famous to be missed.

Hong Kong has more Rolls-Royces per capita than any other place in the world.

Three **day trips** from Hong Kong stand out:

- **Macau,** a former Portuguese colony that returned to Chinese rule in 1999. Macau presents a quieter alternative to the hustle and bustle of Hong Kong, though it's a bit run-down. Several notable temples are here, especially the **Temple of Kun Iam,** with its lovely architecture and landscaping. **St. Paul's Church**—for a long time Macau was the only stronghold of Christianity in all of China—is worth a visit, as well. Macau, which can be easily reached from Hong Kong by hydrofoil, is renowned as a gambling and horseracing centre. The languages of Macau are Cantonese and Portuguese, but English is spoken by many.

- **The New Territories,** an outlying, surprisingly rural part of Hong Kong. One of the area's best known attractions: the **Temple of 10 000 Buddhas,** in **Shatlin.**

- **Lantau Island,** home to **Po Lin Monastery** and the **Giant Buddha,** which is 34 metres high and weighs 220 tonnes. Also on Lantau Island is Disney's newest theme park, **Hong Kong Disneyland.**

POSSIBLE ITINERARIES

Among the best buys in Hong Kong are silks, porcelain, jade, watches, and some electronics.

China is a long way from Canada. Most tourists prefer to see as much as possible on a visit, presuming that they might not be back for a while. Nine- to 15-day trips are typical. The country can be seen starting with three days in Beijing. Heading south, travellers could stop in the Grand Canal area of Suzhou for two days and then on to Shanghai for two more. They could spend two days in Xian. Then on to a few days in Guilin, cruising along the Li River, before ending their stay at Guangzhou and Hong Kong for three days. (Hong Kong is an ideal final stop, since purchases will be made at the end of the trip and not carried around throughout the journey.)

Return visitors, or those who'd like to take more time for their trip, may want to add a visit to Tibet, a cruise along the Yangtze River, and a stop in Macau. Trips to China are also often combined with a host of allied Asian destinations.

LODGING OPTIONS

Be aware that accommodations in most of China range from adequate (in smaller cities) to deluxe (especially in Beijing and Shanghai). Even more impressive: Hong Kong has dozens of outstanding hotels—many experts claim that there are more world-class facilities and better service in Hong Kong than anywhere else in the world.

Shanghai's Grand Hyatt is on the 53rd through 87th floor of the Jin Mao Tower, making it the "highest" hotel in the world.

In Beijing, the best hotels are found near the Imperial Palace and the Agricultural Exhibition Stadium. Those staying in Hong Kong should try to book hotels on Kowloon Peninsula, especially along the Golden Mile down by Victoria Harbour. A room with a harbour view will be worth it—the waterfront at night is an unforgettable sight. In Shanghai, hotels cluster near People's Square and the Pudong New Area. Hotels in other Chinese cities are often scattered about. It's best to try to book a hotel close to each city's centre.

ALLIED DESTINATIONS

More countries (15) border China than any other nation in the world.

China is surrounded by many countries. In fact, it's so large that its allied destinations must be broken down into three separate regions. To the north are Russia and Mongolia (though most of Russia's main attractions are nearer Europe). In the northeast, you'll find South Korea (on the mainland) and Japan (across the Sea of Japan). And finally, there's the Indian subcontinent and Southeast Asia, with such nations as India, Nepal, Bhutan, Burma (Myanmar), Vietnam, Thailand, Singapore, and Malaysia. In addition, across the South China Sea are the Philippines and Taiwan (which for years claimed to harbour the legitimate government of China). Those travelling between Taiwan and the People's Republic of China should check any government advisories on travel and customs restrictions.

CULTURAL PATTERNS

Political regulations can change often. Always check with the China International Travel Service for the latest advisories before you leave.

Hong Kong has always been a key business centre. Now, all of China will take on that status. It has become increasingly important, therefore, to understand the cultural uniqueness of this land.

- The use of full titles when addressing people is important. In addition, remember that in a Chinese name, the family name is listed first. Bowing is common, though a handshake is also acceptable.

- Promptness is much prized in China; it's even praiseworthy to be early.

- The Chinese don't call their country Red China or Communist China, but the People's Republic (of China).

- Discussing business during a meal is considered improper by the Chinese. In addition, be prepared to make a little speech after a more formal occasion as an acknowledgement to the host.

- Use both hands when passing a gift or food. If one person in a business group is to receive a gift, all others within the group must also receive one.

- It's more likely to be invited to a home in Hong Kong than in the rest of the country, where government approval is often required. In any event, bring a small gift. At least taste every dish served.

- Generosity is important to the Chinese. And treat the elderly with respect.

- Social position is critical in China, and embarrassing situations are avoided, allowing people to save face and retain self-respect. Avoid awkward situations.

- Chinese businesspeople are generally cautious and slow in reaching decisions.

- White is the Chinese colour of mourning and should be avoided in such things as gift-wrapping.

- The concept of lining up is foreign to the Chinese.

- Chinese point with an open hand, not with the index finger.

FACTORS THAT MOTIVATE VISITORS

Among the factors that motivate people to visit China are:

- There are remarkable archaeological treasures and sites.

- Chinese architecture and art are beautiful and impressive.

- China is viewed as a "soft adventure" destination by many Canadians.

- Hong Kong, Shanghai, Beijing, and Guangzhou are major business centres.

- The regional cuisines of China are superb and familiar.

- Many Canadians can trace their ancestry here.

- Cruise ships increasingly call on Chinese ports.

- Hong Kong has legendary, world-class lodging.

- There's great shopping, especially in Hong Kong.

North America's largest Chinatown is in San Francisco; the second largest is in Vancouver.

Hong Kong has about one restaurant for every 700 people.

POSSIBLE MISGIVINGS

Because this region is so far away, some people might hesitate to visit. Some of their possible concerns include:

- "China has a repressive government." Events in the late 1980s brought China's politics into the forefront of the news. Though this might concern some people, it had virtually no effect on tourism. Moreover, China seemingly has become a more modern and open society than in the past.

- "The country isn't set up for tourism and the facilities are primitive." Conditions are less developed than in, say, Europe, but China has been welcoming visitors for many years, and the situation is improving rapidly. Taking a fully inclusive escorted tour—by far the most popular option—will go a long way toward making such a trip more convenient.

- "The Chinese don't like Westerners." The Chinese people are very friendly and (though for generations unaccustomed to outsiders) warmly welcome visitors.

- "I don't think I can take Chinese food every single day." Each region in China offers its own unique cuisine. It's possible to have five or six dishes at each meal, three times a day, for weeks, and never eat the same thing twice.

- "The language is undecipherable." Speaking English in Hong Kong is no problem at all. For those concerned about the rest of the region, you might suggest an escorted tour. Many Chinese guides are fluent in English.

Qualifying the Traveller
BEIJING

FOR PEOPLE WHO WANT	HIGH APPEAL	MEDIUM APPEAL	LOW APPEAL	REMARKS
Historical and Cultural Attractions	▲			Especially Great Wall and Imperial Palace
Beaches and Water Sports			▲	Few facilities
Skiing Opportunities			▲	None
Lots of Nightlife			▲	
Family Activities		▲		Mostly sightseeing
Familiar Cultural Experience			▲	
Exotic Cultural Experience	▲			
Safety and Low Crime		▲		Sporadic unrest; petty theft
Bargain Travel		▲		Packages are all-inclusive
Impressive Scenery		▲		In countryside
Peace and Quiet		▲		Crowded, yet calm
Shopping Opportunities		▲		Hong Kong much better
Adventure		▲		
To Do Business	▲			China is a potentially huge market

SALES STRATEGIES

Because of travel restrictions and language problems, China is ideal for all-inclusive escorted group tours (including those that specialize in trekking expeditions). Travellers seeking an upscale experience can book a custom-designed personal tour with driver and guide for a reasonable price. A river cruise adds a lot to an itinerary. You can enhance a visit to the Great Wall and Ming Tombs by booking a helicopter flight over the area. And because China is so distant from Canada, you might suggest that visitors extend their trip, either within China or to allied countries in Asia, often via a cruise. Similarly, you could consider booking a stopover (for example, in Hawaii for travellers going west or in Europe for those flying east) to break up the long flight. Luxury lodging is especially attractive to travellers to this region.

A mysterious businessman from Seattle built a 1/20-sized version of the Forbidden City in Katy, a town 30 miles west of Houston, Texas. Also on display are reproductions of Xian's terra-cotta warrior statues.

TRAVEL TRIVIA

MORE SIGNS, BROCHURES, AND MEMOS ENCOUNTERED BY TRAVELLERS

- Teeth extracted by the latest Methodists. (Hong Kong)

- Visitors must complain at the office between 9 and 11 daily. (Greece)

- Please bathe inside the tub. (Japan)

- To move the cabin push button for washing floor. (Yugoslavia)

- Ladies are requested not to have children in the bar. (Norway)

- Ticket price for 0–2 year ache babys are 10% of normal price. (Turkey)

- The flattening of underwear with pleasure is the job of the chamber-maid. (Yugoslavia)

- Not to perambulate the corridors in the hours of repose in the boots of ascension. (Austria)

- Bodrum Airlines is not able to caryout flight schadule if an unusual thinks take place like bed weather, float, fire, eath queke, war done of elefricity, natural disaster, etc. (Turkey)

- A sports jacket may be worn to dinner, but no trousers. (France)

- The lift is being fixed for the next day. During that time we regret that you will be unbearable. (Romania)

NAME _____   DATE _____

A traveller wants to visit the places listed below. Which number represents each on the map?

PLACE/ATTRACTION	IN/NEAR WHICH CITY?	NUMBER ON MAP
A. The Temple of Heaven	**A.**	**A.**
B. A palace of the Dalai Lama	**B.**	**B.**
C. Star Ferry trips	**C.**	**C.**
D. Terra-cotta statues in the ground	**D.**	**D.**
E. The Imperial Palace	**E.**	**E.**
F. Dramatic and strange rock formations	**F.**	**F.**
G. The capital of Tibet	**G.**	**G.**
H. A famous floating village	**H.**	**H.**
I. Tiananmen Square	**I.**	**I.**
J. The Temple of the Jade Buddha	**J.**	**J.**

CASE STUDY

NAME _____   DATE _____

Terry and Sue Lee want to go on a trip to China. In their late 50s, they've done a bit of independent travelling in Canada and Europe. They could take up to three weeks, but have settled on 17 days, since they know the trip will be taxing.

Circle the answer that best suits their needs.

1. What Chinese attraction might you suggest to the Lees?

    Chiang Mai   Sherwood Forest

    Deer Park   Reed Flute Cave

    Why?

2. The Lees, of course, prefer to go when the weather is at its best, but the tour they were hoping to get on is all booked up. As their second choice, they'd rather have the climate a bit colder than have to deal with the rain. In which month would you *not* recommend they go?

    March   July

    May   November

    Why?

3. The Lees tell you that they want their last stop to be Hong Kong. What would logically be their destination just before getting to Hong Kong?

    Guangzhou   Tibet

    Macau   Singapore

    Why?

4. Which would probably *not* be a useful recommendation to make to the Lees?

    It's worth it to book a room with a view of Hong Kong's Victoria Harbour.

    Rent a car and drive around the Beijing countryside.

    While you're visiting Beijing, by all means visit the Imperial Palace and the Great Wall.

    Use both hands when passing a gift or food.

    Why?

CREATIVE ACTIVITY

NAME _____   DATE _____

Ancient historians compiled lists of the "Seven Wonders of the World" that every traveller should see. Among them were the Great Pyramids, the Colossus of Rhodes, and the Hanging Gardens of Babylon. (Only the Pyramids still exist.) The current government of China has decided that it, too, should boast of its own seven wonders in all of its promotional materials. What would you think these seven should be? Use the Internet to find photos of these "wonders," with URLs. Be prepared to justify your suggestions.

1.

2.

3.

4.

5.

6.

7.

CHAPTER 33

Asia and the Pacific Potpourri

Japan, China, Australia, New Zealand, and, somewhat beyond, Singapore and Thailand—these are the best-known destinations on the far side of the Pacific Rim. But that's just the start. Between the palm-fringed shores of Asia and California float thousands of islands—many quite famous. And beyond that? Well, that's where the public's geographic knowledge really falters. People have heard of Krakatoa volcano, but where is it? In what country is Mt. Everest? And what, for heaven's sake, is a *yurt*?

We omit quite a few Asian countries from this chapter because they're not major tourist destinations. The reasons are many: Warfare in some keeps travellers away; political turmoil is a major deterrent in others; and still others are opening up rapidly, but do not yet warrant their own sections. In addition, some countries, like North Korea and some of the Southeast Asia nations—Laos, for example, and Cambodia (also known as Kampuchea)—have governments with questionable human rights records and, therefore, limited tourist appeal. (Cambodia *is* taking efforts to reinstate tourism to the legendary Angkor Wat ruins.) Interestingly, there are also countries such as Brunei, which, though having perfectly good relations with most countries, aren't especially interested in encouraging a tourist trade. But keep one important fact in mind: All this can change overnight.

MONGOLIA

Mongolia's location—sandwiched between China and Russia—combined with its exotic history, makes this nation an intriguingly offbeat destination. Under Genghis Khan, Mongolia was once a world power. Today, the people of this nomadic, fairly primitive culture are more closely tied to Russia than to China.

Southern Mongolia is made up of the **Gobi Desert;** this arid, mountainous region is surprisingly pretty, with much interesting wildlife. The rainier north is where most of the population lives. **Ulan Bator** (nicknamed U.B.), the capital, has many monasteries and quite a few museums. In Mongolia's countryside are some impressive monasteries, several national parks, and, in some places, astonishing mountain scenery. The historic town of **Karakorum** was the capital during the time of Genghis Khan. Those who visit Mongolia do so to experience an adventurous destination well off the beaten tourist path. Oh, and the *yurts*? They're the traditional wooden-framed tents that are transported by nomads as they herd across the countryside.

The Korean language is closer to Finnish or Hungarian than to any Asiatic language.

Visitors are welcome to watch the peace talks; passes can be set up through the United Nations office in Seoul.

SOUTH KOREA

Separated from China by only North Korea, South Korea covers the southern strip of the Korean Peninsula; Japan is just across the Sea of Japan on the east, and the Yellow Sea borders South Korea to the west. **Seoul** [SOLE], located in the northwest, was host to the 1988 Summer Olympics. **Incheon International Airport** (ICN), about 48 kilometres west of Seoul, is the main air gateway. (**Gimpo** [GMP] is closer to Seoul, but now mainly handles domestic flights.) The national carrier, **Korean Air** (KE), **Asiana** (OZ), and a few North American airlines fly here. Cruise ships occasionally stop South Korea's largest port, **Busan** (formerly Pusan), on the southeast coast.

Most tourist destinations are toward the north, where the climate is humid. Spring and fall are pleasant in South Korea, with daytime temperatures around 20°C and chilly nights; these two seasons tend to be the driest times of the year. Summers are rainy—mid-July to mid-August is a mini-monsoon season—and the highs can soar into the 30s; winters, on the other hand, are cold, with temperatures often plummeting below zero. The official language is Korean, though English is quite common, especially in business.

Important Places

South Korean tourism, fuelled by visitors who seek shopping bargains and business deals, has reached impressive levels—despite its tensions with North Korea. The capital city of Seoul, historically surrounded by nine gates, is rich with temples, museums, and palaces. The cultural and shopping opportunities are excellent. Seoul's two most important designated national treasures are the **Namdaemun Gate** (the Great South Gate) and the **Dongdaemun Gate** (the Great East Gate). These grand, ornate structures are each adjacent to frenetic, popular marketplaces. The **Itaewon district,** which includes underground complexes, is the city's major tourist shopping area, but there are many others.

Interesting **day trips** and excursions include:

- **The Korean Folk Village** in **Suwon,** a village museum where ancient life in Korea is re-enacted.

- **Panmunjom,** in the demilitarized zone between the two Koreas, where peace talks occasionally are held. A tense place, with plenty of soldiers stationed on both sides, Panmunjom enables visitors to experience one of the world's most important and vexing issues.

- **Namhansansong Castle,** a spectacular fortress on **Mt. Namhan. Hyonchungsa** is a notable old temple in the area.

- **The Royal Tombs at Kumgoknung,** a majestic relic of the Yi Dynasty.

Other sites in South Korea include:

- **Kyongju,** the former capital of Korea. Burial mounds, tombs, temples, and a national museum are the attractions here.

- **Cheju Island,** off the southern coast, a resort area famed for its pearl divers. Cheju Island boasts good beaches, major hotels, a casino, and excellent diving. It's reached by air from Seoul or by a slow, 145 kilometre ferry ride from Busan.

Sales Considerations

South Korea is a convenient extension of a trip to Japan or China. Because of the unfamiliarity of the language, escorted tours are popular. This country will appeal to those who love Asian culture, ancient architecture, and bargain shopping. War veterans may also want to return to the site of their battles, under peaceful conditions. South Korea offers beaches and skiing for active vacationers. Business travellers should be prepared for the no-nonsense approach of Koreans. Potential visitors may be aware of political unrest and the history of South Korea's conflicts with North Korea, but for the moment, neither unrest nor conflict is affecting tourism.

TAIWAN

Until the mid-20th century, this 386 by 131 kilometre island was known as Formosa, which in Portuguese means "beautiful." The early settlers from Portugal knew what they were talking about; the island is a glorious one. For years, Taiwan's rulers claimed to represent the legitimate government of China—all of China. (Taiwan still officially calls itself the Republic of China.) Its airline, for example, continues to be called **China Airlines** (CI)—not to be confused with Mainland China's Air China. Taiwan's other carrier is **EVA Airways** (BR). The country is also serviced by a few North American airlines and several Asian carriers. Taiwan is located off the southeast coast of China, slightly northeast of Hong Kong and just north of the Philippines. **Taipei,** its capital and gateway in the north, can be reached via **Chiang Kai-shek International Airport** (TPE). There's also **Kaohsiung International Airport** (KHH) in the southwest, but it's less used. The official language is Mandarin Chinese, but Taiwanese is also widely spoken, as is some Japanese. English is commonly used in business.

China considers Taiwan to be one of its provinces.

Most of Taiwan's tourist destinations are in the north. The weather here is humid; October through December are the nicest months, with temperatures in the mid-20s during the day. January through March is cooler and rainier. The south is drier and warmer, but there's not as much to see. The typhoon season stretches from June to October. Mountain temperatures, of course, are chillier than in the lowlands.

Important Places

All visitors need do is gaze at its many shrines or travel through its lush countryside to discover Taiwan's beauty. One of its top destinations is Taipei—a busy, cosmopolitan capital. There's a wide selection of goods here and many excellent bargains for those who love to shop. The world-class **National Palace Museum** is a must-see. Located just outside Taipei, it has some 600 000 pieces of Chinese art, much of which was brought over from Beijing's Forbidden City when Taiwan's leaders fled the mainland. The classically styled **Martyrs Shrine** is designed after a hall in that same Forbidden City. The **Chiang Kai-shek Memorial Hall** honours the nation's late general and president; its huge complex features a tower more than 20 storeys high. There are many temples to visit in Taipei; the most notable is the historic, 250-year-old **Lungshan Temple.** A popular marketplace is nearby.

Among the **day trips** are:

- **Taroko Gorge,** a major destination, featuring an awesome 19 kilometre drive on its eastern end, known as the "Rainbow of Treasure Island." It's most commonly reached by a short flight from Taipei southeast to **Hualien.**

- **Yangmingshan** (Grass Mountain) **National Park,** noted for its scenic cherry and azalea trees. The trip here from Taipei passes by the **Peitou Mineral Springs.**

- **Yehliu National Park,** reached via an hour's drive to the east through lovely mountains and farmland. Yehliu's strange rocks and wonderful vistas make this a worthwhile half-day excursion.

One major destination far away from the hub of Taipei is **Sun Moon Lake,** created by a dam and offering rich, green, jungle-like scenery. It's Taiwan's number-one tourist destination, with several interesting shrines, temples, and pagodas. Sun Moon Lake is accessed out of **Taitung,** a pretty town two hours away on the southeast coast.

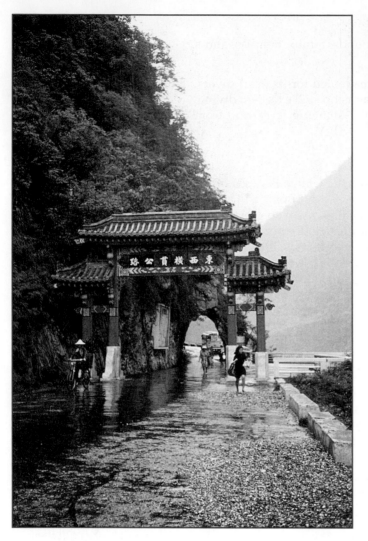

Taroko Gorge, Taiwan
Photo by Justus Ghormley

Sales Considerations

Taiwan attracts visitors because of its scenery, graceful Chinese architecture, and bargain shopping. Since the island is so small, it's easy to sample Chinese cuisine and culture without having to tackle the vastness of Mainland China. Some feel Taiwan is a safer destination than China. Taiwan makes a wonderful extension of any trip to Asia—particularly Japan, the Philippines, and South Korea, as well as China. Because of language problems, an escorted tour or a cruise is a good choice.

THE PHILIPPINES

Less than half of the Philippine islands have names; only around 900 are inhabited.

Comprising more than 7000 islands, the Philippines is located off the southeast coast of China in the South China Sea. It stretches from Taiwan in the north to Indonesia in the south. The main island here is **Luzon** in the north, where the capital of **Manila** is located. **Philippine Airlines** (PR), the national airline, services the country, as do several North American and international carriers, and a few cruise lines. Manila (MNL) is the country's gateway; it also serves as a cruise port.

The climate is fairly steady year-round, with highs averaging in the low 30s, dropping to the low 20s at night. Winter tends to be a bit cooler and more pleasant; March through May are the hottest months. It's rainiest from June to October (when typhoons are most likely to hit). The official languages are Pilipino (based on Tagalog) and English.

Important Places

The Philippines provides historical attractions, scenic sites, popular beach resorts, and good snorkelling and diving. Manila is the political and industrial centre of the country. It's a place of contrasts, with millionaire communities near teeming slums. There's excellent shopping here. (The best-known market is **Pistang Pilipino.**) Visitors can discover Manila's Spanish heritage at **Intramuros,** the old walled city where battletorn Fort Santiago—a former dungeon—is found. **Corregidor** is an island-fortress across **Manila Bay,** with important World War II memorials. Manila has many fine churches. Among the **day trips** from Manila are:

- **Hidden Valley,** which harbours a lush rain forest. Tourists can explore a dormant volcano close by.

- **Pagsanjan Falls,** which inspires visitors with its canyons, rapids, and craggy rock formations. The two-hour drive east of Manila goes through coconut, sugar, and pineapple plantations.

- **Lake Taal** [TAH-AHL], commonly viewed from **Tagaytay Ridge,** 48 kilometres south of Manila. Lake Taal offers a geographic oddity: At its centre is a volcano that, in turn, contains another lake.

Other destinations in the Philippines include:

- **Baguio,** in the mountains 240 kilometres north of Manila, the most popular summer resort centre of the Philippines. (The climate is cooler here.) Nearby, the **Banaue** [bah-NAH-way] **Rice Terraces** are a fascinating attraction: massive, awesome tiers cut into the mountainside.

- **The Visayas,** a cluster of islands in the middle section of the Philippines. Many old churches dot the Visayas, as do beaches and resort developments (especially those at **Cebu**).

- **Zamboanga,** on the southern island of **Mindanao.** Known as the "City of Flowers," this beautiful, active port features hanging gardens, a 300-year-old fort, an impressive mosque, and good beaches relatively nearby. Mindanao has long been a stronghold for rebels, so check the political situation before visits there.

Eighty-seven languages and over 100 dialects are spoken in the Philippines.

If placed end to end, the Banaue terraces would stretch halfway around the world.

Sales Considerations

This tropical island-nation appeals to those who love scenic destinations, relaxing beaches, snorkelling, shopping, history, good value, and a mix of exotic cultures. World War II veterans may also want to return here. The Philippines provides good shopping opportunities. Escorted tours are a popular way to get around from island to island. Budget lodging can leave much to be desired and luxury hotels are a relative bargain. The Philippines is close to Taiwan, Vietnam, Indonesia,

"Peninsular Malaysia" is *not* another term for the "Malay Peninsula." It's the part of Malaysia that's actually on the Malay Peninsula (which also contains parts of Thailand and Burma).

Malaysia, Thailand, and China, creating potentially longer itineraries. Japan and Australia (though more distant) are also potential add-ons. Asian cruises often call on Manila. So far, political turbulence hasn't severely disrupted tourism in the Philippines, though there's always that possibility. Crime and tourist scams are occasionally a problem here.

INDONESIA

Indonesia, with the fourth-largest population in the world, boasts a land area about the size of Quebec and Newfoundland combined. Yet it stretches 4800 kilometres—almost the width of Canada. How can this be? Simple: Indonesia is made up of a spread-out arc of islands (17 508 of them), stretching almost halfway up Peninsular Malaysia on the west and almost to Australia on the east. The largest of its islands, **Sumatra,** lies to the west; **Java,** a densely populated island and the location of the nation's capital, **Jakarta,** is a bit farther east; **Bali** sits at the eastern tip of Java; and the jungles of **Borneo** are to the north. Jakarta (JKT) is the gateway into Indonesia and is reached via the national airline, **Garuda Indonesia** (GA).

Most of Indonesia's landmass lies below the equator, so its seasons—limited as they are—are opposite those in North America. The climate tends to be steamy all year. The driest months are June to early November (but it's still humid and there will be rain), with temperatures around 30°C. Inland temperatures run slightly cooler. Late November to March is extremely wet; the monsoon season is January and February. Bahasa Indonesia is the official language, though many other dialects and languages are spoken. Many Indonesians speak English.

Indonesia is a mosaic of cultures. It's an ancient land: The prehistoric remains of Java Man were discovered here.

Important Places

- **Bali** features lush jungles, volcanic mountain peaks, exotic Hindu ceremonies, unique national parks, mystical temples, pristine beaches, legendary surfing areas, and a culture that expects almost every one of its people to be a craftsmaker, dancer, painter, or other kind of artist. **Denpasar** is the island's main business centre—though most tourists stay at the great resorts near the island's southern tip, which features excellent snorkelling, surfing, and diving. Bali is heavily developed; it's no longer the "primitive" tropical place it was a few decades ago. Terrorists have staged several bombings here. Keep up on the current political situation.

The temple of Borobudur was forgotten for 1000 years and rediscovered by Sir Stamford Raffles (of Singapore's Raffles Hotel fame).

- **Yogyakarta** [jog-jah-KAR-tah] (often shortened to "Yogya"), in the centre of the island of Java, is a major cultural centre. It's known for its batik factories, which are open to tourists. The **Palace of the Sultan** is a complex of elaborate, lavishly designed pavilions. A trip to nearby **Borobudur** [bore-uh-buh-DUR] and its astonishing, spectacular Buddhist temple—built 1200 years ago and recently restored—is a must.

- **Jakarta,** Indonesia's busy and crowded capital, is located on the west end of Java. It has only a few sites of interest. The **National Museum** has some fine art and historical collections. Jakarta is also a good place for shopping and exotic dining experiences.

- **Surabaya,** in east Java, is an area of many volcanoes. The town also operates a good zoo with the famed Komodo dragons, huge lizards that were often used in movies to portray dinosaurs.

- **Sumatra,** a beautiful island with excellent wildlife, is most famous for its Sumatran tigers. Attractions in **Medan** include the interesting **Sultan's Palace** and a native village built on stilts.

- **Krakatoa,** the legendary volcano, rises up on the island of **Rakata**—you can book excursions here. (By the way, there was a movie called *Krakatoa, East of Java.* Krakatoa is actually *west* of Java, but *east* apparently sounded better to Hollywood.)

Sales Considerations

Unless the traveller is going only to Bali, an escorted tour is a great option in Indonesia: Independent travel can be challenging. Indonesia will be popular among those interested in primitive cultures, the religions of the world, water sports, exotic food, shopping, and bargain travel. Cruise ships stop at nearly a dozen different ports. Cruises are also one of the easiest ways to get to see **Komodo Island** and its huge lizards. Parts of Indonesia occasionally suffer from serious political unrest.

When Krakatoa exploded in 1883, it created the loudest sound in recorded history. Some believe that an earlier eruption in A.D. 535 and the global climate changes it caused triggered a plague in the Roman Empire, the Dark Ages in Europe, the abandonment of Teotihuacan, and the rise of Islam.

MALAYSIA

Malaysia is divided into two sections: The most populous region lies on the **Malay Peninsula,** bordered by Thailand to the north and Singapore and Indonesia (across the Strait of Malacca) to the south; the more primitive jungle area sits atop the island of Borneo. **Kuala Lumpur** (KUL), the capital and air gateway, is near the west-central coast of Peninsular Malaysia. It's served by the national carrier, **Malaysian Airlines** (MH), as well as several North American and Asian airlines. (Because Singapore is so conveniently close to Malaysia, some travellers prefer to land there instead.) Malaysia is well situated for cruises: **George Town, Port Kelang,** and **Malacca** are its main ports.

Malaysia has a hot, tropical climate. Daytime highs average around 32°C, with evening lows in the lower 20s. It's humid all year, though October through January is rainiest, whereas March through June is the most pleasant period. Conditions on the peninsula are slightly cooler and drier than on the island of Borneo. Malay is the national language, but English is widely spoken, especially in business.

Borneo has more species of plants than the entire continent of Africa does.

Important Places

A lush country, Malaysia offers beautiful scenery, an austere but intriguing Islamic culture, and some wonderful beaches. Among the most popular destinations are:

- **Kuala Lumpur,** a beautiful city with Moorish architecture. Most notable are the **National Mosque,** the palace-like railroad station, and the twin **Petronas Towers,** two of the world's tallest skyscrapers. The **Central Market** is a busy and entertaining place. Tourists may also enjoy the city's excellent zoo and **National Museum.** Outside the city are the **Batu Caves,** up nearly 300 steps to a Hindu shrine in an exotic grotto, complete with monkeys swinging about. And in the **Genting Highlands** is an upscale resort and recreation area with a very busy casino.

- **Malacca,** three hours south of Kuala Lumpur. This historic port—Malaysia's oldest city—can be seen as a long day trip from Kuala Lumpur. A multi-cultured

Kuala Lumpur is commonly called "KL."

city, it was settled at various times by the Chinese, Portuguese, Dutch, and English. All of these cultures are still in evidence, making Malacca an especially interesting place to visit.

- **Penang Island** is perhaps one of the most interesting and pleasant places to visit in Malaysia. It has great beaches (with windsurfing), intricate temples, historical sites, tropical forests, and architectural gems. Its principal city is George Town.

The British developed the resorts in the highlands to escape from the heat and humidity of the rest of Malaysia.

- **The Cameron Highlands,** on the mainland halfway between Penang and Kuala Lumpur. This recreation area offers waterfalls, tea plantations, wonderful weather, and its famous butterflies. The climate here is cooler than that of the lowlands.

- **Sarawak,** the northwest territory on Borneo. This is the legendary, ancient home of Dyak headhunters. **Kuching,** the capital, features a historical museum, palaces, some fine temples, and several mosques.

- **Sabah,** the northeast territory on Borneo, a region for the adventurous. The capital, **Kota Kinabalu,** has an impressive state mosque and a good museum; the city can serve as a convenient hub for exploring the surrounding tribal area. **Mt. Kinabalu,** rising 4100 metres, is a popular destination for climbers; its hilly national park is filled with exotic birds, flowers, and butterflies.

- **Tioman,** the principal island amid a group of 64 volcanic islands off the eastern coast. With white coral beaches and crystal-clear waters, these islands are being "rediscovered" for their superb snorkelling opportunities and the summer spectacle of hundreds of turtles that swim to shore to lay their eggs.

Sales Considerations

By law, karaoke bars in Malaysia close by 11 p.m. to keep men from staying out too late.

Malaysia is well located for extending trips to Thailand, Singapore, and Indonesia. It's a country for those who love scenery, beaches, shopping (especially batik and brassworks), and tribal culture. It also offers areas that are ideal for the adventurous. You would be wise to upsell hotels rather than book travellers in unpleasant, basic accommodations. Getting around the country can be bothersome, so tours might be appropriate. And, again, Malaysia's proximity to many other nations encourages an expanded trip, often via a cruise.

VIETNAM

For many decades, Vietnam—at war with France and later with the United States—had virtually no tourism. The current government seems far more willing to encourage commerce in general and tourism in particular. As a result, several tour operators and cruise lines have positioned Vietnam as an intriguing destination to visit.

Vietnam—a long, thin country that stretches north to south along the Gulf of Tonkin and the South China Sea—can be divided into three regions. The north is where **Hanoi,** Vietnam's capital, is located. It's an unusual amalgam of ancient temples, colonial French homes, interesting museums, and modern skyscrapers. About 160 kilometres to the southeast is the port of

Haiphong and nearby **Halong Bay.** Halong Bay is Vietnam's natural wonder, with thousands of small islands, beaches, caves, and grottoes. An unusual option: a day or overnight trip in Halong Bay on a Chinese *junk.*

Vietnam's central region is most famous for **Hue** [hoo-WAY], considered Vietnam's most beautiful city. Once the national's imperial capital, Hue's most impressive attraction is the **Citadel,** a huge, moated, partly destroyed complex of structures. Several hours away is **Da Nang,** a port city with many temples and small museums.

Vietnam's southern region is anchored by **Ho Chi Minh City,** more popularly known by its traditional name, **Saigon.** A large, bustling metropolis, Ho Chi Minh City has many French-inspired buildings and more ancient, traditional structures. **Nha Trang,** a developing seaside resort, lies to the city's north.

Most visitors access Vietnam on flights on Asian carriers from Bangkok, or via cruise ships that call on Vietnam's principal ports.

BURMA (MYANMAR)

Sandwiched between India, China, and Thailand, with the Bay of Bengal [ben-GAHL] to the south, Burma—also known as Myanmar [mee-AHN-mahr]—was once a British colony and has retained much of its cultural heritage. The run-down capital of **Rangoon** (also called Yangon) features a gold-and-diamond-encrusted, bell-shaped complex—**Shwedagon Pagoda**—one of the world's most sacred Buddhist shrines and an astonishing sight. **Mandalay,** the former capital, has many historical attractions and several impressive pagodas.

Pagan [pah-GAHN]—yet another former capital—is a uniquely beautiful, fascinating city with the ruins of 5000 pagodas. This was the centre of the powerful Pagan dynasty, until Kublai Khan overran it in the 13th century. **Inle** [IN-lay] **Lake** is a growing resort area.

Burma is an adventure: Lodging is hardly deluxe and there's much political and military turmoil. Most information and arrangements should be secured through Tourist Myanmar, the official agency for all Burmese travel. Burma is usually booked as a two- or three-day "extra" on a trip to the more popular destination—adjoining Thailand.

BHUTAN

Slightly to the east of Nepal and separated from it only by a thin strip of India, lofty Bhutan [boo-TAHN] is known as the "Land of the Thunder Dragon." A country of unspoiled beauty, it's been open to outside

Nearly 100 000 monks live in Mandalay, an important Buddhist centre.

The Burmese celebrate New Year's by throwing buckets of water on one another.

Chapter 33 Asia and the Pacific Potpourri

tourists only since 1974; there continue to be strict limits on the number of tourists permitted yearly. The awesome Himalaya make Bhutan a major destination for treks and mountain climbing.

Paro is Bhutan's largest city. It's home to monasteries and museums, including the **National Museum.** The capital of Bhutan, **Thimphu,** is the folk-cultural centre, with many ancient structures and good crafts shopping. Parts of Bhutan offer spectacular views of the Himalaya. Not surprisingly, the country offers great trekking opportunities.

A *dzong* is a fortress-monastery.

NEPAL

Imagine the most stunning and prodigious mountain range you can. It's likely that you'll be imagining the Himalaya of Nepal. The northern region of this country is perhaps the prime trekking and mountain-climbing destination in the world: This is the land of **Mt. Everest,** the world's tallest peak (8848 metres). Special permits may be necessary for some of the excursions here, so be sure to check with the Ministry of Tourism. Southern Nepal is merely hilly and, thus, more populous. There has been unrest here, which may worry some travellers, so check for government advisories.

Kathmandu is the capital, the main hub for treks, a place of dozens of little architectural, historical, and religious gems. Tourists generally use **Durbar Square** as a hub to visit the city. Near Kathmandu is **Bhaktapur** (once known as Bhadgaon), a cultural arts centre. It was built in A.D. 900 and has retained many temples, monasteries, a famous **Golden Gate,** and the **Palace of Fifty-Five Windows.**

Edmund Hillary and Tenzing Norgay were the first to climb to the top of Mt. Everest.

Tradition states that Buddha was born in Nepal.

Pokhara is the base for treks beginning on the Himalaya's **Annapurna Range.** In the lowlands, **Royal Chitwan National Park** is a popular wildlife preserve, with such rare animals as Royal Bengal tigers and one-horned rhinos. The warm weather and jungle scenery here lend themselves ideally to safaris and rafting excursions. **Tiger Tops** is the area's most famous base camp.

A tiger in a wildlife preserve
Stephanie Kuwasaki/Shutterstock

INDIA

The seventh-largest country in the world, India is slightly less than one-third the size of Canada. It's also the world's second-most populated nation, with over a billion people—more than 30 times Canada's population. The most populous area of India is the fertile plains around the sacred **Ganges** [GAN-jeez] **River;** this lies below the Himalaya, which anchor the northern border in spectacular fashion. India is a beautiful, mystical land of splendour, exotic culture, and heartrending poverty. It's located south of China, bordered on the west by the Arabian Sea and on the east by the Bay of Bengal. The island-nation of Sri Lanka (formerly called Ceylon) rests off its southern tip.

New Delhi, the capital, anchors northern India; it's the main gateway, with flights arriving at **Indira Gandhi International Airport** (DEL). Near the northeast coast is **Kolkata** (formerly Calcutta) (CCU), a major city with a significant port. **Mumbai** (formerly Bombay) (BOM), on the west-central coast, is another important port and a fairly cosmopolitan city. The country is serviced by **Air India** (AI), the national airline, as well as by North American and international carriers.

March through May is a dry and often uncomfortably hot period in India, whereas June through September is the notorious monsoon rain season. It's most comfortable to visit from October to February: The climate in the south ranges from tropical daytime temperatures around 29°C to around 18°C at night. The more mountainous north runs about eight degrees cooler. The Himalaya, of course, can get quite cold. Of the 16 official languages, Hindi is the national language, though English (an associate official tongue) is common in business and government; more than 1500 recognized dialects are spoken across India.

Important Places

Many travellers are attracted to India by some of the world's most historical cities and the Himalaya. Among the country's principal destinations is New Delhi, which is actually made up of the old city of Delhi and a more modern development. Its 17th-century **Red Fort** was built under order of Shah Jahan, who was responsible for creating the Taj Mahal. New Delhi has many landmark mosques, tombs, and temples. One important tomb is the **Raj Ghat,** a memorial to Mahatma Gandhi; it's where his cremated remains rest.

Two essential **excursions** out of New Delhi are:

India is second only to the United States in the length of its road systems.

- **Agra,** home of the **Taj Mahal**—considered by many to be the world's most beautiful building. This exquisite memorial was built by Shah Jahan for his wife. Most people visit it at sunrise *and* at sunset, since it looks very different in different light conditions. (Also, it's much less crowded at sunrise.) For those who take the time to look beyond the Taj, Agra also has some other fine sights, including the **Agra Fort complex.** From New Delhi, Agra is 30 minutes by plane or about three hours by car.

- **Jaipur,** called the "Pink City" for the colour of stone used here. Forts and hills circle the city. **Hawa Mahal** (Palace of the Winds) is in fact no more than a façade with nearly 1000 windows. The **City Palace Museum** has a fine collection of crafts. The **Amber Palace**—Jaipur's principal attraction—impressively overlooks the city. It's also one of several places in India where visitors can experience a ride on an elephant.

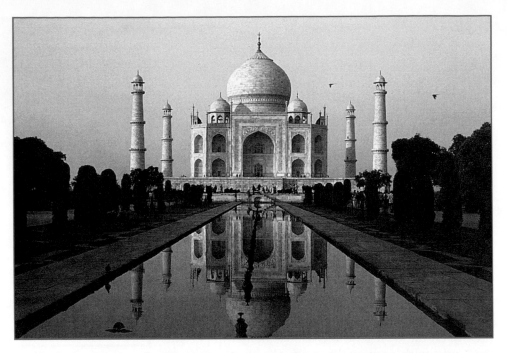

The Taj Mahal, Agra, India
Photo by Justus Ghormley

⊚ Pickled ginger is the most popular pizza topping in India, squid in Japan, and eggs in Australia.

⊚ Where do old cruise ships go when they're decommissioned? They get run aground on India's Alang Beach, where they're taken apart for their valuable metal to be reclaimed.

⊚ Mumbai is home to the "Bollywood" film industry, which produces more feature films than anywhere else in the world. (The name *Bollywood* is a combination of Bombay and Hollywood.)

India's other major destinations are:

- **Varanasi,** also known as Benares. Pilgrims come here to cleanse themselves in the holy waters of the Ganges. Each night an impressive "Sacred Light Ceremony" takes place. It's well worth seeing. Varanasi is the centre of the Hindu religion in India; many sacred temples grace the city. Nearby is the town of **Sarnath,** a major Buddhist centre; it's said that Buddha taught his first lesson here.

- **Kolkata** (Calcutta), the nation's second-largest city. For all its importance, this major port city is painfully squalid. It's not a prime tourist destination, but there are some fine museums, gardens, mansions, markets, and memorials.

- **Madras,** on the southeast coast. The first British settlement was here, at **Fort St. George.** The city is also of major Christian and Hindu importance, with temples, palaces, and religious sites. Outside town are a number of ancient temples.

- **Goa,** a somewhat different sort of Indian destination. Once a Portuguese colony, it's now a tropical beach resort that has a very cosmopolitan feel. The climate is extremely pleasant—even the monsoon season in Goa is relatively mild.

- **Mumbai** (Bombay), the country's business centre. Impressive sixth-century cave temples carved into rock can be found on **Elephanta Island,** reached by ferry.

- **Ajanta** and **Ellora Caves;** these superb ruins lie about 320 kilometres to the northeast of Mumbai. At Ellora, 34 impressive temples are cut out of the rock.

- **Udaipur,** a lovely city where gracefully detailed palaces line a lake.

- **Wildlife reserves,** with some of the rarest creatures in the world. You can book safaris in any number of lush, exciting parks. For over 30 years, India has funded "Project Tiger," a conservation program to protect the endangered tiger. Visitors can see these big cats at many sites throughout the country.

Sales Considerations

India is a large country and its culture (and, especially, the poverty) seems challenging to many; as a result, escorted tours (which help buffer tourists) or cruises are excellent options. In addition, you should up-sell hotel accommodations, since the alternative can often lead to unpleasant experiences. There's even the possibility of staying in a converted palace. Several luxurious train trips are available. The wildlife here is unique and presents an interesting alternative to the traditional African safari areas. India will also attract religious pilgrims, bargain seekers, lovers of early culture and history, and those fascinated by philosophy and mysticism. The people of India are very friendly and welcoming to tourists.

One other point: Sri Lanka (an island-nation south of India that has suffered some political turmoil) and the Maldive Islands (coral islands to the southwest that are a common cruise port of call on the way to Africa) are attractive tropical destinations whose tourism industries have shown considerable growth.

The word *serendipity* comes from the Muslim name for Sri Lanka.

The Maldives constitute the flattest country on earth.

TRAVEL TRIVIA

QUESTIONABLE MENU ITEMS

- "Pork with Fresh Garbage" (Vietnam)

- "As for the tripe served you at the Hotel Monopol, you will be singing its praises to your grandchildren as you lie on your deathbed." (Polish tourist brochure)

- "Chopped up cow with a wire through it (shish-ke-bob)." (Athens hotel)

- "Muscles of Marines/Lobster Thermos" (Cairo)

- "Buttered Saucepans and Fried Hormones" (Japan)

- "Sweat from the Trolley" (Europe)

- "Dreaded Veal Cutlet with Potatoes in Cream" (Europe)

- "Fried Friendship" (Nepal)

- "Beef Rashers Beaten Up in the Country Peoples Fashion" (Poland)

- "Cold Shredded Children & Sea Blubber in Spicy Sauce" (China)

- "French Fried Ships" (Cairo)

- "Roasted Duck, Let Loose" (Poland)

- "Teppen Yaki—Before Your Cooked Right Eyes" (Japan)

- "Goose Barnacles" (Spain)

- "Toes with Butter and Jam" (Bali)

MAP ACTIVITY

NAME _____   DATE _____

A traveller wants to visit the places listed below. Which number represents each on the map?

PLACE/ATTRACTION	IN/NEAR WHICH COUNTRY?	NUMBER ON MAP
A. Mt. Everest	**A.**	**A.**
B. Bali	**B.**	**B.**
C. Elephanta Island	**C.**	**C.**
D. Taipei	**D.**	**D.**
E. The Gobi Desert	**E.**	**E.**
F. The Taj Mahal	**F.**	**F.**
G. Seoul	**G.**	**G.**
H. Kuala Lumpur	**H.**	**H.**
I. Taroko Gorge	**I.**	**I.**
J. Manila	**J.**	**J.**

CASE STUDY

NAME _____   DATE _____

Sandra Durant, in her mid-30s, has wanderlust and enjoys going on adventurous trips by herself. This year she has her sights set on about three weeks in Southeast Asia—Malaysia, Indonesia, perhaps the Philippines, and Singapore. Cost is important to her. The flight over is expensive enough and she'll be looking for bargains along the way. But then, she's always felt that roughing it is the best way to see any country.

Circle the answer that best suits her needs.

1. Which of the following services could you recommend?

    First-class air tickets   A side trip to Thailand

    An escorted safari   Deluxe hotel rooms

    Why?

2. Sandra plans to be on the go for most of her trip, but she wants to find one destination in the area where she can stop and spend a bit more time. Where might you suggest?

    Tahiti   Fiji

    Bali   Bora Bora

    Why?

3. Of the following sites, which would *not* be appropriate for you to recommend that Sandra visit?

    Borobudur   The Taj Mahal

    Batu Caves   Banaue Rice Terraces

    Why?

4. Which of the following tips should you suggest?

    Lodging may be challenging.   Bring a sweater for the chilly nights.

    Convenient transportation is available.   There are major trekking opportunities throughout.

    Why?

CREATIVE ACTIVITY

NAME _____   DATE _____

You work for ACME Cruise Lines, which has decided to inaugurate an 18-day cruise of Asia and the Pacific. The cruise, which will be targeted to culture seekers, begins in Hong Kong at 7 p.m. Your job: to propose an itinerary that will call on at least four ports (you may end the cruise at any port). List the ports you've chosen, indicate what happens each day, and be prepared to justify your itinerary. Remember that the ship shouldn't cruise a distance between ports that would take longer than three days. The ship is capable of speeds of 32 to 40 km/h. Note also that cruise lines usually like to have their ships depart in the early evening and arrive in the early morning so they sail as much as possible at night. (Try to give projected departure and arrival times.) You may have the ship stay at a port for several days or have it merely arrive at a port in the morning and leave that same evening. You may wish to study cruise line brochures to get a few ideas.

Day 1: Embark

Day 2

Day 3

Day 4

Day 5

Day 6

Day 7

Day 8

Day 9

Day 10

Day 11

Day 12

Day 13

Day 14

Day 15

Day 16

Day 17

Day 18

NAME _____   DATE _____

The Matching Game

Directions: Below is a list of cities, attractions, etc., some of which we have covered, some of which we haven't. There are all manner of connections among them. With a group of fellow students, you have exactly 10 minutes to come up with as many connections as possible. (Items may be used more than once.) Write your answers below. Note: There are at least 20 possible connections. For example, Yangtze and Li—both are rivers.

Himalaya	Tahiti	Maldives
Lhasa	Katherine	Great Dividing Range
Japan	Queenstown	Yangtze
Wellington	Canberra	Nepal
Noumea	Vietnam	New Caledonia
Li	Coral	Southern
Darwin	Murray	Palace on Wheels
Brunei	Tonga	Alice Springs
Thailand	Silver Fern	Kuala Lumpur
Beijing	Micronesia	Gold Coast
Taroko	Phuket	Indian Pacific
Blue	Rotorua	Volcano
Truk Island	Shanghai	Western Samoa

Appendix A

Average Length of Stay—Leisure Travellers

The following is a list of major cities and approximately how long the average tourist stays in each (including, perhaps, one day trip) and assuming a leisurely pace. Remember that some visitors may wish to fully explore that city's attractions. Although a city may require only one day to see, a traveller may need two nights' lodging in that city.

CITY	NUMBER OF DAYS	CITY	NUMBER OF DAYS	CITY	NUMBER OF DAYS	CITY	NUMBER OF DAYS
Acapulco	3–4	Geneva	1–2	Niagara Falls	1–2	Vancouver	1–2
Amsterdam	2–3	Guadalajara	1–2	Nice	2–3	Venice	2–3
Anchorage	1–2					Vienna	2–4
Athens	2–3	Helsinki	1–2	Orlando	3–5		
Atlanta	1–2	Hong Kong	2–4	Osaka	1–2	Washington, D.C.	3–5
Atlantic City	1–2	Honolulu (Waikiki)	3–5	Oslo	1–2	Wellington, NZ	1–2
Auckland	1–2	Houston	1–2	Ottawa	1–2	Williamsburg, VA	1–2
Baltimore	1–2	Istanbul	1–2	Paris	3–5	Zurich	1–2
Banff	1–2			Philadelphia	1–2		
Bangkok	2–3	Jerusalem	2–4	Phoenix	1–2		
Barcelona	2–3			Portland, OR	1–2		
Beijing	3–4	Kyoto	1–3	Puerto Vallarta	2–3		
Berlin	2–3						
Boston	2–3	Lancaster, PA	1–2	Quebec City	1–2		
Brisbane	2–3	Las Vegas	2–3	Quito	1–2		
Brussels	2–3	Lima	1–3				
Budapest	1–2	Lisbon	1–3	Rio de Janeiro	2–4		
Buenos Aires	1–2	London	3–5	Rome	3–4		
		Los Angeles	3–5	Rotorua	1–2		
Cairo	1–2						
Calgary	1–2	Madrid	2–3	St. Petersburg, Russia	1–2		
Cancun	3–4	Marrakech	1–2	Salt Lake City	1–2		
Chicago	2–3	Mazatlan	2–3	Salzburg	1–2		
Christchurch	1–2	Melbourne	1–2	San Antonio	1–2		
Copenhagen	2–3	Memphis	1–2	San Diego	2–3		
Cuzco	1–2	Mexico City	2–3	San Francisco	2–3		
		Miami	2–3	Santa Fe	1–2		
Dallas	1–2	Milan	1–2	Savannah, GA	1–2		
Denver	1–2	Montreal	2–3	Seattle	1–2		
Dublin	1–2	Moscow	2–3	Seoul	2–3		
		Mumbai (Bombay)	1–3	Stockholm	1–3		
Edinburgh	2–3	Munich	2–3	Sydney	2–3		
Edmonton	1–2						
		Nairobi	1–3	Tampa/Clearwater	2–3		
Fairbanks	1–2	Nashville	1–2	Tangier	1–2		
Florence	2–4	New York	3–5	Tokyo	2–3		
Frankfurt	1–2	Newport, RI	1–2	Toronto	1–2		

Appendix B

Research Resources

The following resources are available in various formats: print and online.

Intelliguide (formerly *The Weissmann Travel Reports*): Plenty of information on virtually every destination in the world, both well-known and obscure. Intelliguide gives sample itineraries, food and shopping tips, plus all the basics, too.

The World Travel Guide gives enormous detail—including information for business travel—about virtually every nation on earth. Its colour layout is impressive; another essential research tool.

The Star Service analyzes hotels across the world in extreme detail. **The Hotel & Travel Index** (HTI) gives information on thousands of hotels.

Travel guidebook series include the following:

- **Fodor** and **Frommer** are fine all-purpose guides. These publishers also have created separate, more specialized lines of guides.

- **Berlitz Pocket** guides manage to compress an amazing amount of detail into their compact books.

- **The Lonely Planet** series takes a somewhat counterculture look at places many other guidebooks neglect.

- **Access** and **Michelin Green** guides stress history, art, and architecture. Their beautiful graphic presentation makes them especially easy to consult.

- **Insight** and **Eyewitness** guides also examine the history and culture of a destination, but with the added benefit of high-quality colour photographs.

- **The Let's Go**, **Rough Guide, Time Out,** and **Moon** series treat the particular needs of student, budget, younger, and independent travellers.

The Eurail Guide contains handy descriptions of railroad routes—not only for Europe but also for many other countries.

Tourist Attractions & Events of the World is a unique compendium of the world's most popular sites. It gives not only useful descriptions but also opening times, admission fees, and addresses.

The Destination Specialist series, created by the Travel Institute, is an admirable group of texts that focus on destinations.

The World Factbook, published by the Central Intelligence Agency, is a little-known print and online resource that contains a wealth of information. In addition to travel information, it gives statistics on a wide variety of topics.

Travel trade magazines and **tourist bureau** materials are often excellent sources of up-to-date information. In addition to search engines, website addresses for most country and many regional tourist bureaus can be found at www.towd.com.

The Consular Affairs Bureau at www.voyage.gc.ca offers information for Canadians travelling abroad, including travel documents required for Canadian citizens.

Health and political advisories are regularly issued by each province's tourism ministry. You should consult them whenever foreign travel is involved.

Appendix C

Destination-Related Feature Films

Sometimes the ambience of a place is just around the corner, at your neighbour-hood video store. Below is a list of films that capture the essence of—or even spoof—their locations. Historical films are, for the most part, excluded. Those rated "R" are indicated accordingly.

Baltimore, MD	*Diner* (R)	Austria (Vienna)	*The Third Man*
The Catskills, NY	*Dirty Dancing*	Bermuda	*The Deep*
Hawaii	*Blue Hawaii*	Botswana	*The Gods Must Be Crazy*
Hawaii	*Hawaii*	Canada	*The Black Robe*
Hawaii	*Hawaiians*	Canada	*Canadian Bacon*
Hollywood, CA	*The Player*	Canada	*The Fast Runner*
Hollywood, CA	*Sunset Boulevard*	Canada	*Snow Walker*
Hollywood, CA	*The Day of the Locust*	China	*Shoes of the Fisherman*
Las Vegas, NV	*Viva Las Vegas*	China	*The Last Emperor*
Las Vegas, NV	*Leaving Las Vegas*	England (London)	*Notting Hill*
Las Vegas, NV	*Honeymoon in Vegas*	Europe	*National Lampoon's European Vacation*
Los Angeles, CA	*L.A. Confidential* (R)		
Los Angeles, CA	*L.A. Story*	France (Paris)	*A Little Romance*
Los Angeles, CA	*Chinatown* (R)	France (Paris)	*Forget Paris*
Los Angeles and New York	*Annie Hall*	France (Paris)	*Love in the Afternoon*
		France (Paris)	*Paris When It Sizzles*
Miami, FL	*Miami Rhapsody* (R)	France (Paris)	*How to Steal a Million*
Miami, FL	*Miami Blues* (R)	France (Paris)	*French Kiss*
New Orleans, LA	*A Streetcar Named Desire*	France (Paris)	*An American in Paris*
New Orleans, LA	*The Big Easy* (R)	France (Paris)	*Charade*
New York City	*Manhattan*	France (Paris)	*Gigi*
New York City	*The Age of Innocence*	France (Riviera)	*To Catch a Thief*
New York City	*On the Town*	Greece (Crete)	*Zorba the Greek*
New York City	*After Hours*	India	*Heat and Dust* (R)
New York City	*Cocktail*	Italy (Assisi)	*The Assisi Underground*
New York City	*The Clock*	Italy (Florence)	*A Room with a View*
New York City	*The Out of Towners*	Italy (Rome)	*La Dolce Vita*
North Dakota	*Fargo*	Italy (Rome)	*Two Weeks in Another Town*
Pennsylvania Dutch Country	*Witness*	Italy (Rome)	*Roman Holiday*
		Italy (Venice)	*Don't Look Now* (R)
San Francisco, CA	*Bullitt*	Italy (Venice)	*Summertime*
San Francisco, CA	*Vertigo*	Japan (Tokyo)	*Lost in Translation*
St. Louis, MO	*Meet Me in St. Louis*	Morocco (Casablanca)	*Casablanca*
Washington, D.C.	*All the President's Men*	Scotland	*Braveheart*
Australia and New York City	*Crocodile Dundee*	Wales	*The Englishman Who Went Up a Hill But Came Down a Mountain*
Austria	*The Sound of Music*		

Index